Keyframes: Popular Cinema and Cultural Studies

Keyframes: Popular Cinema and Cultural Studies links the study of popular cinema around the world with the transformative effects of cultural studies on film studies.

Combining a film studies focus on the film industry, production, and technology with a cultural studies analysis of consumption and audiences, this book demonstrates the dynamism and breadth of approaches now available for understanding popular cinema. The contributors rethink contemporary film culture using ideas and concerns from feminism, queer theory, "race" studies, critiques of nationalism, colonialism and post-colonialism, the cultural economies of fandom, spectator theory, and Marxism. Subjects addressed include:

- studying Ripley and the *Alien* films
- pedagogy and political correctness in martial arts cinema
- Judy Garland fandom on the World Wide Web
- stardom and serial fantasies: Thomas Harris's *Hannibal*
- Tom Hanks and the globalization of stars
- queer Bollywood
- Jackie Chan and black/African-American audiences
- *Home Alone* and the boy-child video spectator
- *12 Monkeys*, postmodernism, and urban space

Contributors: Rich Cante, Rey Chow, Steven Cohan, Pamela Church Gibson, Inderpal Grewal, Ina Rae Hark, Caren Kaplan, Marcia Landy, Gina Marchetti, Toby Miller, Linda Mizejewski, Meaghan Morris, Diane Negra, Chon A. Noriega, Kevin Ohi, Angelo Restivo, Matthew Ruben, Paul Smith, Eric Smoodin, Thomas Waugh, Sharon Willis, Steve Wurtzler, Patricia R. Zimmermann.

Matthew Tinkcom is Assistant Professor in the Department of English and Graduate Program in Communication, Culture and Technology at Georgetown University. **Amy Villarejo** is Assistant Professor in the Women's Studies Program and Department of Theatre, Film and Dance at Cornell University.

Keyframes: Popular Cinema and Cultural Studies

Edited by Matthew Tinkcom and
Amy Villarejo

London and New York

First published 2001
by Routledge
11 New Fetter Lane, London EC4P 4EE

Simultaneously published in the USA and Canada
by Routledge
29 West 35th Street, New York, NY 10001

Routledge is an imprint of the Taylor & Francis Group

© 2001 Matthew Tinkcom and Amy Villarejo for selection and
editorial matter: individual chapters © 2001 the contributors

Typeset in Galliard by
The Running Head Limited, Cambridge
Printed and bound in Great Britain by
TJ International Ltd, Padstow, Cornwall

British Library Cataloguing in Publication Data
A catalogue record for this book is available from the British Library

Library of Congress Cataloging in Publication Data
A catalogue record for this book has been requested

ISBN 0–415–20282–5 (pbk)
ISBN 0–415–20281–7 (hbk)

Contents

Figures

Contributors

Rich Cante is Assistant Professor of Media and Cultural Studies in the Department of Communication Studies at the University of North Carolina at Chapel Hill. He is currently working on contemporary media pornography from a variety of historical and theoretical angles, as well as a book, *Gay Male AIDS and the Form(s) of Contemporary U.S. Culture*.

Rey Chow is Andrew W. Mellon Professor of the Humanities at Brown University where she teaches in the Departments of Comparative Literature, and Modern Culture and Media. She is the author of numerous essays and articles, and a number of books, including *Primitive Passions: Visuality, Sexuality, Ethnography, and Contemporary Chinese Cinema* (Columbia University Press, 1995) and *Ethics after Idealism: Theory—Culture—Ethnicity—Reading* (Indiana University Press, 1998). She is currently completing a new work, *The Protestant Ethnic and the Spirit of Capitalism*.

Pamela Church Gibson is a Senior Lecturer in Cultural Studies at the London College of Fashion who has published essays on heritage and history, film and fashion. She has co-edited and contributed to *Dirty Looks: Women, Power, Pornography* (British Film Institute, 1993), *The Oxford Guide to Film Studies* (Oxford University Press, 1998), and *Fashion Cultures: Theories, Explorations, Analysis* (Routledge, 2000). She is currently working on a book provisionally entitled *Women and Film: Audiences and Consumption*, which should appear in 2001.

Steven Cohan is Professor of English at Syracuse University. He is the author of *Masked Men: Masculinity and the Movies in the Fifties* (Indiana University Press, 1997) and co-editor with Ina Rae Hark of *Screening the Male: Exploring Masculinities in Hollywood Cinema* (Routledge, 1993) and *The Road Movie Book* (Routledge, 1997). His most recent articles have appeared in the collections *Reinventing Film Studies*, ed. Gledhill and William (Oxford University Press, 2000) and *Out Takes: Essays on Queer Theory and Film*, ed. Ellis Hanson (Duke University Press, 1999). He is currently working on a book on the MGM musical.

Inderpal Grewal is Professor of Women's Studies at San Francisco State University. She is author of *Home and Harem: Nation, Gender, Empire and Cultures of Travel* (Duke University Press, 1996) and co-editor, with Caren Kaplan, of *Scattered Hegemonies: Postmodernity and Transnational Feminist Practices* (University of Minnesota Press, 1994). Along with Akhil Gupta and Aihwa Ong, she has co-edited a special issue of *Positions: East Asia Cultures Critique* entitled "Asian Transnationalities:

Media, Markets and Migration," and is now completing a special issue of *Signs* on gender and globalization.

Ina Rae Hark is Professor of English and Director of Film Studies at the University of South Carolina. She is co-editor of *Screening the Male* (Routledge, 1993) and *The Road Movie Book* (Routledge, 1997), and the author of numerous articles and book chapters on gender politics in film and television.

Caren Kaplan is Associate Professor and Chair of the Department of Women's Studies at the University of California at Berkeley. She is the author of *Questions of Travel: Postmodern Discourses of Displacement* (Duke University Press, 1996) and the co-editor with Inderpal Grewal of *Scattered Hegemonies: Postmodernity and Transnational Feminist Practices* (University of Minnesota Press, 1994) and with Norma Alarcón and Minoo Moallem of *Between Women and Nation: Nationalisms, Transnational Feminisms, and the State* (Duke University Press, 1999).

Marcia Landy is Distinguished Service Professor of English/Film Studies with a secondary appointment in the French and Italian Department at the University of Pittsburgh. Her book publications include *Fascism in Film: The Italian Commercial Cinema, 1930–1943* (Princeton University Press, 1986); *Imitations of Life: A Reader on Film and Television Melodrama* (Wayne State University Press, 1991); *British Genres: Cinema and Society 1930–1960* (Princeton University Press, 1991); *Film, Politics and Gramsci* (University of Minnesota Press, 1994); *Cinematic Uses of the Past* (University of Minnesota Press, 1996); *The Folklore of Consensus: Theatricality in the Italian Commercial Cinema, 1930–1943* (SUNY Press, 1998); *Queen Christina* (with Amy Villarejo) (British Film Institute, 1995); *Italian Film* (Cambridge University Press, 2000); and *History and Memory in Cinema and Television* (Rutgers University Press, 2000).

Gina Marchetti is an Associate Professor in the Department of Cinema and Photography at Ithaca College. She is the author of *Romance and the "Yellow Peril": Race, Sex and Discursive Strategies in Hollywood Fiction* (University of California Press, 1993) and has published articles in *Journal of Film and Video*, *Genders*, *Journal of Communication Inquiry*, and others, as well as *Jump Cut*, where she serves on the editorial board. Her current research involves transnationalism and screen culture in Hollywood and Asia.

Toby Miller is Professor of Cultural Studies and Cultural Policy in the Department of Cinema Studies at New York University. He is the editor of *Television and New Media*, co-editor of *Social Text*, and the author of *The Well-Tempered Self: Citizenship, Culture, and the Postmodern Subject* (Johns Hopkins University Press, 1993); *Contemporary Australian Television* (University of New South Wales Press, 1994); *The Avengers* (British Film Institute, 1997); *Technologies of Truth: Cultural Citizenship and the Popular Media* (University of Minnesota Press, 1998); and *Popular Culture and Everyday Life* (Sage, 1998). He co-edited *SportCult* (University of Minnesota Press, 1999); *A Companion to Film Theory* (University of Minnesota Press, 1999); and *Film and Theory: An Anthology* (Blackwell, 2000).

Linda Mizejewski is a Professor of English at Ohio State University. She is the author of *Divine Decadence: Fascism, Female Spectacle, and the Makings of Sally Bowles*

(Princeton University Press, 1992) and *Ziegfeld Girl: Image and Icon in Culture and Cinema* (Duke University Press, 1999). She is currently at work on a book on the picturing of the female dick.

Meaghan Morris is Chair Professor of Cultural Studies, Lingnan University, Hong Kong. An experienced film critic who has lectured and written widely on action cinema, her books include *The Pirate's Fiancée: Feminism, Reading, Postmodernism* (Verso, 1988); *Australian Cultural Studies: A Reader*, co-edited with John Frow (Allen & Unwin, 1993); and *Too Soon, Too Late: History in Popular Culture* (Indiana University Press, 1998).

Diane Negra is Assistant Professor in the Department of Radio, TV, and Film at the University of North Texas. She is the author of two forthcoming books.

Chon A. Noriega is Associate Professor in the UCLA Department of Film and Television. He is author of *Shot in America: Television, the State, and the Rise of Chicano Cinema* (University of Minnesota Press, 2000) and editor of eight books, including *I, Carmelita Tropicana: Performing Between Cultures* (Beacon, 2000), and *Visible Nations: Latin American Cinema and Video* (University of Minnesota Press, 2000). Since 1996, he has been editor of *Aztlán: A Journal of Chicano Studies*. He has curated numerous art exhibitions, most recently, *East of the River: Chicano Art Collectors Anonymous* (Santa Monica Museum of Art).

Kevin Ohi teaches English at Cornell University, where, having completed a dissertation on aestheticism and sexuality, he received his Ph.D. in 2001. He has also published articles on Henry James, Vladimir Nabokov, James Baldwin, and the film *The Boys of St. Vincent*.

Angelo Restivo is Visiting Assistant Professor at Northwestern University. He has formerly taught in the film programs at the University of Iowa and University of Michigan. His book, *The Cinema of Economic Miracles*, is forthcoming from Duke University Press.

Matthew Ruben earned his Ph.D. in English and Urban Studies from the University of Pennsylvania. His dissertation, "The Cultural Geography of Neoliberalism in the U.S.," examines how political-economic change during the last third of the twentieth century was manifested in popular culture and metropolitan development. He is currently Development Director for Bread and Roses Community Fund in Philadelphia.

Paul Smith is Professor of Media and Cultural Studies at the University of Sussex. His most recent books are *Clint Eastwood* (University of Minnesota Press, 1993), *Boys: Masculinities in Contemporary Culture* (ed., Westview Press, 1996) and *Millennial Dreams* (Verso, 1997). He is currently working on a cultural studies manifesto and a book about the political economy of the new media.

Eric Smoodin is Film, Media, and Philosophy Editor at the University of California Press. His forthcoming book is *A Thousand Pairs of Eyes and Ears: Film Reception and Frank Capra*.

Thomas Waugh has been teaching Film Studies at Concordia University, Montreal since 1976, and has also innovated interdisciplinary curricula on HIV/AIDS and in queer studies. His books are *The Fruit Machine: Twenty Years of Writing on Queer Cinema* (Duke University Press, 2000); *Hard to Imagine: Gay Male Eroticism in Photography and Film from their Beginnings to Stonewall* (Columbia University Press, 1996); and *"Show Us Life": Towards a History and Aesthetics of the Committed Documentary* (Scarecrow Press, 1984, 1988). He has been researching and teaching Indian Cinema since 1988.

Sharon Willis is Professor of French and Visual and Cultural Studies and Director of the Film Studies Program at the University of Rochester. A co-editor of *Camera Obscura*, she is author of *Marguerite Duras: Writing on the Body* (University of Illinois Press, 1987) and *High Contrast: Race and Gender in Contemporary Hollywood Film* (Duke University Press, 1997).

Steve Wurtzler is an Assistant Professor in the English Department at Georgetown University. His work on sound technology has been published in the journal *Film History* and the anthology *Sound Theory/Sound Practice*. In addition to an essay on US radio in the forthcoming anthology *Communities of the Air: Radio Century, Radio Culture*, he is co-editing a special issue of *LIT* on film adaptation.

Patricia R. Zimmermann is Professor of Cinema and Photography at Ithaca College. She is the author of *Reel Families: A Social History of Amateur Film* (Indiana University Press, 1995) and *States of Emergency: Documentaries, Wars, Democracies* (University of Minnesota Press, 2000). She has also worked as a film, video, and new media curator.

Acknowledgments

The editors and publisher would like to thank copyright holders for permission to reprint the following chapters:

Chapter 2: Inderpal Grewal and Caren Kaplan, "Warrior Marks: Global Womanism's Neo-colonial Discourse in a Multicultural context," *Camera Obscura* 39 (September 1996): 5–33. © 2000 Duke University Press. All rights reserved. Reprinted with permission.

Chapter 12: Rey Chow, "Nostalgia of the New Wave: Structure in Wong Kar-wai's *Happy Together*," *Camera Obscura* 42 (September 2000). © 2000 Duke University Press. All rights reserved. Reprinted with permission.

Chapter 14: Kevin Ohi, "Devouring Creation: Cannibalism, Sodomy, and the Scene of Analysis in *Suddenly, Last Summer*," *Cinema Journal* 38 (3): 27–49. © 1999 University of Texas Press. All rights reserved.

Chapter 19: Eric Smoodin, "'Compulsory' Viewing for Every Citizen: *Mr. Smith* and the Rhetoric of Reception," *Cinema Journal* 35 (2) (Winter 1996): 3–23. © 1996 University of Texas Press. All rights reserved.

Preface

Perhaps one of the most pernicious ideologies at work in the world today is that intellectual work is a singular and isolated enterprise, and there is no small irony to the idea that the fantasy of the scholarly "ivory tower" has now officially yielded to the forces under which colleges and universities are becoming increasingly modeled on the corporate sector, all of this in the name of "privatization." Despite this, and despite the plain fact that the work of scholars frequently *does* isolate them one from the other, this volume should stand as proof of the possibilities of collective work, to the degree that its authors all found to be compelling the project of thinking about how the fields of film studies and cultural studies have transformed each other. We thank them all for their tireless energies and their unending patience. We also owe an immense debt of gratitude to Rebecca Barden of Routledge for approaching us with the idea of a project of this size and guiding it through its various stages, and to Alistair Daniel for answering all our questions. The Running Head provided us with a fine copy-editor and shepherded the manuscript through production.

We would also like to thank Georgetown University for its support of this project in the form of a Summer Research Grant and a Junior Faculty Research Grant for Matthew Tinkcom. We thank the A. D. White Society for the Humanities at Cornell University for its support of our collaborative work. We also owe thanks to the administrative staff of Cornell's Department of Theatre, Film and Dance for help in preparing the manuscript for submission. Amy Villarejo's First Year Writing Seminar students in the summer of 2000 gave us thoughtful suggestions for revision of the introduction; we are grateful for their careful readings.

The University of Texas Press and Duke University Press generously granted us permissions to reprint articles from *Cinema Journal* and *Camera Obscura*, respectively.

Numerous friends talked us through the project: Steven Cohan, Anne Cubilie, Cathy Davidson, Pamela Fox, Jamie Poster, Ina Hark, Marcia Landy, Michael Ragussis, Paul Smith, Christine So, Elayne Tobin, Ken Wissoker, Rebecca Schneider, Patty Zimmermann, Marilyn Rivchin (with additional thanks for the title suggestion), and David Bathrick.

Finally, we are grateful to Don and Merna Villarejo, and to James and Alberta Tinkcom, to Matthew Veltkamp, to Andrea Hammer, to Betty, to Slash and to Taag, and to each other.

The degree of possible overlap between **representative** and **representation** in their political and artistic senses is very difficult to estimate. In the sense of the typical, which then stands *for* ("as" or "in place of") others or other things, in either context, there is probably a deep common cultural assumption. At the same time, within this assumption, there is the contradiction expressed both in the arguments about **representative democracy** and in the argument in art about relations between the **representational** and the **representative**.

Raymond Williams, from entry on "representative" in Keywords

Keyframe editing: "One further consideration when making a workprint is whether or not to have it and the camera film coded or edge numbered to make exact matching easy. Professional 16 mm camera film invariably comes with latent image edge numbers (sometimes called key numbers). These numbers are visible—with transmitted light, that is, light which must pass through the film—after the film has been processed, and appear at intervals of twenty or forty frames (every six or twelve inches)." Thus, in the process of filmmaking, the necessity of light, to the goal of a certain kind of precision.

Lenny Lipton, Independent Filmmaking

Introduction

The study of cinema at the university level has become increasingly central in the United States, the United Kingdom, and Australasia, positioned in a number of disciplines such as the history of art, languages and literatures, communications, and emerging work on the histories of mass technologies (film among them). Simultaneously, approaches to film studies which have taken their cue from literary analyses (formalism, semiotics, auteur, and genre theory) have recently seen the challenge of new intellectual work in the form of "cultural studies," an umbrella term for a host of imbricated critical projects such as feminism, queer theory, race studies, poststructuralisms, and materialist analyses. This encounter, of film studies and cultural studies, is the topic of this collection of essays about cinema, with the questions of cultural studies at the foreground.

It should be clear at the outset that, while this collection of essays takes as its mandate the examination of film as it is transformed by the questions of cultural studies, this mandate perhaps already engages with a pernicious assumption that cultural studies, its history and its effects, can be neatly gathered together without attending to the specificity of the very challenges that the field has encountered in its travels during the past four decades in the anglophone academy. Indeed, as we hope to convey, the field is perhaps best understood as a set of engagements with an ongoing set of animating questions: questions about the social distribution of power, forms of social difference, theorizations about the relations between individuals ("subjects") and their social networks, and the role that mass-disseminated commodities and representations play in sustaining the social formations that have arisen in the expansion of the industries that produce popular culture and its ideologies. Frequently, there has been little consensus among even those practitioners of cultural studies about how best to go about the intellectual work of responding to these questions, moving from the concern of what constitutes a worthy object of critical analysis to that of how best to ascertain and understand any given object or text's effects upon those who consume it. As Lawrence Grossberg suggests in an essay on the history of the Centre for Contemporary Cultural Studies (CCCS) at the University of Birmingham (the founding institutional home for the earliest work done in the name of cultural studies), "if cultural studies is seen as an open-ended and ongoing theoretical struggle to understand and intervene into the existing organizations of active domination and subordination within the formations of culture, then the boundaries of the tradition are themselves unstable and changing, sites of contestation and debate."[1]

---

1 Lawrence Grossberg, "Formations of Cultural Studies: An American in Birmingham," in Valda Blundell, John Shepherd, and Ian Taylor, eds, *Relocating Cultural Studies: Developments in Theory and Research* (London: Routledge, 1993), 21–66.

Grossberg describes the Centre's challenges to establish for itself a workable theoretical basis for understanding how cultural productions shape the lives of men and women in industrialized Western societies. Part of the virtue of his account is how, without resorting to any teleological history that would claim to have perfected such forms of intellectual engagement, it helps to recall the fragmented and sometimes tendentious intellectual engagements experienced among the members of the Centre. This volume, in fact, enjoins with Grossberg's sense that cultural studies, at the very least, needs always to renew itself by "requir[ing] us to recognize that it has *always* responded to the *particular* conditions of its intellectual, political, social and historical contexts [where] the result is that within the tradition, theoretical positions have always been provisional takes, meant to give us a better purchase on the world and always implicated within ongoing intellectual and political struggles."

That said, the more pressing question for the present reader might be: why film and cultural studies as the nexus upon which this book insists? The easy answer to this question could take the form of moving the reader to the very opening of this introduction, where the institutional embrace of both film studies and cultural studies among higher education in anglophone settings around the planet would help to remind us that what the volume in hand attempts to convey is how the increased presence of one form of intellectual inquiry, cultural studies, has helped to transform a particular other field, that of the study of the moving image. Simultaneously, one might respond that film studies has summoned its own perfectly adequate critical languages for the analysis of cinematic texts and a variety of historical models for understanding the roles that film has played as a mass cultural form. A perhaps more satisfying answer to this question can be undertaken, though, in conveying how the works included in this book can help students to understand the specificity of each's questions as they press scholars to forge new critical knowledges through the problems of understanding power and social difference, and in the sections that follow, we give more specific accounts of the fields of inquiry included. Here, though, let us offer a more general set of responses. First, the volume offers those interested in the critical scrutiny of film a condensed single source for a number of approaches to film and is intended to be a vital resource for introducing students to the variety of projects possible in film studies, as well as providing those interested in cultural studies the opportunity to situate some of the questions of cultural studies in relation to more specific contemporary cinematic visions. More specifically, the essays demonstrate the possibilities of rethinking recent cinema in light of work in feminism, queer studies, race studies, critiques of nationalism, colonialism and postcolonialism, the cultural economies of fandom, spectator theory, and Marxism and its debates, as these sites of inquiry themselves might be said to cross-pollinate each other and press one another to achieve greater nuance in their approaches to film as formal and social text. Second, this collection is seen as a way for students and scholars to examine the kinds of intellectual work currently being undertaken in the increasingly *hybridized* fields of film studies and cultural studies and as a way of bringing forth the modes of critical work on *production* of cinema that have emerged in film studies while following more closely the movement of such texts to their audiences, a movement in the sphere of *consumption* upon which cultural studies has focused in its emphasis on subcultures and the specificity of the cultural commodity to the formation of social identities and practices.

With this in mind, this collection is offered not as a rejection of more traditional forms of film studies, but as one that builds upon the work of previous critical and theoretical projects. These essays are grounded in the analysis of cinema—its formal organization, its modes of production, its substantial pre-existing theoretical models, and they address the media-specific qualities of cinema as it marks the particular ideological and social formation of the past ten to fifteen years. In short, this volume is intended to offer critical work that is underpinned by close, elegant treatment of cinema as a technological medium. Yet, these formal and technological questions need to be foregrounded as ones also about the labor-intensity and expense of the production of cinema, the circulation of cinema into mutating and often unexpected spheres and contexts of exhibition, and the variety of subject-responses to the meanings of film. Further, such questions of production, distribution, and viewing are always imbricated with material factors of cinematography, editing, sound, lighting, effects, stardom, acting, and publicity, to name a few, and the essays that follow are situated as much in the language and history of cinema as in the theoretical terrain of cultural studies' animating forces.

Complicating matters in new and exciting ways is a sense in this book's essays that the opposition of "mainstream" and "alternative" cinematic production and reception becomes increasingly untenable as a designation of reactionary and revolutionary practices. Part of the immense contribution to the ideological critique of popular culture brought to bear by cultural studies has been the sense that *some* Hollywood cinema, for example, embodies complicated and contradictory social relations and by no means can simply be dismissed because of its corporate roots. At the same time, the move to celebrate "alternative" cinematic visions in a singularly uncritical way has led to a canonization of films that deserve a more thoughtful intervention than the celebratory. Contemporary cinema, that is, needs to be understood in terms of hegemonic (a term we discuss further below) structures, and the best forms of ideological critique, whatever their interest, attend to the complex ways in which films make their appeals to us as viewers in the multiple and specific places in which we as social subjects incorporate cinema into our everyday lives. What cultural studies has sought to understand from early in its own history is how apparently dominant and apparently homogenized commodities—such as corporate produced cinema—can, however momentarily, sustain within smaller social settings ("subcultures") alternative or resistant readings (see again Grossberg's account of the work of Hall, Hebdige, McRobbie, Morley *et al.*); equally worthy of consideration is how the recent emphasis on "independent" cinema demands a healthy suspicion about what kinds of political responses might be summoned—never mind implied—in attempts by some filmmakers to distance themselves from the Hollywood product, all the while that the independent product seems to mimic the formal, economic and political strategies of its more mainstream cousin. In attempting to encompass films that appear in ever more widespread circumstances (the "blockbuster" Hollywood film) *and* films that are less widely available, this book hopes to be able to steer students and scholars of recent cinema to some less commonly known films that students would be well-served to begin to investigate. In so far as this book seeks to capture and display the "state of the art," it has modestly millennial (an oxymoron?) aspirations to assess the most enabling critical work on the academic landscape.

In the sections that follow, we outline the brief history of several different areas of critical inquiry in which we suggest film and cultural studies have been able to inform one another, and one form of engaged debate might be to consider how these areas of critical focus, such as feminism and queer theory, came to be encompassed in film studies and cultural studies without that having been the specific intent of scholars at the CCCS. In that regard, critical inquiry can seldom shape the places to which its commentary takes subsequent practitioners. Nevertheless, in order to understand the kinds of questions that animate critical and historical work on film, the following areas will help students to trace their own positions (and those of their faculty!) as they consider the histories and concerns of these fields.

Marxism

The fact that the philosophical enterprise of the nineteenth century European philosopher Karl Marx (1818–1883) should continue to sustain critics of the current social arrangements beheld locally and globally might come as a surprise to the student of contemporary media culture; after all, with the end of the cold war between the West and the Soviet Union and the emergent dynamic capitalist economy that now extends into seemingly every aspect of modern life, Marx's call for a revolutionary action against capitalism might seem outdated and worthy of what Marx himself called the "scrap-heap of history." Indeed, many of Marx's assertions about the quick decline of capitalism, victim of its own internal contradictions and unable to sustain the promises of a marketplace that would grant to each subject an increased buying power and affluence through his labors, have not come true, and in places where there have been attempts by working classes to seize power and ownership of production, the ultimate fate of those societies seems given over to the dominance of the "magic hand" of the market that Adam Smith so famously enjoined.

Why, then, the renewed interest in how Marx thought about capitalism? It should be pointed out that there has been in Western societies a long-standing interest in Marx that is seldom recorded in popular media beyond trite vilifications or nostalgic sentiment. The "New Left" in Great Britain, fostered by such intellectuals as Raymond Williams and Stuart Hall in the 1960s and 1970s, found in Marx's writings a language for describing the rapid transformation of older forms of life (such as the disappearance of working-class life into new social configurations around consumerism) and the potential role of a stronger state to mete out social benefits, such as education and universal health care (the now apparently distasteful "welfare state"), and advocated a role for working people in the distribution of wealth produced by industrial societies. Intellectuals and activists in the United States, bruised by the aggressive hand of the state in the 1950s in its attempts to ensure that political power not disappear into the hands of those who labor on behalf of profit, discovered vitalizing energies in the work of such expatriate critics from Germany as Theodor Adorno, Max Horkheimer, Bertolt Brecht, and Herbert Marcuse (exiles from the "Frankfurt School" founded in Germany in the 1930s) and their critical approaches to the manufacture of culture for the masses who now discovered their lives saturated by the structures of industrial life demanded by capital (the distinction between leisure and work, the forms of entertainment that seemed like so much distraction from any agency in the shaping of history, and the homogenization of culture on national and global scales). Remarkably, what is often characterized as the "Frankfurt School" approach (a generalization that probably too often steamrolls over the nuances of these critics' works) has left many readers of Marx dissatisfied, to the extent that the apparently unrelenting homogenization of mass forms, detected famously by Horkheimer and Adorno in an essay on the subject,[2] are not necessarily the questions that interest current scholars of Marx, despite the lingering effects of the trenchant comments of these critics.

---

2 Theodor Adorno and Max Horkheimer, "The Culture Industry: Enlightenment as Mass Deception," in Simon During, ed., *The Cultural Studies Reader* (London: Routledge, 1993), 29–43.

Even more pressing for readers of the present volume would be the question of why Marx matters for the analysis of contemporary media. Several factors come into play in order to understand this abiding interest. Marx was profoundly interested in the fact that capital not only dispensed consumer goods by streamlining the cycles of production —whereby raw goods and labor (harvested now on a global scale through the imperial activities of European and, later, American nations) were combined to make cheaper and more accessible the things that capital can produce and innovate—but also had a representational role. This emerges for Marx, among other places, in the writings of the *Grundrisse*, a set of working notes he initially sketched out for himself about the project that would become the lengthy three-volume *Capital.* Here, Marx wonders about how capital might transform human societies in its traffic in things that stand in for other things—i.e. representation. Marx sets out the premise that the value of a commodity is predicated on the labor and raw goods demanded in its manufacture—that its monetary value encapsulates the efforts of humans (labor) which capitalism extracts from masses of men and women. Thus, the commodity represents their labor (for which they are rewarded in the form of wages), but it is an uneasy equation, mainly because labor seems so amorphous and intangible a phenomenon, while the commodity seems to have a fixed materiality in the world: one can hardly recall the labor involved in its making, even as Marx reminds us that the commodity might be read as labor's "congealing." Thus, the value of the commodity seems so common-sensical, while in fact it is founded on something apparently invisible (although it is hardly lived as invisible by those who do the work!). Even more pressing for the problem of representation that Marx theorizes, in order to facilitate the movement of the commodity through its production, distribution and consumption, capitalism becomes a new kind of life for humans because of how it transforms money. Previously, money was assumed to be able to stand in for the things exchanged because it held some value in itself—gold and other precious metals had a kind of appeal because of their own apparently intrinsic qualities of durability, ease of transport, etc. When money becomes the basis for all exchange in the new industrial economies, it takes on another abstract quality that Marx is challenged to pin down— and it is one of Marx's great theoretical flourishes that he maintains that money carries with it two forms of value: money as exchange and money as profit. Workers and owners use money in different ways (the former use it to buy things, while the latter use it to start new enterprises to generate yet more profit) but they seldom recognize currency's dual roles; and in this regard, money's capacity to *represent* value is often thus deceptive.

This short detour through a portion of Marx's critique of capitalism helps us to think about another set of representations, those of the cinema itself. It is perhaps not coincidental that the cinema emerges as a capitalist technology, demonstrating the fact of mass production of moving images that can be moved with relative ease and given to large numbers of people. Even more to the point, the cinema can offer those humans who dwell in industrial capitalist societies images and sounds that help them to make sense of the rapid transformations that they experience—but these images and sounds are not solely to be read as standing in for the world which they record. That is, they are *ideological*—they carry with them arguments for how we might see the world, sometimes in more celebratory fashion and sometimes with more critical weight. (For an excellent summary of this topic, see Mike Cormack's *Ideology*.)[3] We should, however, be

3 Mike Cormack, *Ideology* (Ann Arbor: University of Michigan Press, 1992).

careful in how we think about how ideology works, for it can too easily become an argument for the force of mass imagery as a kind of deception, which renders the recipients of popular forms as theoretically somehow naive when they in fact are probably more sophisticated and, indeed, suspicious of how a film, for example, attempts to offer up a recognizable world. The fact that the bulk of popular cinemas do indeed attempt to show something that approximates our own lives (with a few important exceptions, such as the historical film and the films of science fiction) should, on the other hand, not dispel the fact that they seek selectively to represent our private and social selves back to us. Further, they are made by an industry that has greater purchase upon the now global movement of their product, so that, in the case of Hollywood, the largely white and privileged subjects of Hollywood film now travel to a mostly non-white and increasingly industrialized working population that receives such images.

The question of cinema as an ideological force situates film studies in relation to one of the most important intellectual debates in the Western academy in the 1960s and 1970s, a debate that emerges from French intellectual life and moves out to other settings. In brief, this argument about ideology takes shape around the writings of French philosopher Louis Althusser (1918–1990) and his interest in a way of conceiving how ideology is lived and breathed on a daily basis. Rather than think of ideology as something imposed from above (say, by the state, as in Soviet propaganda), to which individuals are largely hostile but about which they are often complacent, Althusser argued that ideology might be thought of as the sense that could be made of the social world in relation to the subject's material circumstances and which, while not adequately representing the forms of power or alienation beheld in Western societies—as those things too are lived on a daily basis—partially and provisionally satisfies. In this regard, ideology is more like something that one inhabits and constantly has to have renewed, lest one forget or disregard its explanations.

Key to Althusser's notion of ideology are two ways of thinking about ourselves as social beings. The first is the concept of the "subject." By now this term is so widely used, quite often to refer simply to "a person," that we forget the powerful distinctions that Althusser made in addressing individuals as subjects. Subjects have a dual status under capitalism: they are subject *to* its forms of social regulation (such as having to work particular hours or to perform the social role of woman-as-caretaker), but they also have the power to enact themselves as subjects of actions—they have volition and desires and at least ostensibly can participate in Western democracies through their forms of organization and voting. This combined emphasis on the individual as a social actor who is capable of action and yet is acted upon—by ideology—carries with it the dynamic sense of the *subjectivity* of each individual, characterized by such features as sexuality, gender, race, and ethnicity (some of the more heated debates about the worth of the theoretical category of the subject have appeared around the degree to which various features of social difference, such as gender or race, play a role in determining how one experiences subjectivity).

Cinema forms a fascinating site upon which to think through the implications of the concept of the subject, and that is precisely what happened in the writings of the British journal *Screen* in a period of intense critical debate during the 1970s that produced some of the most influential writings about film. The "*Screen* debates," as they are sometimes described, turned on the ways that cinema stages us as subjects—both acknowledging our desires and yet shaping them simultaneously. In its capacity to wield the technologies of the film on a mass scale to shape the experience of subjectivity, cinema came to have a not-too-coincidental status accorded to it as one of the primary sites of modernity that molded masses of people into social subjects. As described in greater detail below in relation to feminism and psychoanalysis, much of the writing in *Screen* during this period embraced not only Althusser's notion of the subject but the refinements of the French psychoanalytic theory which suggested that the experience of subjectivity is not always a reasonable or rational one—we may act and be acted upon, but how we do so and the reasons we make certain choices may emanate from the unconscious as much as from enlightened debate.

The second concept from Althusser that animated interest in the notion of ideology rests on his distinction between forms of institutional coercion. Althusser argues that while there are, of course, direct forms of coercion and expression of the will of the state or of capital's regimentations, institutions he labeled "Repressive State Apparatuses" or "RSAs" (for example, prisons and mental hospitals), most subjects seldom encounter such a direct expression of power. Why, then, are there so many obedient subjects? What produces forms of social compliance without the appearance of repression? There must be other social formations, Althusser reasoned, which are as active in the management of social subjects as the RSAs, and these institutions, which Althusser christened "Ideological State Apparatuses" or "ISAs," take the form of schools, universities, social clubs, organized religion, sports, etc. Even as such institutions take as their prompting the improvement of the lives of the humans who inhabit them, they are powerful conduits for ideas about what constitutes appropriate and inappropriate thoughts, statements, and gestures in subjects. Most subjects do not need to be repressed because, Althusser argued in short, they are taught how to repress themselves through the ways of thinking given to them by various ISAs.

The concept of the subject and the distinction between RSAs and ISAs are provocative ideas, although with apparently serious shortcomings. They give the idea of ideology a kind of priority that makes it seem incontestable as a theoretical model: if it ignores the complexity of our situation as subjects of *multiple* ideologies, the notion becomes unwieldy and simplistic in its rendering of some monolothic set of beliefs that we are said to subscribe to (though Althusser himself distinguishes between a general theory of "ideology"—in the singular—and these multiple "ideologies"). The intent of Althusser's work, in fact, was to counter such a notion of an overarching and determining structure and to suggest how ideologies are multiple and often contradictory. For example, we might consider how the labor of women is crosshatched by ideologies of maternalism about how women are said to function primarily in the sphere of reproduction, as physical and emotional support for the production of new subjects (children), and there are yet other ideologies about how women should express their apparent freedom and creativity by entering the workforce and becoming vital producers in the sphere of industry. There is no reason to doubt the pleasures of motherhood or of work— the important problem here is the remarkable lack of women's say in the ways that their lives are determined through such ideologies, and the paucity of institutions run by and for women in collective fashion. To conclude this example, then, we might wonder at the function of contemporary films which offer to women spectators pleasurable visions of maternalism and work: seldom does one encounter a film that attempts to encompass both those social formations at once.

Althusser's refinement of the notion of ideology, and the fact of mass-disseminated films as a form of representation made by profit-driven corporations, merge with another intellectual strain that appeared on the historical stage at a highly politicized moment in Europe through the work of Antonio Gramsci (1891–1937). Writing in the 1930s, Gramsci, an Italian intellectual of Sardinian descent, wondered at what he understood to be a remarkable choice to be made by the citizens of the nations of the West, a choice among the options of socialist revolution (which he supported), capitalist "democracy," or the wholesale transformation of the relation between the state and capital heralded by the fascism of 1930s Europe. Gramsci refused, in his own historical setting, to regard the historical subjects around him as duped or deceived by what they witnessed in the various political options available to them, but instead insisted that power is achieved by those who enjoy its benefits over other humans through what he labeled "consent." More often than not, according to Gramsci, humans are not coerced into their roles as workers who labor unfairly on behalf of capitalist profit, but rather give their consent to such social arrangements because of other more limited political and material benefits made available, and it is the work of popular representations to remind them of those benefits, or even of just the promise of those benefits. For Gramsci, fascism succeeded in Europe for its duration because it could suggest that the reorganization of the state and capitalist enterprises would eventually be beneficial to those who ostensibly (and often in fact) lost many of their privileges to speak and act as members of a political body (such as the Italian state).

Gramsci's writings were neglected until the 1970s, when critics, many of them working at the Birmingham Centre, found in his work a way of understanding how capitalist societies maintain a delicate balance between, on the one hand, insisting that the people who dwell in such societies have to get up and go to work (or maintain a kind of subsistence on public benefits) and, on the other, forestalling political interventions by the larger masses who do not enjoy the wealth possessed by capital's smaller sector of owners and shareholders. Returning to the idea of popular texts as having within them ideologies (or more properly, being ideological), Gramsci's work offered a strong counter to the notion of all capitalist representations as ideological (itself often frequently elitist: only left-wing critics might claim to know how dire capital's effects were). With this in mind, we discover a new form of complication in the critique of mass-imagery, one sustained by the sense that such imagery does indeed help to gain the consent of those governed by the state and dwelling within capital's social hierarchies, and yet not ignorant (and perhaps even disrespectful) of those political and spectatorial subjects who find in the forms of mass entertainment acknowledgment (even half-hearted or cynical) of the fact of their political and economic subjection. Gramsci's name for this matrix of shaky and hard-won power is "hegemony."

Thus, a film that might seem to some critics as the embodiment of all that is most reprehensible in the forms of popular entertainment could be the central and sole critical engagement with the popular that is available to spectators without access to forms of education that should apparently tell them that such a film ought to be avoided. In this regard, the film offers an image of the social world that appeals to a given subject, even as he or she knows it not to be the sole way of thinking about the world of political and economic subjection in which he or she dwells, and allows us to think of film as *hegemonic*, in its capacity to acknowledge that social injustice is maintained and yet to remind the viewer that he or she might in the short run benefit from such injustices. The viewer acknowledges the parts of a film that maintain an appeal while recognizing that its source—say, Hollywood—hardly cares to represent other less palatable experiences such as racism or exploitation (despite the temporary fix of the "happy ending"). The point for a critic to consider is not simply that the film in question maintains such dissatisfactions, but *how* it seeks to forestall social action by viewers. One critic's poison is another viewer's manna, and part of the intellectual thrust of the most engaged work in cultural studies has been to take seriously the meanings of such a viewer's investments as they can transform the critic's project, all the while steering carefully between the languages of valediction and dismissal.

Psychoanalysis and feminism

Just as surely as we invoke Sergei Eisenstein's theories of montage, any student of cinema in the Anglophone university worth her salt can usually cite Laura Mulvey's essay, "Visual Pleasure and Narrative Cinema," as one of the founding texts of feminist film theory.[4] One of its central contentions, that femininity in classical Hollywood cinema functions as a passive spectacle constituted through the active male gaze, is summoned these days and oft repeated as a truism, through what was literally a form of shorthand in her essay: male/active, female/passive. But any careful reading of Mulvey's piece (not to mention the debates in the British journal *Screen* in which that essay sought to intervene) would show such a shorthand to wobble precariously. In Mulvey's view, as in ours, the psychoanalytic edifice that supports, indeed reinforces, such a clean-cut distinction is precisely the same scaffold that can render it unstable.

In "Visual Pleasure," Mulvey sought, in fact, to wield psychoanalysis as a weapon in the battle for a critical consciousness caught in the ambush of Hollywood's constraining and constricting representations of gender relations. What Mulvey noticed was that, *overwhelmingly* in the commercial narrative cinema of the studio era, the spectator constructed through the look of the cinematic apparatus is complicit with a process of objectification and fragmentation that *is* the representation of woman, and, moreover, such shoring up of the male subject's power is precisely the "visual pleasure" of the classical narrative structure and its "gaze." To confront the violences of this pleasure is to delve into the mechanisms of the unconscious, the myriad strategies upon which the male subject relies for fending off a primary threat (posited in psychoanalysis as the threat of castration), including the replaying of defenses through the male-centered repetitive narratives of the movies. Ultimately, Mulvey calls upon us (intellectuals, filmmakers) to convert passive pleasure into both critical acumen and a counter-cinema. Despite the ways in which her argument and many subsequent to it may appear to reinforce a cleavage between the repressive repetitions of popular (i.e., Hollywood classical) cinema and the liberatory potential of art cinema, the force of Mulvey's gesture—tooling a weapon through careful, energetic intellectual work on an enormously complicated system— sustained and enlivened much of the writing that followed it in the name of psychoanalytic and feminist film theory, and, rather than further embalming "Visual Pleasure," we seek here to follow some of the strands of work on cinema, psychoanalysis and feminism over the past quarter-decade in order to situate the present essays.

The first question must surely be: what does psychoanalysis have to do with cinema? And further, which psychoanalysis? What cinema? It is likely not enough to remind ourselves that the two were born at the same moment, the dawn of the twentieth century, and have both largely been concerned with telling stories about the same delicious preoccupations or themes (desire, the family, sexuality, perversion, prohibition, murder,

4 Laura Mulvey, "Visual Pleasure and Narrative Cinema," *Screen* 16 (1) (Winter 1975), 51–79.

addiction . . .). Cinema has, moreover, often referred to psychoanalysis directly: it abounds with Freud jokes, Oedipal explanations, wise therapists, sibling rivalries and, of course, phallic imagery. But the history of psychoanalysis as an interpretive science that could be brought to bear on cultural objects (art, literature, film) begins in the 1930s in Germany, when readers of Freud (especially Freud's studies of artists such as Leonardo da Vinci, or the book of his pupil, Marie Bonaparte, on Edgar Allan Poe) used psychoanalysis to understand how an artist's or author's personality shaped his or her creative work. The critic functioned as analyst, the artist/author as patient, and the genre of what we now call "psycho-biography" became a respected form, one that now, significantly, overwhelms biographies of stars and other celebrities. From the movement of psycho-biography to America in the 1940s through the present, psychoanalysis has provided a powerful frame not only for understanding aesthetic form and narrative structure, but also for thinking through the ways in which desire and power are produced and reproduced, whether in the individual, the family or socially.

There is a danger, however, in being cavalier about the body of work we refer to when talking about "psychoanalysis" itself as an entity. In reading a film's phallic imagery (the magnificent conclusion, for example, of Douglas Sirk's *Written on the Wind*, 1956), we might bracket the sense in which psychoanalysis functions as the "talking cure," a therapeutic practice that seeks to cure people suffering from real symptoms. Analysts have continued the conversations Freud initiated a century ago, writing reams of case studies and theoretical works; and even the archive he left remains open to contestation and revision.[5] For heuristic purposes, then, let us propose a brief taxonomy of several axes of that to which we refer in talking about "psychoanalysis," before turning to its specific relation to cinema and feminism. We borrow the structure from E. Ann Kaplan's fine introduction to her collection, *Psychoanalysis and Cinema*.[6]

First, psychoanalysis exists as a body of writings, a discourse initiated by Sigmund Freud (the "Standard Edition" of whose work retains textual authority) and continued by many others; those who have been particularly significant to cinema studies include, among quite a few, Ernest Jones, Melanie Klein, Julia Kristeva, Jacques Lacan, and Joan Rivière. Because this set of writings is enormous, and because even for Freud the science of psychoanalysis was an evolving one, nonspecialists often tend either to seize upon one or two suggestive concepts or formulations (the idea of the fetish, for example) without situating them within a broader historical or theoretical context, or to balk at the investment of time a deep knowledge (not mastery) of psychoanalysis requires and thus to reject its utility out of hand. As with Marxism's reliance upon not only the extensive writings of Karl Marx but a long tradition of thought (some of which we have surveyed) and struggle, psychoanalysis has the capacity to breed a certain kind of fidelity ("I am a Freudian who has read the entirety of his writings. In German."), a certain kind of internecine warfare ("I am not a Freudian but a Lacanian.") and a certain kind of animosity ("What bull@#$%."). It is similarly enticing in its complexity, its systematic and totalizing explanation; and, like Marxism, in thinking about the uses to which it is

5 See Jacques Derrida, *Archive Fever: A Freudian Impression*, translated by Eric Prenowitz (Chicago and London: University of Chicago Press, 1995).
6 E. Ann Kaplan, "From Plato's Cave to Freud's Screen," *Psychoanalysis and Cinema*, edited by E. Ann Kaplan (London and New York: Routledge, 1990), 1–23.

put, one wants to ask after the practices of reading and textual attention that determine those uses in any given context.

The second axis of psychoanalysis involves, as we have already mentioned, the therapeutic situation itself, the "talking cure," with the analysand (the "patient," but more properly the one who is analyzed) on the couch, the analyst in the chair and the process of the analysand's speech, his or her recounting of dreams, slips of the tongue and jokes (manifestations of the unconscious) and associations they produce, to which the analyst responds with interpretations. Some of Freud's texts, *The Interpretation of Dreams* and *Dora: Fragment of an Analysis of a Case of Hysteria*, provide models (the latter an admitted failure) of the analytic situation and process, the interpretive work of the analyst and the progress toward cure of the analysis itself. The practice of psychoanalysis as cure seeks indeed to uncover the unconscious source of somatic clues (symptoms): certain phobias, tics, and the like. And the "talking cure" is thus based upon particular understandings of psychosexual development set forth in Freud's *oeuvre*; this is the psychoanalysis to which we refer when we talk, for example, about stages of development, perversions and neuroses, the Oedipus complex or the family romance.

The texts that emerge from the analytic situation can be elegant, engaging and complex narratives on their own (reading Freud's case studies is a pleasure), and, as we all know, dreams in their telling emerge as complicated texts that lend themselves to interpretation as narratives. While psychoanalysis may be used, therefore, to explain relationships, actions or motives *within* films (as works perhaps too nicely with most Hitchcock films), and while it can also be a *theme* of a given film (a film "about" psychoanalysis, such as the 1976 film, *The Seven Percent Solution*), it can also, in our third axis, be seen structurally as an aesthetic discourse in its own right. That is to say, psychoanalysis as a narrative-producing mechanism can be understood as similar to fiction, or to forms of narrative cinema, just as the language of the dream seems to have filmic corollaries (Salvador Dali and Luis Buñuel's 1929 film, *Un Chien Andalou*, is but one example). The aesthetic dimensions of psychoanalysis, in fact, seem particularly congenial to the study of literary language and to cinema, since both often seek to represent the unrepresentable, to render irrelevant the distinction—as do what are called "borderline" subjects— between conscious and unconscious, and to seize upon what is enigmatic, striking, uncanny, arresting.

The fourth axis involves understanding psychoanalysis as an historical, ideological and cultural discourse, an understanding that is crucial to seeing how it may be at work in a given film as a theme or to using it as a grid for reading narrative motivations or actions. One could chart, in other words, how psychoanalysis has changed over time: the attitudes of the psychoanalytic institution toward homosexuality, for example, have moved from pathologization (homosexuality as disease) to a more affirmative position in the 1973 Diagnostic and Statistical Manual III.[7] One can also examine Freud's own moorings in bourgeois, European culture of the Victorian era to shed light on his interpretive moves (his inability, to cite again the example of Dora, to consider *her* homosexual desires). Likewise, in studying American culture of the 1950s, one is struck by how (sometimes watered-down) psychoanalytic language and concepts had become part of everyday speech and culture, "popular psychology" or "pop-psych," influencing

---

7 See Eve Kosofsky Sedgwick, "How to Bring Your Kids Up Gay: The War on Effeminate Boys," in E. K. Sedgwick, *Tendencies* (Durham, NC: Duke University Press, 1993), 154–164.

the ways in which its culture explained the decade's paranoia. On the ideological front, some of the founding presuppositions of psychoanalysis, such as the powerful force of childhood sexuality, have been banished in order to regulate sexuality more generally, while others have become truisms used in the service of misogyny (the assumption, for example, that women suffer from "penis-envy"). While this conception of psychoanalysis as a discourse deployed toward specific ends depends upon a rigorous familiarity with the body of work we mentioned as our first category, it also deepens our understanding of cultural history and the force of the psychoanalytic institution.

Finally, psychoanalysis can be understood as a specific process or set of processes (related to but distinct from the analytic encounter) that can be used analogically to make sense of textual processes or the relations between spectators and filmic texts. One strain of film theory became preoccupied with the following analogy: the spectator is to the screen what the child, in Lacan's theory of subject formation, is to the mirror in the "mirror stage" (the same moment to which Mulvey refers in "Visual Pleasure," at which the child misrecognizes its own image in a mirror as an ideal version—more coordinated, more "with it"—of him/herself). There are obvious dangers to such analogizing, included among them the tendency to literalize the metaphors of psychoanalytic language, but it is not surprising that this last axis has taken hold of quite a bit of work in the humanities, for it positions the reader/spectator in the immensely powerful position of the analyst. As we cautioned above with regard to readings of the psychoanalytic corpus, it does seem important to think carefully about how we position ourselves as intellectuals in relation to the objects we choose to study and to regard presumptions of mastery with suspicion; one strikingly disturbing trend of late has been toward the metapsychology of entire populations or nations, attributing to some, for instance, a generalized "melancholia."

We think, then, that these categories are useful as a heuristic breakdown through which to appreciate the multiple levels on which we make habitual reference to psychoanalysis in relation to the study of the humanities, and yet they fail to include some of the most pervasive language of popular psychology or other strains of psychologistic thought (such as the increasingly prevalent language of self-help) that exert pressure in enclaves of the world not saturated by the discourse of the academic humanities. Given these descriptions, though, we can see how very different elements of the "psychoanalysis" monolith might work in conversation with the "cinema" monolith, an entity that also requires some refining. Because the present volume is devoted to popular cinema (as opposed to art cinema or alternative media), we narrow our focus now to return to one of the ways in which psychoanalysis has engaged that realm.

This important path of academic work has involved examining, as we suggested through Mulvey at the outset and in our discussion of Marxism, how commercial narrative cinema devastatingly reproduces dominant and constraining versions of the world. Whether through narrative pattern, the use of sound, the milieu of the bourgeois family, or the structure of the tripartite gaze, classical Hollywood cinema seems constantly, to take but one element of hegemony, to enlist our consent for patriarchal power. This is not to say that there are not important exceptions, nor is it to suggest that spectators do not differ in their readings, and neither is it to prioritize gender above other dimensions of hegemony (dimensions of class, race, or sexuality, to repeat a mantra). Psychoanalytic processes (such as the account Freud and Lacan, differently, offer of subject-formation and the subject's insertion into the symbolic order) seem to describe well the ways in which spectators are stitched or, to use Christian Metz's term, "sutured" into the symbolic world of the narrative film, while to the extent to which the Oedipal scenario, in the words of Bellour and Rosolato, "supports the entire dynamic of the narrative, puts the identifications into play and activates sexual difference, it as an almost universal principle of the operation of the film in the American cinema."[8] Thinkers such as Pam Cook, the late Claire Johnston, Janet Bergstrom, Constance Penley, Kaja Silverman, Teresa de Lauretis and others have concentrated on the reproduction (through suture and the Oedipal triangle as well as other gendered thematics) of patriarchal worldviews through every conceivable tool of the classical Hollywood cinema, from its use of voiceover to its patterns of shot/reverse shot editing. The complexity of the psychoanalytic system also provided them with a broad intellectual horizon indeed to explore questions of gender and genre (melodrama and the "woman's film" of the 1940s), as well as issues of reception, the role of women directors, the possibilities of independent or alternative cinema and the like. A subset, if you like, of this work was pioneered by Bellour and by his compatriot, video maker Thierry Kuntzel, whose extraordinarily close analyses of single sequences or images of films sought to pursue a lexicon of visual signifiers in order to see how meaning, in the most general sense, is made, how images grab us (in fascination and in unease) and how we might grab them. A final subset of this work turned to the work of American psychologists such as Carol Gilligan and Nancy Chodorow, whose respective accounts of girls' interactive, contextual reasoning processes and of the role of mothering in reproducing female subjectivity, seemed to many Anglophone academics to provide more powerful accounts of female subjectivity than either Freudian or Lacanian psychoanalysis.

We think it important to emphasize that this strain of feminist psychoanalytically informed scholarship has not, in our view, been in any way superseded; we do not endorse the idea of "postfeminist" scholarship, even in the best sense of the term: "everything that comes now is dependent *upon* and indebted *to* feminism." We agree with Constance Penley, too, that the turn to Gilligan and Chodorow, in particular, tended to propose a regressive, limited model of female identification and that Freudian and Lacanian psychoanalytic formulations continue to provide us with immensely complex accounts of identification and desire.[9] The challenges, however, that cultural studies poses to feminist psychoanalytic film theory and to psychoanalysis more generally are several, and those challenges inform the essays collected here. We close this section by gesturing toward them as context for their more specific elaboration in individual essays.

First, as we have suggested, cultural studies (and particularly a cultural studies that follows on the heels of poststructuralism) is a necessarily interdisciplinary, if not antidisciplinary, formation, drawing for its resources and intellectual inspiration upon anthropology and the study of religion as much as upon traditions of literary analysis and cinema studies. While poststructuralist analyses, such as Derrida's *Archive Fever*, tend to inhabit psychoanalytic theory in order to show up its totalizing aspirations or to stage its limits, other limits on its force can be revealed through its status as one explanation among others in a cultural studies project. In so far as cultural studies work

8 Raymond Bellour and Guy Rosolato, "Dialogue: Remembering (This Memory of) a Film," in *Psychoanalysis and Cinema*, 204.

9 Constance Penley, "Feminism, Psychoanalysis and the Study of Popular Culture," in Lawrence Grossberg, Cary Nelson, and Paula Treichler, eds, *Cultural Studies* (London and New York: Routledge, 1992), esp. 479–480.

has endeavored to be resolutely historical and attentive to specificity, psychoanalysis can appear to harbor frighteningly ahistorical assumptions when it is commandeered, say, to address the specific forms of humor in *Hustler* magazine.[10] Not surprisingly, and in keeping with a model of cultural studies as a form of *bricolage*, psychoanalysis has been understood through cultural studies as an historical and ideological discourse more than it has been taken up, *tout court*, as method or totalizing explanation. (We've heard that Laura Mulvey herself abandoned her wholesale commitment to psychoanalysis because it could not explain the Gulf War!)

Similar to its inter- or anti-disciplinary formation, cultural studies has also been a conjunctural one, emphasizing contingency (rather than system or structure) and indebted to a theory of articulation whereby one can explain "the continuing severing, realignment, and recombination of discourses, social groups, political interests, and structures of power in a society."[11] In so far as psychoanalysis tends to banish chance in favor of a necessary systematicity, it involves a considerable balancing act (though not therefore an impossible one) to sustain both attention to the aleatory as it contorts social relations and respect for the kind of structural determinations presupposed by psychoanalysis. The work of Slavoj Žižek is a case in point of an impressive integration of Lacanian psychoanalysis, social analysis and the study of popular culture.

Finally, we have to wonder at the universalizing claims of psychoanalysis, the "discovery" by Freud of a science that explains, as it were, all time and all space. The tendency of cultural studies to treat psychoanalysis discursively, however, may not be of help in our wonder: in the urge to locate it historically and specifically, we may bypass the possibility that its range may, just may, extend beyond Euro-American culture; may, just may, be central to the African-American literary imagination (as it was to black nationalism); may, just may, help us to think about Pokémon, *The Real World* or the former Yugoslavia. The task, it seems to us, is to test it, to read carefully and with attention to a vastly complicated and seductive conceptual language. Not to master, but to enjoin.

Queer theory

One of the most significant changes within the past few decades in the public discourse and university study of sex/gender difference has been the abundance of work on gay and lesbian representation. The most recent incarnation of this work is "queer studies," and the shift between an emphasis on "gay and lesbian" and "queer" as nominations of sex/gender difference itself suggests a different set of concerns in how we think of sexuality and gender (more on that below). While it is increasingly evident that same-sex desiring women and men have, over a longer duration of the past century, been engaged in shaping language and visual culture with non-homophobic intentions, the question of why "homosexuals" matter to modern societies, as something other than anomalies either to be cured or to be punished, only emerges after World War II as a pressing social concern in Western societies. In the United States, the sociological study of sexuality by Alfred Kinsey and his successors in the field of sexology, marked by Kinsey's immensely influential studies, *Sexual Behavior in the Human Male* (1948) and *Sexual*

---

10 See Laura Kipnis, "(Male) Desire and (Female) Disgust: Reading *Hustler*," in *Cultural Studies*, 373–392.
11 Lawrence Grossberg, Cary Nelson, and Paula Treichler, "Cultural Studies: An Introduction," in *Cultural Studies*, 8.

Behavior in the Human Female (1953), announced through its statistical evidence that the same-sex erotic dimensions of the bulk of human subjects are more expansive and coterminous with other more seemingly conventional kinds of sexuality. Despite the fact that these studies' findings and methods for research are still contested, their historical impact remains difficult to overestimate in the sense that the work of mid-century sexology inadvertently, through its seemingly unbiased and scientific tone and approach, placed in the center of American public discourse the fact that there were homosexual men and women enmeshed in the very fabric of all social life. In the United Kingdom, the Wolfenden legislation of the 1950s signaled a public move to rethink the criminal status of homosexuals, as the latter resulted in the need for such dissident sexualities to be maintained as private and concealed—in short, to make a public secret of the fact of homosexuality. In this case, it was largely men who were named as the agents of such sexual dissidence, as women seemed to have been largely omitted from consideration as maintaining homosexual thoughts and practices. The exemption of women probably reflected a longer-standing disavowal of female sexuality more generally—except in the instances in which the government sought to regulate the apparently expanded practice of female prostitution, which was, as Jeffrey Weeks has demonstrated, entwined in the imagination of the Wolfenden Committee with male homosexuality as apparently a symptom of the corruption of British society since World War II. Though the impulses behind such legal reform in the United Kingdom may have seemed to indicate an enlightened impulse to alter the status of homosexual men, changes in the legal status of same-sex erotic practices had, as Weeks has documented, the effect of increasing attempts at regulation and surveillance of sexuality in the public sphere.[12] Be that as it may, if both examples from the United States and the United Kingdom can be made to serve as exemplary of the effects of making more public the fact of previously more privatized sexualities, then what is revealed is the fact that liberal democracies of the West made apparent, at the moment of that sphere's greatest hegemony, the fact that large numbers of men and women were oppressed subjects because of their sexual and gender difference—in short, homosexuality was emerging as a site of knowledge not only for sociologists and biologists, but for politicians as well. While one of the consequences of this "discovery" of homosexuality was the appearance of an expanded importance given to the institutions of the law and of medicine to address, through legal regulation and attempts at therapeutic redress of the "perversion" of same-sex sexuality, the recuperation of the gay and lesbian to a heteronormative model, there was equally a need to invent, by the men and women affected by the expanded popular commentary upon them, more public communities to advocate the decriminalization of private sexual practices.

With this momentum in mind, we discover that the advent of more explicit discussion of homosexuality in post-World War II America and Great Britain happened from "the top down"; that is, homosexuality became political more through attempts at legislating and studying it than through a mobilization by gay men and lesbians. In short, these were not necessarily politicizations of sexuality brought forth by the very citizens most affected by its public articulation; instead, as a response to the aggressive policing and punishment of homosexuality, self-sponsored political formations by gays and lesbians emerged beginning in the 1950s. (An important qualification here is that there

---

12 Jeffrey Weeks, *Sex, Politics and Society: The Regulation of Sexuality Since 1800* (London: Longman, 1981).

had existed more privatized social networks of men's and women's communities prior to the fact of their being identified—but they had not borne the kinds of political weight they now found themselves shouldering.) What emerged were the "homophile" movements of the 1950s, where gays and lesbians tried to shape a public identity for themselves not crafted out of the language of perversion or of the threat of homosexuality to the institutions (the state, the family) that it was purported to undermine.[13] The history of these movements is too long and important to attempt to encapsulate here, but worth emphasizing is their demand for something called "visibility"—and the resonances of this term for students of media should quickly become apparent. The fact that the state deemed it worthwhile to speculate and discover just how many homosexuals were, for example, employed by the US government—fomenting the dismal experience during the 1950s of many men and women's expulsion from their jobs in government service— found its political response among gays and lesbians in a voice that demanded fair treatment under the law, but it also fostered the impulse to wonder at the long-standing ban on representation of same-sex sexuality within the industries of popular culture.

In a sense, the political rejoinder by homophile movements to these efforts to identify and expel them from the workplace can be seen, on the one hand, as an emphasis upon the fact that they clearly had been visualized as one thing—perverse, corrupt— and, on the other, as an effort to call forth another language that made clear that such visibility was only part of the political picture. It is important to recall this history in the context of a discussion of gay and lesbian film because the social movements of the 1950s and 1960s would shape the intellectual work of gay and lesbian scholars and activists in the decades that followed. While those earlier movements (such as the Daughters of Bilitis, a lesbian political group, and the Mattachine Society, populated by men) mostly avoided questions of how representations of gay and lesbian life and sexuality circulated within popular culture, after 1970 the historian of sexuality discovers a flourishing political movement intent not only on changing the law but also driven to reshape the kinds of images and sounds (music was also important) about homosexuality to be found in the forms of mass culture—quite prominently film. This latter impulse can be perceived as having three trajectories: the first to understand how same-sex sexuality has been demonized within the commodities of the culture industries; a second, accompanying, one to discern those (often fragmentary) moments in which such desires did, however obliquely and momentarily, make their appearance; and the third tendency to want to forge cultural productions that gave expression to experiences and new-found languages of lesbians and gay men. In the case of dominant film culture, the first two emphases, whose effects were closely affiliated, can be witnessed in the forms of critical response to be found in the writings about cinema of Parker Tyler, Gore Vidal, and Vito Russo (all, worth pointing out, white American men), while the latter can be found, to take several examples, in the films of Yvonne Rainer, Kenneth Anger, Andy Warhol, and Prathiba Parmar. These three movements mark an important convergence of the political and artistic concerns of the women and men involved, but they also have their limits, the discovery of which marks the more recent formation of "queer studies," work driven equally by a desire to discover those structures of sex/gender oppression at work, but work also informed by a sense of the more loosely affiliated positions of all those

---

13 For an excellent history of this period, see John D'Emilio, *Sexual Politics, Sexual Communities: The Making of a Homosexual Minority in the United States, 1940–1970* (Chicago: University of Chicago Press, 1983).

Figure I.1 John Wilson, Matthew Baidoo, and Ben Ellison in *Looking for Langston* (1989). Courtesy of Sunil Gupta and Sankofa Film and Video

men and women who are affected by such forms of power and representation, not simply those choosing the political nomination of lesbian or gay.

An example will help here. The publication in 1977 of the late Vito Russo's widely influential study, *The Celluloid Closet*, offered a history of Hollywood cinema that attempted to demonstrate how there indeed were representations of male and female homosexuality in cinema appearing even in the earliest moments of the silent cinema and extending up to the present moment of that book's appearance. Although Russo's work undertook a breathtakingly exhaustive treatment of the topic (one that continues to inspire students of the subject), it insisted upon dividing the images that it offered into a binary of either "negative" (i.e. homophobic, stereotypical) or "positive" (pro-gay and lesbian). While this scheme has the virtue of recognizing that the bulk of these images of homosexuals appeared under the duress of censorship (most specifically, the Production Code in Hollywood), it failed to account for how some images, even the most seemingly repellent to a pro-gay stance, carried with them a kind of perverse appeal for viewers not necessarily given to homophobic sentiments. Further, it largely ignored the fact that many viewers already saw Hollywood film at a distance—by virtue of national divisions (British viewers, for example, already could perceive American cinema as something importing foreign modes of representation and an American way of life at odds with their own), class divisions and racial difference. Compounding the matter was that homosexual men and women have served very different functions within the regimes of sex/gender representation, gay men more often seen as weak-willed (coded as effeminacy) or pathological in their capacity to desire other men, while women were capable of romantic friendships and sentimental alliances that need not necessarily carry with them the taint of a perverse sexuality.

The point here is not to vilify Russo's work but to discover how it introduced new questions for scholars attempting to historicize and theorize same-sex sexuality in the domain of popular cinema. Indeed, the challenges to do just that—to offer the historical and theoretical dimensions of Hollywood's treatment of gays and lesbians—appeared simultaneously with other intellectual and political projects taking shape, not least the work of the CCCS and the endeavors of feminist scholars and activists in the 1970s and 1980s. The former could be said to have had a smaller immediate impact for the earliest gay and lesbian studies of film, concerned more centrally as cultural studies was with issues of class, while the importance of the latter cannot be overestimated for its immediate impact for lesbian and gay scholars. Gay and lesbian studies needs to be understood in the light of how feminism made central (specifically to the study of film and other visual media and more generally to all social arrangements) the political dimensions of women's lives, at a time when the idea that there were political aspects to reproduction, mothering, domesticity, work, consumption, and sexuality might have struck even sympathetic ears as a bit of a stretch. The biggest challenge, though, for conveying the intellectual work of feminist film theory to the concerns of gay and lesbian studies, was the choice of a critical method, because the powerful model at hand for feminist writers—psychoanalysis—situated gay/lesbian work in relation to an institution whose discourses and practices were often at odds with the force of a political movement attempting to forge models that did not have to apologize or explain the fact of homosexuality as some form of aberrance. While feminism itself grappled with the contradictions of engaging with psychoanalysis—a language which could express the dynamics of the unconscious and pleasure in looking ("scopophilia") but did so in the framework of a practice given over to the normalization of the female subject in her struggle to make sense of the patriarchy around her—the fact of the constitutionally neurotic female subject did not seem to offer much promise for lesbians and gays who understood all too well how psychoanalysis was deployed to encompass them into the world of a compulsory heterosexuality. Despite the challenges met by feminist scholars of film, psychoanalysis vivified their work (as we discuss later) if solely for one reason: through it they could demonstrate how the very forms of dominant cinema were fundamentally predicated on managing the contradictory status of women spectators—as, on the one hand, desiring subjects whose desires, on the other hand, could serve to rend asunder the very structures of patriarchy which demanded that they not maintain an erotic and pleasured interest in the forms of the narrative moving image. If gay male critical work, as exemplified by Russo, did not manage a more nuanced approach to the images it sought to understand, then the work of psychoanalytic feminism had demonstrated a more complicated way of critically intervening in the Hollywood product through questions of sex/gender difference.

It is striking that, barring a few key examples such as Teresa de Lauretis' work on lesbian film, gay and lesbian critical work initially inherited feminist psychoanalytic work's more careful attention to the subtleties of the film product but not always its faith in the nomenclature and categories of psychoanalysis, in any of its permutations (e.g. Lacanian revisitings of the question of the unconscious). Part of the increased theoretical sophistication and historical scope of gay and lesbian critical inquiry, and its movement toward the name of "queer," has been the impact of its previously named predecessor, the Birmingham Centre, with its innovative study of subcultures and ideological critique.

Further, the expansion of work done in the name of cultural studies to encompass the complications of sex/gender difference suggested that language and representation were not simply ideology as a form of deception (an old and unwieldy way of interpreting the cultural commodities brought forth by capitalism); but also that they were not utopian or compensatory, offering the subjects of capital forms of distraction from the conditions of everyday life (discussed above in relation to Marxism). This form of ideological critique combined with a sense that the "social text" of a film attempted to offer a discernible world to the viewer (unlike, say, an avant-garde film which attempted to express a more private, psychological worldview of the artist) while offering her or him pleasurable resolutions not available in everyday life. When, in his immensely important essay, "Entertainment and Utopia," Richard Dyer elegantly parses the structure of the film musical as bringing together the inadequacies of modern life *and* the feelings of fantastic, utopian solutions to those shortcomings (marked by song and dance), he offers a model for understanding how one generic form of the Hollywood product makes its appeal to viewers—and he then suggests that it is perhaps no coincidence that the musical has been important to gays, adolescents, blacks, and women as film-viewers.[14] It is hard to imagine an account such as Russo's offering this pairing of formal analysis and ideological critique.

It signals a new way of thinking about popular culture when an academic discipline engages with popular entertainment, through questions about how the latter has co-operated with regimes of sex/gender ordering which more usually ignore the presence of gays and lesbians or offer images of them that serve to vilify, while it simultaneously recognizes that many such dissident sexual subjects have found in the things of mass culture ways of interpreting their own presence, however marginal. Alexander Doty, Richard Dyer, B. Ruby Rich, Thomas Waugh, and Patricia White have emerged as strong critical voices that allow for the history of film to be seen as an active element in the organization not only of the regulation of desire but of desire itself.

As noted above, there has been a marked shift recently in the way that work on gay and lesbian imagery and language has merged into a field called "queer" studies; in part this can be explained by the impulse to take what had previously been a name of sexist derision and to disqualify its impulses to degrade gays and lesbians. But the transition is incomplete—and perhaps not a few self-described lesbians and gay men have balked at the idea of embracing a term that previously expressed the fear and ignorance they have been made to bear. The movement to "queer" also suggests a sense of the specificity of "gay" and "lesbian" to European and American history during a particular period, a specificity that might need to acknowledge its own relative privilege in relation to other same-sex desiring men and women who enjoy neither the economic status (too often, middle class and educated) nor the white privilege of the subject tacitly and common-sensically taken as queer. In this regard, the fact of there being immense numbers of men and women, some working class, some people of color, with lives grounded in their same-sex desire and practices, has not been encompassed in the use of "lesbian and gay." Further, the generational shift of "gay" and "lesbian" to "queer" marks the aging of one political movement and its need to acknowledge younger men and women to whom prior historical moments are just that—history! Lastly, if globalization can be

14 Richard Dyer, "Entertainment and Utopia," in Simon During, ed., *The Cultural Studies Reader*, 2nd edn (London: Routledge, 1999).

understood as the historical effect of an increased movement of information and knowl-edge to and from other subjects beyond the West, then we begin to understand how "gay" and "lesbian" might also have a geographic significance as names given to specific individuals and their political/social formations. For example, South Asian men and women living both in their countries of derivation and in diasporic, postcolonial settings such as London or New York (or Leeds or Milwaukee) might discover themselves to be as queer to gays and lesbians as they are "black" to the whites who surround them (as we discuss below). Nevertheless, it remains that all such kinds of identity (and sex/gender difference is but one such example) reflect the social forces at work upon subjects and their responses to those (not always benevolent) forms of power; in that regard, all the names we choose for ourselves begin to reveal themselves as tentative and in need of continual rethinking.

Given our invocation of globalization as a tendency to be understood in terms of its impact on sex/gender, it is a pressing concern for queer studies as it addresses the sub-ject of film culture that dissident sexualities are no longer necessarily produced solely through acts of repression but, in fact, are actively deployed as marketing tools for the industries of cinema. What might once have been seen as the (relatively concealed) same-sex male and female subcultures that interpreted dominant film for their own needs now emerge as niche markets for films that are said to cater to gay men and lesbians, and indeed here one can begin to understand how the distinction between mainstream and alternative film is less about studio finances and more about a way of naming a film so that it will gather substantial enough an audience to garner a profit at the box office. Some readers will recognize this as the concept of "appropriation," a model that ascer-tains how specific styles and concerns of cultural production develop along the margins of social life and find themselves subsequently incorporated into the popular corporate product as so much product innovation—and queer lives are a rich source of examples of such movements from fringe to center. It should be equally clear that what some-times appear to us as the kinds of representations that gay and lesbian audiences thirst for (being largely nonexistent in other popular venues, such as television) function within the marketplace as another tool for product placement. One woman's "appropriation" might be another woman's long-sought-for image of a desire like her own.

Psychoanalysis has aided queer theory in thinking about how such desires work. Our discussion of the reading of Freud in the British/American academic context empha-sizes what both Teresa de Lauretis and Jacqueline Rose have called his "negative theory of sexuality," the contention that healthy adult heterosexuality is rarely, if ever, achieved. Most of us, as even the first Kinsey report noted, emerge from childhood development's complex paths (and their remarkably formative detours) slightly out of whack, whether or not our unconscious quirks appear through debilitating symptoms of neuroses or as fully-fledged perversions. As you can imagine, such a reading of Freud is also congenial to queer theory: first, since it proposes that perversions are healthy rather than neurotic (perversions at least *act* on unconscious structures of desire rather than deny them!); and, second, since it unites all of us in our failure to achieve the adult heterosexual ideal (a necessary fiction of psychoanalytic theory *and* practice). Whether such failure ought to be generalized as "queer" remains an open question (as the category "queer" itself resists specification), but at the very least Freud's "negative" impulses militate against pathologizing a specific minority by contrast with a presumed-stable "healthy" majority.

Anglophone queer theory has, in fact, nurtured an extraordinarily animated discus-sion of the work of Freud, Lacan, and some of the psychoanalytic thinkers whose work we mentioned as important to film studies (Joan Rivière and Melanie Klein, to recall two). There are several correspondences. First, feminist film theory was itself enlivened by challenges to its own heterosexist assumptions, challenges that yielded crucial work on lesbian representation as well as reexaminations of some of its core questions (what does it mean, for example to Mulvey's argument, for a *female* viewer to adopt an active position of desire in relation to a female star image?). And in so far as both women and gay men are marginal to the dominant, patriarchal conceptions of power and desire reiterated by Hollywood cinema, feminist work on cinema (including its psychoanalytic strains) lent itself nicely to modifications and extensions for a queer critique of its sexual politics. At the same time, lesbian work on the contradictory subject-positions of female spectators challenged not only the spare accounts of female subject-formation in Freud and Lacan but also the inability of many feminist readings of those thinkers to see contradiction at work at all.

Second, work on cinema, including but not limited to its psychoanalytic inflections, has been central to the more general projects of queer theory itself. This centrality of cinema to queer life and thought is indebted to cinema's role as a form of modern technology (though one now perhaps yielding its exemplary status to television and digital media), massively deployed toward the reproduction of power and desire, whether in hegemonic or contestatory forms. Queer fandom of "mainstream" or dominant cinema (the legendary affection gay men have for Judy Garland, say) has been a central discourse of gay and lesbian cultural production; more important, queer readings of, or queer presences within, dominant cinema explode the image of commercial narrative cinema as a repressive monster as well as undermine the interpretation of alternative or independent cinema as its necessary (read, liberatory) white knight.[15]

A third correspondence between queer theory, psychoanalysis, and cinema, in certain of their articulations, is that all three are predominantly concerned with the domain of the visible, loosely and, as we shall see, problematically understood. Queer theory quite often takes the visible as a term of political representation: queer efforts toward public presence (whether in Parliament, Congress, or on corporate boards of directors) involve the translation, as Eric Clarke puts it, of "private vices into public virtues." The goal, in other words, of queer politics is to legitimate queer existences publicly, to validate the lives of lesbians and gay men (and bisexual and transgendered and other queer folks) through public acts, and thereby to open public spaces (work, government, media) to queer presence. The motto of gay pride marches, "We are everywhere," is a good condensation of the political-representational valence of visibility. Clarke and others have discussed the extent to which such a desire for visibility necessarily involves a kind of capitulation: to enter the public sphere virtuously is to be a "good queer," one acceptable to those who have wielded the power to keep queers out in the first place. To see a necessary contradiction is not, however, to dismiss the desire to enter. This claim for collective visibility entails, in fact, a more complicated set of questions, including a more individual sense of desire and identification: one can self-identify as queer (after or

15 Patricia White, for example, suggests a lesbian reading of the "mammy" supporting characters in Hollywood cinema, such as those played by Ethel Waters in *Pinky* (Elia Kazan, 1949) and *The Member of the Wedding* (Fred Zinnemann, 1952): *Uninvited: Classical Hollywood Cinema and Lesbian Representability* (Bloomington: Indiana University Press, 1999), 136–193. The essays in the present volume by Thomas Waugh and Linda Mizejewski also speak to this distinction.

during the recognition of one's own desires as in some way queer) in order to join a collectivity that seeks to join the public sphere, but one is also, all-too-often, *called* "queer" (its pejorative sense is its prior one, subsequently taken up and redeployed as empowering through queer politics). Queer, in other words, might be less a matter of rational self-definition than a naming that comes from elsewhere (as, given the history of language, all names in fact do).

Psychoanalytic work on affect (a category of feelings prior to the their contextualization as "emotions") has proven particularly useful to Eve Sedgwick's explorations of what it means to be called "queer," to be on the receiving end of a name hurled in hatred. While her essays, in her previously mentioned book, *Tendencies*, take to task the psychoanalytic institution (what we discussed above as part of the historical/discursive sense of psychoanalysis) for its legitimation of homophobia, Sedgwick nonetheless circles frequently around the affect "shame" as central to queer identity-formation. And whether shame is privileged above other affects for queers, identity-formation must be central to understanding how we come to inhabit the contours of what we understand as queer bodies, how we live queer existences, how we affirm queerness rather than reproduce hatred. Psychoanalysis, again at the very least, provides one account (open to revision, an incomplete project) of how we come to be what we are and, most important, how we come to be desiring and split (in the sense that we exist on at least two planes at once, conscious and unconscious). Identity-formation, it argues, is a matter of a series of acts of identification, of the incorporation of the other into the self, beginning with the primary recognition by the child of the mother as a separate and distinct entity; the end result of these identifications, as fragmented and layered and contradictory as they may be, is the sum total of what we are. One can see how such a series of identifications, again which actually *constitute* what we are, might be said to involve a string of visible recognitions akin to those of the cinema.

Indeed, the common-sense idea of "identifying with" a character is central to the (narrative) cinema's own signifying work, and if queer politics embed an idea of visibility as a representational project (in the sense of representation as delegation or proxy), and if psychoanalysis elaborates an account of identity-formation as a series of recognitions/identifications/incorporations of the other, the cinema provides a place for us literally to see ourselves as others (representation as portrait), caught as we are in the relays of the three looks or "gazes" of the cinema Mulvey describes in "Visual Pleasure and Narrative Cinema." The slippage between the sense of representation as proxy and representation as portrait, however, we think authorizes a conjoining of queer politics with cinema; the task of several of the essays in this volume is, in fact, to pry apart the two projects in order to bring them into a more critical relationship with one another, through and against psychoanalysis.

Cultural studies lineages

We have spent some time discussing the prominence of psychoanalytic theory, largely in order to show readers of the present collection its enormously complicated layers and to suggest that these have often become flattened into a set of commonplaces, at worst clichés, naturalized within the discourse of film studies and reproduced frequently in cultural studies texts. The "Eurocentric" origins of psychoanalysis, as well as some of Freud's racist metaphors, have opened it, as we have also suggested, to criticism on both historical and ideological grounds. In so far, then, as psychoanalysis retains explanatory force, it will have to reckon with the kinds of questions generated by the insistence upon historical and social specificity that characterizes the best work in the cultural studies tradition. Does psychoanalysis claim to explain, through the Oedipal model of the bourgeois nuclear family, people whose unit of social organization is *not* the nuclear family? How might Freud's writings be adapted for the increasing prominence in the US of single parent families? How might Freud's model of memory, figured through a nineteenth century toy known as the "mystic writing pad" (a lot like an Etch-A-Sketch), stand up to the speed of email?

Our reading of a lineage of work in feminist film theory also runs the risk of enshrining thought that has reproduced racial hierarchies (what American film scholar Jane Gaines has called its "color-blindness")[16] even as it sought to explore the dynamics of mastery involved in the cinema's "gaze." Our reading of queer lineages, too, tends to emphasize the largely white and middle-class homophile organizations as a point of departure for contemporary queer struggles for visibility, even while we open the language of visibility to critique. One of the issues we want to foreground in this introduction is thus the necessarily gnarled nature of thinking through cultural studies. To follow but one strand along its history or preoccupations is to forgo the strength of a good knot.

A different place to begin, then, to pry open the relationship between representation, visibility, and cinema is through an examination of race and ethnicity. As with much academic writing on cinema, much of our thinking about race, ethnicity and cinema borrows from work done in other disciplines: the literary scholars Hortense Spillers and Henry Louis Gates, Jr., and the philosopher Cornel West provide models of engaged intellectual work on African-American culture. Another trajectory of thought on race and ethnicity is more indebted to a political formation than an academic one: discussions of what is called "Third Cinema," a term proposed in the late 1960s to describe not simply the cinema of the Third World (itself a term coined in the service of Western power) but a political cinema of decolonization, anti-imperialism, and progressive social change. Debates around Third Cinema (some of which are available in the book, *Questions of Third Cinema*) galvanized some film scholars to pay attention to the extraordinary films produced in Africa and Latin America, as well as to look at some of the independent films of Britain and the US as related, as diaspora, to the political projects of decolonization. Discussions of Third Cinema have also spawned work in film studies on topics as various as the 1930s Hollywood "black cast" musicals, Mexican *telenovelas* and the recent films of Senegalese director Ousmane Sembene.

There is yet another trajectory of work on race and ethnicity that belongs more centrally to cultural studies, and we touch in what follows upon an essay by Isaac Julien and Kobena Mercer that reveals the contradictory nature of attempts to thematize race and "include" it among other ostensible topics. Tracing the lineages it establishes among work in cultural studies, some of which we have already opened in our section above on Marxism, is not tantamount to addressing a significant body of work in a field. Instead, we use moments as symptomatic, as revelatory of tendencies or directions, and we follow only a few of them. To take the work of two black British gay men (about which more below) as exemplary is, however, to pick apart the purity of the categories we have sketched. Moreover, what is most important to us about their work is its conviction,

---

16 Jane Gaines, "White Privilege and Looking Relations—Race and Gender in Feminist Film Theory," *Screen* 29 (4) (1988), 59–79. This is the issue edited by Julien and Mercer which we discuss shortly.

from the start, that visual texts (film, photography, video) be taken seriously in *any* discussion of the terms on our table: "the popular," Marxism, psychoanalysis, queerness, or black culture.

For Anglophone readers outside of Britain, the resonance of "black" requires a few words in advance. In Britain, the word "black" is a political category comparable to its usage in the US: "people of color." Both terms, "black" and "people of color," build connections among people of African, Afro-Caribbean, Asian and Latino origins. Both terms value solidarity. The comparison is not, however, perfect, as the transformation of "black" from an essentializing category to a coalition-building term of solidarity, as Mercer puts it, "remains a political achievement otherwise specific and unique to British conditions."[17] The stakes of that political achievement were to redress the lack of recognition of Asians (particularly South Asians) in cultural politics in Britain and to forge connections between different sources of cultural work. The historical patterns of immigration in Britain produced a generation of Britons who came of age (when Mercer did, in the late 1970s) there as their parents had not, since there was a massive wave of immigration from the West Indies and Asia following the break-up of the British Empire after World War II. This history of migration produced a specific set of political urgencies that are not translatable to the violent origins in slavery of many African-Americans, nor to the patterns of ethnic immigration in the US. Moreover, central to black British cultural politics are issues of the *nation*, of its imaginary and of belonging, a ground for the strong criticism of Raymond Williams' white vision of England found in Paul Gilroy (another important voice in black British cultural studies), whose first book was aptly titled *There Ain't No Black in the Union Jack*.[18] There have been a number of such important criticisms of the unquestioned status of the nation, of Britain more specifically, in the lineages and work of the Birmingham CCCS in the 1970s and 1980s.

The second note is, thus, on lineage: Isaac Julien is a black British gay filmmaker (to whose 1989 film, *Looking for Langston*, we will turn at the end of this section). His work with the film collective, Sankofa, helped to render film central to black British cultural politics in the 1980s, and his work remains central to our understanding of how film itself provides a critical voice in cultural studies. We turn to him, in other words, not further to install "British cultural studies" at the center of our understanding of what cultural studies might mean for our present study of cinema, but to emphasize how film (as the emblem of Americanization *par excellance* but also as a medium for cultural studies intellectual work) functions within the rubric of cultural studies. Kobena Mercer's critical work also emerged in the early 1980s from collective endeavors with the Gay Writer's Group in London; his writings on photography in particular (the work of Robert Mapplethorpe and the Nigerian-British photographer Rotimi Fani-Kayode, to take two examples) are among the most incisive (and delightful to read) critiques of simple identity-based politics in the field of cultural studies. Like Julien, Mercer has made the study of visual culture indispensable to the analysis of "culture." Both Julien and Mercer are deeply indebted to the work of Stuart Hall, who, as we have mentioned,

---

17 Kobena Mercer, "The Cultural Politics of Diaspora," in Kobena Mercer, *Welcome to the Jungle: New Positions in Black Cultural Studies* (London and New York: Routledge, 1994), 28. Mercer's essay in this volume includes revised portions of "De Margin and De Centre."

18 Paul Gilroy, *There Ain't No Black in the Union Jack: The Cultural Politics of Race and Nation* (London: Hutchinson, 1987).

was the driving force behind the CCCS. Hall is reluctant, in his own writings, to find himself at the origin of what we now call "cultural studies" (in this volume, for example), preferring instead rhetorically to install the work of Raymond Williams as the "founder." Rather than search for the "father" of the field, we want instead to position Julien, Mercer, and Hall in a line of thinkers crucial to the projects in this volume, whether or not they are explicitly named as such, by remarking in what follows on the ways in which they have insisted on critical questions, including the analysis of race and ethnicity, with an enormous energy, insistence, and insight from which we continue to learn.

Julien and Mercer wrote a joint introduction for an issue of the same journal, *Screen*, in which Laura Mulvey's influential essay appeared a quarter century earlier. Their introduction sets out a series of relationships among the study of film, the intellectual lineages of cultural studies, and the critical priority of race and ethnicity. Entitled "De Margin and De Centre," it puns by reference to the "centre" as the "Centre for Contemporary Cultural Studies" and yet positions itself in complicated ways in relation to the intellectual work of cultural studies, film studies, and their "centers" (meaning their institutions, their priorities, their exclusions, and their peripheries). Complicating the reference, for example, is the fact that the piece's initial appearance in *Screen* came in a special issue edited by Julien and Mercer and entitled "The Last 'Special Issue' on Race?" Through that title question they sought to make visible a contradiction: while the title foregrounds how the subjects of race and ethnicity are continually relegated to the margins (of institutions as well as of discussions and theories) and are treated nonetheless as urgent in "special issues" of journals, the "special issue" tends to reinforce rather than challenge "the perceived otherness and marginality of the subject itself."[19] From the interstices of this contradiction, Julien and Mercer follow the lines of a shift, initially proposed by Stuart Hall in his essay "New ethnicities," regarding black cultural politics. We find that shift, as well as Julien and Mercer's work, both intellectually central to the work of cultural studies as we see it in relation to the study of cinema, as well as helpful in providing specific explanation for the ways in which race is central to many of the essays in this volume.

In "New ethnicities," then, Hall marks a shift at the end of the 1980s in black British cultural politics. In Hall's view, there became visible in that decade's photography, music, film, painting, and literature a transition from critical and artistic struggles, over what he calls the "relations" of representation, to struggles (also critical and artistic) over what he calls the "politics" of representation itself.[20] Included for Hall among the "relations of representation" are battles over *access* to the rights to representation (access to resources, funding, expertise, exhibition space, critical responses, and the like), as well as a form of contestation over the continuing marginalization, stereotyping, and fetishization of the black image, countered by the assertion of a " 'positive' black imagery".[21] That is, as with some strands of gay and lesbian cinema we have discussed, makers and intellectuals focused on the need to gain access to the tools of cultural production and a need to respond to negative images produced by the mainstream; this work continues

19 Isaac Julien and Kobena Mercer, "De Margin and De Centre," reprinted in *Stuart Hall: Critical Dialogues in Cultural Studies*, edited by David Morley and Kuan-Hsing Chen (London and New York: Routledge, 1996), 450.
20 Ibid., 442.
21 Ibid.

and remains vital, but it has spawned another whole domain of struggle around cultural politics.

Included in Hall's second term (the "politics" of representation), then, are two significant maneuvers: first, an encounter between black cultural politics and a largely white, Eurocentric critical and cultural theory. The names of those theoretical positions are continuously contested, and their contestation has to do with the extent to which they encounter new constituencies, new contexts and new challenges such as that posed by black British intellectuals; they include the various discourses of poststructuralism, postmodernism, psychoanalysis, Marxism and post-Marxism, and feminism. Second, the shift marks what Hall calls the "end of innocence," or the end of the innocent notion of the essential black subject. Hall explains:

> What is at issue here is the recognition of the extraordinary diversity of subjective positions, social experiences and cultural identities which comprise the category "black"; that is, the recognition that "black" is essentially a politically and culturally *constructed* category, which cannot be grounded in a set of fixed trans-cultural or transcendental racial categories and which therefore has no guarantees in nature. What this brings into play is the recognition of the immense diversity and differentiation of the historical and cultural experience of black subjects.[22]

In this passage, Hall is keen to see "black" in terms of its cultural construction, without having to make recourse to an essential ground (whether biological, historical, or otherwise). One can see the importance in such an argument: Hall is seeking to avoid any concept that would ground "black" experience in an eternal nature rather than a mutable culture. If race, in other words, simply "is" (naturalized, essentialized) and is for all time (eternal), then racism can't be eliminated. The careful reader may, however, want to note how Hall's own language slips: " 'black' is *essentially* a politically and culturally constructed category" (our change of italics from the above citation). What we want to underscore here is the sense in which the shift Hall is marking is, strictly speaking, an impossible one. We routinely say, "What I mean is essentially that . . ." and by "essentially" we do mean to get down to some ground. We all inhabit some views of the world that are grounded on essentialism. The question is, what ground, and when is such a move dangerous?

This latter question preoccupies current work on race and ethnicity as well as on gender and sexuality, and has proven to be a sticky one. There are a number of apparent routes out of the essentialist/constructivist debates, the most speedy among them a shift in terms. Hence the proliferation of discussions of hybridity (the cross-fertilization of a number of subject-positions at once: Nigerian-British, black feminist, gay Taiwanese); of *mestizaje* (a Chicano term for "mixing"); of translation (a term favored by Hall as well as theorist Homi Bhabha); or, finally, of the language of crossing borders, deep ambivalence, multiplicity, difference, and the like. A slower route, but a productive one especially in combination with the coining of new concepts and metaphors, is the historical one: one built, as our discussion of Antonio Gramsci's work suggests, on the identification of what he called "conjunctures" and their trajectories.

---

22 Ibid., 443.

Julien and Mercer are conjunctural thinkers, indebted again to Stuart Hall in his discussion of "Gramsci's relevance for the study of race and ethnicity."[23] They urge political criticism by rejecting the "celebratory" mode of reception: as Hall puts it, "[f]ilms are not necessarily good because black people make them. They are not necessarily 'right-on' by virtue of the fact that they deal with the black experience."[24] They reject both a "one-sided" fixation with marginality that keeps race in "special issues" and assumes that "ethnicity belongs to the Other alone,"[25] while at the same time they reject a unitary notion of blackness (or ethnicity more generally) that smothers its internal differences and cultural and social specificity. There is not one racism but many, there is not one ethnicity but many over time, there is not one challenge to dominant discourses but many, and there are equally many (in Gayatri Spivak's phrase) "epistemic violences" (violences at the level of thought) that those discourses have wrought. We return to the problem of what to do with these multiplicities.

Diaspora, postcoloniality, subalternity

Isaac Julien's 1989 film, *Looking for Langston* (Fig. I.2), refracts "blackness" like a prism, refusing a unitary notion of racial (and, for that matter, ethnic or sexual) categories: black culture, both black British and African-American, glimmers in its facets as a complex history, seductive both in its surface's sheen as well as in the substance of its political and aesthetic productions. What "official" black history denies, homosexual desire, the film affirms in abundance; whatever most would want to see as separate, the film conjoins. Julien thus "meditates" (as he tells us in an introductory intertitle) upon the Harlem Renaissance in order to generate multiple connections (Britain and the US, white and black, straight and gay), connections that furthermore introduce queerness into the folds of diaspora (by diaspora, we mean a community of common origin violently dispelled and dispersed).

The film's title summons the American poet, Langston Hughes, a key figure in the effulgent African-American literary and cultural output of 1920s New York City called, in retrospect, "the Harlem Renaissance." To remember the Harlem Renaissance is generally to forget that it was a product of white patronage ("when Harlem was in vogue"), that its artists therefore had to conform to the image patrons held of black expression, including the images of primitivism, hyper-masculinity and heterosexuality. The film remembers otherwise. It literally looks elsewhere; it seeks to open the hidden vaults of black collective memory, to explore the fact of Hughes' homosexuality along with other "closeted" or finessed secrets of sexuality in the Harlem Renaissance. Neither a biography of Hughes nor a traditional period piece, *Looking for Langston* traverses, as does a dream, the distance between "now" (the late 1980s, HIV- and AIDS-related gay-bashing, urban gay life) and "then" (a remarkable but quashed moment of black cultural expression); it also trammels, in that temporal movement, distinctions between black and white, popular culture and avant-garde art and cinema, photography and film, and poetry and prose.

Looking for Langston is not, in other words, a popular film: it is not quite feature-length, has not had a commercial run, is not narrative in form, has not been seen by

---

23 In *Stuart Hall: Critical Dialogues in Cultural Studies*, 411–440.
24 Ibid., 441–449.
25 Ibid., 455.

Figure I.2 Meeting of Two Queens. Courtesy of Women Make Movies

many people (and, not only is it "about" black gay poets but its form prompted one irritated film scholar to complain in *Screen*, "Audiences do matter . . . If you're practical you do want to reach people beyond your buddies").[26] The film does, however, in José Arroyo's reading, "[link] black British culture and black American culture through time and space as a diaspora culture."[27] Musical forms such as the blues join Britain to the US, while British pop star Jimmy Somerville presides as an angel over the internationally popular house music of the film's gleeful conclusive defeat of gay-bashers. What is of more interest to most critics than the cultural forms that provide the diasporic glue for the film are the much-discussed ways in which the film explores desire, voyeurism, fetishism and scopophilia (literally, the love of looking) through the image of the black male body and the loving/desiring gaze of the gay man.

Through its iconography of desire, the film challenges traditional conceptions of racial, diasporic, or postcolonial politics. Instead of fists in the air as the sign of revolutionary fervor, we see an eyebrow raised over a glass of champagne, as one black man cruises

26 Judith Williamson, "Two Kinds of Otherness: Black Film and the Avant-garde," *Screen* 4 (29) (1988), 111.
27 José Arroyo, "Isaac Julien: Look Back and Talk Back," in Michael T. Martin, ed., *Cinemas of the Black Diaspora: Diversity, Dependence and Oppositionality* (Detroit: Wayne State University Press, 1995), 331.

another. Instead of a Soviet-inspired montage of the debased nature of American commodity culture (as in the epic Third Cinematic masterpiece, *Hour of the Furnaces*), we experience an homage to the links between the avant-garde and popular culture through visual quotations. (To mention only photography and cinema, *Looking for Langston* is a citational mecca: it makes, if sometimes oblique, reference to queer filmmakers such as Kenneth Anger, Jean Cocteau, and Derek Jarman; photographers of the male body such as Robert Mapplethorpe and George Platt-Lynes; and the much-loved queer playwright, novelist, and criminal, Jean Genet.) Instead of locating resistance in Africa or in Latin America, Julien pinpoints the capacity for glorious rebellion in dark alleys in the midst of New York (or Sydney, or Dublin). Julien's refusal of the resolute distance of alterity (of struggle and of "real politics") most marks this film as diasporic (as Arroyo seems to indicate in his careful reading of the film's lyrics and poetry). Proximity, the literal cuddling up to the complexity of marginality: Julien takes this path in order to elucidate not only the experience but the fantasies and the desires of the diaspora.

Diaspora, the experience of the migrant (in, say, urban London), is not the same thing as decolonization or the experience of the subaltern (a term Gramsci borrowed from the military to denote the lowest in rank, used by him to mean the lowest in social position), as it were, at home. The work of Gayatri Chakravorty Spivak is often at pains to make a distinction that is often obscured by the kind of "hybridity" talk we noted above. Though she (rhetorically) insists that she is not a film critic, Spivak has read Stephen Frears' 1987 film *Sammy and Rosie Get Laid* precisely in order to make such a distinction visible.[28] What interests her in that film, and what preoccupies her work more generally, is the careful, patient reading of difference: the difference between a Pakistani who has grown up in London and his father who has held power in the Pakistani government following Independence and the Partition of India and Pakistan in 1947; the difference between the labor politics of low-caste women in India and the Western rhetoric of "global feminism"; the difference between how a poem makes meaning and how a film might represent desire. As we suggested above in our remarks on Marx, the apparent ease with which exploitative capitalist forms of organization are devouring the planet should make us all the more attentive to uneven, contradictory, and layered phenomena and perceptions and conceptions of the world, if we are to think about change at all.

Conclusion

To a powerful degree, the contributors to this volume are passionate about change: change as measured through film's histories, change as measured through film form; change as measured through politics as we think of "it" conventionally (electoral, forms of law and government) or change as measured through a more expansive understanding of social and cultural organization. In this introduction we have attempted to follow enough of the threads of intellectual history to make palpable the texture of the collection as a whole. We have, in addition, provided the sections that follow with separate introductory comments, seeking to link the individual essays to these discussions of race, feminism, Marxism, and psychoanalysis. We hope the reader will find them useful.

28 Gayatri Chakravorty Spivak, "*Sammy and Rosie Get Laid*," in G. C. Spivak, *Outside in the Teaching Machine* (New York and London: Routledge, 1993), 243–254.

Part I

Woman as inter/national sign

Introduction

National borders seem so common-sensically self-evident as a defining fact of contemporary life that we only become aware of them in the (often policed and restricted, always political) movement across them. Despite the variety of utopian claims asserted in the name of globalization and the apparent ease of movement of information and goods across these national thresholds, the enduring political and economic conditions of nations mean that subjects of national address find themselves caught in a dual ideological bind of identifying themselves as part of a nation while also discovering the traffic of representations of themselves as national "others." Nowhere is this more pressing than in the situation of women, who in many national rhetorics become the defining emblem of national idealizations of what constitutes appropriate and obedient citizenship—in the making of new national subjects (children), in the production of the household as the model of efficiency and affective stability, and in the willingness to take on subordinate spheres of labor within the larger matrixes of industrial production.

The essays in this section examine the impact of such national identities on women in a variety of spheres, and the first thing to note about them is that they carefully avoid any assumptions about what it means to be addressed as a female subject within any national register without contemplating how specific forms of femininity are continually constituted within an international framework. These essays can therefore be understood as taking seriously Gayatri Chakravorty Spivak's challenge[1] to locate always the woman who is spoken for, and whether the fact of one woman's speaking, say, in the location of American feminist intellectual work, has an impact on how such an argument tacitly assumes another woman elsewhere whose experiences cannot be encompassed in such a moment of theory. The point is not to censure, but to locate the woman who speaks and on what terms. Together, then, these essays ask about how, where, and to what ends images of women are produced and circulated; they help us to think about the relation of gender to genre (types of films such as science fiction or documentary) and also about the protocols for reading films closely. Frequently, that is, these essays ask us to declare as candidly as possible where we stand as readers: making visible our own assumptions about feminism, about the struggles of women beyond but imbricated in "the West," about violence and, just as significant, about pleasure.

As with the other sections to come, we introduce a caveat. Many of the other essays in this volume could equally well be at home in this section, written as they are by feminists,

---

1 For example, see her essay, "French Feminism in an International Frame," in G. C. Spivak, *In Other Worlds: Essays in Cultural Politics* (New York: Methuen, 1987).

for whom gender politics, transnational capitalism, and processes of decolonization are critical and intellectual priorities: Marcia Landy's discussion of Australian adolescent cosmopolitanism, as it imagines Aboriginal organizations of time and space, in *Heavenly Creatures*, or Rey Chow's reading of the "gay" (read, male) film *Happy Together*. Many of the essays in this section, too, might well belong to a separate section on "history," a term we would prefer not to deaden further by relegating it to a compartment of thought; instead, we would ask readers to keep alive an appreciation for both historical contingency (the chance nature of events) and for historical determination. If we learn from the essays we have included in this section that our habitual ways of organizing knowledge require overhauls, that our wisdom is partial and, more significant, *located*, we ought to become better readers of the sections that follow.

1 "You've been in my life so long I can't remember anything else"

Into the labyrinth with Ripley and the Alien

Pamela Church Gibson

The postwar settlement was supposed to mark the dawn of a new era of regulation and control . . . Fueled by a complex of military goals, corporate interests, solid-state economies and industrial-strength testosterone, computers were supposed to be a fool-proof means to the familiar ends of social security, political organisation, economic order, prediction and control . . . All digital computers translate information into the zeros and ones of machine code . . . perfect symbols of the orders of western reality, the ancient logical codes which make the difference . . . between . . . light and dark, form and matter, mind and body . . . And they made a lovely couple when it came to sex . . .

In the 1990s, western cultures were suddenly struck by an extraordinary sense of volatility in all matters sexual; differences, relations, identities, definitions, roles, attributes, means and ends . . . Heterosexual relations were losing their viability, queer connections were flourishing, the carnival had begun for a vast range of paraphilias and so-called perversions, and if there was more than one sex to have, there were also more than two to be.

Sadie Plant, *Zeros and Ones*

Introduction

Twenty years ago, Ripley first encountered the Alien and, the conflict concluded, she sank back, seemingly triumphant, into hypersleep. The "sole survivor of the *Nostromo*" was "signing off"—but not for long. The popular imagination was stirred, a huge fan base generated—and the academy, unsurprisingly, responded swiftly to this extraordinary film with its two unusual protagonists. Here was a six-foot-tall heroine, strong, slim, and resourceful, facing up to her monstrous Other in the darkness of deep space and in a future seemingly dominated by a peculiarly unpleasant militaristic mode of supra-global capitalism. This potent mix provoked fans and film-scholars alike into different modes of activity—and made the studios aware of the vast commercial potential of their new product.

It might seem a straightforward task, to chronicle the subsequent history and relationship of these different players and to follow the saga through the reception of the next three films, charting the reaction of audiences and focusing on the varied activity within the academy—and its uneasy relationship with "spectators," many of whom became increasingly busy within a parallel universe of their own; a flourishing subculture swiftly emerged, focused around comics, computer games, magazines, novels and, latterly, internet activities. It would appear easy enough to outline the history of film theory during the last two decades, and to describe the different strands in the work that was inspired

Figure 1.1 Sigourney Weaver and Winona Ryder in *Alien Resurrection* (20th Century Fox 1997). Courtesy of the Kobal Collection

by these particular films, which was so interestingly prolific at first and is so notable, now, for its comparative paucity. *Alien 3*, it is true, did receive some academic attention—but *Alien Resurrection* (Fig. 1.1), which could be used so effectively to illustrate recent developments within critical theory, has been virtually ignored by those very theorists for whom it could have been made. Audiences, too, were disappointed by this last film—but fans are waiting eagerly for *Alien V*, which they hope will make good the deficiencies of the fourth instalment and will at least put Ripley and Alien back in the frame and on the screen.

However, the task became both baffling and daunting, as if this writer were one of the hapless characters who follow Ripley down those endless dark—and lovingly described—corridors, shafts, and tunnels to where the Alien waits, now poised to eradicate any foolish attempt to impose order, structure, or overview. So complex are the inter-relationships between the players, so tortuous and intertwined the various histories played out over the past twenty years, that the only way to escape is to present a series of reflections. Connecting and guiding threads will, I trust, be visible to guide the reader through the labyrinth.

Weaver, Ripley, and the Alien

In 1979, Sigourney Weaver first took on the role of Warrant Officer Ripley—who was to become her Significant Other, her alter ego, and to remain so for almost twenty years, perhaps for longer. For the films may, of course, continue—fans, who have their own ways of making their voices heard, want the saga to carry on, as indeed it has within their own, independent, activities. Weaver herself, empowered in the last two films as executive producer, has talked of a prequel, possibly involving a return to the planet where the eggs were originally discovered. Weaver as actress is continually recontextualized through this continuing struggle with the Alien, a generalized figure of threatening Otherness—not traditionally a part of the construction and presentation of the Hollywood star, not when that star is a woman. Arguably Ripley's shifting persona and her relationship with this dark Other makes her for Weaver a strangely compelling alter ego, where boundaries of identification can easily become blurred.

She herself is very aware of the extraordinary, and changing, nature of Ripley's feelings for and about the Alien—she has articulated these more freely, indeed, than many academics. Interviewed when *Alien Resurrection* was released, she asked, "Why should you be afraid the alien is going to eat you? I certainly think that what it is going to do to you is sexual." To illustrate this, she described a scene which both she and Ridley Scott wanted to include in the first film, in which she hides naked in a closet. Seeing her exposed flesh, the Alien reaches out to touch and stroke this body with a surface so unlike its own (Nathan 1997: 134). Significantly, this interview was accompanied by a publicity still from the film which shows Ripley stretched out languorously in the Alien nest, the zip of her jerkin undone to the waist, a tentacle protruding from her crotch.

The diaries that she kept during the shooting stress the nature of this sequence and of her delight in the new, part-Alien, Ripley—"What a relief, finally, to let out the monster in myself" (Weaver 1997: 115). Their publication in *Premiere* is illustrated by a photograph taken by Annie Liebowitz, now best known for her *Vanity Fair* cover shots, which shows Ripley posed with hand spread against her thigh to display her long darkly varnished fingernails, in the tight leather outfit, ribbed, studded, and buckled, that she wears in the film—the antithesis of the baggy fatigues seen throughout the first three movies.

Reviewers and academicians alike are happy to give us psychoanalytic readings of the films. But they disregard, overlook, or perhaps fight shy of certain implications of Ripley's repeated confrontations with this creature which gestates In There—both within our psyche and within our bodily cavities—and is discovered Out There, in the recesses of deep space, the product of the desire to probe and the capitalist drive to colonize and possess.

This particular Alien has an extraordinary fascination for audiences and academy alike. It can be understood as "monster from the Id," manifestation of sexual terrors, reflection of xenophobic fears, or as this essay would suggest, all of these and more, tied to the structures of power—the monstrous Other not just of the rapacious "Company" whose covert activities bring it within the "human" sphere of activity, but arguably of patriarchal capitalism itself. This last may seem overly simplistic, or at least a familiar cinematic motif—*Frankenstein*, *The Mummy* and *Godzilla*, to name but three examples, show us something monstrous stirred up by the desire to conquer, the wish to tamper, and post-Enlightenment male-directed scientific activity. What is new and for some disturbing is the symbiotic relationship, with sexual connotations, established and developed in this series between the central protagonist and this unsettling Other. Despite—or perhaps because of—its liberal persuasion, the academy often seems to operate certain repressive or censoring mechanisms when considering certain aspects of sexuality.

It seems imperative, within an academic overview such as this, to try and understand exactly what it is about the shifting relationship between Ripley and the Alien, as the cycle progresses, that activates such censorship, whether unintentional or unconscious. There is a great deal of writing about the psychoanalytic underpinning of the first two films, but there are certain things that this strand of scholarship seems to overlook, and it chooses to eschew almost entirely any discussion of the last two films with their different sexual and political implications. It is safer, it seems, to couch discussion of sexuality in a particular way and to displace certain diegetic elements. Where the die-gesis prevents such evasion, many scholars are happier to evade the challenges of these problematic texts—the critical neglect of the last two films is very noticeable, very pro-nounced. But although these two films were not commercially successful, the audiences—and in particular the hardcore fans—did not shy away from their disturbing portrayal of difference. *Alien 3* and *Alien Resurrection* were more avant-garde in form and con-tent and were less successful commercially, particularly in the United States. However, audiences await the return of Ripley and Alien—any cursory study of fan activity will reveal a fixed, firm, unshakeable belief that there will soon be some cinematic reincar-nation of these two protagonists.

Over the past twenty years, four very different directors have created and used Ripley and the Aliens in very different ways—Ridley Scott in 1979, James Cameron in 1986, David Fincher in 1992, and Jean-Pierre Jeunet in 1997 (see the Filmography at the end of this chapter). Indeed, the only constant is the on-screen presence of Ripley herself. This is only a constant in that Ripley is always played by Weaver—for Ripley mutates, alters, and changes throughout the films in the same way as the Alien. She, too, is Protean—something sometimes overlooked in the multitudinous body of work in which she is studied. For, at first, Ripley and Alien were subject to endless re-examination, using different strategies which sometimes—though not always—reflected development and diversification within critical theory itself. Film scholars scrutinized the earlier films as thoroughly as the scientists of the Company and United Systems Military examined the alien life-forms within the diegesis. This obsessive scrutiny lessened as the cycle of films continued—though there is still a flutter within the laboratories, as elsewhere, when the name "Ripley" is mentioned. But it does seem important to understand exactly why academic interest dissipated, to a point where *Alien Resurrection* was almost ignored within filmic scholarship. There seems to have been some unexpected rupture between *Aliens* and *Alien 3*.

For after the restoration of order so carefully provided—in different ways—within the narrative frameworks of the first two films, and the triumph in both of Ripley as sur-vivor, the audiences and the academy alike were perhaps taken aback by her suicide and self-sacrifice in the closing minutes of the third film. Her spectacular slow-motion dive backwards into the blast furnace filled with molten lead was her solution, her way of escaping the clutches of the Company scientists and denying them access to the Alien infant within her; in the closing moments, the Queen suddenly bursts from her chest, and Ripley cradles the child to her, accepting this final intertwining, during the long, slow fall to their deaths within the fiery pit beneath them.

Once the shock had subsided, explanations appeared. But for Weaver herself, the Ripley of *Alien 3* seemed a logical progression—and that acceptance of her relationship with the Alien is something she wants to stress. She is also keen to explain the motivation here and within the very different context of *Alien Resurrection*.

Although she was not originally part of Fox's plans for *Alien 3*, when the film was finally made, after endless changes of script, director and setting, Weaver was for the first time in the position of executive producer. She talks of her admiration for Fincher who "had a very hard time with the studio," and of her own support for his attempt to make a completely different film. He wanted to "turn it all inside out"; she approves of the fact that "what Jim Cameron built up, Fincher wanted to destroy." She herself felt at this juncture that "if they were going to make a dumb Alien Vs. Predator" (one of the ideas on the Fox drawing-board at this stage) "then I didn't want to be a part of it . . . that's one of the reasons I died" (Nathan 1997: 126). Notably, in this film, there are no guns, after the massive display of weaponry and firepower in *Aliens*. Weaver insisted on this—and she also suggested that Ripley should have her first sexual encounter. An interview with one of the Special Effects technicians, who wanted to remain anonymous, stressed the nature of her input in a magazine interview: "From what I was told she had a lot to do with the script; she was the one who didn't want there to be any guns in this film, she was the one who decided to have the love scene . . . there was no reason for it other than she decided Ripley should get into bed with someone" (Pearce 1992: 68).

The rationale behind and nature of such decisions, the circumstances in which these films were produced, and the difficulties of their gestation—all have been largely ignored by scholarship around the cycle. These seemingly mundane considerations seem to be highly significant omissions. It is surely important that there is another Company—possibly as rapacious as that revealed and depicted within the films. Twentieth Century Fox own what they describe as "the franchise"—and all the profits from the assorted merchandising. But interestingly, were it not for a decision on the part of this Company, Weaver and Ripley would not have survived the first film. The original ending to *Alien* had Ripley beheaded by her adversary—with all the implications thereof—who then, using her voice, transmits a message to Earth, explaining that the last survivor is on the way home. It has recently been revealed that Fox refused "to greenlight such a downbeat ending" (Leigh 1998: 5) and so Ripley triumphed, while Weaver went on to fight a series of battles with executives at the studio.

It seems important to be aware of these extra-diegetic struggles, which inform the relationship between Weaver and Ripley, and within which the on-screen Ripley is conceived. The rebirth of the new Ripley—Clone Eight of *Alien Resurrection*—had Weaver, as always completely identified with this character, as pro-active midwife. In interview, she discusses her collaboration with Jeunet: "He trusted me completely and wasn't deterred by my ideas about the new Ripley." She then presents some of these ideas: "When you come back from the dead, you don't take very much seriously—especially people trying to stay alive. She certainly wasn't concerned with saving people. She has been set free from what I would call human obligations" (Nathan 1997: 130).

Those who know the films well will recall Ash's words about the Alien in the first film—he declares his admiration for this creature unblemished by "delusions of morality." This new part-alien Ripley of the last film, of so little interest it seems to the academy, is not only a "meat by-product" of the cloning process—so General Perez describes her in the text—but also a radical departure from the "human" Ripley, and the joint creation of Weaver, Jeunet, and Joss Whedon. It was Whedon, the screenwriter, who first suggested to Fox that they solve the problem of what to do with the series by bringing Ripley back from the dead. This scientific meddling with choices over life and death appealed to Weaver—"that sort of final liberty no longer exists and I was very curious to play someone who is brought back against her will" (Nathan 1997: 124).

Her diaries show the struggles she had with the Fox studio chairman to keep intact certain graphic scenes, "the coolest and creepiest stuff," and emphasize throughout her feelings for the Alien, now both her "baby" and her sibling—through the incestuous implications of the cloning process—and with whom she will unwittingly produce a whole new life-form, a hybrid: "It's a novel experience for Ripley to surrender. I am supremely lucky because Jean-Pierre really understands the relationship Ripley has with the Alien. The French are great—you just can't shock them" (Weaver 1997: 147).

It is both interesting and ironic that it should be the Hollywood actress, rather than any hovering academic, who is most willing to state explicitly just how transgressive is the nature of the relationship between her on-screen character and her on-screen Other. Weaver certainly understands that some very queer things are going on—and is happy to talk about them. As, indeed, are the fans. To be fair, what critical writing there is on the last two texts has begun to explore the implications of this last phase of the Ripley–Alien partnership—but even then, there is, at times, a crucial holding back.

We should remember, too, that for fans—and Weaver—the Alien species is as important as Ripley herself. Popular literature has described their separate, independent adventures, while a novel written to follow on from the last film showed what one fan happily recognized as "at last . . . the aliens' point of view" (amazon.com homepage 1999: www.amazon.com).

The academy and its activities

Parallel to these cinematic re-creations of Ripley and her oppositional Other, an inordinate amount of critical literature appeared. Cultural readings of films and characters were, at first, spawned as speedily and as prolifically as the alien creatures themselves. For to continue the comparison, just as the aliens swiftly found—albeit unwilling—host bodies for their gestation and rampant breeding, so they and their adversary found an instant welcome within the field of film scholarship. There, the fascination with them has not completely faded.

The academic study of the Alien saga is indicative of the divisions and fissures within the discipline of film theory. It is perhaps disturbing, that, with some exceptions, the political and psychoanalytic readings of the film seem to proceed along parallel tracks, never converging. Some writers who use models of psychoanalysis, such as Harvey Greenberg, Annette Kuhn and Constance Penley, do so from within an overall political and left-wing perspective. However, others seem unaware of the fact that there are very different readings of the Alien itself, which possess a literal and political specificity. Amy Taubin writes of the confrontation at the end of *Aliens* between Ripley and the Queen: "If Ripley is the prototypical upper-middle-class WASP, the alien queen bears a suspicious resemblance to a favourite scapegoat of the Reagan era—the black welfare mother, that parasite on the economy whose uncurbed productive drive reduced hard-working taxpayers to bankruptcy" (Taubin 1992: 9).

Annette Kuhn, in her essay "Border Crossing," has made similar parallels between a fear of "aliens" from elsewhere in the universe and that of illegal immigrants (Kuhn 1992: 13), while for Charles Ramirez Berg, *Aliens* reflects the feelings of the Reagan government that it faced an uncontrollable influx of Hispanic/Latino immigrants. For him, the conflict between the two mothers in the closing sequence shows us Ripley as the "civilized" mother. The Alien mother is "a monster out of the nativist's worst nightmares, procreation gone mad, uncontrollable and unstoppable" (Ramirez Berg 1989: 14). There is something explicit, in the dialogue itself, which supports these readings—furthermore, it's in the form of a supposed "joke" made by the edgy Hudson at the expense of the only Hispanic character, Vasquez: "Hey man, she thought you said ILLE-GAL aliens!"

I am not suggesting that any form of reading is necessarily to be preferred—though arguably the psychoanalytic readings have, in fact, taken precedence. I am, however, concerned that there should always be some critical acknowledgement of different and divergent readings. I am assuming, too, that readers of this article will be aware of the arguments woven around the first two films, and of seminal texts, such as Barbara Creed's work on the monstrous-feminine (Creed 1993: 16–31).

Surely, the reader of this particular piece might justifiably or even wearily conclude, there can be nothing left to say. But there are the strange omissions, the absences, and the academic shunning of the last two films—these things have not yet been addressed. And the films should be contextualized not only within the parameters of critical theory itself, but could now be reviewed, in retrospect, as products of particular political moments which they, in so many different ways, reflect.

Alien was made in the very year that Margaret Thatcher became British Prime Minister—the first woman ever to hold that position, she wrought profound and irreversible social and economic change. The Welfare State was dismantled, the industrial infrastructure permitted to decay, while laissez-faire economics meant that entrepreneurs were encouraged, aided, and abetted in their activities. "There is no such thing as society," Thatcher famously declared. Her Significant Other, a man she admired and supported in all his interventionist foreign activities, was Ronald Reagan. Both these politicians were famously xenophobic, even imperialist, while they shared the same belief in "family values," and an abhorrence of "deviant" social and sexual behavior.

In retrospect, it is easy to see—together with many other things—some fear of this aggressive brand of capitalism and its consequences in *Alien*, and indeed to see in *Aliens* some tacit acceptance of what are now usually described as the "gung-ho" foreign adventures that characterized the era of Reagan and Thatcher. This is not to call for a simplistic one-to-one correspondence between film and political climate—but simply to stress the different political and ideological circumstances that they mirror. The cycle spans two decades—the certainties of Reagan and Thatcher were replaced, as the economic climate worsened in both countries, first by the cautious, ineffectual pragmatism shared by George Bush and John Major, and finally in the 1990s by the centrist, supposedly liberal politics of Bill Clinton and Tony Blair. The final film was released just three years before the end of the millennium, in a climate of political and social uncertainty.

These years also saw changes, if not upheavals, in critical theory. The first film appeared at the very end of the 1970s, a decade in which film study had been dominated by psychoanalysis—and offered itself up almost as a justification of this particular approach. That same decade saw feminism firmly established within the academy—and Ripley, as active female protagonist, was fruitful material for a number of very different feminist interpretations. From the earliest ecstatic embraces of Ripley as feminist icon—with some dissenting voices—she later became the centre of arguments around motherhood, sexual identity, and women's reproductive rights. For during the 1980s, increased debates around and interest in the body again found a focus in these films where bodies, both human and alien, form both backdrop, landscape, and site of conflict.

The most significant developments in the last decades of the millennium, surely, are the work of postcolonialist scholars and queer theorists—and their legitimation within the scholastic arena—and the work of cyberfeminists such as Donna J. Haraway and Sadie Plant. The work of Haraway, Plant, and others is a dramatic rupture within feminist theoretical thought. Yet, while there has been some acknowledgment of the way in which the films might function within the context of recent feminist work, there has been no real seizing of these films—and especially of *Alien Resurrection*—with the zest that could be expected. Throughout the entire cycle some very queer readings suggest themselves, while this last film is almost a *locus classicus* for queer theory. Furthermore, the ending of this film, where a six-foot woman who is part-alien and a small female android bond together, socially and sexually, to save the planet from destruction, could seem almost designed to showcase the potential of the alliances and acknowledgments advocated in "A Manifesto for Cyborgs" (Haraway 1985).

Here, too, a post-patriarchal world is hinted at—during the flight from the aliens, the android Call (Winona Ryder) finally breaks into the mainframe of the ship's computer, "Father," at Ripley's insistence—and crashes the system. So when the unpleasant scientist who conducted the cloning of Ripley and the Alien Queen tries to access the ship's network and escape from the chaos he has created, it is a woman's voice that tells him "Father's dead, asshole." She has already handed the new part-alien Ripley a flame-thrower with which to torch the laboratory in which she was created, which still contained, floating in great glass jars, the grotesque mutants that were Clones One to Six. Alive, and chained naked on an operating table, Clone Seven—with Ripley's face and a dreadfully misshapen body—pleaded "Kill me." This particular aberrant alliance between militarism and science is ended by a feminist blend—machine, human, and alien.

The film teases out all the implications and problems of the cloning process—and the psychosexual dimensions—and does so in the light of recent scientific developments, so it is surprising that there has not been far more interdisciplinary feminist interest in the film. Perhaps it is the way the vision of the future is presented—and the fact that it jars with the very different dystopian vision of *Alien 3*, which is itself unsettling within the context of the cycle. The two films do not sit happily together.

The differences between the two films are as marked, as radical in formal terms as the difference between *Alien 3* and its predecessor. *Alien 3* disrupts the cycle completely —since the *mise-en-scène* is, for the first and only time, constructed to suggest the decaying industrial infrastructure of an Anglo-American present rather than a hi-tech, intergalactic future. Much of the film is set within grim, grey prison buildings—and in these scenes, whether the setting is a bleak, sparsely equipped canteen, a delapidated, Victorian infirmary, a scrapyard full of mouldering, obsolete mechanical parts, or the endless decrepit corridors, the lighting is subdued. The scenes within the "work facility" by contrast, are characterized from the start by the lurid orange light of the vast, spectacular furnace. The factory with its huge turning wheels, endless shafts and ladders, seems almost nineteenth century in appearance and ambience. The settings and story are bleak, dystopian—the music reflects the relentless, remorseless drive toward the unexpected, shocking catharsis. But the opening sequence of *Alien Resurrection* once again takes us back to a gleaming future—various interlocking sets of vast double steel doors slide open, white-coated scientists go about their work, surfaces shine. However, as the film progresses, there are shifts and changes—the sinister scientists on their massive futuristic ship are joined by the piratical crew of the Betty, an ancient, rusty space freighter, with its bas-relief of Betty Grable, as revealed in the closing moments of the film. This knowing glimpse of a mid-twentieth-century icon gives us some clue to the formal strategies of the film. It does seem, in its mix of settings, its deployment of strategies from various filmic genres, and its camp humour, to be self-consciously "postmodern." By contrast with the grim vision presented by the formal strategies at work in the third film, this last film is considerably lighter in tone and mode—and its vision, ultimately, far more positive, even utopian.

The insights of postmodernism, too, have not really been used in the critical work around these films, despite a claim that *Alien* and *Bladerunner* "have become canonical touchstones not just for discussions of difference but also for those engaged in debates about postmodernism and the nature of postmodern aesthetics and representation" (Cook and Bernink 1999: 193). This comment is perhaps predicated more upon the content of the films than upon the strategies at work within the *Alien* canon—but the entire series, in fact, is subjected to a self-referential and gleeful postmodern pastiche in *Alien Resurrection*. This film continually reworks dialogue from the earlier films, and plays with the narrative conventions and the range of characters that have developed within the cycle itself. It consciously makes reference to other films—homage is paid to *The Poseidon Adventure*, *Rio Bravo*, and *Johnny Guitar*, among others—while the whole film is infused with a mordant humour, its dialogue dominated by sardonic comments and wisecracks, all unthinkable in its predecessors.

The changes in the cycle and the pariah status—within the academy—of these last two films, together with their very different reception among the fans of the series, seem to make certain insinuations inevitable. Perhaps fan commentary is more attuned, not only to the films themselves, but also to the new sensibilities that follow from the work of Donna Haraway and Sadie Plant—and which are reflected in *Alien Resurrection*.

Scholars and spectators

There is, in the *Alien* scholarship, a strange absence of work on audience. Given the recent growth of reception studies and the way in which acknowledged audience demands for more instalments have kept Ripley and the Aliens alive—indeed, have brought about their resurrection from the dead—this seems odd. In a recent article, Martin Barker argues that, despite the resurgence of reception studies, there is a need for further work:

> There are issues at stake which film scholars neglect at some peril . . . the serious attention which filmmakers give to their audiences and the role that audience research has in "their" work . . . [and] the simple fact that, however unintended, academic work on audiences already contains assumptions about the "audience"—assumptions which almost certainly will not stand up to rigorous testing.
>
> (Barker 1998: 143)

He describes the problems within the psychoanalytic tradition of criticism, that it posits an "assumed view of the audience" which "should be tested," and concludes, given his own roots in "the traditions of British cultural studies" where audiences "are always, and in complicated ways, social," that the qualitative and ethnographic modes of research found within that tradition can fruitfully be deployed. He concludes: "We badly need a real community of researchers regularly exchanging knowledge and ideas —willing to look at ways to combine different kinds of research; quantitative and qualitative, historical and contemporary, archival and primary" (143).

"Audiences" are not only largely ignored by *Alien* scholars—or, as Barker implies, subject to certain untested assumptions within the proliferation of psychoanalytic work. As Matthew Tinkcom has said, there is also the implicit deprecation of "fandom" within film scholarship. By the very use and notion of the word "spectator," he suggests that "we fall into the habit of prioritizing cinema viewing (and especially the attendance of narrative studio film) over and above other activities that are implied by fandom" (Tinkcom 1999: 273). Some of the fans of these films may actually be antagonized by the activities of academics. The best-selling British film magazine *Empire* is aware of "fandom" in a way that official scholarship is not—it regards some academic work as risible and often takes pleasure in denouncing it. One issue devoted a whole half-page to lambasting the writing on these films in particular: "The *Alien* franchise has been at the centre of more egghead pontificating than any other movies in cinematic history. And all of it is absolute arse . . ." The feature then takes snippets from many well-known, anthologized essays—some of them referred to earlier in this article—and follows each with a facetious riposte. For example: "We say: You can take the concept of 'us' and stick it right up the 'other'" (Freer 1997: 132).

Some of this aggressive derision is perhaps generated by the fact that most academic work on the cycle tends not to discuss in any detail the production designs and special effects which particularly interest *Empire* readers—and indeed those fans investigated by Will Brooker in his essay on internet fandom (Brooker 1999). Exploring different fan constituencies, he finds that fans of this saga form "a large and diverse canon" (65); while it may at times resemble "an online equivalent of the role-playing groups whose popularity peaked in the mid to late 80s" (64), he finds an "in-depth knowledge of technical production detail and appeals to the craft of screenwriting" (64). He also comments on the informed interest shown by his *Bladerunner* fans in the work of Scott Bukatman, comparing this to the *Alien* fans' "silence on the subject of psychoanalytic interpretations": "While Scott Bukatman's essays are treated as key references by *Bladerunner* fans, who subscribe to much the same project of enquiry as Bukatman himself, I have seen no mention of Barbara Creed's equivalent work on *Alien* on any of the sites" (64).

Annette Kuhn asks if this might be explained by the fact that these debates are feminist in nature. Surely the explanation is much simpler: the work of these two writers and their "projects" are completely different. Creed and others have looked at the Alien itself and at the various settings—using psychoanalytic models—as a configuration of male fears, and the Alien thus becomes "phallic mother" (Creed 1993: 16–31). Bukatman, however, discusses the genesis, the history, the making of science fiction films, from pre-production through to the design and realization of special effects. Although writing as an academic—citing Haraway, Jameson, and Foucault among others—he does not, thankfully, believe that this should render his own text opaque. Consequently, his work on science fiction in general—and *Bladerunner* in particular—means that his research is made available to a range of readers, many tempted for the first time into the realm of academic scholarship by his visible enthusiasm for these films—and by the nature and scope of his enquiries.

Brooker concludes his study of his fansites thus:

> All are engaged in acts of enthusiastic and dedicated creation; and all are engaged in a constant process of negotiation as they work within, around and against an existing and ongoing framework, lovingly crafting their own culture in the chinks of the producers' world-machines. (70)

It is puzzling, however, that despite the somewhat narrow field of his research—ten websites in all for three different fan bases—that Brooker did not encounter a single acknowledged lesbian appreciation of Ripley, when any trawl through cyberspace will generate so many hits indicating the size of Ripley's—or Weaver's—avowed lesbian fan base and its various activities.

Matthew Tinkcom, examining active spectatorship, suggests that the theoretical models for addressing spectatorship are too rigid—based as they are on conventional binarism, there is "little room for the mobility of sex/gender difference" (Tinkcom 1999: 273–274). Genderswapping on the internet is not, of course, any solution. But Brooker might at least consider its existence, potential, and scope, rather than attributing gender where it is not possible so to do (Brooker 1999: 49).

Avowed fans of the series—unlike many academics—are invariably familiar with the work of the artist H. R. Giger. Everyone with any interest in the films knows that he created the original designs for the Alien, for which he was rewarded with an Oscar—but to state this, even to describe the designs and then to move on, is to diminish his contribution. He was primarily responsible for the *mise-en-scène* of the first film, including the much-discussed interior of the Alien spaceship, for which the extant scholarship does not really give him credit. Many academics have acknowledged instead the work of Dan O'Bannon, writer of the original story. But Giger's contribution is infinitely greater. The appearance of the Alien—its phallic shape, its vagina-dentata gaping jaws, and the penile inner jaw, also toothed, that thrusts out from within—has been endlessly analysed. So, too, has the appearance of the infant alien—something cheerfully emphasized by Jeunet *et al.* in *Alien Resurrection*. When, in her bizarre caesarean birth, the scientists lift the infant Queen out of Ripley's chest cavity, the snarling head is not visible at first, until what looks like a blood-stained foreskin slides back to reveal the familiar features. Barbara Creed's influential reading of the text is predicated not only on the appearance of the creature and its particular methods of procreation, but also on the appearance of the Alien spacecraft where the eggs are found, with its "vaginal opening shaped like a horseshoe, its curved sides like two long legs spread apart at the entrance . . . a corridor which seems to be made of a combination of the organic and the inorganic . . . this ship is dark, dank and mysterious" (Creed 93: 18).

Obviously it does not matter, for the purposes of interpretation, who designed the ship. But when such images are repeated throughout all of Giger's paintings and drawings, particularly in the "Biomechanoids" series of the mid-1970s, which inspired the designers who first struggled with the appearance of the Alien to invite him to take over the task, it seems odd to ignore his existence so completely. Weaver was, it seems, cast because her jawline matched perfectly that of the creature in one of the paintings Giger produced as the basis for his designs. Yet in all the mass of critical literature, there are only very brief references to his work—indeed, he is sometimes described, rather inaccurately, as a "surrealist painter." It is within the non-academic work around the series that Giger receives his due recognition. But why should he be acknowledged and discussed only within the pages of magazines devoted to special effects, and in the parallel universe of Alien subculture?

This might be because Giger's work is too unsettling, too transgressive, or too phallic. One painting, a vision of a comfortably seated alien, engaged in seemingly consensual penetrative sex both orally and vaginally with a responsive, naked human female, predates the films by three years (Giger 1996: 29). The disregard for Giger's work could also be the result of artistic snobbery—his work seen as second-rate, as not coming within any recognized canon. But really there seems to be a lack of knowledge, rather than a considered judgment, among film scholars. Interestingly, Giger overtly explores in some of the paintings in the "Passages" series his own primal scenes—that favoured critical terrain around the first two films (Giger 1996: 68–69).

Alien 3 and *Alien Resurrection*—transgressive and difficult

John Berger, in a recent essay, "Welcome to the Abyss," writes of the "fragmented, nightmare vision" of the panel representing Hell in Bosch's Millennium Triptych, which he sees as a "strange prophecy . . . the clamour of the disparate, fragmentary present . . . a kind of spatial delirium . . . a puzzle whose wretched pieces do not fit together" (Berger 1999: 7).

Perhaps this dystopian vision is reflected in *Alien 3* and—with a more positive conclusion proffered—in *Alien Resurrection*, while Berger's critique of the globalization which has given us this "fragmentary present" can be extended to the supra-globalism that the entire series depicts. Forays into space are dictated only by the profit motive—the *Nostromo* is a mining ship and refinery, and the exploration of space simply a vast commercial exercise, in which planets are colonized and ravaged for their mineral wealth. In *Alien 3*, the convicts are actually used as slave labour—and there is a sense of defeat missing from the first two films. *Alien 3*, bleak beyond belief, was at first a puzzle, both to fans and the academy—but with the success of Fincher's next film, *Seven*, there was some rethinking in the popular press. In my own primary source research among hardcore *Alien* fans who don't participate in internet activity and therefore can't be tracked in cyberspace (Church Gibson, forthcoming) a surprising number cite *Alien 3* as their favourite film—it's particularly popular with art students.

They admire Fincher's visual style and the *mise-en-scène* of the film, and are particularly impressed by the camerawork in the closing scenes, where the Alien is lured toward the lead mould. The chases along the corridors are shot from what they surmise is the Alien's point of view—at several points the screen tilts wildly and even turns upside down. They cite the "Gothic" nature of the interior sequences, the strange industrial wasteland in and around the prison, and the nature of the cinematography.

Perhaps some feminist critics found the new, vulnerable Ripley, the female intruder in the celibate world of the all-male penal colony, problematic. In this off-world community of former murderers, rapists, and paedophiles, who have now embraced a fundamentalist faith and renounced their former ways, Ripley for the first time meets active, consistent human hostility—especially when the inmates discover that the Alien decimating their fellows arrived aboard her ship. They—and she—are unaware of the foetus she carries within her.

Ilsa Bick's detailed psychoanalytic analysis of *Alien 3* sets out to "investigate the nervousness, the transgressive turning about of the traditional assumptions of power and the crossing of boundaries in the series" (Bick 1994/5). She describes herself as "a woman, a mother, a wife, a writer, a serious lover and critic of film" and, although she does not make it explicit, a conventional analyst—certainly not one interested in, say, queer theory. Whatever "transgressive turning about" may interest her, it is within traditional binaries and the seemingly unproblematic categories she lists above.

Her observations are often incisive—even if she does, strangely, assert that this film is "arguably the least accomplished and visually rich of the films" (50). She asks a vital question—why exactly is Ripley now so vulnerable? Her answer is to suggest that it is because she has been penetrated by the alien—and is penetrated again by Clemens, her doctor, during the course of the film. This act takes place at her instigation, to avoid his probing questions, and the Alien soon comes to punish Clemens for his temerity, leaving the terrified prisoner Gorlick safely alone.

Bick states that here "Ripley and the Alien are again one and the same" but this time the Alien is "an alluring and alien woman who spreads the disease of her own sexuality"

(52). Despite her androgynous appearance, with shaven head and loose clothing, Ripley is still a disturbing presence and a threat. Bick signals her awareness of the other readings of the film—both the claim that it is a Christian allegory, with Ripley as both serpent and Redeemer, and, more significantly, that the film is a metaphorical presentation of the AIDS crisis.

Paul Burston, writing as queer theorist, champions this last reading. Remarking that "the third instalment in the *Alien* saga is not only the most underrated, it is also the most frequently misunderstood," he asks why it was left to Amy Taubin to argue that it is, in fact, "an art-house film" with a particular resonance for women and gay men (Burston 1995: 171–174).

Taubin, writing three years earlier, was surprised by the critical silence around the film: "no-one has written about *Alien 3* in either the gay or the feminist press, despite the fact that the film is all about the AIDS crisis and the threat to women's reproductive rights" (Taubin 1992: 9). She develops this argument persuasively, citing the endless references to contagion within the film, the frequent shots of needles and injections, the iconography of the shaven-headed men. Finally, she links Ripley's "pregnancy" and the scientist's desire to interfere with her "choice" at the end, to the revived US abortion debates, with Ripley as the intruding Alien who secretly brings the foetus with her. She reads the repeated shots of the basement lair as not only showing a fear of the "monstrous-feminine" but also as deeply homophobic, with "uterine and anal plumbing intertwined" (Taubin 1992: 9).

Both Taubin and Bick discuss her alliance with Dillon, the leader of the prisoners and the only black man in the colony. They don't mention the fact that Dillon sacrifices himself in a suicidal hand-to-hand combat with the Alien to stop it escaping up a ladder. It is very similar to the way in which Parker, the only black crew member on the *Nostromo*, makes a similar sacrifice in a bid to save Lambert, while in *Alien Resurrection*, Christie, the only black pirate aboard the *Betty*, gives up his life to save that of the paraplegic Vriess. Dillon, too, rescues Ripley from the three prisoners who are about to rape and perhaps murder her, just as Parker rescued her when Ash attempted to kill her by ramming a magazine down her throat. Without their help, Ripley would not have survived. Yet these parallels have not been made—these coincidences have not been noted anywhere else. Perhaps there is more work to be done around issues of ethnicity in the films.

However, it should be remembered that racial and ethnic differences between the human characters are perhaps minimized when the Alien looms among them as the sign of a difference which threatens them all. Charles S. Dutton, the actor who plays Dillon, has himself been in jail in real life—a fact not mentioned in UK publicity, perhaps because that might reflect poorly, if accurately, the ethnic balance in the American prison population. But there are different ways of interpreting the presence in the films of these particular characters—and perhaps it is worth noting, too, the sardonic heroism and final self-immolation of Vasquez, the only Hispanic character in the cycle.

Burston makes one vital point in conclusion, ignored or insufficiently stressed by other writers. Ripley, he emphasizes, has "learned to love the Alien" (Burston 1995: 174). But there are other factors at work, too, which could be equally unsettling for some; the horrible situations within and around childbirth that occur in both these last, least-loved films, for example.

In *Alien 3*, Ripley feels that she might have incurred some injury. It is when she subjects herself to a CAT scan—with the help of the slow-witted, well-meaning officer Aaron—that the discovery of the Alien within her is made. The scene works as a grotesque parody of the pregnancy scan, routine in modern hospitals. Man sits beside prone woman, both scrutinize a fuzzy image on a screen—here, Aaron recognizes the shape and tells her, "You've got one of them inside you." Ripley is at first disbelieving, then appalled. "What does it look like?" and is told "Horrible." Later, we witness the birth—and Ripley, now, is ready to clasp the child to her breast, as mothers do with newborn babies. In *Alien Resurrection*, the first scene is a terrible travesty of a modern perinatal environment — complete with hi-tech equipment, smiling attendants, the questions about "our patient." And lastly there is the bizarre, protracted sequence in the nest of the Alien Queen. Here, the captured, cocooned scientist, Gediman, tries to act as encouraging midwife while the Queen, now part-human, goes through an agonizing labour. Ripley's "gift to her," through the perilous cloning process, has been a human reproductive system.

Ripley watches in horrified sympathy as a huge creature, half-human and half-alien, emerges from the womb of the Alien who is both her sister and her daughter. Again, the mother attempts to embrace her newborn—but here his response is to attack and kill her. He then turns to look for Ripley who he regards as his "real" mother. An unusually long, penile tongue emerges to lap and caress her face and neck.

Scenes like this—and their implications—may have something to do with the turning-away from this film. The other reason might be the constant emphasis on sex and different forms of sexuality, not only here but everywhere in this film. It's not something we associate with the *Alien* saga.

For this last film is the first in the series to show sexually aware, sexually active space travellers. Vivian Sobchack quite rightly included the Ripley of *Alien* in her essay "The Virginity of Astronauts" (Sobchack 1985/1990: 103–116) and while the Ripley of *Alien* may occasionally flirt with Hicks, she is coy and the marines on the *Sulaco* as asexual as the crew of the *Nostromo*. There is a degree of innuendo in one scene, ignored by all critics of the film, save Charles Ramirez Berg. Here, Hicks tells her, "I want to introduce you to a personal friend of mine . . . feel the weight," while encouraging her to handle and investigate the vast gun carried by all the Marines. (To get the effect he wanted, incidentally, Cameron lashed assault rifles onto Steadicam camera mounts.) Ripley becomes coquettish. "You started this," she complains. "I want to see everything." This seems like a high-school dalliance—but Ramirez Berg reads it differently, seeing it as her conversion to right-wing politics (Ramirez Berg 1989: 174).

In *Alien 3* the sex is perfunctory or violent—Ripley's diversion of Clemens, and the prisoners' attempt to rape Ripley, where they bend her forward over a rail, suggesting that she will be forcibly sodomized. *Alien Resurrection* is the first film where sexual activity is seen as something that might actually be enjoyable. Elgin, Captain of the *Betty*, and his girlfriend Hillard are seen flirting while she docks the ship—and later, he slowly, sensuously massages her feet when she lies comfortably sprawled in her underwear in a luxurious cabin on the *Auriga*. There is a tracking shot of her body, emphasizing its contours and indicating her pleasure. The others have to make do with a home shopping channel, where the items on display are the latest handguns.

Jonner makes crude advances to Ripley when they find her playing basketball. Unaware of who—or what—she is, he propositions her—and Ripley deliberately taunts him, teasing him, enjoying her new-found sexuality. She may not find the thuggish Jonner attractive—but she does like her new powers. Finally, she floors him—she now has super-human strength and reflexes, too, and is happy to show off. "Have we had enough fun?" asks Gediman.

In her first encounter with the female android, Call, Ripley lies in a provocative pose feigning sleep, letting Call creep up to her and slide open her top with a knife to examine

her throat and chest for the tell-tale scar. Only then does she speak. From the very beginning, her relationship with Call is presented erotically. So too is the body of Ripley—
her costumes throughout draw attention to it; they are like a second skin, as are the
outfits worn by Willard. The men of the *Betty* dress like heavy metal fans, or bikers,
with the odd garment borrowed from war movies—Jonner's fur-lined leather flying jacket,
for instance. Only Call wears the androgynous fatigues familiar from the first three films.

The dialogue is very direct. When General Perez asks nonchalantly about Call, Elgin
grins at him. "She is severely fuckable, ain't she?" he replies. Later, when her 'droid
status is discovered, Jonner is appalled. "To think I almost fucked you," he snarls at
her. "Like you never fucked a robot," snaps back Vriess, who—like Jonner—will later
be saved by the extraordinary powers of Ripley and Call in combination. Such
exchanges would be unthinkable on the *Nostromo*, the *Sulaco* or even among the "double Y chromo boys"—as Dillon describes them—of the penal colony.

Colleen Keane, one of the tiny band who discuss *Alien Resurrection* in any detail,
mentions the fact that the film has not been well received, and acknowledges "the aspects
that are played out here—the sexuality, sexual suggestion and imagery." She cites the
work of Haraway in her discussion of the "species interplay and exchange" which here
"becomes full-blown species ambiguity and ambivalence." She suggests that the film opens
up space for "a new, a radically open otherness and hybrid potential." She talks, too,
of the "resonances" of cloning that are explored, and describes not only the eroticized
dialogue between clone and robot but some of the "sensual interactions" between the
mother and alien daughter. However, there are omissions and questions; she asks,
puzzlingly: "In the erotic lesbian charge between . . . Ripley and Call, are we witnessing
a sexual and gender ambiguity that is dangerously perverse?"

She does not explain exactly why it might be "dangerous"—unless it's because she
sees it as "pre-Oedipal." For she has just described Ripley's suction into the nest as "a
perverse version of pre-Oedipal bliss and desire," wrongly believing her to have been
sucked into the "comforting matter that is the body of the alien queen" (Keane 1998:
34). In fact, a careful examination of this scene will reveal that it is not the body of the
Queen at all, but the bodies of various Alien offspring, with one of whom Ripley has a
more than close encounter; some kind of sexual activity is clearly suggested. Catherine
Constable, who has also written at some length on the film, has provided a shot-by-
shot breakdown of this sequence—from Ripley's suction into the nest to the birth of
the Newborn (Constable 1999: 193–194).

It does seem that the problem for academics in studying this film might be the full
range of transgressive sexual activities shown. What behavioral psychologists call "pre-
ventive blanks" seem to have shielded both Keane and Constable in their scrutiny of
the film. Keane sees the lesbianism and some of the incestuous activity—but not what
happens to Ripley on the journey to the nest with her half-glimpsed Alien carrier. Nor,
indeed, does she seem to take in the graphic presentation of Ripley's final embraces with
the horrid, hybrid child, to whom the Queen gave birth "for you, Ripley," as Gediman
explains. Catherine Constable describes not only the sex between Ripley and her Alien
abductor, but also the precise way in which the camera tilts to suggest the full erotic
charge of the embrace between Ripley and the Newborn—her son or grandson—before,
with voiced regret, she is forced to murder him and watch his death throes. Constable
gives voice to the full incestuous implications of this last scene, where "the motif of
sexual intercourse compounds the intermingling of alien and human potentialities"
(Constable 1999: 196). In a long and fascinating essay, informed by both psychoanalysis
and recent feminist philosophy, she somehow ignores completely any lesbian implications

—in activity, dialogue, or narrative. It is strange, since these are so forcibly spelt out. Perhaps the film is so thoroughly transgressive that the complete gamut of its psycho-sexual implications is difficult for academics to acknowledge.

A recent article in *Screen*, which refers to all four *Alien* films, focuses on Ripley as "active woman" and completely avoids such controversial issues. But it is particularly interesting in that its author, Elizabeth Hills, suggests that Ripley in fact becomes "what Rosi Braidotti calls a Post-Woman woman through operating in the productive middle space between binaries" (Hills 1999: 46). Braidotti's work is insufficiently known in both the UK and the US—and, it seems, is virgin territory for the majority of film scholars. Braidotti, on the other hand, is familiar with their work—one of the writers to whom she refers extensively is Teresa de Lauretis. Braidotti's writings, mingling as they do highly sophisticated radical philosophy with an awareness of the practical and economic real-ities of late capitalism, are surely indicative of one way forward for feminist thought and therefore for film and cultural studies. They are also remarkable for their clarity of style, as it ranges across disciplines and registers; there is a worrying tendency within film studies to assume that opacity is synonymous with scholarship.

Conclusion

Whatever needs to be understood or taught can be found in and around these films—conditions of production, authorship, stardom, fandom, psychoanalysis, Marxism, post-colonialism, postmodernism. But some strange self-censorship seems to be at work in the supposedly liberal groves of academe, making the last film almost taboo. In fact the whole sequence has a transgressive potency in its presentation of Ripley's relationship with the Alien. What is notable is that many fans see all this—and are perfectly relaxed about it. But here—as usual—the fans are perhaps more accepting and less censorious. The academy can best cope with all this transgressive activity when it is carefully encoded in the conventional language of psychoanalysis—and that traps us in what Braidotti would describe as "the dualistic conceptual constraints" of phallocentrism. It is time to move around, or beyond, the binaries. It is time, too, to acknowledge the activities of fans—and possibly to learn.

Acknowledgement

I would like to thank Paul Willemen for his encouragement in the writing of this chapter.

Filmography

Alien (1979) directed by Ridley Scott.
Cast: Sigourney Weaver, John Hurt, Ian Holm, Harry Dean Stanton.

Aliens (1986) directed by James Cameron.
Cast: Sigourney Weaver, Carrie Henn, Michael Biehn.

Alien 3 (1992) directed by David Fincher.
Cast: Sigourney Weaver, Charles S. Dutton, Charles Dance.

Alien Resurrection (1997) directed by Jean-Pierre Jeunet.
Cast: Sigourney Weaver, Winona Ryder, Dominique Pinon.

References

amazon.com homepage (1999) http://www.amazon.com.
Barker, M. (1998) "Film Audience Research: Making a Virtue out of a Necessity," *Iris* 26: 131–147.
Berger, J. (1999) "Welcome to the Abyss," *Race and Class*, Institute of Race Relations, November.
Bick, I. (1994/5) "'Well, I Guess I Must Make You Nervous': Woman and the Space of *Alien 3*," *Post-Script* 14 (1/2): 45–58.
Braidotti, R. (1991) *Patterns of Dissonance*, London: Polity Press.
—— (1994) *Nomadic Subjects*, New York: Columbia University Press.
Brooker, W. (1999) "Internet Fandom and the Continuing Narratives of *Star Wars, Bladerunner* and *Alien*," in Kuhn 1999, 50–72.
Burston, P. (1995) *What Are You Looking At?: Queer Sex, Style and Cinema*, London: Cassell.
Constable, C. (1999) "Becoming the Monster's Mother: Morphologies of Identity in the *Alien* Series," in Kuhn 1999, 173–202.
Cook, P. and Bernink, M., eds (1999) *The Cinema Book*, 2nd edn, London: British Film Institute.
Creed, B. (1993) *The Monstrous-Feminine: Film, Feminism, Psychoanalysis*, London: Routledge.
de Lauretis, T. (1987) *Technologies of Gender: Essays on Theory, Film and Fiction*, Bloomington: Indiana University Press.
Freer, I. (1997) "Alien Procrastination," *Empire* (December) 102: 132.
Giger, H. R. (1996) *HR Giger ARh+*, Cologne: Taschen.
Greenberg, H. R. (1986) "Reimagining the Gargoyle: Psychoanalytic Notes on *Alien*," *Camera Obscura* 15: 87–108.
Haraway, D. J. (1985) "Manifesto for Cyborgs: Science, Technology and Socialist Feminism in the 1980s," *Socialist Review* 80: 65–108. Reprinted 1991 in D. J. Haraway, *Simians, Cyborgs, and Women: The Reinvention of Nature*, London: Free Association Books.
Hills, E. (1999) "From 'Figurative Males' to Action Heroines: Further Thoughts on Active Women in the Cinema," *Screen* 40 (1): 38–50.
Keane, C. (1998) "Ambiguity, Perversity and *Alien Resurrection*," *Metro* 116: 30–35.
Kuhn, A., ed. (1990) *Alien Zone: Cultural Theory and Contemporary Science Fiction Cinema*, London: Verso.
—— ed. (1999) *Alien Zone II*, London: Verso.
Leigh, Peter (1998) "In Space No-one Can Hear You Scream," *The Guardian Weekend Guide* (November 28): 5.
Nathan, I. (1997) "*Alien Reincarnation*," *Empire* (December) 102: 124–136.
Pearce, Garth (1992) "Return to the Forbidden Planet," *Empire* (September) 39: 60–69.
Penley, C., Lyon, E., Spigel, L. and Bergstrom, J., eds (1990) *Close Encounters: Film, Feminism, and Science Fiction*, Minneapolis: University of Minnesota Press.
Plant, S. (1998) *Zeros and Ones*, London: Fourth Estate.
Ramirez Berg, Charles (1989) "Immigrants, Aliens and Extra-Terrestrials: Science Fiction's Alien 'Other,'" *Cineaction* (Autumn) 18: 3–18.
Sobchack, Vivian, (1985/1990) "The Virginity of Astronauts," reprinted in Kuhn 1990, 103–116.
Taubin, A. (1992) "Invading Bodies," *Sight and Sound* 2 (3) (November): 9–10.
Tinkcom, M. (1999) "Scandalous!" in E. Hanson, ed., *Out Takes: Essays on Queer Theory and Film*, Durham, NC: Duke University Press.
Weaver, S. (1997) "The Alien Inside Me," *Premiere* (US) 11 (4): 115–118, 147.

2 *Warrior Marks*

Global womanism's neo-colonial discourse in a multicultural context

Inderpal Grewal and Caren Kaplan

> Imperialism's image as the establisher of the good society is marked by the espousal of the woman as *object* of protection from her own kind.[1]
>
> Gayatri Spivak

In the last ten to fifteen years, the fields of colonial and postcolonial discourses have produced a by-now-standard critique of objectification, essentialism, exoticization, and Orientalism as the representational practices of modern Western imperialism. That is, an oppositional power relation between colonizer and colonized has come to be understood as a crucial dynamic at work in the disciplines, institutions, subjects, and practices of modernity. Less understood or less examined in the interdisciplinary cultural studies of colonial and postcolonial discourses are the power relations between the different hybrid subjects produced during centuries of imperialism and modernity. Thus, the center–periphery model, or West/Non-West binary, is inadequate to understand contemporary world conditions under globalization: the relations between gendering practices, class formations, sexual identities, racialized subjects, transnational affiliations, and diasporic nationalisms, etc. Constructing monolithic notions of "Western" and "non-Western" subjects in binary opposition cannot always account for the complex, hybrid, and often contradictory subject positions that mark the era of postmodernity.

We begin with this premise in order to understand the practices, womanist and feminist, that underlie *Warrior Marks* (1993), a film directed by Pratibha Parmar and produced by Alice Walker. Since its first screenings, responses have ranged from celebration to angry denunciation. It has been hailed, on the one hand, as a film that brings to light the misogynistic practice of "female genital mutilation"; and, on the other hand, it has also been condemned as a colonialist narrative that depicts African women as victims of their own culture, a "postcolonial civilizing mission" as Rogaia Mustafa Abusharaf

We would like to thank the many colleagues and friends who shared their own work, suggestions for research, and comments on our work in progress: in particular, Isabelle Gunning, Carolyn Dinshaw, Eric Smoodin, Ella Shohat, Sharon Willis, Jean Walton, Rogaia Mustafa Abusharaf, L. Omede Obiora, Kagendo Murungi, Jacqui Alexander, Donald Moore, Norma Alarcón, Minoo Moallem, Tani Barlow, Lisa Cartwright, Lisa Rofel, Cathy Davidson, Rebecca Jennison, and our students at San Fancisco State University and UC-Berkeley (who gave us lots of excellent discussion, feedback, and support).

1 Gayatri Chakravorty Spivak, "Can the Subaltern Speak?" in Cary Nelson and Lawrence Grossberg, eds, *Marxism and the Interpretation of Culture* (Urbana: University of Illinois Press, 1988), 299.

calls it.[2] Sorting through these divergent responses helps us understand the contemporary transnational formations through which sexuality, race, and gender create new subjects. Under globalization, by which we mean the expansionary economic and cultural processes of advanced capitalism, these subjects participate in the construction of an identity politics that draws upon both Euro-American cultural feminism and global feminism to articulate an anti-racist multiculturalism. Such a multiculturalism, as evidenced by the Walker–Parmar film, remains embedded in the practices of Western modernity. The modernity of this multicultural subject lies in the humanist metaphysics and liberal political formations that comprise its liberatory agenda. In *Warrior Marks*, this modernity produces a global womanism—the belief that the intersection of race and gender creates a homogeneous colonized female body as well as the conditions for the liberation of that body. The Walker–Parmar film assumes that a Euro-American multicultural agenda travels freely across national boundaries. Thus, we need to understand multiculturalism in a transnational perspective in order to come to grips with this relatively under-recognized legacy of colonial discourses at work in contemporary Euro-American feminist and womanist practices.

In *Warrior Marks*, a film made presumably with the very best intentions by two committed feminist activists of color, the articulation of a global version of womanism derived from Euro-American cultural feminism results in a neo-colonial representational practice. US cultural feminism constructed an unproblematic narrative of liberation based on a universalized and essentialist identity as "woman."

This form of cultural feminism, as it has been practiced in the US and in Europe from the 1970s to the present, often turns its attention to "global sisterhood" when faced with the dilemma of transnational feminist politics. This form of "global feminism," as Chandra Mohanty and others have pointed out, can result in imperializing and racist forms of "knowing" those constituted as "others."[3] Our task in this chapter is to investigate the complex positionality of the subjects constructed through this representational practice. In order to analyze the contemporary reach of what we call multiculturalism's global sisterhood, we will examine the genealogies of these practices in colonial discourses about women.

As Martin Jay has argued, within Western modernity's "scopic regime" the "visual" plays a primary role in communication and the institutionalization of knowledge.[4] Western ethnographic and documentary film traditions are fully implicated in the

2 Rogaia Mustafa Abusharaf, "The Resurrection of the Savage: *Warrior Marks* Revisited," paper delivered at the seminar on "The Future of Gender" (2 April 1997), at the Pembroke Center for Teaching and Research on Women, 2.

3 Chandra Talpade Mohanty, "Cartographies of Struggle: Third World Women and the Politics of Feminism," and "Under Western Eyes: Feminist Scholarship and Colonial Discourses," in Chandra Talpade Mohanty, Ann Russo, and Lourdes Torres, eds, *Third World Women and the Politics of Feminism* (Bloomington: Indiana University Press, 1991), 1–47, 51–80. See also, Norma Alarcón, "The Theoretical Subject(s) of *This Bridge Called My Back* and Anglo-American Feminism," in Gloria Anzaldúa, ed., *Making Face, Making Soul: Haciendo Caras* (San Francisco: Aunt Lute Books, 1990), 356–369; and Norma Alarcón, "Traddutora, Traditora: A Paradigmatic Figure of Chicana Feminism," in Inderpal Grewal and Caren Kaplan, eds, *Scattered Hegemonies: Postmodernity and Transnational Feminist Practices* (Minneapolis: Minnesota University Press, 1994), 110–133; and Inderpal Grewal and Caren Kaplan, "Introduction: Transnational Feminist Practices and Questions of Postmodernity," in Grewal and Kaplan, *Scattered Hegemonies*, 1–33.

4 Martin Jay, "Scopic Regimes of Modernity," in S. Lash and J. Friedman, eds, *Modernity and Identity* (Oxford: Blackwell, 1994).

empiricist, realist, and positivist ideologies of modernity, ideologies that Walker and Parmar rely upon in their multiculturalist project. While scholars have begun to examine the ways in which multiculturalism has been co-opted and commodified (limiting its oppositional possibilities),[5] we argue that in a transnational framework, US multiculturalists cannot address issues of inequalities and differences if they presume the goal of progressive politics is to construct subjects, feminist or womanist, that are just like themselves.

Multiculturalism's global sisterhood: reading *Warrior Marks*

After several decades of struggle and resistance to ethnocentric and Eurocentric articulations of feminism, multicultural feminism and its variants such as womanism and global womanism have achieved considerable recognition as feminist practices in the United States. Even within the enabling and demystifying paradigms of feminist multiculturalism, a tendency to elide geopolitical considerations and to promote a universalized identity for women of color can also produce points of alliance with colonial discourses. When Euro-American feminist multiculturalism links with colonial discourses that articulate binaries of tradition and progress, for example, or civilized and barbaric, a powerful form of neo-colonialism recurs in activist and progressive representational practices.

The film *Warrior Marks* and its accompanying coffee-table print version, *Warrior Marks: Female Genital Mutilation and the Sexual Blinding of Women*, are recent examples of contemporary Euro-American multicultural feminism in its imperializing vein as global womanism.[6] Proposing "benevolent" rescues and principled interventions, *Warrior Marks* advocates a return to the interlocking traditions of missionary projects, modernizing practices, and global sisterhood. Claiming to demystify a practice from far away lands that appears to have origins deep in a patriarchal past, the *Warrior Marks* texts remystify genital surgeries in Africa, creating conventional subjects of an anthropological gaze already well-known to Western viewers through ethnographic and documentary cinema and their popular and mainstream counterparts.

Ethnography, as Claude Lévi-Strauss defined it, represents "societies *other* than the one in which we live."[7] This displacement from the location where "we" live to a gaze upon a place where "others" can be observed forms a foundation for representational practices and discourses under the sign of modernity. The ethnographic impulse, that is, the authority conferred upon the observer by modernity's scopic regime, underlies the birth of cinema itself—the films of Lumière have been referred to as "direct" or "actuality" cinema, terms that can be linked to the rhetorical structure of classic ethno-

---

5 See Ella Shohat and Robert Stam, *Unthinking Eurocentrism: Multiculturalism and the Media* (New York: Routledge, 1994); Avery F. Gordon and Christopher Newfield, eds, *Mapping Multiculturalism* (Minneapolis: University of Minnesota Press, 1996); David Theo Goldberg, ed., *Multiculturalism: A Critical Reader* (Oxford: Blackwell, 1994).

6 Here we need to differ from approaches such as Faye V. Harrison's toward Alice Walker's representation of women in a global framework. While Harrison argues that Walker's novel, *In the Temple of My Familiar*, is a "world cultural history from a pluralistic Third World feminist perspective" which "deessentializes gender as well as race and class," we view such projects as recuperating new kinds of global gendered subjects. See Faye V. Harrison, "Anthropology, Fiction, and Unequal Relations of Intellectual Production," in Ruth Behar and Deborah A. Gordon, eds, *Women Writing Culture* (Berkeley: University of California Press, 1995), 233–245.

7 Claude Lévi-Strauss, *Structural Anthropology* (New York: Basic Books, 1963), 16–17.

graphy's reliance upon positivist realism.[8] The rise of modern science and its link to discourses of vision and rationality in the West informs the voyeuristic practices of ethnographic cinema in its documentary mode. Western subjects learn to "see" in a specific set of historically constructed interpretive regimes based upon discourses of unmediated visuality, scientific evidence, objectivity, and the "real."[9]

Ethnographic film as an anthropological practice, David MacDougall has argued, has been defined by its intercultural and interpretive focus, in which foreignness, exoticism, travel, and adventure were necessary elements in constructing knowledge about "others."[10] Visual anthropologists who produce ethnographic films become cultural brokers in what MacDougall calls "the economic exchange of global images."[11] While this tradition has been subverted and critiqued by anthropologists and filmmakers such as MacDougall himself, Jean Rouch, Trinh T. Minh-ha, Laleen Jayamanne, and others, ethnographic cinema, as Fatimah Tobing Rony argues, continues a tradition of "pervasive 'racialization' of indigenous peoples."[12] Such a racialization, according to Rony, denies people of color "historical agency and psychological complexity."[13]

Warrior Marks not only relies on the positivist production of empirical knowledge as documentary testimony but recuperates the racialization and gendered "othering" of non-Western subjects from the ethnographic cinematic tradition. That the cultural producers of this work are two women of color raises important issues about new forms of racialization and power relations between women from First and Third World locations. While we have seen the appropriation and recuperation of positivist visual logics in Third World cultural production (for instance, in nationalist, anti-colonial narratives),[14] what is new here is the construction of a global womanist project framed epistemologically by US multiculturalism.

Given the particular intellectual and political trajectories of both Alice Walker and Pratibha Parmar, respectively, certain questions arise in relation to how *Warrior Marks* continues the tradition of ethnographic visual representation. Walker is best known as an award-

8 Noel Burch, *Life to Those Shadows* (Berkeley: University of California Press, 1990), 16. For discussion of "ethnographic authority" and the history of anthropological cultures of representation see James Clifford and George Marcus, eds, *Writing Culture* (Berkeley: University of California Press, 1986); and James Clifford, *The Predicament of Culture: Twentieth-Century Ethnography, Literature, and Art* (Cambridge, MA: Harvard University Press, 1988).

9 See Denise Albanese, *New Science, New World* (Durham, NC: Duke University Press, 1996); John Berger, *Ways of Seeing* (Harmondsworth: Penguin, 1977); Lisa Cartwright, *Screening the Body: Tracing Medicine's Visual Culture* (Minneapolis: University of Minnesota Press, 1995); and Valerie Hartouni, *Cultural Conceptions: On Reproductive Technologies and the Remaking of Life* (Minneapolis: University of Minnesota Press, 1997).

10 David MacDougall, "Prospects of the Ethnographic Film," in Bill Nichols, ed., *Movies and Methods* (Berkeley: University of California Press, 1976), 136.

11 David MacDougall, "Beyond Observation Cinema," in P. Hockings, ed., *Principles of Visual Anthropology* (Paris: Mouton, 1975), 118, cited in Kathleen Kuehnast, "Visual Imperialism and the Export of Prejudice: An Exploration of Ethnographic Film," in Peter Ian Crawford and David Turton, eds, *Film as Ethnography* (Manchester: Manchester University Press, 1992), 186.

12 Fatimah Tobing Rony, *The Third Eye: Race, Cinema, and Ethnographic Spectacle* (Durham, NC: Duke University Press, 1996), 8.

13 Ibid., 71.

14 See Parama Roy, *Indian Traffic* (Berkeley: University of California Press, 1998); Nalini Natarajan, "Women, Nation, and Narration in *Midnight's Children*," in Grewal and Kaplan, *Scattered Hegemonies*, 76–89; Rey Chow, *Primitive Passions: Visuality, Sexuality, Ethnography, and Contemporary Chinese Cinema* (New York: Columbia University Press, 1995); and Shohat and Stam, *Unthinking Eurocentrism*.

winning novelist and anti-racist activist who has refused the label "feminist" in favor of what she terms "womanist."[15] Instrumental in moving US cultural feminism into discussions of racial difference, sexual identities, and resistance to white supremacy, Walker is a primary figure in the US women's movement in general and the movements of women of color in particular. Parmar, who began as an anti-racist feminist activist in Britain, is an increasingly well-known independent filmmaker whose films have ranged from investigations of racialized sexual identity to profiles of well-known women of color writers and activists. Parmar's interest in coalitions with US women of color and Walker's desire to address a topic with "global" dimensions has led to a collaboration that presents the tensions that arise in multicultural feminism's imbrication within racialized diasporas.

The collaboration between Walker and Parmar forms a compelling and complicated coalition between a US-based writer and cultural figure who has struggled to make a space for African-American women's concerns and a British filmmaker whose family's diaspora includes South Asia and East Africa and who has made a commitment to lesbian feminist and anti-racist cultural production. Their process of building an alliance and finding a method of working together is powerfully depicted in the print text of *Warrior Marks*. Consequently, in discussing Walker and Parmar's collaborative work, we need to refer to both the film and the print text. The book *Warrior Marks* records the production of the entire project in both narrative and glossy visuals, giving more context for the project as a whole and adding appendices that document resources. The print text, then, is interesting in and of itself even as it comments self-reflexively on the production of the film. Framed by maps of West Africa, the book utilizes epistolary devices, organizing sections around letters sent between Walker and Parmar throughout the pre- and post-production period. In this text, the narration is evenly divided between Walker, the film's producer and narrator, and Parmar, the director. A third section of the book is devoted to interviews, informational tables, networking information, and other appendices. This section attempts to provide the "voices" of other women, including African and European activists as well as "native" informants. In this sense, the print text differs significantly from the film, providing the kind of production information that is edited out of conventional film products. Nevertheless, both texts adhere to a set of ideological and discursive formations that produce specific subjects; in this case, victimized females in rural Africa and their First World saviors.

Because Walker and Parmar's work has helped to shape both multicultural and anti-racist feminist practices, the emergence of colonial discourse in their collaborative texts raises important questions for many of us who share their political concerns. Thus, the problem is not that Walker and Parmar are not "post-structuralists" or "postcolonial theorists"—Parmar is the author of a significant contribution to feminist postcolonial theory and Walker is a well-respected public intellectual.[16] Our critique does not cast them outside our fields but, rather, seeks to situate our feminist arenas of activism and political struggle within a transnational framework of cultural production that can never be seen to be apart from the politics of representation. As producers of representations, Walker and Parmar can be held accountable for their choices of genre, format, and discursive practices. Since they chose a documentary form for their film, intending to

---

15 Alice Walker, *In Search of Our Mother's Gardens* (New York: Harcourt, Brace, Jovanovich, 1983).
16 See Valerie Amos and Pratibha Parmar, "Challenging Imperial Feminism," *Feminist Review* 17 (1984), 3–19.

use the techniques of montage, interview, voiceover narration, and travelogue to make a political statement about a set of practices in a distant location, we read the text as feminist cultural critics of the history of modern imperialism. Consequently, we are concerned that such interventions, since they rely on colonial tropes, cannot be effective because they do not provide a socio-cultural and historical context in which activism, as the intersection of gender and agency, can become possible.[17]

The project of *Warrior Marks* is circumscribed at the outset by its rhetorical strategy of global womanism. Given the history of discussions of female genital surgeries in Africa in the anthropological literature and the Western cultural feminist discourses of human rights and domestic violence, the multicultural feminist or womanist approach to the topic cannot escape a colonial legacy. In the history of the multitudinous ways in which the female gender is produced in various cultures, female circumcision has been given an overwhelming and problematic attention in the West.[18] The value-laden terminology justifies and rationalizes interventionist narratives and practices. The surgical removal or alteration of women's genitals is referred to by a range of terms including circumcision, excision, genital mutilation, and clitoridectomy. FGM, the acronym for female genital mutilation, has come to stand for the surgical practice itself in many US feminist/ womanist communities. Given that terms are always political and contingent, we are opting to use the phrase "genital surgeries" following Isabelle Gunning's argument that "mutilation" is ethnocentric and judgmental while "circumcision" is misleadingly benign.[19] The problem of terms marks the social relations that structure the sexual-, gender-, and geo-politics of these discourses. That is, each term is attached to a history of colonialism linked to Enlightenment concepts of individuality and bodily integrity, medicalized notions of "cleanliness" and "health," sexualized notions of the primacy of "clitoral orgasm" and cultural organizations of pleasure. Terminologies produce epistemic violence—the silencing and erasure that specialized language enacts in particular situations in reference to particular inequities.[20] Such problems of vocabulary characterize the fraught terrain of cultural commentary in international and cross-cultural contexts.

Alice Walker has been investigating female genital surgeries (although she would insist upon the term FGM—female genital mutilation) for many years. Her novel, *Possessing the Secret of Joy* (1992), revolves around a circumcised protagonist, picking up one of the narrative threads of *The Color Purple* (1982). *Warrior Marks* uses a documentary format to rally opposition to FGM and enhance the international activist movement for its abolition. In the film, Walker interviews women in Europe and Africa to demonstrate

---

17 For an extended discussion of the importance of "socio-cultural" context for black women cultural producers, see Gloria Gibson-Hudson, "Aspects of Black Feminist Cultural Ideology in Films by Black Women Independent Artists," in Diane Carson, Linda Dittmar, and Janice R. Welsch, eds, *Multiple Voices in Feminist Film Criticism* (Minneapolis: University of Minnesota Press, 1994), 365–379.

18 For a variety of anthropological, legal, historical, and cultural perspectives on female genital surgeries as a question of "tradition" in an era of human rights activism, see Bettina Shell-Duncan and Ylva Hernlund, eds, *Female Circumcision in Africa: Culture, Controversy and Change* (Boulder, CO: Lynne Rienner Publishers, 2000).

19 Isabelle Gunning, "Arrogant Perception, World-Travelling and Multicultural Feminism: The Case of Female Genital Surgeries," *Columbia Human Rights Law Review* 23 (1992), 189. We have been inspired and encouraged by Gunning's interventions in human rights discourse and by her complex, materially grounded theorization of multicultural feminism.

20 For an extremely useful discussion of the history of Western representations of the clitoris see Lisa Jean Moore and Adele E. Clarke, "Clitoral Conventions and Transgressions: Graphic Representations in Anatomy Texts, c. 1900–1991," *Feminist Studies* 21 (2) (Summer 1995), 255–301.

the destructive effects of FGM and to draw a connection between violence against women in general and this practice in particular. The film advocates a global sisterhood composed of diverse women of color living in the US and Europe intervening in order to "save" the lives of women and girls in Africa and African immigrant communities in the First World.

In the print text, Walker outlines clearly her personal stake in this project when she discusses her understanding of the metaphorical link between various kinds of "patriarchal wounds." Drawing upon her own experience of violence in a family setting, Walker describes a terrible childhood trauma. Her brother aimed his BB gun straight at her and struck her in the eye. In Walker's recounting of this frightening event, it is clear that her injury was as deeply psychic as it was physical. Her mother and father's distanced response to her pain and fright only compounded her sense of betrayal and danger. Walker makes a direct association between this betrayal and the role that African mothers and grandmothers play in FGM as reproducers of the legitimating ideology and as colluding participants. Her identification with the African victims of FGM is based on her own experience of the vulnerability of young girls in patriarchal families.

This logic of identification is used in the film to link Walker to the African women and children and to link the film spectators to Walker's point of view. Her practice depends upon a notion of interpretation whereby one subject comes to "know" another or others based on a perceived similarity that precludes any self-consciousness of the contingent and power-laden nature of relations between women. In *Writing Diaspora*, Rey Chow argues that several strands of the word "identification" are at stake in the politics of identifying "authentic" natives: "How do we identify the native? How do we identify with her? How do we construct the native's 'identity'? What processes of identification are involved? We cannot approach this politics without being critical of a particular relation to *images* that is in question."[21] *Warrior Marks* utilizes visual colonial tropes not only to identify the "natives" but also to enable Walker herself, as narrator, to identify with this native. Doris Sommer has argued that a romanticized identification with cultural Others can be "the ultimate violence" as appropriation and can foreclose the possibility of any political alliance or solidarity across identities.[22] Thus, Walker legitimates her view of African genital surgeries by projecting her own tragedy—her brother's assault and her injured eye—onto the bodies of women whom she perceives to be in peril from patriarchal violence. "I chose to be part of the subject of *Warrior Marks* and not a distant observer because I wanted to directly align myself with genitally mutilated women," Walker explains. "Like them, I knew I had a patriarchal wound."[23] Without taking away from the horror of an attack by a family member, how can an analogy be made between such different practices and events? Each has its own complex articulation within a specific patriarchy and a particular historical context that includes race, nation, gender, class, and other social factors. Walker's experience of violence can be read through the lens of a male dominance that is complexly sanctioned within a nuclear and extended family both shaped and constrained by histories of racism and class among other social forces at work in the American South. Her identification with the "victims" of female genital surgeries does not inform us about the nuanced relations

21 Rey Chow, *Writing Diaspora: Tactics of Intervention in Contemporary Cultural Studies* (Bloomington: Indiana University Press, 1993), 28–29.

22 Doris Sommer, "Resistant Texts and Incompetent Readers," *Poetics Today* 15 (4) (Winter 1994), 543, cited in Diana Fuss, *Identification Papers* (New York: Routledge, 1995), 9.

23 Evelyn C. White, "Alice Walker's Compassionate Crusade," *San Francisco Chronicle* (Monday, November 15, 1993), D1.

between men and women, between women and women of different classes, ages, nations, ethnicities, and their differential participation in modernity in contemporary Africa. Like so many acts of identification, it enacts its own epistemic violence and erasures.[24]

As a representational strategy, "identification" requires an elision of material difference in favor of a fantasized similarity. In her section of the print text, Parmar describes how working on the project caused her to become increasingly emotionally swept up into Walker's point of view. She reports that once she arrives in Africa, she wakes up from dreams screaming that she is in danger of being infibulated. This aura of terror and helpless victimization pervades the entire film, contradicting some of the footage itself (which shows local women looking healthy and happy), and punctuating the dry, documentary reportage of health workers, doctors, and activists. Throughout the film, a dancer is used to demonstrate the filmmakers' emotional projections of terror onto the symbolic body of the African victims. The visual logic brings viewer and dancer together into a state of fused identification.

Based in part on these kinds of techniques, the film has generated strong and deeply felt support within particular feminist communities in Europe and North America. The relatively widespread advance publicity and distribution of the film and print text can be attributed to Walker's popularity as a novelist and cultural figure as well as to Parmar's growing reputation as an independent filmmaker. For example, *Warrior Marks* has been picked up for distribution by the influential Women Make Movies group, and flagged for special attention beyond their general catalogue in special flyers on the subject of global feminism tied to the 1995 UN Beijing Women's Conference. We attended the screening of the rough cut of the film at the 1993 San Francisco Gay and Lesbian film festival where a capacity crowd enthusiastically applauded the presentation of a special director's award to Pratibha Parmar. Similarly large crowds greeted with strong emotion the film's opening in several metropolitan locations in the United States. The journalist who covered the Washington, DC, premiere at Howard University for the activist publication *off our backs* described an auditorium-size audience "openly weeping" and "spontaneously cheering," for instance.[25]

The reception of the film in print has been divided between the global womanists (many of whom identified with the film's construction of universalized racial and sexual communities) and those who critiqued the neo-colonial representational practices of the film (many of them Africanists). The film was reviewed positively in most US-based feminist and lesbian-feminist publications, where the global womanist viewpoint was overwhelmingly valorized.[26] The enthusiastic support for the film, reflected in the reviews, may come from an affirmation of the Parmar–Walker project which, at the moment that it constructs the African woman as silent victim or global womanist/feminist, constitutes Western subjectivities. This imperialist subject is affirmed by the film's recuperation of the civilizing project of colonialism within which the figure of the colonized woman as silent victim played a key role.

---

24 Here we disagree with Diana Fuss and other psychoanalytic feminist theorists who argue for a politicized recognition of the erotic and mobilizing powers of identification as a compensation for lost love-objects. While we acknowledge the rigor of these arguments, examples such as *Warrior Marks* demonstrate the cultural and political limits of such an approach. See Fuss, *Identification Papers*.

25 Amy Hamilton, "Warrior Marks," *off our backs* 23 (11) (December 1993), 2.

26 See Diane Minor, "*Warrior Marks*: Joyous Resistance at Walker Film Debut," *National NOW Times* (January 1994), 7; Mari Keiko Gonzalez, "Culture or Torture?" *Bay Area Reporter* (18 November 1993); White, "Alice Walker's Compassionate Crusade," D1; David A. Kaplan, "Is It Torture or Tradition?" *Newsweek* (December 20, 1993), 124.

Although the most prominent mainstream critique of the film appeared as an op-ed piece by Seble Dawit and Salem Mekuria in *The New York Times*,[27] other critiques have built upon earlier responses to Walker's previously published novel on the topic, *Possessing the Secret of Joy*. These reviews argue that Walker's overgeneralizing of African history and culture leads to errors of fact and the reproduction of long-standing stereotypes.[28] Most recently, a special issue of the *Case Western Reserve Law Review* that focused on female circumcision included detailed critiques of Alice Walker's work.[29] For example, while L. Amede Obiora argues that many Western representations of female circumcision ignore the diversity and complexity of this practice, Micere Githae Mugo focuses on Alice Walker's work as an example of a Western "external messiah syndrome" in which activism becomes an invasive practice imbued with unequal power relations.[30]

The construction of knowledge through gendered representations in colonial contexts

The "civilizing" practices of modern European imperialism have generated specifically gendered forms of colonial discourse within which the figure of the "woman" plays a key role in subject constitution. Practices that pertain to women's lives such as *suttee*, seclusion, foot binding, veiling, arranged marriages, and female circumcision have come to symbolize the "barbarism" of non-Western cultures.[31] Singling out such practices as

---

27 Seble Dawit and Salem Mekuria, "The West Just Doesn't Get It," *The New York Times* (Tuesday, December 7, 1993), A27. This piece is an exception to the rule. Most *New York Times* op-ed pieces on the topic echo the tone and approach found in A. M. Rosenthal's "Female Genital Torture," *The New York Times* (Friday, November 12, 1993), A33.

28 Critiques of *Possessing the Secret of Joy* include: Margaret Kent Bass, "Alice's Secret," *CLA Journal* (September 1994), 1–10, and Diane C. Menya, "Possessing the Secret of Joy," *Lancet* 341 (February 1993), 423. Critiques of *Warrior Marks* include Leasa Farrar-Frazer, "An Opportunity Missed: A Review of *Warrior Marks*," *Black Film Review* 8 (1) (1994), 41–42; Gay Wilentz, "Healing the Wounds of Time," *Women's Review of Books* 10 (5) (February 1993), 15–16; and Kagendo Murungi, "Get Away from My Genitals: A Commentary on *Warrior Marks*," *Interstices* 2 (1) (Spring 1994), 11–15; and Abusharaf, "The Resurrection of the Savage."

29 *Case Western Reserve Law Review* 47 (2) (Winter 1997). See in particular L. Amede Obiora, "Bridges and Barricades: Rethinking Polemics and Intransigence in the Campaign Against Female Circumcision," 275–387; Micere Githae Mugo, "Elitist Anti-Circumcision Discourse as Mutilating and Anti-Feminist," 461–479; and Isabelle R. Gunning, "Uneasy Alliances and Solid Sisterhood: A Response to Professor Obiora's 'Bridges and Barricades,'" 445–459.

30 Mugo, "Elitist Anti-Circumcision Discourse," 462.

31 The second wave, Western feminist salvo against footbinding as "gynocide" was fired by Andrea Dworkin in her well-known text *Woman Hating* (New York: E. P. Dutton, 1974), 95–117. Although Elizabeth Gould Davis also outlines the history of atrocities committed against women, reserving special scorn for those from non-European or non-Christian cultures in *The First Sex* (New York: Penguin Books, 1971), it is Mary Daly who is best known for her analysis of patriarchal violence that includes "Indian" *suttee*, "Chinese" footbinding, and "African" genital mutilation. See *Gyn/Ecology: The Metaethics of Radical Feminism* (Boston: Beacon Press, 1978). This approach lent support to and in many ways instigated the contemporary movement to create International Tribunals on Crimes against Women; see Diane E. H. Russell and Nicole Van de Ven, *Crimes against Women: Proceedings of the International Tribunal* (East Palo Alto, CA: Frog in the Well Press, 1984). Lata Mani has documented both British and South Asian nationalist discourses on *sati* (or *suttee*) in "Contentious Traditions: The Debate on Sati in Colonial India," in KumKum Sangari and Sudesh Vaid, eds, *Recasting Women* (New Delhi: Kali for Women, 1989), 88–126. For a more historically complex approach to footbinding in East Asia, see Alison R. Drucket, "The Influence of Western Women on the Anti-Footbinding Movement, 1840–1911," in Richard W. Guisso and Stanley Johannesen, eds, *Women in China* (Youngstown, NY: Philo Press, 1981).

moral anathemas, imperialist discourses condemn entire cultures. Feminist scholarship on colonialism has given us profound insights into the ways in which such isolated tropologies work to mystify histories of social relations, particularly interlocking patriarchal forms and the recastings of various hegemonic formations under colonialisms and nationalisms.[32]

More recently, gendered colonial tropologies are visible in the media as debates over the *hijab* (head covering), in attacks on Muslim fundamentalism, sensationalized accounts of sex tourism, and efforts to legislate against female genital surgeries. These representational practices produce images of Third World women as objects or victims who require First World assistance and direction. Within modernity, First World discourses of the Third World as well as nationalist discourses about its female or subaltern subjects continue such representational practices in a variety of historical contexts. When women are raped during a war, for example, their bodies function symbolically as metaphors for "nation," generating patriotic, patriarchal nationalist responses.[33] Yet, at the same time, local domestic violence and physical abuse do not resonate within geopolitical recuperations of nationalism. For example, the high incidence of rape and domestic violence in the US is not addressed as an international human rights problem in the mainstream press. Our point is not that any of these tropological instances are in and of themselves morally or politically defensible. Rather, their popular representation constructs a binary opposition between West and non-West that disallows an examination of the links between patriarchies in modernity and postmodernity.

For instance, female genital surgeries clearly need to be examined as a problematic social practice within the reconstruction of patriarchies in the context of decolonization. Yet, in Western contexts there is very little discourse on genital surgeries that does not reproduce social relations inherited from European imperialism.[34] Poor women everywhere, especially in the formerly colonized parts of the world, face limited health care and educational opportunities as well as the denial of economic and political agency due to global inequalities, rearticulations of patriarchies in specific regions, and the legacies of colonization. Western discourse on female genital surgeries does not incorporate these

32 In addition to Gayatri Spivak's groundbreaking work collected in *In Other Worlds* (New York: Methuen, 1987) and *Outside in the Teaching Machine* (New York: Routledge, 1993) as well as in Sarah Harasym, ed., *The Post-colonial Critic* (New York: Routledge, 1990), see also Cynthia Enloe, *Bananas, Beaches, and Bases* (Berkeley: University of California Press, 1989); Trinh T. Minh-ha, *Woman/Native/Other* (Bloomington: Indiana University Press, 1989); Shohat and Stam, *Unthinking Eurocentrism*; Chow, *Writing Diaspora*; Lisa Lowe, *Critical Terrains* (Ithaca, NY: Cornell University Press, 1991); Françoise Lionnet, *Postcolonial Representations* (Ithaca, NY: Cornell University Press, 1995); Nupur Chaudhuri and Margaret Strobel, *Western Women and Imperialism* (Bloomington: Indiana University Press, 1992); Jenny Sharpe, *Allegories of Empire* (Minneapolis: University of Minnesota Press, 1993); Kumari Jayawardena, *The White Woman's Other Burden* (New York: Routledge, 1995); Antoinette Burton, *Burdens of History* (Chapel Hill: University of North Carolina Press, 1994); Anne McClintock, *Imperial Leather* (New York: Routledge, 1995); and Helen Callaway, *Gender, Culture, and Empire* (Urbana: University of Illinois Press, 1987).

33 See Mary Layoun, "The Female Body and 'Transnational' Reproduction; or, Rape by Any Other Name?" in Grewal and Kaplan, *Scattered Hegemonies*, 63–75; and Sharpe, *Allegories of Empire*. See also Susan Jeffords, "Fantastic Conquests: In U.S. Military History Only Some Rapes Count," *Village Voice* (July 13, 1993), 22–24, 29.

34 Important exceptions include Vicki Kirby, "On the Cutting Edge: Feminism and Clitoridectomy," *Australian Feminist Studies* 5 (Summer 1987), 35–55; Angela Davis, "Women in Egypt: A Personal View," in *Women, Culture, and Politics* (New York: Vintage, 1990), 116–154; Françoise Lionnet, "Feminisms and Universalisms: 'Universal Rights' and the Legal Debate around the Practice of Female Excision in France," *Inscriptions* 6 (1992), 98–115; and the work of Gunning.

complex factors, but continues to direct a "horrified gaze" toward its colonial and post-colonial subjects.

In order to understand what is at stake in such a "horrified gaze," we have to place female genital surgeries in the context of a long representational history in Western cultures. The ascription of such surgeries as a sign of non-Western "barbarism" requires the suppression of the history of this practice in the West, displacing these surgeries onto an ontological "other."[35] This kind of displacement occurs in accounts constructed by colonial bureaucrats, missionaries, health workers, educators, anthropologists, and travelers throughout the nineteenth and twentieth centuries.[36] Such accounts form an important textual archive as well as a discursive practice of empire that disciplines col-

35 See Terry Kapsalis, *Public Privates: Performing Gynecology from Both Ends of the Speculum* (Durham, NC: Duke University Press, 1997); G. J. Barker-Benfield, *The Horrors of the Half-Known Life: Male Attitudes toward Women and Sexuality in Nineteenth-Century America* (New York: Harper and Row, 1976); Elaine Showalter, *The Female Malady* (New York: Pantheon, 1985), 75–78; John Money, *The Destroying Angel* (Buffalo, NY: Prometheus Books, 1985), 119–120; John Duffy, "Masturbation and Clitoridectomy," *Journal of the American Medical Association* 186 (3) (October 19, 1963), 246–249; J. B. Fleming *et al.*, "Clitoridectomy—The Disastrous Downfall of Isaac Baker Brown, F.R.C.S. (1867)," *Journal of Obstetrics and Gynaecology of the British Empire* 67 (6) (October 1960), 1017–1034; and Isaac Baker Brown, *On the Curability of Certain Forms of Insanity, Epilepsy, Catalepsy, and Hysteria in Females* (London: Robert Hardwicke, 1866).

36 Female circumcision or genital surgery in general has been represented in "modern" discussions of anatomy as well as marked as "culturally significant" in ethnographic discourse. For example, P. C. Remondino's *History of Circumcision from the Earliest Times to the Present* (Philadelphia: F. A. Davis, 1900) combines ethnographic "knowledge," folk legend, and medical "facts." Richard Burton supplied ethnographic data on female infibulation and excision in a lost first version of *First Footsteps in East Africa* (1856) that has been recovered by Gordon Waterfield in a 1966 edition. Burton's characterization of this "remarkable method" of maintaining chastity as "barbarous" is continued in the stringently "scientific" discourse of an article by Allen Worsley published in the *Journal of Obstetrics and Gynaecology of the British Empire* in 1938 in which the author refers to female circumcision as "evil." The practice is referred to in soft-core pornography in 1939 in Felix Bryk's *Dark Rapture: The Sex-Life of the African Negro* (New York: Walden, 1939) as well as in academia in an article by the celebrated Ashley Montague in *The American Anthropologist* in 1945. "Second wave," Western feminist approaches to the topic follow the parameters and tone established by Fran Hosken in her work since the 1970s (gathered in her 1983 *The Hosken Report: Genital and Sexual Mutilation of Females*). See also Henny Lightfoot-Klein, *Prisoners of Ritual: An Odyssey into Female Genital Circumcision in Africa* (New York: Haworth, 1989); Mary Daly, *Gyn/Ecology*; Robin Morgan and Gloria Steinem, "The International Crime of Genital Mutilation," *Ms* 8 (9) (March 1980), 65–69. Third World feminists who have published denunciations of the practice include: Awa Thiam, *Speak Out, Black Sisters: Feminism and Oppression in Black Africa* (London: Pluto Press, 1986); Olayinka Koso-Thomas, *The Circumcision of Women: A Strategy for Eradication* (London: Zed Books, 1987); Asma El Dareer, *Woman, Why Do You Weep?* (London: Zed Books, 1982); Efua Dorkenoo and Scilla Elworthy, *Female Genital Mutilation: Proposals for Change* (London: Minority Rights Group International, 1992); Nawal el Saadawi, *The Hidden Face of Eve: Women in the Arab World* (London: Zed Books, 1980). Female circumcision has also been featured in nationalist and decolonization discourses. See Jomo Kenyatta, *Facing Mount Kenya: The Tribal Life of the Kikuyu* (New York: Random House, 1975). For a stellar discussion of the politics of female circumcision discourse in the decolonization struggle in Kenya, see Susan Pedersen, "National Bodies, Unspeakable Acts: The Sexual Politics of Colonial Policy-Making," *Journal of Modern History* 63 (December 1991), 647–680. We identify significant participation in the discourse of sexual surgery in activist writing generated by groups such as the Intersex Society of North America. See, for example, the ISNA's newsletter, *Hermaphrodites with Attitudes*, and their call for an end to "IGM"—Intersexed Genital Mutilation. See also our work-in-progress for a fuller discussion of this complex site of alliance between queer, transgender, and global feminist activism around sexual surgeries.

onized bodies in historically specific ways.[37] This process of "othering" has constructed colonizing subjects as well. Thus the colonial classifications of racial and ethnic types include notions of "whole" and "fragmented" or "mutilated" bodies. The "mutilated" body is at once an object of fascination, desire, and repulsion, differentiating between colonizer "self" and colonized "other."[38] European modernity utilizes horror, romance, and adventure genres to gain power and to construct a Western identity of a fixed and stable self.

The modalities of such knowledge are visible in the binary division between modernity and tradition, the identification processes of humanist subject formation, the construction of subjects and objects through "ethnographic authority," the descriptive and stylistic genres of cultural productions of "difference" as "otherness."[39] In this context, "knowing" can mean the violent imposition of one's values, perspectives, and agendas on those seen as mirrors of the self rather than as complex, historical subjects.[40] These identification practices proliferate in both visual and print traditions in Western modernity.

Reproducing colonial discourse: global womanism's narrative and visual conventions

Feminist scholarship on colonial discourse has been crucial in pointing out the ways in which imperialist social relations produced the female subaltern as a specifically embodied subject situated in the Third World. Yet, the history of Western feminist ideas and practices includes imperializing and racist formations. Contemporary feminist scholarship on women travelers, for example, has been divided between celebrations of adventurous heroines and condemnations of racist "memsahibs." Such a division in representation can obscure the complicated class and ethnic distinctions that structure Western women's travel and immigration as well as the history of both pro- and anti-imperialist activities on the part of Western feminists. Enmeshed in either the romance of individual achievement over the rigors of travel or a nationalist resistance to European or North American traveling cultures, Western feminist representations of travel remain uneven,

37 See Ann Laura Stoler's work: "Carnal Knowledge and Imperial Power: Gender, Race, and Morality in Colonial Asia," in Micaela di Leonardo, ed., *Gender at the Crossroads of Knowledge: Feminist Anthropology in the Postmodern Era* (Berkeley: University of California Press, 1991), 51–101; and *Race and the Education of Desire: Foucault's "History of Sexuality" and the Colonial Order of Things* (Durham, NC: Duke University Press, 1995).

38 See Ann Balsamo, *Technologies of the Gendered Body* (Durham, NC: Duke University Press, 1995); Jennifer Terry and Jacqueline Urla, eds, *Deviant Bodies* (Bloomington: Indiana University Press, 1995); Cartwright, *Screening the Body*; Kathy Davis, *Reshaping the Female Body* (New York: Routledge, 1995); David Bell and Gill Valentine, eds, *Mapping Desire: Geographies of Sexualities* (New York: Routledge, 1995); and Mary Jacobus, Evelyn Fox, and Sally Shuttleworth, eds, *Body Politics* (New York: Routledge, 1990).

39 See Edward W. Said, *Orientalism* (New York: Random House, 1978); Clifford and Marcus, *Writing Culture*; and Clifford, *The Predicament of Culture*.

40 See Mary Louise Pratt, *Imperial Eyes: Travel Writing and Transculturation* (London: Routledge, 1992); Shohat and Stam, *Unthinking Eurocentrism*; Inderpal Grewal, *Home and Harem: Nation, Gender, Empire, and the Cultures of Travel* (Durham, NC: Duke University Press, 1996); Caren Kaplan, *Questions of Travel: Postmodern Discourses of Displacement* (Durham, NC: Duke University Press, 1996); and Caren Kaplan, "'Getting to Know You': Travel, Gender, and the Politics of Representation in *Anna and the King of Siam* and *The King and I*," in Roman de la Campa, E. Ann Kaplan, and Michael Sprinker, eds, *Late Imperial Culture* (London: Verso, 1995), 33–52.

under-theorized, and deeply troubling. For instance, the presence of African-American missionaries in Africa in the nineteenth and twentieth centuries requires more research into and discussion of these kinds of complex positionalities that cannot be understood fully within the binary of colonizer/colonized.[41] One of the primary technologies which Walker and Parmar use to convey knowledge is a map of their "travels." It is standard practice in colonial discourse to naturalize the social world through representation. Such maps, used in the broadest metaphorical sense, chart the flows of goods, resources, and peoples in the uneven trajectories of capital. *Warrior Marks*, markedly uninterested in class issues, makes a map of ethnic and racial diaspora that is superimposed upon a map of a unified and universal female body. This complex mapping of modern subjects conflates an "African" diaspora with a Western cultural feminist construction of "woman" to argue for a "return" to the mother country, to the body of the mother, to the source of female identity.[42]

This universalized body—whole, unified, and organic in relation to the circumcised body of the "Other"—forms the standpoint for the feminist practices visible in *Warrior Marks*. Such a standpoint prevents recognition of the ways in which Western patriarchies are inscribed on women's bodies through various technologies and disciplinary practices— breast augmentation, liposuction, rhinoplasty, tubal ligations, *in vitro* fertilization, mastectomies, hysterectomies, cosmetic surgeries, etc.—within the context of a lack of health care and reproductive freedom for metropolitan women, especially poor women and women of color.[43] Geopolitics and cultural asymmetries must be included in our analyses of the formation of specific sexed and gendered subjects in various locations. The histories and relations between such subjects are important topics of analysis in our struggle to deconstruct global feminist discourses. Western feminism's essentialist notions of bodies and sexuality pervade the globalizing discourse of "sisterhood," through imperializing representations. *Warrior Marks* is only one such cultural product in circulation, generating neo-colonialisms in the name of multicultural feminism. One response to *Warrior Marks*, therefore, is to begin a discussion of the ways visual representations, identities, and subjects in modernity collude with the power relations of late capital's colonial ventures.

In the film *Warrior Marks*, the primary tropes of travel that centuries of imperialist economic expansion have engendered are easily identifiable. First and foremost, a designated area—here "Africa"—must be emptied metaphorically and made culturally

---

41 See Sylvia M. Jacobs, ed., *Black Americans and the Missionary Movement in Africa* (Westport, CT: Greenwod Press, 1982). See also Sylvia M. Jacobs, "Give a Thought to Africa: Black Women Missionaries in Southern Africa," in Chaudhuri and Strobel, *Western Women and Imperialism*, 207–228.

42 This point is more fully discussed in our work-in-progress as part of the discourse of global feminism whereby a unified and unfragmented female body becomes equated with an ideal "lesbian body." In this context, female genital surgery eradicates or alters a zone that is configured in historically specific ways by contemporary Western cultural and lesbian feminist discursive practices.

43 See Davis, *Reshaping the Female Body*; Jennifer Craik, *The Face of Fashion: Cultural Studies in Fashion* (London: Routledge, 1994); Hilary Radner, *Shopping Around: Feminine Culture and the Pursuit of Pleasure* (New York: Routledge, 1995); Shari Benstock and Suzanne Ferriss, eds, *On Fashion* (New Brunswick, NJ: Rutgers University Press, 1994); Carol A. Stabile, *Feminism and the Technological Fix* (Manchester: Manchester University Press, 1994); Ann Balsamo, "On the Cutting Edge: Cosmetic Surgery and the Technological Production of the Gendered Body," *Camera Obscura* 28 (1992), 207–238; and Cartwright, *Screening the Body*. Walker does mention cosmetic surgeries and pressures on Western women to conform to patriarchal ideal forms in the written text when she is in the planning stages of the project, but this set of crucial ideas drops out of the film (*Warrior Marks*, 9–10).

blank.[44] Thus, the film depicts an overwhelmingly rural Africa peopled only by natives dominated by cultural tradition. *Warrior Marks* acknowledges a few African doctors and activists who work against the practice of genital surgeries but suggests that their actions are ineffectual and can only be strengthened by help from abroad. Both the film and the book present Walker and Parmar on a heroic mission to an Africa that is the site of unspeakable practices against its "women." Indeed, in its portrayal of Africa as a relatively undifferentiated space of "otherness," *Warrior Marks* erases the histories of decolonizations and diverse formations of nation-states including decades of "development," "modernization" programs, and localized strategies of resistance.

Instead, *Warrior Marks* prefers to deploy images that could easily be culled from the magazine pages or documentary footage of *National Geographic*.[45] The world the film conjures for its female heroines to travel through is one in which tradition is drastically differentiated from modernity. This distinction is drawn as a geographical map where some regions remain "dark," unenlightened, and thus more dangerous for women than others. In the print version, this map is rendered literally, complete with insets and scales in a manner reminiscent of such nineteenth-century travel accounts as Mary Kingsley's *Travels in West Africa*.[46] The book is organized into sections that recount the "journeys" of Walker and Parmar. These journeys are further linked to a particular set of Western feminist conventions through the use of epistolary communications: "Dear Pratibha," the book begins.[47] The film also uses the letters between Walker and Parmar as part of its narrative strategy. But before the literary convention of the epistle fully structures our understanding of the film, we see and hear the most typical of colonial discourse tropes—we hear drumming and we see a muscular leg draped in a multi-patterned fabric resembling "native garb." We are from the first instant "abroad." More specifically, the drumming signals "Africa" to non-Africans raised on both Hollywood and standard ethnographic films. That is, we, the viewers, must be assumed to be people who are not living in Western Africa—who are not at home there.

Although Walker's early intention was to make a film to educate and raise African consciousness about genital surgeries, she and Parmar soon discover financial and technical constraints—the cost of subtitling a film made in English and the lack of

---

44 See Pratt, *Imperial Eyes*; Clifford, *The Predicament of Culture*; Shohat and Stam, *Unthinking Eurocentrism*; and Said, *Orientalism*. See also Christopher Miller, *Blank Darkness: Africanist Discourse in French* (Chicago: University of Chicago Press, 1985).

45 See Lisa Bloom, *Gender on Ice: American Ideologies of Polar Expeditions* (Minneapolis: University of Minnesota Press, 1993); Catherine A. Lutz and Jane L. Collins, *Reading National Geographic* (Chicago: University of Chicago Press, 1993); William M. O'Barr, "Representations of Others, Part 1: Advertisements in the 1929 *National Geographic* Magazine," in *Culture and the Ad: Exploring Otherness in the World of Advertising* (Boulder, CO: Westview Press, 1994), 45–72; Tamar Y. Rothenberg, "Voyeurs of Imperialism: *The National Geographic Magazine* before World War II," in Anne Godlewska and Neil Smith, eds, *Geography and Empire* (Oxford: Basil Blackwell, 1994), 155–172.

46 Mary H. Kingsley, *Travels in West Africa 1897* (Boston: Beacon Press, 1988). Kingsley's influence on contemporary "women's travel" literature can be seen in works such as Caroline Alexander's memoir *One Dry Season: In the Footsteps of Mary Kingsley* (New York: Vintage Books, 1991) and in Alison Blunt's critical monograph *Travel, Gender, and Imperialism: Mary Kingsley and West Africa* (New York: Guilford Press, 1994). See also, Katherine Frank, *A Voyager Out: The Life of Mary Kingsley* (New York: Ballantine Books, 1986).

47 For a discussion of epistolary conventions in women's writing, see Linda S. Kauffman, *Special Delivery: Epistolary Modes in Modern Fiction* (Chicago: Chicago University Press, 1992).

screening or viewing facilities, for example. In the film project, the rhetorical effect of "knowledge" must be produced in the face of a profound lack of information on the part of the filmmakers. African women in diverse locations and of different classes become subsumed under the category "African" as the film's shooting sites in Gambia and Senegal become generalizable to an entire continent and the specific practices of genital surgeries are universalized. Although Parmar and her assistant were able to spend only a week in Gambia researching locations and setting up contacts before Walker arrived and the two-week shoot began, the presentation of information in the text is asserted with great confidence as "fact." Yet, without local guides and with elusive and unreliable contacts, the film crew is literally "lost"; none of the visitors speaks the relevant languages, no one has spent time in these places before, and no one is knowledgeable about this part of Africa. While Parmar spent part of her childhood in Kenya, her adult life in England has not been focused on African topics or studies. By the grace of her research for her novel, *Possessing the Secret of Joy,* Walker becomes the production's "expert" on female genital surgeries. The relatively short pre-production period, the great distances and language barriers, and their difficulties in linking up with prominent activists, such as Awa Thiam, mean that such contacts are more haphazard than they are the product of long-term coalitional activity.

The mistrust of some local figures toward the filmmakers may be justified. For in order to create a global subject—"woman"—as victim of generalized patriarchal oppression, Walker and Parmar have to utilize both anti-feminist and Eurocentric discourses in the form of authoritative texts. The "Selected Bibliography and Suggested Reading" section that appears at the end of the print version of *Warrior Marks* is interesting in several regards. The key citations fall into categories such as African nationalists (Jomo Kenyatta), Euro-American popular sexologists (Masters and Johnson, Shere Hite, etc.), randomly selected and uncritiqued ethnographies (Marcel Griaule, Jacques Lantier), and African and Euro-American activists on women's health issues who are heavily identified with the fight against FGM. Absent from the bibliography are feminist histories of colonialism and nationalism or decolonization, critiques of ethnographic knowledge in general or the surgeries in particular, and socio-political accounts of the lives of women in Africa. While Walker and Parmar acknowledge that contemporary practices of FGM may be attributed in part to colonialism, such an acknowledgment disallows any infiltration or impact on their own thinking or ideological formation as Western subjects in modernity. The burden of an oppressive practice falls on an ahistorical "tradition" in an exoticized culture.

The appearance of a binary opposition between tradition and modernity is a primary paradigm of colonial discourse. As critics and historians including Edward Said, Talal Asad, Johannes Fabian, Gayatri Spivak, and Ella Shohat have pointed out, this binary division creates a logic for Western intervention because it constructs a view of modernity as a corrective to tradition.[48] Modernity becomes a signifier for a range of attributes including the enlightened West, progress, civilization, democracy, self-determination, and freedom of choice. Tradition becomes the "other" by which non-Western cultures make

---

48 See Said, *Orientalism*; Spivak, *In Other Worlds* and *Outside in the Teaching Machine*; Shohat and Stam, *Unthinking Eurocentrism*; as well as Johannes Fabian, *Time and the Other: How Anthropology Makes Its Object* (New York: Columbia University Press, 1983); and Tala Asad, *Anthropology and the Colonial Encounter* (London: Ithaca Press, 1973).

their own empowerment socially, politically, and culturally. It is only by deconstructing this binary opposition through historicization and contextualization, that tradition and modernity emerge as constructs of a European world view that emphasizes a teleological and rational course over and above other modes of representing change, difference, and similarity. As two aspects of the same paradigm, then, the oppositional relationship between tradition and modernity masks the power of one term to describe and evaluate cultures that are designated as the "other."

Warrior Marks reinscribes this oppositional relationship that is so central to colonial discourse and Western, metropolitan subject formation. Rural Africa comes to signify "tradition," a destructive environment for women. In the film, the camera utilizes standard ethnographic shots to establish cultural difference. The gaze behind the camera penetrates the social space of the local people, moving in and out of doorways, searching for "secrets." The pivotal scene around which all these issues seem to revolve occurs in Walker's interview with an elderly female "circumciser" (who has no identity or name except "Circumciser 1" in both print and film texts). This scene summons many of the tropes of colonial discourse as it is interpellated through global feminism, especially the missionary discourse of eradicating ritual practices by "outing" them, by bringing "light" onto the subject, as it were.

Following Gayatri Spivak's and Rey Chow's examination of the representation of subaltern subjects in colonial discourse, this scene between Walker and the "circumciser" illustrates the way resistance and silence—often coded as "secrets"—challenge Western, liberal political formations.[49] In the interview, the elderly woman is portrayed as sinisterly withholding information from the interviewer, Alice Walker.[50] This "withholding" is presented as being crucial to maintaining tradition. Walker's "telling," on the other hand, is seen as the key to liberating the prisoners of traditional culture. The struggle between Walker and the nameless Gambian "circumciser" is visually and textually presented as a moral victory for Walker's viewpoint. The camera focuses repeatedly on the crude blade the woman holds in her lap, suggesting its deadly and cruel uses. Many reviewers comment on the powerful impact of the struggle between the "circumciser" and Walker's efforts to force her to reveal her "secrets." Indeed, the *San Francisco Chronicle*'s reviewer referred to the elderly woman as "wizened" and "ominous" while applauding Walker's speech, here termed "giving the woman a piece of her mind."[51]

In this and other scenes, the film makes no effort to question ethnographic authority (as the films of Trinh Minh-ha or Laleen Jayamanne have attempted for over a decade) or to make dialogical or epistemological innovations.[52] An uncritical use of ethnographic texts builds upon the nineteenth-century literary tradition that Mary Louise Pratt refers

49 See Spivak, "Can the Subaltern Speak?" 271–313; and Chow, *Writing Diaspora*.
50 Alice Walker and Pratibha Parmar, *Warrior Marks: Female Genital Mutilation and the Sexual Blinding of Women* (New York: Harcourt Brace, 1993), 301–308.
51 White, "Alice Walker's Compassionate Crusade," D1.
52 For critiques of ethnographic authority in anthropological and cultural discourses see Clifford and Marcus, *Writing Culture*; George E. Marcus and Michael M. J. Fischer, *Anthropology as Cultural Critique: An Experimental Moment in the Human Sciences* (Chicago: University of Chicago Press, 1986); and Clifford, *The Predicament of Culture*. See also, Laleen Jayamanne, "Do you think I am a woman, ha! Do you?" *Discourse* 11 (2) (Spring–Summer 1989), 49–62; and Trinh T. Minh-ha, *Framer Framed* (New York: Routledge, 1992).

to as "manners and customs description," constructing the "native" as object.[53] Walker and Parmar utilize ethnographic materials as "authoritative" when it suits their end. For example, in the print text at the end of the transcript of Walker's interview with "Circumciser 1," the reader finds a "description" of an infibulation from a 1978 medical thesis from the University of Bordeaux.[54] Parmar cites A. M. I. Vergiat's *Moeurs et Coutumes des Manjas* (1937) as the source of a "ritual" song sung by circumcised girls.[55] Many Third World and anti-imperialist feminist filmmakers and writers have struggled against the reproduction of ethnographic colonial discourses in cinematic and cultural practice, critiquing and resisting its representational strategies. The *Warrior Marks* texts reinforce and reproduce colonial discourse through an unproblematized reliance upon and alliance with "authoritative," Eurocentric studies.

In the standard colonial gesture of constructing a "native" through the operation of difference, the elderly circumciser in *Warrior Marks* is depicted as actively evil and passively deluded by tradition. Walker, the interviewer, on the other hand, throws off the mantle of objective questioner to reveal the enlightened metropolitan subject who "knows" all. In "Can the Subaltern Speak?" Gayatri Spivak calls the position and power of the investigator or interviewer into question in order to examine how the "third-world subject is represented within Western discourse."[56] Rejecting the liberal demand that all subjects constitute themselves through public "speech," Spivak argues that social and political movements cannot break the epistemological stranglehold of imperial culture by resurrecting the "shadows" of subjectivity, the categories that imperialism created. Without deconstruction, the "possibility of collectivity itself is persistently foreclosed through the manipulation of female agency."[57]

Read against the grain, as it were, the print text opens up some questions of knowledge production that could have been pursued in the film itself. For instance, "Pratibha's Journey," Parmar's section of the print text, chronicles, among many things, the contradictions and tensions that emerge in the representational politics of the project. Despite Parmar's increasing identification with Walker's "vision," she expresses concern during pre-production and the shoot about making sufficient contact with local activists. Awa Thiam, for instance, remains relatively elusive for reasons upon which Parmar can only speculate. Parmar worries that if Thiam will not cooperate by leading the filmmakers to the "right" contacts in Senegal and elsewhere or by endorsing the project, their work will be hampered logistically and their credibility will suffer. Thiam, as it happens, is in the midst of a pre-election campaign for the opposition political party in her country and does not seem able to drop everything to meet with Parmar. While Parmar presents this situation as Thiam's obstinate resistance, the text leaves the question open as to whether Thiam is playing the powerful diva/native informant or whether she is just a busy professional who has not been asked far enough ahead of time whether the film schedule would be convenient for her.

In an interview included in the print text, Thiam makes it very clear that she agrees with Walker and Parmar on the symbolic import of female genital surgeries. Since Thiam

---

53 Pratt, *Imperial Eyes*, 58–68.
54 See "Alice Walker and Circumciser 1," 301–309 (including the excerpt from Alan David, *Infibulation en République de Djibouti*, 308–309).
55 Walker and Parmar, *Warrior Marks*, 179.
56 Spivak, "Can the Subaltern Speak?" 271.
57 Ibid., 282.

comes from a local group that practices, as she says, "80 percent female circumcision and sometimes infibulation," she views the situation as urgent and agrees with the film-makers on the need to organize internationally. However, her analysis of the practice as an indication of women's subordination that is embedded within the power structures of particular societies leads her, after ten years of working in what she calls the "female circle," to "get involved in the sphere of politics," and to "succeed in convincing the decision makers, both male and female, and to try to struggle for the abolition of sexual mutilation."[58]

Thiam's move toward participation in electoral politics highlights the suppression of such socio-political and economic continuums in *Warrior Marks*. In addition to their fuzzy relationship to both state and non-governmental structures, Walker and Parmar's texts erase many facets of transnational economic factors, mystifying the division of labor that makes possible, for instance, the funding of a film instead of a refrigerated truck. In the print version of *Warrior Marks*, the authors recount an extraordinary anecdote that describes a meeting between a group of women who run a collective garden and the filmmakers. Asked their feelings about FGM, these women respond by asking the "rich Americans" for a refrigerated truck they need badly to get their produce to out-lying areas. The filmmakers, who do not perceive themselves as "rich" by their own cultural standards, joke that they could probably only pay for one tire for such a truck. The request for a truck is not mentioned again. This will to ignore or misrecognize information that does not seem to pertain to their own project marks the imperialist tendencies of this project. The power to set an agenda, to arrive uninvited in a coun-try for a brief period of time, to tell people how they ought to feel and think about their sexuality and their bodies, to assume the right to rescue other people's children, and to use this experience as a yardstick of one's own freedom, is standard operating procedure in the textual tracks of imperialism's cultural production. These gestures and moves are an historical legacy—*Warrior Marks* does not take the opportunity to unlearn or even to question this representational heritage and thus cannot do more than repeat its signs. As Chandra Mohanty argues in her critique of Western feminist discourse on female genital surgeries: "Sisterhood cannot be assumed on the basis of gender; it must be forged in concrete historical and political practice and analysis."[59]

Thus, Walker and Parmar make a film that speaks directly, vividly, and authoritatively to demand a change in the way people conduct their lives in particular locations. Their right to make this demand comes through an unquestioned adherence to Western med-ical science, and, apparently, through their superior ethical positioning (their "knowledge" of right and wrong), that is, they "know better." This positivist ethics is conjoined with an appeal to liberal juridical practices, engendering a powerful set of philosophical, medical, and legal certainties in the effort to "civilize" in the name of a multicultural global womanism.

Multiculturalism's globalizing discourses

It is clear from the work of many scholars in recent years that what we call "imperial feminism" emerged during the nineteenth century to create simultaneously new feminist

---

58 Walker and Parmar, *Warrior Marks*, 284.
59 Mohanty, "Under Western Eyes," 58.

subjects in the West and their objects of rescue in the "periphery"—"sisters" with drastically different material conditions of life. The collusion between some Western feminist practices and colonial discourses has been amply documented in over a decade of emergent critical work. The advent of "postcolonial theory" constructed by diasporas of scholars who settled in Europe or in North America created a new demand for increased attention to the aftermath of colonialism. Furthermore, the politicization of racial minorities through multiculturalism as a social and cultural movement in the United States has gained its voice through the articulation of rights claims against the modern state. These political and cultural movements inform feminist practices in metropolitan locations in a profound and complex manner.

With this complicated social and cultural field in mind, we might see figures such as Walker and Parmar, with quite different historical trajectories, coming together for a project such as *Warrior Marks* through their links with movements that have emerged through anti-colonialist efforts. This means that Walker's concern with the aftermath of slavery in the US and Parmar's participation in anti-racist movements in Britain have contributed to a heightened understanding of present-day gender as constructed through colonized patriarchies around the globe. Multiculturalism, then, has been one way to demand the rights of citizens racialized as well as gendered in particular ways. Yet, when multiculturalism remains fixed upon state remedies, reinforcing national agendas, and placing less emphasis on socio-economic formations, the alliance between "women of color" may become strained.

To a certain extent this dilemma is being addressed by solidarity movements that draw upon a range of ideologies of cosmopolitanism and global unity. Thus, the "global" and "transnational" are all interpellated by feminist subjects who also rely upon a discourse of multiculturalism. Yet differences between subjects of less powerful and more powerful states remain to be addressed. This process conflates the racialized subject of the state with the global feminist or womanist who constructs a universal woman as the paradigmatic female subject of global sisterhood. Thus, Walker and Parmar, in solidarity with this global woman, wish to rescue and include her in the privileges of modernity and its emergent sexual subjectivities and embodied practices. What drops out of this gesture is any recognition that this global woman exists only to reaffirm the metropolitan subject of feminism. The multicultural subject, as it is constituted through such a globalized practice of feminism, may be part of an anti-racist strategy but its only space of negotiation is a modern nation-state.

In order to create a film that satisfies the demands of Western subjectivity and the ethnographic tradition, all the complex negotiations between the multicultural subject and the imperial state fall away so that what remains are the conventional colonial tropes— the very tradition of representation that leads to a racism that the multiculturalism project seeks to resist. To have made a less "popular" film, Walker and Parmar would have had to include many of the tensions and conflicts that emerge in the print text (even if only in passing), such as the links between an analysis of diverse surgical practices as gendered and racialized modes of subject constitution or the difficulty of forging alliances and gaining the cooperation of women activists in the regions of Africa visited by the film crew.

Warrior Marks is just one prominent instance of the difficulties of globalizing a multicultural feminist agenda. It is important to read the texts that come out of the political movements we are committed to not only in a celebratory manner but with an attention to these dilemmas in representational practice and politics. Our aim is not to destroy or take away important icons and cultural practices that support communities of resistance. Rather, we want to generate debate and discussion about our representational practices and politics. In many ways, the dilemma for late twentieth-century multicultural feminists is similar to that faced by late nineteenth-century national feminists—how to work with, around, and against the state. Asking for rights from the nation-state, representing others through identitarian practices, is an inevitable and necessary process for all social movements in modernity. But in acknowledging that inevitability, we should not abandon critique. These are challenges offered by the extremely difficult task of public policy formation and activist work. Our reading of an activist, multiculturalist feminist/womanist film and its accompanying print text is not, therefore, simply one of opposing aesthetic tastes or political correctness. Given that genital surgeries and refugee asylum claims based on FGM are now a matter of governmental debate in the US and Europe,[60] it seems timely and necessary to examine the connections between discourses of human rights, racialized nationalisms, and multiculturalism in feminist and womanist frameworks.

60 See Kay Boulware-Miller, "Female Circumcision: Challenges to the Practice as a Human Rights Violation," *Harvard Women's Law Journal* 8 (Spring 1985), 155–177; Isabelle R. Gunning, "Modernizing Customary International Law: The Challenge of Human Rights," *Virginia Journal of International Law* 31 (2) (Winter 1991), 211–247; Georgia Dullea, "Female Circumcision a Topic at U.N. Parley," *The New York Times* (Friday, July 18, 1980), B4; Marlise Simons, "France Jails Woman for Daughter's Circumcision," *The New York Times* (January 11, 1993), A8; Timothy Egan, "An Ancient Ritual and a Mother's Asylum Plea," *The New York Times* (March 4, 1994), A25; Clyde H. Farnsworth, "Canada Gives Somali Mother Refugee Status," *The New York Times* (July 21, 1994), A14; Jill Lawrence, "Women Seek Asylum in West to Avoid Abuses in Homeland," *The San Francisco Chronicle* (March 21, 1994), A3; Sophfronia Scott Gregory, "At Risk of Mutilation," *Time* (March 21, 1994), 45–46. For a vigorous discussion of the pitfalls of cultural defense arguments and the rhetoric of human rights in the context of racism, see Sherene Razack, "What Is To Be Gained by Looking White People in the Eye? Culture, Race, and Gender in Cases of Sexual Violence," *Signs* 19 (4) (Summer 1994), 894–923.

3 "Daddy, where's the FBI warning?"

Constructing the video spectator

Ina Rae Hark

I

In a "Family Circus" cartoon of the early 1990s the little girl, Dolly, seated with her parents in the multiplex auditorium as the credits roll at the beginning of the feature, turns and asks her father, "Daddy, where's the FBI warning?" A generation of viewers now exists for whom consumption of movies at home on video has always been the norm. What does this shift signal for the spectatorial paradigm governed by notions of the apparatus based solely on theatrical projection? Are the questions of gender that have preoccupied theory about spectatorship different for the person who watches films on home video? And how has Hollywood gone about interpolating such reconfigured spectators into its narratives?

Increased empowerment distinguishes the video spectator from the theatrical spectator. Dolly's anticipated FBI warning replaces similar minatory exhortations in theatrical policy trailers that caution patrons not to smoke or converse and urge them to remove crying babies to the lobby. But if the FBI warning may constrain law-abiding consumers from violating the film's copyright for their own profit and amusement, the divergence from the theatrical preamble reminds them that, when watching films at home, they *may* smoke and talk and treat crying babies however they see fit. More significantly, the home video viewer can fast forward through the warning, the video trailers, and substantial portions of the film for that matter.

Anne Friedberg has distinguished televisual from cinematic spectatorship in five major respects: the non-projected nature of the television image, the "modicum of mobility" and "distracted gaze" it allows, its time-shifting potential, its synchronic and diachronic choice of viewing options, and its smaller image scale (Friedberg 1993: 136–137). John Ellis similarly observes: "TV does not encourage the same degree of spectator concentration. There is no surrounding darkness, no anonymity of the fellow viewers, no large image, no lack of movement amongst the spectators, no rapt attention" (Ellis 1992: 128). While the camera's look and the characters in the diegesis vested the cinematic spectator with a surrogate power, the "virtual mobilized gaze," as Friedberg calls it, came at the expense of a lessening of actual physical freedom. In Baudry's famous example, the cinematic apparatus replicated for its subjects the captive condition of Plato's prisoners in the cave, the necessary conditions of each being "suspension of mobility and predominance of the visual function" (Baudry 1974: 294). With these conditions suspended for the television viewer, the rapt gaze is replaced, in Ellis's terms, by the distracted glance.

Another distinction of films on video is that the spectator relates to the film as a commodity as well as an experience. While few theatrical spectators venture into the projection booth to feed the celluloid through the projection apparatus, video consumers hold the tape or disc in their hands and place it directly into the video player for viewing. Purchased videos, laser discs or DVDs, or films taped off the air, become permanent possessions, finally making films ownable commodities like books, artworks, or recorded music. The owner of a home video commodity may also be compensated for the deficit in image size and quality by various surpluses, among them additional scenes that were cut for theatrical distribution, anniversary special editions containing documentaries on the film's production, additional voiceover commentary on laser discs and DVDs. Unlike the theatrical spectator spellbound in darkness, moreover, video spectators have physical control over the film: they may interrupt, repeat, skip over, go back to, or freeze-frame specific sections of the narrative. If they own the tape, they may edit, erase, or record over any or all portions of it. If theatrical spectators sit immobilized and transfixed, video spectators can make the film wait for them if they wish to walk about.

How do we characterize this newly empowered, video spectator in relation to the classic viewer constructed by theories of spectatorship derived from the conditions of theatrical exhibition? Perhaps the first question to ask is the one we inevitably ask of any newborn: Is it a boy or a girl? A number of theories have identified the spectator constructed by the cinematic apparatus as male and the one constructed by the televisual apparatus as female. Most famously, Laura Mulvey states in "Visual Pleasure and Narrative Cinema": "The determining male gaze projects its fantasy onto the female figure, which is styled accordingly. In their traditional exhibitionist role women are simultaneously looked at and displayed, with their appearance coded for strong visual and erotic impact so that they can be said to connote *to-be-looked-at-ness*" (Mulvey 1975: 19). The scopic regime of the cinema delineated via psychoanalysis in such seminal works as Christian Metz's *The Imaginary Signifier* depends so much on Oedipal dynamics and the operations of castration anxiety that it was difficult to conceive of the spectator constructed by the apparatus as anything but male.

Given the very different style of looking embodied in the glance, television has "a very different relationship to voyeurism" (Ellis 1992: 128) than does cinema. And since television is also "intimate and everyday, a part of home life rather than any kind of special event" (Ellis 1992: 113), it becomes tempting to set up a polar opposition between the male gaze exercised outside the home and the female glance at the television as domestic object. Beverle Houston stated unequivocally in 1984 "that the strategies of the television institution, enunciation, and apparatus that I have been discussing put all its spectators—both male and female—into a situation that is, in many ways, much like the one that has been theorized for the feminine spectator and subject, but which is, in fact, available to all subjects" (189). Lynn Spigel's study of popular discourse about television in the 1950s points out that "unlike the male spectator of classical cinema, who has been represented in terms of mastery and control over the scene, television in these popular accounts was shown to take away authority over the image. It threatened to make men into female spectators" (Spigel 1990: 88).

Films played on television via video apparatuses already challenge this binary by combining the hardware of the televisual apparatus with software originally produced for the cinematic spectator. Lynne Joyrich, cautioning against too easy acceptance of the association of TV spectatorship with emasculation, has in fact noted that television programs, to the extent that they are shot in a more cinematic style, "attempt to evade TV's feminization" (Joyrich 1990: 166). Yet theories derived from television's arrival amid the 1950s ideological project of domesticating entertainment as part of the wider goal of idealizing the suburban nuclear family, which assert the feminizing effect of viewing any text on television, need another look in the age of computerized, digital electronics. The male television spectator who springs to mind today does not lack "mastery and control" over the scene or "authority over the image"; he's sitting there with the remote, channel surfing.

As power over electronic entertainment comes more and more to reside in a hand-held device one aims and shoots, the femininity ascribed to television because it is a domestic appliance fades as the spectator reconfigures himself into that ultimate male icon, a guy with a gun. The shift in computer technology that allows more and more functions to be carried out with a mouse one points and clicks and less and less through typing on the keyboard so long associated with female clerical workers reveals a similar consolidation of male hegemony over what might be viewed as potentially feminizing technology.

Even television's association with the domestic environment is not so automatic a marker of housewifery as it once was. With so many dual-career households and single parents, the person likely to spend the most time at home with the TV and video player is neither husband nor wife, but the child. Indeed we all know the stories of the young-ster summoned to program the VCR for the bumbling parent who just can't get it to stop flashing "12:00." Moreover, the endless repeatability of viewing possible with video appeals most strongly to children; titles for children inevitably dominate the top video sales lists. So if we combine the various markers of the ideal spectator implied by film-on-video technology, a figure emerges whom I will dub "the empowered boy-child."

II

Classical Hollywood also attracted its share of young male spectators, and pre-teen and adolescent boys still make up the largest segment of the theatrical audience. However, since the cinematic spectator wields only virtual power, granted through identification with characters in the diegesis, there was no need to have those characters mirror the actual demographics of the audience. Video-era spectators, on the other hand, have a power over the image that mimics the diegetic power in the hands of the filmed narra-tive's protagonist. During the 1980s, the first decade in which home video achieved a presence in a majority of American households, there was a concomitant rise in the num-ber of empowered boy-children who served as the protagonists of Hollywood features. He figured prominently in blockbusters like *E. T.* and *Back to the Future*, and films fea-turing him would continue into the early 1990s to flood the multiplexes every summer: *Last Action Hero*, *Terminator 2*, *Free Willy*, *Searching for Bobby Fischer*, *Forever Young*, *The Man without a Face*, *Rookie of the Year*, *North*, to name but a few.

The film that probably crystallized Hollywood's awareness of the ascendancy of this boy-hero as identificatory site for video-era film consumers was the 1990s *Home Alone* (Figs 3.1 and 3.2), in which, as Alan Nadel notes, "the idea of empowering the child is taken to its logical limits" (Nadel 1997: 157). The film's incredible, and totally unanticipated, box office success in retrospect looks almost inevitable, for its diegesis contains practically every element necessary to interpolate members of the first video generation. Nadel's *Flatlining on the Field of Dreams* comments on some of the prevailing narratives that dominated commercial cinema in President Reagan's America, films that served as "the consumables of a hyperconsumptive society situated between

Figure 3.1 Macaulay Culkin in *Home Alone* (20th Century Fox 1990). Courtesy of the Kobal Collection

Figure 3.2 Macaulay Culkin in *Home Alone II* (20th Century Fox 1992). Courtesy of the Kobal Collection

two recessions" (Nadel 1997: 4). Two of the narratives that tie in with the switch from cinematic to video spectator are the one of a ghostly or inadequate patriarch seeking an avatar through whom he can reestablish the safety of his family, and, the specialty of *Home Alone* producer John Hughes, "one in which dysfunctional families save themselves through the successful fending off of the invasive strangers who bring the social problems of another time and place to the site of President Reagan's America, which is otherwise fundamentally safe, suburban, and white" (Nadel 1997: 142).

The home into which the video spectator brings a film, watching it under conditions he at last controls, is probably *the* contested site of the 1980s. On the one hand, the family, for whom the home serves as metonymy, was undergoing a major reconfiguration. Divorce rates climbed, both parents of intact couples frequently worked, children subsequently found themselves home alone indeed after school. At the same time, however, skyrocketing real estate prices and rents contributed to an epidemic of homelessness. Nadel quotes statistics to the effect that "fair market rent" in 1979 equalled or exceeded 80 percent of minimum-wage income in only three states and was below 60 percent in forty-five. By 1990 it exceeded 80 percent in ten states and was below 60 percent only in fifteen (163). This specter of failing to retain basic decent shelter made even the most dysfunctional family fiercely protective of the home that marked them off from an urban "outside" roiled by street crime related to the increase in crack cocaine addiction and the emergence of AIDS as a threat to sexual relations. Bringing the movies home in the form of videos was one way of adding them to the provisioning of a domestic site under siege.

However, there is a wider context to this move that derives from long-standing practices in Hollywood narratology. Before it became possible to view films at home on television, studio films tended to associate danger—but also excitement and adventure—with sites far distant from home, either spatially or temporally. Movies made their money by getting people out of the house, after all, and a subliminal message of many of them echoed that of *His Girl Friday* (1940): settling down equalled Ralph Bellamy and Albany, while stimulating adventures and Cary Grant accompanied an unsettled life. A look back at the 1950s shows that home invasion scenarios accompanied the advent of television, and I don't think it's any accident that two of the major films on that theme, *The Desperate Hours* and *Cape Fear*, were remade in 1990 and 1991, respectively. What Vivian Sobchack notes of the transformation of the science fiction and horror genres during the video age applies to much of 1980s cinema in general: "Those exotic *visual sites* of horrific abstraction and revulsion, and of utopian wonder and dystopian anxiety, which characterized and differentiated 'traditional' horror and SF films were explicitly returned to American soil and to that domestic structure of social relations we call the nuclear family . . . [for] in the age of television the drawbridge is always down; the world intrudes. It is no longer possible to avoid the invasive presence of Others—whether poltergeists, extra-terrestrials, or one's own alien kids" (Sobchack 1987: 7–8).

One persistent strain of nuclear family dysfunction in first video-generation films concerned the absent or failed father. Children of the 1980s were frequently the offspring of baby boomer parents whose 1960s idealism had been co-opted by Reaganite greed, or of fathers who had fought in America's first losing overseas conflict. The rising divorce rate made it more likely that a father would be physically absent from the home as well. Sons of such fathers lacked the powerful patriarch against whom to define their Oedipal trajectories, and film after film therefore deals with the efforts of these sons to rewrite the unsatisfactory father, to re-create him as more powerful and more successful or to find a present substitute for him: Nadel's "ghost-patriarch" films, the body-switcher scenarios[1] that find adolescent males in grown-up bodies, even the child-of-divorce-context of *E.T.* Peter Biskind observes of video-era directors that they "wished to infantilize their characters and their audience, [but] they also wanted to re-create the strong father; in fact infantilization demanded the strong father" (1990: 141). That

---

1 A rash of these films appeared in 1987 and 1988, including *Big, Vice-Versa, 18 Again!*, and *Like Father, Like Son*.

the young boy's access to video technology abets such fantasies of rewriting the failed father becomes apparent in *Back to the Future* (1985). Marty McFly's camcorder plays an important part in the plot dynamics, and the whole idea of going back in time to alter an unsatisfactory present reality bears no small resemblance to rewinding a tape and recording over its contents. In Marty's case, his father is erased as the star of a dreary blue-collar farce and cast instead as the hero of a sophisticated comedy.

Home Alone combines the tale of an empowered boy-child who must protect his home in the absence of his father with an alien-invasion or frontier-siege scenario transplanted to the contemporary Chicago suburbs. It thus maintains a balance between film as away-from-home adventure and film as consumable domestic product. As a testament to the ascendancy of the technologically savvy child over the pre-electronic adult that at the same time grants ultimate moral authority to more traditional tools of masculine prowess, as a Christmas fable for the age of two-income yuppie families, couch potatoes, cocooning and commodity fetishism, partaking equally of the culture of the mall multiplex and of the VCR, *Home Alone* was made to go both ways.

III

The first words Kevin McAlister, *Home Alone*'s protagonist, utters are "Mom, Uncle Frank won't let me watch the movie, but the big kids can. Why can't I? It's not even rated R; he's just being a jerk." Access to the VCR is thus established as a major locus of power. At the same time, the film sketches the modified 1980s Oedipal dynamics that Kevin's adventure will invoke. At eight, Kevin is not quite ready for an inter-generational conflict with his father. The primary opponents of this youngest of five children are first and foremost his older siblings, especially his bullying brother Buzz. The adults who threaten him are portrayed as self-absorbed children themselves: the boorish Uncle Frank and the bumbling "Wet Bandits" Harry and Marv. Kevin's real father, Peter, as his name suggests, is neither absent, childish, nor notably emasculated, as are so many fathers in 1980s films. But he remains a cipher, distinguished by his cool refusal to get excited, angry, or panicked by any of the incredible coincidences that strand Kevin at home and prevent the family from regaining contact with him for three days. *Home Alone* essentially writes him out of its psychological equation to concentrate on Kevin's sibling rivalries, especially his competition for his mother's love. Thus, when Kevin remembers the cruel words from his family that caused him to wish them away, he conjures up images of his mother, his brothers and sisters, and Uncle Frank, but not his father.[2]

Kevin at this point in the narrative struggles first and foremost to escape the identity of "baby," a label likely to cling to the youngest of a large family even when he is a precocious eight-year-old. Shut out from the video pleasures of the "big kids," he dreads sharing a bunk with his bed-wetting younger cousin Fuller. This desire to avoid being figuratively and literally stained by association with Fuller leads to his exile to the attic which in turn results in his being forgotten during the mad rush to reach the airport on time.

2 Peter had in fact stood apart by not chewing Kevin out, despite the fact that the boy ruined his new fish-hooks. Nevertheless, it is only to "Mom," and not his Dad, that Kevin calls out during his most desperate moments while in the house alone.

During his first night alone, Kevin gets to play big kid, reading his brother's stash of *Playboy*s and appropriating his life savings, eating junk food, leaving a mess in the kitchen, and watching the forbidden videos. Yet Kevin turns out to share more of the sensibilities of his parents than his older siblings: "Guys, I'm eating junk and watching rubbish," he calls out in mid-orgy. "You'd better come out and stop me." The murder in the parody 1930s gangster film, *Angels with Filthy Souls*, terrifies him into freeze-framing the image and calling out for Mom, who, as if by telepathy, realizes that he has been left behind. The rest of Kevin's adventure will grant him not adolescent, rebellious independence but the mature judgment of a parent and homeowner. He quells his childish fears when he decides to confront rather than hide from the burglars' threat: "Only a wimp would be hiding under a bed, and I can't be a wimp. I'm the man of the house."

The terms under which Kevin accepts this responsibility are of course conventionally patriarchal. Yet his actions as man of the house emphasize the house in a way consistent with the domestication of the adventure narrative that the culture of home film consumption has authorized. He not only takes up arms to defend the homestead, he does the laundry and marketing. The man of the house is equally the ideal coupon-clipping homemaker. When his mother laments that the family has returned to an empty larder, Kevin, who before his rite of passage could not pack a suitcase, reassures her that he has been to the store and brought home "milk, eggs and fabric softener." "What a funny guy," his father responds. He might well have said, "What an eighties kid."

If Kevin wishes away the family that turns a house into a home ("When I get married I'm livin' alone," he grumbles early on), he gets them back only after a struggle to secure the material integrity of the McAlisters' lavishly appointed Winnetka residence. Home in *Home Alone* is compounded equally of domestic sentiments and desire-inducing commodities, thus making it the ideal Christmas movie for the end of the 1980s. Harry himself resembles a greedy child awaiting Christmas morning as he recounts the treasures available in the deserted homes. Product placements within the film were foregrounded, and two companies so featured, American Airlines and Pepsi, placed commercials on the initial video release. Moreover, *Home Alone* is quite aware of itself as a Christmas commodity. The citations of such film classics as *Miracle on 34th Street*, *How the Grinch Stole Christmas*, and *It's a Wonderful Life* (in French) on television at various points in the narrative define the repeatable holiday classic identity the film wishes to appropriate for itself, although the massive sell-through of videocassettes was a bonus probably as unexpected as its skyrocketing into the ranks of all-time box office champions.

A library of films on tape is another marker of the all-sufficient, upscale 1980s home. But they turn out to have a utility that goes beyond entertainment. Kevin is able to deceive the pizza delivery man and temporarily scare off the robbers by careful manipulation via remote control of the *Angels with Filthy Souls* tape. (We would probably see him wielding the home computer and Nintendo joystick as well, if the filmmakers hadn't been careful to keep non-cinematic competitors for home screen attention out of the diegesis.)

Yet the very ease with which children can manipulate VCRs and their companion electronic home appliances becomes a central theme in *Home Alone*. An unarticulated subtext of the film is the status of the latch-key child, and we should realize that the development of home electronics has furthered the acceptability of leaving one's children home alone. While parents would fear disaster should an eight-year-old cook some scrambled eggs on the stove, they can confidently leave him or her a frozen meal to pop into the microwave (the way that Kevin makes his Christmas Eve dinner of nutritious macaroni and cheese). Likewise, while we wouldn't imagine that youngsters could keep themselves entertained with a 16 mm projector, over two-thirds of 1980s households with children had VCRs and tapes with which kids could furnish themselves hours of entertainment.

If advanced technology comes second nature to the 1980s child, then maturity is signified by association with the tools of the father's and grandfather's childhoods. For Kevin to achieve grown-up status in a VCR-era film, he must therefore gain expertise in the mechanical as well as the electronic. His greatest fear is of the ominously wheezing and glowing basement furnace. Succeeding in willing its transformation in his mind from monster to mere mechanism, he can then easily operate the washing machine. His booby traps for the invading thieves utilize weights and pulleys, ropes and gears, and plain, old-fashioned obstacles. The final blow to the burglars, delivered by old man Marley, comes from a sturdy, no-moving-parts snow shovel applied to their crania.

The film's attitude toward consumer electronics is as ambivalent as its attitude toward latch-key kids. For if such machines make it possible for very small children to survive domestically without burning the house down—as Buzz grudgingly congratulates Kevin for doing—they encourage a dehumanizing isolation. The automatic light timers throughout the McAlisters' neighborhood do not deceive the burglars, but they produce an effect of mindless robotic existence with their sequential illuminations. When the McAlisters are frantically trying to contact any friends or neighbors who might check up on Kevin, their phone calls reach "nothing but a bunch of answering machines."

If such technology enables children to perform adult tasks successfully, that is precisely their danger. While part of *Home Alone* assures guilty yuppie parents that their kids will do just fine without them—an attitude shared by the real-life Illinois couple who purposely left their two young daughters home alone while they went on vacation—another part indicts them for abdicating parental responsibility. When Harry arrives disguised as a police officer to case the McAlister residence at the film's opening, he can't find anyone to admit responsibility for the household: "All kids and no parents—probably a fancy orphanage!" This positing of failed parenting also clearly places *Home Alone* as a product of its times. It too traces the regressive Oedipal scenario that arguably distinguishes filmed narratives of the first video generation from those of preceding eras.

In *Home Alone* this plotline is essentially displaced onto the old man Marley subplot. Designated by the video-saturated older boys as their own nightmare on Lincoln Boulevard, the "South Bend Shovel Slayer" who has obliterated all traces of his family, Marley supplants the colorless Peter McAlister as the primary Oedipal menace in Kevin's imagination. However, the white-bearded Marley, as his Dickensian name hints, turns out to be the film's true Father Christmas—"Have you been a good boy this year?" he asks Kevin in the church. Nevertheless, he *has* made his family disappear, a quarrel with his son causing a complete breach. It is Kevin, now acutely aware of the pain that can result from wishing one's parents away, who advises him to try to re-establish the family hierarchy and thus empowers him to do so. In turn, when Kevin, for all his ingenuity, ends up in the burglars' clutches, it is Marley and his shovel that strike the blow to prevent Harry from acting on his castration threats to boil Kevin's *cojones* in motor oil and "bite off his little fingers."

While Kevin and Marley retain phallic power, Harry and Marv are the ones to be castrated. Harry's glistening gold tooth, which clues Kevin in to his duplicity, symbolizes his illegitimate efforts to steal other men's possessions, to usurp their patriarchal authority. He loses it during the battle in the McAlister home, and Peter, appropriately, discovers it when he returns on Christmas Day. Like Marley's restored family, it is a legacy from the eight-year-old "man of the house" who reassumes his position as picked-upon kid brother at the film's conclusion.

If films made for movie-goers used the concluding heterosexual romantic embrace to keep men from going off with their buddies and abandoning home altogether, those made for both theatrical and home consumption keep the convention to heterosexualize the narrative but offer a sizable number of parallel texts resolved by the father–son embrace (in this case projected onto the reunion between Marley senior and junior that Kevin witnesses after his recuperation of his own family) and the restoration of a dysfunctional home that the adventurer may never have left at all.

In the twenty-first century the first generation never to have known a time without the possibility of consuming films on video will be adults, and perhaps the empowered boy-child will give way to another figure of identification, although the continuing evolution of delivery systems may dictate the persistence of the child-expert figure for somewhat longer than we might anticipate. What will be perhaps more interesting to chart is whether the dual sites of film consumption, both mall multiplex screen and family room TV, will persist, given the movie theatre's stubborn refusal to offer the child-expert the mastery s/he wields at home. In *Playing with Power* Marsha Kinder writes of her son:

> To kids like Victor who are raised on television, moviegoing frequently translates into a frightening loss of power. In contrast to television, the oversized movie images and overbearing sounds demand their undivided attention for long stretches of time and deprive them, not only of control over what they perceive, but also of periodic retreat into a comforting domestic background.
>
> (Kinder 1991: 30)

Or as I overheard a mother say to her little girl, on a potty break in the middle of a screening of *The Lion King*, "Don't dawdle, dear. We can't rewind this one."

Gloomy pronouncements that home entertainment would destroy moviegoing have been with us since the invention of radio, and I doubt that even the availability of movies at home on demand is going to close up the theatres. Clearly, however, unlike my generation for whom movies consumed via television were defined by their deviation from an implicitly superior theatrical norm, for that little girl, and Victor, and the cartoon Dolly, movies on video or cable are the superior form, in comparison to which the spectacular but disempowering cinema may be increasingly found wanting.

References

Baudry, J.-L. (1974) "Ideological Effects of the Basic Cinematographic Apparatus," reprinted in P. Rosen, ed., *Narrative, Apparatus, Ideology: A Film Theory Reader*, New York: Columbia University Press, 1986, 286–298.

Biskind, P. (1990) "The Last Crusade," in M. C. Miller, ed., *Seeing Through Movies*, New York: Pantheon, 112–149.

Ellis, J. (1992) *Visible Fictions* (rev. edn), London: Routledge.

Friedberg, A. (1993) *Window Shopping: Cinema and the Postmodern*, Berkeley: University of California Press.

Houston, B. (1984) "Viewing Television: The Metapsychology of Endless Consumption," *Quarterly Review of Film and Television* 9 (3): 183–195.

Joyrich, L. (1990) "Critical and Textual Hypermasculinity," in P. Mellencamp, ed., *Logics of Television*, Bloomington: Indiana University Press, 156–172.

Kinder, M. (1991) *Playing with Power in Movies, Television and Video Games*, Berkeley: University of California Press.

Metz, C. (1977) *The Imaginary Signifier*, Bloomington: Indiana University Press.

Mulvey, L. (1975) "Visual Pleasure and Narrative Cinema," reprinted in *Visual and Other Pleasures*, Bloomington: Indiana University Press, 1989, 14–26.

Nadel, A. (1997) *Flatlining on the Field of Dreams: Cultural Narratives in the Films of President Reagan's America*, New Brunswick, NJ: Rutgers University Press.

Sobchack, V. (1987) "Child/Alien/Father: Patriarchal Crisis and Generic Exchange," *Camera Obscura* 15: 6–35.

Spigel, L. (1990) "Television in the Family Circle: the Popular Reception of a New Medium," in P. Mellencamp, ed., *Logics of Television*, Bloomington: Indiana University Press.

4 Romance and/as tourism

Heritage whiteness and the (inter)national imaginary in the new woman's film

Diane Negra

In this chapter I devote attention to one of the ways in which romance in recent American cinema is implicated with the fantasy transcendence of US borders. Attending to the emergence of a set of films that centralize a narrative of Europeanization, I argue that these texts constitute an important new permutation of the woman's film in the 1990s. Films such as *Only You* (1994), *Four Weddings and a Funeral* (1994), *French Kiss* (1995), *The Matchmaker* (1997), and *Notting Hill* (1999) are bound together by a codified set of narrative protocols which include, for instance, the reluctant or accidental arrival of the protagonist in a nation in Western Europe, the discovery within that national setting of new possibilities for coupling and family formation, and the narrow averting of a return to the US by the heroine, who is instead inscribed within a "happy ending" achievable because of her symbolic acquisition of a foreign nationality.

I argue that these films carry a set of concerns pertinent to the experience of American female spectators at the close of the twentieth century. Among those concerns are:

- The evolution of US culture in such a way that idealized family formation is culturally contradictory, both urgent and impossible. Confusedly responding to the advent of the "New Traditionalism" in American culture, these films register a desire to escape from the strictures of American "family values," although they ultimately re-inscribe those values.
- The superficial stigmatization of whiteness which now must enrich itself through contact with desirable ethnicities. Romance, which has long proposed solutions to social problems, now addresses itself to the provision of fantasy states of whiteness corrective to perceived deficiencies. These fictions specifically redress the disconnection between American whiteness and heritage homelands and give evidence of the way that in recent decades "white ethnicity emerges as a trope of empowerment" (Decker 1997: 207).
- Economic developments which increasingly curtail individual agency and mobility while endlessly celebrating those values. In these romances, heroines are either separated from quotidian economic concerns, or restored to a simplified, purified economic realm. In their adopted national context economic concerns are entirely eliminated, presented as altogether absent, or meaningful only as an expression of coupling. (In *French Kiss*, for instance, an American heroine's romance with a French vintner is enhanced through a mutual entrepreneurial bond.) While romances set in the US increasingly acknowledge coupling as a form of repair for disconnected social relations and ferocious modes of economic competition (*You've Got Mail* [1998] is a telling example), these films absent their heroines from those pressing concerns.

In devoting attention to these films' presentation of imaginary European homelands, I will shed light on the complex interrelations between popular film and tourism as an experiential mode set up to resolve identity problems in late-twentieth-century US culture, and investigate the rescripting of romance to reflect perceptions of American national identity (and American whiteness) in crisis. Analyzing the contiguity of romance and expatriation, I will argue that these narratives rely on a formula in which tourism serves as the antidote for a variety of overtly or tacitly diagnosed social problems. When romance is correlated with the symbolic acquisition of alternate ethnic/national identity, it takes on a powerful new charge.

The tourist romance

Tourism, it is clear, is an ever more important social and economic phenomenon in contemporary life. If, in earlier phases of modern life, tourism was most often constructed as a tranquil, therapeutic respite from one's everyday cares, tourist experience is now most frequently positioned as an opportunity for integration and stimulation that will make up (implicitly or explicitly) for the deficiencies of daily life. Thrill-seeking tourism of all kinds has boomed in the 1990s, with a particular emphasis on conquering nature through extreme sports. Climbing Mount Everest became increasingly popular (in some cases with disastrous results) throughout a decade which closed with the deaths of a number of adventure-seeking tourists in 1999 on a canyoneering tour in Interlaken, Switzerland. As Barbara Kirshenblatt-Gimblett has observed, the rewriting of tourist experience around higher grades of stimulation has produced a crisis for traditional sites of tourist interest: "Museums are experiencing a crisis of identity as they compete with other attractions within a tourist economy that privileges experience, immediacy, and what the industry calls adventure" (Kirshenblatt-Gimblett 1998: 7).

A key development in the recent history of tourism is the recognition on the part of tourist industries that tourists want to feel they know the place they are visiting. Thus, new modes of tourism attach value to those experiences that reflect the closest connection to the place being visited. Stress is increasingly placed on fully immersive modes of tourism predicated on integration in a new environment/culture. At the close of the twentieth century, particular emphasis has been placed on tourism that is personally enriching, with a fuller experience of local culture being demanded by a larger percentage of travelers. Recent tourist practice has been defined by the ascendance of the "authenticity"-driven "special interest," "active," or "adventure" tourism model, which presupposes the desire to integrate as fully as possible into local culture. As the authors of *Tourism: A Gender Analysis* have noted, "Tourism therefore involves the purchase of the particular social relations and characteristics of the host" (Kinnaird and Hall 1994: 13). In a climate emphasizing the postmodern play of identity, touristic pleasure is now more likely to be linked to the performance of those characteristics and the reproduction of those social relations. In *Staging Tourism: Bodies on Display from Waikiki to Sea World*, Jane Desmond trenchantly observes that "The natural, represented by this essential culture . . . emerges as something lost by white, middle-class tourists and briefly rediscovered through invigorating contact with representatives of that culture" (Desmond 1999: 255). As I will show in my discussion of the tourist romances, the desire to experience somatic stimulation and environmental encounters marked out as "authentic" pervades those fictions just as it increasingly factors as part of the appeal of vacation packages.

As it has shifted to a new integrative and experiential model, tourism has also begun to cultivate new constituencies. While the tourism industries maintain a strongly dominant focus on heterosexual couples as their primary clientele, some room is being made in the marketplace for other kinds of travelers, including single women. A 1996 article in *The Minneapolis Star Tribune* reported that:

> Rising incomes, delayed marriage, divorce and longer life spans have produced a burgeoning number of women with the means to see the world, but without husband or family to accompany them. Social change and sheer demographics are shattering lingering taboos that once discouraged women from traveling far without a male protector.
>
> (Dickerson 1996: 5G)

A growing category of advice literature directed toward prospective women travelers has emerged, including titles such as *A Journey of One's Own: Uncommon Advice for the Independent Woman Traveler* (1996, Thalia Zepatos), *Traveler's Tales: Gutsy Women, Travel Tips and Wisdom for the Road* (1996, Marybeth Bond), and *Every Woman's Guide to Romance in Paris* (1998, Caroline O'Connell). In 1999, the top internet destination for women, women.com, added a new travel feature with specialized information about the travel interests and needs of women.

The dynamics of tourism have long implicated the male tourist in the consumption of indigenous femininity, whether overtly designated as sex tourism, or at a more implicit level. When women travel, romance is often presented as a natural outgrowth of immersive tourism. In a recent feature article a female journalist wrote, "While I wouldn't say that the possibility of meeting someone motivated my wanderings, it's always floated in the back of my mind like moonlight on the Taj Mahal" (Spano 1998: E7). The quest for romance is thus discursively figured as equivalent to the destination itself.

The desire to identify with indigenous populations and feel a sense of inclusion within local culture is a key feature of the recent tourist romances which assume that the national/cultural location visited is more "real" than the (inevitably American) culture the protagonists leave behind. *The Matchmaker* posits this distinction by equating American culture with the ersatz world of political "spin" and contrasting it to the comical "authenticity" of rural Ireland. Its heroine Marcy Tizard (Janeane Garafalo) is presented as a woman whose energies are fruitlessly expended in the service of a corrupt American politician. In Ireland, she meets Sean, an Irishman who has abandoned a career in public relations because he perceives it to be morally bankrupt, and has resettled near his family in the West of Ireland. Marcy acquires the ability to critique slick, American-style political showmanship as she gains "insider" knowledge of Irish culture.

Tourism has traditionally operated as a mode of ideological reinforcement—we experience another place in order to return, rejuvenated, to our customary environment.[1] Yet in the tourist romances of recent film, this last link in the traditional social contract of tourism is emphatically severed—the films decisively emphasize the non-return of the native—Kate in *French Kiss* and Faith in *Only You* are narrowly prevented from returning to the US, while at the close of *Notting Hill* the heroine Anna Scott answers

---

1 In Hollywood film, the most emblematic instance of this return is of course Dorothy's discovery in *The Wizard of Oz* (1939) that there really is "no place like home."

the question "How long are you intending to stay in Britain?" with a jubilant "Indefinitely." In all three films, satisfactory narrative closure strikingly hinges on the spectator's agreement that the greatest prospect for a happy future life for the heroine lies in expatriation.[2]

The tourist romance and the burdens of citizenship

Few critics have addressed the flourishing category of cinematic romance in the 1990s. Yet as Catherine Preston (2000) has shown, the romance has played an important role in the cinema of the 1990s and particularly in the filmographies of major female stars such as Julia Roberts, Meg Ryan, and Sandra Bullock. Preston argues that the generic status of the romance is somewhat blurred, and its prominence as a successful film formula is frequently obscured by the fact that it is often grouped with many other kinds of films. Nevertheless there has indeed been what she terms "a steady rise" in the production of film romances since the late 1980s and, further, those films have been among the most successful at the box office. Surveying the box office results for 1990–99, for instance, reveals that at least one film romance was among the top highest-grossing American films worldwide in every year except 1995 and 1998. In key respects, some of the most successful film romances of the late 1980s established precedents that are still being adhered to. From *Moonstruck* (1987) and *When Harry Met Sally* (1989) forward, a large number of cinematic romances have promoted regionalism as an accessory to romantic fusion through camerawork that is highly attentive to the local landscape. Such films would seem to serve as the domestic correlatives to the films I discuss here. I turn now, however, in more specificity to themes of internationalism in the romance.

Certainly Hollywood films have long treated themes of international romance. Postwar American film was particularly adept at thematizing the encounter between Americans and European culture, in films such as *The Quiet Man* (1952), *Gentlemen Prefer Blondes* (1953), and *Roman Holiday* (1953). Taking *Now Voyager* (1942) as another representative case, it is possible to see how earlier films display an altogether different conception of the relation between travel and female identity. In the melodrama, Bette Davis' Charlotte Vale is able to escape her mother's stifling, repressive influence by affiliating herself with the exoticism of travel (in this case to Brazil). Although Charlotte's mother has reproached her in the past, saying "You have all the vigor of a typical American tourist," this film figures tourism slightly differently than in the newer romances. Here, tourism is likewise emancipating, but it confers an identity that is sustainable upon a return trip home. Charlotte's romance on a cruise to Rio de Janeiro with Jerry (a married man also trapped in an unhappy domesticity) will live on after the two have returned to the US. Charlotte's new sense of herself enables her to transform her grim home life, and she is ultimately able to generate an alternative model of maternal behavior from the negative example set by her mother. She continues to wear a camellia corsage as a

2 That the trope of Europeanization inevitably centralizes female transformation is attributable to more than the fact that the romance conventionally tells the stories of women. For a counter-example, consider *The Talented Mr. Ripley* (1999), a film that pathologizes male identity transformation in Europe. This did not, however, prevent the film from inspiring travel-related press pieces advising readers on the towns, cities, and beaches to visit to reconstruct Ripley's travels in Italy. See Rebello 2000, 42–45.

sign of her newly tropicalized identity, and at the close of the film, Charlotte and Jerry fondly recall their time together in Brazil and pledge to protect "that little strip of territory that's ours," as the film celebrates their reterritorialization of their sphere of the American social landscape. *Now Voyager* imagines its heroine spending time overseas to enrich her identity for a more empowered homecoming, in which she reshapes her domesticity to reflect what she has learned. Such returns are largely ruled out in the newer romances.

What I propose is that more recent American films cover much the same terrain, but they do so now under the terms of a new ideological agenda. A crucial shift involves the assumption of dysfunctional gender relations in the American context, and the proposition that US affiliation has become burdensome. Dissatisfaction with the prospects for romance in the US has been provocatively addressed even in romances that (strictly speaking) depart from the model I investigate here. Set in the US, such films nevertheless propose correction for the social problems that impede coupling through an invocation of Europe. In *While You Were Sleeping* (1995), heroine Lucy's (Sandra Bullock) quest to produce a home for herself (the real romance here is with the hero's family and the domestic security they represent) is associated with her fantasy of travel to Italy. An employee of the Chicago Transit Authority whose days consist of a series of anonymous urban encounters in a tollbooth, Lucy is obsessed with Florence, and carries an unstamped passport around as the film's sign of her emotional and geographic confinement. The unspoken mutual feeling between Lucy and Jack (Bill Pullman) appears to be cemented as he gives her a snow globe of Florence, and at the close of the film, Lucy proudly recounts, "Jack gave me the perfect gift—a stamp in my passport. He took me to Florence for our honeymoon."[3] The remake of *Sabrina* (1995) proceeds from the assumption that the titular heroine has found herself through Europeanization, becoming visible as a candidate for romantic attention only after a transformative stay in Paris. Other films, such as *Next Stop, Wonderland* (1998), centralize a heroine paralyzed by a kind of free-floating nostalgia that the film briefly anchors to her reminiscences of a childhood vacation in Ireland.[4]

Up to this point, I have alluded only in rather vague ways to a widely shared perception in contemporary American romances that "social problems" impede coupling, noting that often the resolution of those problems involves the transference of the hero-

---

3 *The Story of Us* (1999) is also imprinted with the notion of Europe as a fantasy ideal. In this film (a diagnostic of an American marriage) a married couple, Ben and Katie Jordan, briefly experience marital reconnection on a trip to Venice. When they return to the US, their problems instantly reemerge and their closeness is revealed to have been a temporary response to their European environment (and mutual rejection of a stereotypical American couple whose saccharine romance disgusts them). Ben laments in voiceover narration, "If only there was a way to bottle that unfettered state of mind that comes with being on foreign soil." He chastizes his wife, telling her that when they were in Europe their relationship "would have come first." The film provides other signs that Ben, in a state of crisis during his estrangement from his wife, links the deficiencies in the marriage to its distance from a vibrant Europeanness. A writer, he plans a book project on his European-born mother, whose marriage and parenting he idealizes.

4 It is interesting to observe the kinds of films high-profile female film stars choose to make at particularly empowered stages of their careers. In the 1990s, these are often travel-oriented romances. Julia Roberts appeared in *Notting Hill* after rejuvenating her career in *My Best Friend's Wedding*, Meg Ryan in *French Kiss* after *Sleepless in Seattle*, and Marisa Tomei in *Only You* not long after winning the Oscar for *My Cousin Vinny*. My purpose here is to investigate how such films marshal a kind of response to the ideological contours of 1990s US culture. If they aren't progressive at all levels, they at least engage fantasies of travel and national redefinition worth analyzing.

ine from the US context to a setting in Western Europe. These social problems remain vague in narrative context because it is the nature of Hollywood film to showcase trajectories of transcendence/resolution rather than to perform sustained social diagnosis. Yet, the tourist romances are bound together by their (muted) critique of a number of dominant features of contemporary US experience—social isolation, gender disempowerment, class difference, body anxiety, and conditions of environmental oppression. These features are brought together as the implicit catalysts for the heroine's identity crisis which is subject to adequate resolution only in a European context. By analyzing these dynamics I will begin to develop a response to the main question which this essay seeks to address: what function is Europe currently made to serve in the American romantic imaginary?

The authors of *The Social Health of the Nation: How America Is Really Doing* maintain that nearly exclusive reliance on economic and business barometers for measuring the national condition have obscured other significant social indicators such as poverty, crime, economic inequality, housing affordability, and access to health care. The authors' gathered data suggest that by many indicators national social health has declined in the 1990s, even while economic health has appeared to be robust through much of the decade. One of their most significant findings addresses the distribution of wealth and highlights the widening gap between poverty and affluence. At the close of the twentieth century, the United States has the largest gap between rich and poor among industrialized nations; in 1996 the poorest fifth of the nation held a mean annual income of $11,388, while the mean income of the top fifth was $125,627 (Miringhoff and Miringhoff 1999: 104). This polarization of wealth has produced extraordinarily competitive social terms in which widespread (and accurate) perceptions of a shrinking middle class have fostered awareness of a two-tiered economy.

In a discussion of work re-engineering and its implications for family life in the 1990s, Sarah Ryan observes that many post-baby-boom Americans feel that the "social contract" that seemed to structure white American life in the post-World War II period has been increasingly violated. Ryan writes that:

> An almost constant sense of insecurity haunts American families in the 1990s. Nearly half the population worries that someone in their household will be out of work in the next year. Parents no longer expect their children to have a higher standard of living than themselves. Most expect large-scale layoffs to be a permanent feature of the modern economy; meanwhile, they experience more stress while at work and are contributing more and more hours to the job. No wonder nostalgia for more prosperous and predictable times is a recurring theme in politics and the arts, even among young people who have embraced the technology and values of the 1990s.
>
> (Ryan 1999: 332–333)

The widely held view that Americans now operate in a "postfeminist" environment in which the concerns of feminism are taken to be irrelevant and/or archaic has largely led to the stigmatization of a feminist vocabulary that might serve as a productive outlet for responding to this state of affairs and its impact on women. The disappearance of mainstream feminist discourse was chronicled in an editorial in *USA Today* in which founder Al Neuharth announced that *Ms.* magazine would soon cease publication. "Reason: Women's libbers are fewer and far less fanatical than 30 years ago" (Neuharth 2000: 12). The decreasing availability of feminism as a responsive mode to the continued disenfranchisement of women means that dominant Hollywood fictions (as well as self-help discourses and the new domestic regimes propounded by figures like Martha Stewart) face little competition in their characterization of women's lives, interests, and concerns in 1990s US culture.[5]

The expatriate romances restore quality of life for American women on terms now viewed as impossible in the US, for any notion of US citizenship in the late twentieth century is thus implicated with these competitive, precarious, social and economic conditions. In addition, definitions of American identity are increasingly bound up with anxieties over the loss of community, and the destruction of a viable definition of place.

In *Country of Exiles: The Destruction of Place in American Life*, William Leach argues for a dynamic of placelessness as a key feature in contemporary US culture. As a function of the preeminence of an intermodal transport system designed to promote the mobility of people and goods to the detriment of human quality of life, the emergence of an economy dominated by temporary modes of labor, and the delocalization of business, he contends that Americans now feel a powerful "need for continuity and stability, and for confident attachment to a place to be from" (Leach 1999: 6). The current emphasis on temporary housing, both in the form of easily resold generic mansions for the executive class and mobile homes for the poor testifies to the way that "For many Americans, rich or poor, the home has been reconceived to accommodate the new flexible patterns in work and management" (Leach 1999: 60).

The 1990s have also seen the distinctive emergence of what Leach refers to as a neo-expatriate class—Americans who seek to make their fortunes overseas, particularly in emergent markets such as Asia and Eastern Europe. As the American Dream has gone global (in many ways, seeming to be most realizable outside of US borders) the definition of expatriation has undergone revision. If the dominant image of the expatriate was once tied to the creativity of the literary figure or artist, it is now tied predominantly to business. As Leach argues, "In the 1990s the thrust of business, reinforced by the state, has been toward flexibility and dissolution of place" (Leach 1999: 85). For those American regions, cities, and towns left by the wayside in the rush toward corporate globalization, tourism has stepped into the breach as a means of economic rehabilitation. By the 1990s, tourism employed 10 percent of the American workforce as American cities and towns repackaged themselves for tourist consumption, selling an ersatz definition of place to compensate for the destruction of their economic, political, and social vitality.

In surprising ways, the tourist romances register the anxieties produced by these new forms of rootlessness and economic competitiveness. For the reasons I've indicated, their perceptions of US social problems are never presented in depth, and they are thus best understood by examining the strenuous efforts made toward their correction. For instance, the films demonstrate that the social isolation of heroines who are imprisoned by fame (*Notting Hill*) or confined by an all-encompassing job (*The Matchmaker*) will be corrected by their incorporation into a warm and enveloping community of friends and relatives when they resettle outside the US.

In some instances the films rely on the most clichéd of strategies to exposit their heroines' isolation, presenting them as real or implied orphans. This is the case in both *French*

---

5 It is worth pointing out that the success of the tourist romances supplies story ideas to women's magazines. An article in the March 2000 issue of *Marie Claire*, for instance, chronicled the experiences of several expatriate American women married to non-American men, inviting reader speculation about whether they would make a similar choice. See Harney 2000, 78–86.

Kiss and *Only You*, which showcase heroines who have virtually no family and look ahead to the families they will gain by marriage. Both protagonists are schoolteachers "marrying up" to professional men (an oncologist and a podiatrist) in arrangements that are implicitly understood to connote their economic/class advancement. In the case of films like *The Matchmaker* and *Notting Hill* a stark incompatibility is shown between work and personal life; if the heroines of *French Kiss* and *Only You* will advance themselves economically through marriage, the protagonists of these films indicate an inverse case in which successful working women must forgo a rewarding personal life. It should be clear that this set of films thus maps out both dimensions of what 1990s popular cultural discourse has defined as women's dominant lifestyle choice—to look to marriage for economic providence or, if choosing a professional path, to expect to be unable to sustain any other type of reward. In the fantasy structure provided in the tourist romance, all such problems of economics/class/social integration are made to dissolve in the European context. Kirshenblatt-Gimblett has written that "Tourists travel to actual destinations to experience virtual places" (Kirshenblatt-Gimblett 1998: 9), and this insight certainly enables us to understand better why the mechanics of tourism are so compatible with Hollywood narrative. In the tourist romances, a false opposition is posited between a US social environment in which women are bombarded with "tough choices" about work and coupling as binarized categories and a Europe in which those categories are brought into a close alignment and rendered no longer problematic.

As I have suggested, one of the most striking features of these texts is that, in stark contrast to the assimilationist credo of earlier Hollywood films, they de-assimilate their heroines. While heritage memory has tended to be eradicated by the "landscape of the temporary" (in Leach's terms) and the ongoing quest for economic advantage in US culture, the films function to reattach white Americans to the designated viable homelands of Europe. As they Europeanize, they shed the constraints of American whiteness, connecting themselves to ideologies and lifestyles the films mourn as lost within our own national context. In this respect we can come to see how these films are part of a broader symptomatology of late-twentieth-century whiteness which has settled into two dominant paradigms: defensiveness and nostalgia. Divorced from its traditional representational moorings in a multicultural environment in which whiteness is less self-evidently valuable than it once was, recent American film, as I have argued elsewhere, manifests a variety of signs of an emergent crisis in the once-stable and self-explanatory definitions of whiteness. Narratives that centralize an embattled white patriarch (*Falling Down* [1992], *Ransom* [1996]) have proliferated in popular American film, while both romances and male melodramas thematize a retreat to an idealized white hometown. Cinematic narratives of hometown return have emerged (*Hope Floats* [1998] and *Practical Magic* [1998]) as well as three recent TV franchises founded on the premise, *Providence*, *Maggie Winters* and *Judging Amy*.[6] Another set of American films focuses

---

6 In the first series, an unusually strong midseason replacement hit for NBC, a thirty something woman abandons her professional life in southern California to return to her parents' house in Rhode Island; in the second, a CBS show that did not survive its first season, a thirty something woman returns home to rebuild her life after a divorce; in the third (also on CBS) a female judge's professional authority is held in bounds by her return to her mother's house. It bears noticing that *Providence* has helped foster a tourism boom in Rhode Island, the state in which the drama is set. A short blurb in *USA Today* on April 21, 2000 noted that "Tourism experts are urging more hotels in Rhode Island, where convention business and the NBC drama 'Providence' are behind a travel boom."

on white ethnic communities defined by social bonds of intimacy, community, and ethnicity as they are imagined to have existed in the past. Exemplary in this regard are *Once Around* (1991) and *Polish Wedding* (1998), ethnic romances where the adult heroine lives in her parents' house. These films face a difficulty, however, because they so transparently fictionalize contemporary social relations. Forced radically to readjust contemporary social experience to carry off their version of ethnic intimacy, such films often feel out of kilter in ways that detract from any credible verisimilitude. This may account for their general failure at the box office despite their star casts.

When we turn to the tourist romances (many of them box office hits), it becomes clear, however, that Europe has become an ideal staging ground for nostalgic fantasies of American whiteness. In essence, these films really reflect a displaced nostalgia. Unlike the US-based ethnic romances, which often exhibit an anachronistic character despite their present-day setting, the tourist romances maintain a contemporary flavor by seeming to reveal to us that the vibrant family and community relations of the past still exist, awaiting our discovery, in Europe. In this way, the surface quest plot of the films facilitates an underlying travelogue which strongly thematizes a European past as a consumable good. American whiteness is now understood as an evacuated category, and the rootlessness of the heroines in the tourist romances reflects this. The single most important gesture of resolution in the tourist films is that they stabilize their migratory heroines.

If in some respects this category of recent film romance might appear progressive in that it undertakes social diagnosis, it must not be mistaken for a searching analysis of contemporary culture. Rather, the films offer a conservative cultural escape route in which American women are coupled with European men who will lead them out of the public sphere. The romances resettle their heroines in ways that finally camouflage the problems that catalyzed their identity quests. One of the ways that this is accomplished is through strong pictorial representations of an idealized harmony with nature. The "right" men in such films are often literally and metaphorically grounded—associated with the land. In *French Kiss*, Luc teaches Kate to "read" nature in a scene in which he cues her to identify all of the contributing flavors in a locally produced wine. In *Only You*, Peter speaks of his love for trees and states that he would be happy doing nothing for the rest of his life but growing them, while in *The Matchmaker*, Sean has opted out of urban life in favor of a retreat to the country. In all of the films, the couples take scenic walks together—walks that seem symbolically to cement their relationship to their environment. In *The Matchmaker*, Marcy and Sean take a crucial walk along the sea cliffs in the Aran Islands that seems to clinch their feelings for one another, while in the hit romantic comedy *Notting Hill*, protagonist pair Anna Scott (Julia Roberts) and William Thacker (Hugh Grant) take an evening walk in the eponymous neighborhood that leads them to a garden retreat. Where they are not directly connected to land itself, the European heroes are at least shown to be in a state of harmonious accord with their environment. In *Notting Hill*, William is depicted as fully a creature of his environment—most evidently in a symbolic season-transcending walk through a freshmarket in his neighborhood. Although this is urban space, it is defined by flowers, fruits, and vegetables, and various natural signs of seasonal change.

In this category of film, European men are distinguished by their willingness to take life at a slower pace, and by a strong sense of identity linked to their environment. If the heroines are dispossessed at a crucial level from place-oriented community (they do not know where they are from) the heroes are inevitably living their lives in just the right place. Their settledness in contrast to the heroines' nomadism is related to their status as representatives of a social harmony that is meant to contrast distinctly with the implied social chaos of contemporary American life.

The tourist romance and the promise of community membership

Fantasies of long-term settlement lie at the heart of the tourist romance. As I have indicated, the heroines are inevitably socially isolated—through romance they acquire membership in a literal or symbolic family. In *Four Weddings and a Funeral* American Carrie (Andie MacDowell) is virtually always alone as is Anna in *Notting Hill*, while in both films British Hugh Grant is incessantly surrounded by a close-knit group of friends. In *The Matchmaker* Sean woos Marcy with a song whose lyrics imply the promise of community membership, "Won't you stay, stay a while with your own ones?"

The films' Europeans[7] are depicted as understanding and honoring the rules of community membership in contrast to a US public sphere in which competition has supplanted community. This is vividly conveyed in *The Matchmaker* when Marcy (with the assistance of the residents of the small Irish town of Bally na Gra) stages an obscene tableau of rural Irish life for her American politician employer that satirizes US definitions of Irish community. By now an insider, Marcy is able to author a scene that reflects her newfound knowledge of the distinction between authentic and fabricated community and legitimately reproach her employer for his desire to manufacture Irish roots for US political gain. Marcy's incorporation into the community is possible because she refuses to exploit it.

Humane local authorities are often key accessory figures in the tourist films, and they frequently act to validate the heroine's emotional agenda. In *Only You* Faith's assimilation into European ethnicity is tellingly signaled by the contrasting outcomes of two hasty searches in airports at the beginning and end of the film. Early on, as Faith bolts through an American airport in her wedding dress hoping to intercept the man she believes she's fated to marry before he boards his plane, she is represented as an object of scrutiny, and the subject of bemused gazes throughout the airport. It is clear that her execution of an emotional agenda in public space is bewilderingly inappropriate to those around her. Making it to the gate, she attempts to explain herself to the American Airlines personnel, who call security when Faith asks them to call the plane back to the gate. The moment is paralleled and corrected at the conclusion as Faith runs to stop another plane from leaving in the Rome airport (this one carries the man coded as "right" for Faith). In this cultural context, intense emotional expressiveness is not seen as aberrant. This time Faith is significantly able to communicate her emotional agenda to the sympathetic Alitalia staff who drop everything to assist her when they understand what is at stake. The film concludes as the closed jetway is reopened for Faith, who reunites with the hero aboard the plane.

Just as the films fantasize hospitable natives as accessories to romance, and a social environment that is uniquely accommodating to the needs and desires of the heroine, they also depict a communal interest in and agreement to the burgeoning romance. This communal interest is most clearly expressed in the endings of the films which characteristically assemble a group of the hero's native friends to bring the couple together

---

7 Such characters are frequently played by a small group of actors whose European identities have become archetypal over the course of their careers (Hugh Grant, Jean Reno, Kristen Scott Thomas, etc.).

(this occurs in *The Matchmaker* and *Notting Hill*) or nominate a local representative to do so (Luc's police detective friend plays this role in *French Kiss*). These characters, whether operating collectively or individually, assist the films in bearing witness to the fact that the onset of modernity has not precipitated the dissolution of community cohesiveness.[8] Emphatically insisting upon the authenticity of their locations, the films employ travelogue aesthetics and fetishistic camerawork to produce a deep and resonant vision of place that effectively compensates for a contemporary sense of American placelessness.[9]

It seems likely that the tourist films' vision of an intense European "placefulness" represents another category of response to the crisis of place discussed by William Leach. Recent American emphasis on various forms of a domestic landscape of nostalgia (commercially reconstructed colonial towns, the emergence of the highly ornamental postmodern Victorian as a major model for the high-end American home, and the invention of an entire Disney town, Celebration, Florida) attests to a widespread desire to simulate the physical and social models of the past. In the tourist romance, intensely romanticized public spaces correct for the culture of retreat that prevails in the late twentieth century US. Symbolically reconciled are the desire for privacy and the desire for communal membership. In *Notting Hill* (a film whose narrative strategies I discuss more fully in the next section), Anna and William's romance is linked significantly to a communal garden symbolic of the European urban paradise that is the staging ground for coupling. Yet, the communal gardens, the defining feature of the Notting Hill neighborhood, according to one recent article, are (despite their name), limited access only:

> It is the communal gardens that make the houses in these streets so special. London is famous for its garden squares, but the Notting Hill gardens are different. Sandwiched in the gaps between the terraces, many of these communal gardens are only glimpsed from the road with access solely through the houses themselves.
>
> (Masey 1999)

---

8 *The Very Thought of You* (1999) hystericizes the formula for the tourist romance. Here a romance between a British man and an American woman interrupts the lifelong bonds of a male friendship group and the desirability of the American woman is represented as such that three British men vie for her attentions. This film leaves its central couple in national limbo, heading on a plane for Iceland, rather than comfortably establishing a life together in Europe. In a notable departure from the notions of community that structure the other films, here the European characters are cast in largely competitive and dysfunctional terms rather than supportive ones.

9 In this regard, it would be interesting to consider *Before Sunrise*, another tourist romance, but one quite different in tone from such films as *French Kiss* and *Only You*. A somber meditation on the transitory nature of human connection, the film derives its pathos in part from the fact that neither member of the protagonist couple (Celine, a Frenchwoman, and Jesse, an American) can stay on in the location in which they have come together. The film simply charts the conversation and growing intimacy of the couple during one night in Vienna. (Jesse is to fly home in the morning, bringing to an end a failed vacation he had begun to visit his American girlfriend in Madrid; Celine is *en route* from a visit to her grandmother in Budapest back to Paris). The film solidifies our tourist sensibility in a closing montage that takes place after the couple's departure. Here, the camera revisits many of the locations through which Celine and Jesse traveled, mourning their absence on one level, but also inscribing the landscape with a powerful, pleasurable nostalgia. Through its deviations from the narrative paradigm of the expatriate romance, *Before Sunrise* underscores the importance of a local figure to the romance formula.

The somatic subtext of the tourist romance: *Notting Hill*

As I have suggested, the contemporary tourist romance is devoted to generating new national contexts that resolve the contradictions and dilemmas of "normative" contemporary American femininity. This mode of redemptive tourism proposes deliverance from the economic and sexual dynamics of US culture. Yet in its search for more stable ground for female identity, this new narrative paradigm focuses continually on the status of the body and the films' criteria for evaluation are consistently tied to conservative, consumer-oriented somatic definitions. Consequently, the films in this category evaluate women's bodies in travel and probe the connection of the body to food, to clothing, to sex, etc. Indeed, a preoccupation runs through the films with somatic versions of national status as the American female body is rendered hysterical (via traces of slapstick comedy in *French Kiss* and *Only You*) or neurotic, or simply problematic (the potentially unruly body of Jeaneane Garofolo serves this function in *The Matchmaker*)[10] in contrast to the European body at ease with itself. Vital to these films' presentation of cultural contrast is their assumption that the European body retains a close bond with the realm of the natural, communing easily with the landscape, with animals, with food, etc., while the American body's relationship with the natural is seem to be disrupted or severed in some way. The establishment of a romance involves the correction of this dysfunctional relation to the natural realm. These preoccupations are developed most fully in *Notting Hill* (Fig. 4.1), in which Julia Roberts' Anna, a major American film star who clearly resembles the actress herself, is defined by her exclusion from the warm modes of community enjoyed by William, a travel bookstore owner whose placement in a warm coterie of friends, and easy, settled relationship to place, are his defining traits. The film deeply fetishizes the pleasures of a geographically defined home, and invests Notting Hill (a suburb of West London) with an enormous amount of narrative power as a source of stability. William experiences no disjuncture between life and work; this is symbolically communicated by the fact that he lives nearly across the street from his workplace. *Notting Hill*'s thematics of refuge work in such a way as also to showcase the communal garden ("they're like little villages," says William) in which there is a wooden bench inscribed by a long-time husband to his deceased wife.

Here, as in many of the other films in this category, the heroine's discovery of homeland involves a reoriented relationship to food. Comfort food is a particularly important element in creating the ground for the fiction. In *Notting Hill*, William is continually associated with comfort foods of various kinds—in the film's first scene he enters his apartment to make toast. He meets Anna briefly in his bookstore and then shortly after they meet again when he inadvertently spills a glass of orange juice on her in the street. On their first date to a dinner party celebrating his sister's birthday (in a scene of remarkable expository efficiency) a final brownie is vied for by the guests who explain in turn why they most deserve the morsel of comfort food. Anna recounts not the stresses and strains of her job, but instead makes a speech whose primary focus is on the status of

---

10 A brief scene in *The Matchmaker*, in which Garofalo's Marcy (having hurt her ankle) is carried into a pub by Sean, gives rise to the only overt anxiety expressed about Marcy's body. A pub patron turns to Sean and says, "She looks a heavy carry," to which Sean replies "No, sure no." Garofalo, whose body fails to conform to Hollywood mandates of size and slimness, had been earlier vividly contrasted with Uma Thurman in a romance entirely centered around body anxiety, *The Truth About Cats and Dogs* (1996).

Figure 4.1 Hugh Grant and Julia Roberts in *Notting Hill* (Polygram Filmed Entertainment 1999). Courtesy of the Kobal Collection

her body, speaking of her plastic surgeries and telling the group, "I've been on a diet every day since I was nineteen, which basically means I've been hungry for a decade."

We meet Jeff King (Alec Baldwin), Anna's callow American movie star boyfriend in just one scene but it is enough for us to glean understanding of his status as an agent of those industrial and cultural forces that police Anna's food intake. In contrast to the time spent together by Anna and William, who are seen comfortably eating together on several occasions, the dysfunctions of Anna's relationship with Jeff are indicated by his admonishment to her "not to overdo it" on her room service order, because "I don't want people saying there goes that famous actor with the big fat girlfriend." His American-ness is underscored in his room service order for cold water "unless it's illegal here to serve water above room temperature." The distinctive sole appearance by Roberts' American boyfriend consists of a reminder to her not to eat too much, and mistaking William for their room service waiter.

The film's obsessive subtext about bodies and food[11] is brought full circle in the character of Bella, William's close friend and former girlfriend. Bella's body has been damaged (she has suffered paralysis as a result of an accident the film leaves mysterious) yet she is nurtured and cared for by a loving partner. The film gives us to understand that even lacking an ideal body, she retains value. The new national context is thus

---

11 *Notting Hill*'s obsessive preoccupation with food runs deeper than I have room (or necessity) to indicate fully here. Indeed, from its earliest scenes, incidents and emotions in *Notting Hill* take place and are expressed nearly exclusively in the language of food. On their first meeting, William attempts to sell Anna a guide-book for Turkey by telling her it features an "amusing incident with a kebab." William's lodger Spike announces that he's "going into the kitchen to get some food. Then I'll tell you a story that will make your balls shrink to the size of raisins." Separated from Anna later in the film, William is introduced to a series of women in turn who are exposited nearly exclusively in terms of their relationship to food and drink. The excessive exuberance of one woman is indicated by her invitation to William to "get sloshed," the rigidity of a second is communicated by her blunt announcement that she is a "fruitarian," and the attractive pragmatism of a third is revealed by her frank assessment of the dinner she is served.

associated with alternative definitions of femininity that are not simply and exclusively oriented around the idealized body. In this regard, *Notting Hill* activates an established contrast between the US as a site of body dysfunction and Europe as a place in which women enjoy an easy, settled relationship to food and an untroubled somatic identity.[12] The film's ending, in which a pregnant Anna relaxes with William in the communal garden, implies that Anna has gained somatic control in a way that contrasts with the public ownership of her body (strict regulation of diet in service of the body that is professionally required, bodily exposure through the publication of nude photographs, etc.) and an unreality defined in relation to American celebrity culture (as Anna tells William "Fame isn't real"). In its connections between a vision of British utopianism and food, *Notting Hill* thus gives evidence of the way that fantasies of the gratified body stand alongside fantasies of environmental integration in the tourist romance.

Romance narratives have long operated as confirmation that our social system is working the way that it should. For recent evidence of this, one need only turn to 1999's *Runaway Bride* where an hysterically "all is made right" method of closure leads strangers to cheer and couples to embrace on the street at the news that the protagonist pair has finally tied the knot.[13] In this discussion, I have sought to show that, despite its enduring ideological conservatism, the genre of contemporary romance has nevertheless given rise to an interesting permutation that distinctly fails the confidence test. The "expatriate romances" are unified in their commitment to staging coupling outside of US borders altogether, and because of this they gesture at (although perhaps not as fully as one might wish) an indictment of contemporary American social and economic structures that has rarely been seen in the genre.

Filmography

Titles are accompanied by the year of US release, and the country in which the major part of the action is set.

Before Sunrise (1995, Austria)
The Matchmaker (1997, Ireland)
Only You (1994, Italy)
French Kiss (1995, France)
Sabrina (1995, France)
Stealing Beauty (1996, Italy)
Next Stop, Wonderland (1998, United States)
Notting Hill (1999, Britain)
Four Weddings and a Funeral (1994, Britain)
Shirley Valentine (1989, Greece)
Local Hero (1983, Scotland)
Tokyo Pop (1988, Japan)

12 In Susan Bordo's useful discussion of the European stereotypes at work in a FibreThin diet pill commercial she details how "a metaphor of European 'difference' reveals itself as a means of representing that enviable and truly foreign 'other': the woman for whom food is merely ordinary, who can take it or leave it" (Bordo 1993: 100).
13 Of course, a more subversive reading of the film's conclusion might stipulate that the excessive celebration is really tied to the fact that the single woman's potential challenge to patriarchy has now been extinguished.

Bibliography

Anderson, Benedict (1983) *Imagined Communities: Reflections on the Origin and Spread of Nationalism*, London: Verso.

Bordo, Susan (1993) *Unbearable Weight: Feminism, Western Culture, and the Body*, Berkeley: University of California Press.

Connor, John and Sylvia Harvey, eds (1991) *Enterprise and Heritage: Crosscurrents of National Culture*, London: Routledge.

Cook, Pam (1998) "No Fixed Address: The Women's Picture from *Outrage* to *Blue Steel*," in Steve Neale and Murray Smith, eds, *Contemporary Hollywood Cinema*, London: Routledge, 229–246.

Culler, Jonathan (1988) "The Semiotics of Tourism," in *Framing the Sign: Criticism and Its Institutions*, Norman: University of Oklahoma Press, 153–167.

Decker, Jeffrey Louis (1997) *Made in America: Self-Styled Success from Horatio Alger to Oprah Winfrey*, Minneapolis: University of Minnesota Press.

Desmond, Jane C. (1999) *Staging Tourism: Bodies on Display from Waikiki to Sea World*, Chicago: University of Chicago Press.

Dickerson, Martha (1996) "Women on the Road: More and More Are Setting Out to Explore the World on Their Own Terms," *Minneapolis Star Tribune*, November 24, 5G.

Dyer, Richard (1997) *White*, London: Routledge.

Gritten, David (1999) "A Familiar Neighborhood," *Newsday*, May 24: B2.

Harney, Alexandra (2000) "American Women Abroad: How Far Would You Go for the Man You Love?" *Marie Claire*, March: 78–86.

Haskell, Molly (1998) "A Touch of the 1940s Woman in the 90s," *The New York Times*, November 15, 1998.

Kaplan, Caren (1998) *Questions of Travel: Postmodern Discourses of Displacement*, Durham, NC: Duke University Press.

Kinnaird, Vivian and Derek Hall (1994) *Tourism: A Gender Analysis*, New York: John Wiley & Sons.

Kirshenblatt-Gimblett, Barbara (1998) *Destination Culture: Tourism, Museums, and Heritage*, Berkeley: University of California Press.

Leach, William (1999) *Country of Exiles: The Destruction of Place in American Life*, New York: Pantheon.

Marshment, Margaret (1997) "Gender Takes a Holiday: Representation in Holiday Brochures," in M. Thea Sinclair, ed., *Gender, Work and Tourism*, London: Routledge, 16–34.

Masey, Anthea (1999) "House & Home: Why Notting Hill is the Star" *London Telegraph*, May 2.

Miringhoff, Marc and Marque-Luisa Miringhoff (1999) *The Social Health of the Nation: How America Is Really Doing*, Oxford: Oxford University Press.

Neuharth, Al (2000) "How New Mags Rate: Oprah's 'O' a Winner," *USA Today* (April 21), 12.

Preston, Catherine L. (2000) "Hanging on a Star: The Resurrection of the Romance Film in the 1990s," in Wheeler Winston Dixon, ed., *Film Genre 2000: New Critical Essays*, Albany: SUNY Press, 227–243.

Rafferty, Jean Bond (1994) "Notting Hill on the Rise: London's New Bohemia Is a Hip Hotbed of the Cheeky and the Chic," *Town & Country* 148 (October 1), 118.

Rebello, Stephen (2000) "Ripley's Italian Seacoast," *Movieline* 11 (7) (April): 42–45.

Riley, Robert B. (1994) "Speculations on the New American Landscapes," in Kenneth E. Foote, Peter J. Hugill, Kent Mathewson, and Jonathan M. Smith, eds, *Re-Reading Cultural Geography*, Austin: University of Texas Press, 139–155.

Ryan, Sarah (1999) "Management by Stress: The Reorganization of Work Hits Home in the 1990s," in Stephanie Coontz, ed., *American Families: A Multicultural Reader*, New York: Routledge, 332–341.

Spano, Susan (1998) "Traveling Romance: Love It or Leave It," *Newsday*, E7.
Urry, John (1990) *The Tourist Gaze: Leisure and Travel in Contemporary Societies*, London: Sage.
Weiler, Betty and Colin Michael Hall, eds (1992) *Special Interest Tourism*, London: Belhaven Press.
Wood, Robin (1998) *Sexual Politics and Narrative Film: Hollywood and Beyond*, New York: Columbia University Press.

5 Race as spectacle, feminism as alibi

Representing the civil rights era in the 1990s

Sharon Willis

The August 1963 March on Washington emphasized the tight connections between the civil rights movement and television, in part through the unprecedented collaboration of the three networks in order to televise as much of the event as possible, but also through the messages protestors produced. In *The Expanding Vista: American Television in the Kennedy Years*, Mary Ann Watson notes that:

> Thousands of signs were carried in Washington that day. One banner—referring to the long-running series "Lassie"—read, 'LOOK MOM! Dogs Have TV Shows. NEGROES DON'T!' Whoever painted the message on that sign intuited the potency of entertainment in shaping values and attitudes. The integration of prime-time television was as important as the integration of public transportation and education.[1]

The reciprocal impact of television and the civil rights movement was apparently evident to the black speaker cited above. But white consciousness about race was also reshaped at the same moment that our collective understanding of the status of images in relation to history was undergoing a profound shift. Television became the vehicle of our imagined access to history in the making through the moment of the civil rights movement, the first mass movement to take place consistently on TV. Television's attention to civil rights produced a dramatic impact, according to J. Fred MacDonald, who argues that "the simultaneous emergence of the civil rights movement and television was fortuitous for those advocating reform in race relations. While radio verbalized matters such as the US Supreme Court decision on school segregation in 1954 and the black boycott of city buses in Montgomery in 1954 and 1955, the mixture of pictures and sound via TV was considerably more impressive."[2] At the very moment that race relations emerge as a permanent "national" discussion and contested terrain, television and the movies are renegotiating the relationships of the media to "history," to public consciousness, and to the "present."

---

1 Mary Ann Watson, *The Expanding Vista: American Television in the Kennedy Years* (Durham and London: Duke University Press, 1990), 59. This sign appeared at the March on Washington, in August 1963, which was also noted for the unprecedented collaboration of the three networks in order to televise as much of the event as possible.
2 J. Fred MacDonald, *Blacks and White TV: Afro-Americans in Television since 1948* (Chicago: Nelson Hall Publishers, 1983), 72.

Figure 5.1 Michelle Pfeiffer in *Love Field* (Orion 1992). Courtesy of the Kobal Collection

Significantly, the importance of civil rights to TV and of TV to civil rights is registering again for a broad white audience, and perhaps especially for those who witnessed this unfolding relationship in their childhoods. But this event now registers in the movies. Several recent cinematic efforts to revisit the civil rights era from the perspective of the 1990s seem distinctly shaped by memories of both TV and the civil rights movement. While I focus here on Jonathan Kaplan's *Love Field* (1992) and *The Long Walk Home* (Richard Pearce, 1990), I read these films in the context of *Pleasantville* (Gary Ross, 1998) and Antonio Banderas's recent *Crazy in Alabama* (1999).

Love Field (Fig. 5.1) and *The Long Walk Home* both plot dramatic upheavals and transformations of white racial consciousness in intimate personal encounters with "black" experience and the inequality it makes visible. By contrast, *Pleasantville* exposes contemporary nostalgias for unspecified "simpler times" in a form that consistently allegorizes the period of the civil rights movement through the emergence of color television. Entering the world of a 1950s family sitcom, *Pleasantville* emphasizes the central importance of race relations and racism to the characters, precisely by highlighting the enormous trouble they took to sanitize that world of all racial references. *Crazy in Alabama* takes a different approach, focusing explicitly on race, as Melanie Griffith's character, an aspiring television actress who appears on *Bewitched*, inspires her teenaged nephew to brave white intimidation to testify against a policeman who has murdered a black youth.

In organizing its allegory around the medium of television, *Pleasantville* sheds some light on the place of TV in collective white racial consciousness and on its apprehensions of recent history. Equally important, the film's interest in television not only echoes, but even amplifies the prominent role that medium plays in the two earlier films. Neither the stories these films tell, nor the films themselves, could take anything like their final shape without the intervention of TV.

It is perhaps not surprising that at the moment television displaces the newsreel to take charge of the "here," the "now," the "real," the "live," and the "present," movies lay claim to the "there," to "History," to the fictional or imaginary, the dead and the past. What is more surprising to me is that contemporary revisions of this moment seem to be more or less consciously preoccupied with this division of representational labor and with its consequences for race relations and racial consciousness. In these films, we can see cinema reclaiming a distanced past through the lens of intimacy that television introduced. In this connection, it is interesting to remember that television has also recently engaged in historical revision through the series *I'll Fly Away* and *Home Front*, both of which premiered in 1991. Discussing the function of history in these "allegedly true fictions," Mimi White observes that, "In one sense, history provides the possibility for distance, enabling viewers to declare at any given moment, 'But that was then, this is now,' even as they identify with the fiction in the present or recognize their own experience."[3] As a consequence, she writes,

> historical fiction can thus serve as a safety net for general social reception, as the programs structurally imply that the problems they address in narrative terms, in particular regarding race and gender, were worse "back then." In this light, such historical dramatizations, indeed the very existence of these programs, propose that the problems have at least been substantially ameliorated in the course of the history—between the diegetic past and the viewer's present.[4]

All three films seem to offer this sort of historical alibi as a format for identifications mediated and attenuated through a reassuring distance, which is marked most intensely and precisely through a white feminine agency they represent as propelled by proto-feminism. Moreover, this proto-feminism is posited as native to the civil rights era. That this feminine agency comes forward in association with television is significant because it casts the white woman as a medium for the transformation of the racial conscious-ness of the men around her.

Love Field organizes its narrative around the irreversible detour a white woman's life takes upon her encounter and involvement with a black man. A Dallas hairdresser and housewife determines to travel by bus to the Kennedy funeral. *En route* she meets a northern black man accompanied by a little girl who turns out to be his newly reclaimed daughter. A series of misunderstandings and mishaps lead Lurene (Michelle Pfeiffer), Paul (Dennis Haysbert), and the little girl to leave the bus in flight from the police, who assume he has kidnapped both the child and the white woman. The greater part of the journey, then, passes in the privacy of a stolen car, rather than in the iconic space that the bus presents for our memories of the period.

Significantly, however, that very encounter is precipitated by an event experienced tele-visually: the Kennedy assassination. *Love Field* successfully captures the unprecedented televisuality of this national event, embedding well-known and much shown contem-porary footage: Walter Cronkite's emotional announcement of Kennedy's death, Mrs. Kennedy and Caroline at the casket, the assassination of Lee Harvey Oswald. Crucially, each televisual intervention into the film's narrative and visual flow is marked by the complete coincidence of the cinematic frame with that of the television. This overlay of

---

3 Mimi White, "Race, Gender, and Popular Memory," in Sasha Torres, ed., *Living Color* (Durham, NC: Duke University Press, 1998), 121.
4 Ibid.

frames is of course all the more disruptive as it produces a stark textual contrast—from color to black and white, from film to video. Historical distance is literally embedded in the images and soundtrack, at the same time that we are pulled into a dizzying proximity with the collective of contemporary viewers as we share their point of view. (It is possible to experience the TV here as a view of its own, as the film gives itself over to the television screen dilated to monumental proportions.)

Love Field casts its heroine, Lurene, as a Jackie Kennedy "fan." Her domestic world and her fantasy life turn on her identification with "Jackie," which she concretizes through her collection of images of the Kennedys. In this fantasy arena, of course, the television figures large, producing a consistency of access to the events of the Kennedys' lives. More literally, however, the television interrupts Lurene's trajectory back from *Love Field* to her home, as a crowd gathered around a television in an appliance store window captures her attention. Upon learning of the assassination, Lurene moves from the public scene of grief before the television in the beauty salon to a private decision to make a pilgrimage—in person—to the live scene of the Kennedy funeral procession.

It is not insignificant that among the many images the film provides to substantiate the utter incompatibility of Lurene and her husband—their complete opposition—is that of Ray sound asleep in front of the TV on the night of the assassination. Later, Lurene will evince as her one moment of identification with Ray their shared inability to comprehend the Spanish language on a trip to Mexico. In the face of his palpable discomfort, she suggests that this may be his only moment of access to her continual state of alienation from her own culture. As Lurene recounts this moment to Paul Cater, "I almost loved him that weekend. I almost felt that, 'cause he wasn't understanding it either, and I thought, 'Honey, now you know.'" The overarching point, of course, is that the real difference between them is that Lurene always knows she is failing to understand fully, whereas Ray is generally oblivious to his lack of comprehension of the events and practices that surround him and in which he participates: "he thinks he's found the center of the universe on the living room couch," that is, in front of the TV. She has fallen out of the framework of privileged ignorance that he comfortably inhabits. Through an elaborate complex of images and identifications, Lurene begins to lend a content to her alienation: "I don't get ordinary life." What she doesn't get, she'll conclude, is precisely the circumscriptions imposed on "ordinary life" by gender and race, and the place of images in their construction.

The film is quite clear in opposing Lurene's relationship with images to her relationship with discourse. Its opening sequence delivers up the images in Lurene's scrapbook: glossy black-and-white and color photographs drawn from magazines memorialize the various poses of the Kennedys, both individually and as a family. This sequence offers a montage that reproduces the staging of ordinary life in the White House. From the retrospective angle of the film's own production date, and its narrative conclusion, of course, these photographs memorialize mourning itself, and all the more so as we learn that Lurene's identificatory obsession with Jackie Kennedy has been enhanced by her own mourning for a lost baby, which she processes through Kennedy's public miscarriage. Much of the film's work seeks to explore not only the status of the public image in private imaginings, but also the transformation of Lurene's relationship to images, as she takes on a voice and a critical position through discursive contact and conflict with Paul and with white culture's responses to him. In this context, it is worth examining Wayne Koestenbaum's assessment of the significance of Jackie Kennedy's own silence as a public figure:

Jackie's silence was profound, proverbial, virtually unbroken. Did we love her silence or resent it? Was the silence, like Garbo's, a willed refusal, or was it self-sacrifice, apathetic capitulation to the misogynist dictate that women be seen but not heard? A speaking Jackie could not have remained the demure and enigmatic repository of our projections.[5]

Part of the appeal of this image, according to Koestenbaum, is its muteness, since "photographs were our primary connection to Jackie."[6] Significantly, for our purposes, Koestenbaum goes on to contend that: "there were two varieties of Jackie silence: her absence of public statements and the intrinsic silence of photographs."[7]

Loquacious Lurene pays homage to her silent idol by imitating her physical appearance. "From the first time I saw her . . . she grabbed me. I'd be eating or in the bathtub or just walking down the street and I'd think of her doing that." Facing the breach between herself and "ordinary" life, Lurene plasters it over with the mediating image, the force of her identification. To the telling vitality of the false detail we find in her Marilyn Monroe hairstyle, platinum blonde, slightly disarranged—a decidedly anti-Jackie sign— the film adds Lurene's propensity to chatter, a compulsive soundtrack over a fantasy life organized by the silent images she collects. As much as Lurene's story is about the place and the use and the meanings of images, it is also about the meanings of everyday speech. While she confesses to an inability to parse ordinary life that matches her bewilderment in Spanish, a foreign tongue in which she cannot even discern word units, like Paul, and the film itself, we spectators must learn along with Lurene which are the significant units in the stream of her comments. Talk though she must, Lurene learns only with difficulty to *say* anything, to tell any story.

Perhaps the most compelling of the film's images of television's impact on Lurene's life comes when she and her companion, hiding out in the home of a white Virginia couple, turn to the television for information about the location of JFK's burial and the procession leading to it. A segment that covers the body lying in state is interrupted by the famous footage of Lee Harvey Oswald's assassination ("pandemonium has broken loose"). Paul and Lurene join hands for the first time as the images of Mrs. Kennedy and Caroline touching the casket pass across the screen. Paul thus acknowledges his sensitivity to Lurene's identification with the First Lady. But this gesture also inadvertently displays their intimacy before a third party as well, rendering public the private rapprochement they have achieved. Television has mediated a moment of extraordinary proximity, and unimaginable contact.

This scene produces an even more shocking effect, however; in their collective astonishment no one in this group seems to notice that a black man has just taken a seat in the bedroom of this white couple to whom he is a complete stranger. But the scene also opens Lurene to the critical scrutiny of the kindly older white woman. That scrutiny will end in a dis-identification between the two white women, with the older woman taking a strict moral distance from Lurene, even though they collaborate in deflecting the policemen seeking Paul at the Enright house. It is as if this moment were meant to figure Lurene's definitive crossing of the border of racial taboo. But why should this

---

5 Wayne Koestenbaum, *Jackie Under My Skin: Interpreting an Icon* (New York: Penguin/Plume, 1995), 43.
6 Ibid.
7 Ibid., 42.

take place before the television, as if the TV itself mediated and facilitated this exchange and the change it effects? Indeed, this televisual interruption precedes the first moments of identification and of extreme dis-identification between Paul and Lurene. More important, however, dis-identification seems to function as the necessary prerequisite to having sex, as Paul demands that Lurene acknowledge the violent social effects of difference.

Unlike *The Long Walk Home*, which is much more conventional in its reliance on a subtext of sight and magic—and on the image of black resistance—*Love Field* works through the contentious intersections of looks and speech. *The Long Walk Home* presents its black female protagonist Odessa Carter (Whoopi Goldberg) as the mute image of black stoicism, while its soundtrack continually deploys choirs singing spirituals to register collective, if passive, resistance. *Love Field*'s intersections mark a plot that proceeds through conflict and interpretation—not resolution. Take, for instance, Lurene's perspective on Kennedy's racial politics, which she tries out on black interlocutors. Stopped in a small town, hoping a mechanic can repair their car, whose engine can't propel them faster than 40 mph (what a metaphor for the progress of integration!), Lurene speculates that many of the town's residents, who are black, will be attending the Kennedy funeral. Met with a resistant silence, she ventures to the mechanic: "he did a lot for your people." "Look around, ma'am," replies the mechanic, "look like he done much here?"

Significantly, the injunction to look reverberates through this sequence, which occurs at the film's precise temporal center. As she retreats, in her typical fashion, to the company of Paul's daughter Jonelle, who is playing on the swing, Lurene's newly alerted gaze will let her see herself through the black men's eyes. As the two black men joke about the dangers of traveling with a white woman in the front seat, Paul asserts that he'd really like to put her in the back, because of the way she "runs her mouth." This is a moment of "truth" for Lurene. And the film emphasizes this by showing the men's conversation from a point it establishes as aligned with her point of view, yet closer to them than she actually is, while the amplified soundtrack lets us hear clearly their distant voices. These displacements into implausibility—what appears to be Lurene's POV allows for a closer view and clearer sound than could possibly reach her—highlight the intensity of her effort to penetrate the meanings of the men's exchange, even as that exchange emphasizes the distance that separates them. More important, however, these displacements inscribe a slight, yet shocking, realignment of Lurene's "view" in general.

Yet the film does not entirely blame Lurene for her inability to process what she sees around her as giving the lie to her conviction that Kennedy "did a lot for the Negroes." After all, Kennedy's progressive racial politics was largely a televisual effect. As television followed the civil rights movement, bringing its major standoffs into the living rooms of northern white people on the one hand, thus crossing geographical distance, and into the living rooms of southern blacks on the other, bridging segregated spaces, a certain political struggle raged around television news coverage.[8] In June 1963, in the wake of

---

8 Lynn Spigel reports on contemporary research into this subject: "Raymond Stewart found that television 'has a very special meaning for invalids, or for Southern Negroes who are similarly barred from public entertainments.' One black respondent in the study claimed: 'It [television] permits us to see things in an uncompromising manner. Ordinarily to see these things would require that we be segregated and occupy the least desirable seats or vantage point. With television, we're on a level with everyone else'" (*Make Room for TV: Television and the Family Ideal in Postwar America*, Chicago and London: University of Chicago Press, 1992, 113).

a partial political victory in the conflict with George Wallace at the University of Alabama, the President went on television to make a definitive statement, one that civil rights leaders had long been agitating for, giving a twelve-minute live-telecast speech on civil rights as a pressing national moral issue. As Mary Ann Watson recounts: "The following afternoon, with the success of the federal government at the University of Alabama likely, the President made an uncharacteristically sudden decision to go on television. At 6 p.m., the White House asked the television networks for a fifteen-minute block of time at 8 p.m."[9] The "uncharacteristic" spontaneity is important here. Just as Kennedy had shown a certain genius for working within the television format in his campaign and throughout his office, his decision to appear on short notice with little preparation suggests that he was well aware that a spontaneous response would help to highlight the state of crisis and his response to it in a performative manner, just as rhetorically the impromptu feel of his speech might read as the spontaneous expression of a more personal, and hence authentic, conviction. But equally important, according to Watson's account of the events, he must have been responding to a televisual event:

> On Sunday, June 9, 1963, a TV interview with Martin Luther King was aired on WPIX in New York City on David Susskind's syndicated talk show "Open End." During the two-hour discussion, King was severely critical of the Kennedy administration's commitment to civil rights. While Eisenhower's approach to civil rights was "miserable," King said, Kennedy's was "inadequate." He called on the President to revive fireside chats and explain civil rights to the nation on television. He asked the President to speak not in purely political terms, but in moral terms.[10]

Kennedy may rise to this occasion. But, of course from the point of view of King and the civil rights movement, he rises to it on a tide created by their struggle. From Lurene's point of view, however, the President's televisual image is that of someone "doing a lot for the Negro," with all that African-Americans were doing for themselves unfolding as a backdrop.

Lurene lives in a world where she makes sense of things by identification and resemblance; Paul, on the other hand, is a vigilant reader of differences and of contexts. Where for Lurene the meanings of things are permanent, if incomprehensible, for Paul they are situational and immediately legible. His original assessment of her consciousness is starkly reflected in his offering her a magazine to read, "one with lots of pictures," *Look*. It is not lost on her that this is a sign of his contempt—not a shrewd reader, she must be confined to the world of glossy images. But the magazine's title might be an injunction: "Look!" This might be the implicit injunction that Lurene's story obeys, as she learns to see through a different lens, one that includes but exceeds identification. As part of her early acquaintanceship with Paul's child, Jonelle, Lurene works entirely through identification: Jonelle is silent, as she herself was as a child; Jonelle's two syllable name sounds like a contraction of two names, perhaps Joan Ellen, just like Lurene's (Louise Irene). Only when Jonelle tries the same procedure, asking Lurene if she's sad because she has lost her mother, like the little girl herself, does Lurene begin to see this child as having a whole history and context of her own. Later, at the film's end, when Lurene

9 *The Expanding Vista*, 105.
10 Ibid., 104.

presents Jonelle with a going away gift, a locket, just like the one she has bought for herself, identification takes a different form—it is a two-way street.

Thus, we might say that Lurene's is an apprenticeship elaborated through looking. This apprenticeship leads her to an awareness of the ambient white gaze that surveys and partitions the social field, as inscribed in segregated restrooms, for example.[11] Ultimately, while the film suggests that racist consciousness may change if its subject learns to see differently, it refuses the metaphor of "seeing through the other's eyes" because it emphasizes that rather than stop at trying to see as Paul does, Lurene goes on to find herself in the visual field as the other of the surveying white gaze. Her and Paul's private encounter is thus irrevocably public in this visual field. Social change, then, cannot be a private or privatized event.

Lurene's basic strategy of apprehension through identification leads her into a discourse of reversibility. When she questions Paul about Kennedy, "I thought the Negroes liked Kennedy," he allows that "some did," forcing upon her a distinction she hasn't seen, and goes on to account for his own suspicion: "I just don't expect much from white people." Lurene's testy response to this is: "I think that's pretty prejudiced if you don't mind my saying so." This incident suggests that the only language she can muster to challenge him is a simple reversal of white racism.

In one of the more brutally excruciating exchanges between Lurene and Paul, after she has bathed his wounds and hidden him from the police, they are arguing about when to make their escape, and whether or not to remain together. In the shadowy light of late afternoon in the barn, shafts of light exaggerate Lurene's pale skin and white blonde hair in a brutal contrast with Paul who is completely shadowed in dark brown to black. Lurene isolates as an explanation for Paul's desire to separate from her her own manipulation of racist language in handling the policeman: "Well, ain't no niggers around here." And she tries to confront the contradictions embedded in her ready access to manipulating the language of racism as she adopts the posture of white Southern womanhood, performing an identification with the policeman's discourse, even in order to subvert his purposes. "I said it, but I didn't mean it."

This precipitates an explosive confrontation in which Paul attacks Lurene on a variety of fronts. To her concern about his child, he responds that when she has a child of her own she can tell him what to do, thus deploying her grief against her. "Until then," he continues, "you can sit tight in your little clean world where the First Lady gives a shit about you." In the face of this grinding attack on her personal symptoms, Lurene ventures, "I thought we understood each other." For his part, Paul attacks the subtext of identification that may underlie her sense of understanding. "Being bored and being black are different . . . I want my child to be free to grow up as bored and stupid and useless as any white woman. We are *not* the same." In this deeply gendered framework, Paul simultaneously makes Lurene stand in for white women in general, and, in turn, makes white women a symptom of whiteness itself. Yet his position provides a glance at a competing reading, which is that it is precisely the alienation Lurene experiences

---

11 Robin D. G. Kelly describes the symbolic importance of Jim Crow in public and consumer spaces for black people in *Race Rebels: Culture, Politics and the Black Working Class* (New York and London: The Free Press, 1994). In this connection it is worth considering the impact of the symbolic surveillance that partitions these spaces as well.

in her domestic situation—which may manifest itself as boredom—that allows her, in whatever uneven and clumsy ways, to meet him at all.

In a complicated way, the more Paul wants to deny that they understand each other, the more he shows a developed knowledge of her intimate landscape, even if only to use it against her. For her part, Lurene's mistake has been to claim that the new understandings she has achieved through reading contexts that are irrevocably changed by her connection to Paul amount to a reciprocal understanding and a shared purview. Indeed, Paul's initial outburst details Lurene's misreadings and miscalculations and their consequences: "Thank you for not meaning nigger. Thank you for calling the FBI. And, baby, thank you for sticking out that thumb and bringing those crackers down on me." Lurene's failure to read their visibility, her failure to realize that the white gaze and white reactions need to be managed, is actively dangerous. On the other hand, Lurene does see Paul, and in ways that reinforce the film's own view of him. Paul is never an image of blackness. He is never a picture: he is a gaze, watchful, vigilant, defensive, scrutinizing, reading. The film gives equal visual attention to Lurene and to Paul, figured most often in conversations delivered through alternating medium closeups, where we watch them talk and listen. We see her listen intently to his voice offscreen. Only in the last third of the film do we see them frequently in two shot. This film works visually to establish and sustain reciprocity, in which Paul does not become an image, and Lurene undoes her self-construction as an icon.

The relationship of images to icons is as central to *The Long Walk Home* as it is to *Love Field*. In both narratives, the bus emerges as a key site of racial interaction and struggle. This is surely because so many televisual memories of the civil rights movement are shaped by struggles for and on the bus, including both bus boycotts, and busing as the primary tool of desegregation a few years later. Robin D. G. Kelly accounts for the concrete and iconic status of the bus in this way: "In some ways, the design and function of busses and streetcars rendered them unique sites of contestation. An especially apt metaphor for understanding the character of domination and resistance on public transportation might be to view the interior spaces as 'moving theaters.'"[12] Kelly continues to elaborate on this metaphor: "Theater can have two meanings: as a site of performance and as a site of military conflict . . . The design of streetcars and busses themselves—enclosed spaces with seats facing forward or toward the center aisle—lent a dramaturgical quality to everyday discursive and physical confrontations."[13]

An important scene in *The Long Walk Home* condenses several lines of force around the televisual image of the Montgomery bus boycott, which is central to the film's drama. At the Christmas holidays—soon to be memorialized by the father (Dwight Schultz) with his new Super 8 camera—the television constitutes both the intrusion of the world into the hermetically sealed refuge of the Thompson home and the momentary sanctuary of fantasy. Seen across the family dining table, a non-reciprocating voice in the family dialogue, the television inhabits the space of a marginal family member, much like the domestics, always present but largely to be ignored. It interrupts the family banter with a mock news report signaling that an "unidentified flying object" has been spotted over the "North Pole." This holiday pleasantry provokes the cynical response

12 Ibid., 57.
13 Ibid.

of the older sister, just home from college, who asks pointedly why they repeat this gag when no one who still believes in Santa Claus is watching. The simple irony, of course, is that the little sister, Mary Katherine, from whose point of view the story unfolds, still embraces this happy fantasy and the violent destruction of her belief is an allegory for one of the film's central narrative pretexts, the systematic undoing of the little girl's—and her mother's—delusions about race. So the big sister interrupts the Christmas fairy tale about the benign grandfatherly figure whose magical powers allow him to trump time and space to reach all the children in the world—equally, as the Santa myth would have it. She interrupts the voice of the television, challenging its claims to truth or reality, apparently insulted by its knowingly celebratory broadcast of fiction as truth. Yet the very next televised segment, a news report on the day's events in the boycott, becomes lost in this intimate and relatively trivial family dispute. The intrusion of "real" news prompts the family to extinguish the set, as the newscaster's voice fades in amplitude. But we also see here the way that television presents a newly intimate "history" in the form of current events taking place in proximate but non-communicating spaces.

Mr. Thompson's theory that to publicize the boycott as newsworthy is to advance black resistance perfectly epitomizes his sense of his world and everyone's place in it. But it also brings into focus the kinds of issues that emerged in and around television in the 1950s. On the one hand, many whites, like Mr. Thompson, actively blamed television for promoting civil rights and inciting demonstrations.[14] On the other hand, within the industry, even as network executives and sponsors worried about losing white—especially Southern white—viewers, others within and around the industry actively sought to promote ideological and material change through representation.[15] J. Fred MacDonald characterizes the impact of television in the period this way: "Images of chanting demonstrators being sprayed by fire hoses and attacked by dogs, freedom riders being abused, sit-in participants being taunted or beaten, and small black children needing military escorts to enter public schools—these pictures made television a powerful propaganda tool for those wanting progressive change."[16] These remain the indelible images associated with the civil rights movement for those who witnessed the original coverage as well as for those gaining access to the period through film and television reframings of these very images as history. This history is decidedly a history of representations for all Americans—across the racial and generational spectrum.

14 J. Fred MacDonald details the repressive force such representations provoked: "Many southern stations refused to accept syndicated and network movies because they felt such films would upset local social standards . . . ABC refused for the 1962–1963 season to air *The Defiant Ones* . . . As reported in *Variety*, Dallas police in 1958 banned Brigitte Bardot's film, *And God Created Woman*, from black theaters. The police explained that the French film was 'too exciting for colored folk.' One year earlier, the Alabama House of Representatives unanimously resolved to ask Alabama theater operators not to exhibit *Island in the Sun*, featuring Harry Belafonte and Joan Fontaine, because, in the words of one legislator, 'the making of such films will be most pleasing to the Communists and other un-American organizations, and to all intents and purposes will amount to another tactic in their campaign to brainwash the American public into acceptance of race mongrelization'" (72–73).

15 One such critic is Robert Lewis Shayon, cited by Philip Brian Harper in his essay, "Extra-Special Effects: Televisual Representation and the Claims of 'the Black Experience'": "In November, 1962, for example, Shayon extolled television's yet unrealized capacity to 'communicate . . . the Negro image to millions of homes,' suggesting the broad dissemination of that 'image' would help improve blacks' social standing in the world beyond the television screen" (*Living Color*, edited by Sasha Torres, Durham, NC and London: Duke University Press, 1998, 63).

16 *Blacks and White TV*, 72.

In this connection, it is worth comparing the relationship of blacks appearing in news reportage and documentary to that of blacks appearing in the framework of entertainment that dominates network television. Philip Brian Harper cites the critique of television by *Saturday Review* columnist Robert Lewis Shayon, in a 1962 article. After indicating that the overwhelming majority of blacks on television are singers and dancers, Shayon "goes on to remark that 'people appearing as themselves' on news broadcasts, informational programs, and educational documentaries—which constituted the category of programming with the second highest frequency of appearances by blacks—'are again merely passing through'—usually without benefit of any fee."[17] Despite progressive impulses, practically speaking, blacks appear as "themselves": entertainers, sports figures, or newsmakers. Within this limited range, we should note that the appearance as oneself takes two forms: one is an exceptional individual, circulating as a star whose features are precisely not generalized, or as the newsworthy individual, usually distinguished by aberration, or one appears as part of massified blackness, in demonstrations. With the exception of political leaders like Martin Luther King or Malcolm X, we might say then that if blacks are rarely seen they are even less often heard, and mostly they are heard as the singing voice, the entertainer or the mass voice singing in church or in protest. In a world where for the white people, blacks are "news" or nothing, invisible unless they make news through an event of resistance, the shift in Mrs. Thompson's (Sissy Spacek) consciousness does not so much bring her maid Odessa into perspective as it brings her into view, at first. And this coming into view is a necessary prerequisite to her becoming Miriam Thompson's teacher, revising her racial perspective. Once Miriam begins to see Odessa, then Odessa has a new job: that of the native informant. Just as the domestics in this film are always shown to be working overtime, caring for two homes and families, and just as the white people insist on making most of their labor disappear, while always expanding the arena of tasks that form part of the official "job," Miriam thinks nothing of enlisting Odessa as her civil rights "instructor." And like her mother, the film's narrator (Mary Steenburgen), the now adult Mary Katherine through whose perspective these events are supposedly remembered, sees nothing out of balance here.

Introducing Odessa as she does the story in the film's opening sequence, the narrator tells us: "This was the first woman to rock me to sleep. There wasn't anything extraordinary about her. I guess there's always something extraordinary about somebody who changes and then changes those around them." Understood at the level of privatized individual consciousness, this statement makes little sense, but it thereby demonstrates the film's fundamental contradiction: that of trying to explain a mass movement and its consequences as a private or familial drama of "change." Most compelling among the film's oversights is that it fails to see that Odessa has not needed to "change" herself. She has needed to engage in active resistance and agitation to change not the Thompsons', or even all of white Montgomery's minds, but rather concrete social practices and institutions. And while the film displays the positive virtue of remembering that people can change their political positions through affective, rather than intellectual, channels, or through structures of feeling, it also promotes a sense that the deep structure of feeling is primary. Of course it is not: it makes no practical difference how

---

17 "Extra-Special Effects," 64.

the busdriver feels about integration, so long as he maintains it on the bus. One key sequence in a film that dismantles and rebuilds white racial consciousness through images involves Miriam's family album. Just after her husband makes his decision to join the Citizens' Council, which would otherwise be known as the White Citizens' Council, arguing that this is his only alternative to the Klan, Martin Luther King's home is firebombed. Notably, Mr. Thompson's decision is filmically precipitated by the evening news: "40,000 local Negroes walk and carpool, while buses run empty on day 49." A long tracking shot takes us past the King house from the point of view of a driver. A cut establishes the next scene in the Thompson house; as is characteristic of these domestic views, we watch the maids in medium long shot, squeezed toward the edge of the frame in the kitchen. This composition is emphatic: the maids are framed in the window formed by the counter, and by the cinematic frame. The camera zooms out slowly to reveal that Miriam is the subject of this contemplative vision of the distant and silent maids arranged in tableau, as they so often are in this domestic space. A temporal lapse figures Miriam's prolonged effort to establish the connection between the King house and her own domestics.

What happens next is more interesting. Later, Mrs. Thompson begins to pore over the family album. We move from medium closeup of her to zoom in—in a sightline match—on a particular picture. As a little girl in a white dress, Miriam stands before her house, holding the hand of a black nurse the top of whose head is cut by the upper frame of the photo. She is emphatically *not* its subject. In a picture on the album's next page, little Miriam holds a black hand but the rest of this body is cropped by the left edge of the frame. Visually, then, the maid is almost part of the frame itself. As the camera focuses on these images, we are in the position to see Miriam seeing them, and what we are invited to believe we are seeing is that, for the first time, she sees herself propped on the maid. Her identity, like her childhood, and like her self-image, has always been, as it is now, propped on that of black women, just as her household is literally sustained by their labor. Equally important, this propping must remain invisible to work. And perhaps the significance of this moment is that Miriam clearly remembers this maid with affection, but not as "part of the picture" of her childhood, because she requires this visual evidence to establish her memory of her presence.

The impact of this restored memory comes across in Miriam's next conversation with Odessa. Miriam's husband has discovered that she has been driving Odessa, and has forbidden her to continue the practice The photo album evokes memories that have remained unprocessed until the moment of photographic contemplation. Explaining her husband's position, Miriam asserts, "Norman's just always been where everything is segregated." Immediately, she offers the following anecdote of a girls' club bus trip to Oregon that she took at age 15 in the 1930s. They had stopped to swim at a public pool, when "some colored boys came down." Twenty club girls scrambled out of the pool, she reports, "we just didn't know any better. Those other kids just kept right on swimming." Her understanding of segregationist ideology suggests that it depends upon what is available to sight. Consequently, *seeing* something different is a prerequisite to *thinking* differently. But she will immediately overturn her own position, contemplating her husband's: "makes me wonder if he saw as much of the world during the war as he thinks."

Captivated by the power of visual impressions—images from the past—the film seems unable to overcome its own drive to construct Odessa as a permanent and fixed image of resistance to match its own project to record day-to-day resistance. Like its white female protagonist, whose gaze primarily mediates our contemplation of the black women in the white interior, the film compulsively either frames them as pictures, or shoves them to the edge of the frame as it focuses on the white characters. In the rigidly coded topography of the white interior, whites alternate between prolonged contemplation of the mute surface of the black face and the structure of the near oblivious glance. This glance catches the black body as a shadow at the edge of the frame, or sees it in instrumental fragments, hands washing dishes or polishing silver, for example, or the body glimpsed as a torso serving rolls or hors d'oeuvres. Here lies the usefulness of the little girl's perspective: materializing the white domestic ideology, she sees the maids at waist level, shadows passing through the room. But an alternation between contemplative and interpretive gazes also characterizes the difference between Miriam and Norman Thompson. Miriam meditates on what appearances can tell her about the interior life of her maid, while Norman sees Odessa's face as a mask that conceals a hostile attitude, telling his wife that the domestic she sees in her home is "not the real Odessa."

In this defensively self-enclosed world, whites observe blacks visually and blacks observe whites by overhearing them. This is the tension played out in the Christmas dinner scene, where Mr. Thompson's mother—the bad Mrs. Thompson against whom the daughter-in-law emerges as heroic—makes a speech about the domino effect of civil rights protest: "next year you'll have to have them sitting here at the table with you." This scene calls attention to the perverse intimacy and the privileges of ignorance that hold this interior together. The two maids are not only within earshot, they are right at hand, serving food all around this table.

The Thompsons' changing world registers on the one hand in the TV images, images of the mass, images in motion, images of mass movement, and on the other hand in the family photo album. By contrast to the TV, photos are still, silent, private memorials that may serve as fetishes, as well as repositories of private interpretations of the past. Significantly, the film's preoccupation with this inscription of public and private through images figures in its own frame. A powerful resonance between the opening and final sequences of *The Long Walk Home* gathers around the shifting shape of images themselves. This film opens with sound on a black screen. Its first image appears to be a still, a black-and-white negative. Gradually, the film lends both color and motion to this image of an empty street, and in the process the largely black-toned screen fills with a whitening light. This could be taken as a visual figure for the whole film—it promises to tell a black woman's story, but it ends up with a white conclusion, and a white future, which follows from the progressive intensification of its focus on the white side of things.[18] Slowly filling with color, from black-and-white to sepia tones, to a full palette, the image resolves into focus on the motion of a bus pulling into the frame. By the time the sequence concludes, as marked by Mary Katherine's finishing her introduction of

18 In this respect, *The Long Walk Home* seems to share the characteristics that Mimi White identifies in *I'll Fly Away* and *Home Front*, which actively produce histories in the fictional representation of private memory: "Public histories and personal memories intersect in narratives and images that can be readily reproduced, especially on television . . . History serves simultaneously as the alibi and the product of these programs, crisscrossing personal memory with public history and historical fiction" ("Race, Gender, and Popular Memory," 134).

both Odessa and the story, we are faced with what could be a still portrait of the black woman standing on the bus, captured in medium closeup contemplating the empty seats beyond the color line.[19]

Striking in effect, the sequence gives the impression that it is reanimating for us a past that had been immobilized, frozen. In so doing, it seems to promise to bring the past back to us, in a move that may be analogous to the distance bridging function of the TV image, especially for this period of intense national conflict that took distinctly regional shapes. Here this film shares some of the complexities of the 1990s historical nostalgia television programming that Mimi White finds exemplified in *I'll Fly Away* and *Home Front*. "Questions of historical 'voice,'" writes White, "are further complicated by the programs' reliance on popular culture and media as integral aspects of the history they deploy. The historical record that grounds these programs is drawn from the popular media; these stories and images have already circulated in the public arena in a variety of forms."[20]

But the film also makes a visual metaphor out of movement and motion, political action and its image in pictures. In this connection, and perhaps only in this connection, does the full visual significance of the film's closing sequence come to light. We leave Odessa, again in medium closeup, raising her voice in song with the mass of black women who have just faced down the white mob at the carpool garage. So, we return to the still, individualized image and the soundtrack, a mass black voice. Odessa's act of resistance is reframed as the *image* of resistance. Through her, the film has put a face on resistance, to be sure. But that face is a picture in a metaphoric family album. As the adult Mary Katherine concludes about this incident in voiceover, the moment when her mother "stepped over the line," the color line, that is, to stand momentarily with the black women against the white men: "It would be years before I understood what standing in that line meant. To my mother, and, as I grew older, to me." Mother and daughter may step over the line, but, contrary to the threats of the white men, they may also step right back.

If the incident becomes fully intelligible to the daughter only after years, we must understand it as stored, an image she revisits as her mother revisited the family album. It is almost as if the film believes the same to be true of white interpretations of civil rights; this is to be understood through private retrospection. Thus the film shares an historical perspective that Mimi White uncovers in the recent television representations of postwar social change through family dramas: "Thus dramatized, the oppressions of the past become the implicit motive and explanation for the subsequent emergence of the civil rights and women's movements. These tacit explanatory frameworks, based in the temporal structures of historical narrativity, are in turn embedded in more

---

19 Robin D. G. Kelly remarks upon the importance of this line, and its instability: "What is more striking than the sheer number of incidents is the fact that, in most cases, the racial compartmentalization of existing space was not the primary point of contention. For many black working-class riders, simply getting on the bus was a struggle in and of itself . . . On numerous occasions, black passengers paid their fare at the front door but before they had a chance to board the bus drove off. The rule itself was not only obnoxious but ambiguous: drivers were instructed to 'collect fares at the front entrance of all vehicles *when they are crowded*' (emphasis added). What was meant by crowded was always subject to interpretation, leading to immense confusion and, at times, intense disagreement' (*Race Rebels*, 59).

20 "Race, Gender, and Popular Memory," 133.

particularized story trajectories which displace and reconstrue these interests in relation to individual, fictional characters."[21] Whether fictionalized or not, as White observes, such efforts to dramatize collective memory are tethered to particular perspectives. Despite its inclusion of the private life of Odessa's own family, *The Long Walk Home*'s perspective on change is unwaveringly attached to the white characters, from whose individual points of view it aims to construct a generalized, collective—but still white—gaze.

We find this effect perfectly crystallized in the final sequence of the film. Marked by the focus-pulling that has persistently dramatized the notion of the field of vision, of perspective itself, this sequence alternates between individualizing and collectivizing, or "massifying" visual gestures. So, the film's conclusion offers us a final and monumental image to commemorate its own, and Miriam's, visual apprenticeship. She, the film, and by extension we spectators, have learned to distinguish one black face from the mass and to reorient our visual field so that the blacks no longer necessarily fade into shadow. Equally important, the film's use of rack focus has helped to dramatize the partitioning of both domestic and public spaces, where blacks and whites inhabit parallel, non-communicating spaces that cannot—literally—be taken in by the same gaze, or focus.

As this last sequence concludes, the film zooms in on Odessa, from medium shot to closeup. As her stoical, tear-streaked face fills the frame, she is effectively isolated from the line of black women around her. A cut brings her into view from the side, and the next shot reveals that it is from Miriam's POV that we study Odessa's face. Miriam directs our gaze to Odessa and symbolically allows all the other women to fade away. Significantly, this scene emphasizes the film's only look exchanges between Miriam and Odessa. But the steadfastness of the film's overarching white perspective and its view of the black community is reinforced by the voiceover: "50,000 people boycotted the buses. I knew one." Mary Katherine and her mother, like the film itself, come to "know" about black people and their legitimate demands by a process of subtraction—isolating one representative—and subsequently by a process that seems strictly additive, "multiply Odessa by 50,000," and you get: change.

From this perspective, we might remember Lurene's way of "knowing," which seems far more sophisticated, because of its internal complexities and her own implication in it: "He wasn't understanding any of it either, and I thought, 'Honey, now you know.'" In this context, it is surely no accident that the film concludes by offering us Odessa's frozen image before fading to black under a soundtrack of voices singing "Marching Off to Zion" and Martin Luther King making a speech. The black mass is pure voice; the mass itself is music, crystallized around the representative cadences of Dr. King. Almost reverentially, the film consigns Odessa back to the image, evanescing her back into the mass black voice, which appears here as a soundtrack to white enlightenment.

Both *Love Field* and *The Long Walk Home* challenge the commonplace and wishful notion that close proximity and exposure to members of a different race erase prejudice, as the problem is overcome by "knowing." Yet in *The Long Walk Home*, the daily intimacy of cross-racial contact amounts to no knowledge. It is as if television, with its introduction of the distant and the elsewhere into the intimate sphere of the home, were necessary to mediate this change. Miriam comes to "know" black people through representations of them. By contrast, in *Love Field*, the couple's proximity seems initially

---

21 Ibid., 121.

to produce more confusion and distance. What shapes Lurene's shifting perspective is the external white gaze on herself and Paul—together. In this gaze, their mere proximity transforms them into an image. Seeing herself seen with him, as part of this image in the eye of the white beholder, is what allows her to see differently. Visually, she is marked in the white field of vision, as her point of view on the world and in the film is aligned in parallel with Paul's. At the same time, even as these films refuse to equate intimacy or proximity with knowledge, both seem to subscribe to another reassuring commonplace of white liberal ideology concerning the elimination of racism. Both films elaborate shifts in white consciousness through the accident, the unforeseen circumstances that establish a connection that leads to solidarity. Such encounters seem to be governed entirely by chance.

In both films, however, what helps to complicate conventional liberal notions of cross-racial "knowing" and of the effects of intimacy is gender. In "stepping over the line," Miriam and her daughter have literally crossed a gender line as well as a racial one—leaving the mob of white men to join the crowd of black women. Thus does Miriam reach the culmination of her journey, which has brought her into a new kind of intimate exchange with her maid, at the direct expense of her relationship with her husband. As the boycott situation polarizes, Miriam, like many historical Montgomery housewives, begins to drive her maid to work. As her husband moves toward the Citizens' Council, the white men's organization, which brings him into solidarity with many local racist businessmen, the public and the private also polarize along gender lines, since Miriam ends by defying her husband in order to transport the maid who will keep the household in running order. Thus, the film articulates gender and racial conflicts together, and it does so in a way that is no doubt historically accurate. But recalling the similarities between Miriam and Lurene, who leaves her husband after meeting Paul, we need to ask what representational work these strikingly appealing, complex, and contradictory white women, figured as proto-feminists, perform.

What might account for contemporary interest in the historical intersections of the civil rights movement and feminism that we see elaborated in these two films, as well as in television? On the one hand, we want to recognize the struggles of white middle-class women, who are not often figured as historical agents. And we certainly need to explore the ways the civil rights movement may have helped to propel the women's movement through political collaboration, or even sympathy. On the other hand, these accounts, founded on "accident" or "circumstance," tend to cast race relations as matters of affect and emotion, just as they cast white women as the locus of sentiment.

In both of these films, white women get deployed both as symptomatic of white consciousness and as emissaries toward blackness. Without wanting to diminish the agency of white women and girls in the 1950s and 1960s, we might want to ask how contemporary gender politics and ideologies allow for the confident assertion of feminism's "natural" alliance with civil rights activism and with progressive racial politics. The films' emphasis on feminist awakening provides a certain reassurance: the white woman enters history as the subject of social change. But at the same time she serves as an alibi for her race, rewriting its history redemptively.

These films advance the premise that history itself is a representational struggle that continues in permanent revisions. But a persistent racial unconscious nonetheless underlies their critical efforts. In depicting white women as political heroes who are more progressive than white men, these films cast their women as representative of their race. Whether sentimental or celebratory, this central focus on the progressive woman downplays white resistance to integration in general, since not only white men but white collectivity recedes into the background behind the woman protagonists.

Garnering political credit through their feminist sympathies, these films nevertheless advance the familiar false analogies between gender oppression and racial oppression that white consciousness so frequently entertains. Credit gained through this false analogy cannot be so easily transferred; the links the progressive woman makes between gender ideologies and racial ones do not automatically guarantee the films' racial politics. As political alibi, then, these white women are symptomatic. Once the symptomatic site of white fantasies about the vulnerability of whiteness to blackness through sexuality, these revised figures of white femininity still serve as the privileged medium of racial exchange. Behind the white feminist as an agent of change is the white feminist as a medium of exchange. This may account for her close association with the figure of television, which became the medium for national racial exchange during the civil rights era. But where television brought social struggle into the private domestic sphere, these films' revisions of the 1950s and 1960s rewrite public political conflicts as privatized, family affairs.

Part II
New constellations: stars

Introduction

The idea of the "movie star" might seem to be such a long-standing feature of film production that we can easily forget that stardom was in fact an early innovation of the Hollywood film studios. The "star" had to be invented as a way of marketing the feature film; as historians such as Richard DeCordova and Miriam Hansen[1] have demonstrated, the film studios were initially resistant to naming their actors in publicity, mainly by reason of not wanting to pay higher salaries to workers who could, nevertheless, potentially draw audiences back to the cinema and thereby expand studio profits. Be that as it may, the star is now such a powerful tool for creating the sense of product differentiation vital to commodity culture that the international movement of stars allows for critics to assess the different meanings of a film as it travels through a variety of spheres of exhibition. Through the star, the critic can access the everyday languages through which we decide that stars have meaning and importance for us: they embody our conventionalized notions of beauty, wealth, behavior, fashion, but not always for the same reason in the different places in which stardom is embraced.

The star is not, in other words, a person. Instead, the writers of the following essays understand the star as a text, as a carefully calculated product with dimensions that reach far beyond the films in which the star appears. Stars, of course, often have other roles: Jodie Foster and Barbra Streisand, to take but two examples, are well known for their directorial roles as well as their star images. But we mean something even larger: stars are precisely our images of them (images that have been sold to us, but images nonetheless). In this larger sense, stars have *personae*, images engineered by publicity and the enormous apparatus of intertexts (texts related to films such as entertainment media, product tie-ins and endorsements, fan discourses and the like) that sustain stardom as a system. Because stardom is vitally dependent upon these intertexts, stars are difficult to isolate for inquiry, but the study of stardom is rewarding to the degree that it reaches the width of film culture's social existence across a number of practices.

Star studies are thus a relatively recent feature of the study of cinema, and the essays that follow embrace the sense that the star, as a site of critical inquiry, deserves greater attention not solely for how his or her popularity mobilizes certain meanings *within* the text of a film, but for how larger social meanings are organized through the appeal of the star in multiple texts, and not solely those of films, but of fan magazines, web sites,

---

1 See Richard DeCordova, *Picture Personalities: The Emergence of the Star System in America* (Urbana: University of Illinois Press, 1990); Miriam Hansen, *Babel and Babylon: Spectatorship in American Silent Film* (Cambridge, MA: Harvard University Press, 1991).

and the commentaries of everyday life shared by friends and workers. One of the arguments cultural studies brings, in fact, to the study of cinema is that films can indeed be read ideologically, not as reflections of the world but as bearing imprints of the social world of which they are a product and which they help to shape. These essays bring the stars down to earth for our critical analysis.

6 Judy on the net

Judy Garland fandom and "the gay thing" revisited

Steven Cohan

It is a truth almost universally acknowledged that a single man in possession of a Judy Garland CD must *not* be in want of a wife. However little known the feelings or views of such a man may be on his first entering a record store, this truth is so well fixed in the minds of the surrounding public that Garland is considered the rightful property of some one or other of Dorothy's friends. "It was no secret," Michael Bronski observes, "that her most dedicated fans were gay men" (Bronski 1984: 103).

In *Heavenly Bodies*, Richard Dyer analyzes how the fifties Garland star text, arising from her attempted suicide in 1950 and subsequent firing by MGM, structured "much of the gay reading" (Dyer 1986: 143) because it heightened "the disparity between the [screen] image and the imputed real person" (156). This star text, he continues, articulates a "gay sensibility" that "holds together qualities that are elsewhere felt to be antithetical"—such as "theatricality and authenticity," "intensity and irony" (154) — primarily through Garland's embodiment of "a special relationship to suffering, ordinariness, normality" (143). Drawing upon Dyer's analysis, Janet Staiger further shows how, prior to the revelations of Garland's professional and personal troubles in 1950, the basis for that gay reception was present in the fan discourse during the MGM years, which promoted a "star image [that] was already at odds with her film roles" (Staiger 1992: 163). With the release of her 1954 comeback vehicle, *A Star is Born*, Garland's star text was fixed enough in the public imagination to determine the reception of both her image and her work through what Staiger calls "alternate readings" of the film that, disregarding the narrative logic, mediated it through the biography.

As far as Garland's star text is read today, it is still widely perceived as the special province of a gay male fandom identified with a pre-Stonewall ethos of camp and abjection, to the point that what were initially alternate readings have since become the preferred or dominant ones. For instance, Wade Jennings assumes the centrality of the alternate reading when he uses Garland to exemplify the formation of cult stardom. He argues that two related factors distinguish her from other stars of her generation. Because of "recorded performance, visual and aural," he first points out, "virtually the whole career is preserved as a whole, an established canon of images and sounds that can be known and shared . . . Even when the career of a performer stretches over a long period and encompasses as many changes as Garland's, all the individual recorded performances interconnect and comment upon one another." At the same time, he continues, her cult standing is dependent upon fans realizing the incongruities of the life and the work, "find[ing] part of their identity in their detailed and considerable knowledge of the contradictions, the differences between the publicized career and the reality . . . In the case of every star who becomes a cult figure, there is some variation of the notion of 'the suffering artist.' " No star, he remarks, referring to what has become a truism about her biography and career as they interacted, "more completely embodied" this abrasive confrontation with and triumphant overcoming of "personal defeat and despair" than Judy Garland (Jennings 1991: 92–94).

This view of Garland as the phoenix-like diva of suffering, often used to account for her strong, cultish appeal to gay fans, dominates how her stardom is now remembered. The media continues to circulate it with every retrospective account in print or on television. But that does not mean as a consequence that Garland's star text is any more coherent or stable today than it was during her lifetime. Her following was and continues to be marked by several major intersections of fan positionings (for example, whether oriented around the Garland of the film musicals, the Garland of the concert years, the Garland of recordings, the Garland of the annual telecasting of *The Wizard of Oz*, the Garland of posthumous reflections and revaluations), and fan positionings do not coincide or overlap, as Jennings proposes, so much as mark fractured points of resistance to the sort of totalizing reading that he describes. These multiple fan formations are evident in the various web pages devoted to Garland on the internet, which provide a valuable opportunity for further inquiry into the ongoing reception of her star text, albeit with some obvious limitations, since whatever demographic picture results includes only those people who have access to the web and an inclination—not to say education, leisure time, and income—to use it. Nevertheless, this resource allows us to witness how contemporary fans read Garland's stardom. Her significance for them is not fixed to the reading that dominates mainstream and critical accounts but, on the contrary, requires their continual negotiation of the meanings Garland is taken to embody.

Focusing in particular on ambivalence about her status as a gay icon in the conflicted efforts of fans to articulate Garland's value as a star, I will concentrate on the two sites that have become most central to the fan community with access to the internet: "The Judy Garland DataBase," the most comprehensive effort of all the web pages to document her career, and "The Judy List," a daily email discussion about her stardom. As in the other fan pages devoted to Garland, the DataBase makes every effort to reconcile the contradictions between life and work, past and present, which Jennings sees as essential to her cult status; and to do so, it practically removes all traces of the features that Dyer argues were central to her association with a "gay sensibility": namely, an androgynous image, camp performing style, and a persona that projects a "special relationship with ordinariness" because it is "saturated" with connotations of normality without being normative (Dyer 1986: 156). The DataBase's effacement of the dominant gay reading of Garland's star text somewhat mirrors the recent marketing of her work on home video and CD, so the prominence on the listserve of debates about "the gay thing," as one poster called it, stands out all the more as a focal point of fan negotiations. The controversial question of whether or not Garland's gay following was and continues to be a significant factor in her stardom has evoked sharp disagreements among list subscribers, most notably (and the timing was not coincidental) prior to and after the cablecasting of the Arts & Entertainment biography special on March 27, 1997. These discussions call attention to the ways that contemporary Garland fans actively and self-consciously read her stardom as a text, often interpreting it with a high degree of critical sophistication—and a determined agenda. In their differing ways, both the DataBase and the Judy List manifest fans' conscious efforts to replace the present dominant reading of Garland, itself originally an alternative account that privileged the biography, with a new and more recuperative interpretation that not only reads the life through the career but does so in response to their own close identification with mainstream consumer culture.

The Judy Garland DataBase: documenting the legend

In 1998 there was enough Garland fan activity on the internet to attract the notice of an Associated Press reporter, who, referring to "the 15 core sites," observed: "the number of elaborate, fan-generated Web sites dedicated to Garland so many years after her death is somewhat remarkable. Her Web presence dwarfs that of many contemporary artists" (Sampey 1998). As I write this essay a year later, that number has doubled; an exact figure is hard to come by since some pages become defunct—downloadable one day, gone the next—while others are reinvented under new names. Some notable sites include "The Judy Garland Media Storage," a site with sound files of songs and dialogues from her films; "The Judy Garland Photographic Page," featuring, along with the many images, a special Memorial Wall on which visitors inscribe testimonials and tributes; and a fan's memorabilia-filled "Judy Room," with photos of the contents that can be sent as electronic postcards. Another site specializes in her live performances and CBS television series, there are two different pages on *A Star is Born*, and the British-based Judy Garland fan club has a link to the president's own pages recording the star's various appearances in London. Still other sites are devoted to more avowed fan worship, offering photos, trivia games, polls, film- and discographies, magazine and newspaper clippings, and so forth. But even these are specialized in one form or another. "Young Judy Garland," devoted to her child stardom, offers "an alternative perspective on this natural artist who's [sic] precocious behavior and beautiful (divine) voice won the hearts of an entire nation"; and "Judy Garland: Forever Beautiful" has, among its many other features, a section entitled "Judy's Guardians," offering fans a chance "to 'own' a certain part of Judy history (only in cyberspace)" by claiming a song, movie, character, concert, or TV appearance as their own (both downloaded September 9, 1999).

Other fan pages devoted to Hollywood stars of the studio era have similar ambitions, but the Garland pages surpass them in the sheer density of their archival documentation. Becoming increasingly "notable for their sophisticated design, breadth of information and intricate multimedia links" (Sampey 1998), as the AP reporter observed, the Garland pages combine fan worship and collecting with an encyclopedic intent that exceeds mere dedication to the star, complicating too simplistic notions of what such strong attachments on the part of fans reveal about their relation to stardom. This phenomenon is amply evident in "The Judy Garland DataBase," which serves as the model for many of the websites already mentioned.

Begun in 1995, the DataBase has grown to the point where, four years later, it comprises "more than 800 pages and nearly 4000 files of information and pictures, occupying 80 Mb of disk space" ("Introduction," downloaded September 18, 1999). It is hosted by baby-boomer Jim Johnson, a former flower-child and self-identified heterosexual in so far as his wife has featured prominently as supporting player in his relation to Garland fandom. Devoted primarily to Garland's MGM years, while still covering her entire career, the DataBase undergoes continual revision and expansion. Despite its additions and subtractions, though, the structure has remained relatively constant, its main contents organized around the obvious topics of Garland's music, films, radio, TV, and videos. These sections are then liberally subdivided to facilitate access to the information Johnson has collated, all elaborately illustrated, documented, and linked to each other through hypertext. The DataBase, moreover, does not stop here. It also features a large section devoted to Garland photos, and another one concerned with her presence in magazines. Johnson does not ignore his passion for collecting Garland memorabilia either, subdividing this section according to type, each with links to online dealers, and featuring a separate page displaying his own "Judy Room" dedicated exclusively to his vast collection, with seven photos arranged so as to simulate a panoramic 360° tour of the space. There are still other sections: a Garland biography; a categorized bibliography; a page about the internet fan community; an album of fans' personal remembrances; an irregularly updated column by author John Fricke (considered by many fans to be the definitive historian of Garland's life); trivia games centering on the star; an archived list of updates; a search engine; a guestbook; and the requisite links to other Garland pages and celebrity web rings.

Johnson explains that he developed the DataBase, dedicated to "a major star . . . considered a legend in her own time," as a "serious hobby . . . I *hope* that it is a place that people can find information pertaining to Judy's career—people who are not particularly Judy's fans, but who are interested in, or curious about, her work" ("Introduction," downloaded April 26, 1997). By 1999 this project had achieved such an indisputable authority for fans that Johnson now presents it as an evolving "reference volume . . . [where] the serious student can find the facts pertaining to Judy's work" ("Introduction," downloaded September 18, 1999). Yet for all this professing of scholarship, the voluminous DataBase inscribes a position of fandom constructed by, rather than reflective upon, movie culture. The contents do not historicize Garland's career but instead try to recover the terms by which MGM regulated her star image during her tenure at the studio in the late 1930s and 1940s. Moreover, addressing Garland fans as consumers of her talent through its ongoing commodification by the home video and music industries, the DataBase assumes that the most dedicated of fans are those committed to preserving her studio-produced image in the name of its historical authenticity.

The DataBase thus acquires its authority from the way that Johnson's archival record of Garland's career equates fan dedication with amateur scholarship, which is probably why, as the site became more comprehensive with each month's updating, he ended up removing all personal references to his own status as a fan in 1999. He eliminated not only his biographical profile but also a section devoted to his participation in Garland fandom. For instance, he had included an account of his 1996 trip to Hollywood with his wife and their friend, the chair of the welcoming committee of the now defunct Garland internet fan club. Johnson described how the trio stay in Hollywood, visit the Chinese theater's famous forecourt to put their feet in you-know-whose footprints, photograph the Capitol Records Building (Garland's label in the late 1950s and 60s), shop in various movie memorabilia stores, met with author John Fricke, and visit another Garland collector in West Hollywood ("Krista, Jim & Kellie go Hollywood," downloaded March 17, 1997). Nevertheless, even with these omissions, traces of the DataBase's fan orientation remain in the attention paid to collecting Garland memorabilia, beginning with the presentation of Johnson's Judy Room, as well as in the fan album, magazine section, and photo gallery. The gallery's cover page, for instance, features a 1944 pinup from *Esquire* magazine, which displays the star in a negligee, lying upside down in a seductive pose ("Judy Garland Photo Gallery," downloaded October 12, 1999). The photo is the sort of glamorous publicity shot that MGM routinely used for Lana Turner and Hedy Lamar but more rarely for Garland.

The gallery photos chronicle a range of Garland imagery, from chubby adolescent to girl-next-door to svelte star to Hirschfeld caricature, but they epitomize how the DataBase as a whole resists what Dyer points out was the ambivalent relation to Hollywood glamour that informed her star image while working at MGM. With a body that did not conform to the regimen of Hollywood glamour and was often difficult to clothe—because of her short-waisted build as well as her unstable weight—a "sense of inadequacy and inferiority" in comparison to her glamorous colleagues features prominently in Garland's biographical profile, and it also works its way into her films through characters who project a difference-within-ordinariness (Dyer 1986: 165). Often expressed in plot terms as a tension between her extraordinary native talent and her lack of glamour, Garland's ambiguous relation to Hollywood's version of normative gender roles as an "in-between" (as one of her early songs puts it) later became crystallized in her signature costumes (the tramp outfit and tuxedo jacket, both adapted from her films), and in the camp inflection of her performing style. These elements were then underscored in Garland's concerts after leaving MGM, their repertoire built primarily around songs from her films recontextualized in the light of her failures and comebacks, and they were foregrounded even more in the wry, demystifying stance she took toward the MGM glamour factory when telling stories about her career on nighttime talk shows. The DataBase's visual treatment of Garland, by comparison, works to normalize her persona by representing it in more conventional movie-star terms consistent with an overriding nostalgia for the presumed stability of the studio era. This view of her stardom effaces reference to the nonconformity of her studio work, viewed as labor as well as product, which, along with the gay fans who responded to it most famously, consequently functions as a crucial structuring absence of Johnson's archival documentation of her history.

Toward this end, the biographical section, unchanged in content despite the site's stylistic renovations, shies away from the turbulent story of failures and comebacks that typically structure accounts of Garland's life. Johnson represents her well-documented personal and professional turbulence according to mainstream perceptions of star labor under the old studio system so that it does not readily connote the kind of "emotional difference born within normality" which Dyer refers to when analyzing the Garland star text and which summarizes its queer signification for gay fans (Dyer 1986: 162). Not surprisingly, mention is never made in the DataBase of Garland's professional debt to and close friendships with the gay men in the Arthur Freed producing unit at MGM, who mentored, directed, choreographed, and costumed her, in effect, shaping her distinct performing style to achieve its camp register. In fact, Johnson, like many Garland fans, pretty much ignores the perspective taken by David Shipman's biography, explicit in drawing out the gay culture in which Garland worked and lived, but criticized by other Garland authors for its sensationalizing treatment, and follows John Fricke's biographical portrait of the trouper whose love of performing and special affinity with her fans always transcended her private demons and conflicts with her studio.

The DataBase's biography of Garland begins with a long quotation from Fricke's book that emphasizes her triumphs in "work[ing] for nearly forty-five of her forty-seven years." The first page recounts the life story in a pseudo-dialogic form as answers to a series of questions, from "Where and when was Judy born?" and "How did Judy get her start in show business?" to "Is it true that Judy was a drug addict?" and "Is it true that Judy was mentally ill?" Regarding her drug use, Johnson replies that, like other performers of her era, she took benzedrine, which was not understood as addictive but considered "the new miracle appetite suppressor of the period," and resorted to sleeping pills in the evening to counteract the drug's effects. Furthermore, he reports, "she did manage to break her habit many times, but often started up again when the pressures of a new film came along." Was she mentally ill? No, she "had emotional problems, possibly including depression . . . Such is often the case with truly gifted people . . . However, it may be that Judy's emotional problems were caused by the drugs that she used." Omitted is reference to her 1950 suicide attempt, although her letter to fans afterward, published in *Modern Screen*, is included in the magazine section. Garland is likewise not fired by MGM in Johnson's account but mutually agrees with the studio to terminate her contract, and, most triumphantly, her "one last comeback" was her funeral, which drew a crowd of "more than 22,000 people" ("Judy Garland Biography," downloaded March 16, 1998).

In succeeding pages, Johnson chronicles Garland's career at MGM with a year-by-year account of her work, contracts, salary, production starts and delays, and so on. However, this attention to the material details of her work life indirectly points out how Garland's star text raises questions about the studio system as it operated to normalize star labor even while glamorizing and financially rewarding it. Historically, Garland can be understood as presenting MGM with an instance of unregulatable, hence abnormal, industrial labor in the late 1940s—a star who did not conform to the production-line practice demanded by the film industry as it adjusted its working conditions to meet major shifts in its economical base and its audience after World War II. According to Fricke, even after being dropped from *Royal Wedding*, usually considered to have been the proverbial final straw, MGM had still wanted to retain her services: "they considered revising her contract for a single picture with options for two more. But President Nick Schenck was afraid the stockholders would claim the studio was running its business on sympathy and not intelligence," and cited her "increased weight" as the reason for letting her go, since she was now "unrecognizable." As Fricke puts it, she "was no longer cost-effective" (Fricke 1992: 122). By contrast, the DataBase's effort to dispel "a legend [that] has grown around Judy which shrouds much of the truth about her" (Biography, downloaded March 26, 1998) effaces even these nonnormative resonances of her star text, revising the alternate reading that has come to dominate public perceptions of Garland since 1950. The detailed chronology underscores the sheer output of her work (vaudeville, films, recordings, radio, and TV), to be sure, and refers to the industrial conditions under which she labored as a contracted performer, but in letting the "facts" speak for themselves, Johnson's DataBase mediates them through a new "legend."

Time-Warner, which now controls most Garland merchandising, has apparently not protested the inclusion of so many stills, posters, and video or CD covers on the DataBase. It is doubtful if Johnson has any direct connection with the corporate owners of Garland's MGM image, whether Turner Entertainment (which owned rights to the studio's catalogue at the time of the DataBase's beginning) or Time-Warner now (through its purchase of Turner), although there may well be some mediation by way of Fricke. Author of two books on *The Wizard of Oz* and one on the star's career, he has had a hand in most recent Garland merchandise, not only the MGM material on laser-disc and Rhino CDs (also now owned by Time-Warner) but the A&E biography, too, which he coproduced. The DataBase's normalization of Garland is consistent with the merchandising of her musicals on home video and CD, which revises her star image with the similar intent, as Johnson puts it, of enshrining "a true living legend" in terms that outwardly evoke the conventions of mainstream stardom. The cover photo of Rhino's double-CD, *Judy Garland: Collectors' Gems from the MGM Films* (released in 1996) features a glamour shot from the 1940s similar to the *Esquire* pinup. The publicity shoot from which that still was taken also provided the illustration of Garland in the 1997 special issue of *Entertainment Weekly*—a Time-Warner publication—on 100 Greatest Stars. (Johnson includes several stills from this series at the top of his gallery, too.)

Nonetheless, the people responsible for merchandising the new Garland product do have some sense of the gay market as its target base, since they have not been able to capture a sizeable crossover audience. Whereas the advertisement for the unsuccessful theatrical release of *That's Entertainment III* featured a stylized drawing evocative of Fred Astaire and Ginger Rogers to define the MGM musical as heterosexual in its appeal, the laser-disc box set substituted a drawing of Garland in her "Get Happy" costume of fedora and tuxedo jacket. Likewise, the liner notes for the laser-disc box set of *Ziegfeld Follies* describes Garland's number, "A Great Lady Has 'an Interview,'" as "a campy novelty" featuring the star dancing with "sixteen anxious 'boys' of the press" (Production notes 1994). The underscoring of "boys" by quotation marks evokes the same resonance that Matthew Tinkcom more explicitly finds in the number in his account of how the gay labor force of the Freed unit manifested itself in its characteristic camp style (Tinkcom 1996: 38–39). Indeed, this number, filmed in 1944, parodies the glamorous posing in those publicity photos of Garland appearing in magazines such as *Esquire* at that time, photos now recycled by Time-Warner and Johnson as emblems of her golden days at MGM.

Responsibility for the restoration and release of the MGM vault material on laser when distributed for Turner by MGM-UA was due to George Feltenstein, who, after Time-Warner gained full control of the Metro catalogue, moved over to that larger company to produce a series of CDs exploiting the studio's archive on its own Rhino label. In the documentary included on the box set of *That's Entertainment III*, when he introduces the outtakes from Garland's aborted *Annie, Get Your Gun* project, Feltenstein says how glad he is to have the opportunity to share the footage with her fans, adding: "As one of the keepers of the archives, I've always searched for a way to present all of this material . . . in a way that would finally release it to the people such as myself who are really crazy about Judy Garland" (*That's Entertainment III: Behind the Screen*). As John Fricke comments in his DataBase column, "George Feltenstein . . . is 'one of us'—a Judy fan, too" ("John's Page," June 1996, downloaded April 26, 1997). Just who comprises that "us"—and whether being a Judy fan is euphemistic of or just coincidental to her gay following—is neither self-evident nor free of controversy, at least not on the daily pages of the Judy List.

Pride and prejudices on the Judy List: preserving Garland's legacy

Inaugurated in October 1996, the listserve devoted to Judy Garland fandom continues to be owned and moderated by its founder, Mark Harris of North Carolina. From remarks made at times by Harris in his posts and to the press, it appears that the Judy List has a subscription base of over 250 members, a few of whom figure prominently (if silently on the list) in the entertainment industry (Sampey 1998). The list has attracted many gay Garland fans of the era Dyer writes about, but the membership is by no means homogeneous in its age, gender, sexual orientation, occupation—or opinions. What appears to unite the Judy List's readers is a shared recognition of Garland's emotional intensity when performing and a hunger for finding a community of similar-minded fans as a means of overcoming what they begrudgingly recognize is her insignificance for mainstream audiences. During the first months of its existence, the list was quickly joined by professional Garland authors Fricke, Coyne Steven Saunders (*Rainbow's End*), and Al DiOrio (*Little Girl Lost*), and several producers of Garland material, such as Feltenstein and Scott Schecter (editor of the US Garland fanzine, *Garlands for Judy*, and publicity consultant for Pioneer's DVD releases of the Garland TV series in 1999). At once biographers and unabashed fans, these specialists represent what I will stress is a crucial interaction between reading and writing the text of Garland's stardom, so their authority tends to dominate the list's contents, particularly when it comes to debating how—or if—her life and career cohere in a legible and transcendent personality. In writing to the list, that is to say, non-professional Garland fans similarly tend to put themselves in the position of producing while consuming an authoritative star image, which has sometimes resulted in heated conflicts and testy public exchanges between the professional and amateur authorities. One poster from San Diego, who as we shall see can always be counted on to generate controversy, claimed this agenda as an important aspect of his fandom when he wrote in 1998:

> One of my goals for the Judy List is to come up with a "politically" correct view of talking about Judy's life, troubles, and attitudes. The "politically" correct point of view may or may not be all the facts. However, it would reflect what most people think is the best "spin" to put on Judy for the enhancement of her legend in the future. As we know, anyone can be made to look good or bad. We have the challenge to be fair and respect Judy's talent and life. I don't believe the truth will ever hurt Judy's legacy. However, errors in stories and false reports could be destructive.
>
> (Judy List daily digest, February 2, 1998)

What's so striking about this post—and exemplary for the list's discussions as a whole—is the writer's self-consciousness of fandom as an interested reading of Garland, one motivated by both ambivalence toward and respect for the authenticating status of facts. In this poster's mind, Garland fans must take an active role in the continual reconstitution of her star text, correcting the dominant readings promoted by the various media and accepted by the general public as "factual." By the same token, the terms for enhancing Judy's legacy from a " 'politically' correct point of view" are not identified, but that is not surprising. For as this goal plays itself out in the correspondence on the listserve, such a viewpoint has to obscure how the position from which fans read with or against dominant readings responds to the market value of Garland product for mainstream audiences, so their readings also reveal their own strong investment in commodity culture as the index of a "politically correct" normativity.

This is well illustrated by the list's major debates about Garland's status as a gay icon. The topic was initially raised as a question by a female graduate student in October 1996, and it resulted in a relatively sympathetic discussion. The list manager cited identification with Garland's "always-evident emotion and indestructible talent," and alluded to her camp, saying, "Judy always came across as a FUN person, and what self-respecting gay man doesn't like to have fun?? <grin>" (October 11, 1996). Another poster referred to the artistic stereotype of gay men and then historicized it: "Particularly in the fifties and sixties when Judy was alive, who had the time to develop a cult? Very young people without jobs and families and gays who weren't going in that direction" (October 15, 1996). My post, in which I talked about the resistance to gender norms in her film persona (October 13, 1996), led someone else to read *Life* magazine's 1954 photo coverage of Garland on the set of *A Star is Born* in contrast with all the other photos in the issue that feature "women as objects used to advertise TVs and other products." Garland, he commented, comes off as "a powerful, action oriented, hard driving person, doing her best to make the movie terrific." "In a sense," he speculated, "maybe she was blacklisted because she wouldn't be a docile, deferential lady" (October 28, 1996). This was followed by someone writing in detail about Dyer's book, "a very good explanation of why Judy appeals to gay men" (December 8, 1996). After someone else announced that he had put up on his own website Vito Russo's explanation of the gay Garland cult (October 13, 1996), another poster offered to share a piece he had written about Garland's gay fan following for the *Washington Blade* (December 26, 1996). This initial conversation, which ran on and off for several months, was clearly dominated by agreement that Garland was and continues to be a gay icon. The writers not only were cognizant that their understandings of her star value amounted to a gay reading, but they were well aware, too, of its mediation by academic and journalistic readings, which they incorporated into their own accounts.

The topic of Garland's gay following came up again in March 1997. That poster from San Diego began by announcing, after watching the Denmark TV interview sent to him by a collector: "Contrary to what people say, I believe the last six months of Judy's life were very happy." Then, almost without skipping a beat, this poster added: "In regards to a question about gays being attracted to her concerts, she went almost berserk with anger." After saying more about that, he reasoned:

> In real life, Judy was good friends with many gay people. Thus, I think she was more upset for her fans than she was for herself. Now, I don't think Judy's fans are upset about the association to gays. Of course, I never did or never will believe that a majority of her fans are gay. Nevertheless, the perception persists and is probably true to some extent. In the recent movie "American Presidents" [*My Fellow Americans*], they have a gay parade that features men dressed as Dorothy. How do people feel about this? Do you think it helps or hurts Judy's legacy?
>
> (March 14, 1997)

How to interpret this question was immediately addressed by a twenty something self-proclaimed straight man on the staff of a large Midwestern university. "Well, I don't think it helps Judy's legacy, that's for sure." After decrying the appropriation of Garland's image by gay pride, he then stated that, if straight people were confronted by that sight in real life, "They might never want to buy a Judy Garland CD or watch *The Wizard of Oz* again. Judy would not have wanted that, and it's not a good thing for us either." Citing the need to increase the Garland audience in order "to see more Garland material released by the CD and video companies," he continued, "I also feel, since Judy herself did not target her work to a specifically gay audience, it isn't compromising her image to let that association quietly fade away into non-existence" (March 15, 1997). In a follow-up post, he clarified his point:

> I don't think it's good for Judy Garland fandom to be perceived as a "gay thing" by the general public . . . See, you have to think about the other side. If the straight

guy down the street thinks he's buying into a homosexual-oriented fetish by pur-
chasing a Judy Garland CD, he's going to be a lot less likely to buy one. And that's
a pretty critical issue. I'm somewhat of an exception to that—if someone wants to
raise their eyebrows at me 'cause I like Judy Garland, let 'em. But an awfully [sic]
lot of my heterosexual cohorts would not feel that way. To them it would make
the difference between buying one of her CDs and not buying it. "I don't want
anyone to think I am gay" is a powerful incentive, folks. To be honest, it is even
for me (to a limited extent), although that's not going to stop me from being a
Garland fan, or from having gay friends if I want to.

(March 16, 1997)

Both posters were in essence repeating what they had written before in the previous discussion of Garland's strong association with gay fandom, when their remarks had gone
without much comment, but by this time the list membership was larger and more diverse
in its demographics—and the list erupted in a heated debate. However, at this point,
because inflammatory posts were being returned for self-censorship, the discussion did
not try to address the homophobia of the two threads, except obliquely (one poster
staged a mock outing) and symptomatically (by the lack of personal revelation). Most
of the respondents accepted the recontextualization of the "gay thing" in what appeared
to be the more pressing question of merchandising Garland to a mainstream audience.
To be sure, the list manager was still quick to point out "that easily 50% on this list
are [gay]—certainly a greater proportion than in the general population" (March 15,
1997). Others wrote to applaud that reminder, and to explain, in some thoughtful detail,
"how this 'Judy myth' is part of our collective culture—it's not something we gay folks
have been, for lack of a better term, 'flaunting'" (March 16, 1997). But more interesting at this point was how the discussion now generated, from both men and women,
so many cautious, contradictory disavowals of homophobic panic about Garland fandom, and how that anxiety became embedded in a need to identify their fandom with
mainstream culture, as if they could reclaim Garland's mass appeal from the 1940s. On
one hand, this controversy was resolved by everyone agreeing that "not everyone likes
Judy, just people with good taste; gay, straight, whatever" (March 18, 1997). On the
other hand, it was punctuated by daily posts from the chair of the internet fan club's
welcoming committee, telling list members how they could order the A&E biography
in advance of its March 27 cablecast.

The mounting excitement about the biography at the time this second debate
occurred clearly resulted from expectations that the show would be presenting two hours
of film and TV clips featuring Garland, some possibly never seen before. But it was also
due to hopes that the program, scheduled at a special time on a Sunday evening when
television viewing is at its highest, would provide a means of reconnecting Garland fandom to mass culture. Enthusiasm about the biography was so high that it seemed almost
like the handiwork of a Hollywood screenwriter when a system crash silenced the Judy
List for 72 hours that weekend, unexpectedly deferring the discussion that had been
anticipated for several weeks, in some large part around the gay issue.

Immediately after the cablecast, Fricke posted his promised behind the scenes commentary, disclosing a disagreement with coproducer Peter Jones over how to end the
biography, whether it would feature the tragic or triumphant Judy. His intention, Fricke
confided, was always to tell "the story of Judy Garland [as] that of a woman who came
back from oblivion three major times: 1951, 1961, and since her death." In other words,

he wanted to give evidence "of the impact Judy has had over the last three decades." At the last minute, Jones, seemingly in conjunction with A&E, presented Fricke with a "fait accompli scripted final act comprising a horrifically negative, downbeat ending." A compromise was reached, as Fricke argued "the finale back from negative to reflective" (March 23, 1997).

The list's discussion was subsequently structured by Fricke's commentary and authorial role. Posters debated the biography's concentration on the life over the work, attacked or defended the treatment of Garland's drug use, and raised the "gay thing" again by complaining about the program's outing of her father Frank Gumm, second husband Vincente Minnelli, and ex-son-in-law Peter Allen, since they are not alive to "defend themselves," and since it invoked that gay orientation of Garland's star text, also acknowledged by the program with its account of her gay following. A contract dancer's reference to Minnelli's "green eyeshadows, purple lipsticks and a tam," as illustration of why no one at the studio ever expected him to marry anyone, particularly rankled. Fricke vigorously defended these revelations, writing:

> The statements we included about Vincente were used as such because—while all the MGM associates were free in discussing it off-camera (remind me in Grand Rapids to quote a little Ann Miller for you!)—that generation doesn't have the contemporary "take" on gay or bisexual lifestyles—i.e. the casualness of admission that is certainly more prevalent today. It WAS important to include in the show if only to demonstrate that, once again, Judy's life (like anyone else's) was NOT black and white—and that, although virtually every other book and commentary "blames" HER for the failure of that marriage, the difficulties and problems certainly did NOT all stem from her.
>
> (March 27, 1997)

Fricke's friend Al DiOrio responded similarly, outing Garland's fourth husband, Mark Herron, for good measure (March 29, 1997). Fallout from the documentary was almost as immediate beyond the confines of the list too. Originally scheduled as a star attraction at the upcoming annual Judy Garland Festival held in her birthplace, Grand Rapids, Minnesota, to which he refers, Fricke was summarily uninvited because "the Luft family was unhappy with [him] (purportedly over the A&E 'Biography' comments about Frank Gumm and Vincente Minnelli)," and had delivered an "'either Fricke or us' ultimatum" to the Festival director (May 23, 1997).

The ambiguity resulting from the documentary's divided viewpoint—not only over *which* biographical narrative to tell but also how to situate Garland's legendary talent in the light of a contemporary musical audience (so that her final comeback in the A&E biography was now not her funeral, as in the DataBase, but her lasting hold on fans), and what to make of the lingering gay connection in both the life and the fans—all of this ultimately worked against normalizing Garland through her life story. That became perfectly clear in two long, detailed and quite extraordinary posts two weeks after the biography special aired.

Both posts reopened the problem of how to negotiate the star text in view of the biographical personality and its inescapable intimations of cultural marginality. One writer, a friend of Mark Herron, professed his longtime admiration of Garland's unique talent but added, "I have always regarded her with an objective, critical eye." For several pages he then stressed the point that he had "been interested and quite disturbed by the reaction to the discussion of Judy's drug addiction in the biography special—since it *was* about her life, and she was a drug addict, totally "responsible for her addiction"— and added that, contrary to that previous post about her being "happy," the last interview in Denmark showed the full extent of her decline. As the final means of authorizing this position, the poster signed his name, adding, "and I am an alcoholic" (April 5, 1997). The next night another long post appeared, arguing against this viewpoint. Citing his authority as a clinical therapist, this writer diagnosed Garland as "probably cyclothymic with depressive features. In layperson's terms, she cycled rapidly between up periods and down periods . . . there was more to Judy's drug use than someone that wants to get a rush or a high. This was someone who wanted to try to feel normal, happy, and productive . . . and was unable to do so herself because of a PRE-EXIST-ING emotional disorder" (April 6, 1997). And he ended with the inscription of a diva snap. From either perspective, the Garland star text remains queer in the sense that it is still resistant to normalization, and as that diva snap suggests, the gay issue brings to the surface the inability of fans to identify with mainstream culture through their fascination with "Judy."

While list contributors did not immediately return to the "gay thing" once the debate about the A&E biography died down, in early 1998 equally contentious discussions began again over issues that feature comparably in Dyer's reading of Garland: the medical or cultural transgressiveness implied by her unstable body; a new Garland revue in New York City featuring a drag impersonator in the star part; and a show sensationalizing her life in E! Entertainment's series, "Hollywood Scandals and Mysteries," which apparently disregarded any efforts on the part of biographers Fricke and Steve Saunders to correct errors. The docudrama, in fact, hired list-member Beverly Shields, a professional female Garland imitator, to play the aged star, complete with death scene on the toilet. So much accusation and blame were aimed at Shields for participating in the project that she eventually unsubscribed from the list, not with a diva snap, but not with a whimper either.

These moments of heated debate in the history of the Judy List should not give the impression that the "gay thing" is a continual preoccupation of writers, for it is not. Daily posts focus more on collecting and hunting down Garland music and videos, recounting reminiscences or anecdotal information, proposing what should be included in the multi-CD that Capitol Records was once planning or who should play Garland on TV or in the movies, posting reviews of books, reporting news of impending DVD releases, recounting personal feelings about Garland, analyzing the source of her appeal or her beauty, polling for her worst costume or hair style, and so on. Inevitably, though, such threads can often turn into discussions about the relation of Garland's biography to her stage or screen persona, the need to promote her to a mainstream audience, and the constitution of her fan following. These issues are ultimately related, symptomatically brought together for the list in resistance to the dominant reading of Garland as a gay icon.

Old and new friends of Dorothy: historicizing Garland fandom

On the day of the biography's cablecast, a female college student, who had complained more than once about her marginal status as a Garland fan among her friends and family, wrote:

Now I know it's old but I want to put my point of view in on the gay thing. For one thing not all gays like Judy. My cousin and best friend Robert is not a fan of hers. And I didn't even know that she was considered a gay icon until this summer. My cousin's cousin on his side of the family is gay, and Rob, me, and his cousin Tom and Tom's husband Gary were at Six Flags in Texas. And they kept talking about Dorothy and *The Wizard of Oz*. Finally I asked why? And they said that most gay men think of Dorothy going over the rainbow into Oz is like gay men coming out of the closet. And I kind of can see their point. So I think it's OK. Like I said, just because you like Judy doesn't automatically mean you're labeled GAY. My ex-boyfriend Chris liked Judy, but then again we think he might be. That's another story.

(March 23, 1997)

The Judy List illustrates how Garland's perceived gay following still structures her star text as an account of her post-MGM stardom, although it's not the same old story from the 1950s and 1960s, responsive to her historically shifting value as a Hollywood commodity that interrupts her fans' relation to mainstream culture. As that young female poster herself exemplifies, moreover, there is indeed yet another story to Garland fandom. A second young female fan wrote in 1999 that she became "Judy crazy" following the telecasting of *The Wizard of Oz* in 1997, after which she spent the entire day watching a Garland birthday tribute on Turner Classic Movies—"and if it had not been for my mother stopping me I would have seen every one of them. I love Judy," she went on, "but my mother is against it. She knows all about the gay men that Judy was with and all the pills and drinks and she doesn't want me to have anything to do with Judy. But I can't just stop lovin' the only person I give a damn about" (March 9, 1999).

Female fans such as these two have traditionally been absent in accounts of Garland's star text, but they seem equally attracted to its marginalizing stance toward mainstream culture, and they are beginning to make their presence evident on the internet, too. A strong, somewhat iconoclastic identification of female fans with Garland is evident in their profiles on the DataBase's defunct Internet Fan Club, in their comments in the DataBase's guestbook, in their effusive testimonials on the memorial wall of another site, "The Judy Garland Photographic Page," and in the increasing number of web pages hosted by young women, such as "Fans 4 Judy," "Mitali's Judy Garland Page," and "Judy Garland: Forever Beautiful," with its all-female "Judy Guardians." Adolescent female fans, like the second one quoted above, discover Garland through the annual showings of *The Wizard of Oz* and encounter the legend only after a connection is forged with Dorothy's nonconformist longing to go over the rainbow. While omnipresent in the internet fan club in 1997 these fans rarely wrote to the Judy List then, if indeed they subscribed to it in any sizeable number. When they did post they were most often placed in an unacknowledged subordinate relation to the male fans who, writing with greater regularity and in more detail, and with more defensiveness about their relation to mainstream culture as Garland fans, dominated the terms of discussion. With the list's gender gap closing, the more active participation of female posters has made more evident how the multiple formations comprising Garland fandom do not overlap but in fact compete with each other in the claims fans make for the authenticity of their own interested readings—readings that are themselves historically situated as articulations of cultural marginality.

The greater heterogeneity of list membership helps to explain why the most recent eruption of controversy in March 1999 shifted the ground of discussion about Garland's being a gay icon, reflecting more of an emergent awareness on the part of some fans of their generational differences from the dominant readings that still surround her star text. The discussion began when a woman wrote to complain about Michael Musto's campy foreword to *Rainbow: A Star Studded Tribute to Judy Garland*, a collection of excerpted publicity, fan magazine, and "serious" journalistic pieces. Noting that Musto's contribution "is not written as a fan so much as a critic," this poster complained about its "Judy-on-the brink" view of the star as both "gay icon" and "tragic chanteuse," asking the list, "Do you use those terms? . . . I don't know about you, but I have NEVER been drawn to her by the drama of her personal life and its effect on her performances" (March 1, 1999). A few days later she elaborated: "I have no problem with Judy's status in the gay community . . . That isn't what bothered me. My question was how many true fans, when discussing Judy, actually use the term 'gay icon' . . . or for that matter 'tragic chanteuse'? Don't you think that perpetuates an image which many in the crowd use as an excuse NOT to explore her talent?" (March 4, 1999, second ellipsis in original).

Aside from the expected explanations of why Garland's status as a gay icon is "pretty inarguable" (March 2, 1999), the discussion that followed generated lengthy, often multiple responses from every segment of the list membership, and it centered upon finding alternate terms for locating her appeal (her talent, her sexiness, her humor, her vulnerability, her delivery of raw, naked emotion). Some respondents made a point of disentangling the "gay icon" label from its cultural embeddedness in "tragic chanteuse." This thread, in turn, led some posters—straight and gay, male and female—to deny that their fascination with the star was related to their sexual orientation at all. But the debate also prompted a number of passionate recollections about how fans first became intensely fascinated with the star (most frequently, but not always, through *Oz*). For all the fans' discomfort with, as one writer put it, "the idea that something about themselves could conceivably have anything to do with something gay" (March 2, 1999), what emerged quite noticeably from these various reflections, which drew upon public myths and critical texts as much as personal narratives, was a greater acknowledgment of the historical dimension of the dominant reading that they contested as well as an articulation of the generational differences among fans themselves, many of them new converts to what the list calls "Judy-ism."

A more self-conscious generational awareness was in evidence among younger gay listmembers, several of whom wrote to the list simultaneously. One writer agreed that "a Garland performance appealed to—in fact, filled a chasm for repressed gay men," but asked: "what about after Stonewall?" In particular, he was rejecting the argument advanced by D. A. Miller in *Place for Us*, namely, "that musicals provided an outlet that subconsciously united all gay men (a thesis that can roughly be transposed to Judy Garland)." For the image that Miller presents "of a 13-year-old boy just coming to terms with his sexuality, crying while mouthing the words to the Carnegie Hall concert in his basement . . . seems completely outdated . . . [it] doesn't seem applicable any more" (March 9, 1999). Another fan agreed, remarking, "it seems to be more of an older generational thing, though there are many [fans] in my generation (early 30s) and younger" (March 9, 1999). A third fan was even more specific:

To the vast majority of gay men in their twenties—and to those now coming out in their teens—Judy Garland is little more than the actress who played Dorothy . . . This is not to deny the inexplicable force she played in the gay psyche during the 50s, 60s, and 70s—just that sometime during the 80s it began to diminish.

Perhaps this is a natural balancing: Judy's heterosexual female following will become more present (it's always been there) and her gay male following will become less so (although it will never disappear), and Judy herself will be more and more recognized for her talent and not for her pathos.

(March 9, 1999)

Trying to come to terms with Garland fandom as it has shifted historically and generationally, these writers bring out what, in his account of the transformation of gay camp during the past fifty years, Daniel Harris has more explicitly argued: "the fact that our love for performers like Judy Garland was actually a learned behavior," "part of our socialization as homosexuals" (Harris 1997: 21). Gay fandom, he comments, "was an emphatic political assertion of ethnic camaraderie, as was the gay sensibility itself, which did not emanate from some sort of deeply embedded homosexual 'soul,' but arose as a way of achieving a collective subcultural identity" (17). Regarding the cult forming around Garland concerts in the fifties and sixties, Harris sees it as a means of achieving community and visibility for her gay fans, concluding, "they liked, not her, so much as her audience" (18).

Harris dismisses the value of Garland herself as the object of intense emotional and increasingly public investment by gay fans, but her significance for them was clearly more complex than he appreciates. Indeed, when placed in conjunction with Dyer's analysis of Garland's appeal to a "gay sensibility," what Harris has to say elsewhere in his book about pre-Stonewall gay fascination with film stars does suggest why the Garland cult was not separable from its object. In a homophobic society that required the invisibility of gay men and defined homosexuality as inverted or compromised masculinity, Garland's star text encouraged strong gay readings because of its potentiality for what Harris refers to as "the aestheticism of maladjustment" (10): that is, fans inhabited a social identity that defined their own "in-between" relation to mainstream culture by transforming it into an identification with marginality as a performance of style, one embodied in the Garland image of difference within normality. As one listmember recalled, after seeing *A Star is Born* in the 1950s, "for the next 3 days, I walked in a haze (which I now realize had a lot to do not only with the stunning display of talent, but with a force and a sense of style I was trying to cultivate in myself)" (March 9, 1999).

The thrust of this return to "the gay thing" on the list was to historicize Garland's gay star text, but most fans nonetheless understood the discussion as evidence of her inherent and timeless appeal to "ALL KINDS of people" (March 6, 1999), "a cross-section of humanity" (March 9, 1999). As in the earlier debates, these posters then tried to close the discussion by concluding that Garland fandom was simply a result of "good taste"—without ever appreciating how "good taste" itself had once supplied a major set of class codes for pre-Stonewall gay men. These fans articulated their historical difference from older generations as a purer appreciation of Garland's transcendent talent, as if there were now no textual mediation of Garland herself, the writers' own commentaries notwithstanding. Writers of both genders and of varying ages, for instance, testified with great passion that being a fan provided them with a principle of continuity for their identity: "Judy Garland has always been a part of my life" (March 10, 1999),

"I have thought about her everyday" (March 10, 1999), "she seemed to fill the void" (March 11, 1999), "she was a constant in my life" (March 13, 1999), "my day is never complete without a dash of Judy" (March 13, 1999). These claims personalize their dedication to Garland, while articulating how, in anchoring their sense of private continuity, their fandom reinscribes the marginalized cultural identity it seemingly assuages. Although each debate about Garland's gay following on the Judy List pushed the controversy in different directions, taken together they highlight the instability of her star text to sustain a coherent, unified meaning historically. The Garland star text, as Dyer wrote of an older generation of gay fans, still speaks of a special relation to ordinariness, but the inflection of this queer signification, what fans take it to refer to in their own lives, has shifted considerably so that it now connotes more than a "gay sensibility." While the anxiety about Garland's gay associations, which galvanizes the list's members into these debates, obviously raises a strong homophobic reaction to the inference that their own fandom may be tinged with gayness, it has increasingly opened up a fault line in the list's discourse that registers as much discomfort with the culturally marginal status of their fan community. Disagreements about Garland and the "gay thing" thus respond to the non-normativity that her star text still signifies, but now recontextualized in the commodity culture of contemporary fans. The need to normalize their dedication is then made most evident when fans read Garland in a way that authenticates both her legacy as a show business legend and the relation of their fandom to the mainstream consumer culture where they find their identities and upon which they depend for her ongoing commodification so as to ensure that she remains a constancy in their lives as product, completing the void they otherwise feel. As one grateful poster exclaimed, when concluding his account of becoming a fan, "I can't believe that I can put Judy on ANYTIME I want to" (March 10, 1999).

Collecting Garland products may secure the star's stability as a continuing source of pleasure, but it in no way guarantees the meanings or emotions attributed to the merchandise and memorabilia that appear to objectify her stardom. Consequently, as each eruption of controversy over her gay associations stresses the instability of Garland's star text, the Judy List also records fans' efforts to normalize both that text and their fandom along the same lines as the DataBase. However, in contrast with monologic fan pages such as the DataBase, which can fix a certain meaning for Garland through their archival concentration on one aspect of her career, the dialogic nature of the listserve—a site dedicated to arguing about her significance—foregrounds the lack of consensus, ideologically and generationally, that makes a star text like hers continually volatile, perhaps even more so now than during her lifetime, when fans did not have an opportunity for such interaction on a daily basis. At the same time that posters insist upon viewing the list itself as a private space, a safe haven from the non-understanding general public, debating Garland's star text in this forum places their fandom, which they understand in deeply personal terms, in a social setting. The public sphere of Garland fandom is continually implied by the intertextual frameworks of criticism, biographies, and media promotion that writers incorporate into their commentaries. For that matter, because of its electronic circulation and presence on the Web in a complete archival record available for anyone to read, the listserve itself makes the public sphere a requisite of membership in the fan community. In the face of their different readings of Garland, the most devoted fans are then compelled to defend the terms by which her star text is made legible for them: continually reinterpreting the relation of her life and her work, repudiating the dominant reading of her gay associations kept in circulation by the media, reconciling the clashing variants of fan formations.

With the marginality of their fandom disturbing their identification with mainstream consumer culture, listmembers' attempts to stabilize a new alternate reading and to authenticate it in "fact" often end up appealing outside fandom to unsympathetic corporate interests as their means of accounting for and redressing the cultural displacement they experience because of their devotion to Garland. The more they concentrate her star text in the value of Garland products as their means of revising the significance of her stardom, the more uneasily these posters have to confront what John Fiske refers to as "the contradictory functions performed by cultural commodities which on the one hand serve the economic interests of the industry and on the other the cultural interests of the fans" (1992: 47). As the debates occurring before and after the A&E biography make especially clear, many Garland fans project an imagined entertainment industry that also has some presumed investment in normalizing her stardom while embracing all possible readings of it, even though in their manufacturing and marketing of Garland products—home videos, CDs, biographies—that industry seems perfectly aware of her audience's marginality despite its increased diversity. Those same fans are just as quick to blame industrial exploitation for Garland's personal troubles *and* for the motives of those, profiting from her work and life today, who keep that dominant reading in place as the "preferred" one. The contradictory premise of this new alternate reading articulates fans' ambivalence toward the consumer culture that fails to appreciate Garland, and it accounts for the privileged status on the list of authors like Fricke and others; as fans and biographers, they are at once inside and outside the Garland industry, producers and consumers of it. This contradiction keeps debates on the list ongoing, reiterating how the Garland star text is just that for fans—an unstable text that continually needs to be read on a daily basis, just like the Judy List itself: "Well so it goes . . .," mused one poster after supplying his fan-is-born narrative, "the dialogue continues . . . and we still love JG! To be continued . . ." (March 9, 1999, ellipsis in original).

References

Bronski, M. (1984) *Culture Clash: The Making of Gay Sensibility*, Boston: South End Press.

Dyer, R. (1986) *Heavenly Bodies: Film Stars and Society*, New York: St. Martin's Press.

Fiske, J. (1992) "The Cultural Economy of Fandom," in L. A. Lewis, ed., *The Adoring Audience: Fan Culture and Popular Media*, London: Routledge, 30–49.

Fricke, J. (1992) *Judy Garland: World's Greatest Entertainer*, New York: Henry Holt.

Harris, D. (1997) *The Rise and Fall of Gay Culture*, New York: Ballantine.

Jennings, W. (1991) "The Star as Cult Icon: Judy Garland," in J. Telotte, ed., *The Cult Experience: Beyond All Reason*, Austin: University of Texas Press, 90–101.

Miller, D. (1998) *Place for Us: Essay on the Broadway Musical*, Cambridge, MA: Harvard University Press.

"Production notes" (1994) *Ziegfeld Follies* (1946) CAV laser-disc box set, MGM–UA home video.

Sampey, K. (1998) "Judy Garland Remains a Big Star on the Web," June 25, 1998, Associated Press, www.Technoserver.com/newsroom, downloaded September 23, 1999.

Shipman, D. (1992) *Judy Garland: The Secret Life of an American Legend*, New York: Hyperion.

Staiger, J. (1992) *Interpreting Films: Studies in the Historical Reception of American Cinema*, Princeton: Princeton University Press.

That's Entertainment III: Behind the Screen (1994) supplement to *That's Entertainment III* deluxe collector's edition, laser-disc box set, MGM–UA home video.

Tinkcom, M. (1996) "Working Like a Homosexual: Camp Visual Values and the Labor of Gay Subjects in the MGM Freed Unit," *Cinema Journal* 35 (2): 24–42.
Vare, E. (1998) *Rainbow: A Star-Studded Tribute to Judy Garland*, New York: Boulevard Books.

Web pages cited (working as of October 12, 1999)

"*A Star Is Born*," http://www.nobby.de/e_mstar.htm.
"An *A Star Is Born* Walkthrough," http://homel.swipnet.se/~w-18501/Bilder/Star/ sib.htm.
"Beverly Shields' tribute to Judy Garland," http://www.flash.net/~nthrjudy.
"Class act," http://www.zianet.com/jjohnson/classact.htm.
"David de Alba's encounters with the legendary Judy Garland," http://www.ctaz. com/~pryner/ jg-enc.htm.
"Fans 4 Judy," http://homepages.go.com/homepages/f/aln/fans4judy.
"Jennifer's Judy Garland page," http://bigsun.wbs.net/homepages/e/s/t/esthersmith.
"Judy Garland club," http://www.btinternet.com/~judyin.london/judyclub.htm.
"Judy Garland DataBase," http://www.zianet.com/jjohnson/contents.htm.
"Judy Garland forever beautiful," http://www.angelfire.com/ri/JudyGarland/index.html.
"Judy Garland media storage," http://members.xoom.com/garland/index.html.
"Judy Garland page," http://users.aol.com/robotb9/private/garland.htm.
"Judy Garland page," http://mitglied.tripod.de/ChristianEckel/Judy_Garland_Seite.htm.
"Judy Garland photographic tribute," http://www.zianet.com/chrisb.
"Judy Garland photos and collectibles," http://www.geocities.com/Broadway/ Balcony/1220.
"Judy Garland reading room," http://www.netins.net/showcase/reading/garland. html.
"Judy Garland showcase," http://wwwjgarland.com.
"Judy Garland trivia page," http://homepages.go.com/homepages/j/d/y/jdygrlnd.
"Judy Garland web ring homepage," http://members.tripod.comljudyring.
"Judy Garland!" http://www.geocities.coml~ppicking/judy.html.
"Judy Garland," http://members.xoom.com/gethappy55.
"Judy Garland: the live performances!" http://users.deltacomm.com/rainbowz.
"Judy in London," http://www.btinternet.com/~judyin.london/judyill.htm.
"Judy list web site," http://wwwjudylist.com.
"Judy lovers homepage," http://www.geocities.comlHollywoodlLot/6502.
"Judy room," http://homepages.go.com/~ozianscott/index.html.
"Judy!" http://members.aol.corn/LizMontFan/Judy.html.
"Megan Kiddie's Judy Garland tribute," http://judygarland.virtualave.net.
"MIDI sing along songbook," http://www.bol.netloverseerS/midisongbook.html.
"Miss show business," http://www.users.bigpond.com/paultassone/jgindex.HTM.
"Mitali's Judy Garland page," http://www.angelfire.com/ny/swingmrcharlie.
"Tribute to one of the world's greatest," http://www.geocities.com/Vienna/Studio/ 7416.
"Young Judy Garland site," http://www.tn.co.za/casale/Jootes.htm.

7   Jackie Chan and the black connection

Gina Marchetti

In his writings on postmodernism, Fredric Jameson is fond of quoting "China," a work by San Francisco based poet Bob Perelman. Jameson describes the creation of the disjointed poem that he uses as an example of the schizophrenic nature of the postmodern condition as follows:

> In the present case, the represented object is not really China after all: what happened was that Perelman came across a book of photographs in a stationery store in Chinatown, a book whose captions and characters obviously remained dead letters (or should one say material signifiers?) to him. The sentences of the poem are *his* captions to those pictures. Their referents are other images, another text, and the "unity" of the poem is not *in* the text at all but outside it in the bound unity of an absent book.[1]

Jameson's encounter with this poem, Perelman's encounter with these photographs in Chinatown, and the present absences, the contradictory feelings of sense and nonsense, totality and fragmentation, unitary address and schizophrenic multiplicity, that both these encounters conjure up parallel the way in which Jackie Chan has been encountered by scholars, fans, and myriad other viewers globally. Jackie Chan seems to be a "material signifier" that may or may not be a "dead letter" to particular viewers. Just as Perelman's "China" represents his own fantasy based on pictures that have other captions in Chinese, Chan seems to represent a "China" that cannot be "translated." Both the Chinese text and the images themselves remain unavailable to those who encounter the poem, and Chan, in his multiple significations and existence as pure image, may be in this same postmodern cultural condition.

I would like to dedicate this chapter to my mother, Frances Marchetti, who passed away while I was writing it. I would also like to acknowledge my African-American Jow Ga kung fu Si-Heng Chris Henderson, Howard Bryant, Tai Brighthaupt, Howard Davis, and Ronald Wheeler, and thank them for their patience and dedication to the martial arts.

1 Fredric Jameson, "Postmodernism and Consumer Society," in Hal Foster, ed., *The Anti-Aesthetic: Essays on Postmodern Culture* (Port Townsend, WA: Bay Press, 1983), 123. This poem is quoted in its entirety by Jameson in "Postmodernism and Consumer Society" (121–122) and again in its entirety in a slightly different context in Fredric Jameson, *Postmodernism, or, The Cultural Logic of Late Capitalism* (Durham, NC: Duke University Press, 1991), 28–29. The poem was originally published in *Primer* (Berkeley: This Press, 1978).

In the essay "Global Bodies/Postnationalities: Charles Johnson's Consumer Culture,"[2] Bill Brown analyzes a 1983 short story by Charles Johnson also called "China." In this story, a middle-aged African-American postal worker living in Seattle discovers martial arts by going to see a Hong Kong movie and, inspired, subsequently joins a kung fu school, much to his wife's chagrin. In the essay, Brown looks at Johnson's protagonist's attraction to Chinese culture through kung fu and martial arts movies within the context of the American black community. Specifically, Brown traces the connection between African-Americans in the military and the rise in interest in Japanese/Okinawan/Korean martial arts after World War II and the Korean War. He further notes the political connections forged between the civil rights movement and the movement against the war in Vietnam that connected those domestic groups to international solidarity work involving the emergence of Third World interests extending beyond Vietnam to China, Latin America, and Africa. Brown continues to trace these connections in popular culture with the rise of the Hong Kong kung fu film in the black community, reaching its apogee with the phenomenal success of Bruce Lee in the early 1970s.

When Johnson published "China" in 1983, what had been called the "kung fu craze" had quieted. However, the appeal of Hong Kong films in the black community continued. As inner city theaters closed, the African-American audience moved to Chinatown cinemas, and, as these closed, the audience continued to rent or purchase legal and pirated Hong Kong martial arts fare on videocassette.[3] By far the biggest star of the Hong Kong martial arts cinema at that time was Jackie Chan. Chan's visibility in the black community throughout the 1980s and into the 1990s is undeniable. Chan's recognition of his appeal to blacks is also evident. The effacement of this connection with the growth of Chan's popularity outside the African-American community and black viewership worldwide seems noteworthy. Like Perelman's book of photos, blackness serves as a present absence that structures Chan's films.

In the current phase of Chan's career that has catapulted him to stardom in Hollywood, Chan continues to appropriate black culture and use it in his films. Four of his recent films involve Africa, the African diaspora, and/or African-American issues: *Rumble in the Bronx* (1995, recut and released in the United States in 1996), *Mr. Nice Guy* (1997), *Who Am I?* (1998), and *Rush Hour* (1998). In order to attempt to understand Chan's black connection, these films need to be analyzed in relation to transnational consumer culture, postmodernism, postcolonialism, and questions of identity. Chan's relationship to black issues and viewers needs to be addressed, as well

2 Bill Brown, "Global Bodies/Postnationalities: Charles Johnson's Consumer Culture," *Representations* 58 (Spring 1997), 24–48. Charles Johnson, "China" (1983) in *The Sorcerer's Apprentice: Tales and Conjurations* (New York: 1987), 61–95.

3 Described by Frances Gateward in "Wong Fei Hong in Da House: Hong Kong Martial Arts Films and Hip Hop Culture," paper presented at Year 2000 and Beyond: History, Technology and Future of Transnational Chinese Film and TV—The Second International Conference on Chinese Cinema, Hong Kong Baptist University, April 20, 2000. Also, this has been my own personal observation of the American Cinema (Chinese owned and operated theater in L'Enfant Plaza in Washington, DC) as well as of the theaters that operated on the North Side in Chicago during the 1980s and New York City's Chinatown theaters during the same period. The clientele at that time was predominantly Chinese, but with a significant percentage of African-American and a lesser percentage of Hispanic and white viewers. I am also familiar with small grocers and merchants in the DC African-American community offering Shaw Brothers and Golden Harvest martial arts films for sale (sometimes under the counter along with X-rated videos).

as the continuing importance of black culture in films that have crossed over into mainstream theaters with very different audiences.

> *"We live on the third world from the sun. Number three. Nobody tells us what to do."*
> Bob Perelman, "China"

In his autobiography, Jackie Chan writes: "The other day, one of my favorite singers, Lionel Richie, came to visit me on the set. Yesterday, Michael Jackson gave me a call."[4] Although Chan includes his encounters with Richie and Jackson as proof of his making it in Hollywood, he says nothing explicitly about the influence of African-American culture in his films or the loyalty of his black fans in his autobiography beyond references to a few black actors (most notably Chris Tucker). His vision of Hollywood, and the American Dream it seems to encapsulate for him, is decidedly white:

> I had long watched American films with envy, wishing I had the budgets and resources they boasted with every frame; I'd danced along with Fred Astaire, hummed to Frank Sinatra and Julie Andrews, laughed at Chaplin and Keaton and Lloyd, the great comics of the silent classics.[5]

Even if he does not acknowledge his black fans in his autobiography and critics who relish the joy of discovery also ignore them, their presence is felt in Chan's films, in his casting choices, locations, themes, and working techniques.

The involvement of the black audience with Hong Kong martial arts films predates Jackie Chan and heralds the rise of Bruce Lee. As Hollywood underwent substantial change owing to the Paramount Decree, television, changing audience demographics, and other factors, and lost its grip on its domestic and international market, the commercial cinemas of the Third World strengthened in India, Mexico, Egypt, and Hong Kong as well as other countries. Italy's spaghetti Westerns and Hong Kong martial arts films, for example, filled the gap in Hollywood's B-movie production.

Always transnational,[6] Hong Kong productions began to cross over from Chinatown cinemas to other "ghetto" theaters. In the case of the United States, Hong Kong provided a cheap product in the form of dubbed martial arts films to inner city cinemas trying to cut costs and develop a new clientele as television and the suburbanization of America eroded the downtown white or racially mixed audience of an earlier generation. In his essay, "The Kung Fu Craze: Hong Kong Cinema's First American Reception," David Desser points out the appeal of the genre to the black audience:

> Outside of the blaxploitation genre it largely replaced, kung fu films offered the only nonwhite heroes, men and women, to audiences alienated by mainstream film and often by mainstream culture. This was the genre of the underdog, the underdog of color, often fighting against colonialist enemies, white culture, or

---

4 Jackie Chan, *I Am Jackie Chan: My Life in Action*, with Jeff Yang (New York: Ballantine, 1999), 336.
5 Ibid., 253.
6 See Sheldon Lu, "Historical Introduction: Chinese Cinemas (1896–1996) and Transnational Film Studies," in Sheldon Hsiao-peng Lu, ed., *Transnational Chinese Cinemas: Identity, Nationhood, Gender* (Honolulu: University of Hawaii Press, 1997), 1–31.

the Japanese. The lone, often unarmed combatant fighting a foe with greater economic clout who represented the status quo provides an obvious but nonetheless real connection between kung fu films and black audiences.[7]

The success of films like the dubbed version of *Five Fingers of Death* (1973) transformed not only American popular cinema but Hong Kong cinema as well. The international co-production *Enter the Dragon* (1973) went on to establish what remains the generic baseline to this day. Directed by Hollywood action veteran Robert Clouse,[8] produced and distributed by Warner Bros. and Golden Harvest, the film co-stars Asian-American/Hong Kong star Bruce Lee, ersatz James Bond John Saxon, and African-American martial artist Jim Kelly. The leading role was split three ways to draw in as much of the international action audience as possible from Hong Kong to black America.

Kelly plays Williams, a former soldier who runs a karate academy in the black community. When he arrives in Hong Kong, he verbalizes an immediate solidarity with the impoverished Chinese. Seeing the floating slums in the harbor, he remarks, "ghettoes are the same everywhere; they stink." This moment establishes an immediate link between audiences in Hong Kong and the black ghetto, and it creates an imaginative solidarity that continues to be exploited in action films. For example, this scene is echoed in *Lethal Weapon IV* (1998) when Danny Glover emotionally notes the connection between illegal Chinese immigrants being smuggled in on a boat and the Middle Passage endured by his African ancestors.[9]

Everyone involved in *Enter the Dragon* recognized the importance of Lee's connection to the American martial arts subculture and the crucial import of the popularity of martial arts and Hong Kong film in the black community. Lee knew America well after spending years in the States as a college student, kung fu instructor and competitor, and television personality. He admired black athletes like Mohammed Ali and had several famous black students, most notably Kareem Abdul Jabbar, who fought with his instructor in Lee's last film, *Game of Death* (1978) (Fig. 7.1).

Jackie Chan certainly knew what Lee knew. Chan worked as a stuntman on two productions with Lee, *Fists of Fury* (aka *The Big Boss*, 1972) (Fig. 7.2) and *Enter the Dragon* (1973), so Chan knew firsthand Lee's formula. Like Lee, Chan refers to black culture in many of his films. In *Police Story* (1985), for example, Chan mimics Michael Jackson's moon-walking in order to get some dog manure off his shoes. In *City Hunter* (1992), Chan break dances and quotes Bruce Lee's fight with Kareem Abdul Jabbar from *Game of Death*. In *Armour of God* (1986), Chan confronts a line of black women martial artists dressed in black leather bustiers, high heels, and black silk stockings, and coiffed with fluffy "Afro" naturals. Chan solidifies his ties to the martial arts subculture and

7 David Desser, "The Kung Fu Craze: Hong Kong Cinema's First American Reception," in Poshek Fu and David Desser, eds, *The Cinema of Hong Kong: History, Arts, Identity* (New York: Cambridge University Press, 2000), 38.
8 Clouse has written about his experiences making the film in Robert Clouse, *The Making of Enter the Dragon* (Burbank: Unique, 1987). Clouse also went on to make *Black Belt Jones* (1974), a film that attempted again to exploit the connections between blaxploitation and the kung fu film. David Desser describes the role Warner Bros. played in marketing both blaxploitation and Hong Kong martial arts films in his essay, "The Kung Fu Craze."
9 This scene was eloquently described by Gayle Wald, "Same Difference: Reading Racial Masculinity in Recent Hong Kong/Hollywood Hybrids," Society for Cinema Studies Conference, Chicago, IL, March 10, 2000.

Figure 7.1 Bruce Lee in *Game of Death* (Golden Harvest/Paragon 1978). Courtesy of the Kobal Collection

to the American black community by including African-American kung fu practitioner Marcia Chisholm[10] and karate champion Linda Denley[11] in this transnational production.[12]

> *"It's always time to leave."*
>
> Bob Perelman, "China"

Although it appeared new to mainstream American audiences when it opened in 1996, *Rumble in the Bronx* represents a fantasy that has played well in Hong Kong film

---

10 Marcia Chisholm was trained by Dennis Brown, one of the foremost promoters of Chinese martial arts in the Metro Washington, DC, area, known nationally for his annual tournament, the Capitol Classics. According to Master Brown, Marcia Chisholm was and still is a black belt with his school. Email correspondence dated June 13, 2000.

11 Bey Logan, *Hong Kong Action Cinema* (Woodstock, NY: Overlook Press, 1995), 73.

12 Although Chan had worked in the US previously, *Armour of God* represents his first major foray into international location shooting with himself at the helm as director. Shot primarily in Yugoslavia with Europeans in black face to represent African natives, the film is perhaps best known for nearly occasioning Chan's premature death from a blow to the head during a stunt gone wrong.

Figure 7.2 Fists of Fury aka *The Big Boss* (NGP 1972). Courtesy of the Kobal Collection

for decades. As a colony, Hong Kong has been populated by successive generations of immigrants from China or from other places within the diaspora. Jackie Chan's family, for example, came to Hong Kong from Shandong in Mainland China, leaving some family members behind, moved to Australia to work, and maintained connections with Hong Kong through their son Jackie, who could not adjust to life abroad. For most Hong Kong viewers (and many Asian viewers who were not ethnic Chinese), these stories of immigration, economic struggle in a foreign land, racism and brotherhood in an unfamiliar environment struck a responsive chord. Likely, many in the black audience, who also had an intimate understanding of racism, colonialism, and diaspora, could feel that same connection to these narratives.

Given this environment, it is not surprising that Chan sets so many of his films in places other than Hong Kong. In fact, Chan follows the route laid down by the British Empire and the Commonwealth for many within the Chinese diaspora.[13] Of course, scores within the African diaspora know this route or similar ones from the periphery to the center as well. The movement in all these films is from Asia (the Third World) to the West (First World). In *Rumble*, Chan moves from Hong Kong to the Bronx

13 On the relationship between the Chinese diaspora and the legacy of European colonialism in Asia, see Lynn Pan, *Sons of the Yellow Emperor: A History of the Chinese Diaspora* (New York: Kodansha International, 1994).

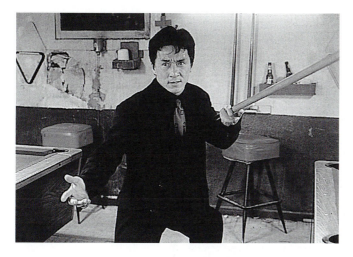

Figure 7.3 Jackie Chan in *Rush Hour* (New Line Cinema 1998). Courtesy of the Kobal Collection

(obviously Canada with the mountains of British Columbia looming in the background of several shots standing in for New York City). *Mr. Nice Guy* takes place in Melbourne, Australia. *Who Am I?* moves from South Africa to Holland, following a Dutch Afrikaner connection, with the jungles of Malaysia (former British colony and one of Chan's and the Hong Kong industry's favorite locations with a roughly 35 percent ethnic Chinese population) opening the film. *Rush Hour* (Fig. 7.3) finally delivers Chan to America, and Chan symbolically clings to the United States by hanging on to a Hollywood sign. Chan travels the globe with a purpose, choosing locations where English is spoken, production costs are low, and labor is available. From Vancouver to Melbourne to Johannesburg to Los Angeles, Chan, in his recent films, has worked in locations that would be considered possible sites of relocation for his Hong Kong Chinese audience or familiar places of residence for those in the black diaspora.

"The train takes you where it goes."

Bob Perelman, "China"

In 1992, four white policemen captured on videotape beating a black man, Rodney King, were freed. Violence broke out in Los Angeles, destroying several Asian-owned businesses in the black community. In *Immigrant Acts: On Asian American Cultural Politics,* Lisa Lowe describes the media depiction of these events as follows:

> The dominant U.S. media construction of the Korean Americans in the L.A. crisis has generally reduced and obscured them as "middle men" within U.S. race and class relations, situating them in an intermediary position within capitalist development and suggesting they are more threatened by Blacks than by corporate capitalism.[14]

14 Lisa Lowe, *Immigrant Acts: On Asian American Cultural Politics* (Durham, NC: Duke University Press, 1996), 93–94.

In *Margins and Mainstreams: Asians in American History and Culture*, Gary Okihiro poses the question, "Is Yellow Black or White?"[15] In fact, there is a long history of Asians serving as "buffers" or "middlemen" between blacks and whites in American and in many colonial situations globally. The Chinese grocer, for example, has played this role in both rural and urban America, and Third World Newreel's documentary *Mississippi Triangle* has explored the triangular nature of race relations in the American South by focusing on several Chinese groceries in the Mississippi Delta.[16] The documentary shows a range of attitudes and feelings among the various communities, from identification across racial lines, kinship, and close relations to misunderstanding, bigotry, and suspicion.

Rumble in the Bronx takes up this feeling of kinship as well as ambivalence. Even the dare-devil Chan would not actually go to the South Bronx to make his film: "I'm no stranger to taking risks, but making a movie on location in the Bronx seemed crazy even to me."[17] The film fashions a vision of the American ghetto that allows for the violent destruction of the Asian grocer as well as the solidification of cross-ethnic affiliations, multicultural understandings, and interracial contact. It flatters the global Asian middle class while not forgetting its debt to the black community frustrated with ghetto life.

Rodney King and the Los Angeles uprising also figure as a present absence in *Rush Hour*. Lee (Jackie Chan), the inspector from Hong Kong, and Carter (Chris Tucker), a police officer in Los Angeles, both have an ambivalent relationship to the American justice system and its relationship to people of color. Obliquely referring to Rodney King and the numerous other instances of black abuse at the hands of the LAPD, Tucker/Carter quips, "This is the LAPD—we're the most hated cops in the free world. My own Mama's ashamed of me. She tells everybody I'm a drug dealer."

Acting as Lee's (and, implicitly, the white viewer's) guide to the black community in Los Angeles, Carter serves as an ambassador of ill will at the outset. In fact, Carter initially appears to be a bigot.[18] He calls Lee a "Chunking cop" and "Mr. Rice A Roni," and he has an argument with a Chinese carryout vender about his "greasy food." When he meets up with the principal Chinese villain at the film's climax, he says, "I've been looking for your sweet and sour chicken ass." The tensions between the Asian and black communities are palpable throughout the film.

"I'd rather the stars didn't describe us to each other; I'd rather we do it for ourselves."
Bob Perelman, "China"

15 Gary Okihiro, *Margins and Mainstreams: Asians in American History and Culture* (Seattle: University of Washington Press, 1994).
16 See my essay "Ethnicity, the Cinema, and Cultural Studies," in Lester Friedman, ed., *Unspeakable Images: Ethnicity and the American Cinema* (Urbana: University of Illinois Press, 1991), 277–307. For more on the Mississippi Chinese, see James W. Loewen, *The Mississippi Chinese: Between Black and White* (Prospect Heights, IL: Waveland Press, 1971).
17 Chan, *I Am Jackie Chan*, 332.
18 Carter is also presented as being sexist. He makes several smutty remarks to his colleague, Johnson (Elizabeth Pena), about her underwear and her sexual reputation. However, she never quite manages to get her own back in the same way as Lee.

Figure 7.4 Enter the Dragon (Concord/Warner Bros 1978). Courtesy of the Kobal Collection

Although an uneasy alliance, the experience of the ghetto links the Chinese with the black community.[19] In *The Star Raft: China's Encounter with Africa*, Philip Snow notes a Chinese exchange student's reaction to Harlem: "It was wrong to criticize them [*hei ren*; literally "black people"], as some people did, for thronging together in ghettoes. She could understand their need to live in poor areas: she was poor herself."[20] Stuart Kaminsky has described Bruce Lee as a "ghetto figure"[21] and described kung fu films as "ghetto myths."[22] In *Kung Fu: Cinema of Vengeance*,[23] Verina Glaessner also talks about the ghetto roots of the genre in the poverty, crime, and social unrest of Hong Kong in the 1960s. The portrait of the Bronx presented in *Rumble* offers nothing in the way of verisimilitude; however, it does offer a certain understanding of the ghetto that seems to strike a responsive chord across races and cultures.

As far as Chan moved away from Bruce Lee and the "ghetto myth," it is interesting that *Rumble in the Bronx* should bring him back full circle with a vehicle that shows a remarkable similarity to *The Way of the Dragon* (1972, aka *The Return of the Dragon*), a film that Lee made before his breakthrough international co-production *Enter the Dragon* (Fig. 7.4), but released worldwide after the latter film proved successful.

"Folks straggling along vast stretches of concrete, heading into the plane."

Bob Perelman, "China"

19 Other scholars have added other things, including religion, spirituality, family obligation, and a constant struggle for survival to this list. See Gateward, "Wong Fei Hong in Da House."
20 Philip Snow, *The Star Raft: China's Encounter with Africa* (Ithaca, NY: Cornell University Press, 1988), 211.
21 Stuart M. Kaminsky in Thomas R. Atkins, ed., *Graphic Violence on the Screen* (New York: Simon and Schuster, 1976), 59.
22 Attributed to Kaminsky by Peggy Chiao in Chiao Hsiung-Ping, "Bruce Lee: His Influence on the Evolution of the Kung Fu Genre," *Journal of Popular Film and Television* 9 (1) (1981), 30–42.
23 In Verina Glaessner, *Kung Fu: Cinema of Vengeance* (London: Lorrimer, 1974).

Rumble's resemblance to this Lee vehicle (one which Lee also directed and wrote) is uncanny. Like *Return*, *Rumble* begins with its protagonist arriving at the airport. In both films, the protagonist is immediately coded as a bumbling foreigner who goes to the West to help with a business problem. These businesses represent Chinese outposts in the wild and violent West, where the Chinese must accommodate themselves to an alien and threatening environment. In both films, flamboyant street thugs (multiracial and multiethnic armed gangs) and avaricious capitalists in well-tailored suits harass the Chinese entrepreneurs. Chan and Lee function to preserve the Chinese presence in the West, while maintaining their own intention to return to Hong Kong.

However, while Lee offers up stylishly dressed black antagonists as part of the Roman milieu in *Return*, Chan actually sets his film in the Bronx and creates out of snippets of Toronto and Vancouver a vision of martial arts multiculturalism in a ghetto environment. Mick LaSalle, a critic for the *San Francisco Chronicle*, asks the following question about the choice of location for *Rumble*:

> American discomfort about racial issues puts a squeeze on the film. Keung fights a white street gang in the Bronx, but in the real Bronx a white street gang would have long ago moved to the suburbs. "Rumble" throws Chan into the middle of an unrecognizable, cartoonlike version of America, then makes him look silly by forcing him to take it all too seriously . . . If they wanted neither to film in the Bronx or to tell a real Bronx story, why bother setting the story there?[24]

The answer to this question seems clear. The Bronx provides an imaginative meeting ground for an audience composed of nervous Hong Kong residents, African-Americans, and those within the Asian diaspora. *Rumble* attempts to revive and revitalize Lee's ghetto myth in the aftermath of Rodney King and the Los Angeles crisis.

"The landscape is motorized."

Bob Perelman, "China"

The skyline of New York City punctuates the film, and the Statue of Liberty appears with the World Trade Center towers as the physical emblems of America. The twin promises of freedom and material prosperity through a capitalist market economy thematically frame the film's rather disjointed narrative. New York represents the ideological extremes of a global economy out of control in a way that few other locations do.

As Keung moves from the impressive prosperity of Manhattan to the poverty of the Bronx, *Rumble* continues to rely on internationally known icons. *Fort Apache, the Bronx* (1981) made the South Bronx a global symbol of the crisis of the American inner city, of racial and ethnic tensions, and of the decay of the American Dream. *Rumble* relies on these expectations to play with what the ghetto signifies as well as what ghetto fantasies can promise.

When Keung arrives at his uncle's market in the Bronx, he learns that Uncle Bill (Bill Tung) is literally trying to whitewash the place to prepare to fleece the new buyer, Elaine (Anita Mui). Bill attempts to put his best foot forward, but it is abundantly clear why he wants out of the ghetto as the graffiti reappear and various gangs come in for protection money, shoplifting, and general vandalism.

---

24 Mick LaSalle, "Film Review—Chan Takes a Fall in 'Rumble': Weak Film Might Lose Potential U.S. Viewers," *San Francisco Chronicle*, February 23, 1996.

"Bridges among water."

Bob Perelman, "China"

However, just as the viewer may begin to think Bill is a bigot, a counter-discourse emerges. Bill makes a point of reminding Keung that a white thug killed his father.[25] The grocery functions as a multiracial enterprise. It has a white female cashier, African-American stock clerk, black and white painters, as well as the Asian management. Also, Bill's fiancée, Whitney (Carrie Cain-Sparks), is African-American.

As the wedding of Bill and Whitney symbolizes the marriage of blacks and Asians, *Rumble* carefully creates an image of the ghetto as a place of multiracial and multicultural possibility. Although comedy takes the edge off any uneasiness created by the interracial marriage, Bill and Whitney's wedding devotes screen time to a celebration of black and Asian solidarity. Carrie Cain-Sparks sings a soul-inspired song written by Tim Dang and Nathan Wang, "You Are the One," with black female back-up singers, as she walks down the aisle as Whitney to marry Bill. Later in the sequence, she performs a comic duet in Cantonese with Bill.

Bill and Whitney's interracial marriage points to a significant change from Lee's *Return of the Dragon*. In *Return*, the emphasis was on maintaining a Chinese presence in a hostile environment. *Rumble*, on the other hand, attempts the Chinese facilitation of a transformation of the ghetto into a multiracial and multiethnic community. Clearly, this fantasy has an appeal outside Asian viewership, acknowledging the importance of racial harmony above nationalism, and nodding in the direction of the black audience.

"The sun rises also."

Bob Perelman, "China"

For those who comment on the lack of verisimilitude in the film, the depiction of the gang ranks with the Canadian landscape as one of the most absurd elements in the film. However, Keung's relationship with Tony and his gang provides the structure for the preponderance of the action sequences in *Rumble* and the location of Keung's power over his ghetto environment. Although the reviewer for the *San Francisco Chronicle* misrepresented the gang as entirely white, the gang's leader, Tony (Marc Akerstream), and main henchman, Angelo (Garvin Cross), are white. Indeed, Angelo's bleached white hair and the whiteness of the tattooed buttock emphasize his whiteness as he exposes his rear for Keung to kiss in one of their confrontations.[26] Other members of the gang are Chinese, Hispanic (indicated by the "que pasa" in the New Line version), black, and, possibly, Native American (indicated by buckskin and hairstyle). The importance of the multiculturalism of the gang to Chan's renewed ghetto myth cannot be overemphasized.

Keung embodies all sides of the contradictions that form the foundation of ghetto culture. Like Rodney King, he is a man of color victimized by violent whites. As an Asian storekeeper, he represents the "model minority" victimized by mob violence. Clearly, Chan could not symbolically embody this contradiction if the gang members were black.

---

25 This information is left out of the re-dubbed version distributed by New Line.

26 This again harkens back to *Return of the Dragon* in which Chuck Norris's whiteness as Colt, the fighter for hire, is emphasized in the fight he has with Lee in the Roman Colosseum when he takes off his shirt to reveal a hairy chest that proves his undoing when Lee rips the hair off his chest and blows it into the wind with a look of disgust during the battle.

He would move from representing a ghetto myth to acting as a possible locus of racist sentiment. Keung becomes part of the spectacle of violence against Asians in the American ghetto and survives to show that the "dregs" of American society (who very often, demographically, form the bulk of Chan's young American fans) can be redeemed and drawn into a Greater Chinese[27] vision of solidarity that may even enlighten those outside the Chinese community.

In his essay, "Jackie Chan and the Cultural Dynamics of Global Entertainment," Steve Fore describes Chan's heroic posture as follows:

> In keeping with fundamental principles of the martial arts tradition, he is never the aggressor; he fights in defense of his body, in defense of the social community of which he is a member, and, frequently, in order to demonstrate the superiority of his community's value structure; and (unlike U.S. movie action heroes) he never gloats over a fallen opponent, and may even offer the opponent an opportunity to redeem himself by acceding to the values of Chan's community.[28]

Fore goes on to describe the end to Keung's climactic fight with Tony and his gang. Keung lectures the gang in English (in the New Line version): "Why lower yourself? Don't you know you're the scum of the earth?" Switching to Cantonese to express himself, Keung continues: "I hope the next time that we meet we won't be fighting each other. Instead we'll be drinking tea together."

The switch to Chinese is significant. Keung offers a positive sign of "Chineseness" in the allusion to the social ritual of tea drinking to the primarily non-Chinese gang members. Like martial arts films over the decades, *Rumble* proffers what is marked as a particularly Chinese path to survival in a hostile environment. If, as Jim Kelley said in *Enter the Dragon*, "ghettoes are the same everywhere," Keung supplies a remedy from a different ghetto (i.e., the slums of Hong Kong) and a different ghetto culture.

"Everyone enjoyed the explosions."

Bob Perelman, "China"

Jackie Chan's starring vehicles in the 1980s and 1990s devote considerable screen time to the destruction of property.[29] The captain in *Rush Hour* seems to speak on behalf of

---

27 There has been a great deal of controversy in recent years surrounding a constellation of related issues involving Chinese identity in the diaspora, global Chinese ethnic ties, Confucianism, and so-called Asian values. Many of these positions have been put forward by Tu Wei-Ming and can be found outlined in his anthology, *The Living Tree: The Changing Meaning of Being Chinese Today* (Stanford: Stanford University Press, 1994). The concept of "Greater China" has a certain validity; however, when coupled with a resurgence of Confucianism linked with capitalism it takes on a more questionable aspect.

28 Steve Fore, "Jackie Chan and the Cultural Dynamics of Global Entertainment," in Sheldon Hsiao-peng Lu, ed., *Transitional Chinese Cinemas: Identity, Nationhood, Gender* (Honolulu: University of Hawaii Press, 1997), 255.

29 I have discussed elsewhere the relationship between working-class film and television fantasy and spectacles of destruction. See Marchetti, "Class, Ideology and Commercial Television: An Analysis of *The A-Team*," in Ian Angus and Sut Jhally, eds, *Cultural Politics in Contemporary America* (New York: Routledge, 1989), 182–197. For more on class and the action genre, see Chuck Kleinhans, "Class in Action," in David E. James and Rock Berg, eds, *The Hidden Foundation: Cinema and the Question of Class* (Minneapolis: University of Minnesota Press, 1996), 240–263.

action filmmakers generally when he remarks, "Every once in a while we've got to let the general public know we can still blow shit up."

Rumble in the Bronx offers this fantasy of destruction of commodities to its viewers. When Keung trashes Tony's hideout, he uses the purloined commodities against the gang, stuffing one hoodlum into a refrigerator, crowning another with a television, and manipulating overstuffed chairs, shopping carts, and skis as weapons. A running joke throughout the film involves the destruction of Elaine's market and its contents and the lessening of her will to make it rich with a ghetto enterprise. The store is trashed five times in the narrative. A sign at the entrance saying, "Thank you and come again," hangs ironically over the scenes of destruction and rebuilding.

However, tensions surrounding the positioning of various classes in relation to consumerism and commodities threaten to split the film's viewership. The potential divisions between small business and the working classes and the poor heal quickly with the introduction of White Tiger (Kris Lord). As in many action adventure plots, the principal villain provides a fantasy of capitalism out of control. His riches come from horrific exploitation, violence against the poor and laborers, a disdain for and manipulation of the justice system pointing to the ineffectiveness of police and the government, and a ruthless ability to crush his competition. He establishes himself as a racial threat to multicultural harmony initially through the destruction of his black contacts and their purple Cadillac. White Tiger represents a male, white, bourgeois establishment that immediately alienates virtually all members of the audience, and the villains in *Mr. Nice Guy*, *Who Am I?*, and *Rush Hour* are virtually identical to him.

> *"A sister who points to the sky at least once a decade is a good sister."*
>
> Bob Perelman, "China"

In addition to the white, male, bourgeois villain, Chan's films also feature African-American and Hispanic/Latina women. Even when most of Chan's opponents are white and his possible love interests generally Asian, Chan manages to include black and Hispanic women in his casts. Sexy opponents as in *Armour of God* or comedic local color as in *Rumble in the Bronx*, these women generally take up a marginal role in the narrative that becomes a central role of potential identification with the fiction for black fans.

Mr. Nice Guy's Lakeisha (Karen McLymont) provides a case in point. Primarily through her name and accent, Lakeisha appears to be African-American. However, the whys and wherefores of how an African-American woman ended up in Melbourne, Australia, as an assistant to a Chinese cook (Jackie, played by Jackie Chan) on television remain obscure. She is a black presence in the film, but her history is completely absent. Along with Jackie's Chinese girlfriend, Miki (Miki Lee), and a white Australian female news reporter, Diana (Gabrielle Fitzpatrick), Lakeisha forms part of a multiracial female chorus around Jackie.

On the periphery of the central action of the plot, Lakeisha mainly functions as a physical presence, a thin, colorfully dressed, stylish black woman. She provides an entry into the action for black viewers, and, because of her gender, decorative qualities, and marginality within the narrative, she does not threaten the rest of the audience in any way.

> *"Run in front of your shadow."*
>
> Bob Perelman, "China"

The presence of the black female martial arts adept, like *Mr. Nice Guy*'s Lakeisha, puts into play a tension involving questions of racial, gender, and sexual identity in Chan's films. Critics have been divided over whether Chan (and the Hong Kong action genre generally) embodies a remasculinization of castrated, marginalized, colonial/postcolonial subjects or whether he represents a postfeminist androgyny that transcends traditional gender binaries. Yvonne Tasker has commented: "Chan's 'softness' does not consist in a lack of muscularity or an inability to fight, but more in a refusal either to take the male body too seriously or to play the part of Oriental other."[30] Mark Gallagher notes: "Chan's films rely on comic treatments of escape and flight, feminizing his characters while reinscribing his antagonists as caricatures of 'serious masculinity.' "[31] Kwai-Cheung Lo notes this dialectic in play between the representation of Chan in the narrative and in the concluding credit sequences featuring outtakes: "Significantly, it is precisely the outtakes of the flubbed stunts that create the myth of Jackie Chan. Portrayed as a comedian, a common man in the films, Chan becomes a superhero in his outtakes."[32]

The fact that Chan fights along with/against women of color in these films links race and gender together as part of a single problematic. Like black women fighters, the "soft" Chan can represent those doubly marginalized because of their bodies demanding justice through physical action. In contrast to the women fighters, the "hard" Chan symbolizes a dominant masculinity that takes on mythic proportions extratextually through press on his mastery of stunt work.

Lakeisha's presence in *Mr. Nice Guy* also conjures up intertextual associations that may create additional meaning and/or pleasure for some viewers. As the stylish proponent of martial arts, Lakeisha seems to be cast in a mold similar to the blaxploitation heroines of a previous era. Her appearance calls up associations with *Cleopatra Jones* (1973) and *Coffy* (1973), and she alludes to a nostalgia for the Hong Kong martial arts film's twin genre of blaxploitation and female action stars like Pam Grier.

"Pick up the right things."

Bob Perelman, "China"

In "Postmodernism and Consumer Society," Jameson links the "nostalgia film" and "pastiche" as characteristics of postmodernism. A master of both pastiche and nostalgia, Chan self-consciously refers to Hollywood films from all eras in his oeuvre, ranging from Indiana Jones in *Armour of God* (I and II) to the Frank Capra remake of *Pocketful of Miracles/Lady for a Day* in *Mr. Canton and Lady Rose* (1989) and the borrowing from Jean-Claude Van Damme's *Double Impact* in *Twin Dragons* (1992) as well as his more famous re-creations of Lloyd and Keaton stunts in *Project A* (1983) and *Project A: Part II* (1987). Ramie Tateishi has discussed Jackie Chan's oeuvre in relation to pastiche in his essay, "Jackie Chan and the Re-invention of Tradition."[33] It seems useful to expand

30 Yvonne Tasker, "Fists of Fury: Discourses of Race and Masculinity in the Martial Arts Cinema," in Harry Stecopoulos and Michael Uebel, eds, *Race and the Subject of Masculinities* (Durham, NC: Duke University Press, 1997), 334.
31 Mark Gallagher, "Masculinity in Translation: Jackie Chan's Transcultural Star Text," *The Velvet Light Trap* 39 (Spring 1997), 29.
32 Kwai-Cheung Lo, "Muscles and Subjectivity: A Short History of the Masculine Body in Hong Kong Popular Culture," *Camera Obscura* 39 (September 1996), 117.
33 Ramie Tateishi, "Jackie Chan and the Re-invention of Tradition," *Asian Cinema* 10 (1) (Fall 1998), 78–84.

on Tateishi's observations and look at Chan's recent work in relation to postmodern aesthetics.[34]

Rumble in the Bronx, *Mr. Nice Guy*, *Who Am I?*, and *Rush Hour* all rely on the pastiche characteristic of the nostalgia film for their aesthetic foundations. As Jameson points out, the nostalgia film does not invoke a sense of an authentic historical moment that may conjure up memories of the past for those who actually lived through that history. Rather, as the postmodern aesthetic announces the "end of history," the nostalgia film relies on knowledge of past styles and mediated images from the mass consumer culture of previous eras to evoke a sense of nostalgia for films, television shows, and the popular culture of the past. Pastiche involves a "blank parody" that relies on direct quotations, literal recreations, and simulations of past media experiences that make no attempt to satirize or offer a political commentary on the earlier historical moment and its relationship to the present.

The invocation of *Return of the Dragon* in *Rumble in the Bronx* has already been discussed, but it is worth noting further that *Rumble* conjures up the kung fu and blaxploitation films of the early 1970s in even more direct ways. In the marketing of *Rumble in the Bronx*, for example, New Line took advantage of the nostalgia for the 1970s circulating within the cinema at that time, most notably through the revival of 1970s style with Afro hairdos, platform shoes, and polyester in Tarantino's *Pulp Fiction* (1994). Kung fu in a ghetto setting seemed to call out for the 1975 funk/disco hit by Carl Douglas, "Kung Fu Fighting," and this song was featured in trailers for the film (even though it is not on the film's soundtrack). Technically, the film also conjures up memories of the earlier Hong Kong martial arts imports through its dubbing.

Similarly, *Rush Hour* is riddled with references to earlier African-American culture. Carter is first introduced in the film dressed as an urban dandy with a black leather coat, earrings, and conspicuous jewelry, driving a sporty black Stingray that seems to complement his outfit. Images of Shaft and Superfly immediately come to mind. Moreover, the coupling of Tucker with Chan recalls the Eddie Murphy/Nick Nolte vehicle *48 Hours* (1982) in which Murphy pays homage to Bruce Lee in a Chinatown alley.

Carter and Lee find common ground with another blast from the past, Erwin Starr's "War," a rock and roll/soul/rhythm and blues crossover hit from 1970. Lee and Carter bond, communicate across linguistic, racial, national, and cultural borders, and reconcile their personal differences through this song that calls for an end to war (most directly the American war in Vietnam). Although Lee is presented as ignorant of African-American life, he knows "War" by heart and can enunciate every grunt. Similarly, although Carter pleads ignorance of Chinese culture, he clearly knows Hong Kong well enough through its film exports to remark, "You sound like a karate movie." Their bond solidifies through direct references to the "ghetto myth" of the Hong Kong martial arts film that Chan takes up from Bruce Lee by playing a character surnamed Lee.

It is through the two most globally visible aspects of each other's cultures that Lee and Carter can find common ground. Black music and Chinese kung fu share a common cultural currency that circulates transnationally. The Asian and the African diasporas meet in this scene through a recognition of globally circulated images and sounds in the form of mass-mediated consumer culture. Ironically, the capitalism that the fantasy

34 For a detailed discussion of postmodernism and contemporary Hong Kong cinema, see Evans Chan, "Postmodernism and Hong Kong Cinema," *Postmodern Culture* 10 (1) (May 2000), http://www.muse.jhu.edu/journals/pmc/v010/10.3.html.

angrily rails against becomes the conduit for the building of these bonds based on familiarity with a song and an image from the ghetto culture of the 1970s.

> *"Hey guess what? What? I've learned how to talk. Great."*
>
> Bob Perelman, "China"

Most critics of the international action film have hypothesized that part of the transnational appeal of the genre comes from the fact it relies on physical spectacle rather than dialogue for its appeal. Given this truism, it is interesting to note that all four of the Chan vehicles under consideration here explicitly deal with language, translation, communication and miscommunication within a polyglot environment. Made within the context of colonial Hong Kong and the Chinese diaspora, the multilingual nature of the films should come as no surprise. They map the frustrations of translations, mistranslations, mispronunciations, and malapropisms that even the most fluent speakers of second and third languages encounter outside their native tongues.

Because of Chris Tucker's background as a verbal comic, *Rush Hour* offers some particularly telling instances of the use and abuse of language. *Rush Hour* was marketed with the following taglines: "The fastest hands in the East meets the biggest mouth in the West," and, "They come from different cultures. But on a case this big, they speak the same language."[35]

The film is book-ended by two pieces of comic repartee. When Carter confronts Lee about hiding his ability to speak English, Lee retorts, "Not being able to speak is not the same as not speaking. You seem as if you like to talk. I like to let people talk who like to talk. It makes it easier to find out how full of shit they are." Carter remains confused, "What the hell did you just say?" At the end of the film, on their way to Hong Kong, Carter surprises Lee with a few words of Mandarin to the stewardess. Solidifying their bond, Lee moves immediately into black argot, "We can hang in my crib—I'll show you my 'hood.'" Lee's command of African-American slang has advanced considerably from an earlier scene in which he gets into a fight with a large bartender when, following Carter's lead, he says with a grin and a pronounced Chinese accent, "What's up, my nigger?" This naïve use of this racial slur also highlights Lee's own crisis of identity in America. Neither black nor white, he represents a vacuum of signification that exists at the center of many of his other starring vehicles.

> *"Don't forget what your hat and shoes will look like when you are nowhere to be found."*
>
> Bob Perelman, "China"

Made a few months after the return of Hong Kong to Chinese sovereignty, *Who Am I?* uses its amnesiac hero, Jackie/Whoami, as a walking symbol of this postmodern, postcolonial crisis of identity. When Jackie goes to a South African hilltop and screams out over the vast and uncaring landscape, "Who am I?," it has a particular resonance for Chan's Hong Kong audience facing the uncertainty of their new identity under the sovereignty of the People's Republic.[36] In "Muscles and Subjectivity: A Short History

---

35 Quoted in the *Internet Movie Database*, http://us.imdb.com/Taglines?0120812.
36 Sheldon Lu, "Hong Kong Diaspora Film: From Exile to Wrong Love to Flexible Citizenship and Transnationalism," paper presented at Year 2000 and Beyond: History, Technology and Future of Transnational Chinese Film and TV—The Second International Conference on Chinese Cinema, Hong Kong Baptist University, April 19, 2000.

of the Masculine Body in Hong Kong Popular Culture," Kwai-Cheung Lo examines the bodies of Hong Kong martial arts stars like Jackie Chan as bodies that "occupy an empty space without any positive content or intrinsic meaning, and their void can only subsequently be filled through the specificity of their particular historical milieu. What they indicate is only the impossibility of fixed definition."[37] In *Who Am I?*, blackness is used as a way to explore this identity crisis. In light of Chan's career-long links to the black community, it seems fitting that he ends up in Africa in this search for identity. In fact, at the end of the film, Jackie returns to the African village that gave birth to "Whoami" to search for his "roots."

Who Am I?'s narrative revolves around power dynamics involving the First and the Third World. In this case, Chan's character is involved in the same racial construct that exists in *Rumble*. As an Asian, he serves as a racial middleman within multinational relations between the East and the West, Africa and Europe. His personal identity crisis parallels the uneasy geopolitical relations that characterize transnational capitalism. Jackie mediates between the "primitive" world of the black African village and the sophisticated, cosmopolitan cities of Johannesburg and Rotterdam. He moves from the skin shacks of the dry African plains to the postmodern glass edifice of one of Europe's most architecturally daring buildings. He wears the feathers and paint of his adopted African village, dances in their communal rituals, and is mistaken for an African "native" on more than one occasion in the film. However, he also commands computer screens, mobile phones, and state-of-the-art racecars.

Armed in his travels with a fist full of passports and an impressive understanding of sophisticated technical equipment, Jackie presents an action fantasy version of what Aihwa Ong has termed "flexible citizenship," a term she uses to refer to "the strategies and effects of mobile managers, technocrats, and professionals seeking to both circumvent *and* benefit from different nation-state regimes by selecting different sites for investments, work, and family relocations."[38] He may not know who he is, but Jackie/Whoami comes out of the Third World able to function in the global arena. He has a consciousness of the poverty, isolation, and marginality of the Third World coupled with a Westernized technical education and ability to roam the globe freely. He represents the contradictions of global capitalism and the new politics of race in a transnational consumer society. However, flexible citizenship puts into question fundamental aspects of identity, and this crisis underlies Chan's screen persona.

> *"You look great in shorts. And the flag looks great too."*
>
> Bob Perelman, "China"

The postmodern emptiness that film critics have noted at the core of the Hong Kong martial hero may be due to the formation of the figure within a global image industry honed by the domination of Hollywood and the cultural imperialism of bourgeois American ideology. Transnational stardom, in many respects, traps Chan. As a conflicted, fragmented, hybrid figure, Chan does not ultimately transcend the powers against which his characters struggle. He is hemmed in by the constraints placed on him as an Asian

---

37 Lo, "Muscles and Subjectivity," 107.
38 Aihwa Ong, *Flexible Citizenship: The Cultural Logics of Transnationality* (Durham, NC: Duke University Press, 1999), 112.

man, and he seems quite conscious of these limitations as he pokes fun at his own vulnerabilities in his films.

Certainly, this does not represent any new understanding of the racial dynamic within bourgeois, colonial ideology. In many respects, his image seems to echo what W. E. B. Du Bois, at the turn of the previous century, termed "double-consciousness." In *The Souls of Black Folk* (1903), Du Bois states:

> ... in a world which yields him no true self-consciousness, but only lets him see himself through the revelation of the other world. It is a peculiar sensation, this double-consciousness, this sense of always looking at one's self through the eyes of others, of measuring one's soul by the tape of a world that looks on in amused contempt and pity. One ever feels his two-ness,—an American, a Negro; two souls, two thoughts, two unreconciled strivings; two warring ideals in one dark body, whose dogged strength alone keeps it from being torn asunder.[39]

In *Black Skin, White Masks*, Frantz Fanon makes strikingly similar observations about this dualism based on his experiences of being black under French colonialism.[40] The way in which Chan operates in his films parallels the fragmentation and self-consciousness described by Du Bois and Fanon.

Sometimes, Chan's characters represent bodily the forces of colonialism. He plays royal Hong Kong police officers and international spies at the service of Western powers. At other times, he appears to be an emblem of authentic "Chineseness," chauvinistically celebrating the superiority of Chinese culture and the power of Chinese kung fu. Chan's body becomes the place where this racial/colonial battle is played out. He can be comic, pathetic, and awkward, but also potent, heroic, and triumphant.

A mercurial, "flexible citizen," Chan plays many roles in his films that acknowledge and sometimes flatter the white norm. Chan can be the bumbling policeman, the clueless tourist, the "F.O.B." ("fresh off the boat") immigrant, and the unsophisticated, parochial bumpkin. He presents a self-deprecating humor, appreciated by the marginalized, that can also make him less threatening to an empowered audience. When in Africa, he champions the Third World. In the West, he finds acceptance as an entrepreneur or technocrat. He slides between Cantonese, Mandarin, and English, and transcends national borders. Blackness acts as a foil to Chan's pallor and as a support for his color in the racial symbolic in which he operates. The ghetto structures his place within Hollywood's global entertainment environment through the twin genres of blaxploitation and kung fu.

Chan exists somewhere between the two notions of ethnicity Stuart Hall describes, in his influential essay "New Ethnicities," as follows:

> What is involved is the splitting of the notion of ethnicity between, on the one hand the dominant notion which connects it to nation and "race" and on the other hand what I think is the beginning of a positive conception of the ethnicity of the

39 W. E. B. Du Bois, *The Souls of Black Folk*, edited by Henry Louis Gates, Jr., and Terri Hume Oliver (New York: Norton, 1999), 11.

40 Frantz Fanon, *Black Skin, White Masks*, translated by Charles Lam Markmann (New York: Grove Press, 1967), 110–111.

margins, of the periphery . . . This precisely is the politics of ethnicity predicated on difference and diversity.[41]

Chan effortlessly accommodates himself to the commercial system by navigating a path between nationalism and what Hall calls "diaspora-ization," "the process of unsettling, recombination, hybridization and 'cut-and-mix.' "[42] This process that Hall describes in relation to black culture forges an inextricable link between Chan and experiences of people of color globally. As a "new ethnic," Chan enacts race and ethnicity in a way that goes beyond the borders of Asia, China, or Hong Kong.

> *"If it tastes good we eat it."*
>
> Bob Perelman, "China"

One of the most important contributions of cultural studies in recent years has been its critique of the relationship between postcolonialism and postmodernism currently debated within critical theory. In *The Post-colonial Studies Reader*, the editors, Bill Ashcroft, Gareth Griffiths, and Helen Tiffin, point out: "The intensification of theoretical interest in the post-colonial has coincided with the rise of postmodernism in Western society and this has led to both confusion and overlap between the two."[43] The schizophrenic decentering of the subject has much in common with W. E. B. Du Bois' notion of "double consciousness" as well as Frantz Fanon's description of "black skin" in "white masks." Jameson's description of nostalgia strongly resembles Fanon's discussion of one of the phases in the process of decolonization in *The Wretched of the Earth*.[44] In their essay, "De Margin and De Centre," Isaac Julien and Kobena Mercer note:

> Ethnicity has emerged as a key issue as various "marginal" practices . . . are becoming de-marginalized at a time when "centred" discourses of cultural authority and legitimation . . . are becoming increasingly de-centred and destabilized, called into question from within. This scenario . . . has of course already been widely discussed in terms of the characteristic aesthetic and political problems of postmodernism. However, it is ironic that while some of the loudest voices offering commentary have announced nothing less than the "end of representation" or the "end of history", the political possibility of the *end of ethnocentrism* has not been seized upon as a suitably exciting topic for description or inquiry.[45]

Many theorists have argued that postmodernism exists exclusively in the West, and that it only has significance in the East/Third World as an instance of cultural imperialism.[46]

41 Stuart Hall, "New Ethnicities," in David Morley and Kuan-Hsing Chen, eds, *Stuart Hall: Critical Dialogues in Cultural Studies* (London: Routledge, 1996), 447.
42 Ibid.
43 Bill Ashcroft, Gareth Griffiths, and Helen Tiffin, eds, *The Post-colonial Studies Reader* (London: Routledge, 1995), 117.
44 Frantz Fanon, *The Wretched of the Earth*, translated by Constance Farrington (New York: Grove, 1963).
45 Isaac Julien and Kobena Mercer, "De Margin and De Centre," in David Morley and Kuan-Hsing Chen, eds, *Stuart Hall: Critical Dialogues in Cultural Studies* (London: Routledge, 1996), 451.
46 This position is summarized in Kuan-Hsing Chen, "Post-Marxism: Between/Beyond Critical Postmodernism," in David Morley and Kuan-Hsing Chen, eds, *Stuart Hall: Critical Dialogues in Cultural Studies* (London: Routledge, 1996), 309–323.

Certainly, just as Perelman's "China" haunts Jameson's essays on postmodernism, issues involving race, colonialism, and imperialism disturb postmodern theory. In so many ways, the postmodern condition mimics the postcolonial condition, although "China," and all that it represents, remains on the edges of this theoretical discourse. In fact, as in the case of Perelman's poem, postmodernist discourse seems to be built on an absence of "China," i.e., the East, the Third World, the postcolonial, the "feminine,"[47] and the racial/ethnic/cultural Other. Although the center of white, bourgeois patriarchy may be vacant, "China" is not present. It remains an absence that shadows the postmodern presence of crisis.[48]

In the films under discussion here, Jackie Chan seems to exemplify that same present absence of race, ethnicity, and nation found in postmodernist theory. He exists at the cusp of the postmodern and the postcolonial, and he can be read as one or the other depending on the circumstances of exhibition and reception.

If examined in this light, the pastiche that characterizes Chan's films can easily be seen in terms of Homi Bhabha's notions of hybridity and mimicry.[49] He can slip effortlessly between imitations of James Bond, Indiana Jones, and other white masters of global order and Michael Jackson's moon walk or Chris Tucker's version of playing the "dozens." He takes on various racial roles as masks; however, no authentic self is promised behind the persona. Chan turns the image of the Asian cook or houseboy on its head as the polished television chef Jackie in *Mr. Nice Guy*, who can change the kitchen utensils that marked a subordinate status in earlier media images into weapons of ethnic empowerment.[50] However, although Chan may turn ethnic and racial stereotypes on their head and he may mimic the white hero, he does so from a position of uncertainty and questionable power. His deracination frees him in many ways, but limits his legitimacy in other ways. He easily shifts form and position, but, ultimately, accommodates himself to the postmodern condition without much critical footing.

> *"The people who taught us to count were being very kind."*
>
> Bob Perelman, "China"

It is at this stage that it is important to take into account Chan's sudden embrace by the mainstream American public with the success of *Rumble*. Despite earlier failures, New Line Cinema felt that the time was right for the commercial exploitation of Chan in the American market, and the company put considerable time and money (in re-editing, re-dubbing and massively advertising *Rumble*) into this endeavor.[51]

---

47 Rey Chow and many others have pointed out that the "Orient" occupies a "feminized" space in Western discourse. See Rey Chow, *Woman and Chinese Modernity: The Politics of Reading between East and West* (Minneapolis: University of Minnesota Press, 1991).

48 The best-known critique of Jameson's conception of the Third World can be found in Aijaz Ahmad, "Jameson's Rhetoric of Otherness and the 'National Allegory,'" *Social Text* 17 (Fall 1987), 3–25. See also Jameson's response and an interview with Jameson by Anders Stephanson in the same issue.

49 Homi K. Bhabha, *The Location of Culture* (London: Routledge, 1994).

50 For some provocative thoughts on the Asian cooks that Chan models himself after in *Mr. Nice Guy*, see Phebe Shih Chao, "Gendered Cooking," *Jump Cut* 42 (December 1998), 19–27.

51 The details of Chan's relationship with New Line are outlined in Fore, "Jackie Chan." Later, Miramax picked up some of Chan's other films.

Rumble takes up a postmodern style that operates on familiarity with and a faux nostalgia for Hong Kong kung fu films and blaxploitation films of the 1970s. Tarantino had already revived these genres in films like *Pulp Fiction*, and audiences were primed for films with disjointed narratives, opaque characters, pastiches of earlier formulae, spectacular violence, and vague references to ethnic, racial, and cultural alterity displacing the centrality of white, bourgeois males. *Rumble* struck a responsive chord in a cost-effective manner, and *Rush Hour* followed suit as a low-budget Hollywood vehicle for Chan. Video and limited theatrical release also brought in cash in white middle-class communities for *Mr. Nice Guy*, *Who Am I?*, and several other Chan vehicles produced by Golden Harvest and picked up for US distribution.

The use of "blackness" as a signifier in each of these vehicles enhances their marketability across various audiences, including white, middle-class, suburbanites who can place Chan within the defined parameters of "multicultural" spectacle found in the Hollywood action genre. In fact, one of the most striking aspects of *Rush Hour* involves the film's relationship to hip-hop/house culture, primarily associated with urban African-American youth, but popular worldwide. Although the film's director, Brett Ratner, a graduate of New York University, came up through the ranks making music videos featuring African-American rap performers like Public Enemy and Wu Tang Clan before directing Chris Tucker in *Money Talks* (1997), contemporary black youth culture takes a back seat in *Rush Hour* to nostalgic evocations of the 1970s. Rap and hip-hop seem to be there and not there in Tucker's banter and in the background music and culture. Although there is an intimate connection between rap and Hong Kong film,[52] this connection exists only on the edges of *Rush Hour*, since perhaps too close an alliance with a subversive subculture would alienate the newly won mainstream American audience.

With *Rush Hour*, Chan has transformed himself into a Hollywood star, without severing his ties to Hong Kong, Japan, and his non-Western fans, by creating a new "ghetto myth" of transnational multiculturalism. His longtime associate Sammo Hung's imitation of the concept of a Chinese policeman paired with an African-American LAPD renegade on network television's *Martial Law* pays tribute to the fundamental popularity of this formula. As an Asian businessman in the United States, Chan represents the new American Dream of "flexible citizenship," and, as an icon, he symbolizes a whitewashing of ghetto culture for global, postmodern consumerism.

> *"Time to wake up. But better get used to dreams."*
>
> Bob Perelman, "China"

In conclusion, Chan seems to appeal to a wide array of viewers because of his ability to link concerns associated with the postcolonial to those connected to the postmodern. Chan's white, middle-class, male, Western fans, who must navigate the uncertainty of identity within the postmodern destabilization of the bourgeois, patriarchal norm, see a fantasy of control over race, gender, and class. The ghetto myth that once appealed

---

52 Many scholars have examined this connection in detail. See Cynthia Fuchs, "Slicin' Shit Like a Samurai: Hiphop, Martial Arts, and Marketing Styles," paper presented at the Society for Cinema Studies Conference, Chicago, IL, March 10, 2000; Gateward, "Wong Fei Hong in Da House; Grace Wang, "What's Asia Got to Do With It? Asian Sampling in Hip-Hop Culture," paper presented at the Association for Asian American Studies Conference, Tucson, AZ, May 2000.

primarily to those on the margin now becomes available to those who occupy what used to be the center.

In this regard, Chan's black connection becomes a critical part of this ideological operation. Chan's presence signifies racial difference in a way that seems to allow for transcultural exchanges. He manages the chaos of the ghetto and creates a fantasy in which harmony can be created. Although this harmony is illusory, it has an allure for audiences globally. Chan operates in multiple spheres in which he must appeal to a heterogeneous audience across class, racial, and national borders. He represents a dream of physical empowerment to those in the audience who may be oppressed because of the physical differences of race and gender. He can offer a sort of transcendence to those who may be confined to manual labor by showing that the education of the body through martial arts can bring liberation. Chan manipulates his own identity and can be admired by those who have difficulty mastering a similar fluidity. Like Hong Kong itself, Chan is sometimes Chinese, sometimes colonial, and always transnational. He can be chauvinistic and self-deprecating almost simultaneously. He can make fun of the powerful and identify with the status quo. He represents a postmodern figure of contingency, crisis, and alienation that belies any political certainty alluded to in his films. Ultimately, Chan concretizes contradictions played out globally within the postmodern and the postcolonial conditions, and he manages to profit from the fantasies spun around racial otherness and the tenacious presence of its absence.

8   Stardom and serial fantasies

Thomas Harris's *Hannibal*

Linda Mizejewski

The most prominent celebrity serial killer of the twentieth century may have been a fictional one: Hannibal Lecter, the character created by novelist Thomas Harris and portrayed most notably by Anthony Hopkins in Jonathan Demme's 1991 adaptation of *The Silence of the Lambs*. In 1999, closeup images of Hannibal Lecter's face appeared on the covers of both *The New York Times Book Review* and *Entertainment Weekly*, suggesting a wide range of cultural audiences for whom the newly released Thomas Harris novel, *Hannibal*, was a major event.[1]

These two magazine-cover images offered cultural directives about reading the novel; they also encapsulated the issues of visibility, stardom, and transformation that I want to address in this essay. The *NYT* cover was a sketch of Hannibal's face as a ghastly mask, partly human and partly mechanical; its affinities are cyborgs, Terminators, and transformer toys—powerful bodies capable of infinite adaptation. The *Entertainment Weekly* cover, in contrast, announced the return of Hannibal more "realistically," with a photo of Anthony Hopkins from the 1991 film. "HE'S BACK!" the headline read, creating a reading strategy that makes the character in the new novel instantly imaginable and tangible because it has been previously embodied.

In the past decade, the novelization of a popular film—a book version that appears in the wake of the movie—has become a common device that both commodifies the original text and extends it as a new or parallel cultural artifact. However, Harris's *Hannibal* creates even more complicated questions about the uses of the film text in culture. The book *Hannibal* functions in some ways like a novelization, in that at the time of its publication, its characters were already widely identified with the actors from the previous Demme film—Anthony Hopkins and Jodie Foster (Fig. 8.1), who portrayed the FBI agent Clarice Starling.[2] Yet this previous film is not a literal source of the book so much as a cultural source, a reading grid and field of references and expectations. In

---

1 Lecter first emerges in Harris's 1981 novel *Red Dragon*. Played by Brian Cox, he appears in one scene of its 1986 film adaptation *Manhunter* (Michael Mann). My focus here, however, is the better known portrayal of Lecter in Demme's film version of *Silence of the Lambs*. The two magazine covers are *NYT Book Review* (June 13, 1999) and *Entertainment Weekly* (May 7, 1999).

2 This positioning is evident in the headline tease for the *Entertainment Weekly* cover story "He's Back!": "Hannibal Lecter has been missing in action for the last 10 years. Now America's favorite cannibal is back in *Hannibal*, Thomas Harris' long-awaited sequel to *The Silence of the Lambs*—and everyone in Hollywood is gearing up for a feeding frenzy." See Nashawaty 1999, 23. Also see *New York Times* critic Janet Maslin's comments (1999) on *Hannibal* as a "spinoff" of the Demme film.

Figure 8.1 Jodie Foster in *The Silence of the Lambs* (Orion 1991). Courtesy of the Kobal Collection

effect, the *Hannibal* book arrived in popular culture suspended between two movies, the formidable reputation of one and the anticipation for the next one.

Stardom and the star images of Hopkins and Foster are key elements in this grid of expectation and visual cues. The Lecter character, who dominated the publicity for the novel (He's back!), clearly illustrates the invitation to read literature via cinema. Nevertheless, the focus of this essay is the character of FBI agent Clarice Starling, whose picturing is more problematic in cinema history.[3] Serial killers, after all, boast a long list of film credits, from Fritz Lang's *M* (1931) through *American Psycho* (2000). Lecter's excesses and eccentricities, no matter how distinctive, fall into line with the campy terrors of Norman Bates, Jason, and Michael Myers. In contrast, the female investigator makes far rarer cinematic appearances; as the professional woman in a conventionally masculine role, this character is already aligned with lesbianism and feminism, positions not favored in mainstream cinema. So given Foster's previous screen and off-screen personas, her character in Demme's *Silence of the Lambs* played for different stakes from Lecter's. The role came with high expectations on the part of female and lesbian audiences and with the risks of deliberately playing against the traditional Hollywood heroine's framework of romance, heterosexuality, and glamour.

Not surprisingly, then, though both Hopkins and Foster won Academy Awards for their performances, Foster's portrayal did not generate the comedy, quotations, and imitations that Hopkins's did.

Starling's lesser visibility illustrates the wider problem of transferring the woman investigator from fiction to film. This female character—as detective, policewoman, FBI agent, bounty hunter, medical examiner, and so on—continues to gather momentum and avid readers in the popular-fiction market. The number of novels featuring a professional female investigator has tripled every five years since 1981 and remains a booming market.[4] Yet

3 See my previous discussion of this character, "Picturing the Female Dick" (Mizejewski 1993).
4 Walton and Jones give these figures and additional charts of the rise of the female detective in fiction (1999: 29–30).

despite this trend and despite the prestige of the 1991 *Silence of the Lambs*, the number of feature films about female investigators remains relatively small—in fact, scarcely a handful over the past decade: *Impulse* (1990), *Blue Steel* (1990), *V. I. Warshawski* (1991), *A Stranger Among Us* (1992), *Copycat* (1995).

As fictional detectives often point out: to find the motivation, follow the money. The scarcity of films is a clue about contemporary Hollywood's hesitation to invest major dollars in projects featuring a female character whose embodiment and *picturing* work at odds with many cinematic conventions. For example, as the casting began for the movie version of *Hannibal*, there was considerable speculation that *only* Jodie Foster could play Clarice. When Foster announced early in 2000 that she refused the role, one of the trade rumors was that the new movie *Hannibal* could not be made without her. An unnamed "head of a rival studio" was quoted in *Entertainment Weekly* as saying "Jodie is synonymous with the part . . . I don't think I would do it [now]. It's too much risk on a costly investment" (Fierman 2000: 13). In truth, the *Hannibal* film project is larger than Foster's identification with it, and Julianne Moore took the part offered by Universal Studios. My point is that the "risk" involves not only the departure from the previous casting but also the ability of another actress to negotiate the sexual and gender issues which both Foster and the Starling character bring to bear.

The casting controversy about the film version underscores the significance of the Harris novel *Hannibal* as a literary text deeply imbricated with stardom. While stardom is usually associated only with popular visual texts, this novel suggests how star institutions, especially in their articulation of sexuality, operate as a reading strategy across other media. In later years, readers may come to this novel "picturing" Julianne Moore, but I would argue that the celebrity persona of Jodie Foster is inscribed into this text in important ways. Though the novel's focus is Hannibal Lecter, its treatment of Clarice reveals repeated themes of stardom; the public image of this character, its interrogation, and its incitement to discover its private counterpart constitute a powerful subtext of Harris's *Hannibal*.

In this novel, both Lecter and Starling can be understood within the overlapping paradigms of stardom, visual technologies, and what critic Mark Seltzer calls "seriality"—the lure of repeated, cliffhanging episodes typical of certain popular narratives and also of the serial killer's repeated fantasy (1998: 64). The serial killer has a unique and privileged place in cultural representations. As an historical figure, he aims for notoriety through repeated media exposure, so textuality constitutes his very identity. Seltzer emphasizes how this figure serves as trope and material vehicle of reproduction (multiple crimes, multiple media texts) and also of audacious consumption (bodies, sensationalism, journalism).

The consuming habits of capitalism are in fact perfectly matched to the narrative of serial crime. In popular fictions, the serial killer often taunts the hard-boiled detective who may resolve the individual case but not the inevitable reappearance of another sequence of crimes. Accordingly, the serial killer is a recurring theme in television crime shows, films, and pulp detective fiction.[5] Steffen Hantke has pointed out that the story constitutes a subgenre with specific narrative traits: the mythical killer, the stalking sequence, the sexualized milieu, and the eventual discovery and exploration of a terrible, private killing space.

---

5 Television series such as *NYPD Blue*, *Homicide*, and *Law and Order* use this plotline often; *Millennium* used it as its major premise. Recent serial killer films include *To Catch a Killer* (1992), *Henry, Portrait of a Serial Killer* (1989), *Kalifornia* (1993), *Jennifer 8* (1992), and *Seven* (1995).

Hantke's emphasis on the killer's "fantasy of privacy" is particularly relevant to the fantasies of stardom in *Hannibal*. For Hantke, the issue of privacy drives the appeal of the serial killer story. On the one hand, our culture equates privacy with our most personal and meaningful identity; on the other hand, the private self is increasingly under siege by global, electronic, and media technologies and surveillance. If even our private spaces—the desks where we sit at our computers—are linked to elaborate monitoring systems each time we use the internet or email, then our most basic concept of a private self is being eroded. Little wonder, then, that we might "glorify the serial killer as a defender of private space" even as we fear the terrifying effects of his isolation (Hantke 1998: 188). In short, the serial killer subgenre thrives on tensions about personal identification and about what constitutes the boundaries between a private/public self. These tensions also constitute stardom, which likewise relies on relationships between public images and the private person, with questions of how much of the "real" person is visible in his or her representations and public appearances.

The other controversial technology of identification often featured in the serial-killer subgenre is profiling. Popular cinema has in fact taught us a great deal about forensic profiling as a tracking device for criminals—literally, a way of picturing the suspect before he has materialized. The opening of the film *Copycat* shows Sigourney Weaver as a psychologist lecturing on the type of white male who is most likely to be a serial killer. In Demme's *Silence of the Lambs*, Starling is quizzed by her supervisor on profiling when he asks her to characterize the murderer they have not yet found. The profile of the serial killer as a white male, often focused on white female victims, has coincided with the rise of the female detective in popular fiction. Two transgressive fantasies with sexual and gendered inflections are joined in this narrative: the out-of-place woman who dares to embody the law; the man out-of-control whose trail of bodies dares the law to intervene. Two visual dynamics intersect here as well, in the "profile" of the criminal as knowable, even scientifically delineated, and the figure that is in some ways unimaginable, the female dick.

As the 1990's most visible example of this duo, Starling and Lecter are defined by questions of visibility—more specifically, by questions of embodiment, exposure, disguise, adaptation, and transformation (remember the symbolic and narrative importance of the chrysalis and the moth in *Silence of the Lambs*). In *Hannibal*, these issues operate on three levels: within the text itself; as a reading strategy; and as media representation of the book through its most prominent reviews. Although my primary interest here is the production of Clarice Starling, my argument links that production to that of her criminal co-star and object of pursuit, Dr. Lecter. The narrative of *Hannibal* is actually the progression of Starling's and Lecter's stories from mutual pursuits of one another into their common outlaw status eluding the FBI.

At the end of *The Silence of the Lambs*, Starling graduates from the FBI academy as a heroine, having single-handedly tracked and killed the serial murderer Buffalo Bill. In the film version, Starling proudly accepts her badge as multiple cameras flash to capture the moment of triumph. At the beginning of *Hannibal*, we learn that this eminent visibility has rendered her vulnerable to the FBI's worst sexism and petty politics; seven years after her moment of heroism, she is stalled in her career and relegated to dreaded assignments such as drug-busting. In the novel's grim opening sequence, Starling survives a badly planned bust by shooting five people in self-defense, including a woman who was shielding herself with an infant. The horrifying photo images from the shootout create a publicity nightmare for the Justice Department, which then targets

Starling as scapegoat. So the episode instantly morphs from a criminal case into a publicity case marked by sensationalism, exploitation, and misleading public images. The headlines of the *National Tattler* (the conflation of popular tabloids used frequently in Harris's novels) render Starling as both disembodied and mechanical: "DEATH ANGEL: CLARICE STARLING, THE FBI's KILLING MACHINE" (Harris 1999: 19). The news stories characterize her as former star of the FBI, probably at the end of a career which had begun with "fifteen minutes of fame" (19).

As we later discover, the FBI's targeting of Starling similarly involves an inability to imagine her outside of stereotypes and one-dimensional images: man-hating lesbian (denizen of "some goddamned dyke den," 339) or simply woman out of place; the Assistant Director is caught musing that "there was an emotional element in women that often didn't fit in with the Bureau" (360). Starling's professionalism, we are told, had earned her the respect of other women agents. "All the girls—the women know about you, I mean everybody does, but you're kind of . . . kind of special to us," a female colleague tells her (312). In contrast, her record as the FBI's "interservice combat pistol champion three years straight" had won her the moniker, among the men, of "Poison Oakley" (7). In terms of the key cause-and-effect triggers of the narrative, Starling's beauty gets the attention of exactly the wrong man at the Justice Department who then ruins her career. She has previously refused the advances of the Deputy Assistant Inspector General, a married man, who is now happy to humiliate her. He calls her "cornpone country pussy" (265), earning himself one of the novel's worst death scenes.

On a more public level, Starling's torrid new stardom in the tabloids eventually gets the attention of the disguised Hannibal Lecter, on the lam in Italy, and these images prompt him to get in touch with her for the first time since his escape. Lecter sends her a private letter instructing her to disregard the portrayals of herself by the FBI and the public media, and instead to look at herself reflected in a "black iron skillet" (30) of the kind she would have known from her West Virginia home and family. While the public pictures of Starling are warped and unreliable, Lecter hints, this iron mirror is more "true" because, by proffering only rough shapes, it allows her to search for the more authentic self.

This letter, which activates the main plot of the two characters tracking each other, clearly introduces the theme of public image versus the private self; the letter is also curiously a fan letter, with Lecter positioning himself as the "insider" addressing the celebrity whose image has been tarnished by the press. Indeed, at this moment in the narrative, media images of Agent Starling threaten her identity and career. Press photographs and television coverage chart her demise; eventually, the local news runs embarrassing footage of Starling getting a speeding ticket as she flees the scene of her Justice Department hearing. Eventually, too, the novel suggests that only Hannibal Lecter has the imagination to *picture* Clarice Starling without reductive caricature, but this requires a departure from realist portraiture, photos, film, or even mirrors. Though Hannibal is an artist, his sketches of Clarice are impressionistic rather than realist. In *Silence of the Lambs*, he had drawn her as a Christian madonna and shepherdess; in *Hannibal*, he sketches her as a version of the little sister he had lost during World War II (256).

Lecter's obsession with the lost sister is represented as a primary motivation for his murders and also for his attraction to Starling, so that his pursuit of the latter hovers between courtship and a mad dream of resurrection or reconstitution of the dead and the past. When the pursuit and rescue plot lines have ended, *Hannibal* takes a turn toward the poetic and the surreal. Lecter begins studying astrophysics to find a way to reverse time and make broken teacups fly together again (362–364); the novel's grue-some revenge scene is a bizarre Mad Hatter's gourmet dinner/tea party. In short, the novel moves from straightforward action thriller (the opening shootout sequence in a grimy DC neighborhood) to a far more dreamy style and *mise-en-scène*. Its conclusion in Buenos Aires resembles South American magical realism, with Starling as chrysalis-turned-butterfly, freed from the nasty misogyny of the FBI and suddenly located far from the narrative structures of crime/detective/investigation fiction. Transformed, Clarice Starling is no longer tethered to realist problems of representation. In the final pages, Lecter positions Starling in front of an antique mirror that is "slightly smoky and crazed" (466) so that even though we get details of what she is wearing, her actual image eludes us, except that Lecter proclaims, ominously, that she is "a delicious vision" (466).

Starling's journey from law to outlaw, from realist character to poetic embodiment, illustrates the problematic "picturing" of the fictional female investigator, the licensed woman with authority and a gun, whose transgressive presence shifts the genre and the story. The sexuality of this character—the female dick, the female body in the place of the male law/authority/agency—is a key element in this picture. *Hannibal* implies that in the previous seven years, only one other man was seriously interested in Starling; this was an FBI shooting instructor whom she apparently liked and respected very much. "A long time ago John Brigham had asked her something and she said no. And then he asked her if they could be friends, and meant it, and she said yes, and meant it" (27).

The opacity of this description—and the novel never gives us more detail—is capped by Brigham's death. He is one of the fatalities in the opening shootout, so that partic-ular subplot closes before the main plot line gets underway. The next time the novel references their relationship, when Starling visits his grave, the tactic is repeated nearly word for word: "She felt a bond with Brigham that was no less strong because they were never lovers . . . He asked her something gently and she said no, and then he asked her if they could be friends, and meant it, and she said yes, and meant it" (246). More than 200 pages later, we have not gained any more information about the question between them, its context, or what exactly it implied.

The ambiguity of these passages suggests two possible characterizations. On the one hand, if the "something" Brigham had asked was commitment, romance, or sex, then FBI-agent Starling may be categorized among the fictional female investigators who are poised forever in an impossible heterosexuality, always having lost or about to lose a desirable man (Cornwell's Scarpetta, Grafton's Mahone, *Profiler*'s Sam, etc.). On the other hand, the "something" Brigham asked might be more basic: whether or not she dates men. *Hannibal* curiously avoids the heterosexual characterization of Starling so evident in Harris's *Silence of the Lambs,* in which there are references to boyfriends and even a concluding scene with Starling in a man's bed. Instead, this novel's Starling resembles that of the Demme movie, which refrained from categorizing her sexuality; it eliminated references to dating, clothed her in drab colors, and framed her so that her body faded into the *mise-en-scène.*

The Starling of *Hannibal* has clearly had a tough seven years that seem to have iso-lated her from most relationships and certainly from heterosexual ones. The novel does not explicitly portray her as a lesbian, but does deploy the lesbian stereotype of same-sex romantic love.[6] In shades of the nineteenth-century Boston marriage, Starling shares

---

6 Judith Mayne pointed out to me this common stereotype and its matching stereotype of the super-masculine butch, in the character of Margo, the villain's sister (whose femme partner is never represented at all).

Figure 8.2 Jodie: An Icon. Courtesy of Women Make Movies

a duplex with her closest friend Ardelia; and at the end of the novel, she sends Ardelia a ring in which both their initials are engraved, a gesture that can easily be interpreted as more than friendship.

In significant ways, then, Harris's *Hannibal* follows the oblique sexual characterization of Starling in the Demme film. My argument here is that this previous cultural "picturing" works as a reading strategy to fill in the gaps in the new novel, the "something" the text refuses to reveal. In the long run, this suggests for cultural studies further thinking about the visual technologies operating in literature. Certainly the novel *Hannibal* is concerned with celebrity and public images as themes within the text; its extratextual association with cinema—its historical positioning between two film texts—further invites readers to draw on their cultural knowledge as film fans and film spectators in order to envision the world of *Hannibal*.

Jodie Foster brings very specific cultural information to this picture. Most obviously, her casting in the film version of *Silence of the Lambs* had drawn on Foster's extracinematic reputation for intelligence and also for fierce privacy concerning her personal life. Though not outed until 1991, her tomboy/lesbian image and reputation had been long established, as cited for instance in Pratibha Parmar's documentary *Jodie: An Icon* (1996) (Fig. 8.2). In the years following that film, Foster gave birth to a son but—as I write this in 2000—still has no obvious relationship with any man, nor any public identification with lesbianism in spite of her enthusiastic lesbian fans and readings.[7]

Stardom relies on cultural concepts of a "real" or private person in relation to a public persona. Writing of classic constructions of stardom, Richard DeCordova uses Foucault's concept of how sexual discourses circulate through a "will to knowledge," a cultural positing of sexuality as a "truth" that is endlessly divulged and explored, precisely because it has been positioned as a secret. Stardom is often organized within a "logic of secrecy," says DeCordova, as a succession of deepening levels of revelations. Fans are incited to peel away public and textual images in order to discover the private or "real" person underneath (1990: 140). The sexual secret is posited as the ultimate truth, so that "The sexual scandal is the primal scene of all star discourse, the only scenario that offers the promise of a full and satisfying disclosure of the star's identity" (141).

However, for some bi- or homosexual actors and actresses whose sexuality has been constructed by gossip and innuendo, I would argue that this model of layering is reversed, with "the sexual scandal" itself operating as the code or incitement to read the films. Jodie Foster's refusal to refute or even address the "scandalous" lesbian rumors ensures the endless continuation of fan "incitement" or "will to knowledge." But as Parmar's documentary makes clear, the "primal scene" of disclosure is no longer the object of knowledge, because fan knowledge has already authorized and validated certain film readings.

Foster's respected accomplishments as actress, director, and producer also challenge DeCordova's paradigm because her power is institutional rather than phantasmic; Foster's established position relies not only on image but on her ability to fund and produce her own projects. Moreover, her intelligence and integrity allowed her to emerge unscathed from the embarrassing scandal of the would-be assassin Hinckley; like Clarice Starling, Foster does in fact have an extensive background at the FBI. My point is that readers who imagine Foster as Starling in the new *Hannibal* have a vivid way to picture the more complex traits of this character: powerful, competent female authority; beauty without glamour; and a sexual attractiveness that eludes easy categorization. The 200-page gap between the two descriptions of Brigham's question and the very repetition of that question's empty signifier—"something"—become readable (as in comprehensible, familiar, logical) through a concrete image, face, body. Moreover, the sexuality of Starling which the novel *Hannibal* refuses to address (the "something" which is also the ideological problem of the female investigative agent) is more acceptable if read through Jodie Foster, whose persona makes some of these unanswered questions acceptable.

Foster's stardom provides a rich point of reference for this novel in other ways as well. First, stardom as an institution and as a reading device thrives on contradiction, as many scholars have pointed out. While star appeal depends on connection and identification, for example, it also depends on adulation and glamour; fans simultaneously need to imagine the star as fully human and ordinary, but also larger than life and extraordinary. Similarly, the star must maintain a distance or absence in order to achieve mystique, but also must be perceived as omnipresent, on-the-scene, in the moment. These contradictions are related to the larger ideological contradictions embedded within individual films.

7　See Clare Whatling's extensive analysis of Foster's reputation and publicity, including a description of how film texts are used as accumulated material for the "invested" viewer's fantasies and desires (1997: 134–159).

The more troubling subtexts of those films are naturalized or glossed over by the coherency of the star's body and presence. Thus the assuring presence of John Wayne in a Western film may assuage that genre's uneasiness about "civilizing" the frontier through uncivilized acts of genocide.[8] My suggestion here is that the sexuality of Starling which the novel *Hannibal* refuses to address (the "something" which is actually the ideological problem of the female investigative agent) is more acceptable if read through Jodie Foster, whose persona makes some of these contradictions or unanswered questions acceptable.

Again modifying DeCordova's concept of the chain of secrets, I would argue that when an erotic revelation about Starling does occur in the last pages of the novel, its sexuality eludes categorization as a particular kind of "scene." The revelation only confounds the question of what exactly constitutes sex for Starling and Hannibal Lecter, the cannibal who respects no boundaries or categories. Critics of the Demme film have often read the campy, aesthete Hannibal as gay, but this classification may be too simple.[9] After all, the "sex scene" in *Silence of the Lambs*, Lecter's seduction of Clarice and his intimacy with her, is the powerful through-the-bars interview scene in which he penetrates her mind and memory, and makes her touch herself in her most vulnerable place, with the recollection of her childhood story. In *Hannibal*, the concluding chapters suggest that the sexual relationship of Hannibal and Starling is based on incest taboos. Yet when their relationship is described in the final pages, the sexual terms are notably ambiguous:

> Their relationship has a great deal to do with the penetration of Clarice Starling, which she avidly welcomes and encourages. It has much to do with the envelopment of Hannibal Lecter, far beyond the bounds of his experience. It is possible that Clarice Starling could frighten him. Sex is a splendid structure they add to every day. (483)

The following paragraph begins: "Clarice Starling's memory palace is building as well" (483). That is, "sex," as a "splendid structure" similar to memory, is open here to any number of biological, cultural, philosophical, and psychological definitions. Queer theory has shown us that sexuality, sex, and gender are not always symmetrically aligned and that sexuality is not easily categorized by the sexes of the couples involved.

Anthony Hopkins's stardom also functions in this novel around questions of visibility, though in pointedly different ways. In the plot line of *Hannibal*, Lecter's survival depends on *not* being visible or recognizable; for seven years, he has successfully eluded authorities through artful changes of appearance and nationality. The joke is that Lecter is actually hiding in full sight as a socially active academic, the European "Dr. Fell," currently of Florence. Unlike Clarice, he controls and manipulates his public images, proving himself a competent actor, performance artist, and master of disguise. In Italy he is a translator and curator; in transit to the States, he is a middle-class tourist; later he poses as a funeral director, a surgeon, and a hunter—all dark metonymic references to his private interest in highly specialized "renderings" of the body.

8 See Britton 1991, Dyer 1979, and Ellis 1992 on the cinema's uses of contradictory star elements in narratives and genres.
9 Critics have referred casually to Hannibal Lecter as a "campy gay aesthete" (Robbins 1995: 44) or to his "pronounced swish" (Tharp 1991: 111). Diana Fuss argues more extensively for "the specter of a perverse and monstrous homosexuality" connoted by his image as "an insatiable oral sadist" (1993: 195).

The problem with picturing this changeable character is solved, nevertheless, with a narrative assurance of visual continuity. Although Lecter's new faces are not the ones registered on the FBI's most-wanted posters, we are assured that he looks both different and the same as he had in the previous texts: "No current likeness of Dr. Lecter's new face exists in the world. It is not so different from his old face—a little collagen added around the nose and cheeks, changed hair, spectacles—but it is different enough if attention is not called to him" (248). This indicates he could be recognized with prior cuing; that cuing, moreover, has actually been offered to readers via the Demme film. The narrative description implies that we can easily picture the disguised Lecter as Anthony Hopkins, with the kind of appearance changes made possible by Hollywood makeup.

Like Jodie Foster, Hopkins provides a number of stabilizing star qualities for a slippery character who is both criminal and hero in this book. A respected British Shakespearean actor, Hopkins is renowned for his versatility. His roles have included monsters (Quasimodo in a 1982 film of *The Hunchback of Notre Dame*), disillusioned professionals (the doctor in *The Elephant Man* [1980]), fanatics (*The Road to Wellville* [1994]), platonic or grieving lovers (*Remains of the Day* [1993], *Shadowlands* [1993]), and—as a combination of the above—Richard Nixon (*Nixon* [1995]). His ability to embody both class (he is *Sir* Anthony, knighted in 1993) and camp, both monstrosity and human depth, offers a coherent image for the Dr. Lecter of *Hannibal*, who is alternately frightening, tender, and mad. The sustained tension in the novel, after all, is whether he wants to save Clarice from the FBI or cook and eat her.

However, the differences between these two star images are also important in their dimensions of accessibility and legibility. Unlike Foster, Hopkins has acquired no layerings of secrecy, gossip, or ambiguities that propel curiosity about his private life. Hopkins's numerous honors as an actor have not placed him on the same lists and polls of "most popular" stars or "top stars" in which we regularly find Foster, lists that usually connect star and sex appeal. Stardom has often been described through its psychosexual dimensions of narcissism, fetishism, and voyeurism; some critics argue that stars are objects of obsessive investigation precisely because of these psychoanalytic dynamics of sexual difference and identification. Yet certainly not all stars function within this sexualized paradigm; many excellent and respected actors/actresses—and I would include Hopkins in this group—maintain high visibility, popularity, and celebrity through other kinds of identifications and appeals (Tim Robbins, Harvey Keitel, Stockard Channing, Whoopi Goldberg, etc.).

Hannibal draws on these different versions of stardom to stabilize the character of Lecter, on the one hand, and to endow the character of Starling with a certain volatility, on the other. The narrative also offers a familiar cultural story of stars and their fans and stalkers. After Clarice Starling's sudden rise in the media and her sensationalistic exploitation by the FBI and headline-selling journalists, she is pursued by her single most ardent fan, Dr. Lecter. Lecter begins by sending her mail, and then small gifts; he starts to follow her and spy on her while she is jogging; he breaks into her car just to sniff the air and gain approximate physical contact. He exemplifies, in short, the obsessive fan who becomes the stalker and the trespasser. I am thinking, too, of Mark Seltzer's characterization of the serial killer as the seeker of progressively more fulfilling fantasies. Dr. Lecter's career as a serial killer occurred previous to the plot lines of the Harris novels, but this new novel follows his growing fixation on Starling which leads him into escalating levels of recklessness and finally into entrapment.

In the final pages of *Hannibal*, Dr. Lecter's various therapies with Starling seek to discover her ultimate secret, the "something" that would explain the most private level of her being. Yet what Lecter extracts is also what he most needs for himself, accomplishing a fan's most ardent desire: that the fantasies of the star and the fan perfectly coincide. He finds in Starling "the incestual taboo," an attraction only to "good" men like her father, and thus her inability to have a sexual relationship to them (453). Throughout *Hannibal*, we learn that Lecter's own most important fantasies center on family and loss, primarily the loss of his sister, whom he increasingly conflates with Starling. Her long-awaited transformation is also clearly transference; the powerful therapist, who has figured like a father to her in her past, releases her from the incest taboo and becomes the object of desire.

This move may be poetic and surreal, but it can also be read as a suspiciously smug male fantasy. For other fantasies about female power, the move is disappointing. Lecter has plucked Starling away from all public realms in which she could function as an image—for the female colleagues, for example, for whom she was "kind of special." And here is where the text's issues of stardom/visibility overlap with these as extratextual issues—or rather, where they cannot be separated in terms of the cultural meanings of this novel. In the plot line of *Hannibal*, the character Starling had assumed a legendary status organized around the axes of presence/absence, accessibility/inaccessibility, publicity/privacy—that is, the tensions that also produce the stardom of Jodie Foster. The significance of *Hannibal* as a narrative about serial fantasy, male criminality, and female investigation, then, is its turnaround into the investigation and exposure of that highly controversial image, the female agent/authority/detective/dick. The investigation ends with her public disappearance and a startling shift in the stakes of visibility, for in Starling's new status as outlaw, her faces cannot match the ones currently being sought by the FBI. We can picture her as versions of Jodie Foster, but picturing her will always be the problem/investigation itself.

I want to conclude by pointing out how the structure of Starling's investigation/secrecy has also functioned in the book's reception. Early reviewers hinted heavily that Lecter is alive and well at the end of the novel, and even quoted from or described the novel's shocking cannibalistic "Mad Hatter" scene at its conclusion. In contrast, those first reviews had been reluctant to divulge the fate of Clarice Starling—and for good reason. The novel's "surprise twist" ending—a major lure for the reader—has nothing to do with Lecter's survival or cannibalism and everything to do with Clarice's transformation. It could be argued, moreover, that this reviewing/reception strategy is built into the novel itself, in the same way the single "surprise" of *The Crying Game* created its own mechanism for teasing reviews and advertisements.

In his *New York Times* review, Stephen King pointed out that Harris leaves the door open "just a crack" for a sequel, though King himself "would rather see him bar this door and go down a different corridor" (1999: 6). For those of us with certain serial fantasies, this would be a disappointment, for investigative characters such as Starling are "kind of special" to women scholars investigating the genre. Starling's new incarnation as outlaw certainly has its pleasures—at least for this obsessed fan—but I remain suspicious of Hannibal Lecter's consumerist and paternal desires which the novel instructs us to believe are now Starling's desires as well. Lecter teaches Clarice about desire in *Silence of the Lambs*: "We begin by coveting what we see everyday" (227). Thus Clarice's disappearance leaves the world a little less interesting.

Acknowledgments

My thanks to Judith Mayne, the First Draft Group of the English Department at Ohio State University, and the audience at the 2000 Society for Cinema Studies conference, for comments and suggestions about early versions of this chapter.

References

Britton, Andrew (1991) "Star and Genre," in Christine Gledhill, ed., *Stardom: Industry of Desire*, London and New York: Routledge, 198–206.

DeCordova, Richard (1990) *Picture Personalities: The Emergence of the Star System in America*, Urbana and Chicago: University of Illinois Press.

Dyer, Richard (1979) *Stars*, London: British Film Institute.

Ellis, John (1992) "Stars as a Cinematic Phenomenon," in Gerald Mast, Marshall Cohen, and Leo Braudy, eds, *Film Theory and Criticism*, 4th edn, New York: Oxford University Press, 614–621.

Fierman, Daniel (2000) "Lamb Chops," *Entertainment Weekly*, January 14: 12–13.

Fuss, Diana (1993) "Monsters of Perversion: Jeffrey Dahmer and *The Silence of the Lambs*," in Marjorie Garber, Jann Mattock, and Rebecca L. Walkowitz, eds, *Media Spectacles*, New York and London: Routledge, 181–205.

Hantke, Steffen (1998) " 'The Kingdom of the Unimaginable': The Construction of Social Space and the Fantasy of Privacy in Serial Killer Narratives," *Literature/Film Quarterly* 26 (3): 178–195.

Harris, Thomas (1988) *The Silence of the Lambs*, New York: St. Martin's Press.

—— (1999) *Hannibal*, New York: Delacorte.

King, Stephen (1999) Review of *Hannibal* by Thomas Harris, *New York Times Book Review*, June 13: 4ff.

Maslin, Janet (1999) "Cultural Cross-Pollination: A Thousand Markets Bloom," *New York Times*, August 26: B1ff.

Mizejewski, Linda (1993) "Picturing the Female Dick: *The Silence of the Lambs* and *Blue Steel*," *Journal of Film and Video* 45: 6–23.

Nashawaty, Chris (1999) "The Hunger," *Entertainment Weekly*, May 7: 23–27.

Robbins, Bruce (1995) "Murder and Mentorship: Advancement in *The Silence of the Lambs*," *UTS Review* 1 (1): 30–49.

Seltzer, Mark (1998) *Serial Killers: Death and Life in America's Wound Culture*, New York and London: Routledge.

Stacey, Jackie (1994) *Star Gazing: Hollywood Cinema and Female Spectatorship*, London and New York: Routledge.

Tharp, Julie (1991) "The Transvestite as Monster: Gender Horror in *The Silence of the Lambs* and *Psycho*," *Journal of Popular Film and Television* 19 (3): 106–113.

Walton, Priscilla and Manina Jones (1999) *Detective Agency: Women Re-Writing the Hard-Boiled Tradition*, Berkeley: University of California Press.

Whatling, Clare (1997) *Screen Dreams: Fantasising Lesbians in Film*, Manchester: Manchester University Press.

9   Learning from Bruce Lee

Pedagogy and political correctness in martial arts cinema

Meaghan Morris

Film is a mirror, not of reality, but of the act of regarding it.

Rohdie 1995b

Set the images all in your head. Then believe them. And know it can't be stopped.

"Bruce Lee," No Retreat, No Surrender

In recent years I have been troubled by the return of a ploddingly sociological approach to cinema in academic as well as media criticism. By plodding, I do not mean a sociology which goes out to explore the dense social contexts of film consumption today; in cinema as distinct from television studies, we've had very little of that. I mean a strictly armchair way of seeing or not-seeing films which first views them as evidence of some social or political mess, then treats them as guilty stand-ins for that mess—and wages a war of attitude on other viewers.

In the early 1990s, neo-conservative rhetoricians gave a catchy new name to this and other long-established modes of public cultural activism: "political correctness." Outlasting the furor it created on campus, the term passed into ordinary language where it continues to thrive today. Now, whatever one thinks of the diverse attitude wars and thorny institutional issues mashed together as "PC" by the myth tanks clearing the way for George Bush Sr. in the US and then Prime Minister John Howard in Australia (my own views on PC matters are quite mixed), it is the case that a hissing moral outrage has greeted just about every decent film of recent years from *Silence of the Lambs* and *Natural Born Killers* to *Romper Stomper* and *The Heartbreak Kid*. But the hissing comes from all sides, and the outrage is not new. That puritan fear of the aesthetic which damned the theatre in the eighteenth century and warned in the nineteenth that novel-reading would addle women's brains has now given us film critics who can't see any difference between *The Lion King* ("Orientalism," racism) and *The Good Woman of Bangkok*.[1]

Troubled by this but also provoked, made to think about my own basic values, I've often wanted to mass-distribute copies of Dr. George Miller's short film, *Violence in the Cinema . . . Part 1* (1972).[2] Thirty years ago, in another time of anxiety about the power

---

1 On the controversy surrounding Dennis O'Rourke's *The Good Woman of Bangkok*, a fictionalized documentary about the white Australian director's love for a Thai prostitute, see the dossier of debate included in Berry, Hamilton, and Jayamanne (1997).

2 Dr. George Miller is the Australian director of the *Mad Max* trilogy, along with numerous Hollywood films including *The Witches of Eastwick*, *Lorenzo's Oil*, and *Babe: Pig in the City*.

of representation, *Violence in the Cinema* presented two arguments about the "effects" of violent films. One was a lecture delivered by a social expert on screen. The other was the lesson of the film itself; as I remember it, the speaker's body starts exploding and splattering in the visual field until his head comes off while on the soundtrack his voice drones on, lucid, boring, relentlessly making sense. The combination explained more vividly than anything else I've seen that cinema involves film*making*, make-believe, an aesthetic situation. Violence in the cinema lets you have a talking-headless lecturer. Violence in the classroom doesn't.

Of course I'm not alone when I recoil from the moralistic sampling of film themes, scenes, and bits of dialogue which now prevails from the newspaper op-ed page to the cultural studies textbook. Just reading around my neighborhood I find Adrian Martin (1998: 28) renewing the topic of cinephilia ("an experience of the *materiality* of the medium, something quite beyond literary abstractions of theme"), and Lesley Stern (1995: 220) reaffirming the fiercely aesthetic over "movies which merely elicit recognition" and "reproduce boring and often nasty social relations." The most uncompromising restatement of critical principles I've come across, however, is an essay by Sam Rohdie (1995b) on "Sixth Form Film Teaching in Hong Kong."

First given as a talk to teachers in response to a film syllabus more focused on society than on cinema, Rohdie's essay spells out some classic tenets of film formalism. Filmmakers are expert in the cinema, not social theory; film worlds are fictional, they are realms of fantasy and desire in which the process of make-believe itself is of central concern, and the "worthy issues" we call social themes are often alibis for what really moves us in the cinema, "the wonderful asocial wish to do whatever you please" (1995b: 5). In short, films reflect on looking, not reality at large: "the cinema, primarily, is not a commentary on life, but a commentary on cinema" (8).

I am always moved and delighted by these principles, founding as they do a vocation on the necessity for critics to do what pleases *us* most, namely, commenting on cinema. Rohdie expounds them beautifully; I share his belief that aesthetics is fundamental to film teaching and faced with the syllabus he describes I would have argued, with far less dexterity, much the same thing. Yet something here troubles me, too. Rohdie's is a *too* fundamentalist take on film interpretation. In its impulse to purify cinema of worthy concerns ("they take us away from the film"), and to cast the dreaming individual Oedipus ("you can sleep with your mother, murder your father . . .") as the ideal film spectator, his pedagogy restores and renders absolute those great divides between "art" and "society," "fiction" and "reality," which the social critic, a bad film spectator, all too flatly does. In doing so, it precludes, say, Stern's more questioning exploration of a phantasmatic "connection" between films and other realities, perhaps between spectators: for Stern (1995: 219) "movies are not imaginary; they constitute part of my (our?) daily life." And it has little in common with Martin's (1997: 223) loving acceptance of all that cinema is: the "boring and nasty in conventional narrative film," he notes, is "maybe 99.9% of cinema as we know it."

Compared with an aesthetics of connection and porous subjectivity, Rohdie's is a hard-edged modernism in which art is an autonomous realm of freedom. Like dreams, he says in another essay, the cinema is not bound by the social any more than "Bruce Lee or Jackie Chan can be kept still, confined by a banal goodness, the dull gestures of an everyday reality" (Rohdie 1995a: 27), even when such banality is the "message" of their films. In this understanding, "cinema" is always less than the films which are its medium. You subtract the dross (themes, issues, messages) to touch the aesthetic spirit.

Before modernism, the Romantics called this spirit "Imagination"—and its muse or vehicle they called "Inspiration."

This is powerful stuff. Policed as we are these days by a code of truth to Experience— a mutation of another Romantic principle—many people do long for some untrammeled talk about art. I'm one of them. Yet in being provoked, made to think, by PC criticism (let me use that abusive term for a while), I've also come to accept that a purist aesthetic ignores not only too much cinema but also 99.9 percent of the ways in which films matter to people, both in and out of school. Since the "art" and "reality," formalism and Marxism debates of the early 1970s (not to mention the 1920s), forests have died to promote the model of representation staged by *Violence in the Cinema* in a few hilarious minutes, and the theory of the imaginary shaping Rohdie's elegant text. Yet all that writing falls beside today's controversies. It comes close, then misses the point.

Something has changed. In spite of the publicity accorded a few sensually challenged persons who see violation in each beautiful body displayed—to the joy and solace of the rest of us—in public advertising space, in spite of efforts to blame videos for massacres and violent crime (Barker and Petley 1997), in spite of all the rote deconstructions of race–class–gender–sexuality coming off the cultural studies presses: denying the imaginary is not what the fuss is about these days. Most PC critics, whether we are students, teachers, community activists, or casually interested citizens, know all about the differences between fiction and other realities. Rather, it is the very power of art and imagination—more exactly, a politics of gaining access to some of the freedom and power to make-believe—that is now at stake.

A make-believe world: *No Retreat, No Surrender*

Such power is explicitly at work, as Rohdie teaches us, in the most formally banal cinema. Take a scene from Corey Yuen's roughly made, badly acted and (re-released on tape) barely visible but immortal US martial arts classic, *No Retreat, No Surrender* (1985).[3] Nothing artistically transcendent here, plenty of nasty social relations. Late one night in suburban Seattle, a bruised and dejected white boy—the Outsider, the new kid in town— sinks down to rest in the shrine he's reconstructed in an empty house after a tearing fight with his father. His black sidekick, "R.J.," has gone home. Sad, tired, lonely, resentful of his wounded father's cowardice, shamed himself as an incompetent fighter in front of his would-be girlfriend, Jason Stilwell (Kurt McKinney) takes comfort from the icons around him, settles under the covers of a Bruce Lee book, and gently falls asleep.[4]

3 The film's screenwriter has noted of his first script that "*NRNS* is no great masterpiece . . . but it captured people's imagination. It got a widespread theatrical release, and played all over the country. I still have people come up to me to tell me that *NRNS* is their favorite movie of all time. I find that hard to believe, but it makes me feel good all the same" (Strandberg 1997). The "text" of *No Retreat, No Surrender* is a bit unstable, differing in various editions. The version I am calling "barely visible" was re-released by Filmpac on PAL as the "Original Unedited Version" (as packaged in 1986 by Filmways Australasian Distributors). Small but significant differences from the version now available in the US are indicated where necessary.
4 This scene is worth comparing to the brilliant sportswriter Davis Miller's (2000: 27) description of the "sustenance" that he drew as a young man from Lee's image: "I cut the best pictures from . . . magazines and pasted them to pieces of black construction paper, which I taped to the wall beside the Ali poster opposite my bed, where I'd see them each night before I went to bed and each morning when I woke."

Figure 9.1 Bruce Lee

In the murk on screen we glimpse the stuff of his dreams. This boy's inner life is made of film stills. Stills, and the forms they give to other Bruce Lee paraphernalia: books, magazines, a huge poster restored from its shredding at the hands of Jason's father, and, extending the icon's power into the bodily everyday, props for becoming like Bruce Lee: sandbags, a wooden man, ropes. More than an expression of fandom, this place is a *sanctum* for an ideal which is—however kitsch, suburban, crass, narcissistic, exploitative, American, cartoonish, tacky (pick an insult from any pile of reviews)[5]—aesthetically shaped and ethically practical. It is also, in this scene, furtive, relegated to secret, childish places: wildlife in suburbia.

Even harder for critics to deal with unhysterically, the handling of spirituality in this and many other US martial arts films is humorous, and self-parodying too. We're invited to laugh and groan and gasp with disbelief as Jason prays at Bruce Lee's grave ("My name is Jason Stilwell and I just moved here from Los Angeles and I'm a martial artist too . . ."). This is melodrama, real melodrama, not the tortuous allegory of a Freudian case-study world which feminism found in the "woman's film," but festive, romping, participatory popular melodrama. "What should I *do*?!" cries Jason's father in his hospital bed, when crippled by evil Mafia men who want to take over his dojo, and as he inwardly sighs the wrong—"There's nothing else to do but . . . leave!"—the unspoken right answer is clear: "Fight back! Fight back!"[6]

With its call-and-response communalism, melodrama is didactic about the import of narrative conventions and genre rules as well as ethical decisions. When Jason is roused from his slumber by weird music and a bright white light, the "Bruce Lee" who appears to him is both a didact and a special generic figure—the Muse of US martial arts

5 Julius (1996: 140) uses this vocabulary at the friendly end of the range: "A teenage boy learns to overcome his problems with the spectral assistance of a celebrity stiff in this cheap and cheesy but basically harmless fantasy."
6 This scene is missing from the currently available US edition.

cinema.[7] In literary mythology, a Muse empowers as well as inspires the mortal artist she deigns to visit. Bruce Lee not only explains the rules of the fantasy role which Jason wants to embody (to be a hero he must begin to learn all over again, train obediently and give up on revenge) but gives him the knowledge and coincidence he needs to bring his ideal self-image "to life."

Briefly played by Kim Tae Chong, this Muse for suburban Americans is flagrantly a spin-off from the cult video world. A podgy-faced caricature of Lee-clone who brings into the film the jerky English dubbing of old kung fu movies, the spirit who visits Jason is a product rather than a symptom of what Teo (1997: 120) calls the "cult worship" of Lee after his death, which made him "an object, even a fetish."[8] *No Retreat, No Surrender* comments on this worship rather than simply catering to it. As his Muse and teacher, Lee unblocks Jason's powers as a martial artist by helping him transcend his fascination with Bruce Lee images, his fix on Lee the fetish.

Understood as a positive pedagogy, something more than Orientalist mumbo-jumbo (although it certainly is that too), Lee's teaching here bears directly on what Rohdie calls the "act of regarding" reality, and on the proper use of images in a *media-shaped* reality. Jason learns to create images of his own, mental videoclips starring himself, and to believe in them so powerfully he can act them out in the world—or, more exactly, carry their power into the world ("it can't be stopped"). In this way, he learns that positive thinking is the key to success in the classic American tradition. More than self-help hype, however, he learns how to gain access to aesthetic power in bad existential conditions—in this film as in reality, a trickier, more strenuous proposition than idolizing Bruce Lee.[9]

Learning from Bruce Lee

Why "fetishize" a *teacher* as the ideal action hero? The overwhelming concern with "the body" in recent cultural criticism can obscure this aspect of (Western) Bruce Lee worship and narrow unduly our approach to action cinema in general.[10] Consider the persistence of the training film in Hollywood cinema from John G. Avildsen's *Rocky*

---

7 Although *No Retreat* is not simply an "American" film (see the next part of this essay), in referring to "US martial arts cinema" I follow Desser (2000a; see also 2000b) when he argues that "the force and popularity" of kung fu films in the US during 1973–75 "would lead to a genre we might call martial arts, a genre which arose in the U.S. only after the kung fu craze had passed." As Desser notes, Chuck Norris was a key figure in the genre's early definition, with the success of *Good Guys Wear Black* (1978). Strandberg (1997) can also justly claim that *NRNS* started a "resurgence of interest in martial arts films" from the mid-1980s; still a theatrically oriented film, it paved the way for *Kickboxer* (1989), a hit fully able to take advantage of an expanding video market. On the importance of tape in widening the circulation of Hong Kong and other Asian popular cinema, see Server (1999).

8 For a good guide to clones that distinguishes "homages" to Lee from films trying to "steal his persona," see Weisser (1997: 221–222). On the Lee-clone industry generally, and on Kim Tae Chong [aka Kim Tai Chung] in the dreadful *Game of Death* movies completed after Lee's death, see Meyers, Harlib and Palmer (1991: 34–44).

9 For an excellent discussion of how action cinema in general and Steven Seagal's films in particular appeal to working-class experience (especially through "a core fantasy in which one does the right thing without having to calculate economic hardship"), see Kleinhans (1996). See also Tasker (1997) on martial arts films as popular fantasies of physical empowerment responding "to the *constitution of the body through limits.*"

10 As every student of Hong Kong cinema knows, teachers are fundamental to the kung fu universe. The dominant approach to Western action cinema has different concerns: see Trasker (1993).

(1976) to Ridley Scott's *G.I. Jane* (1997). Hollywood heroes tend to be self-impelling, their teachers "family" figures; true friends or antagonists who turn out to be helpers (Mickey in *Rocky*, Master Chief in *G.I. Jane*), they are motivators rather than Muses. However, the training film offers more than a spectacle of fabulously self-made bodies acting out their masochistic reshaping routines. It also frames and moralizes this spectacle as a pedagogical experience. Training films give us lessons in using aesthetics— understood as a practical discipline, "the study of the mind and emotions in relation to the sense of beauty"[11]—to overcome personal and social adversity.

Consider also the complexity of the vast cultural networks in which this pedagogy thrives. To some extent in industrial reality as well as in formalists' dreams, the training genre links the Hollywood blockbuster economy of "global" success to the low-budget, transnational martial arts cinema with its direct-to-video fables of exemplary personal attainment (see Mark DiSalle and David Worth's *Kickboxer*, 1989, and Worth's *Lady Dragon*, 1992). Martial arts videos in turn connect diverse circuits of cult activity, sports fandom, gym, street and self-defense culture, identity politics and self-improvement philosophy to worlds of home entertainment. And both "cinemas" translate and circulate the *formal* influence of the great Hong Kong pedagogy films of the 1970s: among those long available in the West on tape, Chang Cheh's *Shaolin Temple* (1976), Liu Chia-Liang's *36th Chamber of Shaolin* (aka *The Master Killer*, 1978), and Lo Wei's comedy with the young Jackie Chan, *Spiritual Kung Fu* (1978).[12]

Typically described by one writer (Shone 1995) as "a strange twilight zone" and "a critic-proof mud" lying "fathoms below the critical nets through which mainstream films have to swim," martial arts films today compose a fuzzy space between the critically visible grandeurs of "Hollywood" and "Hong Kong." Entrepreneurially transnational in most instances, their ancestral text is neither *Rocky* nor, say, Lo Wei's *Fists of Fury* (aka *The Big Boss*, 1972), honored though these are, but Robert Clouse's unsettling hybrid, *Enter the Dragon* (1973). Starring Bruce Lee, John Saxon and Angela Mao, introducing the African-American karate champion Jim Kelly, produced by Fred Weintraub and Paul Heller for Warner Bros. in association with Golden Harvest's Raymond Chow, *Enter the Dragon* was a "kung fu James Bond film"—like the spaghetti Westerns, overtly a work of translation—pitched with legendary success to a genuinely global audience.[13]

With far more modest means and aspirations, *No Retreat, No Surrender* is a translation in this tradition; Jason's Muse is Lee as he appears in the prelude to *Enter the Dragon*, tenderly cuffing a student. With an American writer (Keith Strandberg), a mini-international cast, and US urban locations (Los Angeles, Seattle) important in the

---

11 *Macquarie Dictionary*. Despite its polemical tone and title, Eagleton (1990) is a useful introduction to this practical understanding of aesthetics.

12 These directors' names are given in the Wade-Giles forms widely used on PAL video boxes. For further reference, "Chang Cheh" (occasionally "Chang Che") = "Zhang Che"; "Lo Wei" = Luo Wei, "Liu Chia-Liang" = "Liu Jialiang" and "Lau Kar-leong."

13 For a discussion of the film as an "uneasy amalgamation of antithetical East–West sentiments," see Teo (1997: 117–118). In some ways this was a cruel inheritance. Since *Enter the Dragon*, the legend of Lee's success has been used by Western critics as a structure of expectation crushingly imposed on ambitious video stars and vastly accomplished Hong Kong artists alike: "can Jean-Claude Van Damme ever make a real film?" and "can a real Jackie Chan film make it in America?" were treated as equivalent problems. They aren't: much more complex obstacles lay in Jackie Chan's path, not least his creative relationship to an older Hollywood cinema consigned now to film study classes and to cable TV.

Figure 9.2 Jean-Claude Van Damme in *No Retreat, No Surrender* (Entertainment Film Productions 1986). Courtesy of the Kobal Collection

legend of American Bruce Lee, *No Retreat, No Surrender* was promoted on its release as a rehash of two Hollywood training hits, Avildsen's *The Karate Kid* (1984)—which translated *Rocky* from big league boxing in the Rust Belt to baby martial arts in California—and Stallone's "self-made" *Rocky IV* (1985). *No Retreat* stole swathes of plot from *The Karate Kid*, replacing the latter's "Mr. Miyagi" with Bruce Lee's ghost. Its debt to *Rocky IV* can seem esoteric now, dated as that film is: as "Ivan the Russian," the villain Jason faces in the final tournament bout, a young Jean-Claude Van Damme kittenishly mimics Dolph Lundgren's Soviet-man-on-steroids (Fig. 9.2).

In style and industrial genealogy, however, *No Retreat* was closer to the Shaolin ped-agogy films than the white-ethnic working-class Hollywood of Avildsen and Stallone. A film made to make it in America, it could also be called a "make-believe" American film. Reversing the *Enter the Dragon* formula (US power and money, "exotic" stars and scenes), it was produced by Ng See Yuen from a story developed with Corey Yuen, aka Yuen Kwai. A Hong Kong industry stalwart, Ng had produced Jackie Chan's first big hits, *Snake in the Eagle's Shadow* (1977) and *Drunken Master* (1978), as well as Tsui Hark's *The Butterfly Murders* (1979).[14] An action choreographer and former Opera School class-

14 On Ng See Yuen, see Lui (1980: 143–148) and Teo (1997: 277).

mate of Jackie Chan and Samo Hung (see Chan 1998), Yuen Kwai is probably best known today for directing *Above the Law* (aka *Righting Wrongs* [1987]) with Yuen Biao and Cynthia Rothrock, and *Yes! Madam* (1987) with Rothrock, Michelle Yeoh, and Tsui Hark in a cameo role, and for his recent remakes of Hollywood hits (*The Bodyguard from Beijing*, 1994) and Hong Kong classics (*Fong Sai-Yuk*, 1993, *Fist of Legend*, 1995), starring Jet Li.

Within a hard-edged allegory of the text as a reflection of its own creative process, *No Retreat, No Surrender* could plausibly be seen as a Hong Kong film that cleverly accessed a US market by retelling the classic Hollywood success story ("Outsider makes good"), using Bruce Lee, the ultimate migrant cross-over star, as its *mise-en-abîme* of accomplishment. The film's canny makers clearly understood Lee's special role in US martial arts *film* culture: neither a "body" nor a generic action hero, Lee is first and foremost an iconic film teacher. In a mythology still being elaborated by countless martial arts magazines and by "secrets of Jeet Kune Do" videos and books, Lee figures as both a great martial arts teacher who struggled against adversity to become a great film star *and* an exemplary martial artist who used film as a pedagogical medium—on both scores, inspiring others to do likewise.[15]

Jason is an emblematic consumer of Lee's media pedagogy. An alienated white boy from Bruce Springsteen territory, he is also the ideal spectator defined by the film. He doesn't want to sleep with his mother (glimpsed for two seconds taking groceries up the drive),[16] but he'd like to impress his girlfriend while getting his father a life—a plain if perfunctory Oedipal fantasy. However, a film's ways of involving viewers in fantasy are not always well described by psychoanalytic models of identification, whether with images or looks, and a messier line of thought gets us closer (in my middle-aged female opinion) to the core of this odd film's appeal.

It is a matter of the formal content of the film's media pedagogy, the DIY philosophy expounded in its patchy training sequences and practiced as it works over the lessons of other films. Instead of seeing *No Retreat, No Surrender* as a Hong Kong ripoff passing as American, we can just as well say that it remade *The Karate Kid* for people who like Hong Kong movies. The copy changed its model by stripping the gloss from its realism: with ultra-low-budget values, physical humor, exclamatory music and minimal interest in character, *No Retreat* lavishly added passages of farce, comic melodrama, pathos, and unabashed playacting with rude stereotypes to the sweet suburban story of the Kid.

Low-key by domestically oriented Hong Kong standards at the time (see Yuen Kwai's own *Lethal Lady*), these features of the film are conducive to noisy collective enjoyment without inhibiting private dreams; they are festive ways of sharing "asocial" wishes and fantasies with lots of other people. Theories of popular "appropriation" abound these days, but imitation does not always imply a furtive or hostile ethos of cultural theft and transgression. If *No Retreat* is composed of borrowed elements mixed in a porous industrial space ("martial arts cinema"), it seeks *affinities* between them, it sifts the training

---

15 The density of this mythology probably owes something to the fact that Lee's students in the 1960s included Hollywood people, among them James Coburn and Steve McQueen. See Desser (2000a) and Abbas (1997: 16–47). Trasker (1997: 322–328) offers an interesting discussion of Lee's use of his knowledge of the Hollywood and Hong Kong film industries.

16 The recent US version has altered this, re-Oedipalizing Jason by adding incoherent footage of a sweet domestic scene between Jason, his mother, and his girlfriend.

film and kung fu comedy together in a loose, rubbly way which is open to the sympathetic laughter of viewers.[17]

This, too, is aesthetic work, and the role of "Bruce Lee" is to explain its basic principles. These bear, as I've said, on the act of regarding reality, but they are mainly concerned with the power *in* reality which images can have. Two techniques of empowerment are demonstrated by parables enacted in Jason's home-made gym. The first is *pragmatic variation*, or, "never can succeed without a surprise"; teaching Jason not to give visual warning of the action he intends, Lee breaks Jason's grip with a move he doesn't foresee (while being himself the film's "surprise" to the Hollywood training formula). The second technique is *productive repetition*, or, practice makes perfect (expressed as the double bind, "from now on, be spontaneous"). When Jason complains of not feeling "natural" using an exercise machine, Lee throws him an apple; catching it, Jason learns that active effort enables effortless action and natural movement presupposes cultivation.

These are clichés of martial arts cinema, as of many self-development regimes, and as compositional principles they refuse autonomy to art. In innumerable films opposing "fluid" to "rigid" styles of fighting (*Dragon*, the *Kickboxer* and *Bloodfist* films), strong, flexible bodies to muscle-bound hulks (*Rage and Honor, Bounty Tracker, Best of the Best 2*), humane to fascist authority (*Showdown, Sidekicks, Only the Strong, Watch the Shadows Dance*), and improvisational to mechanistic training (*Rocky IV, The Karate Kid, Best of the Best*), the point of a pragmatic aesthetic pedagogy is always to shape a socially responsive as well as physically capable self that can handle new experience—brutes and bullies, in these films, are inadaptive—and creatively engage with strangers. Stamped on *No Retreat, No Surrender*'s opening scene, when Jason whirls out of the stiff routine of his father's karate class, this is the trademark ethic of the experimental art of Bruce Lee.

It is also one of those banal messages which, according to Sam Rohdie, fail to confine in their "goodness" the energy of cinema and dreams. For Rohdie, banality is a constraint; fantasy frees us from the everyday, the marvelous flees the mundane. In most martial arts films, banality is a source of power, as practice, repetition, training, the "dull gestures of an everyday reality" intimately *form* the martial artist and bring wonder into the world. Like the soup stirred and the fire stoked by novices in the kitchen of *Shaolin Temple*, the wax applied by the Karate Kid to Mr. Miyagi's car, even the wood Rocky chops in *Rocky IV* for (suitably grateful) peasants, the apple Lee throws Jason is banal in just this way: it marks a ground and a beginning, not a limit.

Affirmative action: *Dragon*

As spectators, we can take this message or leave it. But if cinema primarily comments on cinema, as Rohdie has it, then films may comment on economic problems of composition (often posed in training films, where the socially striving self, not just the body, is raw material for work) as well as on matters of style. Films may reflect, too, on cinema as an *industrial* field of dreams, transnationally producing and distributing acts of regarding reality; therefore, on collective and even geo-political fantasies of doing "whatever we please." And in the ordinary course of a narrative or an image unfolding

17 On the popularity of kung fu comedies in Hong Kong in the late 1970s, see Stokes and Hoover (1999: 92–93).

in time, films may reflect on the blockages and frustrations which desires, even in cinema, do encounter.

Take a scene about the act of regarding reality from Rob Cohen's glossy and engaging romantic biography, *Dragon: The Bruce Lee Story* (1993). It takes place in a West Coast cinema in the early 1960s: recently arrived from Hong Kong but a US citizen by birth, Bruce (Jason Scott Lee) is sitting with his white girlfriend, Linda (Lauren Holly). Deft vignettes have already established the strength of the couple's attraction and the hostility they face: in the preceding scenes, we've seen them obliquely denied service at a restaurant and we've briefly watched Bruce at his everyday training, a simple *mise-en-scène* emphasizing just how gorgeous and powerful he is.

A cut takes us outside a theatre advertising a "Laff Fest Revival." There follows a beautifully intimate study of film spectatorship as a sometimes lonely crowd experience, moving and unpredictable as it differs between people and subtly alters relationships. It begins by positing those familiar imaginary units, "the audience" and "the couple." Potentially from the latter's point of view, the first shot looks up across rows of heads to take in a scene from *Breakfast at Tiffany's*; Audrey Hepburn elegantly scrabbles at a door as Claude Stroud arrives left, asking her the question which *Dragon* reframes as a question about the scene itself; "Hey, baby, what's going on here?" In the reverse shot a happy, expectant Linda, her face framed by others in similar spirits, leans right to whisper that she "loves this movie so much." Bruce winces "Oh yeah?" in reply; it seems that he, too, has seen "this movie" before.

The couple loses unity and abstraction: Linda brightens, Bruce darkens, they part toward opposing edges of the frame. With the audience still in the picture the next shot is of a grossly made-up Mickey Rooney bolting upright in bed to bang his head on his own idiotically positioned lamp. The audience then drops out of the image but swells the sound with "laffs" as we all watch the cartoon "Oriental"—mammoth buck teeth, raucous voice, singsong "Ah So" English—fall over his own photographic equipment as he crashes to the door in a slapstick performance of perfect incompetence. An extreme closeup snaps Linda, full face, laughing, nested in the pleasure around her; we share her gaze to the screen as the beautiful Hepburn looks upwards, and we all look with Hepburn at "Mr. Yunioshi" hideously rasping down the stairwell "Miss Golightly! I prote-e-e-st!"

The next shot is again of Linda in closeup but holds her face a little longer; she turns right to share her pleasure and her smile suddenly fades. Only then does the camera pan left to reveal the solitude of her partner, who sits unsmiling as Rooney shrieks "You disturba me! You must have a key made!" When it pans back to Linda, she is still looking in Bruce's direction. Slowly she looks back to the screen, her own face now unsmiling (in a medium closeup which sets her in contrast with those around her) as Rooney screeches: "I'm an artist! I must have my rest!" When she turns back to Bruce, the couple is framed together for the first time since she declared her love for "this movie." They look at each other, and Linda says, "Let's get out of here."

This is a defining moment in the love story organizing *Dragon*, a sanitized as well as hagiographic interpretation of Bruce Lee's life as authorized by his widow. But with its fluid intercutting of varying "points of view" on *Breakfast at Tiffany's*, this scene is also a rhythmically exact little story about people being differently "moved" (Rohdie's term) in the cinema, their wishes and dreams diverging and then, on this occasion, reaching new empathy as responses of others around them—the sociable dimension of cinema—inflect and color their own. So clear is the scene's affirmation of the diverse collective nature of film experience that it could be said to deconstruct the very idea of "*the* spectator" (that wishful critical projection) and its attendant generalizing rhetoric about "what really moves *us*."

I'm content to claim that it suggests a definition of "political correctness" in cinema. PC is not primarily a code regulating expression but a spectators' revolt. Aesthetically focused but social in resonance, PC is an act or a movement of criticism initiated by groups of people who develop shared responses to particular cultural conventions, and begin to form "an" audience in the marketing sense: by articulating a collective "commentary on cinema," they announce themselves as an audience. And they vocally object to the quality of something which cinema provides.[18] Understood this way, PC as a critical formation has less in common with the grim radicals of media bad dreams (real as dreams may be) than with those highly respectable "consumer movements" which have, through the very same media, powerfully influenced business and advertising practices in recent decades.

Dragon, too, is a respectable and ethically moderate film. The scene I've discussed is didactic (it shows us "how to read a film"), but it teaches neither a hardline identity politics nor an unforgiving war on Linda's sense of humor; it is a parable of change and reciprocity. The scene's premise, after all, is that people routinely sit through a film they dislike in order to please their loved ones, not fun but no big deal; and the editing credits *Dragon*'s audience with a capacity for involvement in more than one way of seeing. Looking with Linda we can see the beauty and lightness in *Breakfast at Tiffany's*, and then see what her partner sees—coarse racism dressed as refinement. Looking with Bruce we see this coarseness go unremarked, as though we ourselves were invisible to those closest to us. From a third position, we see Linda come to understand and share Bruce's revolt, or, since that word is a bit too strong, his revulsion.

If this scene "mirrors" an act of regarding reality, it does so by reflecting back to its audience the mixed, porous, and eventful nature of cinema's own reality. It also assumes a triangular rather than dualistic model of what happens when people watch films. In *Dragon*, film study is more than a matter of "negotiating your subjectivity with the subjectivity of the film" (Rohdie 1995b: 11); cinematic negotiation involves you, the film, and other people. However, while it has three terms this is nonetheless a model of imaginary experience. *Dragon* is not a debunking of fantasy in the name of social realism or the law-abiding Symbolic of psychoanalysis. On the contrary: when Linda suddenly connects the Chinese man beside her, the "Oriental" on screen, and her pleasure in both, she makes an imaginative leap outside the logic of her own familiar dreams which allows her to experience something new. Putting "herself" in another's position, she finds that her companion lives a connection between his body and the grotesque parody on screen—one fictionally modeled in a fleeting moment of cinema but relayed and sustained in his everyday life by the gazes (and the voices) of other people.

Linda returns to *Breakfast at Tiffany's* with the eyes and ears of a critic, or so I like to think; as a student, she is certainly able to "enter into" another subjectivity in the way that Rohdie advises us to do (1995b: 11). No doubt, I'm sketching here my own ideal spectator: I love the experience Linda has, that jaw-dropping jolt of astonishment at how the world shifts when you see, or believe that you can see, what someone else

---

18 For an interesting account of a formalized group of this kind, the Media Action Network for Asian Americans (which picketed Philip Kaufman's *Rising Sun* after failing to influence the script), see Payne (1996). On the long history of such protests, dating back at least to 1911, see Shohat and Stam (1994: 181).

is seeing. This in no way prevents me when I watch action films from taking pleasure in murdering everybody, never mind just Dad. The point is simply that many things move people in the cinema, "worthy issues" included, and that fantasy can impel us toward others as well as deeper into ourselves.

Of course, an imaginative leap can always fall flat. *Dragon* promotes the utopian potential of cinematic negotiation; reconciliation and deeper mutual understanding follow from going to the movies with Bruce Lee. In wider reality, precisely because cinema is sociable, an empathetic movement may equally well meet rejection, indifference, misunderstanding, or dissent. For some viewers, *Dragon* itself is a provocation to criticism; blurring Lee's overt and distinctive cultural nationalism into a generalized "reaction against racism" (Teo 1997: 113), it transfigures a Hong Kong Chinese hero as flexibly "Asian"-American. Nowhere in the film is this effected more clearly than in the *Breakfast at Tiffany's* scene, in which we watch a white American woman empathizing with a Chinese-American man identifying with a *Japanese* stereotype as embodied by an Irish-American actor.[19] Now, as Teo (1997: 111) points out, Lee's Hong Kong films not only were nationalist in an "abstract" way unrelated to a government or state (manifesting "an emotional wish among Chinese people living outside China to identify with China and things Chinese") but they also had a "xenophobic streak" (113)—in particular, toward Japanese.[20] Accordingly, Teo suggests that "Western admirers of Lee view him differently from his Eastern admirers, and the difference revolves around his nationalism"; for Westerners, like the English critic Tony Rayns (1980), the narcissism (and homoeroticism) of Lee's body-culture is his most distinctive trait.[21] These two modes of viewing converge on the figure of Lee in that he can, in Teo's words, be "all things to all men" (1997: 110), but they do not really communicate: "to his many Western viewers, Lee's nationalism is a non-starter" (113).

My view is that the term "Western" is way too large for the complex tensions of spectatorship here. As a Western but Australian participant in these, I can't help but see that a US identity politics, uninterested in any but American social conflicts and burdens, often ignores or refuses to *imagine* that things are "different" for people elsewhere. No doubt there is ample evidence for a "Western" post-nationalist view of Lee, at least in his later life; such compilation tapes as *Bruce Lee: The Legend* and *Bruce Lee: Curse of the Dragon* contain plenty of interviews in which Lee tells Western audiences what Teo thinks we want to hear—universalizing humanist messages exalting the individual and renouncing national "styles." Yet I suspect that far from being a "non-starter" for Western admirers, Lee's modeling of an empowering cultural nationalism detached from any specific

---

19 Screening *Dragon* in Australia, I have found that this moment in the film often creates controversy. People wishing to judge the film's historical accuracy (or to stake a claim to be able to do so) express incredulity that the real Bruce Lee would ever have "seen himself" in a Japanese stereotype at all.

20 Lee's films were not remarkable in this respect. Japanese were widely made targets of hostility and caricature in 1970s Hong Kong cinema (as indeed in many other national cinemas, including Hollywood, in the decades after the Pacific war). See Meyers, Harlib, and Palmer (1991: 64–66) on "cinematic hatred of the Japanese" as expressed in the films of Wang Yu, the 1960s Hong Kong superstar displaced by Bruce Lee's success; paradoxically but also routinely for the times, Yu made anti-Japanese films while working with Japanese filmmakers. While noting the "extremism" of Yu's cinema, Meyers, Harlib, and Palmer have their own problems about Japan. First published in 1985, their book begins a chapter on "Samurai Swordsmen and Karate Killers" by matter-of-factly calling Japan "the nation built on hypocrisy" (1991: 163).

21 For an interesting discussion of these issues in terms of a distinction between Hong Kong and American martial arts cinema, see Trasker (1997).

political state is exactly what makes him inspiring for the comparably abstract and cul-turalized ethnic "nationalisms" that flourish in the US and other densely multicultural Western nations. After all, as Desser (2000a) points out, the American "kung fu craze" of 1973 that launched Lee's global success began in inner city cinemas frequented by black and Hispanic audiences that maintained their interest in martial arts culture long after the craze had passed.

However, unless we see how the narcissism serves the nationalism (and vice versa), all this remains an argument about representation and the fiction/reality relation. What makes *Dragon* so rich a commentary on cinema is rather that it frames its "critique" of *Breakfast at Tiffany's* as an episode in a broader narrative about Bruce Lee's dream of making martial arts films himself; there is an overtly Chinese artist as well as a Western critic in the *Breakfast at Tiffany's* scene. In fact, Lee was able to direct only one com-plete feature, and that in Hong Kong rather than Hollywood: *The Way of the Dragon* (aka *Return of the Dragon*, 1972) is one of the most famous martial arts films ever made. *Dragon* touches lightly on this achievement; a fairytale of star-crossed love in more ways than one, it is mainly interested in the hero's *desire* to gain access to the enchanted castle of Hollywood, and the obstacles he has to overcome.

Focusing on legendary stories that Lee wore a mask as Kato in *The Green Hornet* series to shield American audiences from his "Oriental" face, and was replaced as Caine in *Kung Fu* by the safely white David Carradine—of whom Chuck Norris has reportedly said, "Carradine's as good at martial arts as I am at acting" (Meyers, Harlib, and Palmer 1991: 221)—*Dragon* interprets Lee's life not only as a battle against Western prejudice and, as Teo (1997: 113) delicately notes, a "fatal destiny" obscurely attributed to "Chinese superstition," but also as an affirmative struggle for the freedom and power to "make believe." Whatever the truth of these stories, and however mytho-poeic and American-centered its approach to biography may be, *Dragon* is one of the more powerful treatments of institutionalized racism in a film *industry* (as well as in film images) that US cinema possesses.

Formalism complements materialism here. Those legends of adversity are incipient in the *Breakfast at Tiffany's* scene, held there in potential along with the grief which Linda will have from her mother over marrying a Chinese man; the near-fatal opposition Bruce will encounter from local kung fu masters for taking students who are not Chinese; along with the birth and prefigured death of Brandon Lee. What loads this eventfulness into the scene, framing it as a prediction of Bruce Lee's future in film history as well as a critique of Hollywood's past, is a design effect so delicate as to be almost impercep-tible. The sleekness and tone of Linda's long hair, the make-up and lighting of Lauren Holly's fine-boned features and the crowning touch of her hat, all visually echo (though they do not mirror) the styling of Hepburn as she laughs, hair swept up, castratingly at the "dear little man" above who wails about being an artist—promising to "let" him "take pictures."

As Linda and Bruce push out of their seats, silhouetted against the screen, Mr. Yunioshi asks Holly Golightly: "*When?*" This is what the hero of *Dragon* will ask of Holly-wood, before despairing of an answer and returning to Hong Kong. As readdressed to *Dragon*'s audience, however, this expression of aesthetic yearning is something more than a critical "complaint" about representation ("what's going on here?"). It is a prac-tical demand: the political question of who does, who can, and who wants to be able to "take pictures" has pointedly been raised.

Afterthoughts on PC

Does this make *Dragon* a "politically correct" film? I don't think so. A feminist so inclined could have merciless fun with its gendered division of labor, and like many other anti-racist US martial arts films (for example, Richard W. Munchkin's extraordinary *Blood and Steel: Ring of Fire 2*, indeed almost anything starring Don "The Dragon" Wilson), *Dragon* has little interest in negotiating more complex roles for Asian or black women. *No Retreat, No Surrender* is certainly not PC; with a fat boy, a black boy with a great sense of rhythm, and a hulking Russian bear, its palette of stereotypes is no more shaded by sensitivity about "difference" than that of *Breakfast at Tiffany's*—or, for that matter, *Fists of Fury* and its immediate model, Wang Yu's *The Chinese Boxer* (1970), in which simian Japanese graze their knuckles on the ground.

My argument is not about whether a film or a genre "is" whatever we mean by PC. I'm suggesting on the contrary that "PC" is a term that can't settle on a stable content, a smooth spectrum of complaint, a single "orthodoxy" or dogma. Like any good insult it is slippery, but not meaningless: whether we like the term or not it continues to be in use, and terms in use make meaning. I suspect it has come to name a critical *technique* practiced by and across many different kinds of audiences—restrictive and bureaucratic in some instances, creative and anarchic in others. Whether the term itself will have currency for much longer, I have no idea. However, I am sure of at least one thing: the questions raised in *Dragon*'s scene of PC revolt are not only of academic interest, and they will not go away.

The assumption that every film can be usefully "read" for its performance of social issues certainly is an academic idea, more attuned to the needs of an education and publishing industry than to the economy of popular entertainment. This doesn't make it a bad idea, but its provenance helps to explain the aura of extremism successfully attached to PC in the media, and so inappropriate to a film like *Dragon*. Academic debates about representation generally *are* more "extreme," and sometimes more reductive, than those which arise in socially diffuse moments of aesthetic and ethical revulsion. Popular debates occur sporadically, when enough people are enough annoyed to make a fuss, or to bother responding when someone else does. Academic debates occur on principle: it *must be possible*, our training tells us, to look at this film this way. This interpretive drive can be creative (the technique of "queering" is its liveliest recent manifestation) but also blinkered and narrow in its relentlessness; hence the direct hit scored by Robert Hughes' (1993: 72) famous pot-shot, "the world changes more widely, deeply, thrillingly than at any moment since 1917, perhaps since 1848, and the American academic left keeps fretting about how phallocentricity is inscribed in Dickens's portrayal of Little Nell." However, these modes of discussion are not sealed off from each other, not least because the training of filmmakers as well as bureaucrats, teachers and critics now takes place, like the shaping of subjectivities, in a world where fantasy makes money and images have force. The economic redefinition of art and entertainment as news— serious news (Morris 2000)—is inexorably redistributing the desire and the power to criticize make-believe in this society. While it is true that only a mandarin caste of critics spends much of its time "interrogating" texts, it is no longer true that only mandarins ask textual questions. This is a wide, deep, thrilling change in the world which Robert Hughes has missed. *If* only academics still feel angst about Little Nell (and I have my doubts about that), fretting over phallocentricity is now a popular occupation.

Acknowledgments

This chapter resulted from invitations to speak by the Australian Screen Directors Conference in 1995, and by the Australian Teachers of Media association (ATOM) in 1996; a first version was published in *Metro* 117 (1998), 6–15. My thanks to David Desser, Adrian Martin, and Hank Okazaki for their help.

References

Abbas, Ackbar (1997) *Hong Kong: Culture and the Politics of Disappearance*, Minneapolis: University of Minnesota Press.

Barker, Martin and Julian Petley, eds (1997) *Ill Effects: The Media Violence Debate*, London and New York: Routledge.

Berry, Chris, Annette Hamilton, and Laleen Jayamanne, eds (1997) *The Filmmaker and the Prostitute: Dennis O'Rourke's* "The Good Woman of Bangkok," Sydney: Power Publications.

Chan, Jackie with Jeff Yang (1998) *I Am Jackie Chan: My Life in Action*, New York: Ballantine.

Desser, David (2000a) "The Kung Fu Craze: Hong Kong Cinema's First American Reception," in Fu Poshek and David Desser, eds, *The Cinema of Hong Kong: History, Arts, Identity*, Cambridge: Cambridge University Press, 19–43.

—— (2000b) "The Martial Arts Film in the 1990s," in Wheeler Winston Dixon, ed., *Film Genre 2000: New Critical Essays*, Albany, NY: SUNY Press, 77–109.

Eagleton, Terry (1990) *The Ideology of the Aesthetic*, Oxford: Blackwell.

Hughes, Robert (1993) *Culture of Complaint: The Fraying of America*, New York: Oxford University Press.

Julius, Marshall (1996) *"Action!" The Action Movie A–Z*, Bloomington and Indianapolis: Indiana University Press.

Kleinhans, Chuck (1996) "Class in Action," in David E. James and Rick Berg, eds, *The Hidden Foundations: Cinema and the Question of Class*, Minneapolis: University of Minnesota Press, 240–263.

Lui Shi (1980) "Ng See-Yuen: An Interview," in *A Study of the Hong Kong Martial Arts Film*, Hong Kong: The Urban Council, 143–148.

Martin, Adrian (1977) "Call It Scorsese," *The UTS Review* 3 (1): 216–223.

—— (1998) "Euphoria and Liberating Laughter: The Cinema of Sergio Leone," *Metro* 113/114: 25–34.

Meyers, Richard, Amy Harlib, and Karen Palmer (1991) *From Bruce Lee to the Ninjas: Martial Arts Movies*, New York: Carol Publishing Group.

Miller, Davis (2000) *The Tao of Bruce Lee*, London and Sydney: Vintage.

Morris, Meaghan (2000) "Globalisation and Its Discontents," *Meridian* (Australia), and *Sekai* (Japan), forthcoming.

Payne, Robert M. (1996) "Total Eclipse of the Sun: Interview with Guy Aoki," *Jump Cut* 40: 29–37.

Rayns, Tony (1980) "Bruce Lee: Narcissism and Nationalism," in *A Study of the Hong Kong Martial Arts Film*, Hong Kong: The Urban Council, 110–112.

Rohdie, Sam (1995a) "The Independence of Form: The 19th Hong Kong International Film Festival," *Metro* 103: 24–30.

—— (1995b) "Sixth Form Film Teaching in Hong Kong," *Metro Education* 4 (in *Metro* 102): 3–11.

Server, Lee (1999) *Asian Pop Cinema: Bombay to Tokyo*, San Francisco: Chronicle Books.

Shohat, Ella and Robert Stam (1994) *Unthinking Eurocentrism: Multiculturalism and the Media*, London and New York: Routledge.

Shone, Tom (1995) "Can Van Damme Kick It?" *Sunday Times Magazine* (UK), January 1.

Stern, Lesley (1995) *The Scorsese Connection*, London and Bloomington: British Film Institute and Indiana University Press.

Stokes, Lisa Odham and Michael Hoover (1999) *City on Fire: Hong Kong Cinema*, London and New York: Verso.

Strandberg, Keith W. (1997) "15 Years Making Action Films," http://www.cyberfilmschool.com //articles/action.htm, as available May 1998.

Tasker, Yvonne (1993) *Spectacular Bodies: Gender, Genre and the Action Cinema*, London and New York: Routledge.

——(1997) "Fists of Fury: Discourses of Race and Masculinity in the Martial Arts Cinema," in Harry Stecopoulos and Michael Uebel, eds, *Race and the Subject of Masculinities*, Durham, NC and London: Duke University Press, 315–336.

Teo, Stephen (1997) *Hong Kong Cinema: The Extra Dimensions*, London: British Film Institute.

Weisser, Thomas (1997) *Asian Cult Cinema*, New York: Boulevard Books.

10 "Waas sappening?"

Narrative structure and iconography in *Born in East L.A.*[1]

Chon A. Noriega

"The best way to make a statement is you slip it in the coffee so they don't taste it, but, they get the effect."

Richard "Cheech" Marin[2]

Coffee? When, on August 21, 1987, Universal Studios released Cheech Marin's directorial debut, *Born in East L.A.* (Fig. 10.1), it seemed as if the studio did not know what to do with the film. After all, it was unlike the sex, drugs and rock-n-roll, and more drugs, of the Cheech and Chong "occasions-on-film" that had earned almost $300 million since *Up in Smoke* (1978). Even so, Marin's past reputation conflicted with the "just say no" ethos of the Reagan era.[3] To make matters worse, Universal changed studio heads mid-film, which all but guaranteed a lackluster promotion, since the film's success would accrue to the old, and not the new person in charge. And so, *Born in East L.A.* was dumped on the national market without the usual advance press screenings.

Caught off guard, the local press nonetheless responded favorably to the film, particularly in the Southwest, where the *Los Angeles Times* critic even concluded: "It has more drive and energy than *La Bamba*."[4] Coming one month after the box office success of Luis Valdez's *La Bamba*, statements such as these fueled speculation about the emergence of a "Hispanic Hollywood."[5] But in the national press, *Born in East L.A.* hit a brick wall, receiving only two reviews. *People Weekly* dismissed the film as "a string of uneven skits," while *Cineaste* prefaced its interview with Marin with the high-minded assessment that the film was "well-intentioned," "progressive," but little more than "loosely

1 Reprinted from *Studies in Latin American Popular Culture* 14 (1995). A much shorter version of this article appeared in the media arts issue of *Tonantzin* (February 1991), a tabloid magazine published by the Guadalupe Cultural Arts Center in conjunction with its annual CineFestival. I want to thank Tomás Ybarra-Frausto, Mary Louise Pratt, Kathleen Newman, and Ana M. López for their insightful comments on earlier versions of this essay.
2 Ruben Guevara, Interview with Cheech Marin, *Americas 2001* (June–July 1987), 18–21, 18.
3 According to Pat Aufderheide, "Cheech Marin says, Universal Studios funded *Born in East L.A.* to clear up his doper image at a time when antidrug hysteria has gripped American culture." "Reel Life," *Mother Jones* (April 1988), 24–26, 45–46, 46.
4 Kevin Thomas, "'East L.A.' Gets the Green Card," *Los Angeles Times* (August 24, 1987), sec. F: 1, 4.
5 See Chon A. Noriega, "Chicano Cinema and the Horizon of Expectations: A Discursive Analysis of Film Reviews in the Mainstream, Alternative, and Hispanic Press, 1987–1988," *Aztlán: A Journal of Chicano Studies* 19 (2) (Fall 1988–90), 1–32.

Figure 10.1 Cheech Marin in *Born in East L.A.* (Universal 1987). Courtesy of the Kobal Collection

strung together shticks and vignettes," and, in the final analysis, "politically naive."[6] These very different publications—one popular and conservative, the other elite and "left-of-center"—nonetheless shared a common assumption: namely, that the film lacked a coherent narrative when judged against the correct aesthetics and politics.

Still, *Born in East L.A.* was the second highest grossing film in its first week, and would be the number one film in the Southwest for nearly four weeks.[7] But aside from the "surprise" box office revenue, the film's social impact was not spoken about outside the Chicano and Spanish-language press. When the film premiered in East LA, the *barrio* newspaper *La Opinier* described the event as the reclamation of a ceremonial ritual, and a collective reunion.[8] *La Opinied, Unidad*, and *Americas 2001* also praised the film as an alternative and risky look at a "highly controversial issue" then dom-

---

6 Tom Cunneff, "Born in East L.A.," *People Weekly* (September 14, 1987), 14; and Dennis West and Gary Crowdus, "Cheech Cleans Up His Act," Interview, *Cineaste* 16 (3) (1988), 34–37. *Cineaste* at least provided a forum for Marin to express his views, although the preface to the interview uses later questions as statements that in no way engage, let alone acknowledge, Marin's responses.

7 Information gathered from *Variety* (August 26, 1987; September 2, 1987; September 9, 1987; September 16, 1987; and September 23, 1987).

8 Juan Rodríguez Flores, "En el estreno de la película 'Born in East L.A.,'" *La Opinidr* (August 22, 1987), sec. 3: 1.

inating the news: the expiration on September 1, 1987 of the "grace period" for undocumented workers to apply for "amnesty" under the new immigration law.[9] Indeed, the film represents a calculated use of humor to respond to the Simpson-Rodino Immigration Reform Act and California's successful English-Only Initiative (both 1986). But if the Hollywood film's political significance did not register outside of the Hispanic press in the United States, it did become a turning point for reconsidering oppositional cinema in Latin America.

In December 1987, *Born in East L.A.* won four major awards at the Ninth International Festival of New Latin American Cinema in Havana, Cuba, including, ironically enough, the Glauber Rocha award, given by Prensa Latina, an international press organization based in Havana.[10] The irony is twofold in so far as New Latin American Cinema represented a counter-cinema *vis-à-vis* both Hollywood and the national industries in Latin America that followed in its footsteps. Furthermore, New Latin American Cinema did not just speak *to* an underlying issue of underdevelopment, it transformed underdevelopment into an aesthetic logic aimed at *concientizacig* and cultural decolonization. In this manner, Glauber Rocha, an early filmmaker and theorist of Cinema Novo in Brazil, spoke of an "aesthetics of hunger" and an "aesthetics of violence" as revolutionary responses to colonial oppression: "The moment of violence is the moment when the coloniser becomes aware of the existence of the colonised."[11] In the 1960s and 1970s, such an aesthetics stood outside commercial industrial production, outside humanist, rationalist discourse, and outside a strictly nationalist politics.

But, by the time the festival was established in 1979, New Latin American Cinema had entered into a crisis, brought on by military coups and repression, crippling international debt, and the limits of social transformation in the face of the mass media. The festival represented an attempt on the part of Cuba to provide an institutional mooring and industrial model for New Latin American Cinema that—in some ways—brought the movement into alignment with the national industries. From the start, Chicanos were part of this vision, with Chicano cinema understood as a "national" category, allowing a paradoxical situation when Chicano filmmakers were able to work within *their* national industry, Hollywood. Thus, the awards received by *Born in East L.A.* were a sign at once of a strategic shift within New Latin American Cinema toward more popular and commercial forms, and of the continuing presence of "Chicano cinema" within Latin American film festivals since the 1970s. What the awards suggested, then, was that the political ideals and goals of New Latin American Cinema could now be expressed through Hollywood, with the troubling implication that perhaps the opposite could also be true.[12]

9 Maggie Cardenas, "Born in East L.A.," *Unidad/Unity* (October 12, 1987), 12; and *Americas 2001* (cited above). On the end of the "grace period," see Marita Hernandez, "Amnesty—The First Wave Battles Red Tape," *Los Angeles Times* (September 1, 1987), A9, A16; and Jess Bravin, "No Mass Firings of Aliens Seen as Exemption Ends," *Los Angeles Times* (September 1, 1987), B3, B16.

10 This included: "Tercer Premio Coral" (third prize) in fiction, the "Premio Coral" in screenwriting, the "Premio Coral" in set design, and the Glauber Rocha award. Teresa Toledo, *10 as included: "Tercer Premio Coral"* (Madrid: Verdoux, S.L., 1990), 575. Also, Paul Lenti, "Broad U.S. Presence at Havana's New Latino Fest," *Variety* (December 23, 1987), 5.

11 Glauber Rocha, "The Aesthetics of Hunger," translated by Julianne Burton, in Michael Chanan, ed., *Twenty-Five Years of the New Latin American Cinema* (London: British Film Institute/Channel Four Television, 1983), 13.

12 For an extensive discussion of these historiographic issues, see Ana M. López, "An 'Other' History: The New Latin American Cinema," in Robert Sklar and Charles Musser, eds, *Resisting Images: Essays on Cinema and History* (Philadelphia: Temple University Press, 1990), 308–330.

Since its release and appearance at the festival, *Born in East L.A.* has generated considerable interest among Chicano scholars, who have elucidated Cheech Marin's role as the *pelado* and "Chicano Moses" of American popular film.[13] Why, then, has *Born in East L.A.* been all but forgotten in the US mainstream—in fact, Marin and Valdez have been unable to direct other feature films in the intervening seven years—while it has such resonance within the Chicano community (and the New Latin American Cinema Festival)? Can this resonance itself be explained as a cultural sensibility that allows Chicano audiences to fill in the narrative gaps; that is, to make exceptions for the film in the absence of other Chicano-themed or -produced feature films? Or, does the film have a coherent structure, after all? While the emphasis so far has been on narrative structure or coherence, the iconography of the Chicano Movement (especially in murals and graphic arts) has had a significant impact on Chicano film and video, and provides an important key with which to answer these questions. *Born in East L.A.*, for example, lampoons the Immigration Reform Act and English-Only Movement, but does so by situating its critique through bicultural iconography within the *mise-en-scène*. Thus, while the industry genre classification—comedy, musical—provides some sense of the episodic structure, it is iconography and *mise-en-scène* that provide an overall logic with which to assign meaning to the narrative.

In *Born in East L.A.*, Rudy Robles (Cheech Marin) is deported to Mexico, although he is a third-generation Chicano who does not speak Spanish. The film's premise is based on a newspaper account that Cheech Marin read in the *Los Angeles Times*, as he also listened to Bruce Springsteen's "Born in the U.S.A." on the radio.[14] Thus the narrative is first and foremost about the ephemeral status of Chicano citizenship, and not, as many non-Latino critics assumed, "wetbacks" and "illegal aliens." But unlike the earlier accommodationist politics among Mexican-Americans in which American citizenship and Mexican immigration were placed in opposition, *Born in East L.A.* conflates Chicano nationalism (which is inherently pro-immigration) with the national ideology of America as a land of immigrants.[15] As a critique of the English-Only Movement, *Born in East L.A.* reveals race and not language to be the underlying factor, especially in so far as official language movements often walk hand-in-hand with immigration politics.

13 See Rosa Linda Fregoso, "*Born in East L.A.* and the Politics of Representation," *Cultural Studies* 4 (3) (October 1990), 264–280; Eddie Tafoya, "*Born in East L.A.*: Cheech as the Chicano Moses," *Journal of Popular Culture* 26 (4) (Spring 1993), 123–129; and Christine List, "Self-Directed Stereotyping in the Films of Cheech Marin," and Víctor Fuentes, "Chicano Cinema: A Dialectic of Voices and Images of the Autonomous Discourse versus Those of the Dominant," in Chon A. Noriega, ed., *Chicanos and Film: Representation and Resistance* (Minneapolis: University of Minnesota Press, 1992), 183–194, 207–217.

14 Interview by author with Richard "Cheech" Marin, October 16, 1990, Malibu, California.

15 On the split between Mexican-American and Chicano politics, see Carlos Muñoz, Jr., *Youth, Identity, Power: The Chicano Movement* (New York: Verso, 1989). In many ways, this dichotomy has been a self-serving one within Chicano historical revisionism, and does little to explain, for example, the combined Mexican nationalism and anti-immigration politics of the United Farm Workers Union. For my purposes here, I want to show how immigration functions as a trope around which *Born in East L.A.* conflates cultural nationalism and structural assimilation. In his case histories of the Mexican-American Generation, Mario García complicates the above initial assessment, which reduced the wide range of political activism to a question of accommodation. See *Mexican Americans: Leadership, Ideology, and Identity, 1930–1960* (New Haven, CT: Yale University Press, 1989). See also David G. Gutiérrez, "*Sin Fronteras?* Chicanos, Mexican Americans, and the Emergence of the Contemporary Mexican Immigration Debate, 1968–1978," *Journal of American Ethnic History* 10 (4) (Summer 1991), 5–37.

As Dennis Baron notes in *The English-Only Question*, "so central is language to political organization that in many societies defining language has become tantamount to defining nationality."[16] But this itself often obscures an implied equivalence between language, nation, and race/ethnicity. As Baron concludes, "Americanism evidenced by the adoption of English is not always enough," since official language legislation "inevitably [expresses] a nativism which rejects certain groups of Americans no matter what language they speak."[17] In some respects, Chicano nationalism made an end-run around such nativism in so far as its pro-immigration stance is based on prior claims to the Southwest that are rooted in pre-historical myths as much as in the Mexican nation. In this manner, Chicanos are equated with the Southwest in a move that places them outside of history in order to proclaim the rights of US citizenship.[18]

In the final analysis, *Born in East L.A.* places these issues about the relationship between race and citizenship within a spatial logic more than a narrative one. In other words, the emphasis is on being somewhere (East LA) rather than becoming someone (a good citizen). After Rudy is deported, the film depicts his various attempts to reason, purchase, and sneak his way back across the border. Like the deracinated character of another musical fantasy, Rudy pleads on several occasions, "I just want to go home now, okay?" I refer, of course, to Dorothy in *The Wizard of Oz* (1939). But the allusion is not entirely facetious, since it foregrounds the role of "home" within the otherwise picaresque adventures, and—in the end—reveals these two spaces (home and exile) to be one and the same. As a picaresque hero, Rudy experiences a number of unrelated adventures without an essential transformation of character. Instead, through his romance with Dolores, a would-be border crosser from El Salvador, Rudy—like Dorothy—makes a series of simple realizations that empower him to cross the border through sheer willpower or desire. In between deportation and return, Rudy comes to realize that (1) American society views him as more Mexican than American, (2) Mexicans see him as American or *pocho*, and (3) his attitudes toward women and immigrants have been callous. The latter act of lateral identification follows upon the first two realizations, and leads to Rudy's return. What organizes these picaresque scenes—or, "loosely strung together shticks and vignettes"—is an overarching satire on the paradox that Rudy must struggle to return to a position that remains a birthright. In this sense, he is like Dorothy in that he never left "home," since he never stopped being an American. But it is a birthright that is both entrenched (acculturation) and tenuous (citizenship), adding a racial dimension to Springsteen's working-class lament on citizenship in a postindustrial economy.[19] In effect, the picaresque or "loose" nature of the narrative mirrors the

16 Dennis Baron, *The English-Only Question: An Official Language for Americans?* (New Haven, CT: Yale University Press, 1990), 6.
17 Ibid., 62.
18 For a recent example, see Rosa Linda Fregoso's contention that the US conquest of the Southwest as a result of the Mexican-American War was *illegal*, and, therefore, Mexican immigrants must be given the *legal* status of citizens. Without recourse to some notion of international law, Fregoso makes a reified "historical standpoint"—the fact that California was part of the Mexican nation between 1821 and 1848—the basis for a law (and citizenship) that stands outside of history and historical processes. The "law" that she conjures can only exist within the realm of moral discourses, while the laws that do exist—such as the Treaty of Guadalupe Hidalgo—are never examined as a way to deconstruct the US legal system. *The Bronze Screen: Chicana and Chicano Film Culture* (Minneapolis: University of Minnesota Press, 1993), 85–90.
19 On the political ambiguity of the song's lyrics and reception, see John Lombardi, "St. Boss: The Sanctification of Bruce Springsteen and the Rise of Mass Hip," *Esquire* (December 1988), 139–154, esp. 146.

protagonist's own ambiguous status as citizen, while the iconography and *mise-en-scène* continually frame these scenes within a bi-national logic that works against stereotypical expectations. In so far as the lost "home" is also a literal domicile shared with his mother, sister, and her children, Rudy's status and birthright as the "man" within the family is also called into question. His deportation, then, signals a crisis of citizenship and patriarchy within the *barrio*.

Because *Born in East L.A.* questions space or location, it places more attention on constructing "borders" that will frame events than it does on character and plot development. In the remainder of the essay, I will focus on the opening and closing scenes of the film as well as a comedic framing device that separates these from the narrative proper. These brief scenes use highly charged *mise-en-scène* in order to provide an interpretive structure with which to read the "body" of the film. In the end, the "loosely strung together shticks and vignettes" are neither incoherent nor "politically naive," but rather overdetermined by the paradoxes and contradictions of Chicano birthright.

In its establishing shot, *Born in East L.A.* challenges Hollywood conventions of the *barrio*, initiating a shift from public to private space as the source for Chicano representation in Hollywood films. The film begins with a shot of the Los Angeles skyline, pans to the left to East LA, tilts down and—through a series of dissolves—comes to rest on a house beside a church. Thus the home, with its fence, well-kept yard, and a tree, becomes the defining unit for the *barrio*, rather than—as in *Colors* (1988) *et al.*—a montage of graffiti, gangs, drug deals and so on that signifies "problem space." In essence, East LA is identified as an appropriate site for the American Dream. Similar shot sequences have been used to locate the *barrio* within Los Angeles in social problem films since the 1950s, but these work against either metonymic or metaphoric associations between East Los Angeles and Los Angeles (and America).[20] Instead, these films impose mimicry as a model for Chicanos, who are not seen as a part of or equivalent to American, but rather as "like but not quite" American.[21] As I have argued elsewhere, this supports an argument for ideological assimilation coupled with *barrio* segregation, both of which are depicted as choices made by the male protagonists.[22]

In its next shot, however, *Born in East L.A.* moves beyond a mere alternative to the usual external depictions of the *barrio*, when it zooms in and cuts to the interior of the home. Inside, we see a household that cuts across several "borders" in terms of language usage, generation, popular culture, and cultural identity *vis-à-vis* Mexico and the

20 In *The Ring* (1952), the film begins and ends with a montage sequence centered on another public *barrio* space, Olvera Street, a tourist market that becomes the preferred symbol of social contact between Anglos and Chicanos (rather than boxing). In the Chicano gang film *Boulevard Nights* (1979), the opening sequence stops briefly on a house, where two Chicano youths emerge (depicted in long shot) and walk down into the nearby LA riverbed to meet other gang members (with the camera tracking after them). See also Ilene S. Goldman's discussion of the opening sequence in *Stand and Deliver* in her article in Chon A. Noriega and Ana M. López, eds, *The Ethnic Eye: Latino Media Arts* (Minneapolis: University of Minnesota Press, in press).

21 Homi K. Bhabha, "On Mimicry and Man: The Ambivalence of Colonial Discourse," *October* 28 (1984), 125–133.

22 Chon A. Noriega, "Internal 'Others': Hollywood Narratives 'about' Mexican-Americans," in John King, Ana M. López, and Manuel Alvarado, eds, *Mediating Two Worlds: Cinematic Encounters in the Americas* (London: British Film Institute, 1993), 52–66.

United States.[23] These "borders" are represented as a gentle conflict between Rudy and his mother, initially over her baroque interior decor, then over his duties to extended family members. The two argue as Rudy eats breakfast in the dining room. Rudy's mother wants him to pick up his cousin Javier, an undocumented worker who has recently arrived in the United States, since she and Rudy's sister are going to Fresno for the week. Rudy refuses, revealing that he doesn't speak Spanish and making several snide remarks about Mexican immigrants, but eventually he relents. Throughout the scene, the full shots of Rudy and his mother register details of the interior decor: devotional items, family photographs, kitsch lamps and other objects, a home altar. Once Rudy relents, the camera frames him at the table in a medium closeup in which the background consists of a home altar atop a bookcase filled with an encyclopedia set. Here in one concise image we see their argument both expressed and resolved within the *mise-en-scène*: below, the encyclopedias represent the immigrant's rite of purchase into the objective knowledge of American society; while above, the altar with lit *velas* (candles) is an active and personal engagement of spiritual belief. In this scene, the *mise-en-scène* establishes a hierarchical conflict between mother and son that works on a number of levels: gender, generation, class, and culture of origin. But it also suggests a resolution that favors the mother's side of the equation.

This is literally acted out in their initial struggle over cultural expression within the home when Rudy gets into an argument with his mother over her placement of a dual-perspective picture of Jesus Christ in front of the telephone niche. It is this humorous, playful struggle between the mother's *rasquachismo* and her son's middle-class disdain that establishes the Chicano family and community as the initial context for the narrative conflict. Tomás Ybarra-Frausto defines *rasquachismo* as "an underdog perspective . . . rooted in resourcefulness and adaptability yet mindful of stance and style."[24] Here, making do with what's at hand upends middle-class notions of good taste, decorum, and pragmatism, expressing instead a highly baroque decorative style. Given its working-class sensibilities, "*rasquachismo* suggests vulgarity and bad taste, a sense of being *cursi* (tacky),"[25] rather than its subversive potential. Indeed, Rudy responds to his mother's decorative style with an exasperated roll of the eyes.

But Rudy is not without his own contradictions. In the next scene, he leaves for work in a lowrider fashioned from a pink Volkswagen bug with the license plate "Pink Luv." Thus, Rudy parodies even as he partakes of the masculine expressive culture that stands as a counterpart to that of his mother. But whereas his mother places belief over knowledge and technology (literally) within a *rasquache* aesthetic, Rudy conflates the two within

23 In defining "border culture," Guillermo Gómez-Peña states, "Whenever and wherever two or more cultures meet—peacefully or violently—there is a border experience." "The Multicultural Paradigm: An Open Letter to the National Arts Community," *High Performance* 12 (3) (Fall 1989), 18–27, 20. In *Born in East L.A.*, "border culture" is first depicted as operative *within* the Chicano home, then between Chicanos and Mexicans, and, finally, between Chicanos (and Mexicans/OTMs) and Anglos (and the state). For a critical overview of Gother gang members (with the camera tracking after them). See also Ilene S. Goldman's discussiuillermo Gno home, the *Border Brujo* (1988, 1990)," in Noriega and LChicanos an *The Ethnic Eye*, 228–243.

24 Tomás Ybarra-Frausto, "Rasquachismo: A Chicano Sensibility," in Richard Griswold del Castillo, Teresa McKenna, and Yvonne Yarbro Bejarano, eds, *Chicano Art: Resistance and Affirmation, 1965–1985* (Los Angeles: Wight Art Gallery/UCLA, 1991), 155–162, 156.

25 Ibid.

a second- or third-degree kitsch. In other words, for Rudy objects no longer index and interrelate the ineffable (God) and the alienated (mass society), but become either self-referential commodities or acts of postmodern recycling and hybridity within an assimilationist discourse.[26] The conflict between mother and son, then, expresses itself as a split between private and public, sincere and parodic, form and function, resistance and assimilation. Thus, the film poses much more than the question, "How will Rudy get home?"[27] Instead, home itself is at first called into question, until the film "deterritorializes" Rudy, refiguring home as his object of desire. The film then asks, "How will Rudy be reconciled to domestic space?" This question places the issue of his relationship to women—initially, his mother and sister—within a familial context in which the absent father and wife suggest a failure on Rudy's part to perform his expected gender role. The parodic lowrider, then, marks Rudy's simultaneous *machismo* and assimilation as a threat to the home, one that is acted out and must be resolved in the public sphere.

In between the first and last scenes—the home and a Cinco de Mayo parade—and the narrative itself is a sequence in which a "sexy" French woman walks through the *barrio*.[28] These two sequences overlap with the opening and closing credits, and coincide with the two times in the film in which Rudy occupies the public space of the United States. Thus, despite the brevity of her appearances, the French woman plays a complex allegorical function that frames the picaresque narrative, prefiguring Rudy's deportation and return on sexual, political, and cultural levels.

Her appearance marks a shift in Rudy's behavior between home (mother's *rasquachismo*) and the public sphere (son's kitsch), and between the familial and the sexual. As he drives to work, Rudy pursues the French woman in his pink lowrider, issuing catcalls out of earshot. Whenever he loses sight of her, he stops to ask men on the corner if they have seen a red-headed woman in a green dress. In unison the men point the way. The scene, modelled after the opening sequence in *The Girl Can't Help It* (1956) with Jayne Mansfield, reveals the woman's effect as an uncontrollable "object of desire" on both Rudy and the entire male *barrio*, who—as such—become paralyzed and objectified by their own "gaze" at the woman. Two brief scenes with lowriders provide a doubling with Rudy and his parodic lowrider, blurring the boundaries between the lowrider as cultural identity, nationalist icon, and object of parody. In the first, we see the French woman walk alongside a mural, passing an approving *vato* (dude) squatting in front of a lowrider painted on the wall. In the next, an "authentic" lowrider with four *vatos* bounces up and down in an excited phallic manner as the French woman crosses the street in front of them. This doubling reveals the limits of Rudy's parody, suggesting class-based assimilation and not masculinity as its real object.

The sequence ends with the French woman walking toward the camera and into Rudy's car shop. Behind her is a spray paint mural of the Mexican and United States flags with

---

26 While I borrow Celeste Olalquiaga's distinction between the three degrees of kitsch, I do not want to suggest the class-based historicism that is implicit in the way she privileges postmodern recycling and hybridity. *Megalopolis: Contemporary Cultural Sensibilities* (Minneapolis: University of Minnesota Press, 1992), 36–55.

27 Fregoso, *The Bronze Screen*, 55–56. Fregoso continues, "The film poses an even more scathing question: what type of society deports its citizens merely on the basis of the color of their skin?" While Fregoso focuses attention solely on the role of "institutional racism," I want to show how the film interrelates questions about the Chicano home and US citizenship.

28 The woman steps from a bus marked "Civic Center" and crosses a bridge over the Los Angeles River, which separates downtown from East LA. (The bus route [35] terminates in Beverly Hills.)

lowriders beneath them heading toward the Mexican side of the mural. As she approaches, her body increasingly occupies the space between the two flags, acting as the border. Both the border symbolism and the woman's allegorical status are reinforced in her iconographic coding. She has white, almost alabaster skin, red hair and a green dress: the colors of the Mexican flag. These colors, in addition to her heavy French accent and reappearance during the Cinco de Mayo parade at the end of the film, link her to the French occupation of Mexico in the 1860s. Cinco de Mayo, after all, celebrates the battle that initiated Mexico's overthrow of the French on May 5, 1862. The allusion works on two levels. First, it posits an historical connection between the Chicano *barrio* and Mexico on the basis of colonialism, with the French woman serving as an allegorical figure for French colonialism in Mexico and, by extension, internal colonialism in East LA.[29] Second, Cinco de Mayo celebrations in the United States speak directly to the history of deportation as well as civil rights struggles since the 1930s. During Depression-era repatriation, the Mexican consulates sponsored Cinco de Mayo celebrations as fundraising activities for their efforts to represent the Mexican and Mexican-American communities.[30] Since the 1960s, these celebrations, along with Day of the Dead and Mexican Independence Day, have become symbolic expressions of Chicano cultural affirmation, resistance, and maintenance within the United States.

The French woman functions as a border symbol, embodying the dual or double-edged notion of "liberty" the French acted out in the Americas in the mid-1800s. In addition to the occupation of Mexico, of course, the French also presented the Statue of Liberty to the United States as a gift of freedom to the world (dedicated in 1886). On an iconographic level, the French woman shares the "exaggerated and slightly vulgar" stride of the statue; while her position between the two flags and her red-white-and-green color scheme imply that for Chicanos and Mexicans the colonial experience still prevails over notions of universal liberty.[31] Thus the French woman negotiates a complex relationship between Mexico and the United States, one that calls into question the symbolic purity of the Statue of Liberty in identifying the United States as a nation of immigrants. Within four years of the statue's dedication, the US Census Bureau would declare the frontier closed, the borders set. Those borders, however, had been reached at the expense of Mexican and Native American lands, a fact which set in motion the contradiction between a Jeffersonian sense of Liberty spreading around the globe, and an American expansion and exceptionalism that took liberties with other peoples' sovereignty. In referencing the period between 1862 and 1886, *Born in East L.A.* shifts the discourse on Chicano citizenship from its usual origins in the Mexican-American War and the Treaty of Guadalupe Hidalgo (1848). As I discuss later, this places emphasis on the politics of immigration within an international and multiracial context rather than on the counter-nativist claims of Chicano nationalism.

29 For a review of internal colonialism, see Tomás Almaguer, "Ideological Distortions in Recent Chicano Historiography: The Internal Model and Chicano Historical Interpretation," *Aztlán: A Journal of Chicano Studies* 18 (1) (Spring 1987), 7–28.

30 Francisco E. Balderrama, *In Defense of La Raza: The Los Angeles Mexican Consulate and the Mexican Community, 1929 to 1936* (Tucson: University of Arizona Press, 1982), 45–46.

31 On the statue's stride, see Marina Warner, "The Monument (New York)," in *Monuments and Maidens: The Allegory of the Female Form* (London: Weidenfeld and Nicolson, 1985), 3–17, 8. Warner captures the bipolar terms of the statue's symbolism: "Perceived either as a lie, or as a statement of truth, the claim that the Statue of Liberty makes on behalf of the United States defines the nation's self-image" (11).

After approaching Rudy's garage (and the camera) against the backdrop of the mural, the French woman turns and leans against her car. Situated on the right side of the screen, the car is on the US side of the mural. With her legs spread, her left hand folded across her waist, and her right hand raised to the side of her head with a burning cigarette, the French woman strikes a pose similar to the Statue of Liberty with its tablets and torch. Here, positioned in front of the two flags, she suggests a welcome to Mexican immigrants in which the original invitation to assimilate is framed in sexual terms, seemingly addressed to *male* Mexican nationals. But, contrary to this reading, the bottom portion of the mural itself depicts Chicano lowriders driving from the United States to Mexico, with the *mise-en-scène* implying that they have passed between the woman's legs. It is at this point—in the film's most vulgar sight gag—that the *mise-en-scène* foreshadows Rudy's deportation and the terms of his eventual return. Rudy, who had been working beneath the car, slides out on his back in such a way that his head emerges between the French woman's feet. Taken as an allegory of citizenship, Rudy passes beneath the Statue of Liberty on his way to Mexico.[32] The joke here is that the Statue of Liberty does not face Mexico, but Europe hence the mutual surprise of Rudy and the French woman, captured in shot/reverse-shot to show his pleasure and her shock. Passing beneath the Statue of Liberty against the backdrop of the mural, then, presages Rudy's deportation, and precludes his return within the usual terms of immigration and assimilation.

When linked with the lowriders in the earlier scenes (including Rudy), this scene establishes a causal relationship between desire (for white women, for lowriders) and deportation (from citizenship). Chicano masculine desire is figured as a contrarian form of assimilation in which the desire to "consume" is freed from the object's ostensible function within a Protestant family and work ideology: procreation (woman), transportation (car). The film conflates these two objects of desire around an idea of the foreign-ness of "American" public status symbols (lowriders, white women) in the *barrio*. After he emerges from beneath the car, Rudy leaves the French woman for a moment in order to pick up his guitar from a friend standing next to Rudy's pink lowrider. In response to a question about what he will do over the weekend, Rudy responds, "Probably just sit home and 'Wang Chung,' man." The suggestion of masturbation (and womanlessness) is spoken over a full shot of the red-headed woman leaning against the hood of her black Peugeot. Opposite her on the left half of the frame is a poster of a Zoot Suiter dressed in black and standing in front of a red lowrider; the poster reads: "In East L.A.— where every car is a foreign car." As a symbol of defiance, the image of the Zoot Suiter coopts and exaggerates American popular culture itself, making the car and clothing into a sign of foreign-ness. This symbolic use of the Zoot Suiter provides a counter-discourse drawn from the militarism of the Zoot Suit Riots (voiced by sailors and journalists), while the red-and-black colors posit a genealogy of resistance from the Aztec warrior to the United Farm Workers.[33] Thus, the juxtaposition of these two red-and-black tableaux,

32 Consider Warner's sexualized description of a visit to the Statue of Liberty: "When we enter into her, we are invited to merge with her, to feel at one with her." She concludes: "The female form tends to be perceived as generic and universal, with symbolic overtones; the male as individual, even when it is being used to express a generalized idea." Hence, citizens can be *represented* by (as well as occupy, possess) the Statue of Liberty, but *identify* with Uncle Sam. Warner, "The Monument," 11–12.

33 The UFW banner is a red-and-black Thunderbird. For an account of the militaristic discourses of the Zoot Suit Riots, see Mauricio Mazer, *The Zoot Suit Riots: The Psychology of Symbolic Annihilation* (Austin: University of Texas Press, 1984).

and Rudy's earlier pun contrasting the woman's "black Peugeot" (pubic hair) with her red-headedness, constructs a Chicano masculine ideal of a defiant stance and its rewards that Rudy desires, yet cannot replicate: owing to a continuity error in the film, his much smaller, pink (as in less red) lowrider even disappears in the final shot of the scene with the French woman. Rudy never does get to "Wang Chung" at home, since he is deported in the next scene, when he attempts to pick up his cousin after work.

The last scene of the film, which depicts Rudy's return "home," provides the second half of this narrative frame. While in Mexico, Rudy had taught a group of "Indian" and "Chinese" workers—called OTMs for Other Than Mexican—how to pass as Chicano in order to avoid deportation. In addition to the obvious irony that Rudy himself could not "pass" as Chicano (and that many of the OTMs are played by Latino actors), these scenes, which are punctuated by stereotypical "Chinese" music, allude to the Chinese Exclusion Act of 1882, which lasted until 1943 (the same year as the Zoot Suit Riots), and represented the first denial of the right of free migration to the United States as well as one of the first victories of the emergent labor movement (as it sought to define its working-class agenda in racial terms as "white"). The Chinese Exclusion Act and subsequent laws prohibiting foreign contract labor resulted in a decisive shift within the unskilled labor force from Chinese to Mexican migrants. Mexican nationals—exempted as "foreigners *temporarily* residing in the US"—provided a cheap labor pool for the rapid industrial development in the Southwest; and, between 1880 and 1920, the Mexican population in the United States would increase ninefold, while the national population would double.[34] Given that Rudy identifies himself as the third generation born in the United States, he places his family history at the tail end of this period. In this manner, *Born in East L.A.* establishes the limits of US immigration policy and ideology with respect to racial others, revealing a hidden dynamic at the level of the working class that places various racial and ethnic groups in competition with each other.

In the end, Rudy leads a massive multiracial and multinational assault on the border. The scene visualizes Anglo-Americans' worst fear about illegal aliens swarming across the border to take away jobs, drain welfare funds, overburden social services, and increase urban crime. Marin, however, undercuts these associations, visually coding the scene as humorous, and using music as an added counterpoint. Neil Diamond's "America," which was played at the rededication ceremonies for the Statue of Liberty, describes these new immigrants: "Got a dream they come to share. They come to America . . ." As with Marin's parody of "Born in the U.S.A.," the sincerely ironic use of Diamond's "America" does not so much shift the discourse as expand it to include non-European-descent citizens and immigrants. It is noteworthy, then, that the rededication of the Statue of Liberty occurred in the same year in which the Immigration Reform Bill and California's English-Only Initiative passed into law. Likewise, "America" replaced—literally, in the 1986 rededication—the Emma Lazarus lines inscribed on the statue's base in 1903:

---

34 Rodolfo Acuiver, *Occupied America: A History of Chicanos*, 3rd edn (New York: HarperCollins, 1988), 127; and James D. Cockcroft, *Outlaws in the Promised Land: Mexican Immigrant Workers and America's Future* (New York: Grove Press, 1986), 47–48. According to Cockcroft, "The migration of Mexicans during the first third of the twentieth century shifted an estimated one-eighth of Mexico's population north of the border—one of the largest mass movements of a people in human history."

> Give me your tired, your poor,
> Your huddled masses yearning to breathe free,
> The wretched refuse of your teeming shore.
> Send these, the homeless, tempest-tos't to me,
> I lift my lamp beside the golden door!

The status of these earlier immigrants suggested that they brought nothing with them. Their names were changed, and like empty ciphers, they were expected to acculturate; that is, to acquire the "American" language and culture. Diamond's song, especially in the context of *Born in East L.A.*, reveals a different set of expectations on the part of immigrants as well as inevitable cultural hybridity. For example, Dolores does not want to cross the border until she has saved enough money to be independent—i.e., not on welfare. In cross-referencing "American" popular culture, the film constructs its argument out of contradictions and conflicts within the "mainstream" itself.

While "America" adds an ironic twist to the border crossing, the next scene further undermines the great fear of the mid-1980s, often expressed in the mainstream press as the fear of "Latinization." Rudy and the OTMs are shown running down a hill into the United States, only to emerge in the next scene from a sewer hole into the *barrio* of East LA. In other words, they move directly from the Mexican border to the Chicano *barrio*, invisible in the social space in between, which includes "white flight" suburbs and the military industrial complex. While immigration discourses often invoke and contend over a generic, "American" public space and its attendant rights, the actual struggle is more geographically specific, as the film suggests. After all, it is because the Mexicans and OTMs (Asian and Central American) will have to adapt and fit into the *barrio* and avoid other social spaces that Rudy is able to earn money in Tijuana teaching the OTMs *rasquache* coping strategies.

Having stormed the border, in the next shot, Rudy reemerges from a sewer amidst the Cinco de Mayo parade in East LA with Dolores and the OTMs. The Chinese OTMs quickly blend in as Chicanos—at least as far as the police are concerned. It is at this point that the French woman reappears, causing the parade watchers—men, women, children—to freeze.[35] Does this scene reveal a culture paralyzed by the gazed-upon "white" woman, a sexual-political Medusa who represents the promises and pitfalls of *barrio* aspirations *vis-à-vis* citizenship, cultural maintenance, and racial difference? Does her final look (and smile) into the camera freeze us, make us complicit, or free us from the gaze? The next and final shot of the film suggests the latter: Rudy and Dolores are animated, embracing in front of a priest upon a church float. But if her look frees us from the gaze that she constitutes—that is, from one particular sexual-cultural positioning—on what terms? On an obvious level, the French woman is the whore to Dolores's Madonna. In fact, "dolores" means "pains" or "sorrows." The film conflates the sexual dichotomy with cultural nationalism, so that the whore also tempts Rudy with assimilation (pleasure), while the Madonna ensures cultural affirmation (pain). Although that conflation leads to Rudy's apparent reform, it also relieves him of responsibility. As a *pícaro*, Rudy does not change as much as his circumstances change around him. It is

---

35 The television broadcast of the film contains an additional fifteen minutes with a "cloak-and-dagger" subplot that takes place after the parade scene. Since the standard movie length for a two-hour broadcast is one hundred minutes, shorter films often contain extra footage not included in the theatrical release and video versions.

Dolores, after all, who baptizes Rudy with a pail of water after a sexist remark, and who stands in silent witness to his subsequent acts of charity toward two women, a young, single *mother*, and an older *wife*. These characters mirror or double Rudy's own sister and mother—not just in terms of their familial characterization (Rudy's sister also has two children), but also in the scant screen time given to each. What these brief scenes allow, then, is for Dolores to act as the "witness" or mediation point for Rudy to resolve his Madonna/whore complex, first toward (working-class) Mexican women, then, by extension and implication, toward the (middle-class) Mexican-American women in his own family and community. This is most apparent in the scene with the poor single mother and her two children. After Rudy gives the woman his cart of oranges, the rack focus pulls back to reveal Dolores watching Rudy's act of charity on the other side of the street. Dolores, however, stands in an awkward posture that accentuates both her breasts and her buttocks: facing away from the camera, she twists her torso toward Rudy. In other words, for the viewer, she is framed in order to be seen watching him. Rather than act as a point of moral identification, Dolores becomes the site of an acceptable sexual gaze, but only *after* her role as a moral guardian has been established—first for the viewer, then for Rudy. In the end, Dolores makes it possible for Rudy's spiritual return to the domain of the family, which he had taken for granted, if not ridiculed, in the opening scene. In addition to the mother's religious belief, Dolores facilitates a *latinidad* or pan-ethnic "Latino" identity characterized by her insistence that Rudy learn Spanish.

In this manner, the first and last scenes in the film provide a narrative frame that moves from the private to the public symbols of the *barrio*: the home and the Cinco de Mayo parade. Both spaces are defined in relationship to the church. This shift in social space brings about a corresponding shift in the configuration of familial relations, from mother–son–sister to "father"/priest–son–wife.[36] But this is not necessarily a shift from private to public as defined by Richard Rodriguez in *Hunger of Memory*, or as represented in *The Ring*:[37] that is, a shift from the language of a minority culture to that of the political and economic "mainstream." Instead, the film constructs East LA as an alternative public sphere in its own right, one that stands between the ethnic family and dominant culture.[38]

The overall message, as Marin notes, was *chicanismo*, often translated as Chicano pride.[39] According to Marcos Sánchez-Tranquilino,

> Chicanismo was a complex of nationalist strategies by which Chicano origins and histories, as well as present and future identities, were constructed and legitimized. Furthermore, it provided a context for historical reclamation of the self through the affirmation of Chicano cultural narratives while resisting Anglo models of assimilation.[40]

---

36 This contrasts with an earlier film such as *Bordertown* (1935), in which the padre (church) and mother (home) frame the protagonist's return. See my article, "Internal 'Others' " (cited above).

37 Richard Rodriquez, *Hunger of Memory: The Education of Richard Rodriguez* (New York: Bantam Books, 1982).

38 Ricardo Romo and others describe the *barrio* both as a culture in its own right and as a mediation point between two national cultures that allows recent immigrants to adapt to "American life" on their own terms. Romo, *East Los Angeles: A History of a Barrio* (Austin: University of Texas Press, 1983).

39 See West and Crowdus interview in *Cineaste*, 37 (cited above).

40 Marcos Sánchez-Tranquilino, "Murales del Movimiento: Chicano Murals and the Discourses of Art and Americanization," in Eva Sperling Cockcroft and Holly Barnet-Sánchez, eds, *Signs from the Heart: California Chicano Murals* (Venice, CA: Social and Public Art Resource Center, 1990), 90.

Sánchez-Tranquilino goes on to connect the initial articulations of *chicanismo* through activism, scholarship, literature, and the arts to the concurrent call for a Chicano home-land based on Aztlán, the mythical Aztec homeland: "The renaming of the American Southwest as Aztlán within the national Chicano community [in 1969] was an impor-tant initial step in reclaiming the land-base upon which further development of this Chicano world view [*chicanismo*] could take place."[41] In *Born in East L.A.*, there is not a call for a nationalist "homeland" that exists within and against the United States itself as an ideological overlay, but rather an attempt to make "East LA" synonymous with "U.S.A." and, hence, with citizenship. This is achieved through a rhyme that establishes metonymy between *barrio* and nation, "I was born in East LA," and thereby signifies two seemingly opposite birthrights: Mexican descent and US citizenship.

While negotiating between nationalist and assimilationist conceptions of social space, *Born in East L.A.* attempts to solve its problems of space through a "conservative" cul-tural politics at the level of gender. Thus, if *Born in East L.A.* stresses *chicanismo*, it is a message that is structured around female allegories (French woman) and stereotypes (Dolores) and the threat of homosexual rape (in prison), and ultimately leads to tradi-tional Latino gender roles.[42] It could be argued, however, that *Born in East L.A.* is not a realist drama, but a comedy, and "[c]omedy always and above all depends upon an awareness that it is fictional."[43] Indeed, it is hard to explain several scenes in terms of realism or non-fictional narrative conventions. Did the mariachi performance of Jimi Hendrix's "Purple Haze" *really* happen, or was it a fantasy on the part of the protag-onist? The film repeatedly collapses not just narrative space, but geographical space, as well. First of all, *Born in East L.A.* collapses the space from Tijuana to the south in its representation of Dolores, who works three jobs in Tijuana, but lives in a trailer in El Rosario about 200 miles south. Next, the border crossing scene that ends the film, and which recalls the fatal crossing in *El Norte*, humorously collapses the 100-plus mile dis-tance between Tijuana and East LA. Herein lies the film's logic: in collapsing the space between Dolores's and Rudy's homes, and between Tijuana and East LA, the film draws attention to the erasure of history (how people get from one space to another) within public discourse and the popular imagination. When one considers the fact that Rudy's mother and sister are visiting family in Fresno—about 200 miles north of Los Angeles—the film can be seen to map out a generic Chicano family history that moves from Mexico (underemployed) to the agricultural belt (working class) to the urban cen-ter (middle class).[44] But, at the same time, the film constructs desire within these very

---

41 Ibid.

42 In fact, in response to questions about the "sexist images of women" in the film, Marin argues that his message was about *chicanismo* and not about women, suggesting that issues of gender and cultural affirma-tion are two different things. See West and Crowdus interview cited above. See also the discussion of *chicanismo* in Ramón Gutiérrez, "Community, Patriarchy, and Individualism: The Politics of Chicano History and the Dream of Equality," *American Quarterly* 45 (1) (March 1993), 44–72, 46.

43 Stephen Neale, *Genre* (London: British Film Institute, 1980), 40.

44 These movements to the north and south leave the house empty, except for Javier (Paul Rodriquez), who must mediate between the mother's and the son's contradictory configuration of the home: the Jesus Christ picture over the phone versus Rudy's beer and cable television (Playboy channel). When Rudy calls home for help, Javier mistakes him for Christ and covers the television. On the spatial contrast between Rudy and Javier, see Fregoso, *The Bronze Screen*, 57.

same terms, conflating space and history around the French woman who enters the *barrio*, symbolizing assimilation and internal colonization.[45]

If anything, then, *Born in East L.A.* manifests the ways in which Chicano expressions have understood cultural resistance and affirmation within oppositional terms that center on the role of women, family and the home as sites of either redemption or betrayal. Ultimately, what the film argues is a familial, collective identity over and against a masculine, individual one, presenting this shift in nationalist terms as an alternative between assimilation with deportation versus cultural maintenance within the *barrio*.[46] While this itself is framed within the patriarchal terms of a madonna/whore dichotomy, the film also uses these terms to register a subtle shift from Chicano nationalism to a pan-Latino identity. The implication of marriage between an assimilated Chicano and an "illegal alien" reveals how the immigration continuum both sustains and diversifies *barrio* culture. The fact that Dolores is from El Salvador alludes to the impact of recent Central American refugees; while Rudy's repeated utterance of Ronald Reagan's name in Tijuana serves as a reminder that it was his Central American and immigration policies that are, in large part, responsible. In the end, to be born in East LA is no longer equated with Mexican descent (let alone descent from a single country of origin, if we imagine that Rudy and Dolores have children). The fact that the Spanish-language float is for an Evangelist church suggests other recent changes in the *barrio*. The reference to Evangelical Christianity first occurs in the prison scenes in Tijuana, where the jail guard Feo ("ugly") uses Evangelical-style sermonizing to frighten the inmates.[47] This keeps the inmates from raping Rudy, a "favor" that Feo uses to exploit Rudy for financial gain. These two references (prison and float), then, establish a complex counterpoint to Catholicism and Liberation Theology *within* the representation of Latino cultural politics. These cracks in the image of a monolithic Chicano/Mexican-descent culture may, in fact, explain the film's progressive appeal for Chicana and Chicano critics: it is seen to destabilize the essentialist underpinnings of Chicano nationalism while still offering a critique of dominant culture.[48] But while the film destabilizes internal and external stereotypes of the *barrio* in terms of culture, language, religion, and country of origin, it does so through traditional gender roles that reproduce the *barrio* as *barrio*, while equating that space with citizenship.

45 The film reinforces this conflation of spatial and historical references through an ambiguous time frame for the narrative. While Rudy's brief time in the United States is defined by a 9-to-5 workday which ends in deportation, it is unclear how many days he is in Tijuana.

46 This is implicit in Tafoya's reading of the film in light of Latin American Liberation Theology. In *The Bronze Screen*, Fregoso explicitly links this "political/religious metaphor" with a "sense of collectivity" that "resists ideology of individual heroism" (61).

47 See Tafoya, "Cheech as the New Moses," 127.

48 In "*Born in East L.A.* and the Politics of Representation," for example, Rosa Linda Fregoso stresses the film's cultural affirmation and critique of dominant ideologies, but chooses not to raise gender issues in the non-Chicano publication *Cultural Studies* (1990). This was her explanation given at the roundtable discussion cited in note 1. In *The Bronze Screen*, Fregoso takes up the iconographic elements and gender critique that I raised in *Tonanztin*, but sets these "apart" from the film's "effective indictment of dominant official discourse" (54). See also Tafoya's article (cited above) and Sandra Peña-Sarmiento, who speaks for a new generation of Chicano and Chicana filmmakers, identifies *Born in East L.A.* as the only feature film to question "the Chicano Experience."

Returning to Marin's coffee metaphor, it is fitting, then, that David Avalos, one of the original founders of the Border Arts Workshop/Taller Arte Fronterizo (BAW/TAF), extends the metaphor to account for *mestizaje* as well as the use of comedy for hidden messages. In his installation piece *Café Mestizo*, which rejects the notion that "two halves makes less than a whole," Avalos depicts that process as coffee and cream poured side by side into a cup, while a caption reads, "A grind so fine . . . you give in to the pleasure."[49] Unlike other Chicano writers and artists, Avalos extends *mestizaje* both as metaphor (cultural hybridity) and as literal act (miscegenation) in locating Chicanos within the United States. Interestingly, though, *Born in East L.A.* argues against *that* pleasure from the perspective of the state and of the *barrio*. Indeed, Rudy taught the OTMs how to be Chicano by way of a *posture* of desire for the white women (two blonde tourists) who entered *their* public space. But when the OTMs actually run after these women, rather than cruise them from a street corner or lowrider, Rudy stops the OTMs. This is his contradiction, which becomes defined as that which paralyzes the entire *barrio*, and is resolved (if also transformed) only through a Latino marriage. Thus, the picaresque—with its emphasis on the material aspects of existence and its parody of social institutions—finds its resolution within the terms of melodrama wherein religious devotion and couple formation overcome the "outside" threat to the home.[50] While this process registers cultural shifts within the *barrio* itself, the film is unable to pose this in either ambiguous or intercultural terms *vis-à-vis* the national culture. In other words—despite Marin's contention that "American culture and Latino culture are inextricably bound, and there is no history of one without the other"—these cultural shifts must nonetheless be recontained within the *barrio* or risk moral ambiguity about deterritorialization.[51] In the end, Rudy's trademark question remains a rhetorical one: "Orale vato, waas sappening?"

49 David Avalos, *Café Mestizo*, exhibition catalogue (New York: Intar Gallery, 1989).

50 In this respect, *Born in East L.A.*, like the slave narrative, "is a counter-genre, a meditation between the novel of sentiment and the picaresque, oscillating somewhere between the two in a bipolar moment." Henry Louis Gates, Jr., *Figures in Black: Words, Signs, and the "Racial" Self* (New York: Oxford University Press, 1987), 81. In so far as this is also "set in motion by the mode of the confession," the film becomes a site of quasi-autobiography. Indeed, the film represented a decisive break in Marin's career, albeit one that was negotiated within the generic limitations and expectations of Hollywood.

51 Quotation from West and Crowdus interview, *Cineaste*, 35. See Gates, *Figures in Black*, 87.

Part III
Moving desires

Introduction

The title of this section harbors, of course, a double suggestion, of desires in motion (the abstraction, "desires," meaning something like "sexualities," changing over time and across space) and also of desires that are moving, in the sense of producing emotional response. As it happens, there are further senses: of the illusion of movement that is fundamentally the precondition of cinema in the sense of "moving pictures," and, as one of our students remarked in a *noir* reading of the phrase, a picture of a guy with a porkpie hat and a trenchcoat hurrying down an alley. All the better: discussions of sexuality and popular cinema ought, we think, to traverse the resolutely concrete and the realm of fantasy, the requirements and specificities of national film industries, and the real but difficult to grasp transnational affinities of what we might in a too-confident Anglophone certainty call queer desires.

The last decade might have made a movie-goer seeking films dealing with same-sex desires and sexualities think that at last a new era of filmmaking had commenced, one in which an open-minded approach to the fact of gay, lesbian, bisexual (and, to a much lesser degree, transgender) people actually existing as something besides predatory monsters or pathetic victims could now be admitted, and indeed there has been a greater number of film productions claiming to offer "tolerance" to the subject of dissident sexualities. Beyond the idea that such folks, loosely named as queer subjects, could find their place in the realm of cinematic representation by being tolerated, such a movie-goer would be disappointed to discover that the men and women offered were largely affluent, urban, white, and privileged enough in certain measure not to have to worry about how their sex/gender difference might jeopardize in wholesale ways their very livelihood.

Out of this tension, between expectation and disappointment at the outcome of the "liberalization" of attitudes toward dissident sexualities in the mass-market product, a more subtle attention to the function of such sexualities for the forms of current widely disseminated film can reveal the degree to which such sexualities disrupt many of the assumptions we have about how cinema can bring the meanings of sex and gender to our attention. In large measure, the differences in cinema around queer desires and practices need to be registered by noting that such desires do not arise as identical phenomena in all spaces on the local and global levels, and one way of knowing the importance of these emergent forms of representation lies in the path of perceiving them, like so many things, as increasingly globalized and increasingly made available through unconventional (i.e., not solely Hollywood) forms of cinema. The writers of the essays in this section fix their attentions upon the structural importance of other forms of "otherness" —race and class for same-sex desiring subjects—and in these essays we come to see how dissident desires are not only embedded in other dynamics of difference but in measure co-constituted with them. Yet, these forms of difference are not solely those of, say, racialized socializations, but also the forms of cinema itself, so that video (as in the case of pornography) or national cinema (as relates to Hong Kong cinema) have a bearing upon how desires arrive before us in film. The point here is not that such sexualities become ancillary or incidental to other dynamics of film, but that they are densely entangled with them.

That entanglement is also historically determined; our grids for reading and responding are built from our pasts, both individual and collective. What we see, what can be seen, and what can be shown to us are as much products of the dynamics of difference we have mentioned as they are of battles fought in the past (over censorship, for example) or battles waged in the present over how to name these differences politically (the discussion over the term "transgendered," for example, in relation to the film *Boys Don't Cry* [Kimberly Pierce 1999]). The essays in this section engage those various histories as much as they move us, elsewhere.

11 The voice of pornography

Tracking the subject through the sonic spaces of gay male moving-image pornography

Rich Cante and Angelo Restivo

The aim of and the assumptions underlying this essay fall largely in line with Leo Bersani's necessarily almost "defensive" comments on queer critical method in the passage below. In a conversation with Tim Dean, Hal Foster, and Kaja Silverman, he suggests that

> The problem with queer politics as we now define it is that, however broad its reach may be, it is still a micropolitics focused on numerous particular issues which there is no reason to believe will ever be exhausted if the fundamental types of community and relationality out of which such issues spring are not themselves questioned and attacked. And that activity has to be, at least for the moment, an activity of the intellectual imagination—one for which the micropoliticians often have no use or patience, but which seems to me no less an activity and no more of a luxury than our immediate and our, of course, vital concrete struggles.[1]

Elsewhere in this very illuminating conversation, a line from *Homos* (about a character of André Gide's) is quoted in order to coax Bersani into explicating the somewhat enigmatic project of all of his work with Ulysse Dutoit. The line reads, "His sexual preference is without psychic content; there are no complexes, no repressed conflicts; no developmental explanations; only the chaste promiscuity of form repeatedly reaching out to find itself beyond itself."[2] Indeed, the Gide quotation very effectively condenses, especially when read in relation to Bersani's attitude toward queer politics, the project of Bersani and Dutoit's writing: developing a descriptive theoretical poetics of what they call the "formal" aspects of sexuality, and of homosexuality in particular. The main idea here is that the ego functions primarily as a "form." Therefore, textuality's connection to the deep interiorities of subjectivity are enacted in what Bersani and Dutoit call "communication of forms," a mysterious mode of "communication" (a word which is used very unconventionally here, as will be clearer in a moment) essential to all sexual pleasure and, more generally, to the experience of all sexual acts.

For Bersani, "the homosexual might be crucial for constituting a relationality not based on identity . . . for imagining the possibility of nonidentitarian community . . . and a peculiar notion of non-identitarian sameness."[3] This is because, when sexuality is conceived

1 Tim Dean, Hal Foster, and Kaja Silverman, "A Conversation with Leo Bersani," *October* 82 (Fall 1997), 3–16, 11.
2 Ibid., 9.
3 Ibid., 13.

formally, "Identity boundaries are violated not only as a masochistic phenomenon, but also as an effect of reaching toward one's own 'form' elsewhere."[4] Both this "elsewhere" and the "reaching" itself, then—as the terms themselves suggest—have everything to do with *fantasy*.[5] A specifically homosexual enactment of "reaching for one's own form elsewhere," or a specifically homosexual form of *fantasy*, leaves especially interesting psychic and empirical "traces" in its wake. Or, alternatively, the specificity of homosexuality can only be imagined by recourse to the especially interesting histories (both phylogenic and ontogenic, both psychic and social) of such available traces in the first place.

For Bersani, as for many other theorists, both (sexual) fantasy and actually existing sexual "acts" always involve a movement toward "self-shattering" in that they both involve reaching for one's own form elsewhere and are produced by and as the available "histories" of sundry previous reachings. What is original and important about Bersani's particular account of all this is the extent to which he insists that we understand such movements as functioning beyond the limiting psychoanalytic concepts of primordial masochism and castration, not to mention beyond the logic of some of the specific terms in which Foucault laid out his sexual ethics in Volumes II and III of the *History* and in the various interviews on homosexuality.[6] It is with this more particular aim that the (phantasmatic) form(s) which compose the "homosexual ego"—and among which that ego cavorts in enacting itself—are thus addressed in Bersani's writing with Dutoit.

At one point in the *October* conversation, Timothy Dean transposes this project into different terms. Dean tags it as being indebted to the idea that "interpersonal relationships don't determine relationality or sociality,"[7] and thus as being about "how desire gets attached to persons [in general]."[8] Consequently, both Dean and Kaja Silverman are quick to articulate the primary benefit of such an approach with/as its potential for a "radical de-anthropomorphicization." "It helps us to understand that what we are at the level of the ego may be a much more complex issue than we are accustomed to imagining," says Silverman. "And it permits us to begin conceptualizing relationality outside the usual human categories, which have become very reduced in recent years through the insistence on race, class, gender, etc."[9]

---

4   Ibid., 15.

5   Laplanche's and Pontalis's description of fantasy is also highly formal: fantasy is for them the "*mise-en-scène* of desire." It is a *scenario* in which the subject is invariably present, such as in the primal scene—where the subject is present not simply as the gaze, but as that "object" whose presence/gaze interrupts the sexual act. Therefore, the *mise-en-scène* or *scenario* that is the fantasy "space" is essentially characterized by always already having taken the subject's gaze into account. In this sense, this is clearly an important concept for the analysis of moving-image pornography. Indeed, given the fundamentally atemporal nature of desire, we can take this a step further and say that fantasy is a *sequence* in which the subject always has a role to play, even though that role may be continually effaced in the subject's own experience of all this. And it is this role and this experience in relation to which the subject performs himself or herself *vis-à-vis* desire. Thus, fantasy is simultaneously what stages the desire in which the subject performs its social role and/or desire in the first place; in this sense, fantasy and desire continually (re)produce the various sorts of objects around which the subject's trajectory across space and time is charted.

6   For an excellent analysis which tries to re-place Foucault's thought on the ethical self-fashioning (*aeskesis*) of homosexuality from the margins to the center of his contribution to "philosophy," see David Halperin, *Saint Foucault: Toward a Gay Hagiography* (New York: SUNY Press, 1995), Chapter 2.

7   "A Conversation with Leo Bersani," 15.

8   Ibid.

9   Ibid., 9.

Later, it is Dean who also explains the organic(ized) theoretical connection between the communication of forms and homosexuality in different terms, which are more explicit than Bersani's own. Commenting initially on how notions of the romantic "couple" get implicitly transformed by this account into something very different than we might be prepared for, Dean says to Bersani:

> It's not really a couple at all, or, if it is, it's one person coupled with something else that isn't another person. You pose a non-reciprocal relationship [read: a relationship to a *form*] as the basis for relationality; there's a kind of depersonalization there. And the reason that homosexuality seems to work as a model is precisely because in certain kinds of gay sex (though not only there), there's a kind of depersonalization of sexuality, even a dehumanization—which is, of course, always an object of intense criticism. Isn't it that relation—not between persons but between a person and something that is non-human—that you want to build?[10]

Bersani's response: "Very much so . . . the homosexual as a model not only for the intersubjective, but for the relation between the human and the non-human."[11]

The reason we turn to this particular explication of Bersani's work at the outset of the present essay involves more than an aspiration toward drawing the idiosyncrasies of Bersani's thought and language into our own argument. As we previously suggested, the particular litany of terms and ideas mobilized in the course of this conversation— e.g., reciprocity, depersonalization, de-anthropomorphicization, and nonhumanity—is itself symptomatic of a point we wish to address. As should be clear to anyone who has lent even the most tentative ear to any of the various "public debates" about film and video pornography which purportedly base themselves in "ethical" and "moral" considerations, the key terms and ideas of this conversation clearly converge with those of these other debates, despite a fundamentally different conception even of, say, "ethics" underlying the ways they are differentially operationalized in each context. While one might rationally assume that this convergence is an effect mostly of the extent to which the work of individuals like Bersani, Dean, and Silverman is engaged from the outset in a Foucauldian attempt to "reverse the discourse" of various contemporary notions of (homo)sexuality, we would like to assert otherwise. We think this convergence is, at least partly, *an effect of the conversation's very aspiration toward addressing that particular mode of relationality, and the phantasmatic communication of forms, which is contemporary homosexuality.* In other words, we think this convergence occurs partly because of something about homosexuality itself, something about it which discursively encircles debates about pornography in general: something about hardcore, moving-image gay pornography—gay male pornography, to be specific (though not only gay *male* porn)— which, to borrow the old Lacanian formulation "in you more than you," makes it *more pornographic than pornography.*[12]

10 Ibid., 11.
11 Ibid.
12 In this regard, the theoretical intervention we are attempting in the analysis which follows could plausibly be presented as an extension of Lauren Berlant and Michael Warner's assumptions in their article "Sex in Public." Lauren Berlant and Michael Warner, "Sex in Public," guest editor Lauren Berlant, *Critical Inquiry* "Intimacy Issue," 24 (2) (Winter 1998), 547–567. For considerations of related issues with more empirical and sociological angles, see the pieces collected in William Leap's anthology *Public Sex/Gay Space* (New York: Columbia University Press, 1999).

In particular, we'd like to illustrate with what follows that the phantasmatic communication of forms whose traces (now) mark the movement of the "subject" of contemporary US homosexuality across American history since the late sixties—and now (indirectly) maps that movement into the massive, ever-expanding, and increasingly omnipresent socio-psychic archive that is the history of gay male moving images—*always already implants the very "public realm" from which the terms of this (counter)conversation seem initially to have been borrowed at the heart of the homosexual communication "forms," and at the heart of both contemporary moving-image pornographic aesthetics and real gay men's phenomenological experience of pornotextuality (in the particular as well as in the abstract) across the range of media in which these texts have been conventionally incarnated during this historical period*. In other words, we would like to argue that what distinguishes the textual system of "all-male"[13] media porn, and the subject historically attached to it from a myriad of oblique angles, from those of other pornographic orientations, since the advent of the filmic-feature in this genre is a particular and necessary sort of "passage through publicness" involved: a "passage," or phantasmatic *sequence*, via which the specificity of the gay male relation to something "nonhuman" appears to involve a certain relation to "publicity" itself.[14]

13 We use this anachronistic term here polemically. However significatorially unstable is the term "all-male" (of the three "canonical" pieces of homosexual porn to which we will turn our attention in the next section, only one actually contains no images of women), those instabilities are eclipsed by the ambiguities and incoherences of the most readily available alternative, which we will use throughout the remainder of the chapter nonetheless: gay male porn. We do this because—as our particular argument will, as an effect, ultimately allow us to assume with little exegetical scandal—such instabilities of reference are, paradoxically, in this case productive of rather than intrusive to generic coherence. (Just as, say, female–female sex acts are a conventional component of what can just as unproblematically be called "heterosexual moving-image pornography" nonetheless.)

14 We shift immediately from "publicness" to the less familiar and seemingly more awkward term "publicity" here in order to heed Kluge and Negt's warnings about Jürgen Habermas' (in)famous conceptualization of the "public sphere." In their *The Public Sphere and Experience*, from which Peter Labanyi translated and published selections in 1996 (not coincidentally, also in *October*), the opening paragraph—from Kluge and Negt's foreword—ends with the observation that "The real social experiences of human beings, produced in everyday life and work, cut across divisions between the public and the private" (60). This is one of the key observations for which they want to account in their revisions of Habermas. They write: "Something that is purely private is regarded as public simply because it belongs within the ambit of a public institution or is provided with the stamp of public authority. Something that counts as private, such as the rearing of young children, is in reality of the greatest public interest" (66). *Experience* thus becomes a central concept for Kluge and Negt (and, in a certain way, for critical social theory in general) as the nexus between the public and the private in contemporary media society. "It is via the unified life context, which man experiences publicly and privately," they write, "that he 'absorbs' society as a whole, the totality of the context of mystification" (70). In Kluge and Negt's account, it is what they call "fantasy"—"not a particular substance, as when one says 'so and so has a lot of imagination,' but the organizer of mediation, a specific process whereby libidinal structure, consciousness and the outside world are connected to one another" (80)—which ultimately organizes all experience, and which thus guides the grafting of subjective interiority and civic sociality onto publicness and privateness. Thus, the functioning of the public sphere is very different for Kluge and Negt than it is for Habermas; it works through "the organization of collective experience" (66), via "the workings of fantasy as the form in which authentic experience is produced" (76). It is for this precise reason that translator Labanyi notes that a better translation for the key category (*Öffentlichkeit*) they are writing about than "public sphere" might be "publicity," since in the original language Kluge and Negt use the term in three different senses, and often dialectically, in the three different senses simultaneously. These three senses are: "1) as a spatial concept denoting the social sites or levels where meanings are manufactured, distributed, and exchanged; 2) as the ideational substance

I

Other critics attempting to do for gay pornography something equivalent to what Linda Williams did for heterosexual porn in *Hardcore* (1990) have also invoked Bersani in the course of their arguments. John Champagne's chapter on videoporn in his 1995 book *The Ethics of Marginality* is exemplary.[15] Here, the author sketches the conceptual importance of "non-productive expenditure" to gay videoporn. In Champagne's terms, this is a passion for "waste" and the "unnecessary" that is embodied by gay videoporn's dominant conventions, and is in turn related to the "sovereign subject" that dominant conceptions of "sexuality" posit—though this is typically posited along with little illusion about the shabby pretensions of that very positing. The well-known fictivity of this nonetheless supposedly-generally-believed-in "sexual sovereignty" thus becomes the tarmac over which our endless "ethical struggles over intelligibility" occur in the realm

which is processed and produced within these sites; 3) as a 'general horizon of social experience'" (60). Labanyi writes: "Whereas 'public sphere,' which has become the established translation, adequately if inelegantly renders sense (1), it cannot grasp (2) and (3)" (60). We use the term "publicity," then, because while our ensuing analysis will indeed focus on pornotextual space, it will do so in a way—through its simultaneous focus on sound and voice in pornographic textuality—which aspires further to harness the exegetical power of senses (2) and (3) for textual media studies. Furthermore, while the particular *notion* of fantasy that emerges in the remainder of Kluge and Negt's analysis is one we find reductive and problematic, it is not at all incompatible with the notions of fantasy we have so far discussed in addressing either Bersani's (reaching for one's form elsewhere) or Laplanche and Pontalis's (the scenario and the sequence) formulations. Kluge and Negt quote Ferruccio Rossi-Landi here: "What we call private is so only in that it is public. It has been public and must remain public precisely in order that it can be, whether for a moment or several thousand years, private" (68). Ultimately, then, it is in the sense of Rossi-Landi's statement that we choose to describe the textual element and effect of pornography on which we have our finger here as a "*passage* through publicity."

15 John Champagne, *The Ethics of Marginality: A New Approach to Gay Studies* (Minneapolis: University of Minnesota Press, 1995), 28–57. See also Earl Jackson Jr.'s chapter on pornography in his book *Strategies of Deviance: Studies in Gay Male Representation* (Bloomington: Indiana University Press, 1995), 126–179, in which he tries to discuss the "subject of [gay] pornography": an attempt which differs significantly from ours in that what Jackson ends up discussing is, simply put, the function of "character" in gay porn (which is not an altogether uninteresting project in and of itself, given pornography's interesting relationship to both "fiction" and "non-fiction," just one which is not appropriately nominated by his title). Also, it is important to note John Champagne's later argument elsewhere, in "Stop Reading Films!: Film Studies, Close Analysis, and Gay Pornography," *Cinema Journal* 36 (4) (Summer 1997), 76–98, that approaching the study of pornography from within the confines of media studies (and, in particular, film studies) really gets at the impossibilities of the disciplinary formations thus involved in that, according to Champagne, it makes no sense to "read" pornographic texts. This is because, when we account for particular viewing situations, spectators aren't really "watching" the texts. Champagne is particularly concerned with the video arcade, but is interested as well in other contexts in which the text becoming a pretext to sociality of one sort or another, rather than its "meanings" occupying a central place in its "reception." For a broader consideration of such contexts in contemporary US urban gay everyday life, see Cante, "Pouring on the Past: Videobars and the Emplacement of Gay Male Desire," in *Queer Frontiers: Millennial Geographies, Genders, and Generations*, edited by Queer Frontiers Collective (Madison: University of Wisconsin Press, 2000), 135–166. In the chapter in Champagne's book, however, this later argument is merely nascent, finding its way primarily in the manner in which Champagne takes to task Richard Dyer's article on gay videoporn *as video*, especially its assumptions about media spectatorship, "narrative structure," and the relation of both to the liberatory possibilities of gay sexuality and "politics." See Richard Dyer, "Coming to Terms," in *Out There: Marginalization and Contemporary Cultures*, edited by Russel Ferguson, Martha Gever, Trinh T. Minh-ha, and Cornel West (New York: New Museum of Contemporary Art and Cambridge, MA: MIT Press, 1990), 290–302.

of queer signification. In moving toward an apprehension of the role of both this sovereignty and these interpretive struggles in gay pornographic pleasure, Champagne fixes upon a litany of objects and acts which he puts forth as Foucauldian "technologies of the self." His list includes cock rings, vacuum pumps, objects used to penetrate and manipulate the anus, spanking, fisting, and watersports.[16]

For Champagne, these qualify as Foucauldian "acts" with such technologies—acts around which all sorts of *scenes* are then staged—because they "are done to the self, often by the self, and are often accomplished through the intervention of devices and machines ... In other words, they foreground the production of pleasure as an 'unnatural' act, and refuse certain humanist understandings of sexual desire and excitation as resulting from natural biological urges and drives."[17] While (rightly) suspicious of the "possibilities" too many other queer writers continue to blithely assume are attached to such objects, acts, and scenes, Champagne is nonetheless clearly insistent on integrating these into his discussion of gay pornography as Foucauldian "affirmations of non-identity." More specifically, he is insistent upon reading their presence in particular repertoires of gay sexuality in relation to conventional "narratological" aspects of gay videoporn. He still proceeds to assume, in other words, that these are technologies with which one potentially "de-subjectifies" oneself—if only, in Foucault's own qualifications, "to a certain point, perhaps not radically . . . but certainly significantly." For Foucault, a sort of pleasure in sexuality which is "desexualized" is thus potentially produced. For Champagne, this is thus waiting to be activated in spectatorial relations to gay porn—however unlikely is, for whatever reason, the actual spectatorial incarnation of the contained "non-productive" potential.

Champagne's argument is an important one in the scheme of other work on gay porn because, while it insists on their connection via "technologies" like those above, it refuses to collapse sexual desire/pleasure with the desire for pornography/pleasure in pornography. Likewise, it allows us to remember that pornographic sex is not the ontological equivalent of "fake" sex despite its being staged for the camera; we cannot allow its existence to institute a realm of the sexual supposedly ontologically prior to pornographic sexual action, although porn's formal characteristics do thus lie—as does the pleasure spectators take from it—partly in the self-consciousness of that "staging" itself.[18]

---

16 Indeed, when the entire list is looked at, its strain for unity almost approaches the famous "list" by Borges which Foucault quotes at the beginning of *The Order of Things*. While this indeed poses a major problem for Champagne's assertion about these "technologies" to go very far in addressing pornotextuality itself, this is not a problem which the integration of Champagne above imports into our own analysis. Indeed, the point of that importation is ultimately a more solid movement into the text project into which Champagne ends up making relatively little progress.

17 *The Ethics of Marginality*, 54.

18 This being, generally, the major point of difference between academic analyses of gay pornography and straight pornography, and what generates the very different "tone" and particular poetics of such analyses. And that's fine, given certain scholarly agendas which wish to account for certain arguments within feminism, whatever the sorts of porn they are looking at. What is disturbing is the utter blind spot toward the grounds from which an assertion like ours arises to be found in certain work. For instance, see Bill Nichols *et al.* on "pornography and ethnography," wherein the authors argue that both "paradigms" are "indefensible." This is an heteronormative argument if ever there was one: not in (or not only in) the sense that it doesn't account for gay experiences of pornography in the least, but in the sense that it doesn't account for already existing gay writing on, and other cultural "testimony" about, pornography and the tone and experience attached, described in and through that.

The voice of pornography   213

Champagne clearly *wants to allow* the *medium* which intervenes there to float appropriately to the top of his argument. It's just that he can't quite figure out how! The implicit conception of the "text" which circulates through media studies and cultural studies, then, is the point of blockage he hits in appropriately dealing with specific pornographic texts, or even in appropriately dealing globally with "conventions" of gay male porn in toto. In this regard, Champagne's (in)famous demand that we "stop reading [pornographic] texts," a demand set forth in a separate but related essay, and that we instead account for the social situations in which both the pornographic apparatus and any discrete text make themselves relatively unimportant to their "viewers," finally appears for what it apparently is: a self-conscious, preformatted denial of the need a talk about the text and the medium in detail. And a denial which has nothing to do whatsoever with spectatorial "responses" to these things, but with a much broader, harder to locate entity nonetheless attached to the field of discourse encircling such texts even if no one is watching them. This is precisely what we mean by the "subject" of gay male pornography, a slightly but very significantly different entity from what other writers mean with this similar term, and different from the "subject" automatically attached to related notions such as "fantasy" in these analyses. Indeed, our own analysis is ultimately bound up with very different assumptions about how the text can possibly be "traversed" as a cultural document, and about where its points of entry lie.[19]

We mean a subject which is not necessarily attached to a spectator or even a spectatorial position within the text in the manner in which so much "film theory" still insists on conceiving the subject relative to the spectator, and we mean something that is not necessarily attached to character. We mean something that arises as a result of a continual phantasmatic self-shattering whose mechanisms and effects sublate the distinction between interiority and exteriority, and between "privacy" and "publicity," within the

---

19 For instance, Mandy Merck has written about one of the specific texts we will address in the readings that follow, ours thus being sort of an extrapolation from and extension of her argument and understanding of this text's general project which nonetheless ends up manufacturing *More of a Man* as a very different cultural object (even, in other words, if it ends up looking like a similar *media* object to the one Merck seems to be discussing). For us, it is these aesthetic dimensions which finally bring that text in line with the "history" in which we will emplace it in our argument. Likewise, writers on gay porn like Daniel Harris and Thomas Waugh (besides the already discussed Earl Jackson Jr.) have written pieces with a scholarly aim similar to ours, however different the language, but which either never make it to dealing with individual texts in detail (Harris, like Champagne) or never deal with texts via the sorts of theoretical ideas and techniques we use here (Waugh). Likewise, Laura Kipnis's brilliant culturalist analysis of pornography as signifying practice generally pushes toward the same ends as does our argument here in its wish to discuss the "subject," but never deals substantively with moving-image media as media which specifically produce certain sorts of phantasmatic effects, subject effects, and aesthetic evidence. See Mandy Merck, *Perversions: Deviant Readings* (New York: Routledge, 1993), Laura Kipnis, *Bound and Gagged: Pornography and the Politics of Fantasy in America* (New York: Grover Press, 1996), Thomas Waugh, *Hard to Imagine: Gay Male Eroticism in Photography and Film from their Beginnings to Stonewall* (New York: Columbia University Press, 1996), and Daniel Harris, "The Evolution of Gay Pornography: Film," *The Rise and Fall of Gay Culture* (New York: Hyperion, 1997), 111–134. In other words, our piece is a synthesis of: (1) works on gay and straight pornography, and (2) works which fall on both sides of the (phantasmatic) culturalist/formalist divide which is now doing, and recently has done, such harm to film and television studies in the US. (Of course, this is largely media studies' own fault, for its practitioners *invented* that divide as a disciplinary divide sometime during the 1980s, partly owing to the embattled history of film studies and its lingering impulse to maintain disciplinary specificity by recourse to the insular specificity of its objects and methods—and then proceeded to act on the presumed existence of this divide in all sorts of questionable ways.)

textual economy at the same time—and via the same methods—that they sublate the distinction between the interiority and the exteriority of the text itself.[20]

In order better to grasp this entity's precise sort of amorphousness, we want to discuss the way in which sound (the voice being one component of that) functions in gay porn texts in particular as the marker of all that is exterior but is nonetheless lodged into the deep interiority of the sexual subject. This focus ties this project directly back to *Hardcore*, though ours is distinct in the manner in which it attempts to revise our understanding of sound and voice in relation to gay experience, gay culture, and the specificities of gay pornographic texts. Put another way, the mechanisms by which sound (and the voice in particular) and space insert themselves in both gay pornographic textuality and the gay experience of pornographic textuality in such a way that they become the primary (along with the medium carrying them) "technologies" of the self which Champagne (mistakenly) tries to pin to his own list of objects and acts. They become especially important placeholders, in other words, for the realm of experience which pornography mobilizes in its play(s) with our affect, and our affective plays with it, by shattering and reinstating the very public/private divide which effectively structures such experience. Therefore, we will be treating sound and space as objects crucial to the function of porn and *vis-à-vis* which the subject of porn both materializes and continually dissolves in all its homosexual specificity—materializations and dissolutions so impossible but important to track because they don't just cross but, by crossing it, continually instantiate the limits of our fields of sensation themselves.

20 Perhaps the two best models for this kind of reconceptualization of the relationship between subject and text in recent critical theory who do actually read media texts in significant detail, in a manner which thus gets around the old problem of the formulation of a spectator in most currently existing film theory, are Slavoj Žižek and Toby Miller. While Žižek's recourse in doing this is mostly to the Lacanian concept of the "real" and a rigorously dialectical understanding of psychoanalysis in general, Miller's recourse is to a more Adornonian "culturalist" methodology which also attempts to account for negativity, in order that the emphasis of Miller's work can (ostensibly) fall on notions of citizenship. It should be noted that the two projects are not at all far apart in scope or product, as is the connection of this mode of exegesis to the work of people like Berlant and Warner, despite the grounding of the latter in literary rather than media textual operations (which sometimes causes problems when they deal with film). In another context (discussing the related challenge for the transnational turn in gay and lesbian studies, the challenge of accounting for the "noncorrespondence between discursive, psychic, and practical orders"), George Chauncey and Elizabeth Povinelli put the project on which we're trying to put our finger—and which we are trying to explicate further and contribute to in this article—this way: "How do we produce our undoing as we attempt to follow our desire? After all, in doing what we will to do, we do 'a thousand and one things we hadn't willed to do' and so 'the act is not pure.' We leave traces and, in wiping away these traces, we leave others. In Levinas' words, it is 'like an animal fleeing in a straight line across the snow before the sound of the hunters, thus leaving the very traces that will lead to its death.' It is this travail of the subject, fashioned far afield from itself, that globalization studies has yet to track." Indeed, that travail of the subject is what we are arguing textual studies only very recently began to track in the important work of figures like Žižek and Miller—whose more or less unpopular work is essentially reviving the possibilities of, say, film theory within the context of a rigorous theoretical culturalism by developing a mode of textual analysis which indeed "traverses textuality" in previously unimaginable ways, and through previously unimaginable points of entry. For particular examples, see Slavoj Žižek, *For They Know Not What They Do: Enjoyment as a Political Factor* (London and New York: Verso, 1991), and Lauren Berlant, "National Brands/National Body: Imitation of Life," in J. Hortense Spillers, ed., *Comparative American Identities: Race, Sex, and Nationality in the Modern Text* (New York: Routledge, 1991), 110–140. For their argument in its entirety, see George Chauncey and Elizabeth A. Povinelli, "Editors' Introduction," *GLQ* 4 (5) (Autumn 1999), 1–19, special issue on *Thinking Sexuality Transnationally*.

Sound is connected to the articulation of (real and phantasmatic) space in and out-side of such textual systems and can lead us to the mechanisms through which public and private are "inscribed" (or not inscribed) in gay texts, and the mechanisms through which that specific (non)inscription distinguishes both the texts themselves and the sub-ject floating around their existence from other "orientations" of media porn. We are interested in the manner in which the sound system of these texts functions to articu-late and delimit the physical spaces (both public and private) across which a specifically gay brand of fantasy assembles itself as being a largely sonic one in the first place. These aesthetics carry important cultural traces of the particular way in which both the voice and space can come to appear as objects of utter exteriority (the Law, the other, the voice of the text itself, the voice of "culture") inhumanly lodged in the interiority (sites of phantasmatic enjoyment, at which the subject dissolves but at which the individual is still always an agent) of gay-subjectivity-as-form—and thus at the interiority of gay sexual "relationality" in general.[21]

This, then, is what we respond to, phenomenologically, in "responding" to the aes-thetic astonishments of gay porn: the voice can become the "site" for these mechanisms in gay porn only because of the particular relation to space, place, and site which becomes attached to voice in the phantasmatics underlying the fixations of such sites and such responses. Thus, we call this essay the "voice of pornography" because we are tracing something here about the general rhetorical system of gay pornography in the manner in which Bill Nichols tracked the same thing for documentary in his classic article from which we borrow the titular formulation. But also in the more specific sense, in which that general rhetorical aspiration gets implanted in the "mouths of [gay] pornographic babes" via the fantasy system which articulates their very vocations with a visual system of display. And we mean by this the way in which gay pornography "speaks us" and "speaks to us" as spectators and as analysts of media, of culture, of texts of all material sorts, and of the social structures to which all three are always already related.

II

This project subsequently becomes an historical one only in a very specific sense of that term, and a sense which is best explained—as are its methodological implications—by situating our take on the three texts we will discuss below in relation to Linda Williams' take on her own objects of analysis in *Hardcore*. Williams' model is characterized by an understanding that the sex act staged by the text is not a "pure" one, and her analysis does take into account the camera's, and ultimately the spectator's, gaze. However, the problem is that this observation is eclipsed as Williams adopts what is essentially a melo-dramatic analytic framework. In such a framework that which is not representable within the diegesis—the invisible "truth" of sex, and the pleasure of Woman in particular—is displaced into two "superficial" textual conventions: those governing the emplacement of the come shot in the sex sequences, and those governing the use of the ecstatic female voice in the text's sound design (just as in melodrama, where the music and ruptures

---

21 For the theory underlying such an approach to the voice within the theoretical parameters we have cre-ated so far, see in particular Mladen Dolar, "The Object Voice" and Slavoj Žižek, "I Hear You With My Eyes; or, The Invisible Master," both in *Gaze and Voice as Love Objects*, edited by Renata Salacl and Slavoj Žižek (Durham, NC: Duke University Press, 1996), 7–32 and 90–129.

in the *mise-en-scène* are displacements of the deep truths of the characters' psychic lives, or of the deep symptoms of the way the psyche, and subjectivity, operate in general). Thus, Williams' approach privileges the continual manufacture of a continuously "pornotopic" space which is not unlike the diegesis of classical Hollywood cinema in its ideological function. What gets ignored by this framework is the "excess kernel of enjoyment" which arises out of, and is an effect of, the exhibitionistic, preformatted aspect of pornotextuality: that porn is, by definition, enacted for a "third gaze."

Since this model is developed in relation to heterosexual, feature-length, narrative-oriented porn and is closely related to the one Kaja Silverman lays out in *The Acoustic Mirror*, it "makes sense" that Williams ends up privileging one over the other. But, had she looked at the history of gay porn she would have come to very different conclusions. There's an important reason for this which often gets lost in the banality of the preceding assertion, or which has not yet been articulated with that assertion: Williams' argument implicitly models—and this is precisely where John Champagne's impulse to argue with her comes from, despite his argument never going very far because of the way his "technologies of the self" assertion is so readily connected back to the voice in a model like this—a spectator who is engaged by the text and sutured into it via the model of "screen theory."

Williams is writing just as video is emerging as both a dominant production material and a dominant home-viewing pattern for pornography. In fact, this is what allows her to construct the filmic-feature genre the way she does. This it to say that, as Williams herself prominently notes, the engaged spectator this model assumes is already, at the time of *Hardcore*'s publication, a nostalgic thing of the past. Likewise, Williams' fixation upon—by exhaustive employment of—the notion of the fetish in order to theorize the conventions involving the come shot and the female voice reinscribes into her mode of exegesis the very "phallic economy of the one" in the service of which she so rightly tags these conventions as operating. Even if she had taken, say, S/M porn as more central to her analysis than she did, our hunch is Williams' critical methodology would have had to look significantly different than it does in order to account for the (specific brands of) "dehumanization" and "self-shattering" here being textualized—brands to which Bersani draws our attention as constituent of all sexual subjectivity. So, we are now in a position not only to draw these gay texts back from the center to the margin of such a project —a drawing back which has still yet to be done as gay male scholars have apparently been comfortable assuming *Hardcore* has little to say on the realities of gay porn (and basing their own analyses on other, far less theoretically astute arguments)—but also to create a model of pornographic space as fantasy space which takes into account the predominantly videographic modes in which most commercial porn is now produced and consumed, and which will ultimately be able to say something about pornography's current and impending further digitization too.

Let's assume for argument's sake that, in general, the feature-length gay porn film which emerged along with the straight ones Williams discusses, in its narrative incarnations,[22] resembles fairly well those on which Williams builds her model. These texts are heavily reliant upon the manufacture of a unified story space and the delimiting of its

---

22 For an interesting, related argument from the *Intimacy Issue* Berlant edited, which is about sexual activity, gender, and talk and which relates voice to the complications of (queer and non-queer) "publicity" through its attempts to formulate a "depersonalized intimacy," see Candace Vogler, "Sex and Talk," *Critical Inquiry* 24 (Winter 1998), 328–365.

boundaries through their employment of the come shot and particular sound–image relations in order to manufacture the "visible evidence" of the truth of *desire* which is then experienced by the spectator as staged in(to) these scenes. In effect, then, what these films finally make visible is nothing less than the figure of the post-Stonewall "male homosexual" that is emerging contemporaneously as an historical entity—a visible entity simultaneously being implicitly attached to particular notions of social positionality via the dispersal of this entity. Since "coming out" narratives often organize the spaces of such narrative films, as well as the temporal relations among these spaces, the coming out narrative can here be seen as a production process through which these texts make continual ideological and formal passage—the "product" of both this coming out and this passage through the coming out narrative being both a visible marketable entity and a version of the "gay male subject" which doesn't empirically exist in the same way as the former but is still simultaneously marketed as now suddenly existing as a novel "privately public" entity. Think of all those signifiers of style, behavioral or sartorial, and the modes of reception that developed around them, which aspire to writing "gay male desire" on to the surface of the body: most famously, various historical incarnations of the "clone style." These engage us in exactly the visual logic of the melodramatic text, and this is precisely why Williams' assumptions *are* so useful for gay porn, though only in a predictably twisted fashion: that it is the formerly repressed "deep truth" of the subject which is finally fated to compose its visible surface.

The specific problem with this in these "gay" texts is that, just as, say, the police uniform can't give the clone the (same) "power" that the uniform itself signifies, the display of the come shots here, and the use of the sound conventions, can't hold the rhetorical system together for reasons different from those of straight porn (where Williams argues they essentially *do* hold the system together anyway). The come shot cannot function in any stable way as the visible evidence of an "authentically" gay male desire if the gay male figure here can't function as the woman functions in the heterosexual texts: as placeholder of all the invisible pleasure deep inside the penetrated subject, the subject being always already penetrated (of course) by the "language" which the voice embodies by its seeming nonetheless to originate from deep inside. In other words, we have "too much" in these gay texts visually, rather than "too little," as is the case once there's a woman.[23] The phallic economy of the one—to the extent that it does seem important given these texts' continual production of *the* newly emerging gay male as an always already unified discursive and social entity, if only for "marketing" purposes (if often political marketing concurrently with the other type, given the affiliations of those making gay porn at this time)—cannot be emplaced within the figure of an other the same way: every one of the bodies in the thick of this scenario has a penis, and every one of them has an anus.

In this sense, as Williams recognizes, it is the rhetorical brilliance of *Deep Throat* that its gimmick—the placing of the clitoris in the female "protagonist's" throat—allows for the condensation of the come shot with open-mouthed signifiers of feminine enjoyment, as well as the sounds "emanating" to the soundtrack, into the space of the closeup. It allows, that is, for the movement toward an apparent "simultaneity" whose "lack" in the pornographic scenario is bound always to be a problem (though a problem generative, of course, of desire). In the gay male case, such hetero-simultaneity is unimaginable

---

23 To use Linda Williams' own terms, that is, from her separate but related article which deals, more generally, with "Body Genres": horror and melodrama as well as porn.

because the combination of two male genital "systems" is supposed in this culture not to automatically produce orgasms for both actants (read: the insertee) where intercourse is concerned.[24] Thus, the couple's pleasure must now be spread across any number of spatial and temporal positions precisely because of the "extra penis" always haunting gay male porn. In other words, the temporal preformatted breach of the gay couple cannot possibly be covered up as it is in the straight porn, and this is partly because the particular productive breach itself is gay male desire at its essence, an underlying component of its particular range of available scenarios for "reaching for one's form elsewhere" in the first place. Thus, what "comes out" in these coming out narratives of the gay male filmic features and the broader historical movement of which they are now evidence can be nothing other than the inherent instability of the identity position which was once supposedly "deep inside the [secret gay] subject"—or evidence of the particular incompatibility of this "new" identity position with all systems of visual representation, including the pornography charged with the burden of continually ascribing to the male homosexual a place in visual culture.[25] And these deep innards get splattered all across the space and time of late consumer capitalism. If, according to Laplanche and Pontalis (as well as, implicitly, Bersani), fantasy is always sequenced, this is partly because in the relationship of some originary sequence to any particular restaging of it there is always a "gap." If fantasy inevitably fixates on particular temporal intervals in the restaging of such a sequence—and binds its energies around particular spaces (and sonic "scapes" too, of course) in the process—there is an essential difference in the way cinema facilitates this and the way electronic media do. With the economically driven proliferation of new forms of pornotextuality which emerge with the "video revolution" (paradigmatically, the compilation tape and the screen test tape) and, concomitantly, with the changes in spectatorial practice video also ushers in (paradigmatically, the masturbatorial viewer who takes numerous things into his own hands, including the "voice" of the pornographic text itself via the remote control), we do indeed end up with, in Richard Dyer's terms, a spatial/temporal textual mode which isn't necessarily as teleologically genital, or orgasmically oriented, as it had become by the generic reification of the narrative feature.

The identity of porn's historical reader thus aspires to the possibility of being nothing but a disembodied entity, a sequence of disconnected engagements across time and space (with any variety of objects) whose inscriptions into texts would seem naturally to gravitate phantasmatically toward the sonic rather than the visual, given these changes in technology which also accompany the move to video (for example, the easier access to sound synchronization which gets written into conventions affects a presence while the manner in which remote control fast-forwarding officiously "wipes away" the soundtrack of entire portions of a tape at the spectator's command erases the presence of a

---

24 Thus the ubiquitous tendency toward an increasing frenzy of "finishing onself off" for both partners when ejaculation is not internal—though we should note there's no necessary aesthetic reason why we've latched on to such self-manipulation as the convention in this country, and the relation to non-pornographic sexual practice of such conventions is of course an extremely complicated one. We will have more to say about this soon, in the third textual/analytical section of this essay.

25 After all, doesn't pornography—especially today in the rampant nature of its production and reception by gay men as well as its enormous archivalization—represent the gay male more than any other media genre? (We can imagine hearing no complaints about the lack of gay representation once porn is taken into account; but need it be said that most of the ideologues who still tend toward such complaints aren't quite likely to take to such an accounting system!).

form which, by definition, is bound to be in and of itself insufficient to individual scopic/sonic "desire").[26] Still, in other ways the very ludicrousness of such "disjunctions" between sound and image and also between the intentions and effects of pornographic sound–image relations more generally is bound, after video, to expose the problematic underlying the gay male text: namely, the invocation of the universal function of representing (or, at least, allegorizing) the "communication of forms" which is sexuality generally in texts which exists solely as a result of the politics and production process of the *particular*, and in order to produce the gay male particularly and send him traveling through post-WWII America's commodity chains. And gay porn's repeated and necessary "accidental documentation" of that leftover penis is bound to make this continually manifest whatever the technology at hand.

III

In the final section of this essay we offer an analysis of a more recent gay pornographic text; in a more expansive version of this argument we would treat the (comparatively) longer history of the genre by examining texts from different historical moments since the emergence of the gay filmic feature which interests us in terms of how sound and the voice function relative to the above considerations. These are different historical spaces related to both the real social world and the phantasmatics of the gay historical subject via the relation between public and private through which they are inscribed (or not inscribed) into the text. It is these various disruptions to the system of pornography and gay pornography in particular—historical, textual, theoretical—which institute the present analysis, and which guide our selection of particular texts and moments in the first place via the way in which they thus become assimilable to Bersani's conception of sexuality to the functions of "publicity" in queer culture discussed above. Thus, we are relying on the reading of the texts we have chosen because of their idiosyncratic qualities as texts and less their representative qualities as cultural documents, not vice versa (as film studies has tended to do in recent years). And to the extent that our approach to these documents is indebted to psychoanalysis, that usage of idiosyncrasy makes perfect sense.

This is an historical project primarily in that historicity is conceived as retroactivity; in the sense that we are tracking the emergence of the subject of gay male pornography in the first text and its continual reemergence in other forms in the second two, that first emergence becoming "originary" only retroactively and phantasmatically, and these texts becoming the "tracks" left by gay subjectivity on the way in which they appear to us now, given the changes in the pornographic apparatus and in culture and society at large in the intervening years.

---

26 Of course, it is now a historiographical commonality—and therefore a not-a-bit dubious interpretive premise— that pornography was essentially the underlying logic driving the development of the home video market: the possibility of viewing porn in "private" being the unspoken "surplus" driving the consumer purchase. Even if true, this is necessarily working differently phantasmatically and socially historically for "straights" and "gays," once you consider the reception contexts in the "public sphere," like the porn theaters which Champagne discusses as male–male sex sites and which *Night at the Adonis* also self-reflexively seems to want eventually retroactively historically to mythologize as such given the "sense of an ending" always attached to it. In this regard, the tag line we will discuss from that film, "There's always the Adonis," becomes an interesting "affirmation" (thus its repetition) in the face of some potential, unspoken threat to the very possibility of the Adonis' continuance—a threat which, of course, will ultimately have its place held in the symbolic order by the emergence of AIDS, and in the systems of gay hardcore by the (continually effaced) presence of the condom.

The centrality of the transition from film to video in this argument thus appears not only in terms of the way the sound technology itself becomes different with this shift, but also in the sense that the apparatus of gay pornography itself—as institution, as text, as technology, as consumption practice, as "representation," etc.—is the very thing which enables the ultimate existence of the archive which renders our particular sort of gay subjective history possible, that archive first taking the form of the video store and later being grafted gradually into cyberspace. In other words, we are particularly interested in these disruptions in all these components of the apparatus in and of themselves, for they too are now productive of desire—though differently than they originally were—as disruptions in the history of porn, homosexuality, and human subjectivity which are themselves bound to be repeated and invoked in all sorts of manners in pornography's future, and the (phantasized) future of the "subject" attached to this entire apparatus of vision, sound, and feeling.

The impulse to focus on sound here, then, arises not just from an organic element of interest in these and other texts in this archive but also from a number of related factors guiding this impulse. For instance, with the transition from film to video we also get the emergence of the full-blown AIDS epidemic and the popularity of a phenomenon like "phone sex" which accompanies it. And in some sense our argument is propped on an argument about shifts from image dominance to sound dominance which recent sound theorists have made, a shift made possible only by the phantasmatic imaginings of film and video technology by gay male porn. We wouldn't want to discount the manner in which such an historical development motivates this analysis and the degree to which the "passage through the public" which gay porn always effects via its sonics topples out of the text and into everyday life via such broader developments and changes in sexual culture.

Likewise, there are any number of other "external" and/or culturally compelling reasons for our wishing to turn our attentions to sound. For instance, beyond being a melodramatic one, we notice that Linda Williams' model is essentially grounded in conventions of the musical. Indeed, this is where she gets her terms for the distinction between the sex scenes and the rest of the narrative filmic feature, the split between the "narrative" and the "numbers." Beyond what we've already addressed about her model's use of voice, the fact that its swollen music is one of melodrama's primary mechanisms of fixation for the ruptures of its "troubled" textual system makes Williams' a model more deeply indebted to notions of the sonic than it might at first glance appear. And it is of course this focus that arises from the same discursive field out of which the sonic conventions we describe are imagined and experienced in the first place and out of which "phone sex" can become a popular phenomenon too. And all of this while surprisingly (or, if one buys psychoanalytic dialectics, not surprisingly at all) the explicit focus on porn sound in its specificity seems to us a notable lacuna in studies of porn at the same time, and especially of gay male porn.[27]

27 For example, the early existence of the Wakefield Poole feature *Bijou* (1972), in which Poole, working on double system 16 mm film, manages to secure enough money to install one magazine of sync sound into his film and then chooses (almost as with Warhol) to use the sync to record the ambient sounds of a character in his room as he listens to a radio, does his toilette, etc., which could have been done almost as easily without the sync as most of the sounds emanate from off-screen sources—rather than to "emplace" any dialogue in the mouths of his characters or even to use the sync during a "number" alone makes it seem like there's something very, very interesting going on here.

Similarly, one could argue that with the emergence of clone styles the problem of the "sameness" haunting gay male porn (and, in different ways, the idea of a "gay culture" in general), of the "extra one," becomes intensified so that the voice is charged with an extra burden toward "differentiation" of whatever sort as the visual system fails to perform this mandate. Indeed, is sound not where, after all, we continue to look for the "femininities" we assume to have been relocated elsewhere after self-consciousness puts the kibosh, on both the "encoding" and "decoding" ends, on limp-wristed pre-formatted "embodiment?"

Likewise, Justice Potter's famous makeshift, solipsistic definition of pornography—"I know it when I see it"—gets things wrong, or only gets half the story, in that isn't it the case that, just as often, we know it when we *hear* it? In fact, if anything distinguishes the textual aesthetics of porn at the level of "style" (as opposed to the realm of "content"), isn't it the conventional, cheaply produced, repetitive music which accompanies the scenes and mimics their visual machinations in such an interesting way? Also, there are other sound conventions in porn that are easily noticeable and recognizable even to the novice viewer: one of them being a particular use of language we will call "porno-performativity," and the other being the very interplay between sync and non-sync sound which characterized the texts for years and years. These are all particularly important in gay pornography for specific reasons. (And none of this even mentions the manner in which pornographic "acting styles" are finally carried by voice and ambient sound to such a great extent—the dead silence, or the buzz of video under the scene character-izing the pornographic status of the text as much as its supposedly more central sonic elements).

The importance of pornoperformative dirty talk is exemplary here. Such vocatives must be understood as a component of an interactive spatial system whose fantasy scenar-ios—those scenarios which aspire to desubjectivization, and paradoxically individuate us in the process—involve "publicity" to an extent and via mechanisms that straight porn simply doesn't. The male who, while being fucked, incessantly exclaims to his partner "fuck me" or "suck his dick" seems totally self-conscious—both as a performer and as a sexual actant—that he is producing what the communication theorists call "phatic" communication. His "desire," as vocally expressed, cannot be heeded to the extent that it is already being heeded, and that is what's commissioning the vocatives in the first place: it is then, strictly speaking, nothing less than a formally dialectical psychoanalytic *desire* being vocalized here through the very language outside of whose code desire always lies. It is in that sense that we mean that the dimensions of both language and the experi-ence of it (its role in the communication of forms, the self-shattering attached to that communication, the agency which nonetheless stays attached to the body, and the non-human thing to which we are related by sexuality—which is here language itself once its "meanings" no longer function as such despite their apparent "presence") are "passed through" with each repetition of such a convention.

In the textual model we are developing here—in trying to remember that the "third gaze" is always part of fantasy itself, and that fantasy is a sequence and is thus based on the imprecation of sound not as "monads" but as having "durations," and where there is thus always a gap via recording technology between the spoken and the heard to boot—these vocatives function therefore not so much as inter-character exchange but as address to the spectator himself. The specific of its usage in gay porn is perhaps clearest in the history of the "porn star" since the development of the filmic feature, a version of "stardom" really only imaginable after the movement to video via modes of talk: Jeff

Stryker as the active top, Joey Stefano as the voracious but still vocally active bottom (an innovation at the time), etc. In fact, the movement within porn discourse—both in the industry and for spectators—from calling porn participants "actors" to calling them "performers" to calling them "models"[28] seems connected in some interesting if indirect way to the manner in which the conception of identity fundamentally connected to porn stardom changes significantly over the years from the filmic-feature to the present, and the role of the voice is key in all this (via, of course, the conception of "image" implicitly attached to and propagated by certain such notions of voice).

Unlike in the melodramatic conception of the media text, where what can't be photographed in the pro-filmic is registered in the extra-diegetic realm (prototypically, as the "swollen music"), here we have the reverse: the text implanting its voice into the pro-filmic—and, particularly, onto the image of the actors—because the only reasons these utterances are made are for the demands of the pornography itself (however much that demand is welcomed by the actants as actants). In other words, such utterances are bound to come off as being directed and responsive to the "third gaze" as a sonic point of surveillance (and/or to the "director" himself). But in gay pornography they play an extra function about giving us "information" about the pleasure being "enjoyed" by the actors too, thus supplementing the visual information of erections while being fucked, come shots, other movements of the body and face, etc. These sounds lead us toward pondering the question, in other words, "is this actor really gay?," especially because so much of the industry discourse circulates around so many stars being "trade." (And these days both "top trade" and "bottom trade"!) There is simply no equivalent set of "questions" toward which we are directed with straight porn, just as the question (a narrative one) of "what's gonna happen" is not a question in straight videoporn, just as the narratological question for "what's going to happen" is not the same sort of question in straight porn. In the gay textual system and its experience by real spectators, who will be fucked is always the question at hand, one way or another (especially given American gay porn's rigid distinction between top and bottom performers in the age of video in general, which is itself a change from the era of film).

Thus, it is in this sense that the sonic serves to glue the spectator into the fantasy space of the text. So, Champagne's argument might have been more concerned with who was "listening" to the text rather than who was watching it. Video technology, with its economic sync recording and editing potentials, facilitates this. And finally, given all of the above, an element such as pornoperformativity is conventionalized in gay videoporn. Given that, in the seventies, porn in general is plagued by the "problem of sound," new and important historical connotations thus become potentially retroactively entangled with the sound aesthetics of the older texts in the present discursive fields of pornographic reception, and the field delimiting the very historically specific and medium-dependent idea of pornography itself. Just as the issue of exhibitionist pleasure exposes the inherent ambiguity in the enunciative regimes of pornography, the gay male

---

28 A recent move made by Jocks studio in this regard—its marketing ploy of calling its performers "athletes"—is particularly interesting the way the shift in the locus of "activity" is linguistically displaced from voice to image just as sound technologies in video make the location of such activity in voice all the easier. (A paradox not unrelated to the tendency to VCR zap by fast forwarding whole sonic sections of the text while the soundscape itself becomes so important to the desire for the experience for porn. Anyone who has tried to watch video porn without sound, so a neighbor doesn't know, probably knows the "disappointing" aspect of this.)

videotext exposes this particular ontological ambiguity via its fixation on dirty talk, which is only an imaginable convention after the accessible sync of video. If the come shot can't signify anal pleasure, and the erection (or even flaccidity, to be contrarian) can't do this either, even though there is this central surplus in the textual system because ejaculatory truth IS possible within the textual economy relative to straight porn, it would indeed seem to be anal pleasure that the voice is standing in for—for there is still the temporal gap in ejaculation caused by penetration (and later, by the necessity of the condom too). This is especially overdetermined given the aforementioned tendency to look for "effeminacy" in the actors' voices. The "real" sexual identity of a performer aspires to being read, as does the "authenticity" of his "enjoyment" of particular acts, not only in relation to his dialogue and his delivery of it in both the numbers and the narrative but in the actual *grain of his voice.* The visible evidence is supplanted by the invisible evidence of sounds; these preformatted acts—and maybe the whole identity category encircling the gay texts which paradoxically creates this possibility as a "surplus of enjoyment"!—don't necessarily betray the identificatory pleasures with which they are ostensibly simultaneous once the voice, and "simultaneous ambience," intervenes the way it does with the move to video.

And this is precisely what we mean by the problematic of the universal and the particular in gay porn, the more general tension which emplaces the role of "publicity" which our analyses will uncover. As Joan Copjec notes (after Pascal Bonitzer), the particular is what "ruins the possibility of the Universal." In other words, it is precisely the *embodiment* of voice that spells "the death of meaning," the loss of the universal in the particular (voice or utterance). In so far as the grain of the voice has no particular content, but is—as Barthes formulated—simply the friction produced by language's materiality, then the grain of the voice becomes the mark of desire NOT in the speaking subject, but in the listener/spectator instead. Video's embodied voice, then, allows for the production of a "surplus" which can activate the viewer/listener's desire even as it marks the actor/speaker/text's with mortality, with death, and with a strange (and somewhat mysteriously related) "inauthenticity" within the economy of porn. But this desire of the listener is ultimately undermined by the pornotextual's move away from the logic of "desire" over the course of the seventies, eighties, and nineties—a move we can put in the language of Slavoj Žižek—and toward the logic of the *drive, a cultural shift which does not accidentally accompany the recent advent and history of the gay male as a category of US public and private agency.* As Copjec writes, under the regime of the drive, "the intimate core of our being, no longer sheltered by sense, ceases to be supposed and suddenly becomes *exposed.*" Yet, this "exposure of self" cannot be understood in the terms of any depth model of psychology. "What is made audible—or visible—is the void as such, contentless and nonsensical." And, perhaps we can also add, queer.

Finally, our impulse to talk about pornographic sound in the way we are addressing it here relates back to the psychoanalytic notion, from Laplanche and Pontalis (among others), that the "primal scene" is the *sine qua non* of phantasmatic space. Considering the manner in which image–sound relations in gay porn today are, as previously discussed, always bound to return us to one "primal scene" or another, we would have to concede that psychoanalysis still understands fantasy primarily as image construction—as scenario staging. Yet, in the contemporary bourgeois family, the child is much more likely to have *heard* the parents' sex act than to have *seen* it. As a result, we might say that the primal scene comes to be built around a "sonic core" which itself partakes of the Lacanian real in that it is the unsymbolizable element upon which the fantasy edifice in general is now often constructed.

Michel Chion, in theorizing what he calls the "soft revolution" in cinema sound, develops the notion of *rendu*, a notion which would seem logically useful here. This is the filmic rendering of sound in a kind of immediacy that marks it as outside the enunciation of the film. Chion argues that, with the increasing complexity of sonic design, the soundtrack has come to replace the function of the establishing shot, so that it is the soundtrack which orients us in relation to the floating fragments of images. Slavoj Žižek then makes the crucial move of arguing that this "sonic aquarium" stands in for nothing other than the Real of psychic life itself: we are oriented not through visual signifiers of externality, but through aural signs which seem to be *internal*, and which therefore seize us *immediately*.

Ultimately, *rendu* must be seen as a pure form which expresses the logic of the content of a particular historical moment. This is why it is an important concept for our purposes. In terms of electronic media pornography, we can say that the primacy of sound serves precisely to "seize" us in that it evokes the Real core around which the primal scene is constructed. After all, it is precisely an "arrest of movement" that marks the subject's position as witness to the scene here, not unlike the masturbating spectator's compulsive repetition before the videotext. Thus, if the fantasy scenario of the image always risks "losing" the spectator in the sense that it diverges too far from the phantasmatic of a particular subject (a "risk" which John Champagne addresses as crucial to the ideological effects of gay pornography), it is the sound which can keep him plugged in. It is in this precise sense that the "passage through publicity" which we will show to characterize gay porn latches onto the sound as the conduit for its self-performance, and becomes the nexus between the text and its own publicness in a way that the image can't possibly pull off given its very queer "surplus."

IV 1989: *More of a Man*

By the late eighties, when *More of a Man* was made, video had replaced film as the medium for the production and distribution of pornography, and the site of reception has been relocated to within the private space of the home. Given video's electronic "marriage" of sound and image, one might expect to find a change in sound/image aesthetics concomitant to the shift to video. In film, sound and image are constitutively separated, so that a synthetic operation is always required in constructing a mimetic representation of the world; the strategies that gay male film porn adopted were integrally connected to an awareness of public space as that necessary backdrop against which the gay subject can emerge. Fundamental to this argument, of course, is that the particularities of sound aesthetics in low-budget film porn have a more than incidental or utilitarian meaning: that it in fact becomes conventionalized and can so be read symptomatically. This methodological assumption receives its best vindication when one notices that in video porn, vestiges of these older conventions survive. Thus, while it would seem that video would allow for a more widespread use of synchronous sound and the total elimination of "semi-sync," in fact much video porn still contains a large number of shots taped without sound; and it also resorts to the post-production re-creation of bodily noises and voices, especially in group scenes. Of course, the video soundtrack does generally contain more synchronous footage; and overall, the soundtracks are less "rough." From a production point of view, the persistence of the older conventions can be explained by reasons of utility: the need to use voice to direct the actors, etc. But underlying this, one can argue that the problem of situating the gay subject in relation to public space remains a central problem in eighties porn, as a tape like *More of a Man* attests.

More of a Man is set in LA—which by the eighties has become not only the center of a thriving porn industry, but also the cultural landscape which most often is the backdrop for the porn tapes themselves—and so one would expect to see a significant change in the way public and private spaces are configured, given LA's position as a postmodern "edge city" modeled on suburban notions of space and privacy. The narrative of *More of a Man* is constructed around the convergence of the stories of the two central characters, who end up a "couple" (or at least, end up "coupling"); one is the coming out story of the character played by Joey Stefano (Vito); the other is the story of an AIDS activist (Duffy) in LA's gay community, whose lover breaks up with him early in the film for, as the lover puts it, being a "professional homosexual" to the detriment of their relationship. What is most interesting about this scenario is the way in which "uneven development" is now located in the intangible domain of gay male subjectivity itself. Joey Stefano even goes so far as to engage in a gay bashing early in the film, after an anonymous sexual encounter in a train station tearoom. Stefano is clearly marked as an Italian ethnic subject, not only by name, but by his obsessive Catholicism: the tape begins with a rack focus into an extreme closeup of rosary beads, as we hear Vito in voice-off telling God that he will do "absolutely anything" to get "all of these impure thoughts out of my head." Clearly, much of his turmoil comes from an internalization of the mentality of the ethnic enclave: so that at least part of the film's project is to present coming out as a kind of homogenization, where what remains of the ethnic is its appearance, its use-value in the erotic combinatoire. This psychic "uneven development" has important repercussions in the text's sense of history: as if the linearity of the history of gay "progress" embodied in the activist is always confronted with the circularity of repetition, as yet another generation, another ethnic enclave, must reconquer for itself—through its own coming out process—the gains achieved by the past.[29]

But the spaces of the film mimic as well the uneven development at the level of consciousness. While the activist lives in a glossy, fashionable apartment hung with Keith Haring prints, Stefano's character, for the first half of the video, is associated with such outmoded, "residual" spaces as the bus (or train)[30] station and the dark, seedy shack of a tattoo artist. The video's sound design, in fact, repeatedly resorts to layering in of ambient tracks of "the public," in a manner reminiscent of the semi-sync techniques of film pornography. In the tape's first sex number—the scene in the men's room of the bus station, which follows immediately Vito's credit-sequence promise to God that he will "do anything"—an ambient soundtrack of the echoing voices of the crowd is layered over what is clearly a studio set: the stalls of the tearoom where the sex act occurs. This sound technique will occur in three more sequences, including the final one at the LA Gay Pride parade. In this narrative where the central issue is the coming out of the main character, it is more than anything else the soundtrack which will bear the

29 A similar argument is made by Jameson in relation to the uneven development of realist modes of representation. See Fredric Jameson, "The Existence of Italy," in *Signatures of the Visible* (New York: Routledge, 1996), 156.

30 A symptomatic ambiguity: the ambient sound clearly announces the arrival of a bus, but repeatedly announces departures from "gates." This further confuses our sense of place, since gates are used at airports.

weight of the passage through publicity that we have argued as constitutive of gay porn. This is so even though the penultimate scene of the film is a scene of "public sex," where Vito, having gone to a gay club called "Another World" in order to see the performance of his mother-surrogate, drag-queen Chi Chi LaRue, ends up in a four-man orgy at the bar, in full view of all the bar patrons. But this scene is "odd" for a number of reasons: unlike the public sex in *Night at the Adonis*, here it is blatantly unrealistic: for even the most "notorious" of bars in real life do not occasion such well-lit sex, unless this is a private party.[31] The tape here falls into an ambiguity over the very public/private divide, so that it "feels" as if this orgy scene is in a private space.

It seems then reasonable to conclude that it is the institutionalization of gay subjectivity itself—in the form of a "community" with rituals, parades, flags, etc.—that then decisively reframes the question of identity in terms of an "inner search" for some hidden truth about oneself. In the tape, this is reflected in an early scene between Vito, Chi Chi, and Duffy, in the local tavern which serves as their hangout. Vito leaves after complaining to Chi Chi that "faggots" keep hitting on him (this after he himself lured a man into the wild bus-station tearoom romp); whereupon Duffy looks at Chi Chi and says, "He doesn't know?" It is thus the truth about himself that Vito disavows, in the same way he can disavow that Chi Chi isn't really a woman. However odd this version of fetishism is—for in this case the mother does indeed possess a penis—it is nevertheless fetishism; and once seen in this light, explains the way that this tape presents us with fetish objects from beginning to end. In Vito's second sex number, the fetishism is even doubled: he goes to a tattoo parlor and the tattoo artist brings out, in addition to his tattooing instruments, two vacuum pumps for them to use while he does the tattoo. We've already noted that the tape opens with a shot of rosary beads; but in the final sex number, when Vito finally affirms his gayness by having sex with Duffy inside a float at the Pride parade (about which more will follow), one would think that the fetish object would be abandoned. But not so: after having almost completely stripped Duffy, Vito goes to remove the last remaining garment—his athletic tube socks—when Duffy insists that Vito leave them on; and the sex scene proceeds with both of them clad in socks. Of course, this is yet another displacement, of the condom itself, which plays an uncharacteristically visible narrative role in this scene. Vito says of the condom, "It's against my religion," and Duffy replies, "Well, it's not against mine": so that in one stroke, the last vestige of Vito's old identity is cast aside, while at the same time Duffy confirms his lover's earlier assessment of him, that homosexuality has indeed become his "religion." The tape ends with a shot the mirror image of the first shot: a closeup of the rosary, now discarded and lying beside a condom.

Certainly one could argue that this fetishization of the condom is in fact part of the political project of the tape: via a series of substitutions, the condom, which otherwise would be a barrier or hindrance to sexual pleasure, is made to acquire an erotic charge in the interest of AIDS education. What is perhaps not as obvious is the self-reflexivity of this strategy. That is to say, by the late eighties, the condom had become a virtual requirement of gay porn, yet the convention was to treat it as if it weren't there:[32]

---

31 Which it clearly isn't, since Chi Chi tells Vito he left a comp for him at the door.
32 As indeed is still the dominant convention today. Thus, *More of a Man* represents a significant departure from convention, specific to a historical moment in the development of gay male porn, undoubtedly connected to the state of the AIDS crisis in the late 1980s.

usually by showing a shot of the unsheathed penis about to be inserted, then a cut to a more distant angle with the (sometimes imperceptibly) condomed penis already "in action." By visibly investing the condom with the energy the text had slowly built up and displaced from object to object, *More of a Man* reveals the already fetishistic—because disavowed—conventions surrounding the condom in gay porn in general.

But ultimately, one could argue that, in so far as fetishism plays itself out around the binary of presence/absence, the final image, of the "unfilled" condom, is decisive; and that it is substituting for the very unrepresentability of that "passage through the public." This returns us, then, to the issue of public space; and specifically, to the use of sound in the film's final scene at the Gay Pride parade. The scene begins with exterior documentary footage of the preparatory moments of the parade: the onlookers gathering, the floats lining up, and so on. Laid over this is an obviously faked soundtrack of the crowd. Vito walks through the street looking for the float for the bar "Another World," where Chi Chi and Duffy will be. The float has a huge plastic globe of the earth, and when Vito arrives, Duffy takes him "into" the plastic globe, where they have the sexual encounter described above. During this encounter, the sound design replicates almost exactly that of the first scene in the bus station: a voice-off of the crowd runs continually through the scene. But this time, the crowd is cheering the passing float, and is thus now charged with the additional weight of conveying the director's editorial comment on the scene at hand. And so the overall trajectory of the work becomes a move from the anonymous, unknowing gaze of the bus station to the knowing gaze at the parade. And it is precisely this transition from an ignorant Other to a perverse, knowing Other that renders so ambiguous in *More of a Man* the distinction between the public and the private. For ironically, much as the sound might try to compensate, *More of a Man* ends with the couple enclosed within a cocoon, in a space correlative to the stall Vito occupies in the opening scene. Thus it would seem that the utopian project has fundamentally shifted terms: and the project of enframing the world—the "already-existing" world—by homosexual desire has been replaced by the enclosure within "Another World."

12 Nostalgia of the new wave

Structure in Wong Kar-wai's *Happy Together*

Rey Chow

In one of the earliest discussions of poststructuralism to appear in English, "Of Structure as an Inmixing of an Otherness Prerequisite to any Subject Whatever," Jacques Lacan puts across a notion of structure that would henceforth have significant ramifications on the way identity is theorized across the human sciences. This was during the late 1960s, when structuralism, having been an intellectual trend in Europe for some time, had belatedly crossed the Atlantic and become controversial in select North American academic circles. Lacan, like his younger contemporary Jacques Derrida, was working against the more traditional and widely accepted philosophical assumptions about structure, which tended to see structure as the systematic relation between the part and the whole, with the whole being given priority as a *unitary* or central governing totality. Unity, Lacan writes, has always been considered "the most important and characteristic trait of structure." Instead of unitariness, Lacan introduces the possibility of thinking about structure in terms of otherness, which he explains in part by appealing to Frege's parsing of numbers. In even the most elementary process of counting, he argues, it is always a subsequent number that holds the meaning of the one preceding it:

> When you try to read the theories of mathematicians regarding numbers you find the formula "*n* plus 1" ($n + 1$) as the basis of all the theories. It is this question of the "one more" that is the key to the genesis of numbers and instead of this unifying unity that constitutes two in the first case I propose that you consider the real numerical genesis of two.
>
> It is necessary that this two constitute the first integer which is not yet born as a number before the two appears . . . the *two* is here to grant existence to the first *one*: put *two* in the place of *one* and consequently in the place of the *two* you see *three* appear . . .[1]

Lacan's confusion of logical sequence with temporal sequence is a deliberate provocation. Albeit still in the heyday of structuralism, what he is arguing here is of course already a poststructuralist way of understanding structure itself as a temporal process governed by non-identity (or difference). Accordingly, a structure (such as an integer), no matter

1 Jacques Lacan, "Of Structure as an Inmixing of an Otherness Prerequisite to Any Subject Whatever," in Richard Macksey and Eugenio Donato, eds, *The Structuralist Controversy: The Languages of Criticism and the Sciences of Man* (Baltimore and London: Johns Hopkins University Press, 1970), 186–200; emphases in the original.

how integrated (as one) it appears, must be understood to be the effect of retroaction —a belated conferral of meaning on an event (such as the number 1) which does not have such a meaning until it has been repeated in an other, subsequent event (the number 2). The non-italicized word "two," then, stands in Lacan's passage both as the number/integer 2 and as the second, deferred space of a repeated event. The phrase "one more," which Lacan uses to describe the genesis of numbers, Jacques Derrida would, in his own equally famous arguments, call "supplementarity" or "play," which tends to be repressed or restricted within the normative understanding of structure. Whereas Lacan problematizes the unity or oneness attributed to structure, Derrida would problematize the notions of origin and center, and their accompanying metaphysics of presence.[2]

The point of these brief and simplistic recalls of otherness (with its vast implications for the subject) and supplementarity (with its vast implications for language and the text) is not to instigate another round of debate about the master theorists of poststructuralism. It is, rather, to use them as a kind of historical and theoretical shorthand with which to examine what may at first appear to be a rather distant event, a contemporary film from Hong Kong. If the major epistemological rupture introduced by early poststructuralism can be summarized by the formula $1 = 1+$, how might this rupture inform the reading of a cultural work such as a film, a love story between two men?

Although this operation ("applying theory to practice") may come across as naive, it is nonetheless relevant as a way to counter the analytically reductionist readings, ubiquitous inside and outside the academy, of non-Western cultural work. I am referring to the tendency, whenever a non-Western work is being analyzed, to affix to it a kind of reflectionist value by way of geopolitical realism—so that a film made in Hong Kong around 1997, for instance, would invariably be approached as having something to do with the factographic "reality" of Hong Kong's return to the People's Republic of China. While a detailed analysis of such a tendency and its complicity with a specific type of cross-cultural interpretative politics can only be made on a different occasion,[3] it would be salutary to attempt a kind of analysis that consciously departs from it. The brief references to Lacan and Derrida serve, then, as a means of introducing certain prevalent epistemological problems—the problems of structure and its accompanying metaphysics—that are, I would argue, interestingly set into play in the film *Happy Together* (1997) (Fig. 12.1), which brought Wong Kar-wai the Best Director Award at the Cannes Film Festival of the same year.

"Let's start over again": nostalgia for a mythic origin

Let me begin by suggesting that *Happy Together* can be seen as a nostalgic film. This may surprise some readers for the simple fact that nostalgia is most commonly under-

2 See Jacques Derrida, "Structure, Sign, and Play in the Discourse of the Human Sciences," in *The Structuralist Controversy*, 247–272.
3 Interested readers are asked to see Rey Chow, "Introduction: On Chineseness as a Theoretical Problem," *Boundary 2* 23 (3) (Fall 1998), 1–24. In this essay, I analyze the manners in which certain kinds of ethnicity (such as Chineseness) are explicitly or implicitly imposed on non-Western literary or cultural texts, as if such texts would make sense only if they can be shown to speak in a documentary mode—from within their *a priori* ghettoized backgrounds. Instead of simply focusing on identity politics *per se*, then, my point is to underscore the way identity politics is, in such contexts, always already embedded in habits of literary criticism and reading that may be termed coercive mimeticism.

Figure 12.1 Tony Leung and Chang Chen in *Happy Together* (Hong Kong 1997). Courtesy of the Kobal Collection

stood as the sentiment of homesickness, which may extend into a tendency to reminisce about old times or to romanticize what happened in the irretrievable past, whereas Wong's film is decidedly a work of Hong Kong's "New Wave Cinema"[4] both in terms of its technical aspects—its avant-garde, experimental use of image, color, sound, and editing —and in terms of its content—a love affair between two men.[5] Unlike many contemporary Chinese films, Wong's work does not seem to be emotionally invested in the usual sites of nostalgia such as rural life or the remote areas of China, or, for that matter, anything having to do with the ideologically oppressive but visually spectacular Chinese cultural tradition. How can a film like this be described as nostalgic, and what is its relationship with the old and with the past as such?

The first clue, I think, lies in the titling of the film itself. The Chinese title, *Cheun Gwong Tsa Sit/Chunguang zhaxie* (in Cantonese and Mandarin), literally meaning the "unexpected revelation of scenes of spring," is a metaphor for the surprising display of

4 Stephen Teo, for instance, writes of Wong's work in the following terms: "As the latest new wave auteur, Wong may be said to have brought the Hong Kong new wave into the 90s by combining postmodern themes with new wave stylistics." In Wong's films, "the accent on style conveys a feeling of sharp-edged excitement and a sense of high-octane elation recalling the impact of the French new wave in Europe." *Hong Kong Cinema: The Extra Dimension* (London: British Film Institute, 1997), 196 and 197.

5 Some critics in Hong Kong consider *Happy Together* to be a love story rather than a love story between two gay men. Wong Kar-wai himself shares this view. When asked during an interview the reason he had chosen to deal with the theme of male homosexual love in this film, he said: "As far as I am concerned, this was not planned in advance . . . in fact, homosexual love is not any different from heterosexual love." (Interview in Cannes by Peng Yiping, *Dianying shuangzhoukan* [*City Entertainment*] 473 (1997), 42). Naturally, other critics disagree. For instance, Jiang Yingsheng writes: "Happy Together takes homosexual love as a point of departure but also tends to idealize paternal power. For the character Lai Yiu-fai, traditional family values and his own homosexual identity constitute two incompatible forces" ("Let's Start Over Again— A Brand New Wong Kar-wai," *Dianying shuangzhoukan* 473 (1997), 70). Translations from the Chinese are mine.

erotic sights, and as a film title it is borrowed from the Chinese translation of Michelangelo Antonioni's *Blow Up* when the latter was shown in Hong Kong in the 1960s. In many ways, of course, the phrase *cheun gwong tsa sit* is entirely apt for the sensual aspects of Wong's film, which indeed amount to a revelation of the erotically charged relationship between two men. However, although the Chinese title focuses on the eroticism of the relationship, it is, as I will argue, the English title, *Happy Together* (with the subtitle *A Story about Reunion*), which more precisely reflects the nostalgia embedded in the story, loosely adapted from the little-known novella *A Buenos Aires Affair* by Manuel Puig. Indeed, the bilingualism and multiway translations of the film title raise some interesting questions: what is this film really about, and what is the relationship between the erotic as such—the so-called "scenes of spring"—and the state of being happy together? If eros has customarily been construed as "2 becoming 1" (or 1 + 1 = 1) in classical philosophy, what does it tell us about the metaphysics of structure? Do eros and happiness complement each other, or are they incommensurable events?

Like some of Wong Kar-wai's other films, the story here revolves around a melodic popular song with a catchy refrain:[6] the state of being happy together is thus literally a theme both in the musical and in the narrative sense. At the same time, narratologically speaking, this theme is a frustrated one: despite the suggestiveness of the music, it is clear from the narrative that being happy together is a difficult, perhaps impossible, project. In this regard, the music itself, while being familiar, seems to be a signifier with no real referent; it is as if the more readily we recognize the tune "happy together," the more we must notice the actual gap, the discontinuity, between what we hear and what we experience through the film narrative.

The film narration begins with the voiceover of Lai Yiu-fai (played by Tony Leung Chiu-wai) telling us about his ongoing relationship with Ho Bo-wing (played by Leslie Cheung Kwok-wing).[7] The two lovers have traveled from Hong Kong all the way to Argentina, hoping to see with their own eyes the famous Iguazu Falls. Like many lovers, Fai and Bo-wing often quarrel bitterly and break up, but after being separated for a while Bo-wing usually suggests. "Let's start over again." In this manner, the tortuous relationship continues.

In terms of our discussion about structure, the plea to start over again bespeaks a certain desire for a new beginning, a fresh point of departure. This seemingly simple and innocent plea, nonetheless, already contains its own contradiction, for the wish to start anew often turns out to be a wish to repeat, to revisit something familiar, something that has already been lived through before. The desire to begin from the origin—from "the first" as it were—is thus haunted by the inherent duplicity of its own articulation: the figure of 1, even as it is being invoked as a way to clear the past, inevitably derives its meaning from that past. 1 is always already a *reiteration*, which makes sense only in the supplementarity of 1+.

This fundamental otherness of structure is staged in the film through the handling of eros. Near the beginning of Fai's narration, a scene of the two men having sex appears. This scene, shot in black and white, is the only one in the entire film in which

---

6 The version of the song "Happy Together" Wong had in mind was the one by Frank Zappa. See Zhong Yitai, "From The Turtles to Wong Kar Wai," *Dianying shuangzhoukan* 474 (1997), 71.

7 To avoid confusion, I will hereafter follow the English subtitles of this film and refer to the two main characters as Fai and Bo-wing.

the physical coupling of the two men is presented thoroughly without constraint, and in which they seem to climax together. It is entirely possible to interpret this erotic scene as part of an act of recollection—as part of a memory of what has supposedly already receded into the past. Even so, it would be insufficient to conclude that such remembrance alone is what constitutes nostalgia. As we will see, the nostalgia projected by the film complicates the purely chronological sense of remembering the past as such.

The series of black-and-white shots featuring the physical entanglement of the lovers is, in terms of effects, quite distinct from other scenes in the film. It is, for sure, a moment of erotic passion, but it is also what we may call a moment of indifferentiation, a condition of perfect unity that was not only (perhaps) chronologically past but also seemingly *before difference and separation*. A moment like this, placed at the beginning of the film, cannot but be evocative. It brings to mind myths of origins such as that of Adam and Eve in the Garden of Eden. Are these images of passionate togetherness, then, indeed a recollection of something that actually happened, or are they part of a fantasy, a metaphysical conjuring of something that never took place? We do not know. In terms of narrative structure, therefore, these images of copulation constitute not only a remembered but an enigmatic other time, an other-worldly existence. They are unforgettable because their ontological status is, strictly speaking, indeterminable.

But whether or not this series of "primal scenes" actually took place, both men apparently desire to return to the reality they conjure. This desire to return—to some other life that is imagined as a primal union—is I believe the most important dimension of the nostalgia projected by this film. Nostalgia in this case is no longer an emotion attached to a concretely experienced, chronological past; rather, it is attached to a fantasized state of oneness, to a time of absolute coupling and indifferentiation that may, nonetheless, appear in the guise of an intense, indeed delirious, memory. From this perspective, Wong's style of nostalgia differs significantly from other contemporary Chinese directors' in aim. Among the Fifth Generation Chinese directors from the People's Republic, for instance, nostalgia usually assumes the form of cultural self-reflection, by way of stories about traditional China, stories which receive their sharpest focus in the rural countryside or in remote geographical areas beyond Han Chinese boundaries. Directors from Taiwan and Hong Kong, on the other hand, often convey nostalgia in the form of a sentimental fascination with legendary eras with clear moral divisions, such as are found in martial arts (kung fu) movies. There are also the works featuring modern and contemporary society with their typically contradictory feelings about the rural or colonized past, which is at once idealized and resented: we may include here not only those films about diasporas, exiles, and emigration to the West, and about "home" visits to China, but also those films in which a particular form of traditional art (such as Beijing or Cantonese opera) is being thematized. Nostalgia, in other words, can be found everywhere in contemporary Chinese cinema, but the object of nostalgia—that which is remembered and longed for—is arguably often in the form of a concrete place, time, and event.

The nostalgia that surfaces in Wong's films is of course also traceable to concrete places, times, and events (e.g., the gangsters' haven of Mongkok in *As Tears Go By*; the protagonist's journey to the Philippines to look for his birth mother, or the clock pointing at three in *Days of Being Wild*; the derelict, crime-infested Chungking Mansion and the fetishized canned pineapples with their "use by"-dates in *Chungking Express*; the claustrophobic tunnels, dark alleys, tiny apartments, bustling shops and restaurants in Hong Kong in *Fallen Angels*, and so forth). But the concretely situated happenings in his stories seem at the same time to give way to something more elusive and intangible. As Wong himself puts it, all of his works tend to "revolve around one theme: the communication among human beings."[8] With this predominant interest in human beings, the nostalgia expressed in his films is, we may surmise, not simply a hankering after a specific historical past. Instead, the object for which his films are nostalgic is what we may call the flawless union among people, the perfect convergence between emotional and empirical realities—a condition of togetherness in multiple senses of the term. This is a condition which can never be fully attained but which is therefore always desired and pursued. In *Happy Together*, this nostalgic pursuit of what is ultimately unreachable is clearest in the relationship between Fai and Bo-wing. In terms of personalities, they are opposites. One is earnest and faithful; the other is an irresponsible scumbag. How could there be a long-lasting union between two such different people? And yet, it is precisely on their impossible, indeed hopeless, encounter and entanglement that Wong constructs the fantasy of being "happy together."[9]

This wishful imagining of, or insistent gesturing back to, an originary state of togetherness—a kind of Edenic perfection in terms of human relationships—against a profound understanding of the tragic differences that divide human beings is characteristic of a certain irreverent and Romanticist tendency in what may be termed high modernism. (The plays of Samuel Beckett, Eugene Ionesco, Harold Pinter, and their contemporaries come to mind.) In this light, the English title of Wong's film, *Happy Together*, is arguably more appropriate than the Chinese title because it accurately captures this Romanticist and modernist structuring of desire. Etymologically, the word "happy" in English can be traced to roots such as *hap* and *fit*. Apart from its common meaning of feeling good, "happy," also carries connotations of happenstance, coincidence, good luck, and the felicitous fit. These connotations suggest that happiness is, philosophically speaking, an expression of the metaphysical condition of unitariness—a condition that is supposedly prior to separation, difference, and conflict; a condition that is, in biblical terms, before the Fall.

Once these implicit connotations of happiness are foregrounded, a place that appears frequently in Wong's films takes on special significance. This is the home. As Shi Qi writes:

> Wong Kar-wai's films are characterized by a basic structure . . . apart from the bond between men, there is also a tenacity expressed toward old, decrepit homes, which serve as a refuge from the wild and dangerous jungle outside, and as the only kind of place belonging to oneself and one's loved ones . . . Few directors have made use of the home as frequently as he . . . whether it is Mongkok, the Central District in Hong Kong, the wilderness, or Argentina, the home [in Wong's films] looks more or less the same, providing a personalized space in the midst of a foreign land.[10]

8 Interview by Peng Yiping, *Dianying shuangzhoukan*, 473 (1997), 44.

9 The contrast between the two characters has been well noted by critics. See, for instance, Xu Kuan, "*Happy Together* as a Continuation of *Days of Being Wild*": "The male characters of Wong Kar-wai's works all follow a consistent pattern, which can be divided into the killer-type and the policeman-type. The former is decadent, unruly, and highly sexed; the latter is innocent, straight, and nearly platonic by inclination. In the film which brought him fame at Cannes, this principle continues to hold." (*Xin bao* [*Hong Kong Economic Journal*], Overseas Edition, May 27, 1997, 9). Similarly, Shi Qi writes that the typical subjectivity explored in Wong's films is "actually a journey of self-exploration . . . there is often an introverted, conservative character as opposed to an unruly and decadent one. This can be regarded as two faces of a single person." ("The 'I' in Wong Kar-wai—a Third Discussion of *Happy Together*," *Ming Pao Daily News*, June 5, 1997). Translations mine.

10 Shi Qi, "The Home in Wong Kar-wai—a Second Discussion of *Happy Together*," *Ming Pao Daily News*, June 4, 1997.

What is the home? Why is there such an obsession with the home and with homelessness in so many modern and contemporary works, East and West? (The current theoretical fascination with the themes of diaspora, exile, travel, migration, and their like is, properly speaking, part and parcel of this obsession as well). Is it possible to argue that, much like happiness, the home is, from a modernist perspective at least, the wishful sign of a primary unitariness, an origin that is felt to be repeatedly threatened and destroyed by human conflict? Home in this modernist construction is not a mere matter of the family or family system; and, even though personalized (as Shi Qi's remarks suggest), it also functions as much more than a personal residence and refuge. Signifying an ideal of a primordial togetherness, the home is, epistemologically, already the product of a binary opposition, the opposition between myself or ourselves (as one unit) and the hostile world outside.

To this extent, the partners involved in an erotic relationship, in so far as they can be considered as a single unit, may be regarded as members of a certain kind of home. The relationship between Fai and Bo-wing can be thought of as a home which, despite its many breakups, both attempt to maintain. Ironically, it is the unfaithful one, the one who is always leaving, who most frequently desires to "start over again" and rebuild the broken home. By agreeing, however reluctantly, to begin anew, Fai is in effect repeatedly submitting to Bo-wing's tyrannical demand that the *two* of them *remain one*—that, rather than remaining as two distinct individuals, they indefinitely perpetuate the dream of the home as the merging of two people into a single entity. And yet, as things never quite work out, this home remains no more than the occasion for a certain metaphysical longing. As unitariness always eludes the two lovers, eros gives rise to a profound nostalgia or homesickness.

To complicate things a little, it would be pertinent to recall at this juncture one of the most imaginative theories about the home—Freud's argument about the uncanny (1919).[11] Freud's thesis, we remember, is that the feeling of uncanniness is not necessarily the result of what is strange and frightening, but rather the result of some emotional affect (from an earlier time) which one has repressed yet which, somehow, recurs fatefully to haunt one. For Freud, the uncanny is thus associated with an inner repetition-compulsion, an involuntary return to what was once a familiar, or homely, place. In the context of our lovers, this compulsion to repeat could easily be identified in Bo-wing's frequent suggestion that they "start over again." But there is still the question of what exactly it is that demands repetition. What is it that Bo-wing needs to have start over again?

In a theoretical move that was to make his essay controversial, Freud would go on to suggest that, for his male patients at least, the uncanny *par excellence* is the female genitals, which stand as reminders of "intra-uterine existence," of the former home where "everyone dwelt once upon a time and in the beginning."[12] The wish to start over again, for Freud, would be the wish to return to this maternal origin, a wish which, tragically, can only be fulfilled through conscious or unconscious substitutes (of the mother). What this means is that, by virtue of its intense intimacy, an erotic relationship—even when it is an erotic relationship between two men—is inevitably haunted by an uncanny, because

11 Sigmund Freud, "The 'Uncanny,'" in *Collected Papers*, vol. 4, authorized translation under the supervision of Joan Rivière (New York: Basic Books, 1959), 368–407.
12 Freud, "The 'Uncanny,'" 397–399.

repressed, memory of the primary bond with the mother. In this regard, it would be possible to see the scene of erotic indifferentiation staged at the beginning of *Happy Together* in terms of a mother–child dyad, and to interpret Bo-wing's constant plea to "start over again" accordingly as a wish to revisit this familiar home. Should this line of reasoning that is so powerfully elaborated by Freud be followed, the biological mother–child bond would by necessity become the ultimate figure of the primeval union to which all erotic relationships, be they homosexual or heterosexual, seek to return. At the same time, for the simple fact that being-one-with-the-mother is already an irretrievable loss (as Freud repeatedly reminds us), this line of reasoning and the desire that accompanies it remain largely fantastical—and trapped within a nostalgic and metaphysical structure.

Another sense of home: the banality of everyday life

In retrospect, what seems most redeemable about Freud's argument is not his masculinist musings about the female genitals *per se* (as the home to which we all seek to return) but rather his imaginative introduction of the figure of woman in a discussion about the home. By equating the homely and the familiar not just with anything or any place but specifically with the mother, Freud has, unwittingly, provided us with a means of deflecting the age-old trajectory of nostalgia and shifting the discussion from a metaphysical into a social frame. (To be sure, he did not actually do this himself, but his argument, if only because it is so noticeably simple-minded about the mother—namely, that she equals her uterus—forces us to change the terms of the discussion fundamentally.) Rather than thinking of the mother simply as the child-bearing biological organ (and hence as the ultimate origin, the site of a primal union), then, it is also necessary to think of the mother as a worker, a caretaker, and a custodian of the home in the sociological sense. This theoretical shift, which deconstructs the metaphysics attached to the origin as such at the same time that it places woman at the center of thinking about the home, opens up a significantly alternative dimension to intimacy and happiness.

Importantly, in *Happy Together*, the shift from the metaphysical to the sociological understanding of the material is enacted in a relationship between men, which further confirms my suggestion that the maternal as such need not be essentialized and tied to the biologically female body, but should instead be considered as the outcome of specific social configurations, of preferred arrangements of intimate bonds across or within biological groups (that is, among men and women, among women and women, or among men and men). In this regard, the numerous small, unremarkable details in the film that fill the mundane experience of actually living together become highly revealing. What is the status of such details in relation to the erotic, on the one hand, and the quest for happiness and togetherness, on the other? Let us look at a few examples.

When the two lovers try looking for the waterfall, we remember, their car breaks down; there is the usual petty, bitter quarrel, and another separation. The waterfall is nowhere to be seen. After this incident, Fai works at a tango bar in Buenos Aires and lives a rather boring life; Bo-wing, meanwhile, continues his promiscuous adventures and is seen going in and out of the bar with different partners. Although they pass each other, they do not talk. One day, Bo-wing is badly beaten up and comes begging to be reunited with Fai, who, though reluctant, once again allows him to stay.

Later, Fai tells us that the period when Bo-wing is recovering from his injuries is the happiest time they have spent together. (This is also the time when the film changes steadily from black-and-white into color) This recovery period may thus arguably be considered as the heart of the matter of Wong's (ambivalent) portrayal of happiness. Crucially, *this portrayal is from the perspective of the faithful partner*, the one who is repeatedly betrayed and stuck at home, and who is, moreover, *forced to assume the maternal role of caretaker* when the promiscuous partner comes stumbling back. Certainly, nothing groundbreaking happens during Bo-wing's recuperation. Only the most trivial, indeed oppressive, of domestic routines transpire when Fai and Bo-wing are together in the apartment—with Fai, in the manner of an exploited but loyal wife/mother/servant, cooking for and spoon-feeding Bo-wing (while Bo-wing remains critical and bossy in attitude), cleansing and dressing Bo-wing's wounds, spraying insecticide around the bed because Bo-wing complains of fleas, and going out in the middle of the night to get Bo-wing some cigarettes. The boring and tedious nature of tending to one's beloved comes across unmistakably, but, to Fai, the chores he is obliged to perform also bring about a sense of rhythm and security. This sense of rhythm and security makes it possible to endure even acts of cruelty from the beloved. For instance, one bitterly cold morning, Bo-wing forces Fai to go jogging with him. Fai catches a cold and falls into a feverish sleep. In his typically selfish manner, Bo-wing feels no compunction about waking Fai up simply because he is hungry and wants to eat. Albeit annoyed, Fai not only does not resist but gets up immediately—in the next scene we see him standing by the stove, shivering under his blanket, cooking. This remarkable scene is not at all visually glamorous. In its plainness, however, it communicates a compelling message about love in all its ambiguities, its lack of a clear distinction between submission and abuse, between sacrifice and slavery.

As Bo-wing is confined to the apartment, he becomes for the time being Fai's captive, and Fai takes this opportunity to hide his passport. This detail, needless to say, is once again ordinary but at the same time precise in its reflection of the contradictory mindset in which Fai finds himself: the man he loves happens to be a jerk who fucks around, and comes and goes as he pleases. Apart from literally taking advantage of his temporarily vulnerable condition and treating him like a domesticated animal, what else can Fai do to ensure that Bo-wing will not again leave? Confiscating Bo-wing's passport is of course by no means a reasonable or even practical move, yet its madness also embodies a kind of groping, a desperate attempt to be constructive in the midst of a destructive relationship.

Describing Wong's subtle use of details, Pan Liqiong comments: "The profundity of the film *Happy Together* lies precisely in its 'shallowness'—different kinds of bric-a-brac, sounds, fragments of life all help to expose the difficulty of two lovers living together." Although it is sensitive and perceptive, Pan's view in the end is that these mundane details are what typically destroy romance—in other words, that there is a certain incompatibility, indeed incommensurability, between erotic love and everyday life as such; that romance, being such a delicate phenomenon, cannot really coexist with the banal.[13] By thus preserving a kind of aura around the notion of romance (and eros)—namely, that this is something so precious that it is susceptible to being destroyed by the vulgar realities of everyday life—Pan's reading, despite its insights, falls largely within the metaphysical structure of thinking about origins.

Seen from Fai's perspective, on the other hand, these mundane details do not indicate, as Pan does, that ordinary life destroys love, but rather that ordinary life in all its

---

13 Pan Liqiong, "Ordinary Life Murders Love—*Happy Together*," *Ming Pao Daily News*, June, 1997, C3.

banality is an indispensable part of a love relationship, in which even quarreling must be understood essentially as a way of communicating. The Romanticist, metaphysical meanings of the home, the origin, and happiness are, in this perspective, punctured and deflated into quotidian, almost ritualistic, domestic practices, which bring about a different kind of illumination and equilibrium. For Fai, happiness and togetherness need not be tumescent ideals in the form of a masculinist heroic other time and other life. Instead, they have to do with all the little things that he can do for his beloved in the here and now.

Interestingly, it is during the period of Bo-wing's recovery, when the two lovers reestablish their intimacy, that another male character enters the story. While working at a Chinese restaurant, Fai becomes friends with Chang (played by Chang Chen), a young fellow from Taiwan who seems more interested in men than in women. Perhaps more so than his relationship with Bo-wing, Fai's relationship with Chang is conducted almost exclusively around the banal and mundane—they get to know each other in the kitchen, amid the menial labor of food preparation—without the punctuation of a sexual encounter. In the rest of the film, while his character remains largely undeveloped, Chang's presence nonetheless provides the intriguing suggestion of an alternative kind of relationship, one in which Fai's "maternal" way of loving would, it seems, become a mutually shared practice and in which Fai, too, can feel he is being taken care of.

Rather than becoming one with Bo-wing, then, Fai's character and the affective possibilities that revolve around him stand in effect as an irreducible other(ness) in the structure of eros, the 1+ that dissolves the aura of erotic unitariness, revealing the latter to be a fragile kind of tyranny. In contrast with Fai's nurturance, we see for the first time that romantic love, as personified by Bo-wing, is no more than an act of self-aggrandizement, the point of which is not to sustain intimacy with an other but rather to overcome, to destroy the other's resistance. For the romantic, the other is desirable only in so far as he functions as an impediment to be conquered. Once this conquest is made—once the other gives up resisting and succumbs—he will no longer be valuable and must be abandoned for a different target. Even so, as the romantic repeatedly takes flight toward ever newer objects of desire, his carefree loitering is forever structured by a parasitical dependency on the other's seeming stability, conventionality, and homeliness—hence his pathological compulsion constantly to "start over again." Fai's definition and expectation of love and happiness, based as they are on attentiveness, self-sacrifice, and a need for sustained intimacy with the other, are decidedly different in kind and in quality.

Through the repetitive, lack-luster details of the home, and the accompanying tedium of feminine caretaking as personified by Fai, Wong Kar-wai has, one may argue, introduced a rift within the structure of the all too familiar, nostalgic yearning for togetherness. Without fanfare, Fai's faithfulness and domesticity, and different perspective on happiness stand as a force which has the potential of displacing and dismantling the Romanticist and metaphysical ideals. How successful is this force? To answer this question, we will need to turn to another aspect of Wong's filmmaking—the images, produced and assembled by cinematographer Christopher Doyle.

The order and function of images: returning to nature

At the most basic level, Wong's style—with its trademark of experimentation, its bold deployment of speed and color, and its technically sophisticated methods of shooting and editing—is indeed what has already been widely acknowledged as "new wave" and "avant-garde." However, in the case of *Happy Together*, these labels do not tell us very much. To get at the manner in which Wong's images signify, it is necessary to move beyond such facile labeling.

We notice that many shots, made with a hand-held camera, are in the style of the documentary. Recall, for instance, the multiple scenes around Fai's living quarters—the cold long corridor leading to the public bathroom; the shabby-looking kitchen shared by all the renters; the interior of Fai's apartment, which is neither tidy nor clean. There are also the cold and deserted streets near the bar where Fai works; the kitchen of the Chinese restaurant where Fai calls home to Bo-wing every day during the recovery period; the abattoir where Fai later takes another job; the small side street where Fai, Chang, and their friends play soccer in the shadows of the afternoon sun; and finally, the crowded commercial district in Taipei where Fai looks for Chang. None of these scenes is, strictly speaking, visually spectacular. On the contrary, they often convey the impression of things and people being captured in a drab, matter-of-fact manner. Like the ordinary and fragmented nature of the two lovers' life together, the reality displayed unobtrusively by these images appears unremarkable and unattractive.

In the midst of this unremarkable and unattractive reality, meanwhile, some memorable visual moments surface, such as when Bo-wing tries to teach Fai to tango first in the apartment and then in the shabby kitchen. Between Bo-wing's experienced movements and Fai's awkward gestures, the dance becomes a unique image of love. There is also the cheap lampshade printed with the waterfall the lovers want to see but never manage to see together. Placed in Fai's sparse, impoverished apartment, the incandescent tones of the lampshade bring to life a kind of other-worldly picture bathed in warmth and light. These visually striking images seem to imbue the love story with a kind of magic, inserting in the mundane reality of the documentary-like fragments a dreamlike world.

I would therefore suggest that the images of this film are a structural corollary to the erotic and emotional entanglement between Fai and Bo-wing. However, while a logical comparison, working by the assumption of correspondence between image and content, might want to associate the drab, documentary images with the banality of the home (understood from Fai's perspective), and the brilliant, magical images with the eroticism of romance (as embodied by Bo-wing), let me offer a somewhat different kind of reading, one in which visuality functions in a more ample manner than simply being a mimeticist reflection of the content. Conceptually speaking, it would perhaps be more productive to think homologically (rather than analogically) and argue that the coordination between the documentary-style images and their dreamlike counterpart is not unlike the relationship between a promiscuous lover and his faithful partner. On the one hand, like the promiscuous lover, the documentary-style images pick up things and people ubiquitously and indiscriminately, including even the basest kind of everyday sights such as a slipper, a rag on the floor, a public bathroom, or animal blood from an abattoir draining into the gutter. By simply making them visible, this documentary style establishes a casual, flirtatious liaison with each of these phenomena, a liaison that is replete with all the ambiguities of the actual significance of such arbitrary encounters. (How important is a rag on the floor? Why does it have to be included? Why does it have to be captured and seen?) On the other hand, there are the images which, like the faithful partner, simply keep being there because they are deeply ingrained in memory—and in fantasy—so deeply ingrained as to defy verbal articulation. These other images, such as the lampshade, the waterfall, the tango, and so forth, suggest that in the midst of a messy, degenerate reality there is a wondrous moment, a moment which has become eternal simply because it has not been abandoned casually for something newer or more exciting.

These two complicit orders of images slide from one into the other and back, creating a visual ambience in which the audience must learn to accommodate two different yet complementary emotional perspectives, which are, in the end, indistinguishable from and interchangeable with each other. After the final breakup, for instance, we see Fai having sex with a stranger in a movie theater, and he tells us in the voiceover that to his own surprise, he is much more like Bo-wing than he previously imagined. As Fai plans on returning to Hong Kong, we also hear him speaking exactly like Bo-wing, wondering whether he can "start over again" in his relationship with his own father. Last but not least, there is the astonishing scene in which Bo-wing, returning again to Fai's now empty apartment, begins to scrub and clean the apartment's floor in a manner that literally makes him resemble Fai.

At the metanarrative level of the film as a whole, what is conjured by these at first alternating but ultimately amalgamating image-orders is, I would propose, a kind of superhuman agency. In the case of the lovers, this superhuman agency lies precisely in its ability to yoke together—to render into a unity—entirely incompatible or incommensurate universes (such as promiscuity and fidelity, *flânerie* and domesticity), so that what begins as difference eventually turns into sameness. By the end of the film, precisely the kinds of details that used to distinguish the two men—having casual sex with strangers and performing tedious domestic chores—have become instead the means of *visually conflating them*. Each man has, it seems, internalized the other to the point of changing places with the other.

Alongside the integration of the characters, the superhuman agency of the metanarrative can also be detected in a kind of childlike wishful thinking embedded in the use of certain images, a thinking that says: "If I want something to happen, it will happen." Consider the part when Fai mentions how much he misses Hong Kong: remembering that Hong Kong and Argentina are at two different ends of the globe, he wonders aloud as to what Hong Kong would look like if it could be glimpsed upside down. Following the infantile logic of Fai's free association, the camera immediately gives us scenes from the streets of Hong Kong turned upside down, as if this animistically willed, inverted order of things were indeed what the city would look like from the far end of Argentina. At a moment like this, the screen has, in effect, taken on the status of a magic wand, which is capable of making something "come true" simply because it has been fantasized and voiced, in a manner free of the constraints of the empirical world. In this omnipotence, this fairy-tale fluidity in which they can become whatever they want to become, the images project themselves—to use the language of poststructuralism—as sites of logocentrism, of *unmediated presence*.

As Shi Qi comments, "Fai keeps searching for stability in the midst of his losses. Whenever he fails, he throws himself into work and play. However, he cannot forget the romance associated with the waterfall."[14] Before departure, Fai once again heads for the waterfall. As we watch the swelling torrents fill the entire screen, we are reminded

---

14 Shi Qi, "*Happy Together*—Straightforward and Stylistically Unusual," *Ming Pao Daily News*, June 2, 1997.

that this is the dream that first inspired Fai and Bo-wing to take their trip together.[15] Now the lovers are separated, presumably for good, but the dream stands there in its abundance, seemingly unperturbed by what has transpired in the human world. The visual fullness of the waterfall brings the animistic logic of the image to its crux: it is as if the screen image, an artifact though it is, has in these final moments physically merged with and become part of the origin that is the natural universe.

To this extent, we may argue that the "romance" mentioned by Shi Qi has extended considerably beyond the romance between two men to become the romance of man losing himself in nature. From the perspective of this latter union, the human stories seem paltry. When Fai stands by himself next to the surging waterfall, no viewer knows what will happen to the human stories going on around him. What will become of his friendship with Chang? Will Fai find Chang again? Will Chang, after depositing his unhappiness at the end of the world, return to his former life situation in the boisterous streets of Taipei?[16] What will happen after Fai returns to Hong Kong—how will he relate to his father, who was silent when Fai called him long distance from Buenos Aires? What about Bo-wing, who does not appear to have family and who is grief-stricken by Fai's departure?[17] All of these questions remain loose ends, but none seems particularly important. Against the changefulness of the human stories, the image itself has apparently reached a sublime eternality.

Despite the attention he compellingly bestows on the mundane details of everyday life so as to render the metaphysics of a primeval union untenable, by the end of the film Wong has, to my mind, doubled back to an affirmation of the Romanticist ideal of happiness and togetherness precisely through the fantastical omnipotence he attaches to the image. In the tumescent form of the waterfall, image has now become All, exuding an overpowering feeling of oneness that seemingly transcends the interminable, volatile human narratives around it. Isn't this return to, and integration with, majestic nature—the divine home—the ultimate wishful sign of a lost plenitude and the final meaning of nostalgia in Wong's film? Doesn't the throbbing presence of the nature-image foreclose

---

15 In the words of Charlotte O'Sullivan: "Foaming like a chocolate malt milkshake—a calm maelstrom, whose spiralling steam the camera respectfully trails." "*Happy Together/Chunguang Zhaxie*," *Sight and Sound* 8 (5) (May 1998), 49.

16 Some critics in Hong Kong consider the character of Chang to be an inspired creation and suggest that what takes place around this character can easily lead to the making of another film. Indeed, if the love story of Fai and Bo-wing can be said, in the conventional manner of describing romance, to form a single unit, then what Chang's presence stands for is precisely the "1+," the "one more" that carries with it the unpredictable possibilities of an open-ended structuration. It is in this light that the suggestive use of sound and voice brought by Chang (who likes to understand people through listening), in contrast to the dominance of the image within the diegesis, may be understood. Be that as it may, as a character, Chang remains, as I already mentioned, undeveloped and lacks the vitality of the mutually implicated affinities of Fai and Bo-wing.

17 When an early version of this essay was first presented at the symposium on Visualizing Eros at the University of California, Irvine, in May 1998, some members of the audience commented that Chang has a family to return to in Taipei, whereas Fai's acceptance by his father is uncertain and Bo-wing does not seem to have any family links at all. These familial reminders, they suggested, could be interpreted in conjunction with the announcement of the death of Deng Xiaoping (which is made during Fai's brief stay in Taiwan at the end), with Fai's return to Hong Kong, and with Hong Kong's return to China in 1997. As I indicated at the beginning of this essay, I am not too enthusiastic about this line of inquiry because it would require one to reduce all narrative and imagistic significations more or less to a "national allegory" type of reading and thus, by implication, to confine the film work within an ethnic ghetto.

the sociological alternatives and affective possibilities that the film has otherwise opened up? As the almighty waterfall leaves the indelible impression of its discharge on our memory, these are the questions that reverberate with the sappy musical refrain, "Happy together . . ."[18]

18 Several groups of people must be acknowledged for the contributions they have made to this essay. Leo Tak-hung Chan generously provided, in Summer 1997, copies of some of the Chinese publications mentioned. Sneja Gunew's highly perceptive feedback to the first version (Spring 1998) helped me considerably in my revisions. An enthusiastic audience at Brown University, who heard a subsequent version in Fall 1998, raised questions that helped complete some of my arguments. Finally, my thanks to the editors of *Camera Obscura*, in particular to Lynne Joyrich, for a set of responsive and meticulous suggestions.

13 Mario Lanza and the "fourth world"

Marcia Landy

I borrow the term "fourth world" from a recent film, *Heavenly Creatures* (1994), that prominently features Mario Lanza's movie image and his operatic and ballad singing. His star persona is central to the film's exploration of the problematic connections between everyday life and fantasy. The two young women in the film, Juliet Hulme (Kate Winslet) and Pauline Parker (Melanie Lynskey), brutally murder Pauline's mother and are forever separated from each other as a consequence. For them, Mario Lanza's music is associated with romance, creativity, and freedom from the restraints of education, familial discipline, and sexual repression associated with the materialism, pragmatism, and snobbery of Anglophile New Zealand culture. The film plays with movie stars as fetishes (e.g., Mario Lanza, James Mason, and Orson Welles) configured in the clay figures created by the young women's imagination. These life-sized effigies of the stars and the young women occupy the fourth world where they engage in a frightening drama expressive of the double-edged character of fantasy.

Because of their powerful hold on the imagination of audiences in determining national and, in many instances, local standards of beauty, sexuality, work, social comportment, and talent, the narratives of stardom embed a number of elements that comprise the star as a powerful cultural commodity. The material and historical conditions of their production are inherent to star narratives, both biographical and cinematic, textual and extra-textual. The economy of stardom is never completely effaced. In its operations, it exposes how the commodity is produced, how it circulates, and how it rises and falls in value according to its moment in time. The biographical and cinematic texts of and with stars expose the interventions of entrepreneurs, agents, managers, and patrons in directing the career of the performer both in the narratives of discovery and in the subsequent shaping of the trajectory of the star's career. But acknowledging the material dimensions of stardom does not yield the secret of its seemingly mystical and protean power. In this essay, I examine the production of Mario Lanza's star persona in the 1950s and its current fate. Lanza was still part of the myth-making apparatus of Hollywood that persisted into the post-World War II era, and I discuss how his appearance in the films he made in the 1950s unabashedly reveals and celebrates his exchange value as a star. I identify the terms and conditions of his rise to stardom within the social and cultural milieu of that earlier time in Hollywood as a prelude to assessing the status of his image at the present time. After half a century Lanza's persona continues to circulate in a fashion relevant to the culture and politics of the 1990s. Lanza offers an exemplary instance of how myths of earlier Hollywood stars have altered to suit new economic and cultural exigencies. These myths have not disappeared but have entered into a realm of fantasy— a fourth world—and into other permutations of commodity fetishism.

Figure 13.1 Mario Lanza

Lanza in the mythic world of Hollywood stardom

From his first to his last films (from 1949 to 1959), from the height of his adulation to the more negative assessments of his talents, Lanza's image was tailored by the studios and by the press to conform to the conditions of stardom with its value-creating apparatus. The value-laden aspect of the production of stars involves the expenditure of time and money to produce wealth—presumably for the star but more for the studios and recording companies. The Lanza myth was built on familiar Hollywood ingredients— his social class, his Italian-American identity, and his combination of good looks and exceptional singing talent. In the narratives of his films with their familiar scenario of "poor boy makes good," he is identified first with humble working-class origins, then, by virtue of his unique and powerful voice, is transformed into a star.

His labor is evident through his performances on film, recordings, and personal appearances. Signs of his labor are also evident through the operations of studio publicity, the press, and audience reception reflected in box office receipts. Labor was also evident in his off-screen behavior and publicized by the press. Contemporary accounts of his life reveal the work expended in producing the portrait of a tormented man, insecure and unable to meet the demands of fame in managing his income, his personal affairs, and the obligations of his contract. His personal struggles with the studio, his weight, the law, and an adverse press became part of the star image. The tenuousness of success was a necessary ingredient of stardom and testifies to its competitive dimensions as well as to a constant effort on the star's part to refashion his image according to the dictates of the studio. Lanza's biography and the conflicts portrayed in his films involve the role of the press first in predicting his success and then in capitalizing on his personal and legal problems. Publicity plays a key role in the projection of Lanza's image in its transformation from a simple celebration of talent to a portrait of cynicism.

These extra-cinematic demands are not divorced from economic considerations. They are essential to the production of value, since stardom must capture the imagination of audiences who pay with their time, bodies, and money for sharing in the melodrama of creating the persona of the star. Lanza's narrative is not merely a case of failure to meet the demands of fame but a revelation that the specter of defeat is inevitably part of the star scenario. George Custen has indicated how competition and the threat of non-acceptance are inherent to the process.[1] The value of the star is not merely his or her success but the inevitability of defeat due to internal conflict, ambition, illness, and death.

Lanza's cinematic persona was established in his first two films, *That Midnight Kiss* (1949) and *The Toast of New Orleans* (1950), in which he starred with Kathryn Grayson. In these films as in the two that followed (*The Great Caruso* [1951] and *Serenade* [1956]), he was cast as a worker (e.g., truck driver, shrimp fisherman, street singer, and peasant worker in the vineyards). The melodrama focused on a well-worn and successful Hollywood myth: would success in the form of love for upper-class women, wealth, and recognition for a lower-class man spoil vitality and musical talent? Lanza's ethnic identity bore traces of an earlier Hollywood tradition in its neglect of specificity regarding Latin ethnicities.[2] Italian and Mexican-American stars were often called upon to play Mediterranean and Latin-American roles interchangeably. However, Lanza's Italian origins would ultimately play a different role in the consolidation of his stardom. This difference is evident when his image is compared to Rudolph Valentino, a major Hollywood star of the 1920s who was also Italian. Valentino was associated with an aura of exoticism. He was identified with Otherness of the immigrant and invested with the mantle of the Latin lover. The taint of Mediterranean ethnicity, particularly effeminacy, was primary to his image. Miriam Hansen writes that

> Valentino ... bore the stigma of the first generation, non-Anglo-Saxon immigrant
> —and was cast accordingly. He began his career as a seducer/villain of dark complexion. When female audiences adopted him, despite the moral/racist injunction, he developed the persona of the Latin lover, marketed as a blend of sexual vitality and romantic courtship.[3]

In the late 1940s cinema, the Italian-American graduated from Latin seducer, dancer, gangster and prizefighter to musical personality with certain corresponding changes in

1 George Custen, *Bio/Pics: How Hollywood Constructed Public History* (New Brunswick, NJ: Rutgers University Press, 1992), 72–73.
2 Chon Noriega, "Internal Others: Hollywood Narratives 'About' Mexican-Americans," in John King, Ana M. López and Manuel Alvarado, eds, *Mediating Two Worlds: Cinematic Encounters in the Americas* (London: British Film Institute, 1993), 52–66.
3 Miriam Hansen, "Pleasure, Ambivalence, Identification: Valentino and Female Spectatorship," in Jeremy Buder, ed., *Star Texts: Image and Performance in Film and Television* (Detroit: Wayne State University Press, 1991), 287–288.

the mythology of masculinity and ethnicity. The popularity of Frank Sinatra, Dean Martin, and Frankie Laine among others was a mark of this transformation, and Lanza was exemplary of the move from Latin exotic other to a mainstream national figure. Although, like these legendary vocalists, Lanza was rebellious, tough, and ambitious, his popularity and his brand of masculinity were also connected to the opera (mainly Italian opera and particularly to the arias of Verdi, Puccini, Bellini, and Giordano), an art form not conventionally identified in Hollywood with major male stars.

From the outset of his rise to stardom, the film narratives in which he appeared paralleled his own life. Lanza, born Alfredo Arnold Cocozza, was from a working-class family of Italian immigrant parents in South Philadelphia. According to biographies and reminiscences, he was intractable, unwilling to be disciplined, a feature often repeated in his film characters and a major aspect of his off-screen persona according to the press. Prior to his arrival in Hollywood, he made a name for himself on the concert stage. When he performed at a Hollywood Bowl concert, he was "discovered" by Louis B. Mayer. (Actually Mayer had already heard Lanza on a recording and was impressed with his voice, but the overwhelmingly enthusiastic response to the concert was the evidence Mayer needed that Lanza had star potential.)

A screen test followed and Lanza's movie career was launched. With the aid of the publicity department at MGM, he was to become a "singing Clark Gable," combining good looks and a powerful voice.[4] While the specific comparison with Gable was not part of Lanza image-making, reviews acknowledged that Lanza combined handsomeness with musical ability. Reviews for *That Midnight Kiss* were extremely laudatory about both his looks and his singing talent. In a review of "Toast of the Town," *Newsweek* proclaimed that "Lanza's first picture was too big a hit to keep him under wraps any longer."[5] The *Christian Century* praised the second film, *The Toast of New Orleans*, for "Its excellence of musical portions that compensates for stereotyped plot and situations."[6] The Lanza myth was consolidated through comparisons between Lanza and the Italian tenor Enrico Caruso as a preliminary to his starring in Caruso's biopic, and the identification with Caruso was to follow him in life and continue after his death. Lanza was skeptical about the comparison, but, as Derek Mannering asserts, "the attention lavished on Mario and the numerous comparisons resulted in the reawakening of the Caruso legend. With the introduction of the LP [format] in 1949, more of Caruso's recordings were sold after 1950 than for many years before."[7]

The cloning of Caruso as Lanza was to remain a constant feature in Lanza's publicity and in his films where he is constantly referred to as "Caruso." His film performances gave every indication of a grand career paralleling "grand opera." Fan mail rolled in, and reviews were by and large enthusiastic. Money followed, though shortage of funds was to dog him for the rest of his life. *Newsweek* commented that *The Great Caruso* was a "Technicolor natural for exploiting the sudden and tremendous popularity of Mario Lanza who taught himself to sing by playing Caruso's records over and over."[8] The review praised his "natural and remarkably powerful voice."[9] *Time* found that the "film

---

4 Roland L. Besette, *Mario Lanza: Tenor in Exile* (Portland, OR: Amadeus Press, 1999), 68.
5 *Newsweek* 37 (March 5, 1951), 84.
6 *The Christian Century* 69 (December 29, 1950), 1439.
7 Besette, *Mario Lanza*, 99.
8 *Newsweek* (May 14, 1951), 98.
9 Ibid.

is weak in fact and weaker on fiction," but that "Lanza is in fine voice."[10] Repeatedly, reviews of his films offered snippets of Lanza's biography, praised his voice, but found the plots banal.

Lanza's myth relies heavily on his working-class origin. His overcoming of the limitations of his social class are linked to changing conceptions of masculinity and ethnicity. In *That Midnight Kiss* (1949), Italian-American Johnny Donetti (Lanza) owns a truck for hauling. He is discovered by Prudence (Kathryn Grayson), granddaughter of a Philadelphia socialite, Abigail Trent Budell (Ethel Barrymore), when he sits down at the piano he has delivered to the Budell mansion and sings, thinking that no one is at home. His presence is fortunate for Prudence, since she, also an aspiring opera singer, balks against singing with imperious fat Italian tenor Guido Betelli, played by Thomas Gomez. Betelli is a familiar movie stereotype of the opera singer that will in the film as well as in the culture of the 1950s be erased by Lanza's image. Lanza/Johnny's combination of brashness, musical talent, and good looks are more to Prudence's liking. The Italian-American wins out against the Italian Betelli, and Johnny, after many misunderstandings and obstacles to a romantic union with Prudence, is assimilated into Philadelphia Main Line society. His family too is elevated in status.

In *The Toast of New Orleans* (1950), his class identity is again responsible for the formation of his musical and acting persona, and one that he forgets at his peril. He has to learn the social graces and to smooth over the more exuberant aspects of his public demeanor; that is, he cannot speak too loudly or appear too enthusiastic and his clothing must be less flamboyant and he strains against conforming to the new exigencies of his social life as an opera singer. The uncouth, even vulgar, aspects of his character become a burden to his manager and his operatic co-star as he is rudely initiated into the social manners and values befitting a successful opera star. He progressively succumbs to gentrification at the hands of his managers and co-star only to learn that he has lost his virility in the process. Only when he is reminded that his ethnic and working-class identity are the source of his power as a performer is he able to make contact with the emotional wellspring of his talent and thus reassert his masculinity. He does not revert to his earlier forms of behavior, but, in his work as a performer, he is able to combine his new mannerly behavior with the "passion" of the worker.

The motif of embattled masculinity in *The Toast of New Orleans* is shared thematically with other films—biopics, social problem films, musicals, and melodramas of the 1950s. In keeping with the terms and conditions of stardom, Lanza's persona had to offer both familiar and unique properties. His singular gift was his voice and his dramatic delivery. Lanza's contribution to popular cinema was his ability to endow the male opera singer with an attractive and accessible identity. He was one of the first prominent movie stars to make opera respectable and profitable on screen, though male and female opera singers had long appeared in the movies. Prior to Lanza, the opera singer in Hollywood of the studio years was not a major drawing card, though there are films that star such divas as Lily Pons and Grace Moore. In contrast to Lanza, singers such as Lauritz Melchior and Leo Slezak (who appeared often with Deanna Durbin), are seen not as divos but as father figures, or, as a *Saturday Review* article describes:

10 *Time* 57 (May 21, 1951), 116.

Great tenor voices come in rather unpresentable male packages . . . When a great tenor moves from opera house to movie screen his character is adjusted to accord with the visual rather than the acoustic image. And so Lauritz Melchior ceased to be Siegfried and became Foxy Grandpa as Leo Slezak before him turned from high tragedy to low comedy.[11]

In the 1950s, Lanza was to make the image of the opera singer romantic, glamorous, and profitable, and his popularity signals the disappearance of the stigma of effeminacy usually associated in Hollywood with the image of the operatic singer. His assuming the role of Enrico Caruso in *The Great Caruso* (despite Dore Schary's, the head of MGM, resistance to him as too young and too uncultivated)[12] was a landmark in Lanza's career, helping to consolidate an image of him as a musical prodigy and as heir to the genius of Caruso. The film was important for establishing his dramatic talent as well—as helping to eradicate the image of stodginess typically associated with opera singers. *The Great Caruso* drew huge crowds, becoming MGM's biggest money-maker for 1951. Reviews of the film were generally favorable though there was some dissent on the part of critics who complained about the simplistic narrative and unfavorable comparisons between Lanza and Met singers.

The folklore of Lanza's greatness and his popularity do not rest solely on the many opera arias he sang in films. His repertoire, like that of "the three great tenors" popular today—Pavarotti, Carreras, and Domingo—also contained popular songs, in particular Neapolitan street songs. In *The Great Caruso*, Lanza not only sings arias from *Aida*, *Il trovatore*, *Rigoletto*, *La bohème*, *Cavalleria rusticana*, *Tosca*, and *Lucia di Lammermoor* in conjunction with Metropolitan opera divas Dorothy Kirsten, Blanche Thebom, and Lucine Amara, but he also sings such popular songs as "Marecchiare, "Funiculi funicula," and "A vuchela." His combination of opera and popular music not only identified him as a versatile performer, but offered an image of the Italian-American as more than a Mafioso, prizefighter, and failure.

In Cold War America, the Lanza persona was an expression of the power of "people's capitalism" touted in ads of the time, an embodiment of the myths that were forged in post-World War II culture and politics. Lanza offered an image of a clean-cut, naive, and unaffected young man as opposed to the image of the "alien" often identified with Communist subversion, anti-capitalism, and Jewishness. "[F]ar from the caricatured opera tenor, he is a nice-looking youngster of the average American boy school,"[13] said one review.

Another aspect of the Lanza myth that circulated was his generosity to those in need. The story of his contribution to many causes is recounted by Roland Besette: "Though the press wrote them off as cheap publicity stunts, Lanza performed good deeds for no purpose beyond the pleasure he derived from them."[14] Besette lists Lanza's contributions to charitable organizations and describes the star's donating his time willingly to telephone people in hospital. Biographies recount the story of a young girl, Raphaela Fasano, dying of leukemia, whose mother phoned and asked Lanza to sing to her daughter.

11 *Saturday Review* 39 (September 29, 1956), 34.
12 Besette, *Mario Lanza*, 102.
13 Ibid., 80.
14 Ibid., 115.

According to the story, Lanza phoned the ten-year-old, and then invited her at his expense to visit at his home in Los Angeles. He gave her a silver medal with which she was buried.[15]

Unfortunately, Lanza was often conned by agents, lawyers, and hangers-on. Exploitation by unscrupulous individuals eager to take advantage of the newly found success of the star and of his inability to handle sudden wealth is also part of the mythology of stardom. These dramas circulate in the ubiquitous biographies and press reviews that capitalize on the trials and tribulations of personalities and in the content of biopics and musicals that focus on the various crises in the birth, rise to fame and fortune, and decline of the star, a reminder that melodrama reigns in myths of stardom. Stardom and melodrama are companions: both thrive on adversity, and Lanza's career was increasingly to become a public melodrama.

The Lanza love affair with the critics and the public took a rapid downward turn. The press began to circulate critical reviews of his personality and of his film career. In a cover story of the tenor in 1951, *Time* was one of the first to predict failure. From this review and others to follow, another dimension of the Lanza myth was forged. The negative reviews attacked his lack of training and discipline, and his popularization of opera as a form of vulgarization. A persistent myth about Lanza is that the powerful voice attributed to him was merely the consequence of electronic manipulation. *Time* described him as having a voice of

> natural power and quality, though not of training and polish, a voice that many experts rank with the titans of opera. The voice sells Lanza, but Lanza also sells the voice with curly-haired good looks and a paradoxical combination of beaming boyishness and hairy-chested animal magnetism. He is at once the delight of bobby-soxers, song lovers, and the despair of musical highbrows who believe that a great singer's goal should be the Metropolitan, not Metro-Goldwyn-Mayer.[16]

The article further depicts the "onetime street wise guy who never did a day's work until he was 21" as a "Dead-end Kid" from South Philadelphia, and as gorging himself to the point that he once weighed 300 pounds and with as large an ego, constantly referring to him condescendingly as "Freddy" (Americanized Alfredo). The article ends with a discussion of Lanza as "another American tragedy." He is presented as a classic instance of an artist squandering his gifts, as a performer for whom Hollywood has "been his Frankenstein."[17] (This article was written well before the trouble that arose between Lanza and Dore Schary [who by then had replaced Louis B. Mayer as head of MGM] and before the events that were to cause the suspension of his contract and keep him from acting in *The Student Prince*, though he was featured on the musical soundtrack).

Lanza's career at this point once again reveals that the economic and cultural scenario of stardom is not seamless and untroubled. The performer must constantly compete with others and with himself to maintain his popularity. The test of the star's value resides in overcoming (like the stock market) the possibility of a crash. He must constantly live up to the greatness of his reputation and, in the case of Lanza, to the comparison with

15 Ibid., 115.
16 *Time* (August 5, 1951), 60.
17 Ibid., 60.

Caruso. He must not only prove himself "after a series of hard trials, earned through hard work or apprenticeship,"[18] but he must continue to repeat his triumphs. Equally important to the star persona is the validation of his greatness by a reigning figure, one who assists the newcomer in gaining recognition. Yet the star cannot rest on his past triumphs. The star's value is always threatened—on screen and off—by his own refusal to conform to expectations (as for example in *Serenade*, a film that did less well at the box office).

By 1956, Lanza's star image had undergone alteration. *Newsweek*, in a news report entitled, "The New Lanza," wrote

> Right after the entertainment halls resounded with his vocal derring-do in "Because You're Mine," Mario Lanza's career started downhill and traveled fast. His great popularity in 1952 gave him a big head, which made him difficult on the set (when he deigned to show up on the set) and a big tummy (nearly 300 pounds). About the only thing Hollywood considered him for was another lawsuit.[19]

The most problematic aspect of Lanza's screen presence became, as this review indicates, his physical appearance. He was threatening to recapitulate the caricatured portrait of the fat Italian opera singer in *That Midnight Kiss*. While his physical appearance remained "boyish," "unaffected," and "ruggedly handsome," his body weight began to fluctuate in ways unacceptable to the studio with its insistence on slimness. Having been hired to present a new streamlined image of the opera star, his increased weight threatened to undermine that image and to expose the behind-the-scenes and unglamorous aspects of the production of stardom. Since the body is the manifest sign of the cultural economy of stardom and slimness, an index to the star's exchange value, the battle over Lanza's weight exposed how little control the star has over his or her body. His weight became most troublesome to the studio after the filming of *Because You're Mine* (1952) and was to constitute an ideological battleground between Lanza and his employers. In his resistance to controlling his weight, he was challenging the studio system's insistence on absolute power over every aspect of a star's persona.

Lanza's appearance in the film ranges awkwardly from shots of his bulging, corseted figure, to those in which he is considerably slimmer. The film stars Lanza as an army draftee, Rinaldo, who is accorded special favors (e.g., leaves and release from strenuous activities) by his sergeant, Batterson (James Whitmore). Batterson is a fan of the opera singer, but the sergeant is also eager to help his sister, Bridget (Doretta Morrow) forge a career in opera. At first Batterson indulges the recruit but then turns on Rinaldo when he assumes that the singer has manipulated him merely to get a leave to sing in a concert. In this film, the singer's ability to perform is never in question. Rather the film capitalizes on the protagonist's personality, whether he is an opportunist or genuinely eager to advance Bridget's career, and whether he experiences true affection for her.

Lanza's weight had risen to 250 pounds and he had to go on a crash diet (one of many to come) to get down finally to 160 pounds in preparation for his filming of *The Student Prince*. At the same time, his relationship with Schary, who had replaced Mayer as head of production at MGM, was one of constant antagonism. A businessman with

18 Custen, *Bio/Pics*, 67.
19 *Newsweek* 47 (April 9, 1956), 116.

a concern for keeping production costs down, Schary did not handle the star with kid gloves and was quite overt in his disdain of Lanza. Lanza's situation at the studio reached a climax with *The Student Prince* (1954). His weight soared dramatically and the film was delayed while he was supposed to bring it down. He had already recorded the score. When a slimmer Lanza appeared on the set, his troubles were not over. New difficulties arose when the film's director, Curtis Bernhardt, found fault with the star's acting style. Again the film was postponed and again Lanza's weight soared. Upon finally returning to the set, he and Schary again quarreled and Lanza walked out of the studio. He was sued by the studio and prohibited from singing publicly. He was replaced by a British actor, Edmund Purdom, who mimed Lanza's singing.

The absence of the star and the appropriation of his voice by another is obvious to the viewer. One expects to see the Lanza image that corresponds with the recognizable voice and instead finds a more urbane, sophisticated star, the image of the prince but with a powerful voice that signals a different personality, one that is more vital, more supple than the visual image. Certainly, the absence (or the off-screen presence) of Lanza carries other associations for those who are fans of the star or knowledgeable about his struggles. Even more, what might be concluded from this unnatural superimposition is the question of property (who owns the voice) and of the enigma of the star's representation.

This substitution of Purdom for Lanza was publicized broadly and attributed to Lanza's difficulties not only with the studio but with his overeating, his own problems with controlling his image. Since the star is a complex union of visual as well as aural properties, Lanza was shorn of a major source of his appeal—his engaging physical presence. Several reviews (mainly mixed about the film's virtues), comment adversely on the merging of Lanza's voice with Purdom's acting. For example, Moira Walsh in a review of the film for *America* commented on the "disparity between off-screen voice and on-screen personality . . . disconcertingly evident every time he [Purdom] opens his mouth to sing."[20]

Newsweek also complained that "Although Lanza's voice is dubbed in expertly, there is, nevertheless, a jarring contrast between his flamboyant tenor and Purdom's more conservative style."[21] Purdom had this to say about acting to Lanza's voice: "His voice was an absolutely tremendous experience . . . It was enough to make you sweat, just listening to the voice, particularly at a very high level."[22] The substitution of Purdom for Lanza mitigates a major dimension of Lanza's contribution to the cinema. The star's body is revealed as expendable, an indication of the magic of cinema and of the power of the studios, and even as a prolepsis for the ultimate disappearance of Lanza. Two years were to pass before Lanza made another film—*Serenade* (1956). During this time, he did a minor amount of recording and fell back into the habit of drinking and heavily overeating. He appeared on a live television broadcast, sponsored by Chrysler, which was to be the source of another scandal, since he mouthed recordings made a couple of years earlier. The press detected this cover-up, and rumors began to circulate that the tenor had lost his voice. He appeared in a second Chrysler show and revealed that, though physically overweight, his voice was intact, the rumors of his failing talent unfounded. His failure to meet an obligation to appear in Las Vegas set off another round of speculations about his reliability and even talent as a performer.

20 Moira Walsh, "Films," *America* 91 (June 12, 1954), 306.
21 *Newsweek* 43 (72) (June 18, 1954), 73.
22 Derek Mannering, *Mario Lanza: A Biography* (London: Robert Hale, 1996), 81.

Serenade (based on the James M. Cain novel) was a Warner Bros. production in which Lanza again portrays a worker becoming an opera star as he did in *The Toast of New Orleans* and *The Great Caruso*. *Serenade* opens when Damon Vincenti, played by Lanza, is performing his last day's work in a California vineyard. He is on his way to audition in an Italian restaurant in San Francisco. A wealthy patroness of the arts, *femme fatale* Kendall Hale (played by Joan Fontaine), accompanied by another Italian-American, Marco (Vince Edwards), loses her way on the road, and encounters Damon when the couple stop for directions. Damon directs the couple to the right road. The looks exchanged between Kendall and Damon foreshadow his amorous desires and subjugation to her fatal charm.

Damon and Kendall meet again at Damon's premiere at the San Francisco restaurant, where she and an impresario, Charles Winthrop (Vincent Price), happen to be in the audience and, after hearing Damon sing, they offer to assist his career. Kendall abandons her prizefighter and begins a relationship with Damon. Unable to balance his attraction for her and his desire for a career, the remainder of the melodrama portrays Damon's fatal (and masochistic) attraction to Kendall and its effects on his artistry and masculinity. Distraught over her acquisition of a new lover, a sculptor this time, Damon walks off stage during the last scene of a performance of Verdi's *Otello*. He tries to retrieve his career but, during an audition for the role of Don Ottavio in *Don Giovanni*, he discovers himself blocked and unable to perform. He travels to Mexico, and almost destroys himself with drink until he is saved by a Mexican woman, Juana (Sarita Montiel). They fall in love, and she aids him in recovering his wounded masculinity so that he can return to the opera stage. The narrative sets up an analogy between Damon and Juana's father, a bullfighter who was fatally gored, having been disappointed in love, but through Juana's nurturance Damon is saved from a similar fate.

The following year, Lanza went to Italy, where he was to make only two more films before his untimely death—*The Seven Hills of Rome* (1957) and *For the First Time* (1959). *The Seven Hills of Rome* portrays him as a singer who comes to Rome not for his career but to win back the love of an American heiress (Peggy Castle). He befriends a young Italian woman, Rafaella (Marisa Allasio), who has no place to stay in the city, joins forces with his cousin, and forges a career for himself and his cousin, Carlo (Renato Rascel), in Rome. He almost ruins his cousin's and his own career in his quest for romance, however. Finally he abandons his love for the socialite in favor of Rafaella. The reviewers of the film were more taken with the "topography" of Marisa Allasio (the reviewer's euphemism for her shapely body) than with Lanza's performance, and with helicopter shots of Rome which one critic described as "fascinating . . . the viewer gets some wonderful views of the hills of Rome," though Lanza is described in less complimentary terms: "As the man gets fatter, the voice gets thinner."[23] The reviewer commented though that Lanza's acting "shows . . . considerable improvement." References to Lanza's weight had by now become an essential ingredient of most reviews.

Two episodes in *Seven Hills of Rome* are exemplary of other aspects of Lanza's stardom. Twice in the film, he performs spontaneously; as befitting the musical, life is made to appear as a stage. First, he appears on a Rome street with a child (an actual street singer) who sings for passers-by, and he considerably enlarges her profits for the day. Consistently, in his films, he is portrayed as offering his talents freely, often in

23 *Time* 71 (80) (February 3, 1958), 80.

opposition to his managers. Second, he performs for a group of young people jitterbugging on the street, doing impersonations for them of other Italian-American and African-American singers, namely Dean Martin, Perry Como, Frankie Laine, and Nat King Cole. This episode illustrates Lanza's talent, namely, as a comedian and mimic, situating him in the company of popular vocalists.

Lanza's persona is thus "one of the guys." Whether he is playing as the Great Caruso or as the shrimp fisherman in *The Toast of New Orleans*, he is portrayed as generous, with his gifts—singing on the street, in restaurants, at festivals, or outside the concert hall—proffered for free. *The Great Caruso* identifies Caruso and Lanza by extension as appealing to the masses and expressing their bond with their audiences by performing spontaneously without charge. Thus, like the musical form generally and like Lanza's legend, episodes like these set up a distinction: the familiar and mystified connection between use value and exchange value where, in the final analysis, exchange masquerades as use value. That is, the wealth and profit derived from Lanza's off-screen performance are presented on-screen as having intrinsic value derived from its seeming naturalness and usefulness. Lanza's performance is the product of labor and his performance is a commodity exchanged for money. His labor appears to be given voluntarily without regard for compensation and bearing no sign of its monetary value.

For the First Time was a melodrama that appears strikingly different from his earlier films, both in the transformation of his earlier exuberant persona to a subdued if not worldly performer and in the obvious bid to a young audience as reflected by the on-screen teenage audience. In this film, which also stars Zsa Zsa Gabor, he has the reputation of an irresponsible performer, one who does not meet his obligations. Lanza is no longer a worker to be discovered but a disgruntled celebrity hiding from his public—though not completely hardened to the pleas of fans, especially young people. His irresponsibility is supposed to be due to an excess of love for his audience, especially for those who cannot get tickets to his performances, but his behavior is also consistent with rebelliousness. As the audience waits for him to appear inside the Vienna opera house, he stands outside and sings to those who have been turned away, causing the opera to be canceled. A young deaf woman, Christa (Johanna Von Koszian), with whom he falls in love, restores his belief in performance by giving him a goal for which to strive: to earn the money through appearing in concerts in Europe to pay the medical expenses for restoring her hearing. A melodrama, the film has the familiar fifties thematic of troubled masculinity expressed in Lanza's changed star image. That the object of his love is unable to hear allows the film to play with Lanza's restored screen image and of his voice as the instrument of restoration. Similar to *The Seven Hills of Rome*, *For the First Time* shifts the emphasis from his appeal to older and upper-class audiences to youth: an appeal based on changing audience demographics. Hence, the emphasis on opera is more restrained.

Lanza in the fourth world

Lanza's films capitalized on the melodramatic nature of star mythology: the incompatibility of career and personal satisfaction, the seductive but cynical and opportunistic role of managers and patrons, and the impossibility of a successful resolution to these dilemmas except in the realm of folklore and fairy-tale. His films increasingly capitalized on Lanza's growing reputation as a troubled and an unpredictable performer, a star whose body was out of control, an ageing performer who came late to performances or did not appear at all, a man who had slipped from the dazzling heights of fame. Lanza's star biography thus encompassed the full melodramatic trajectory of stardom, beginning in promise, realizing an exceptional talent, being the center of adulation, and then inevitably slipping from the pinnacle of success through self-destructive behavior or through natural causes—alcoholism, psychic instability, illness, and ageing. The underside of success can also be a source of value and after the star's death become part of the regeneration of his or her image in the realm of the fourth world.

Lanza's death of a heart attack produced predictable hysteria on the part of his fans, though not as great as that expressed by fans for either Valentino's death or later Elvis's. Lanza's funeral which took place in Los Angeles where he was buried, was attended by co-stars from his films and admirers. Death is not alien to the fourth world of fantasy. In Wheeler Winston Dixon's view, "What the cinema does, what photography and popular culture hope to accomplish . . . is nothing less than the retrieval of the dead and the reentry of their phantom presences in the realm of the living."[24] Almost immediately, the fantasy grew that Lanza's death was the consequence of a Mafia vendetta, since he had been friendly with Mafia figures, though this was never documented. Another fantasy that circulated was that he had committed suicide. Despite medical reports that attribute his death to heart failure, neither of these fantasies has been laid to rest.

In 1962, three years after his death, the Mario Lanza Institute was formed, and it has continued to grow since then. The Institute is located in the same building in South Philadelphia that also houses the Mario Lanza Museum, containing artifacts from the singer's life and career. The Institute sponsors competitions for young singers, an annual Spring concert, an annual ball, a scholarship fund, and a web site (http://www.mario-lanza-institute.org). The web site contains a number of Mario Lanza fan clubs active in the US and throughout Europe, and especially in Britain, Australia, Italy, the Netherlands, and Germany. Anecdotes, appreciations, and information on Lanza's life and work can be downloaded from the web and several book-length biographies are available for purchase; the two most recent are Derek Mannering's *Mario Lanza* (1996) and Roland Besette's *Mario Lanza: Tenor in Exile* (1999).

In the last decade, Lanza's singing has undergone reevaluation in the testimonials of opera stars such as Richard Leech and Placido Domingo, who have acknowledged Lanza's influence on their careers in opera. These testimonials have countered the prevailing view that Lanza was no opera singer and that he made no impact at all on the world of opera. For example, Leech has stated that "it was Mario Lanza's voice booming from my parents' hi-fi, that was my first exposure not only to opera but to the tenor voice itself."[25] Lanza's name also appears among responses to an *Opera News* questionnaire addressed to prominent opera singers, "What Is the Greatest Voice You Ever Heard?" Leech asserted, "His passion became the reason I sing. Because of *The Great Caruso*, he became a role model, not only for me but for countless American kids."[26] And Eric Meyer writes:

> When a voice becomes recognizable enough to be used on the soundtracks of Mercedes-Benz commercials, it is truly consecrated. Mario Lanza reached that exalted

24 Wheeler Winston Dixon, *Disaster and Memory: Celebrity Culture and the Crisis of Memory* (New York: Columbia University Press, 1999), 27.
25 Ralph Blumenthal, "50 Years Later, Lanza Booms Forth," *New York Times* (June 23, 1998), E5.
26 *Opera News* 64 (3) (September, 1999), 58.

status last summer. Fifty years after the fact, consumers are hip to what Lanza fans have known since his heyday in the '50s: the troubled but gifted Italian-American tenor was, simply and indisputably, one of the century's greatest vocal phenomena.[27]

Some of the praise for Lanza is associated nostalgically with the 1950s as a contrast to the present time where, in Florence King's words, "We have carried egalitarianism to such a maniacal extreme that we regard beauty as an affront." According to her,

> Lanza's success began in the hearts of teenage girls but it went straight to the heart of something much deeper. As a music critic of the time put it: "Mario Lanza is the symbol of America's cultural democracy." Because of him, anyone who was in high school in the early Fifties stands an excellent chance of being an opera lover regardless of background or education.[28]

King's comments offer one explanation for Lanza's return in the 1990s; namely, that the 1950s have come to represent a watershed, the last gasp of an innocent and uncomplicated world, a black-and-white world that the film *Pleasantville* satirizes as repressive and bigoted. A large share of the current encomium for Lanza is devoted to the influence of his voice on opera and popular culture. The appearance of Lanza impersonators— though not to the same extent as Elvis impersonators—is testimony to the vitality and endurance of Lanza's persona. Victor Lanza claims to be the star's son, to the dismay of the family, and has made a career out of performing the Lanza repertoire. Charles GaVoian has gathered admirers for the effectiveness of his Lanza singing style and mode of performance.

For many social critics and filmmakers, Lanza's star image, like those of other popular film and recording artists, has become part of a contemporary fascination with revisiting the past. In this moment of "postmodernity," the Lanza phenomenon for many entrepreneurs serves to reinvigorate the value of the star as a commodity through new technologies and through the reissuing of films on video and DVD and re-recordings of music. A glance at current releases suggests that the Lanza revival has not peaked. CDs by BMG of *Mario Lanza in Hollywood* and Victor's *Mario Lanza: Opera Arias and Duets* and *Mario Lanza at His Best* contain selections from his film soundtracks, from earlier records of his operatic arias as well as his singing of many Neapolitan and operetta songs. These reissues of Lanza's recordings also contribute to restoring the sagging reputation of opera for a new generation of audiences.

Lanza's never totally forgotten but now reinvigorated star image is not a unique phenomenon in the 1990s: it unites commodities and profit to an inordinate investment in the past—what Jacques Derrida has called archive fever.[29] However, the dizzying replication of images, the resurrection of these images in new technical forms, calls attention to the need to rethink the notion of history as it is being rapidly transformed through the contemporary electronic world of speed, instantaneity, and reproduction. The new technologies will ensure that his biography, his films, and his recordings—as well as the world of the 1950s in which they are embedded—will be circulated at a dizzying pace and to ever-larger audiences and to ever-increasing testimonials to his greatness. They

---

27 Eric Meyer, *Opera News* 63 (9) (March, 1999), 38.
28 Florence King, "The Misanthrope's Corner," *National Review* 47 (20) (October 23, 1995), 68.
29 Jacques Derrida, *Archive Fever* (Chicago: University of Chicago Press, 1999).

do so, however, to an emptying of critical meaning and analysis and, hence, to a reconfiguration of the fourth world of fantasy.

The growing interest in, vitality of, and presence of stars from the past such as Lanza (through remakes and morphing) can be traced to a large body of critical writing on the role of stardom that seeks to rethink ethnicity, masculinity and femininity, sexuality, and the role of memory as a means of altering cultural values. According to these studies, stars "personalize social meanings and ideologies" and stardom is implicated "in the critique of individualism, consumerism, and social stereotyping."[30] While these studies add important psychological and sociological insights on the nature of the star image in relation to its impact on gendered, racial, sexual, and class oppression, they often fall short in neglecting to provide a broader theoretical analysis of value formation. They fail to grasp the slippery and elusive form of the star commodity as it, like the mythical creature, Proteus, changes forms through production, circulation, and consumption, and it is not merely the different forms that the star commodity expresses, but the more fundamental (and abstract) character of how value is assigned. In this context, value belongs to another realm where the seemingly concrete nature of the commodity reveals itself as illusory. The fourth world does not give up its secrets easily.

Heavenly Creatures is a tantalizing text to explore the character of this fourth world and its relation to the phenomenon of stardom and value, particularly since it is an important current evocation of Lanza's stardom. Moreover, the film is significant for its return to the 1950s (as in *Pleasantville*). The film's recourse to the 1950s is evidence of unfinished cultural business (again as in *Pleasantville*), where Cold War conceptions of family, social class, gender, and sexuality are revealed to be in crisis. This period of time is portrayed not as an idyllic black-and-white world without conflict but as a source of antagonisms that cannot be contained. The film's focus on two young women's love for each other and on the forces that ultimately separate them—parents, class differences, and the white, snobbish, Anglophile New Zealand world—are revealing of antagonistic forces that cannot be constrained by parental authority and the disciplining dimensions of education, religion, and psychotherapy.

In contrast to films of social realism that focus on "problems" generated by social non-conformity (e.g. youthful delinquency, sexual promiscuity, aggressive behavior, etc.), *Heavenly Creatures* adopts an anti-naturalistic style, comprised of contrasting sequences between the everyday world and the world of imagination associated with music, cinema, monochrome and colored episodes, and the dissolving of the natural landscape into a brilliantly colored paradisal panorama. This style enables the spectator to move between the grotesque character of the "real" world that the girls inhabit and a fantasy world that offers other, affect-laden gratification as they conflict with their everyday world. The music of Mario Lanza, so popular with female teenagers in the 1950s, particularly his recording of *The Student Prince*, is associated with an enigmatic fourth world. In contrast to the other movie icons invoked in the film—James Mason and Orson Welles—Lanza's image, identified with working-class and with ethnic identifications, is radically other to the strait-laced British heritage in the 1950s world in which the young women lived.[31]

---

30 Christine Gledhill, "Introduction," in Christine Gledhill, ed., *Stardom: Industry of Desire* (London: Routledge, 1991), xiv.

31 For a detailed discussion of the social and historical circumstances of Parker and Hulme, see Julie Glamuzina and Alison J. Laurie, *Parker and Hulme: A Lesbian Impression* (Ithaca, NY: Firebrand Press, 1991).

Figure 13.2 Kate Winslet and Melanie Lynskey in *Heavenly Creatures* (Wingnut/Fontana 1994). Courtesy of the Kobal Collection

Heavenly Creatures shares with many other films of the nineties a concern with the past and with rewriting history to include the role of cinema and popular culture, specifically as it raises the issue of lesbian love and associates it with the fourth world. The flights of fantasy in the film invite a meditation on how cinema has shaped the spectator's understanding and experience of the world in order to make socially disallowed desires appear comprehensible and manageable. Unlike the geographical and cultural designation of First, Second, and Third Worlds, the fourth world belongs to the realms of myth, religion (the hymn-singing in the film), and fetishism (the kingdom of Borovnia) where it becomes abstract and ahistorical, seemingly independent of labor and the state.

In their study of the two women, Parker and Hulme, Glamuzina and Laurie provide a gloss on the fourth world that connects it to Maori beliefs. Summarizing a discussion with a Maori Tohunga, they write that "He said that the saints [expressed through the invocation of the movie stars] and the use of the numbers seven and ten could be interpreted as gatekeepers to the fourth world."[32] This view of the fourth world is identified with spiritual forces that stand in stark opposition to the legalistic and restrictive apparatus of the state predicated on normative conceptions of sexuality. While not negating the force of this interpretation, my use of the fourth world proceeds in another direction.

I identify the fourth world with desire and need, with what can be called "affective value," a form of value that is normally considered outside the circuits of capital. However, I regard the fourth world as containing the possibility of exposing the false dichotomy between desire and economic production and its relation to the state. In this context, the cinematic commodity of the star appears to hold the key to a demystification of what Marx called commodity fetishism, "where the products of the human brain appear as autonomous figures endowed with a life of their own."[33] The enigma of stardom

32 Ibid., 148.
33 Karl Marx, *Capital*, vol. 1 (New York: Vintage Books, 1977), 165.

has continued to challenge film critics who regard the cinema's creation of "heavenly creatures" as a key to open a door to the perennial fascination with the affective power of the human face and body and with prevailing norms of belief and action.[34] Relations between myth, folklore, and the misty realms of religion are not direct, since, as Marx has written, value has never had "its description branded on its forehead."[35]

The heyday of star mythology in the pre-World War II world and in the decade to follow had powerful currency. It conveyed an appearance of naturalness and functioned as an object of value closely aligned with the social and material forces from which it emerged. The mythology of stardom was saturated with belief in the world that produced it. In the 1950s, Hollywood cultural and political mythmaking via the manufacture of the star capitalized on pressing anxieties linked to the Cold War and to the threat of nuclear disaster. Inherent to these myths was the refashioning of images of masculinity, ethnicity, and social mobility to suit new circumstances. Lanza's persona belongs to this labor to reinvigorate belief in an America of opportunity, an enterprise that was not seamless and transparent but that exposed, if often indirectly, the antagonistic conditions that underpin this cultural capital. Lanza's star commodity is no longer identified in terms of the labor of creating, adhering to, and emulating a myth of power and singularity: it now belongs to a fourth world of fantasy uprooted from its earlier context in the world of the 1950s. Lanza's star appeal in the 1990s belongs to the fourth world, a seemingly impenetrable region. In it, the commodity is evident as commodity; its value is more blatantly translated into monetary terms and into accumulation. The quest to unite the material object to the world of imagination, affect, and belief is yet another form of alchemy, of transforming base metals into gold. The commodity and imagination cannot be reconciled, since one negates the other. The recognition of the antagonism between the economic production of the commodity and its personalized consumption saturated with affect suggests that, instead of seeking reconciliation between the two, the critic of stardom should focus on their incompatibility.

Instead of finding a psychological or anthropological origin for the desire generated by the star, one might better acknowledge that stardom functions in the absence of concreteness, commensurability, and meaning. It survives on its memory and on its commercial viability which it now blatantly and opportunistically announces through the ever-expanding media. Thus, unraveling the mysteries of the fourth world leads in two directions. One direction leads to escape, vicarious pleasure, immersion in the power of the commodity itself to the annihilation of the external world. Another, more difficult direction leads to critical reflection on the sources for the antagonism between desire and realization, its mode of construction, its ephemeral and insubstantial character through the media.

Cinema and television continue to refashion folklore, but this folklore is now recognized—as in the case of the circulation of Lanza's image and voice—as a form of nostalgia, a nostalgia that denies the present and any possibility of belief in the world. In Gilles Deleuze's words:

> There are no longer grounds for talking about a real or possible extension capable of constituting an external world: we have ceased to believe in it, and the image is

---

34 See Richard Dyer, *Stars* (London: British Film Institute, 1986); Buder, ed., *Star Texts*; Gledhill, ed., *Stardom*; Gaylyn Studlar, *This Mad Masquerade: Stardom and Masculinity in the Jazz Age* (New York: Columbia University Press, 1996).

35 Marx, *Capital*, 167.

cut off from the external world. But the internalization or integration of self-aware-
ness in a whole has no less disappeared.[36]

Thus Lanza's image offers a meditation on the vanity of trying any longer to connect
the star to the affective dimensions of identification and belief that belong to a vanished
world. In the fourth world of today, stardom has a different life. Shorn of myth, its
virtue and its profitability lie in the power of memory and repetition, in the "fourth
world," where fantasies can be transmitted and consumed electronically and otherwise.

36 Gilles Deleuze, *Cinema 2* (Minneapolis: University of Minnesota Press, 1989), 277.

14 Devouring creation

Cannibalism, sodomy, and the scene of analysis in *Suddenly, Last Summer*

Kevin Ohi

Based on the play by Tennessee Williams, Joseph L. Mankiewicz's 1959 film, *Suddenly, Last Summer*, outlines a double narrative: the traumatic death of Sebastian Venable and the psychotherapy of his cousin, Catherine Holly (Elizabeth Taylor). Through analysis, Dr. Cukrowicz (Montgomery Clift), a psychiatrist from Chicago specializing in lobotomies, helps Catherine to remember the events leading up to her cousin's death. Catherine, her mother, and her brother George, are poor relations of Sebastian's wealthy mother, Violet Venable (Katharine Hepburn), and the story suggests that Sebastian, a gay man, used first his mother and then Catherine as "bait" to attract young men in Europe. The film remains rather vague about how exactly this transaction works, but the magnetic sexual appeal of Catherine and Violet somehow translates into gay sex for Sebastian.[1] After Catherine is raped at a Mardi Gras ball, Sebastian invites her to take Violet's place in their summer travels. Traveling in Europe the summer before the film begins, Catherine witnesses the death of Sebastian, who is killed and cannibalized by hungry young boys in a Spanish town called Cabeza de Lobo. Seeking to suppress the story of Sebastian's death (and the desire that seems to have led to it), Mrs. Venable promises Dr. Cukrowicz the funds for a new mental hospital in return for lobotomizing Catherine. Dr. Cukrowicz, however, champions a talking cure for Catherine. The film

I would like to thank Chris Pye and Ellis Hanson; their comments on earlier drafts of this essay helped me substantially to revise it. Thanks also to Amy Villarejo, Matthew Tinkcom, Richard Stamelman, Leah Shafer, Kolin Ohi, Bonnie Blackwell, and two anonymous readers at *Cinema Journal*. This essay was originally published in *Cinema Journal* 38 (3) and appears here with the permission of the University of Texas Press.

1 D. A. Miller's recent account of the film, "Visual Pleasure in 1959," in Ellis Hanson, ed., *Out Takes: Essays on Queer Theory and Film* (Durham, NC: Duke University Press, 1999), 97–125, explores, among other things, the oddity of this transaction. "Consider," Miller writes, "after all, the striking paradox, contradicting common sense and practical experience alike, that we are here being asked to accept: through their sexual attraction to a woman who looks exactly like Elizabeth Taylor, a town's whole population of toughs turns queer" (112). Particularly in its dazzling readings of several sequences in the film, especially during Catherine's therapeutic narration of Sebastian's life and death, Miller's essay points to the eroticism and disorientation of a structure of desire—enacted visually in these key sequences—that Miller calls "the Gay Male Woman." She is not presented in *Suddenly, Last Summer* as the perhaps familiar construction of a female front covering or crowning gay male desire, but rather, "we regard it in its other, far less familiar aspect, as a woman with a homosexual behind." "Far from dispelling the nightmare of homosexuality," Miller writes, "this woman makes it uncannily intimate with heterosexual dreaming" (115), and to this precarious proximity Miller attributes Catherine's sex appeal in the film—an appeal that evaporates, he argues, when she is cured of the male homosexuality from which she paradoxically suffers.

ends with her recounting the story of Sebastian's death, an apparently curative catharsis for Catherine that leaves Mrs. Venable to lapse into madness.

The film ostensibly sets up two competing methods for the curing of Catherine's madness: the lobotomy and the talking cure. This contest, however, screens a more anxiety-ridden cure that attempts to heterosexualize the desire generated within and by the film; this contest, moreover, must also screen the fact that both the lobotomy and the talking cure end up enacting the gay desire they would occlude. Such a tendency toward reenactment also implicates the heterosexualizing cure in the very desire it would cure, for it relies on Sebastian's method for seducing boys: it seduces by using a beautiful woman as bait.[2] Central to the sexual and spectatorial economies of the film, baiting is its key concept; it is both the film's subject and its method. As much like "jail bait" as fish bait, bait in the film nearly always works to entrap desire. Sebastian uses

2   To use a beautiful woman as bait might offer one way of describing the way that certain feminist theorists, following Laura Mulvey, have understood the operations of cinema as conterminous with ideological structures of gender adumbrated through power relations condensed as relations of vision and visibility, and it would no doubt be possible to emphasize in my reading of *Suddenly, Last Summer* its intertwining with and reliance on that tradition. As I hope to show, however, baiting operates in the film—even when it is a woman's body that is ostentatiously given to be looked at—more to disorient than to establish heterosexualized orthodoxies and to theorize the alluring place of gay male desire within the film's libidinal and spectatorial economies. See Laura Mulvey, "Visual Pleasure and Narrative Cinema" in *The Sexual Subject: A Screen Reader in Sexuality* (London: Routledge, 1992), 22–34. For an overview of feminist accounts of spectatorship, Matthew Tinkcom has recommended to me Judith Mayne, *Cinema and Spectatorship* (New York: Routledge, 1993). Recent gay critics have sought to complicate Mulvey's account of gender and cinema. D. A. Miller points out, "To be necessarily blunt about it, the male bearer-of-the-look is never himself invisible, or visible only as his look: the ontology of his being on film means that he is never *not* given 'to be looked at,' with all the potential implied in that offer to capture the screen or captivate our own look, with his bodily presence or its sexual objectification. And of anyone who hasn't seen that potential abundantly realized in the screen appearances of Clark Gable, Cary Grant, Marlon Brando, William Holden, or Montgomery Clift, to go no further forward than 1959, it is safe to say that, instead of going to the movies, this person must have stayed home reading Laura Mulvey" ("Visual Pleasure in 1959," 109). Miller offers an extended reading of Mulvey, of the one moment in her essay that mentions homosexual desire, and of the limits of her model for gay readings of cinema in notes 5 and 6 to "Visual Pleasure in 1959," 122–123. Lee Edelman also offers a critique of Mulvey and Mulvey-oriented feminist film criticism, in part for installing as indubitable a grounding opposition between male and female in a castration logic of either/or that secures itself by occluding its reliance on a foundational blindness to both anality and to the grounding role of a foreclosure of this anality in making possible castration and, by extension, vision as it is structured by binaries in the Symbolic. This logic is unsettled by the anus as a figure for the Real's recalcitrant unraveling of certainties of Symbolic binaries structured around logics of opposition. More simply, the reifying tendency of such feminist work can make it conterminous with homophobic logics, not necessarily by reiterating any explicitly homophobic attitude so much as by failing to question a structuring of gender and its grounding by and of homophobia as a structure that makes meaning itself possible. See *"Rear Window*'s Glasshole" in *Out Takes*, 72–96, esp. 72–73 and 90–93. Edelman writes, for instance: "Seeing so very clearly the difference that sexual difference can make, the feminist insight can risk reproducing the razor-sharp optic of a Symbolic vision positioned on the side of the social 'reality' it offers as 'naturally' self-evident, as unambiguously clear, so that anyone but the silliest goose knows how, with a single gander, to distinguish—before they are carved up and served up in a blood-colored sauce of Bing cherries deemed, axiomatically, good for them both—the gander from the goose," 72–73. Ellis Hanson argues that Mulvey-influenced criticism can obscure or foreclose the pleasure (even for lesbian and feminist viewers) of vampire films (among others) by a reification of a male gaze. As he writes of Andrea Weiss's "The Vampire Lovers" (in *Vampires and Violets: Lesbians in the Cinema* [New York: Penguin, 1992]), "A lesbian is watching a film in which two women do the nasty together, and all she can think about is men? The 'male gaze' of camera angles is evidently stronger than we guessed, since it can even define the parameters of a feminist's pleasure" ("Lesbians Who Bite," *Out Takes*, 186–187).

Catherine to lure boys in Europe just as the film attempts to use her to bait its viewers. The overdetermination of baiting in the film, as well as its specific references to gay sex, sets up a double bind for the film's attempt to establish and secure heterosexual desire. Attempting to exorcize the spectacle of gay male sex, the film ends up enacting Sebastian's desire, leaving open to view the very spectacle it would occlude. Figured through an ecstatic scene of cannibalism, the spectacular scene of (un)seen sodomy becomes the fuel and figure for cinematic absorption, which, unfolding through layers of baits and cures in this film's curiously redounding self-reflexivity, proves difficult to escape, if such an escape is, in the end, to be desired.

Madness, lobotomy, and the talking cure

> When one announces the fundamental psychoanalytical rule to the patient . . . and then waits for him to pour forth a flood of information, the first thing that happens often is that he has nothing to say. He is silent and declares that nothing comes into his mind. That is of course nothing but the repetition of a homosexual attitude, which comes up as a resistance against remembering anything. As long as he is under treatment he never escapes from this compulsion to repeat; at last one understands that it is his way of remembering.
>
> (Freud, "Recollection, Repetition, and Working Through")[3]

A number of recent critics have pointed to the difficulties gay male desire generates for psychoanalytic narratives such as the positing of the primal scene, to the disruptive recalcitrance of this desire that potentially unsettles the most basic processes of identification and acculturation. Among the most elegant of these arguments is Lee Edelman's "Seeing Things," which presents a dazzling reading of Freud's case history of that famous traumatized viewer, the Wolf-Man.[4] Edelman places broad questions of heterosexualization in the context of relations of spectatorial identification, pointing, most generally, to the perhaps inevitable disintegration of opposed identificatory positions in viewing such a spectacle and the potential collapse of theoretical distance from the primal scene this disintegration invites.

The primal scene, where the infant "sees" the anatomical difference that will retrospectively be interpreted as the castration caused by the mother's submission to the father's desire, is a scene of coitus *a tergo*. While this position allows the infant to get a "clear

---

3 Sigmund Freud, "Further Recommendations in the Technique of Psychoanalysis (1914): Recollection, Repetition, and Working Through," in *The Standard Edition of the Complete Psychological Works of Sigmund Freud*, 24 vols, translated by James Strachey with Anna Freud, Alix Strachey, and Alan Tyson (London: The Hogarth Press, 1958), vol. 6(b), 160–161.

4 Lee Edelman, "Seeing Things: Representation, the Scene of Surveillance, and the Spectacle of Gay Male Sex," in *Homographesis: Essays in Gay Literary and Cultural Theory* (New York: Routledge, 1994), 173–191. For the Wolf-Man, see Freud, "From the History of an Infantile Neurosis," in *Three Case Histories*, edited by Philip Rieff (New York: Collier Books, 1963), 161–280; also printed in vol. 27 of the *Standard Edition*. There are several other readings of the primal scene in recent queer theory, but none, to my mind, is as nuanced as Edelman's. See, for example, Kaja Silverman, "Too Early/Too Late: Male Subjectivity and the Primal Scene," in *Male Subjectivity at the Margins* (New York: Routledge, 1992), 157–181, and Leo Bersani, "The Gay Daddy," in *Homos* (Cambridge, MA: Harvard University Press, 1995), 77–112. For a convincing critique of Silverman, see Eve Kosofsky Sedgwick, "Is the Rectum Straight? Identification and Identity in *The Wings of the Dove*," in *Tendencies* (Durham, NC: Duke University Press, 1993), 73–103, esp. 73–74, 78, 95, 97–98.

view" of sexual difference, it also figures the operation of psychoanalysis, which is similarly structured as a return to traumas that can be seen clearly only from behind (and are in fact constituted through this very movement of return). Metalepsis, the rhetorical term Edelman calls "(be)hindsight," is thus an index of the temporal logic (a reversal of cause and effect—or a causal circularity that makes a cause the effect of its own later effect) that guides both psychoanalysis and the primal scene, a precarious reflexivity whose danger appeared when Freud's critics charged him with projecting his own fantasies onto his patient and the Wolf-Man accused him of wanting to "use him from behind." Freud was charged with effecting a reversal in analysis that merely repeated the reversals of the primal scene.

If, among other things, the psychoanalytic theorization of the primal scene attempts to exorcize the specter of gay male desire from its account of heterosexual acculturation, the difficulty is thus, in part, that the exorcism seems inevitably to enact the very desire it attempts to obliterate. Edelman convincingly argues that Freud's attempts to exonerate himself inscribe him within the Wolf-Man's own problematic, and he points in particular to ways that Freud's case history reenacts the Wolf-Man's identificatory uncertainties. Logically preceding (because it catalyzes) the castration complex, the primal scene becomes coherent only in retrospect, only in light of the differential gender identity secured by the castration complex itself. The infant viewing the primal scene identifies with both the penetrating and the penetrated partner before he knows that they are, in Edelman's words, "(op)positions."[5] Similarly, gay male sex potentially undermines such identity-producing oppositions by making visible the possibility of being penetrated without being castrated, threatening to undermine the threat of castration on which heterosexual masculine identity is built. Freud's irresolution in the case history paradoxically validates and reenacts the "confused"—even queer—split identification of the infant watching the primal scene. *Suddenly, Last Summer*, with its staging of a talking cure that enacts the gay desire it would put to rest, offers a cinematic representation of the disruptive power of gay male desire: the precarious proximity of psychoanalysis's "(be)hindsight" to the traumatic spectacle it would theorize is enacted in the film by the proximity of the traumatic scene Catherine witnesses to the curative modes it calls into action.

In light of the questions of precarious distance and unstable spectatorial identification that the film raises, its own explicit treatment of madness and the considerably lower-octane version of psychoanalysis it provides prove to be something of a distraction. *Suddenly, Last Summer*, however, in presenting several cures for several madnesses, does, in more or less oblique ways, point to the disruptive centrality of gay male desire in the psychic disturbances of its characters. Madness in the film nearly always circulates, in more or less explicit ways, around homosexuality. Before exploring the circumnavigations of the film's cures, then, we might more simply ask where to locate its madness. The film's only diagnosis is one of "dementia praecox," which Dr. Cukrowicz tells Mrs. Venable is a meaningless term. ("Such a pretty name for a disease," she responds, "Sounds like a rare flower, doesn't it? Night-blooming dementia praecox."[6]) Because of its ties

---

5 Edelman, "Seeing Things," 183.
6 As I have not been able to locate a published copy of the film script, this and all following quotations from the film are taken from my transcription of the videotape version released in the United States (Burbank, California: Columbia Tristar Home Video, 1992). The film, co-written by Williams and Gore Vidal and produced by Sam Spiegel with Horizon Pictures in Great Britain, was originally released in the United States through Columbia Pictures.

to paranoia, dementia praecox provides an oblique reference to homosexuality; at least from the Schreber case on, paranoia is linked in psychoanalytic writing to homosexuality, whether as something caused by it or as a complex developed to defend against it.[7] Referring to dementia praecox rather than paranoia, however, does more than further refract its reference to homosexuality; the reference indicates the history of the disease, though less in any specific psychoanalytic sense than in a generalized sense of confusion.

For dementia praecox might be called an "utterly confused category,"[8] and it was used, especially in the late nineteenth and early twentieth centuries, to denote what Freud later grouped under schizophrenia, paranoia, and, to his ears, the etymologically more elegant term, "paraphrenia."[9] The exact definition of dementia praecox fueled one of the livelier disputes in the emerging field of psychoanalysis; the term seemed to inspire a form of category crisis, denoting any number of the forms of madness from which the institutionalized of the turn of the century were said to suffer. Introduced by Benedict Augustus Morel in 1860 and picked up again by Emil Kraepelin in 1898, dementia praecox was important enough for one early analyst to remark, "The history of dementia praecox is really that of psychiatry as a whole."[10] The relation of dementia praecox to *Suddenly, Last Summer*, however, is perhaps not to be found in any specific psychoanalytic genealogy of the term.[11] Rather, its importance might lie in the very sense of confusion it introduced into analytic practice.

That dementia praecox was nonetheless seen as a peculiarly acute threat and one that analysts of the period often couched in sexual terms probably grew in part out of this ambient sense of confusion: dementia praecox seems to overwhelm the categorizing analytic mind because its symptoms are so broad as to make it almost, in Dr. Cukrowicz's

7 Thus "dementia praecox" also serves clinically to mask the film's reference to homosexuality (and to symbolize this masking), which could not, under censorship codes, mention by name. According to Laplanche and Pontalis, "as for Freud, he is quite prepared to see certain so-called paranoid forms of dementia praecox brought under the heading of paranoia . . . As is plain from his account of the case of Schreber . . . this case of "paranoid dementia" is essentially a paranoia proper in Freud's eyes . . . It should be noted . . . that paranoia is defined in psychoanalysis, whatever the variations in its delusional modes, as a defense against homosexuality." (J. Laplanche and J. B. Pontalis, *The Language of Psychoanalysis*, translated by Donald Nicholson-Smith [New York: Norton, 1974], 297.)

Other psychoanalysts have challenged Freud's overt positioning of homosexuality in the Schreber case, particularly in readings of psychosis. See, for example, Jacques Lacan, "On a Question Preliminary to Any Possible Treatment of Psychosis," in *Ecrits: A Selection*, translated by Alan Sheridan (London: Tavistock/Routledge, 1977), 179–225. See also Mikkel Borch-Jacobsen, "Crime and Punishment," in *Lacan: The Absolute Master*, translated by Douglas Brick (Stanford: Stanford University Press, 1991), 21–42. Briefly, in Freud, homosexuality is the root or cause of paranoia (paranoid delusion is a flight from repressed homosexuality), while to Lacan, homosexuality is a symptom of paranoia's structure.

8 This is Michel Foucault's phrase for the confused discourse around sodomy. See *The History of Sexuality, Volume 1: An Introduction*, translated by Robert Hurley (New York: Vintage, 1978), 101.

9 See the Schreber case ("Psychoanalytic Notes on An Autobiographical Account of a Case of Paranoia [Dementia Paranoides]," vol. 12 of *The Standard Edition*), 75–76.

10 A. Meyer, "The Evolution of the Dementia Praecox Concept," in *Schizophrenia (Dementia Praecox)* (New York: n.p., 1928). Quoted in Ida Macalpine, introduction to *Memoirs of My Nervous Illness*, by Daniel Paul Schreber, translated and edited by Ida Macalpine and Richard Hunter (Cambridge, MA: Robert Bentley, Inc., 1955), 14.

11 Analysis, as it is "practiced" in *Suddenly, Last Summer*, seems much closer to American psychology than to Freudian or post-Freudian psychoanalysis, however American psychologists in the 1950s may have conceived of their relation to Freud. It has also frequently been noted that some of Williams' bitterness toward psychiatry may have been a reaction to the lobotomy of his sister.

terms, "meaningless."[12] In the context of the film, the symptoms Leopold Bellak gives for dementia praecox can, at various moments, describe nearly every character as well as the film script and camera themselves. Often characterized by an almost autistic inward-turning of the psyche, dementia praecox, in Bellak's account, is a failure of the reality principle, an acquiescence to the mad fantasies of a deluded inner world. Symptoms include a paranoid fear of food poisoning, an inability to concentrate on exterior events, megalomania, erotomania, a failure of logical connections or rigor (even if the memory and judgment are left unimpaired), and even excessive use of alliteration (which characterizes the script of *Suddenly, Last Summer*, with its flies flown in at great expense, parcel post from Pensacola). One common thread of these symptoms is an obsessive self-reflexivity; alliteration, for example, attests to a signification system that has begun, arbitrarily, to refer not to anything "outside" itself but only to itself and to its own internal structure. Dementia praecox's obsessive self-reflexivity runs through the whole texture of this mad film, and this self-involution, along with the disease's absorptive definitional breadth, is perhaps more important to madness in the film and its connections to figures of cannibalism and gay male sex than is either the precise symptomatology of dementia praecox as a diagnostic category vague to the point of uselessness or the precise outlines of the dispute that surrounds it in the history of psychoanalysis.

More impressionistically, then, what or who appears mad in *Suddenly, Last Summer*? First, masculinity and femininity have gone awry; gender, refracted and exaggerated, often figures madness. Thus when Catherine enters the men's "drum" (the asylum's recreation room which the doctor insists is not a "torture chamber"), madness is figured as a heterosexualized manliness gone out of control: a non-productive, parodic, almost aimlessly ravenous desire for women seems to spur the wild gropings of these men. Similarly, Catherine's attempted suicide in the women's drum figures a leap into a parodic femininity and, as I will suggest, threatens a debunking and strange foreknowledge of her cure. More striking, perhaps, is the opening shot of a woman, in an obsessive parody of motherhood, holding a doll up to the light, a light whose movement up the wall is too quick to be sunlight and thus seems to be manufactured by the filming itself and its lighting, suggesting that her madness comes in part in its staging for and prompting by the camera. Diagnosed with "acute schizophrenic withdrawal" (thus tying her illness to paranoia and dementia praecox), she is lobotomized by Dr. Cukrowicz under the rapt gaze of Dr. Hockstader and a group of medical students. Her rather bereft doll, framed this time in a light that does not flee, unlike the light earlier and the lights on the operating table, testifies to the woman's cure (notably before the operation takes place, when the effects of the anesthesia prefigure those of the lobotomy). In both drums and in the shots of the woman and her doll, masculinity and femininity, as the end points of sexual maturity, turn back on themselves and look like their opposites: mature sexuality becomes indistinguishable from a terrifying infantilization.

The initial cure for unhinged gender is the lobotomy, as the striking shot of the bereft doll suggests. The film thus posits an opposition: Violet's cure for Catherine—the lobotomy,

12 See, for example, Leopold Bellak, *Dementia Praecox, the Past Decade's Work and Present Status: A Review and Evaluation* (New York: Grune and Stratton, 1948). Bellak calls dementia praecox "the most important single psychiatric category" (xiii), and he is emphatic (even paranoid) about its threat to the health of the nation. As a diagnostic category, however, dementia praecox has little to offer in the way of clarification; the very confusion the term introduces into analytic practice unsettlingly parallels the disease's own exorbitant threat to the organization of individual psyches.

a forcible silencing of gender insubordination—versus the doctor's—the talking cure, a more peacefully staged return to placid silence and forgetfulness. According to Mrs. Venable, Catherine "babbles":

Dr. C: What form does her disturbance take? [. . .]
Mrs. V: Madness, obsession, memory. She lacerates herself with memory. [After her experience in Europe . . .] she was taken straight to St. Mary's. And now they can't keep her there. They can't help her or cope with her fits of violence, her babbling, her dreadful obscene babbling.
Dr. C: What kind of babbling?
Mrs. V: Fantastic delusions and fantastic babblings of an unspeakable nature, mostly taking the form of hideous attacks on the moral character of my son, Sebastian.

"You've got to cut this hideous story out of her brain," Mrs. Venable tells the doctor later, but he feels that Catherine must be made to babble more: Catherine, he contends, must overcome her blockage of memory by remembering, repeating, and working through the trauma of Sebastian's death in the contained space of analysis. "She's going to have to be made to remember," he asserts. "She can't remember: that's her illness."

That hideous story has a particular content, and the energies around Catherine's madness and the conflicting curative modes that it calls into action are thus generated by the possibility that she might suddenly fling open the closet door to reveal Sebastian's unspeakable desires and the lurid story of his death. The relation of gay desire to the film's cures, however, is not simply a dialectic of obfuscation and revelation. Neither cure can simply be celebrated as the ally of an unambiguously liberatory revelation; rather, each partakes of variously valenced pleasures and panics of both revelation and obfuscation. The lobotomy and the talking cure, as well as the struggle between them, by blurring the distinction between veiling and unveiling, between curative, even diagnostic, "success" and "failure," all undermine the security of heterosexuality in the film, for all can be shown in various ways to partake of the very desire they would cure by putting them safely to rest.

Most simply, the discursive struggle over Catherine's cure pits Mrs. Venable and the lobotomy against Catherine, the doctor, and the talking cure. This contest over which stories—and the stories of which desires—will be told, is staged as a quasi-Oedipalized confrontation between two women, and it often feels like a contest between Catherine and Violet over who will babble the other into silence and madness. Catherine's talking cure at the end of the film is thus undermined by its peculiar and almost violent transitivity; as if by an unspoken law of the conservation of madness—maintaining a certain "amount" of madness within any given emotional milieu—Catherine is cured by a projective babbling that exchanges her madness for Mrs. Venable's. Moreover, by suggesting that Catherine has perhaps never been mad, the film makes us think that this vindictive outcome may have been the very motive of the talking cure. When Dr. Cukrowicz returns to Catherine in the garden (after assuring her mother and brother that she has been cured), her gaze as she turns around to greet him is one not merely of apparent sanity but of complicity as well. Moreover, her words restage her disturbance after the rape at the "Dueling Oaks": "She's here, Doctor, Miss Catherine's here," echoes both her third-person diary and her words at St. Mary's in her first scene in the film. The doctor, however, looks only relieved and happy—the symptoms of her madness now signify differently. Resignifying her earlier moments of madness, this moment reminds us that Catherine's claim to sanity has always been her ability to talk about and to stage her own madness.

If the talking cure is compromised by this knowingness, so too is the lobotomy, and Mrs. Venable is no less knowing in her slips of madness than Catherine is. The lobotomy, Mrs. Venable's cure of choice, is also often figurally associated with her. The disorientingly self-reflexive structure that ties (even confounds) madness with its cure is thus suggested again by the lobotomized woman's illness: her obsession with her doll mimics Mrs. Venable's relation to Sebastian. Always chanting "My son Sebastian," she looks like a similar parody of motherhood, overdoing a mother's "natural" love for her son, and this obsessive love echoes (but overdoes) folk wisdom that a mother can inadvertently make her son gay by loving him "too much."[13] Motherhood in the film is seemingly synonymous with obsession, and more or less refracted versions of mother-hood appear throughout *Suddenly, Last Summer*. Thus, for example, Sebastian's poetry composition also looks like a parody of motherhood that mirrors Mrs. Venable's rela-tion to him and the madwoman's relation to her doll. Resting nine months (which even Dr. Cukrowicz notes is the period of a pregnancy), he produces just one poem a year. The film's obsessive figuration of motherhood thus starts to redouble obsessive mother-hood, and it is therefore not surprising that many of the film's symptoms of madness circulate around Mrs. Venable, that most charismatic of mothers. More than her obses-sive love for Sebastian, the madness of the dominating and obsessive Mrs. Venable is figured by strange eruptions in her speech, perhaps most luridly demonstrated when, in a discussion with Dr. Cukrowicz, she celebrates the glories of the lobotomy with a sudden reference to the peace to be purchased through the operation:

Dr. C: . . . it will be years before we know if the immediate benefits of the operation are lasting or maybe just passing or perhaps . . . There's a strong possibility that the patient will always be limited. Relieved of acute anxiety, yes, but limited.

Mrs. V: But what a blessing to them, Doctor, to be just peaceful. To be just suddenly peaceful. After all that horror, after those nightmares, just to be able to lift up their eyes to a sky not black with savage devouring birds.

Dr. C: You said a sky filled with savage devouring birds?

Mrs. V: Did I?

Leaving aside momentarily these savage devouring birds, the deceptive ease with which Mrs. Venable can be pronounced mad perhaps baits the viewer into overlooking the staginess of these mad slips. Confronting Catherine in the asylum's sun room, Mrs. Venable seems to feign a faint; the camera catches a very knowing glance toward the doorway Catherine has left vacant—a glance that seems to impel Catherine's suicide attempt. This knowing glance inflects her slips of madness earlier in the film: with these slips, she thus seems stagily to bait the diagnostic acumen of both the gullible (and obtuse) Dr. Cukrowicz

---

13 This is also, of course, Freudian wisdom: it is merely a simplified (although not all that simplified) version of Freud's account of the etiology of male homosexuality in the Leonardo case. See *Leonardo da Vinci and a Memory of his Childhood*, translated by Alan Tyson (New York: Norton, 1961). Briefly, because Leonardo's mother loved him so overwhelmingly much, he looks (narcissistically) for another man whom he can love as his mother once loved him.

and the viewer of the film. Moreover, her slips form part of her more general strategy of rhetorical domination: I cannot help but feel that Mrs. Venable discloses exactly as much as she wants to disclose, and her mad interruptions cut off and control the conversation when it takes a turn she would prefer to avoid. From the first appearance of Mrs. Venable, it becomes difficult to tell madness from its feigning, even as the self-reflexivity of this feigning, which blurs the line between madness and sanity, starts to figure madness and to undermine any secure position from which madness could, without self-betrayal, be diagnosed in another.

If *Suddenly, Last Summer* initially suggests two alternatives for the curing of madness—the talking cure and the lobotomy—that both cures are undermined by the knowingness by which the madness they would cure is staged and deployed is perhaps the least of the difficulties. The first double bind is perhaps already apparent: whether via talking or via surgically imposed silence, these two cures, in the context of the film, amount to the same thing. Both allow the patient serenely to forget. It is not difficult to be horrified by the lobotomy, and the film clearly privileges the talking cure as the more enlightened. The difficulty for the talking cure (as for the film) is that the two cures become harder and harder to tell apart as they converge in silence. To my mind, the silence or forgetfulness is what is important because it makes both cures look like repetitions of the very madness they would cure. For the film initially seems most silent about what exactly needs curing; it is around this luridly silent forgetfulness that the surprisingly underspecified babbling of the film's madness turns—so much so (and all the more if we buy into the talking cure's curative speaking of trauma) that the very "content" of madness seems to be an inability to talk about the content of the madness. The converging silences of the two cures thus seem to screen an anxiety in the film, an anxiety about the marked silence that the alternative cures seem able only to repeat. If, again, the cure coincides with the disease it would cure, why is there talk of a cure in the first place? What needs to be cured and what do the talking cure and the lobotomy screen in the film?

Cannibalism, sodomy, and the heterosexualizing cure

A *Time* magazine review of the period hardly minced its words in expressing its irritation with the film:

> Showman Spiegel . . . has shrewdly presented the whole morbid mess as "an adult horror picture" about a woman "who is suddenly too old to procure boys for her son." Says Spiegel: "Why, it's a theme the masses can identify themselves with." . . . [T]o wonder about this story is to realize that it is nothing more than a psychiatric nursery drama, a homosexual fantasy of guilty pleasure and pleasurable punishment. The dead hero is really no more than a sort of perverted Peter Pan, and the cannibalism itself nothing more than an aggravated case of nail biting.[14]

The knowingness of *Time*'s review begins to suggest one answer to these questions: the review attempts to diffuse the threat of gay desire by implicitly asserting that there is simply nothing to know. The hero is "*really no more* than a sort of perverted Peter Pan,"

14 "Cinema: The New Pictures—*Suddenly, Last Summer*," *Time* 75 (2) (11 January, 1960), 64, 66.

and the film's cannibalism is *"nothing more* than an aggravated case of nail biting." Moreover, the film's morbid "theme," *Time*'s irony asserts, is certainly not one with which any of its readers are in the slightest danger of finding themselves "identifying." One would be hard pressed to specify how a "perverted Peter Pan" would differ from Barrie's original condensation of wish-fulfillment, but the more striking difficulty for this review's knowing pose appears in the tendentiously maintained distance between the attribution of a flighty (homosexual) effeminacy in the mock-serious form of an "aggravated case of nail-biting" and a catty inhabitation of such effeminacy. An uncontrollable overidentification, in other words, is precisely the problem. Knowingness is, moreover, never a safe location in the film; Dr. Hockstader's turns him into a buffoon, and Dr. Cukrowicz's proves to be insulating only when it merges with a baffling obtuseness. Catherine and Mrs. Venable are the only characters who carry such knowingness off with any aplomb, but both do more to expose than to obfuscate Sebastian's gay desire. Both, but especially Catherine, throw a wrench into the curative mechanics of the film. Knowingness, we recall, is perhaps the central feature of Catherine's madness. Asked, for example, whether she had unjustly accused "an elderly gardener of great virtue" of sexual harassment, she responds, "Of course I accused him unjustly. After all, I'm insane. It's the sort of thing an insane woman would do. Besides, doctor, haven't you noticed how oddly I've been looking at you?" As if she can put on and shed her madness at will, the knowingness of Catherine's attesting to her sanity by talking about and staging her insanity not only undermines the necessity of a talking cure but also takes into account the doctor's desire, his libidinal investment in finding her sane. After Dr. Cukrowicz responds to her plangent "Help me" with, "Don't, don't talk like that," she asks, "Why not? Now I sound insane, don't I?" But the film seems as invested in Catherine's sanity as the doctor is, and, to both, the panicked search for a cure grows out of a panic about errant desire.

We might initially posit, then, the trauma that the film must speak to be cured: the film seeks to rid itself of the haunting specter of gay male desire, an expurgation that can take place, according to the film's logic of curative catharsis, only by mentioning it. The film must, but cannot, explicitly articulate this desire; obliquity only makes the desire more omnipresent. Because, that is, they can only be indicated through connotation, homosexuality and, more specifically, the spectacle of gay male sex are signified throughout the film.[15] We might then rephrase in explicitly sexual terms the double bind the film faces as it tries to differentiate the lobotomy from the talking cure: it attempts to differentiate indistinguishable forms of silence, to differentiate, within a homophobic framework, a refusal to denote gay desire from a reticence-as-indication that is designed specifically to denote gay desire. For the "whole morbid mess" of this film, the madness of heterosexuality's reticence derives from the difficulty of distinguishing that which does not discuss itself from that which cannot—but must—discuss itself, to distinguish, that is, the lurid silence around what I will call its "heterosexualizing cure" from the lurid silence around its evocation of gay male sexuality. The content of the memory Catherine must speak figures this supposedly unspeakable trauma: Sebastian's death stands in for his own "unspeakable" tendencies. While the lurid content of Catherine's mem-

---

15 On connotation, see D. A. Miller, "Anal *Rope,*" in Diana Fuss, ed., *Inside/Out: Lesbian Theories, Gay Theories* (New York: Routledge, 1991), 118–141, esp. 129–130.

ory makes its cure more complicated, we should dwell first on the cure that the film, equally luridly, explores.

The rigors of this cure are suggested in another of Catherine's knowing comments after the doctor has begged her never to try to escape: "Must I take off my pretty dress?" The film, that is, seeks not to find a cure for Catherine but to cure itself through a heterosexualizing of her and of its own gaze that projects her madness onto Mrs. Venable. Madness, in this movement, is the counterpoint of desire: for the women in the film, madness (and an erosion of their discursive authority) arises from the withdrawal of male desire. If madness is often a figure for an excessive or hyperbolic sexuality, it is equally a figure for the absence of sexuality; madness, furthermore, appears in the film as the difficulty of distinguishing between an excess and an absence of sexuality. The blurring of this opposition thus compromises the libidinal movement of the film. Mrs. Venable's dazzling first descent into the film, speaking as if "from the wings" to an already rapt audience, marks the high point of her power. The contrast between her initial descent and her descent for the cure sequence, where her self-staging is sabotaged by the doctor's covert rearrangements, prefigures her eventual (at least ostensible) abjection as, babbling, she ascends, staring into the eyes of her dead son. Her loss of authority encapsulates the larger movement of desire, both of the characters in the film (notably Dr. Cukrowicz) and of the film itself, a transfer of libidinal investment from Katharine Hepburn to Elizabeth Taylor.

When Dr. Cukrowicz first meets Mrs. Venable, his discomfitingly bald stare in facing her beauty acknowledges his awkward rapture; after he meets Catherine, however, his longing stares are reserved for her. The film itself also follows this libidinal movement: the camera becomes less and less interested in Hepburn and more and more interested in Taylor. In the terms of my earlier discussion of the discursive struggle between Catherine and Mrs. Venable, then, Mrs. Venable's lapse into madness seems not only an attempt to stabilize the unsettling transitivity of madness set up in the counterplay of her madness and Catherine's. The ending's perhaps willful assertion of a localizable madness also allows and is allowed by a concomitant assertion of heterosexualized desirability that posits Catherine as an object of (presumptively male heterosexual) desire. In the interplay of madness between these two charismatic women, the film brings together its explicit thematization of madness and its implicit thematization of desire.

The film figures its own search for a cure through Dr. Cukrowicz, perhaps the character whose desire most needs to be straightened out.[16] The film pairs him with Sebastian: the oblique shots of Sebastian make him look remarkably like the doctor, who shares his penchant for the color white, and whose looks and dedication to his "art" remind Mrs. Venable of her son. While this taint of homosexuality puts pressure on the doctor's professional and desexualized altruism—Sebastian, as George snickeringly informs us, felt no desire for Catherine—the doctor cannot simply distance

16 That the good doctor was played by Montgomery Clift, whose oddly blank and unreadable allure in the film is no doubt generated in part by his aura of sexual ambiguity and by his status as a gay icon, is no doubt significant. One contemporary review noted that "Dr. Clift, whose gestures have in recent years been more and more reduced to twitches, sometimes looks even queerer than his patient, but on the whole he comes off as 'glacially brilliant'" (*Time*, January 11, 1960, 66). The logic of this (twitchy) formulation is a bit evasive, confounding, among other distinctions, the doctor's and the actor's "art," to say nothing of Clift's well-earned medical degree. Also interesting is the slippage between Clift, Dr. Cukrowicz, Catherine, and Sebastian—who is queerer than whom?

himself from Sebastian by desiring Catherine, for thus to assure himself of his hetero-sexuality would be to take Sebastian's bait. It is striking in this context that Catherine seems to desire him not only as a new-and-improved heterosexual version of Sebastian, but also as Sebastian would have desired him; as she awakens from anesthesia, she con-fuses the doctor with the "items" on Sebastian's "menu": "This one's eyes are so blue." Similarly, a flashback in Catherine's talking cure features an especially telling cut: the camera fades from a shot of the doctor to a closeup on the crotch of one of the men lured by Catherine. This is a delicious moment, no doubt, and one that seems to bait gay male desire. For the moment, however, I would note that the film here makes visible the trap set for the doctor. Making the places of desiring Catherine and being seduced by Sebastian oddly interchangeable, the film places the doctor in a double bind: just as his putatively desireless retreat into his art brings him into uncomfortable proximity with Mrs. Venable's vision of Sebastian, the positing of a curative heterosexual gaze puts the doctor in the position both of Sebastian and of the boys Sebastian seduces.

This double bind entraps not only the doctor but the film as well; both seem to choose Elizabeth Taylor, leaving the talking cure to screen the double bind they would hope to escape. Just as the doctor turns to Catherine as the saving heterosexual object of desire, the film presents Elizabeth Taylor as an erotic object for the camera and for the audience. ("I want you to know that I can look attractive, if I have my hair done," Catherine rather inexplicably says after she has inexplicably kissed the doctor and begged him to help her remember.) As part of her cure, in fact, she is dressed up and has her hair done: it is curiously important that she look attractive. Visually, then, the film seems at times to co-star Elizabeth Taylor's breasts, which, crammed into the most improbable dresses, often quite literally precede her, an effect accentuated all the more by the lighting, which often cuts Taylor across the chest. Even her mother is forced to stare at them, and Catherine's magnetic sexual appeal makes doctors at Lion's View turn around to look at her, not as a patient, but as an erotic object.

For the heterosexual desire that would secure itself from the temptations of queer recidivism, the moment of the cure is thus not the telling of Sebastian's death but the scene just before the telling begins, the scene, with its mysterious injection, that allows Catherine finally to put behind her the Sebastian who did not desire her. "You know what I think you're trying to do?," Catherine says, "I think you're trying to hypnotize me. You're looking at me so *straight*. You're doing something strange to me with your eyes." The doctor's heterosexualizing hypnosis allows Catherine to enter normal het-erosexual relations (no longer parodying them by leaping into the drum) and allows her officially—by stating her need, her lack—to take her place as the camera's, the doctor's, and, ostensibly, the audience's object of desire: "Hold me. I've been so lonely." The kiss that follows (oddly not disturbing to Dr. Hockstader, who interrupts it), with its accompanying music, seems staged as a filmic climax. But, as important as this positing of Elizabeth Taylor as the film's object of desire is, it is not a cure that can be openly acknowledged. The film thus needs the scene of analysis to mask the heterosexualizing cure; it needs the talking cure to make us forget the filmic climax—a crescendo of music leading to a passionate embrace—that we have just witnessed. For to admit the impor-tance of Catherine's position as an object of desire is to implicate the film in the gay desire it is trying to cure by admitting that Sebastian and the heterosexualizing cure are using the same bait. Like Sebastian the previous summer, the film, when it shifts its focus from Hepburn to Taylor to lure the desire of its audience, discards Violet, as Catherine remarks, like "an old toy." Discarding Violet as soon as she is too old to "attract," the film merely repeats Sebastian's mode of seduction. The cure that would establish a heterosexual gaze, in other words, can only repeat the gesture with which Sebastian's gay gaze ensnares boys; it can only offer up the spectacle of Catherine as a desirable object for the famished delectation of its precariously heterosexualized viewers.

Even before exploring the complications this baiting introduces into the film, it is striking that there are many ways the heterosexualizing cure simply does not work. Most simply, it cures too much. Thus, for example, in whatever improbable costume she appears, Taylor generates desire in excess of the heterosexual stability demanded of her. One thinks, for example, of the nurse who embarrasses Dr. Cukrowicz with her extended (and oddly enraptured) speech about Catherine's beauty. What is this wayward and utterly tangential character doing expressing so incontinently her desire for another woman? It seems that desire, once it is set loose, needs to be controlled like Catherine after she is accused of attacking the elderly gardener: in Mrs. Venable's words, "She fought. She screamed. It took four nuns to control her." Even the smallest details in the film bait the viewer with incongruous and excessive images of almost parodic scenarios of desire. The back of the magazine Mrs. Venable picks up in the sun room at Lion's View, for example, features an image of a busty woman in a bathing suit and a leering and groping man. Desire, once posited, seems by necessity to be posited in excess: desire, especially healthy heterosexual desire, becomes indistinguishable from its parody in the drum at Lion's View.

More important, perhaps, this excess of heterosexuality becomes indistinguishable from the homosexuality it would hope to cure. If the busty and increasingly coiffed Taylor is put forward as an irresistible spectacle for (presumptively heterosexual) cinematic consumption, she again coincides structurally with that other lurid spectacle in the film. What is the spectacle that the film so luridly deploys? Two of the film's most spectacular moments—Mrs. Venable's description of the turtles on the Encantadas and Catherine's description of Sebastian's death—return us to the film's obsessive self-reflexivity most often figured through the trope of cannibalism. Mrs. Venable, in the shade of the *garçon-nière* ("an old New Orleans convenience, a place where the young men of the family could go to be private"), describes what she and Sebastian witnessed on the Encantadas. Like Herman Melville, they travel to the Galapagos Islands, but they "see something that Melville hadn't written about":

> We saw the great sea turtles crawl up out of the sea for their annual egg laying. Once a year, the female of the sea turtles crawls up out of the equatorial sea onto the blazing sand beach of a volcanic island to dig a pit in the sand and deposit her eggs there. It's a long and dreadful thing, the depositing of the eggs in the sand pits. And when it's finished, the exhausted female turtle crawls back to the sea, half dead. She never sees her offspring.

Violet and Sebastian do see the turtle offspring. The hatching of the sea turtles spawns a feeding frenzy, and the Venables return

Mrs. V: . . . in time to witness the hatching of the sea turtles and their desperate flight to the sea. The narrow beach, the color of caviar, was all in motion. The sky was in motion, too, full of flesh-eating birds. And the noise of the birds. Their horrible savage cries as they circled over the narrow black beach of the Encantadas, while the new-hatched sea turtles scrambled out of their sand pits and started their race to the sea . . . [t]o escape the flesh-eating birds that made the sky almost as black as the beach. And I said, Sebastian, no, no, it's not like that, but he made me look, he made me see that terrible sight.

Dr. C: What was not like that?

Mrs. V: Life. I said, no, no. That's not true. But he said it is. He said, look, Violet, look there on the shore. And I looked and saw the sand all alive, all alive, as the new-hatched sea turtles made their dash to the sea while the birds hovered and swooped to attack, and hovered and swooped to attack. They were diving down on the sea turtles, turning them over to expose their soft undersides, tearing their undersides open, and rending and eating their flesh.

This description proleptically figures Sebastian's death and thus becomes a figure for cannibalism, which in turn figures gay sex. The flesh-eating birds that feed on the newly hatched sea turtles, that is, are not, strictly speaking, cannibals, but this feeding frenzy evokes the frenzy of Sebastian's death when he is devoured by a flock of famished boys at Cabeza de Lobo. Cannibalism in turn seems here to be a figure for gay male sex acts, whether that means anal sex or, perhaps more to the point in this relentlessly oral film, analingus or fellatio. Mrs. Venable's description, that is, evokes a luridly sexualized form of feeding-as-cannibalism that brings to mind Sebastian's obsessively oral metaphors for sex: boys are "delicious" or "not delicious," Sebastian becomes "famished" for blondes, and Catherine describes his cruising as the perusal of a "menu." With an oral rapacity worthy of Melanie Klein's phantasmagoria, her description seems to figure gay male sex through, in part, the intensity of its fixated revulsion. Whether oral or anal, the "depositing of the eggs in the sand pits" and the ravenous tearing open of "undersides" seem to figure sex acts charged with the fascinating allure of taboo. The cannibalism as a figure for gay male sex, rooted here in a scene of exhausting, arduous, and tragic motherhood, brings to mind less any specific sexual act than the category of sodomy, with all of its moralistic, legalistic, and religious overtones. The dire tones of Mrs. Venable's figuration of gay male sex evoke a sense, above all, of infraction.

As infractions of the "law," how are cannibalism and sodomy related?[17] In the language of *Suddenly, Last Summer*, they are related through their imagined operation as non-regenerative, self-consuming, and self-reflexive acts.[18] Just as cannibalism is notori-

---

17 Sodomy, that "utterly confused category," is of course in no way simply equivalent to any given sex act. I also hope that it has been clear that I am aware of the punitive and legalistic history of the word *sodomy*, a word that, outside of the world of Tennessee Williams, describes, I hope, few people's sex lives. I have chosen to use the word for several reasons. First, it seems appropriate to describe the sexual dynamics around male homosexual panic in the late 1950s in America. Second, perhaps because of all of the confusion around the term, it expresses precisely the kinds of representational disturbances that animate and disrupt the film. Finally, the word's campy sententiousness seems quite at home in *Suddenly, Last Summer*.

18 David Bergman suggests this intertwining at the beginning of "Cannibals and Queers" (in *Gaiety Transfigured: Gay Self-Representation in American Literature* [Madison: The University of Wisconsin Press, 1991], 142), where he argues that "[t]he correlation of homosexuality and cannibalism is quite old." He quotes, for example, from Epiphanius, who accuses the Gnostics or Borborites of violating many taboos, including homosexuality and cannibalism. Practicing "all non-procreative sexual acts," the Borborites, according to Epiphanius, when a woman does become pregnant, cut up the aborted fetus and eat it, "declaring the meal 'the Perfect Passover'" (97–98). "The central act of the Borborites," Bergman writes, "is a feast in which 'the woman and man receive the male emission on their hands,' and standing with 'their eyes raised heavenward,' offer their semen to God and eat it" (86). (Bergman quotes from Epiphanius of Salamis, in James M. Robinson, ed., *The Panarion of Epiphanius of Salamis,* translated by Frank Williams, Nag Hammadi Studies, vol. 35 [Leiden: E. J. Brill, 1987].) Less luridly, while Bergman turns to Aquinas and the "category" mistakes of cannibalism and sodomy, it also seems that the intertwining tropes of cannibalism and sodomy are linked through their (non)generative or (non)productive status (as well as the way that sodomy and cannibalism seem implicit in and to parody the sacrament of the Eucharist, the taking of the Lord into one's mouth).

ously vitamin-deficient (human flesh is not nutritious, as my high school health coun-selors almost obsessively reminded their students—as if nutritional concerns were all that prevented us from wolfing down our classmates), sodomy is a non-procreative "spilling of seed." Sodomy and cannibalism, in other words, are forms of what Mrs. Venable calls a "devouring creation." This devouring creation is figured even in the location of the turtles, which sodomitically recasts the narrative of evolution. For Melville is not the only famous visitor to the Galapagos Islands: the turtles on these islands supposedly led Darwin to posit his theory of natural selection, and the film casts the violent, non-regenerative feeding Sebastian and Violet witness as the essence of evolutionary generation itself. As Mrs. Venable says, "Millions of years ago, dinosaurs fed on the leaves of those trees. The dinosaurs are vegetarians. That's why they became extinct. They were just too gentle for their size. And then the carnivorous creatures, the ones that eat flesh, the killers, inherited the earth. But then they always do, don't they?" Violet and Sebastian "went back . . . In time" to witness what will have been the forward move-ment of evolution.

Evolution, however, is not simply read backwards; its very narrative, already inverted, unreads itself. If, in other words, evolution no longer progresses in a narrative that can be read in a "forward" direction, the essence of its procreative generation appears here as a non-regenerative, non-procreative devouring. Just as motherhood—the deposit-ing of the eggs in the sand pits—becomes a figure less for procreative regeneration than for sodomitical penetration, evolution becomes a figure for sodomy and cannibalism. As "life" in Mrs. Venable's description slides into the frantic swarming of sea turtles as they are devoured, making the sand look "all alive, all alive," aliveness becomes not the end-point of evolutionary development but the repulsive symptom of its self-involution. And the more one probes *Suddenly, Last Summer*, the more one sees how aptly Mrs. Venable characterizes a viewer's relation to this self-consuming, consuming, inescapably alluring film when she asserts that "we are all of us trapped by this devour-ing creation."

The lurid figure of sodomitical penetration, figured through the violence of canni-balism, repeats itself throughout the film. The "boring of a hole into the skull" in the lobotomy, for example, which itself seems to repeat the violence of the rape at the "Dueling Oaks," can be read as another such sodomitical reenactment. Moreover, it is around a scene of lobotomy that the film first figures its audience's precarious distance from the film's various cuts. In one of the many mishaps in the early lobotomy scene, one of the railings in the gallery of Dr. Hockstader's "operatin' theater" gives way; the danger for the rapt medical students figures that of the film's audience. Tumbling over the railing, the audience finds itself enclosed behind the brick wall that opens the film, lying on the operating table to be lobotomized, and pinned in the place of the sea turtles, the boys Sebastian has sex with, and Sebastian, lying "torn and crushed" on the "broken stones" at Cabeza de Lobo.[19] At the end of the film, a rather overstated homonym figures this viewerly implication. Catherine, describing the band of boys that serenades them with a music made of "noise," repeatedly refers to the boys' "cymbals," the "bits of metal

19 As an anonymous *Cinema Journal* reader pointed out to me, the figural connection between the lobotomy and Sebastian's death is also emphasized in the name Cabeza de Lobo. The encrypting of the lobotomy in Cabeza de Lobo thus reasserts the figural chain connecting the lobotomy, cannibalism, and sodomy in the film. The name thus again asserts that the lobotomy fails properly to be curative because it merely repeats the trauma it would cure; the difficulty for the talking cure then is to show just how it avoids being another such repetition.

and other bits of metal that had been flattened out and made into cymbals . . . tin cans flattened out and clashed together . . . cymbals." The boys use these very "cymbals" to cut pieces of Sebastian away before they stuff him "into those gobbling mouths." The viewer's use of "symbols" to read symbolically represents spectatorship as the famished devouring of Sebastian's body, figuring the viewer's implication in the lurid figure of the sacrifice that it simultaneously reenacts. The film's anticipation of its audience, more-over, undermines any positional certainty through which the spectator might attempt to stabilize the slide into the film. The film's viewer, in other words, takes the place of both Sebastian desiring and the boys he desires, of both the boys who devour Sebastian and Sebastian being devoured, of both the lobotomized and the lobotomizer, of both the viewer and viewed, the reader and the read.

The staging of a precariously perched spectatorship in the early lobotomy scene is one figure that suggests that a viewer's distance from the film might be undermined, and this potential collapse of distance is both one possible effect of and a figure for the film's often disorienting self-reflexivity. The film's staging of its own viewing, in other words, both figures self-reflexivity and is a self-reflexive instance that perhaps precipitates a view-er's fall into the film. This self-reflexivity relates thematically and figuratively to the film's exploration of madness. For example, the madness of Mrs. Venable's language grows out of a similar non-regenerative recursive structure (like the alliteration that is a symp-tom of dementia praecox). Both Mrs. Venable's rhetorical domination and her seeming madness grow out of the way her lines turn back on themselves:

> She was with him the day he died, and it was that day, the day he died, that she lost her mind.
>
>   Strictly speaking, his life was his occupation. Yes, yes, Sebastian was a poet. That, that's what I meant when I said his life was his work. Because the work of a poet is the life of a poet, and vice-versa, the life of a poet is the work of a poet. I mean you can't separate them. I mean a poet's life is his work, and his work is his life. In a special sense. [Dr: Are you all right?] Right as rain, however right that is.
>
>   I know it sounds hopelessly vain to say, but we were a famous couple. People didn't speak of Sebastian and his mother or Mrs. Venable and her son. No, they said, Sebastian and Violet, Violet and Sebastian . . . And every appearance, every time we appeared, attention was centered on us, everyone else eclipsed.

The recursive structure of Mrs. Venable's speech—the way her words turn back on and repeat themselves in self-mirroring formulations, an effect emphasized by Hepburn's inim-itable delivery—connects the madness of Mrs. Venable's obsessive motherhood to the "devouring creation" figurally linked to sodomy and cannibalism. More important, these recursive formulations start to figure the movement and cure of the film itself.

The texture of the film is marked throughout by such recursivity. Thus the symbol-ism of the film feels mad less because of its sudden links and arbitrary associations than because of its overdetermination. Even the sun room at Lion's View, for instance, comes freighted with overlapping associations, and, as such, it begins to figure a symbolism of madness and a madness of symbolism in the film. The "sunlight" to which the woman holds up the doll, the sun room in the asylum, the sun room at the Venables', the blinding sun in the Encantadas Mrs. Venable tells the doctor about, and the suffocat-ing sunlight at Cabeza de Lobo and its white glare, all seem to signify madness (or the driving of people mad) within the film, and the condensation of images of sunlight also—through the blankness of this white glare and the overdetermination of light in the film's symbolic structure—makes the film itself appear mad and the experience of viewing it one potentially of madness as well: the white glare might symbolize a viewer's blindness, and the portability of its symbolism the frantic, even mad, traversal of the movement of its overdetermination. The obvious pun on "son," for example, equates the mother's suffocating and homosexualizing gaze not only with the sun at Cabeza de Lobo but with the "son" himself, and the white glare at Cabeza de Lobo not only is cast on Sebastian but seems to emanate from him as he flees in his white suit, his white Panama hat, his white tie, and with his white handkerchief and his white pills. Not only, then, does each element in the chain of symbolic associations refer to every other element; each symbol also symbolizes the cumulative effect of the overdetermination of the chain as a whole. The symbolic elements of the film thus converge in a meta-symbolical linkage connecting madness to the film's famished orality, cannibalism, and sodomy. Orality, that is, both figures the symbolic overdetermination of the film as the different symbolic elements absorb or devour one another and links its symbolism to perverse desire. Thus the sexual overtones of Mrs. Venable's transfixed description of the sea turtles are generated not only by the description's content but also by her traversal of a symbolically overdetermined structure. The very slide, in other words, from the sea turtles by way of motherhood to cannibalism and sodomy both symbolizes the self-involution and recursivity of madness, cannibalism, and sodomy in the film and provides an instance of that recursivity.

Such a self-reflexive return also figures the viewer's relation to the film. Madness as a figure for the film's cure stands in for both the film's own mad symbolization and the viewer's mad traversal of its overdetermination. For the viewer, the reenactment of the film's sodomitical orality takes place more strikingly through another site of symbolic condensation: the structure of baiting, which marks Sebastian's use of Violet and Catherine, Violet's use of the doctor, and the film's use of Catherine and its viewer. Baiting thus structures both the relations among characters within the film and the viewer's relation to the film. To analyze the dynamics of bait within the film, therefore, reenacts the very structure it would analyze. Baiting as an erotic structure, that is, acts as a lure for the viewer, a self-reflexive return that in turn figures the erotics of baiting. To begin to clarify this oddly contagious structure, we should return to Catherine's cure. What does she tell about in her talking cure? She tells, in short, of how Sebastian "died at a place called Cabeza de Lobo." While I cannot say with authority, as Dr. Cukrowicz can, that "I read Spanish," my Spanish dictionary tells me that "Cabeza de Lobo" literally means "wolf's head," but, colloquially, it means "something flaunted to attract favor." The place of Sebastian's death is conflated, in a beautiful (if not terribly subtle) metonymic slide, with Catherine, who, like Mrs. Venable before the previous summer, was used as bait: "We both . . . we were decoys . . . He used us as bait . . . We procured for him." This slide undoes the cure that leads to the heterosexualizing of Catherine, the doctor, and the audience, for this heterosexualizing is shown to work just as Sebastian does, similarly using Catherine as bait. The metonymic slide between Catherine and Cabeza de Lobo makes the curative object of desire interchangeable with a scene of cannibalism and gay male sex. On the one hand, this is hardly surprising, as the scene at Cabeza de Lobo luridly depicts the sacrifice of the homosexual; the appearance of Elizabeth Taylor as the object of desire would then condense the figure of this desire's disappearance. On the other hand, this cannibalistic scene figures the lurid emergence of sodomy itself.

The sacrifice, in other words, participates in the very desire it would sacrifice, and, as the disappearance of the homosexual, it would mark his more lurid reappearance.[20]

Once again, as soon as the male heterosexual gaze is directed toward Catherine, it starts seeing, as if this were what it wanted to see all along, a scene of gay male sex. Like the Venus Fly Trap, "a devouring organism, aptly named for the goddess of love," the film seems to lure its audience, and its self-involuted cures and self-reflexive sym-bolizations converge in a scene of ecstatic cannibalism and gay male sex. Trying to cure itself of homosexuality, it cannot differentiate straight love from sodomy, even as the spectacle of sodomy and of the sacrifice of the sodomite itself starts as well to take the place of bait. "Cabeza de Lobo" thus condenses Catherine (as the putatively curative heterosexual object of desire) and Sebastian's death (as a lurid figure for gay sex troped as cannibalism and as the expunging of this figure) together in an ever more lurid and absorbing structure of baiting.

This baiting structure precipitates the viewer's fall into the film. The spectator's impli-cation in the spiraling lures of *Suddenly, Last Summer* is perhaps most forcibly figured in the film's most scandalous lure: the paradoxically hidden and outrageously overt spec-tacle of its final sacrifice, the death of Sebastian that is simultaneously the film's end point and its desire-fueling origin in trauma. This scene is what the film must seek to cure, and in relation to this scene, we sense why the film's attempt to cure itself through the heterosexualizing of desire is placed in such a paradoxical position. On the one hand, this cure cannot, for the reasons we have noted, be openly acknowledged. On the other, the film seems to thrive on the cure's lurid, even scandalous *un*masking and the prox-imity of this unmasked cure to the equally lurid, if obfuscated, scene of sodomy as sacrifice and the scene of the sacrifice of sodomy at Cabeza de Lobo. The talking cure, which does (and does not) take its place, which screens (and fails to screen) the heterosexu-

---

20 The paradoxical status of the "sacrifice" of Sebastian is one of the reasons I depart from the readings of other critics. Critics, who have for the most part examined the play rather than the film, have focused on economic questions, often reading the play's obsession with cannibalism, as well as Sebastian's "using" of people, as allegories for capitalism gone awry. Sebastian's "using" of European boys is then indistinguishable from Mrs. Venable's economic exploitation (her "using") of her town and poor relations, and Sebastian's homosexuality is, at best, incidental, and, at worst, a sign of the decadence and moral decrepitude of the (southern) upper class. (See, for example, Steven Bruhm, "Blackmailed by Sex: Tennessee Williams and the Economics of Desire," *Modern Drama* 34 (4) (December 1991), 528–537.) Such accounts often rely on an unexamined and potentially homophobic metaphor: most bluntly, they equate being exploited eco-nomically with being fucked. They assume, that is, that being the so-called passive partner in intercourse necessarily entails being disempowered. This logic (the logic, incidentally, of one reading of the castration complex) is precisely what is thrown into question by the film.

   This perspective marks even explicitly antihomophobic projects. Thus David Bergman, in "Cannibals and Queers," argues that gay writers have "transfigured" an initially homophobic "screening" of sodomy by cannibalism into a vision of sodomy as equality between men. To read *Suddenly, Last Summer* in this light, he must first argue that Sebastian's "purchase of sexual partners" is the "ultimate expression of cap-italism's decadence and corruption" (154). Sebastian's death thus becomes a reparative "sacrifice" for homo-sexuality that makes possible "equal" relations among men and atones for the Venables' exploitation of the underclasses. Bergman ends with a peculiarly impacted vision of sacrifice and redemption, destruction and grace, realized in an equalizing moment of gay male sex that surpasses and annuls the economic and sexual inequality through which it takes place. "In Tennessee Williams," he writes, cannibalism "becomes part of the metaphorical cross homosexuals have to bear, and which by confronting—even to their destruc-tion—they achieve a grace that would otherwise be excluded from them" (161). If the politics of these dyspeptic Christian metaphorics are, in themselves, somewhat unpalatable, Bergman is right, I think, to pick up on a tonality of sacrifice at the end of *Suddenly, Last Summer*, but, as I have suggested, if Sebastian's death is a sacrifice, its relation to homosexuality is more vexed than Bergman's argument suggests.

alizing cure, is similarly caught up in the reenactment of the scene of gay male sex it attempts (and does not attempt) to elide. Most overtly, the content of the memory Catherine must speak is a sodomitical encounter figured as cannibalism, and it explicitly calls to mind Mrs. Venable's description of the sea turtles, referring, for example, to the gobbling greedy little boys as a "flock of plucked birds." Catherine's story of Sebastian's death suggests that what is transferred with the male heterosexual gaze (moving from Mrs. Venable to Catherine), the desire that gives women in the film rhetorical power, is the power to speak about a scene of sodomy:

> I heard Sebastian scream. He screamed just once. [. . .] I ran. They let me run. They didn't even see me. [. . .] Cousin Sebastian . . . He . . . he was lying, naked, on the broken stones. And this you won't believe. Nobody, nobody, nobody could believe it. It looked as if, . . . as if they had devoured him. As if they had torn or cut parts of him away with their hands or with knives or those jagged tin cans they made music with. As if they had torn bits of him away and stuffed them into those gobbling mouths. There wasn't a sound any more. There was nothing. But Sebastian, Sebastian, lying on those stones, torn and crushed.

As the exorbitant emergence of an ecstatic orality, this speech marks the appearance of sodomitical rapture in the very movement that would mark its expurgation. Like the sun symbolism and the description of the Encantadas, the relations among the talking cure, the heterosexualizing cure, and the scene of cannibalism as gay sex at Cabeza de Lobo set up a slide of tropological equivalences that enacts the very disturbance the film would cure. The talking cure screens, but also figures, the heterosexualizing cure, which screens and figures the cannibalistic orgy at Cabeza de Lobo, while the slide between these terms enacts the corrosive leveling of differences in the cannibalistic act (as well as in the slide between cannibalism and gay sex).

Such a slide is also enacted in the figurative movement of Catherine's speech. The speech marks the attempt to expel the threat of sodomy by talking about it, an effort figured in Taylor's delivery of the speech: moving toward its climax, she leans over as if to vomit the line, "As if they had devoured him." This attempt to expel sodomy enacts the very confusion in orifices that sodomy itself figures, a confusion figured in the condensing here of cannibalism and sodomy in the oral and anal pleasures of gay sex. The result is the lurid unveiling of the spectacle of sodomy, which Taylor's speech enacts through the movement of its figurative language: the speech marks a literalizing of a figure—Catherine speaks of Sebastian's death "as if" he were being cannibalized until the last moment of the speech, when Sebastian's body, "torn and crushed," marks the concrete appearance of this figure in its mute and lurid materiality. In these redounding layers of unveiled spectacle, the film cavalierly gives itself away. It dramatizes its own attempt to expel the scene of sodomy and its failure to do so, scandalously placing to view, in lurid reenactment after more lurid reenactment, the spectacle of sodomitical rapture. The material remainder—Sebastian's body—attests to (and figures) the way this lurid spectacle fuels the desire of the film.

The trappings of allurement

It is thus possible to argue that *Suddenly, Last Summer* undermines determinations of difference that underlie heterosexual identification in spectatorship and, through such leveling of difference, makes visible the lurid spectacle of gay male sex. As D. A. Miller and Lee Edelman have argued, such too are the stakes of the spectacle of the primal scene, which both establishes and threatens to undermine the differential gender identity on which heterosexuality is built.[21] This differential gender identity relies on a willful act of reading, one that would sacrifice anal pleasure to the demands of the castration complex in the establishment of heterosexual masculine identity. The identification that founds gender identity might be considered one of the infant's first acts of (mis)reading, the act of (mis)reading that makes all subsequent reading possible. *Suddenly, Last Summer* allows a viewer to realize the (impossible) pleasure of seeing and experiencing the excruciating moment when the system of binary oppositions underlying gender and sexual identity, as well as hermeneutic activity and representation, starts to unravel. Such a viewer is potentially forced into the same kind of split identification that inscribed Freud in the primal scene he would theorize. The failure of "theory" to maintain its distance from that which it would theorize—figuring and enacting the hermeneutic conundrum of the primal scene itself—as well as the identificatory uncertainties highlighted in this failure of distance, is thus enacted by the kinds of spectatorial reversals engaged by the baits and lures of *Suddenly, Last Summer*. The film self-consciously stages such generalized conundrums of theoretical distance and identification as problems engaged by the act of cinematic spectatorship.

Thus the film seems to compromise straight viewers by entrapping them within a spectacle of sodomitical rapture that would unravel stable heterosexualization secured through the castration complex. The very virulence of the need to expunge gay male sexuality and to make graphically visible the punitive traces of this desire's disappearance leads to the lurid materialization of the very desire that would be expunged in a graphic and alluring imagining of a scene of gay male sex. Heterosexual acculturation thus impels what Julia Kristeva might call a "hallucination of nothing."[22] The paradoxical effect of this injunction is an intense cathexis of seeing itself—of seeing the very "nothing" that cannot be seen, the spectacular scene of (un)seen sodomy that turns heterosexual identity inside-out. The double-edged cure of *Suddenly, Last Summer* dramatizes a double bind that leads its audience to reenact its sodomitical disruptions; it attempts to cure itself and the structures of heterosexuality from the taint of sodomy by positing a putatively heterosexual object of desire for the camera, the doctor, and the audience, while realizing perhaps that this heterosexual cure implicates it in the scene of sodomitical rapture it attempts to occlude. This disruptive structure keeps replaying itself, marking one layer in the film's unfolding of repeating self-reflexive double binds.

Such is one possible reading of the lure of this film, a lure which, for the anti-homophobic spectator, potentially undermines spectatorial relations securing heterosexual positioning. Like the erotics of gazes and display in any men's locker room, however, such a reading perhaps depends on the possibility of a straight viewer who will not be scandalized at all, who will remain both secure and oblivious. Moreover, this reading perhaps depends on the imminent threat of homophobic recuperation. Thus, while it might be possible to stress the subversive potential of the constitutive failure and incoherence of the cultural narrative of heterosexuality, *Suddenly, Last Summer* demonstrates the perhaps inevitable recuperation of this disintegration through the pleasure generated by the unfolding of narrative itself. If the spectacle of gay male sex is an affront

21 See Miller, "Anal *Rope*" and Edelman, "Seeing Things."
22 See Julia Kristeva, *Powers of Horror: An Essay on Abjection*, translated by Leon S. Roudiez (New York: Columbia University Press, 1982), 42–43, 46.

to the "primary narrative"[23] that orients the straight man's sexuality, *Suddenly, Last Summer* dramatizes not only this disruption but the way that gay male sex, as a lurid and disconcerting spectacle, can be deployed.

The film's double binds, that is to say, are discomfitingly overt, and the film seems to figure sodomitical disruption and seemingly self-subverting straight implication in scenes of gay male sex as the lurid spectacle deployed as the fuel of cinematic absorption. It is not merely that the dramatization of the straight viewer's implication in these lurid and disguised spectacles of sodomy figures the spectator's losing of himself to cinematic pleasure, paradoxically guaranteeing the spectator's distance from the film by shoring up the very identity that is so rapturously to be lost. More important, perhaps, the reassurance of an antihomophobic reading lures us into a false sense of security about the ease with which the film's structure of baits and lures might be eluded. Just as the spectacle of sodomy might act as the bait that seduces the viewer into cinematic (and perhaps sodomitical) rapture, my own reading of the paradoxical structure and self-subverting heterosexualizing cure of the film seems to have been counted on by the film, and this reading may have only taken the bait.

The spectacle of sodomy is quite overtly used as bait, and sodomy, especially through the lurid sacrifice of Sebastian, lures the viewer bent on interpretation as the master key to the film. Cannibalism, madness, psychoanalysis, lobotomy, even heterosexual rape, come into legible view through the rubric of sodomy. My own argument would then seem to lure itself; having posited sodomy, it begins to see it already there, wherever it looks, and we are left with the uncanny feeling of being radically excluded from and anticipated by a film that has begun to read us. My own argument's positing of gay male sex, then, as the term that makes the film's symbolic movements legible, would merely enact the contagious tropological slide it noted within the film's structure. The reading would enact, that is, the movement of the symbolism of the white glare in the sun room and at Cabeza de Lobo, the slide from turtles to motherhood to cannibalism to gay sex in Mrs. Venable's description of the Encantadas, the slide from cannibalism to gay sex in Catherine's description of Sebastian's death, and, more generally, the slide between the lobotomy, the talking cure, the heterosexualizing cure, and the sodomitical spectacle within the film's structure. Positing gay male sex provides my argument with its own bait, and taking it starts the whole structure moving. The allure of the bait then replays the absorption that the film locates in the spectacle of gay sex as the figure for one's rapt attention to the unfolding of a narrative film.

Perhaps the only way to escape the double binds here that seem implicit not only in the baiting of the film, but perhaps in the field of visibility itself, is paradoxically to give ourselves over wholeheartedly to the film's lure, to relinquish ourselves to its blinding rapture. That would be to become Sebastian beneath the rapt and ravishing gaze of the one character perhaps left unimplicated in these multi-leveled and replaying visual binds and the madness of representation they introduce, the character who is labeled mad at the end of the film: Mrs. Venable, as she ascends to a place the camera cannot see—to whatever unspecularizable gustatory paradise forms the locus of the film's digestive *jouissance*—is, unlike the other characters and the audience of the film, left free to be blind. For the film never quite succeeds at transferring the libidinal energy from this ravishing center of blindness, a figure that forms, perhaps, the most seeing point of all.

23 See Edelman, "Seeing Things," 185.

15 Queer Bollywood, or "I'm the player, you're the naive one"

Patterns of sexual subversion in recent Indian popular cinema[1]

Thomas Waugh

Introduction: pelvic thrust, fluid terrain

Indian cinema is no doubt similar to the commercial entertainment industries that exist in many "modernizing" societies of the South, in that queer things are going on there. In fact Indian cinema has traditionally been more than hospitable to same-sex desire—regardless of the fact that it has never been so named—whether within institutions of publicity, stardom, fan culture, and reception, or within narrative worlds in which the borders around and within homosociality have always been naively and uninhibitedly ambiguous. The groundwork for a more "modern" proliferation of explicit erotic iconography—including the *homo*erotic—has been laid over the last decade: the "liberalization" of the Indian economy and the transnationalization of media have stepped up the cross-border importation of Northern erotic commodities and identity ideologies among the elites. The latest censorship brouhahas around the diasporic films *Bandit Queen* (Shekhar Kapur, 1994), *Kama Sutra* (Mira Nair, 1997), and *Fire* (Deepa Mehta, 1998) are reminders that the state censorship apparatus can hardly keep pace with, let alone contain, the proliferating sexual discourses in parallel films such as these, much less in Bollywood and regional popular cinemas. In these popular cinemas, ingredients from rape narratives and the newly merged vamp/virgin heroine to pelvic thrust dancing and "lewd" lyrics have been out of control for more than a decade.

The Indian cinema has not developed a recognizable domestic queer vector to the extent of, say, even Taiwan or the Philippines—at least "recognizable" to Northern eyes. Yet urgent critical attention is called for by the last decade's ferment within the sexual and gender discourses of Indian cinemas, and the shifting sexual alignments within the framework of masculinity that this ferment reflects. In such a complex landscape as that of contemporary Indian cinemas, there is no shortage of directions for future research. One could well explore several distinct fields:

1   The state-subsidized parallel cinema, where the bricolage of cosmopolitan queer iconographies is increasingly evident in recent films. One might have expected from the growing visibility of what Lawrence Cohen calls middle-class metropolitan

1 I am grateful to Saleem Kidwai and Dipti Gupta for having helped me navigate unsubtitled Hindi movies over the years, and to both of them as well as Shohini Ghosh, R. Raj Rao and Deepa Dhanraj for their helpful feedback on this article. "Bollywood" of course is the affectionate domestic shorthand for the commercial narrative film industry, traditionally cantered in Bombay (now Mumbai), but over the last generation spreading to the regional centers of the southern states, chiefly Madras (now Chennai) and Hyderabad.

movements and identities, especially in Mumbai and the other large urban areas, that they would have made more and earlier inroads into the parallel cinemas rooted in these urban cultures. But the parallel cinemas until very recently were remarkable for their timidity, no doubt stemming as much from the self-censorship and stagnation that marks this traditionally social realist sector, dependent on government bureaucrats, as from the tenuousness of those "imported" identities. Nevertheless, an increased momentum is hopefully augured by a whole slew of recent parallel works, however anxious and tentative they sometimes seem: Riyad Wadia's self-financed and anomalous 1996 short, *Bomgay*, fascinating for its recognizably cosmopolitan urban queer landscapes and identities (but an essentialist and reductive translation of R. Raj Rao's defiantly queer poetry); and the feature films *English August* (Dev Benegal, 1996), *Daayra* (*The Square Circle*, Amol Palekar, 1997), *Adhura* (Ashish Nagpal, 1996), *Darmiyaan* (*In Between*, Kalpana Lajmi, 1997), and *Karvaan* (*Shadows in the Dark*, Pankaj Butalia, 1999).

2 The diasporic cinema, which must rightly be seen for fifteen years now as a laboratory where the sexual discourses of metropolitan South Asian cultures are unpacked with a freedom and energy unknown at home. The dialogue between metropolitan and diasporic discourses is increasing, as is evidenced by the huge impact of Deepa Mehta's ongoing work.

3 The independent documentary cinema, which over the last two decades has amply documented the overall crisis in gender politics that is the necessary context for the findings of this chapter, while it has studiously avoided, true to its puritanical Griersonian heritage, the sexual subversions this crisis entails even when they have been staring it in the face. (The authoritarian voiceovers and expository rhetorics of mainstream documentary still largely preside over a political hierarchy in which the subjective and personal are overridden by collective agendas.[2]) Recently, tentative suggestions that this may be changing may be found in such works as Deepa Dhanraj's *Something Like a War* (1991), a film featuring an interclass women's "consciousness raising" group exploring sexual practices and fantasies; Balan's *Male Flower* (*Aan Poove*), a 1996 video documentary on a female-to-male transsexual in Kerala; Shyamal Karmakar's pioneering *Myths—A Dialogue on AIDS* (*Kimvad antiya*) on people with HIV in Madhya Pradesh (1994); and most recently *Summer in my Veins*, Nishit Saran's autobiographical coming out video of 1999.

4 The problematic of female homosociality and lesbian countercurrents across the cinematic landscape as a whole. This problematic is distinct from that of gay male and male homosocial discourses (although *Fire* has demonstrated a certain level of inextricability), given the male domination of both the cinematic apparatus and the public sphere of South Asian society as a whole, where male sexual expression straight or queer is the common currency of the realm, and female sexual expression is a highly charged and continuously challenged "problem" as well as a potent but invisible parallel, private sphere (as Dhanraj's work has suggested). This problematic has been broached with very interesting results by such critics as Ruth Vanita

---

2 For an exploration of a generation in revolt against the post-Independence documentary of the government Films Division, modeled both institutionally and aesthetically after John Grierson's imperial antecedents, see my "'Words of Command': Notes on Cultural and Political Inflections of Direct Cinema in Indian Independent Documentary," *Cineaction!* (Toronto), 23 (Winter 1990–91), 28–39.

and Shohini Ghosh; thus my decision to focus exclusively on male–male patterns of desire and exchange in the present forum, however regrettable, is appropriate both intellectually and strategically.[3]

But since this brief chapter has the space to explore only one direction, I will concentrate on the profuse and richly ambiguous indigenous male–male sexual iconographies in commercial popular narratives of Bollywood cinema of the 1990s, and explore others of these four directions in future work.

In this task, I have found little help in postcolonial theory, which I find all too often constrained by frameworks of race, class, and gender which cannot account fully for sex, indispensable as they are. Much of the theoretical attention to postcolonial culture and politics I find still squeamish by and large about same-sex practice or identities,[4] and much of the recent proliferation of breakthrough scholarship on Indian popular cinemas hardly less so. These two literatures I find limited in their applicability to a navigation of queer and homosocial South Asian textual practices; hence my own bricolage of eclectic sources ranging from Foucault to diasporic queer journalism to first-person narratives to literary fiction. However, for this initial scouting of the territory, I am most indebted, paradoxically, to ethnography, that most colonially constructed of disciplines. In particular here I rely most on queer American anthropologist Lawrence Cohen for having staked it out in terms of lived experience in two seminal articles on "third gender" and homoerotic political caricature respectively, based on field research in Varanasi.[5] This work confirms how helpful queer ethnography can be in its insistence on seeing sex where other disciplines see only the mantra of race, class, and gender, bound by their institutional genealogies of literary analysis or socio-political theory. Cohen's salutary stress on the local and corporal stakes of such research, real places and real bodies, is a lesson for our study of images and fantasies, reminding us of the importance of the sexed spectatorial body in the darkened cinema whether in Varanasi or Patiala. (A personal digression may be necessary to explain why I make symbolic use of this Punjabi city, where I once enjoyed many a movie, both Hindi and "English" [foreign], to keep alive a memory that I suppose is the genesis of this article, and to remind us of the strategic importance yet elusive substance of spectatorship. As a then closeted 22-year-old volunteer English teacher in advanced culture shock, I retreated in 1970 or 1971 to a Sunday showing of then closeted Franco Zeffirelli's *Romeo and Juliet*. All I

---

3 Ruth Vanita was a principal film critic for the Delhi feminist magazine *Manushi* in the 1980s and is co-editor with Saleem Kidwai of the anthology *Same-Sex Love in India: Readings from Literature and History* (New York: St. Martin's Press, 2000). For Shohini Ghosh's work, see "The Cult of Madhuri," *Gentleman* (Mumbai), October 1998, 26–28; "From the Frying Pan to the Fire," *Communalism Combat* (New Delhi), January 1999, 16–19; "The Troubled Existence of Sex and Sexuality: Feminists Engage with Censorship," in Christiane Brosius and Melissa Butcher, eds, *Image Journeys: Audio-Visual Media and Cultural Change in India* (New Delhi: Sage, 1999), 233–259.

4 An exception to the "squeamish" rule is Margaret Jolly and Lenore Manderson, eds, *Sites of Desire, Economies of Pleasure: Sexualities in Asia and the Pacific* (Chicago and London: University of Chicago Press, 1997). Symptomatically, this rich interdisciplinary collection has no South Asian content.

5 Lawrence Cohen, "Holi in Banaras and the *Mahaland* of Modernity," *GLQ* 2 (4) (1995), 399–424; "The Pleasures of Castration: The Postoperative Status of Hijras, Jankhas, and Academics," in Paul Abramson and Steven Pinkerton, eds, *Sexual Nature Sexual Culture* (Chicago: University of Chicago Press, 1995), 276–403. The holy city of Banaras on the River Ganga was called "Benares" by the British and usually "Varanasi" in post-Independence Indian English. Its inhabitants are called "Banarsi".

remember is the moment Leonard Whiting's Romeo unveiled his glorious buttocks, and the pandemonium that broke out in the theatre at that sight, a cacophony of male voices catcalling hysterically from galleries and stalls alike, letting me in on a certain disturbance around male sexuality and masculinity that was already in motion.)

I take to heart the cautionary methodological notes Cohen has sounded, though they are less easy to honor in the cultural studies field, where hybridity is the object, than in ethnographic research, where cultural purity somehow too often remains the unspoken agenda. He warns that we must avoid reducing our analysis "to a set of categories and incitements all too easily grounded in a globalizing heterosexual/homosexual opposition"; we must further avoid immobilizing this exploration "within a set of static tableaux frequently trotted out when Indian and sexual difference are narratively linked,"[6] specifically:

1   the disproportionate focus on the easy target of the hijra, the highly visible intersex persona often called a "eunuch" in English, whose public claim to difference in the Indian public sphere has been the dream of every Northern anthropologist and gay liberationist, "essentialized icons of India."[7] But the hijra has also recently become a Bollywood stock character, the most clamorous marker of sexual stirrings of the nineties screen, replacing perhaps the female avenger of the eighties as a cinematic weathervane, and I therefore cannot avoid coming back to this figure and her related brothers and sisters in a moment.

2   A second must to avoid: the unbalanced syndrome of colonial homoerotics inherited from Northern queer writers such as E. M. Forster. I am afraid this prohibition is equally impossible, and not only because I must confess at the outset my unquenchable Forsterian lust for three successive generations of Bollywood beefcake, tainted with Orientalist objectification and First World intellectual tourism, culminating in Akshay Kumar (Fig. 15.1). (Even within colonial cultural studies, the Forster and J. R. Ackerley connections are far from exhausted, given that the silencing of homosexual cultures and histories has only ended recently and there is still much catching up to do.) But in general, more seriously, representations of sexuality in the South cannot be artificially isolated from their historical backdrop of colonial relations. If all Northern discourses of the South are intrinsically founded on desire for the Other—in fact all intercultural knowledges—there is also, for all this imbalance, much reciprocity in the erotics and homoerotics of these discourses and knowledges. It would be absurd to dismiss the core of subaltern agency in the Hindophone audience's traditional obsession for the aura of the foreign in Bollywood delineations of sexuality, in the Calcutta johns' demands for blow jobs inspired by smuggled porn mags, which the sex workers are said to call "English sex," and in the craving by Indian Anglophone queers for diasporic and "foreign" knowledges, networks and bodies. Traditionally it is the parallel cinema rather than Bollywood that has broached most explicitly the colonial or transcultural sexualities in question, at least in constrained historiographical and literary generic form, but, as I have said, my excursion there must be undertaken at another time.

6   "Holi," 401, 422 n. 5.
7   "Pleasures," 279.

Figure 15.1 Beefcake poster of star Akshay Kumar: phallic coding and fan culture is more than hospitable to same-sex desire. Unidentified fan poster, collection of the author

3   Thirdly, Cohen's caution about domestic queer cravings, in terms namely of middle-class metropolitan movements and identities—which I shall henceforth call MMMIs—and their marginality to the larger landscape, is a useful one. Here again, I have to confess, the flesh is weak, for these cravings have provided me with the South Asian informants, networks, translators and, yes, friends and lovers without whom I would and could not have undertaken this research. In the MMMI dynamic, the incredibly lively diasporic queer movement has been deeply implicated. Diasporic queer culture, profoundly inflected by the MMMIs of its various host cultures, is a key presence on the global mediascape of South Asian sexuality—and not only among Anglophone elites, foreign-returned and otherwise. It inventories and dissects, interpellates and reclaims from its partial distance that which is unspoken back home up close, those alibis and buried energies of the metropolitan homosocial.[8] Indeed I am indebted to the brilliant listmaking of Aniruddh Chawda of *Trikone* for transmitting in print the obsessive oral culture of queer Bollywood

8 Gayatri Gopinath's paper, "Queer Diasporas: Alternative Sexualities and Popular Indian Cinema," presented at the same 1998 Society for Cinema Studies conference in San Diego where this presentation was originally tried out, focused on and provided a challenging assessment of diasporic iconography.

spectatorship, the Wisconsin diasporic proclaiming the canons that I have heard only excitedly whispered in Delhi.[9]

In insisting on methodological rigor and cultural integrity in transcultural studies of sexuality, one must not go so far as to assume the mythical purity of sexual cultures hermetically sealed from all external interaction—across class as well as cultural boundaries. And in assessing the marginality and privilege of MMMI cultures, one must not go so far as to deny either the indigenous cultural authenticity or the agency of those extensive communities inhabiting those cultures. We must not forget what Margaret Jolly and Lenore Manderson call "the deep histories of sexual contact and erotic entanglement between Europeans and 'others' . . . cross-cultural *exchanges* in sexualities— exchanges in meanings and fantasies as well as the erotic liaisons of bodies . . . 'sites of desire' formed by confluences of cultures, be they the tidal waves of European colonialism or the smaller eddies of sexual contacts and erotic imaginings created between cultures . . . this border crossing, this fluid terrain in the exchange of desires . . ."[10] Within the fluid terrain of a South Asian mediascape where Michael Jackson is demonstrably one of the most important choreographic influences of the last generation, and where Australian cricketers are the idols of millions of boys and men who have never spoken a word of English in their lives, who can say where the imported MMMIs end and the indigenous authentic begins?

Men with heart: neo-cons, buddies, and marginals

Arriving then at the principal task prescribed by Cohen, that is, the "local delineation of hegemonic forms of homosociality and of the multiple sites, modes and practices of their subversion, introjection and collapse,"[11] this is clearly a job for an observer of the popular cinema, despite the foregoing methodological traps. For Bollywood, in its incoherently heteroglossic and enigmatic spontaneity, its compulsive flirtations with the forbidden and addiction to the familiar, its foundation on same-sex audience formations, in Patiala as elsewhere, has always been the ideal locus for crystallizing the cultures of homosociality, both textually and contextually. The discourses of male bonding, mentorship, friendship, violence, rivalry over and sharing of women—in short of homosocial desire—cement this cinema across every generic category from multi-starrer action flick to social/family melodrama, and constitute a rich, volatile, and pluralistic site for recent unsettlings and resettlings.

Consider within this fluid or rather turbulent terrain of 1990s Bollywood, three parallel generic dynamics, each soliciting a specific audience constructed along gender and class lines, but all bound together in inextricable discursive alliance.

1   The resurgence of **neo-conservative romances** like the megahits *Hum Apke Hain Kaun* (What Am I to You?, Sooraj Barjatya, 1994) and *Dilwale Dulhaniya le Jayenge*

9 Aniruddh Chawda, "Cracks in the Tinsel Closet," *Trikone* (January 1996), 25–29; "Entering the Third Dimension" *Trikone* (April 1996), 18.

10 M. Jolly and L. Manderson, "Introduction: Sites of Desire/Economies of Pleasure in Asia and the Pacific," in *Sites of Desire*, 1.

11 Cohen, "Holi," 401.

(literally, Men with Heart Take the Bride, Aditya Chopra, 1995), which endlessly spectacularize and celebrate the rituals and resolutions of traditional marriages and families, and whose spinoffs are still piling up in 2000 without any sign of letting up. These films feature not so much the *new* man (since Indian male stars have always had permission to weep and recite poetry) as the revival of more traditional romantic conceptions of gender roles, the romantic hero having edged out the super-man rebel of the seventies and eighties as the most saleable icon of the nineties. At least seventies star rebel Amitabh Bachchan would have got angry in every film rather than ask parental permission to marry as these timid films would have his compliant successors do.[12] The mild gender transgression afforded by the neo-con films' resort to the occasional opportunity for comic drag interludes and pumped up beefcake is small compensation indeed (In the latest *Dilwale* spinoff hit, *Hum Dil De Chuke Sanam* [Straight from the Heart, Sanjay Leela Bhansali, 1999], buff and chiseled Salman Khan spends virtually the first half of the movie naked, but the whole thing ends up affirming arranged marriages, parental tyranny, and female sacrifice all the same).

2   **Male friendship films**: the growing ambiguity and complexity, playfulness and boldness, of this traditional homosocial formula *par excellence* become increasingly self-conscious, even parodic, in such films as *Main Khiladi Tu Anari* (I'm the Player, You're the Naive One, Sameer Malkan, 1994). The formula is often syncretized with the heterosexual neo-romances, though women's roles in the male bonding films are maintained only to the degree necessary to offset panic and maintain the momentum of the star system.

3   The new **sexual marginality film** of the nineties. This pattern encompasses several subgenres, most notably

– the action films where transgenders and more "recognizable" gay men have emerged as charismatic film-stealing villains (as in *Mast Kalandar* [Ballad of Intoxicating Joy, Rahul Rawail, 1989] or *Sadak* [Mahesh Bhatt, 1991] respectively);

– the melodramas with hijras as matriarchal heroines or supporting players, such as *Bombay* (Mani Rathnam, 1994) and *Yaarana* (Comradeship, David Dhawan, 1995). *Adhura*, a TV melodrama, even has a MMMI-constructed gay man as hero. And all this is not to mention, of course, a multiplication of old-fashioned comic cross-dressing in romances and comedies; for example, veteran bit-part comic Rajendra Nath's flaming character in *Raja Hindustani* (1997), the latest in a hoary comic tradition of epicene sidekicks and minor characters. Despite Cohen's warning, I see the hijra (and her sisters and brothers, for they are interchangeable on a certain level, as neither filmmakers or non-hijra spectators make the sharp taxonomical distinctions made by hijras themselves) as an emblematic sign of something stirring, beyond her former *Mrs. Doubtfire*[13] role of maintaining rigid sexual difference. The hijra can now be promoted from her previous status as background figure or low comic diversion—a status still maintained in many films, incidentally—to the complementary narrative functions of supermenace or supermother.

12   See Ashwani Sharma, "Blood, Sweat and Tears: Amitabh Bachchan, Urban Demi-God," in Pat Kirkham and Janet Thumin, eds, *You Tarzan: Masculinity, Movies and Men* (New York: St. Martin's Press, 1993), 167–180.
13   Interestingly, knockoffs of *Mrs. Doubtfire* have now appeared in both Tamil and Hindi.

Figure 15.2 Paresh Rawal as hijra supermother Tikoo in the hit melodrama *Tamanna* (depicted with real-life Tikoo, right). Courtesy of *Trikone*, April 1996

Hijra Tikoo, melo supermother

Let us linger briefly in this melodramatic landscape of the heart, before circling back to the male buddy action territory. The most interesting of several key films of the nineties, *Tamanna*, Mahesh Bhatt's 1996 hit (reportedly based on a real story), can be seen as a melo hybrid of *Les Cages aux folles* and *Stella Dallas*, in which Paresh Rawal stars as Tikoo (Fig. 15.2), an adopting hijra parent to an ingenue romantic heroine, Tamanna. This film is intensely and explicitly linked, perhaps not so paradoxically, to the cinematic reaffirmation of kinship happening elsewhere at the box office, for it details the adopted daughter's fanatical search for and confrontation with her supervillain biological father and suffering biological mother before returning to embrace her alternative family. Tikoo is sanitized to be sure, despite the grating shriek of her disembodied voice. She refuses to belong to the more flamboyant sisterhood of the streets, now that she has a daughter to bring up within the respectable institutions of the middle classes, as the narrative repeatedly makes clear, and her former sisters in struggle are bitchily disdainful of what they see as her treacherous upward mobility. Interestingly, Tamanna finds out the truth about her adoptive parent only when the class contradictions become fiercer than the contradictions within the gender/sex system: Tikoo has had to go back on hijra dancing duty to keep her daughter in her posh private school, and can't cover all her tracks well enough. Gay and lesbian Indian observers have found it especially significant that Tikoo has an implied domestic partner/boyfriend in the person of a Muslim shopkeeper named Saleem, an additional trope of social subversion and reconciliation—across religious communal boundaries this time—which cements the alternative familial structure to which Tamanna will eventually return at the film's happy end.[14]

Other transgendered characters, minor in most cases, have appeared in at least two other melodramas hinged on exacerbated class violence, *Bombay* and *Raja Hindustani*, and one wonders if their supporting dramatic role in these films, as well as in *Tamanna*, somehow partakes of the traditional hijra ritual function as social mediator of hetero-conjugality (especially at births and weddings). In any case, Tikoo deftly encapsulates popular culture's problematization of sexuality, family, and gender in one overdetermined body and vividly performs its interpenetration with socio-economic dynamics and class anger. Is Tikoo, the angry and tender castrated mother, the rebel Amitabh of the nineties?

Akshay and Saïf: homo play

I now want to leave aside the female generic framework of the social melodrama, where sexual otherness seems to cohabit the traditional familial sex–gender system without too much stress, and circle back to the male genres, the friendship and action films, starting specifically with *Main Khiladi*. An action film, I said, but it's really a male romance in more respectable guise. This 1994 hit is a *Lethal Weapon*-style buddy-buddy caper film, starring my Akshay as a macho but upright cop and Saïf Ali Khan as a decadent movie star recruited to his gangster-busting activity (Fig. 15.3).[15] Along with *Tamanna*, *Main Khiladi* has been widely recognized as the most vivid site of big things happening, both by the Mumbai gay circle around the magazine *Bombay Dost* and by local and foreign queer academics.

On screen, the two stars Akshay and Saïf enact male companionship at its most playful and physical, and symmetrically embody antinomies of masculine style and identity that replicate gender difference on the homosocial axis. In the Akshay vs. Saïf opposition, we have the not unfamiliar oppositions of

butch vs. dandy
lean vs. pudgy
hairy vs. smooth
square vs. odalisque
Hindu vs. Muslim
fighter vs. dancer
naked vs. clothed
mature vs. ephebe
authentic vs. glamorous
techno-warrior vs. hysterical klutz

14 Ruth Vanita, "Trauma of Being 'Different,'" unidentified English-language Indian press clipping, c. 1996, kindly provided by the author; Saleem Kidwai, unidentified publication in Indian English-language media, c. 1996, manuscript kindly provided by the author.
15 *Main Khiladi* was so successful that it led to the sequel *Tu Chor Main Sipahi* (You're the Thief, I'm the Officer, 1998), in which Akshay Kumar reprised his role but Saïf Ali Khan apparently thought better of the idea.

Figure 15.3 Akshay Kumar and Saïf Ali Khan in *Main Khiladi Tu Anari:* homosocial male romance and playful antinomies of masculine erotic style

teetotaler prude vs. promiscuous drunk
self-controlling law-enforcer vs. impulsive actor
heterosocial vs. homosocial
family man vs. bachelor (with valet!)
offscreen cockteasing vs. offscreen homosexual panic

Offscreen? The plot thickens: offscreen, a third party was recruited to cement a three-way confrontation between *three* modes of masculine desire. *Bombay Dost* interviewed Akshay Kumar and got him to acknowledge and welcome his gay fans, running a beef-cake pic of him in a towel alongside (Fig. 15.4).[16] But this baring of onscreen dynamics was one kind of fan discourse that got Saïf so very very upset that he punched out the gay critic who spoke the unspoken, Ashok Row Kavi, journalist and intellectual, the most visible homo in India, and very epitome of MMMI.[17] If Saïf was protesting too much

---

16 Reported in *Trikone* 12 (2) (April 1997), 13. I am told that Saïf suffered homophobic fan gossip at the time of his marriage earlier in his career.

17 See such publications as Kavi's "The Contract of Silence," in Khushwant Singh and Shobha Dé, eds, *Uncertain Liaisons: Sex, Strife and Togetherness in Urban India* (New Delhi: Viking Penguin, 1993), 147–174; the Saïf incident was reported by Chawda in "Cracks," 26.

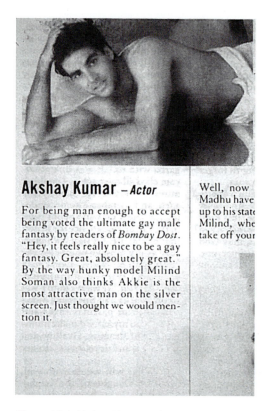

Akshay Kumar *– Actor*

For being man enough to accept being voted the ultimate gay male fantasy by readers of *Bombay Dost*. "Hey, it feels really nice to be a gay fantasy. Great, absolutely great." By the way hunky model Milind Soman also thinks Akkie is the most attractive man on the silver screen. Just thought we would mention it.

Well, now Madhu have up to his stat Milind, whe take off your

Figure 15.4 Akshay Kumar in his towel acknowledging his gay fans, seen through queer diasporic eyes. Courtesy of *Trikone*, April 1996

in his offscreen macho role, it may be because onscreen he personified his half of the romance with winking gusto, far beyond the call of duty, expressing an adolescent crush on the macho cop with a wide-eyed "Wow!" at each one of his martial feats, and sharing practical jokes, jealousy fits, touching and cuddling with his co-star throughout. The two men also traffic in women, or at least, Saïf acts as mediator between Akshay and leading lady Basanti, actively orchestrating their courtship by liquoring up the upright cop who would otherwise not succumb. (Akshay wakes up naked and disoriented [as I did after the screening], wondering whether he has drunkenly deflowered the virginal Basanti, leading, for me at least, to the question of who had disrobed him and put him to bed, and to a comparison with the role drunkenness plays in Northern coming out narratives.) The role of panderer is reversed in the musical number, as we shall see.

The jokey juvenilization of the male figures in this friendship narrative is a standard dynamic with almost all unmarried male characterization in Bollywood representation— as if homosocial play is OK among kids and heterosexual marriage soberly awaits them when they grow up. This is inscribed most vividly and symptomatically in the musical dance duet the two heroes perform. Musical numbers in the nineties still crystallize much of the creative and technical energy of the Bollywood apparatus (followed closely by combat scenes and other spectacle set pieces). The *Main Khiladi* duet, acquiring even more significance as the title piece of this film, is situated about a third of the way into the narrative. The heroes have just had a little spat, sensitive Saïf makes Akshay beg forgiveness for some childish offense or other, and the two tearfully reconcile through a hug with Saïf caressing Akshay's hair, cheeks and ears, staring into his eyes. At this point the musical number literally bursts onto the screen and none too soon, preventing the kiss that reasonable spectators—at least I—might have expected logically to ensue. The song's function is thus not only to consolidate, probe, and ultimately celebrate the friendship that is at the core of the film, but also to deflect any inappropriate inference. The initial discourse of the lyrics is about the two friends' individual uniqueness as "player" and "naive one" respectively. This discourse of friendship, initiated by Akshay's singing, admits to occasional quarrels, which are mockingly reenacted throughout the rest of the song, and which seemingly have the same role that conflict has as a dramatic obstacle in Northern narratives of heteroconjugality. This friendship discourse is nonetheless somewhat paradoxical, since most of the lyrics sung by Saïf in answer are sidetracked by the problematic of women. Saïf exults in the uncontrollable "firecrackers" that he feels in the presence of the red cheeks and slim waists of attractive women, whom he wants to kiss and eventually live happily ever after with. We're thus back to the familiar homosocial triangle, for Akshay has to share his volatile buddy with the girls.[18] The two discourses alternate, the interrogative musing about the origins of such strong heterosexual attraction vs. its implications for male homosocial commitment, the hope that Saïf's attraction to women, seen as uncontrollable and puerile, will not interfere with their mutual recognition of each other as friends.

Within the choreography as well, a dialogue between male friendship and distracting heterosexual courtship unfolds. The lines of female chorines, jerking and galloping, posing and pouting, however vivid in their red and yellow sequined tutus and tights, are strictly backdrop to the performance, lyrical and dance, by the male duet, amazingly athletic and unrestrained in their interaction with each other. (Such a male–male dance duet has been absolutely inconceivable within Hollywood culture since at least the early fifties male duets of Fred Astaire and Gene Kelly, etc.). At one point Akshay sets up Saïf with a chorine, and resumes the tolerant exasperation that he displays at several points in the number whenever his impulsive buddy gets waylaid with his rivals. Often, their interaction is strictly macho, faux pugilistic, or competitive.

At other times the choreography is a surrogate for courtship behavior: Akshay lifts Saïf at the hips and carries him down the chorus line toward the camera; later the supine Saïf, seen laterally, thrusts his groin upwardly toward the center of the frame, while Akshay, standing above him, is making similar pelvic thrusts toward the camera, so that the low angle perspective of the frame brings their thrusts together; toward the end of the number, the two dancers face each other and grasp each other's shoulders and Saïf walks backwards vertically up a handy pillar, supported by Akshay, as the two maintain eye contact. They literally can't keep their hands off each other: Akshay puts his tie on Saïf, slaps his ass, even seems to touch his groin. But it is the larger, symmetrical bodily movements themselves that most play up the physical intimacy of the friendship bond, as they high kick in sync and prance together down the gauntlet of nautch girls.

18 Homosocial triangulation is a narrative structure that is arguably more prevalent in Bollywood than in Hollywood, Howard Hawks notwithstanding, with many precedents ranging from Raj Kapoor's classic *Sangam* (1964) to Surendra Mohan's Hindu–Muslim variation in *Aap Ke Deewane* (You Are My Everything, 1980).

How can we account for all of the winking that is going on, who is doing it with/to whom, and on how many levels—choreographer? songwriter? performers? director? spectators? In comparison, an earlier generation's epochal male duet, "Yeh Dosti" (This friendship), sung between Dharmendra and Amitabh Bachchan in *Sholay* (1975), evoked univocal innocence and crystalline unself-consciousness. In that pioneering "curry western" megahit, the duet took place on a motorcycle and sidecar, occupied alternately by the star duo, who clutch and caress each other's hands, shoulders, head and thighs more consistently than the handlebars, all the while excitedly declaiming,

> We vow to remain friends;
> We'd rather die than sever our friendship.
> Your victory is my victory,
> Your defeat is mine as well.
> Your distress I share
> Just as you share my joy.
> Our love is reciprocal.
> At the risk of my life, for your sake
> I'd incur the enmity of others.
> Though two in body
> We're one in soul—
> Never shall we be separated.
> We eat and drink together
> We'll live and die together.

No need for disavowal and deflection here. A mid-song interlude suffices, where a winsome village woman, complete with water jar, flirts with the two singers at the roadside and the two briefly compete with each other over who goes first—before jointly abjuring hetero skirtchasing in deference to male friendship. The whole song bursts with the freedom of the road, the luxury of the landscape, and the physical exultation in male bonding—the final stanza has Dharmendra perched on Amitabh's sturdy shoulders as the two ride off into the horizon. There is perhaps no better index of Bollywood's evolution between the seventies and the nineties than the comparison of this *anari* duet with the *khiladi* duet twenty years later. Both articulate an over-the-top playfulness, but *Main Khiladi* adds layers of winking semiotic play to the layers of musical and choreographic play.

I am not arguing that play is the alibi for same-sex desire in any simple way (though it may well be on some level in the latter case). Rather I am seeing in these duets an echo and confirmation of Cohen's finding that play, whether corporal, social, or semiotic, is a prevalent axis of same-sex desire in North Indian homosocial culture, along which the gradations between sociality and eroticism are both relative and finely coded. Participant-observed by Cohen in the "real world" of friendship networks and cruising parks of Varanasi, this axis of erotic play is allowable both there and in Bollywood's parallax world because situated within a predominantly heterosexual framework:

> Most of the Banarsi men I know [situated on this axis] . . . focus their erotic attention on women. Their *nazar*, their desiring look or gaze, rests more often on the passing bodies of women than of men. But of this "mostness," this majority, those I know well have played with other men from time to time, in adolescence or on

occasion thereafter. These men speak about same-sex sex and desire in two ways. Intimately, among family and close friends of one's generation, sex is play, or *Khel*. It is about joking around and about friendship, *Dosti*. Different men may articulate the boundaries of friendship and play differently. For most, penetrative sex is seldom an idiom of play and in fact marks its boundary. The boys and (to a lesser extent) men who play around with friends their own age and of similar background must negotiate this mutual terrain of play.[19]

No wonder Saïf panicked when the most famous homosexual in India trumpeted out his onscreen "play" as something un-playlike—stigmatized, foreign, penetrative, and very serious!

Maharani and Pinko: homo violence

Cohen's other axis of same-sex desire is also very serious, associated with the adult world, involving power dynamics of violence, often intergenerational, that can also be detected and confirmed in the movies, specifically in the action pictures:

Less intimately, framed within the world of older and younger or more and less politically powerful men, sex between men is about violence, manliness, and dependency. Dependency can be framed positively or negatively, but the language of most men, including many of those who regularly cruise for sex in the city's parks, is a negative language of using and getting used, of the law of the fishes: eat or be eaten . . . the bodily violence of social difference that frames the alien Other as one who must take his desire through you or be taken by yours.[20]

The intergenerational dynamic is transferred to the cinematic universe primarily in the conventional character of the elder gangster supervillain, usually inspired by the Northern James-Bond-style megalomaniac bad guy, who with snarling excess traditionally hounds the toothsome young heroes to the final conflagration. And indeed in *Main Khiladi*, the villain sends his humungous Mohawked henchman to mow down Akshay with his monstrous phallic gun at the very climax of the cabaret duet *jouissance*—now that's disavowal! Akshay and Saïf may escape that one, but eventually both take their turn to be done *to* at the end of *Main Khiladi*: Saïf is tied to a chair like Pearl White, but the bare-chested Akshay is suspended by his wrists above a frothing pit in an endless display of nude masochistic suffering.[21] The escalation of male nudity seems to be part of the male friendship/male violence formulas, for this is not the first time that Bollywood has saved the naked star torso for an ultimate fleshly mortification and spectatorial delectation at the climax. Leading man Sanjay Dutt gets a similar moment, literally crucified, at the end of *Sadak*, and it is to this somewhat nastier action film, similarly set within Mumbai's gangster/smuggler milieu, that I would now like to turn.

---

19 "Holi," 417.
20 Ibid.
21 Does the fact that Akshay has his luxuriant armpits shaved and unshaved in alternating shots in this suspension scene signify anything more than Bollywood's traditional contempt for continuity and its delectation for frequent costume changes within a single "number"? A subject for further research.

Figure 15.5 *Sadak*: Sadashiv Amrapurkar as rampaging and phallic hijra supervillain Maharani
and the cowering institution of heterosexuality she's out to get (video jacket)

Sadak's villain is the implausibly rampaging and phallic hijra pimp Maharani, played by Sadashiv Amrapurkar (Fig. 15.5). Maharani clearly embodies Cohen's second model of desire, despite her dubious gender credentials. No doubt hijras are associated, in popular culture as well as in anthropological research, with prostitution, but the character of megapimp Maharani is more than an ethnographic treatise. She is so successful in performing the contradictory horror and attraction of the same-sex violence model that the narrative incoherence of her role as simultaneous penetrator and penetratee hardly matters. Maharani's setpieces are neither Tikoo's hysterical revelations nor Akshay's musical extravaganzas, rather monumental concatenations of over-the-top menace and violence, wreaked with weaponry that seems even more parodically phallic than the usual Bollywood variety. In one endlessly protracted scene for example, the quivering Sanjay and his ingenue co-star flee Maharani's rage and super-shotgun in an underground parking garage, as if it is the institution of heterosexuality itself that is her target. Honored by the Indian Oscar equivalent, the *Filmfare* Award, Maharani's ferocious charisma, bedecked with as many signs of revolt and marginality as jewelry and makeup, clearly constitutes what we used to call within MMMIs a negative image.

So does Pinko. Of all the queer villains of the last decade, the charismatic male-gender-identified villain of *Mast Kalandar*, incarnated by respected and popular

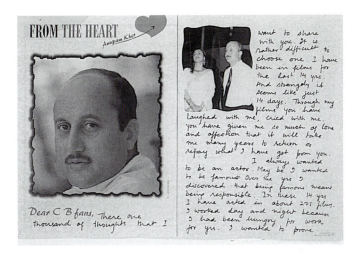

FROM THE HEART

Anupam Kher

want to share with you. It is rather difficult to choose one. I have been in films for the last 14 yrs. And strangely it seems like just 14 days. Through my films you have laughed with me, cried with me, you have given me so much of love and affection that it will take me many years to return or repay what I have got from you. I always wanted to be an actor. May be I wanted to be famous. Over the yrs I discovered that being famous means being responsible. In these 14 yrs I have acted in about 275 films. I worked day and night because I had been hungry for work for yrs. I wanted to prove

Dear C B fans, There are thousand of thoughts that I

Figure 15.6 Star fan profile of Anupam Kher: "serious" heterosexual construction of actor who was catapulted to fame playing swishy queer villains. Courtesy of *CineBlitz* (Bombay)

"character star" Anupam Kher (Fig. 15.6),[22] is the presence most closely matching the MMMI stereotype. A middle-aged man with shaved skull and mustache who is set up as a weak daddy's boy to his supervillain father, Pinko has what it takes and flaunts it as defiantly as any hijra—but as a swishy man rather than as a crossdresser. Pinko openly comes on to men onscreen, namely the other minor character actors who are put in place as his "love interest," fellow villain Prem Chopra and ineffectual corrupt cop Shakti Kapoor, since the leading man is apparently off-limits. Pinko may be effeminate, but like the Kali-esque Maharani, he is full of cinematic and sexual power, heir to generations of cabaret bad girls who always used to lose the hero and often their lives but win the movie. Pinko has one show-stopping setpiece, predictably a cabaret scene not dissimilar to that which would show up in *Main Khiladi*, for cabarets have been the site of exotic (i.e., Northern) and illicit sexualities since the colonial period. Here Pinko is most associated with the modes of parody, excess, and reversal, an interesting analogue to Northern camp sensibilities. Flouncing across the parking lot for his cabaret scene, irrepressible in his pink suit and jewelry, Pinko is already singing the parody of a Bollywood torchsong standard, reversing the pronouns. On the way he has to berate two women onlookers for making fun of him, asking them if they don't have brothers at home and are not ashamed to tease a man in public. More love-song parodies ensue once inside the club, with Pinko leading a full-blown gender-reversal version of "Ik Do Tinn (One, two, three)," a famous hit song about a female singer's passion, seconded by lineups of waiters/chorus boys in yellow satin shirts. The outrageous parodies of

22 *Trikone* has for some time had its approving eye on the subsequent career of Kher who seems in danger of typecasting: in *Zamana Deewana* (Ramesh Sippy, 1995) he plays "a bumbling police detective, who resorts to drag to establish a truce between quarreling old-time (and old) friends, Jeetendra and Shatrughan Sinha." There is also a dream sequence that shows Kher in "gorgeous outfits" doing a slow dance first with one then the other. The 1994 Filmfare awards also featured him in drag (Chawda, "Cracks," 28).

conventions continue to pile up in the number, e.g., a poker game where Pinko winkingly wonders whether he'll get the king, sitting in the lap of his anointed, poor frazzled Prem. The comedy of gender reversal is a standard in Bollywood, as in many popular cultural forms around the world, but here the inflection is pushed to the limit of sexualized marginality, in opposition to the commoner sanitized version.

In the final scene, Pinko naturally gets his comeuppance. But as a relatively harmless second-string villain, he is only jailed rather than blasted to smithereens like Maharani, and in any case is happy to end up in jail with his love interest. He winks boldly at the audience through the cell bars in the last shot of the film, signaling his amorous intentions with regard to his cellmate. *Mast Kalandar* may be one of the earlier films to wink this boldly, to deploy knowingly a postmodern multiple address of this kind: such an excessive invocation of MMMI codes implies a familiarity with them in at least part of the audience, and for spectators not familiar with Northern images of homosexuality, the film is content to transmit a generalized polyvocal message of illicit, exotic sexual thrills—and unabashed, slapstick cinematic pleasure.

Yes, pleasure, for villains aren't necessarily bad, and Pinko and Maharani both stole their respective films. Indian audiences gleefully identify villains with the stable of broadly performed character actors who have specialized in them generation after generation, so much so that many of the generic megalomaniacs consistently outshine their rather humdrum leading men. That queer villains should be a trend of the nineties may well reflect Bollywood's insatiable passion for Northern-flavored novelty, the iconographic spinoffs of global transculturation, but it clearly also reflects something more. The fact that the two most memorable queer villains are the hijra Maharani and the daddy's boy Pinko no doubt helps contain and deflect the "eat or be eaten" model of sexual predation that haunts masculinity in Varanasi. But such charismatic queer villains equally clearly provide both the Indian queer spectator, silent and alone with his buddies in the crowded stalls in Patiala cinemas, and the queer denizens of the Bollywood assembly line, both the flouncers and the discreet ones, with the pleasurable consolation of visibility. They offer a hook for what Foucault would call a reverse discourse, a language and frame for resistant self-definition. The politics of the "negative image" may well be beside the point in a culture based on a pre-political terrain of simultaneous visibility and invisibility, polyvocality and ambiguity.

The charismatic queer penetration model articulated by Maharani and Pinko functions, I would argue, in dialogical counterpoint with the play model in the romances and friendship films, together constituting what Cohen calls "split masculinity."[23] In fact the two patterns can surface in the same films, with the violence and spectacular marginality of the penetrator counteracting the childlike intimacy of homosocial play—and vice versa. If homosociality is indeed a continuum whose gradations toward the homoerotic are volatile, culturally determined, and highly nuanced, violence can be at either end of this continuum, a ritual of male bonding that calls for an enamored "wow!" at one end and the enactment of sexual possession at the other, and the pleasures of recognition and novelty at both ends. In the universe of the cinema, unlike the Varanasi cruising park, the roles of the player and the naive one are not separate, but simultaneous and often interchangeable.

23 "Holi," 421.

Clearly something queer

It is dangerous to offer monolithic generalizations in such a pluralistic field as Indian popular culture, but something queer is clearly going on in Bollywood. This is true certainly within the increasingly brazen and devious Mumbai studio subcultures, which Ashok Row Kavi has called the gayest in the world, and apparently also within the spectators who are watching . . . or at least within some of the spectators who are watching . . . or at the very least within some unconscious part of some of the spectators who are watching. Since the realm of fantasy and desire is hardly as measurable on screen as behaviors are in a social network, the popular cinema only obliquely and contradictorily registers the flux of socio-cultural shifts, unlike ethnography, and the cultural texts of star performances, which have been the most salient vehicles of queer stirrings within Bollywood to date—Akshay/Saïf, Tikoo, Maharani, Pinko—provoke a response that is not directly and literally translatable as ethnographic data or social meaning.

Nevertheless, it is tempting to entertain the too symmetrical cross-cultural comparisons that automatically come to mind between the respective modernizations of sixties Hollywood and nineties Bollywood, between the "something queer going on" in the sixties North and the "something queer going on" of the nineties South Asia. For each industry responded to the sexual revolution at its backdoor with frantic and contradictory cycles of visibility and deflection, alterity and domestication. Such comparisons may well risk imposing Northern-centric and teleological readings on autonomous Indian trajectories, along the lines of Martin F. Manalmansan IV's admonition about imposing globalized Northern models of identity on third sexualities "within a developmental and teleological matrix."[24] But we would be remiss in not at least trying the comparisons on for size. Ultimately, though, in comparison with an earlier and distant sexual revolution that had something to do with Leonard Whiting's buttocks, and even in comparison with the more recent elite and diasporic discourses of the Indian MMMIs and art cinema, the Indian popular cinema's discourses of same-sexuality and fluid masculinity are not so much developmentally far behind or way ahead but in another galaxy. Who's the player and who's the naive one?

24 Martin F. Manalansan IV, "In the Shadows of Stonewall: Examining Gay Transnational Politics and the Diasporic Dilemma," *GLQ*, 2 (4) (1995), 424–438, 428.

Part IV

Production notes

Introduction

Any member of a contemporary industrial society can easily lose sight of the fact that no commodity (including that of cinema) can ever be said to be entirely finished until it reaches the hands (or eyes and ears) of a consumer. Marx took great pains to remind us of the fact that the consumer is as responsible for "making" the commodity as the more customary set of actors whom we identify as its "producers"—in this case, the vast array of writers, cinematographers, software designers, directors, musicians, publicity personnel, actors, projectionists, video distributors, and myriad other workers who labor on a film. Despite our sense that viewing is too often conceived of as a form of passivity, the recipient must produce a film through his or her intellectual endeavors of making sense of a film and deciding that its meanings coincide with or differ from a world-view that the spectator thinks of as his or her own.

The essays that follow can be understood as focusing their energies on the more usual spheres of production, but they do so in order to comprehend how that arena of cinematic enterprise is necessary for understanding the film that shows up on our cinema screens or televisions. To gather a fuller understanding of how cinema's meanings are forged in our daily lives, we need to discover how cinema is made, beyond the massive reportage of fan magazines and entertainment guides, whose usual fare relies almost entirely upon the form of star biography and directorial intent as guideposts for claiming to know about cinema. These forms of star journalism—what goes under the more usual name of "gossip"—themselves cannot be disregarded or scorned simply because they might seem to represent what the corporate cinema wishes its recipients to think about films, but they also need to be framed in a larger scope of the matrix of social relations needed to make movies, a matrix that the industry would be at pains to reproduce in its self-generated reportage.

Recognizing that spectators, as Marx wrote more generally about consumers in the cycle of industrial production, "put the finishing touches on the commodity," though, should not make us naive about the fact that we cannot usually make an infinity of meanings out of a given film, but are constrained by what a film offers; and what it offers depends in great measure on who made it and under what conditions they did so. One of the more unhelpful assumptions offered by the film industry when queried about how it decides what films are produced and what films reside in moribund fashion in that area of production called "turnaround" is that the industry is simply giving audiences what they want—but how do they know what they want if not based on prior instances of film-viewing? The spheres of production and consumption co-constitute each other in more complicated and intimate fashion, and as a first step to knowing how it is that we consume, we need to know how it is that we produce, or in even more daunting fashion, to knowing how it is that "we"—filmgoers in that too nebulous category of the "audience"—rarely have access to the industrial modes of production, the undemocratic fact that we do not in point of fact (and pay attention to the shift of emphasis in this paragraph from that of the first) produce cinema.

In line with our preceding remarks regarding history, however, we may find ourselves on a more complicated path than we might have conceived with regard to the production of cinema. The line, that is, between amateur-produced cinema and commercial cinema is less rigid than it once was, owing entirely to the fact that "independent" cinema (films produced relatively inexpensively by, say, film-school students) has the capacity to generate enormous profit when inserted into the circuits of corporate distribution. The more utopian claim that digital technologies, access to "pro-sumer" level equipment and computer editing capabilities, will produce more genuinely "popular" films is likely true only to the extent to which such films can continue to generate profit at current or better ratios. At the same time, film-school students and scholars of cinema at all levels know that piracy, agitation, sampling, agit-prop, and ambushes produce *and* circulate change.

16 Cinema studies doesn't matter; or, I know what you did last semester

Toby Miller

I want to lower the tone of academic discussion in this chapter, to engage in a shameless polemic. My target is currents within cinema studies as practiced in the United States and the United Kingdom. I am not commenting on other countries. Nor am I suggesting that cinema studies in these two places is a closed shop in which there is no room for dissent or difference. (The Department where I teach, for example, did not employ me because of my standing within conventional cinema studies as parlayed in business-as-usual journals and talkfests, but out of a desire to include cultural studies in its work.)

Let's begin with three investigations. First, an anecdote about a content analysis of tobacco and alcohol use associated with heroic characters in feature-length animation films released between 1937 and 1997. The study was published by the American Medical Association (AMA) in March 1999 (Goldstein, Sobel, and Newman). It received major public attention via a press conference, AMA endorsement, formal replies from Disney, massive TV and newspaper coverage, and so on. Such a paper references some long-standing English-language concerns of cinema studies. These concerns should have made cinema studies part of the AMA's discourse and the media discourse on the report, as well as exciting the attention of cinema studies mavens. But how many cinema studies professors or graduate students read it? How many were asked to comment on it in the media?

My second investigation concerns a related hardy perennial of the screen—the violence debate over whether the screen drives people to commit crime, has a cathartic effect that releases social-psychological tension, or narcotizes viewers away from sensitivity to suffering. It reemerges all the time in the media. Not long after the AMA's moral-guardian content analysts released their report, there was a mass shooting during a screening of *Fight Club*. A medical student walked into a São Paulo cinema in a middle-class mall and fired a submachine gun at the audience. Three people were killed and five wounded. Fernando Henrique Cardoso, an inspirational figure in sociological dependency theory from the 1970s but now a neo-liberal President of Brazil, attributed the incident to the "globalisation of cultural patterns of behaviour" via the media, violence, and international exchange (quoted in "Unnatural" 1999). Similar tales could be told, of course, in the US and elsewhere. What part has cinema studies played in this crucial topic of public debate? Zero.

My third investigation is this: how many people teaching Hollywood film can name the number of publicly funded film commissions that underwrite the United States' so-called *laissez-faire* industry? The figure is 196, including the Palm Beach Film & TV

Office, which advertised in the Society for Cinema Studies' 1999 conference program booklet. But if most of us were asked to comment on the implications of these bodies for cultural policy, or for the claims of neo-classical marginalist economic ideology, I doubt we'd have much to offer the public. Why is this so, and what does it tell us? That is my concern in this chapter.

Norms

I own a how-to book called *Going to the Cinema*. It's part of a British series from the 1950s that instructs middle-class readers on how to enjoy culture. Noting that film "has to cater for millions, and to do so, must make no demands on the public . . . Films are easy to understand," the book promises "increased powers of perception," developing spectators' pleasure to make them more discriminating. A list of "Films everyone should see" is even included, in best Leavisite/*Rolling Stone* fashion (Buchanan and Reed 1957: 13, 155–157). That's remarkably like most of the graduate syllabuses and textbooks that I see, albeit with textual politics the latter-day alibi that displaces a supposedly transcendental taste formation.

Both political and transcendental projects of taste formation reiterate longstanding concerns of film theory, from the silent era's faith in what Vachel Lindsay called "the moving picture man as a local social force . . . the mere formula of [whose] activities" keeps the public well-tempered (Lindsay 1970: 243); through 1930s research into the impact of cinema on American youth via the Payne Fund's ethnographic and sociological studies (Blumer 1933; Hauser 1933; Shuttleworth and May 1933; Forman 1933); to post-World War II social-theory anxieties over Hollywood's intrication of education and entertainment and the need for counter-knowledge among the public (Powdermaker 1950: 12–15; Mayer 1946: 24; also see Mayer 1948).

Myths

This remarkable continuity is secreted from most students today, in favor of a heroic, Whiggish narrative of teleological development. We are sometimes told that, to quote one recent film-theory anthology, there has been "a general movement in approaches to film from a preoccupation with authorship (broadly defined), through a concentration upon the text and textuality, to an investigation of audiences" (Hollows and Jancovich 1995: 8); or, to paraphrase the fifth edition of a widely used anthology, that there has been, consecutively, a pursuit of knowledge about film form, then realism, followed by language, and, finally, cultural politics (Braudy and Cohen 1999: xv–xvi).

Excuse me? These teleologies approximate the history of some humanities-based academic work, but forget the staples of popular cinema criticism, social-science technique, public discourse, social-movement activism, and cultural policy as applied to the screen via (i) the analysis of films; (ii) identification of directors with movies; and (iii) studies of the audience through psychology and psychoanalysis. All of these have been around, quite doggedly, for almost a century (Worth 1981: 39). The twin tasks of elevation identified in *Going to the Cinema*—addressing spectators and examining texts—have always informed film theory (Manvell 1950). But you wouldn't know to read today's primers. There are honorable exceptions among the anthologies (Hill and Church Gibson 1998; Cook and Bernink 1999) but the dominant US trend is clear: rent-seeking amnesia, a form of historiography that is self-serving and developmentalist in its assumptions and claims.

To repeat, the tasks of elevation have long addressed audiences and textual ranking. Over time, of course, they both branch out and converge. Audience concerns include psychological, physiological, sociological, educational, consumer, criminological, and political promises and anxieties. Textual ranking involves authorship, genre, form, style, and representational politics. The two tasks cross over in the area of mimesis, with audiences interpreting films against their own worlds of race, gender, class, region, age, religion, language, politics, and nation.

The questions of pleasure and suppression have become central over time, in ways that represent a development. Progressive cultural studies has sought to account for and resist narrative stereotypes and exclusions in order to explain "why socialists and feminists liked things they thought they ought not to" (Dyer 1992: 4), and why some voices and images have been excluded or systematically distorted in mainstream culture. Difficulties over pleasure, presence, and absence account for film theory being highly critical of prevailing representations, but never reifying itself into the Puritanism alleged by critics of political correctness. The extraordinary diversity of latter-day film anthologies organized by subjectivity makes this point clear. Contemporary feminist film anthologies certainly focus on issues of representation and production that are shared by many women, but they also attend, routinely, to differences between women of race, history, class, sexuality, and nation, alongside and as part of theoretical difference (Carson, Dittmar, and Welsch 1994; Pietropaolo and Testaferri 1995; Thornham 1999), while black film anthologies divide between spectatorial and aesthetic dimensions (Diawara 1993), and queer anthologies identify links between social oppression and film and video practice (Gever, Greyson, and Parmar 1993; Holmlund and Fuchs 1997).

Concerns about representation and audience are, then, relatively stable across time, but with some distinct changes of focus away from the implicit and explicit masculinism, Eurocentrism, and universalism of earlier theory, as social movements and third and fourth world discourses have pointed to silences and generated new methods (Shohat and Stam 1994; Carson and Friedman 1995). Even here, though, there is a long history of protest at, for example, Hollywood's portrayal of foreigners and minorities, dating back to the African-American print media and many foreign governments during the silent and early sound era (Vasey 1997).

What is left out, though, in today's dominant discourse of US cinema studies—by which I include major journals, book series, conferences, graduate programs, discussion groups, and editors? Returning to my anecdotes about the AMA, *Fight Club*, and film commissions, those stories point to: (i) a lack of relevance in the output of cinema studies to both popular and policy-driven discussion of films; (ii) a lack of engagement with the sense-making practices of criticism and research conducted outside the textualist and historical side to the humanities; (iii) a lack of engagement with social science. (As an aside, or perhaps a fourth investigation, when was the last time you saw a humanities paper or book on stardom that addressed the excellent work that appears on that topic in economics [Simonet 1980; Rosen 1981; Adler 1985; Wallace, Seigerman, and Holbrook 1993; Chung and Cox 1994; Albert 1998; de Vany and Walls 1999; Sedgwick and Pokorny 1999] and sociology [Peters 1974; Peters and Cantor 1982; Levy 1989; Baker and Faulkner 1991]?) How *do* people get away with this?

Disciplines

This is how they get away with it. Despite the continuity of textual and audience axes within film theory, latter-day lines have been drawn in the US that divide media, communication, cultural, and film studies for reasons of disciplinary academic professionalism—on all sides. The theorization of production and spectatorship relations between film and television, for instance, continues to be dogged by the separation of mass communication's interest in economics, technology, and policy from film theory's preoccupations with aesthetics and cultural address. Attempts are underway to transform both sides of the divide (Balio 1990; Hill and McLoone 1997). And the division of labor encouraged by that rent-seeking is imperiled by the excellent work done by the likes of Thomas Nakayama (1994, 1997; Nakayama and Krizek 1994; Nakayama and Martin 1999) and Oscar Gandy (1992a, 1992b, 1998; Gandy and Matabane 1989), and by the fact that so many college jobs in film come not from the usual suspect—a literature department in search of a partial make-over—but also from communication and media studies.

Perhaps the most significant intellectual innovation that we need here can be seen at work in cultural history and cultural policy studies. These areas have witnessed a radical historicization of context, such that the analysis of textual properties and spectatorial processes must now be supplemented by an account of *occasionality* that details the conditions under which a text is made, circulated, received, interpreted, and criticized, taking seriously the conditions of existence of cultural production (for cultural policy studies, see Cunningham 1992; Miller 1993; Bennett 1998; for a critique, see Miller 1998: 64–97). The life of any popular or praised film is a passage across space and time, a life remade again and again by institutions, discourses, and practices of distribution and reception that make each uptake of a text into a specific occasion. We must consider all the shifts and shocks that characterize the existence of cultural commodities, their ongoing renewal as the temporary "property" of varied, productive workers and publics, and their condition as the abiding "property" of businesspeople (see Bennett, Emmison, and Frow 1999).

The need for a radical contextualization of interpretation is underlined by a surprising turn—the early history of film as part of a vaudeville bill is being reprised. The moving image is again part of a multiform network of entertainment, via CD-ROMs, computer games, the Web, DVDs, HDTV, and multiplexes. The brief moment when cinema could be viewed as a fairly unitary phenomenon in terms of exhibition (say, 1920 to 1950) set up the *conceptual* prospect of its textual fetishization in academia, something that became technologically feasible with video cassette recorders—just when that technology's popularity compromised the very discourse of stable aestheticization! Now that viewing environments, audiences, technologies, and genres are so multiple, the cinema is restored to a mixed-medium mode. At this crucial juncture, the division between the analysis of text and context must be broken up. The who, what, when, where, and how of screen culture—its occasionality—must become central to our work.

Alternatives

So let me focus my polemic prior to making some proposals. Screen literature and teaching need an overhaul. They frequently fail to consider the following key areas that should be prerequisites to any publication or teaching that makes claims about texts and audiences: engagement with related political and social history and social theory on the human subject, the nation, political economy, cultural policy, the law, and cultural history. In place of this, the current orthodoxy is: (i) use of certain limited, seemingly arbitrarily selected, forms of subject-formation theory; (ii) solitary or classroom textual analysis of film that is actually conducted on a TV screen, an analysis that magically stands for other audiences, subjectivities, cultures, and occasions of viewing; and (iii) neglect of cultural bureaucrats and industry workers in favor of attention to individuals, collectives, or (by magical proxy) social movements, because artists are privileged over governments and unions, and scholarly critics decree themselves able to divine meaning for whole classes of the population, while spectacularity is inordinately prized over the mundane. Such readings are interesting things to do, but they are insufficient as political-economic-textual-anthropological accounts, and their politics is all too frequently limited to the Academy. Let me offer a snapshot of what an account of screen texts that followed other protocols might look like. I have chosen a popular film series, James Bond pictures, in keeping with the remit of this volume.

We'd want to know about the culture that nestles the films—not in order to make unsupportable claims about the films reflecting society, but to engage with ancillary commercial forms that tell us about how producers conceive of their audiences. So, we'd not just note that Bond was an imperialist (an easy mark) but look closely at the 1999 offer from Puerto Rico's El San Juan Hotel & Casino of a "James Bond Package," featuring 007 bathrobes, *From Russia With Love* martinis, and a secret-agent pen personally delivered by a room-service worker called "Q" (MSN Expedia).

This would tell us about the class and gender address of the films, their uptake by affiliated enterprises, and the realities of present-day neo-colonialism. Similarly, auctions such as Christies' 1998 sale of *objets* Bond (the top price paid was $102,000 for Oddjob's bowler) complicate assumptions about the British legacy of racism—the second-highest figure was paid by Houmayoun Sharifi for the right to use "007" as the license plate for his Bentley (Swart 1998). Do we regard this as false consciousness, a sign of a cross-racial form of power identification, an individual quirk, or of no significance for a geopolitical audit of the series' meaning? If the answer to any of these questions is clear, why is it clear, and how is that preferable to other answers?

The 1997 dose of the franchise, *Tomorrow Never Dies*, broke new ground in product placement: Smirnoff, Heineken, Avis, Ericsson, Gateway, BMW, Brioni, Omega, and Visa were all party to payments that meant the film recouped its $100 million budget without selling a ticket, video rental, or an actual item of merchandise (PS 1997). The "laddish" magazine *Maxim* advertised a Visa pack that included a license to kill, a photo of an Asian woman, a driver's and assassin's license, and a computer wallet ("Mostly ladies' numbers") ("007" 1998). A US commercial saw Bond requiring a Visa Check Card as ID and also promoted the upcoming film—a form of reciprocal endorsement. Crucially, it first appeared during ABC's *Monday Night Football*—a clear instance of audience targeting. Banks became sites for the promotion as well, rewarding frequent customers with Bond give-aways ("Visa"). A full-page advertisement in the *New York Times* directly interpellated the male viewer of the new film as a power-mongering, objectifying, wealthy, straight, hedonist: "FAST CARS. DANGEROUS WOMEN. HIGH-TECH GADGETS." The ad promised a "James Bond Secret Agent Kit" of digital phone, calculator, accessory kit, and digital wireless service. Dos this "make" the films sexist or commodified? If so, what does that imply for the purely narrational or diegetic analysis of the texts? And should the advertisements themselves be read literally and damned for political incorrectness and objectification—or are their meanings somehow not to be found on a literal level? Should they be interpreted symptomatically, as critiques of that which they seem to endorse, or as signs of wider capitalist processes? If not, why not?

At the level of political economy, it certainly makes sense, for example, to look at the relative presence in the French market of Gateway 2000, CD-ROMs, Omega watches, and Bond videos to account for the meaning of *Studio* magazine's offer to "Soyez Bond! [Be Bond]" by winning these items in a 1997 contest. Similarly, undifferentiated speculations about spectators to Bond films might be complicated by interviewing, for example, the hundred Americans who pay $1,500 per day each year to attend Bond conventions in Jamaica (Borrows 1997) and distinguishing them from ordinary punters watching the films in rerun on TV, complete with commercial breaks, or from 1970s Italian fans, who received a different set of promotions for *Live and Let Die* from the rest of the world because interracial sex was airbrushed out (Lisa 1994: 9). Or can cinema studies practitioners simply watch a few video tapes from their local store and know the meaning of the films, for all times and in all places?

Conclusion

We should acknowledge the policy, distributional, promotional, and exhibitionary protocols of the screen at each site as much as their textual ones. Enough talk of "economic reductionism" without also problematizing "textual reductionism." Enough valorization of close reading and armchair accounts of human interiority without establishing the political significance of texts and subjectivities within actual social movements and demographic cohorts. Enough denial of the role of government—teaching classes on Hollywood without consideration of the undergirding provided by 196 film commissions. Enough teaching classes on animation, for instance, without reference to effects work, content analysis, and the international political economy that sees the episode of *The Simpsons* decrying globalization actually made by non-union animators in South-East Asia (Lent 1998). These issues—industry frameworks, audience experiences, and cultural policy—should be integral.

I propose two foci to future work. First, we need to view the screen through twin theoretical prisms. On the one hand, it can be understood as the newest component of sovereignty, a twentieth-century cultural addition to ideas of patrimony and rights that sits alongside such traditional topics as territory, language, history, and schooling. On the other hand, the screen is a cluster of culture industries. As such, it is subject to exactly the rent-seeking practices and exclusionary representational protocols that characterize liaisons between state and capital. We must ask: is screen culture expanding the vision and availability of the good life to include the ability of a people to control its representation on screen? Or is screen culture merely a free ride for the culturalist fraction of national, cosmopolitan, or social-movement bourgeoisies? And is cinema studies serving phantasmatic projections of humanities critics' narcissism, or does it actively engage social-movement politics?

Second, there must be a focus not merely on the texts conventionally catalogued as those of the cinema, but on the actual screen experience of citizens—to what extent does the cinema engage them versus TV and other media? The political audit we make of an audiovisual space should focus on the extent to which it is open, both on-camera and off, to the demographics of those inhabiting it. No cinema that claims resistance to Hollywood in the name of national or social-movement specificity is worthy of endorsement unless it attends to sexual and racial minorities and women, along with class politics. Is there a representation of the fullness of the population in the industry and on the screen? The work of Jeffrey Himpele (1996) on Bolivia and Preminda Jacob (1998) on India is exemplary here—but I doubt we'd find them, or the AMA authors writing about drug use and animation, referenced by the hegemons and obedient graduate students of cinema studies. And nor do I think we'd see engagement with their methods or questions.

Returning to my title: what would it mean for cinema studies to "matter"? Here is my list

(i)   influence over public media discourse on the screen;
(ii)   influence over public policy and not-for-profit and commercial practice;
(iii)   academically, not generating the reproduction of a thing called "cinema studies," but instead promoting the doing of work that *studies* the screen, no matter what its institutional provenance.

Business as usual is not good enough. When it comes to key questions of texts and audiences—what gets produced and circulated and how it is read—the methods of cinema studies are sadly deficient. Policy analysis, political economy, ethnography, movement activism, and use of the social-science archive should matter to cinema studies. Because they don't, cinema studies is largely irrelevant outside its tiny cloister of academic parthenogenesis. In short, it doesn't matter.

References

"007," *Maxim*, January 1998: n.p.

Adler, M. (1985) "Stardom and Talent," *American Economic Review* 75 (1): 208–212.

Albert, Steven (1998) "Movie Stars and the Distribution of Financially Successful Films in the Motion Picture Industry," *Journal of Cultural Economics* 22 (4): 249–270.

Baker, Wayne E. and Robert R. Faulkner (1991) "Role as Resource in the Hollywood Film Industry," *American Journal of Sociology* 97 (2): 279–309.

Balio, Tino, ed. (1990) *Hollywood in the Age of Television*, Boston: Unwin Hyman.

Bennett, Tony (1998) *Culture: A Reformer's Science*, London: Sage.

Bennett, Tony, Michael Emmison, and John Frow (1999) *Accounting for Tastes: Australian Everyday Culture*, Cambridge: Cambridge University Press.

Blumer, Herbert (1933) *Movies and Conduct*, New York: Macmillan.

Borrows, Bill (1997) "Dr Doh?" *Loaded* 42 (October): 115–119.

Bourdieu, Pierre (1984) *Distinction: A Social Critique of the Judgement of Taste*, translated by Richard Nice, Cambridge, MA: Harvard University Press.

Braudy, Leo and Marshall Cohen (1999) "Preface," in Leo Braudy and Marshall Cohen, eds, *Film Theory and Criticism: Introductory Readings*, 5th edn, New York: Oxford University Press, xv–xviii.

Buchanan, Andrew and Stanley Reed (1957) *Going to the Cinema*, London: Phoenix House.

Carson, Diane, Linda Dittmar, and Janice R. Welsch, eds (1994) *Multiple Voices in Feminist Film Criticism*, Minneapolis: University of Minnesota Press.

Carson, Diane and Lester D. Friedman, eds (1995) *Shared Differences: Multicultural Media and Practical Pedagogy*, Urbana: University of Illinois Press.

Chung, K. and R. Cox (1994) "A Stochastic Model of Superstardom: An Application of the Yule Distribution," *Review of Economics and Statistics* 76 (4): 771–775.

Cook, Pam and Mieke Bernink, eds (1999) *The Cinema Book*, 2nd edn, London: British Film Institute.

Cunningham, Stuart (1992) *Framing Culture: Culture and Policy in Australia*, Sydney: Allen & Unwin.

de Vany, Arthur and W. David Walls (1999) "Uncertainty in the Movie Industry: Does Star Power Reduce the Terror of the Box Office?" *Journal of Cultural Economics* 23 (4): 285–318.

Diawara, Manthia, ed. (1993) *Black American Cinema*, New York: Routledge.

Dyer, Richard (1992) *Only Entertainment*, London: Routledge.

"FAST CARS. DANGEROUS WOMEN. HIGH-TECH GADGETS," *New York Times*, January 12, 1998: A11.

Forman, Henry James (1933) *Our Movie Made Children*, New York: Macmillan.

Gandy, Oscar H., Jr. (1998) *Communication and Race: A Structural Perspective*, London and New York: Arnold and Oxford University Press.

—— (1992a) "The Political Economy Approach: A Critical Challenge," *Journal of Media Economics* 5 (2): 23–42.

—— (1992b) *The Political Economy of Personal Information*, Boulder, CO: Westview Press.

Gandy, Oscar H., Jr. and Paula Matabane (1989) "Television and Social Perception among African Americans and Hispanics," in M. Asante and W. Gudykunst, eds, *Handbook of International and Intercultural Information*, Newbury Park, CA: Sage, 318–348.

Gever, Martha, John Greyson, and Pratibha Parmar, eds (1993) *Queer Looks: Perspectives on Lesbian and Gay Film and Video*, New York: Routledge.

Goldstein, Adam O., Rachel A. Sobel, and Glen R. Newman (1999) "Tobacco and Alcohol Use in G-Rated Children's Animated Films," *Journal of the American Medical Association* 28 (12): 1131–1136.

Hauser, Philip M. (1933) *Movies, Delinquency and Crime*, New York: Macmillan.

Hill, John and Pamela Church Gibson, eds (1998) *The Oxford Guide to Film Studies*, Oxford: Oxford University Press.

Hill, John and Martin McLoone, eds (1997) *Big Picture Small Screen: The Relations between Film and Television*, Luton: University of Luton Press and John Libbey Media.

Himpele, Jeffrey D. (1996) "Film Distribution as Media: Mapping Difference in the Bolivian Cinemascape," *Visual Anthropology Review* 12 (1): 47–66.

Hollows, Joanne and Mark Jancovich (1995) "Popular Film and Cultural Distinctions," in Joanne Hollows and Mark Jancovich, eds, *Approaches to Popular Film*, Manchester: Manchester University Press, 1–14.

Holmlund, Chris and Cynthia Fuchs, eds (1997) *Between the Sheets, in the Streets: Queer, Lesbian, Gay Documentary*, Minneapolis: University of Minnesota Press.

Jacob, Preminda (1998) "Media Spectacles: The Production and Reception of Tamil Cinema Advertisements," *Visual Anthropology* 11 (4): 287–322.

Lent, John (1998) "The Animation Industry and Its Offshore Factories," in Gerald Sussman and John A. Lent, eds, *Global Productions: Labor in the Making of the "Information Society,"* Cresskill: Hampton Press, 239–254.

Levy, Emmanuel (1989) "The Democratic Elite: America's Movie Stars," *Qualitative Sociology* 12 (1): 29–54.

Lindsay, Vachel (1970) *The Art of the Moving Picture*, New York: Liveright.

Lisa, Philip (1994) "Everything He Touches Turns to $$$," *Hollywood Collectibles* 1 (9): 5–9, 14–19.

Manvell, Roger (1950) *Film*, Harmondsworth: Penguin.

Mayer, J. P. (1946) *Sociology of Film: Studies and Documents*, London: Faber and Faber.

—— (1948) *British Cinemas and Their Audiences*, London: Dobson.

Miller, Toby (1993) *The Well-Tempered Self: Citizenship, Culture, and the Postmodern Subject*, Baltimore: The Johns Hopkins University Press.

—— (1998) *Technologies of Truth: Cultural Citizenship and the Popular Media*, Minneapolis: University of Minnesota Press.

MSN Expedia Staff (1999) "Puerto Rico Package for 007 Fans," *Microsoft Expedia Travel News*, http://www.msn.com.

Nakayama, Thomas K. (1994) "Show/down Time: 'Race,' Gender, Sexuality, and Popular Culture," *Critical Studies in Mass Communication* 11: 162–179.

—— (1997) "Dis/Orienting Identities," in A. Gonzalez, M. Houston, and V. Chen, eds, *Our Voices*, 2nd edn, Los Angeles: Roxbury, 14–20.

Nakayama, Thomas K. and R. L. Krizek (1995) "Whiteness: A Strategic Rhetoric," *Quarterly Journal of Speech* 81: 291–309.

Nakayama, Thomas K. and Judith N. Martin, eds (1999) *Whiteness: The Communication of Social Identity*, Thousand Oaks, CA: Sage.

Peters, Anne K. (1974) "Aspiring Hollywood Actresses: A Sociological Perspective," in P. L. Stewart and M. G. Cantor, eds, *Varieties of Work Experience*, Cambridge, MA: Schenkman.

Peters, Anne K. and Muriel G. Cantor (1982) "Screen Acting as Work," in James S. Ettema and D. Charles Whitney, eds, *Individuals in Mass Media Organizations: Creativity and Constraint*, Beverly Hills, CA: Sage, 53–68.

Pietropaolo, Laura and Ada Testaferri, eds (1995) *Feminisms and the Cinema*, Bloomington: Indiana University Press.

Powdermaker, Hortense (1950) *Hollywood: The Dream Factory*, Boston: Little, Brown.

PS (1997) "007: Licensed to Sell," *Bulletin* 25 (November): 27.

Rosen, S. (1981) "The Economics of Superstars," *American Economic Review* 71 (5): 845–857.

Sedgwick, John and Michael Pokorny (1999) "Movie Stars and the Distribution of Financially Successful Films in the Motion Picture Industry," *Journal of Cultural Economics* 23 (4): 319–323.

Shohat, Ella and Robert Stam (1994) *Unthinking Eurocentrism: Multiculturalism and the Media*, London and New York: Routledge.

Shuttleworth, Frank and Mark May (1933) *The Social Conduct and Attitudes of Movie Fans*, New York: Macmillan.

Simonet, T. (1980) *Regression Analysis of Prior Experience of Key Production Personnel as Predictors of Revenue from High Grossing Motion Pictures in American Release*, New York: Arno Press.

"Soyez Bond!" *Studio*, December 1997: n.p.

Swart, Sharon (1998) "Bond Booty Gone," *Variety* 21–27 (September): 124.

Thornham, Sue, ed. (1999) *Feminist Film Theory: A Reader*, Washington Square: New York University Press.

"Unnatural Brazilian Killer," *Economist*, November 13, 1999: 36.

Vasey, Ruth (1997) *The World According to Hollywood, 1918–1939*, Madison: University of Wisconsin Press.

"Visa Bonds with 007 in Product Tie-In," http://www.ianfleming.org/007news/articles/visa-bond.html.

Wallace, W. Timothy, Alan Seigerman, and Morris B. Holbrook (1993) "The Role of Actors and Actresses in the Success of Films: How Much Is a Movie Star Worth?" *Journal of Cultural Economics* 17 (1): 1–27.

Worth, Sol (1981) *Studying Visual Communication*, edited by Larry Gross, Philadelphia: University of Pennsylvania Press.

17 *12 Monkeys*, postmodernism, and the urban

Toward a new method

Matthew Ruben

So let me offer a proposal. What is necessary, I would argue, is a way of discussing film as a social practice that begins by considering how social relations are spatially organized— through sites of production and consumption—and how film is practiced from and across particular sites and always in relation to other sites.

Hay 1997: 216

The lure of the postmodern

Cole:	"This is October, right?"
Psychiatrist:	"April."
Cole:	"What year is this?"
Psychiatrist:	"What year do you think it is?"
Cole:	"1996."
Psychiatrist:	"That's the future, Cole. Do you think you're living in the future?"
Cole:	"1996 is the past."
Psychiatrist:	"1996 is the future. This is 1990."

James Cole says he comes from the year 2035 and that he has been sent back in time to gather information on the outbreak of a virus that killed 99 percent of the earth's population in 1997. Dr. Kathryn Railly, his psychiatrist, thinks Cole is delusional. Cole explains that he was supposed to land in Philadelphia in October 1996, just before everyone started getting sick. Unfortunately, the scientists who rule the authoritarian society of the future haven't quite perfected their time portal technology, and he has arrived in Baltimore six and half years earlier. So Cole thinks he's in the past, and Dr. Railly thinks that Cole thinks he's in the future. Later on, when Cole does manage to get to Philadelphia and to 1996, Railly comes to believe his time travel story even as he starts to question his own sanity. Having convinced him he is mentally ill, she tries to persuade him that she was wrong and that he is in fact sane. They work together feverishly to pinpoint where the virus came from, and how, when and where it got—or will get—released. They figure it all out, but it seems they're too late to save humanity. Or perhaps they're not too late after all. It's all very confusing.

Confusion is indeed the overarching theme of Terry Gilliam's 1996 film *12 Monkeys*. Neither time nor sensory perception can be counted upon. The plot is circular, with numerous blind alleys and false villains, and the meaning of its outcome is uncertain even after repeated viewing. Nor is it a particularly pleasant film. Part sci-fi tale, part dramatic thriller, and part dark comedy, *12 Monkeys* mixes different styles to lay out an apocalyptic scenario in which humanity is destroyed by its attempts to dominate and manipulate nature. Nothing the hero does can prevent the disaster, and the only aspect of societal organization that survives from the present into the future is government repression.

These various aspects of *12 Monkeys* make it exemplary of what many film critics and culture scholars call postmodernism. Postmodernism is a theory of social change based on economic, social, and aesthetic destabilization. Since the 1980s postmodernist theory has been arguing that we are living in a new era, facing a new "condition" of consciousness and existence. In this new postmodern era, the theory goes, older economic process and arrangements associated with the Enlightenment and capitalist industrialization no longer obtain. Neither government nor organized religion nor any other large-scale social system commands unquestioned authority or legitimacy. Faith in the possibility of revolutionary social change has been lost. We experience "incredulity toward meta-narratives" (Lyotard 1984), a pervasive skepticism and cynicism in which old ideologies of nation, family, and morality no longer provide the security or universal life-guidance they once did. Increased mobility, new information technologies, and new patterns of living are said to have fractured society, increasing the pace of everyday life and altering our very perception of reality.[1]

As might be expected, theories of postmodernity make the job of the film scholar quite difficult. The reason for this is that the question of representation—the relationship between film and reality—has always been the central problematic of film criticism. As critics like Gayatri Spivak (1986) have argued, there are two kinds of representation: portrait and proxy. Representation-as-portrait entails the depiction of people, places, and events in some kind of text, whether it be filmic, spoken, or written. Representation-as-proxy entails speaking about, or in the name of, constituencies in a political context, whether it be as an elected official, community leader, or intellectual. Film scholars are located at the intersection of these two definitions of representation. We offer interpretations aimed at providing an understanding of how to get from text to reality and back again. Yet our interpretive practice also has a political dimension. When we write about what movies mean, we speak to, for, and about the people who watch films and are portrayed in them. Academic film scholars in particular seek to make our interpretations of films resonate with socio-political issues and trends that circulate through and around contemporary movies.[2]

Postmodernist theory argues that the very nature of reality has become more uncertain, more difficult to apprehend or depict with any degree of accuracy. In this scenario, it becomes well nigh impossible to determine the precise relationship of a film to any reality. Many film scholars—along with media scholars, culture scholars, and academics in general—have responded to the postmodernist challenge by focusing on "postmodern"

1 This brief account of postmodernity is intended as an introductory summary of the main currents and claims of postmodernist theory. It does not begin to capture the breadth or complexity of postmodernism. For a selection of influential works on postmodernism (both for and against), as well as a source of references for further study on the topic, see, for example, Baudrillard (1988), Callinicos (1990), DeBord (1994), Jencks (1984), Harvey (1989), Jameson (1984; 1991), and Lyotard (1984).

2 This problem of representation is of course not limited to film studies. It is endemic to all intellectual, artistic, and political work. Moreover, the problem of representation did not originate with postmodernism. The rise of postmodernist theory has, however, brought new prominence and urgency to questions of representation, particularly within the academy.

characteristics of contemporary cultural texts. As opposed to reading stable texts of modernity, the film scholar is faced with reading a postmodern text that consists of multiple sub-texts, of multiple times and places, and hence has the job of reading texts rife with contradiction. The films of the current period are read as mixing and matching different aesthetic styles and different kinds of symbolism in a process known as pastiche—in the same spirit in which Gilliam characterizes *12 Monkeys* as "a jigsaw puzzle" (quoted in Fuchs 1996: 17) and Cynthia Fuchs notes its "combination of genres and tones" (12). Postmodernist texts' references to other films and texts—such as Chris Marker's nuclear apocalypse film *La Jetée* and Hitchcock's *Vertigo* and *The Birds* in the case of *12 Monkeys*—are cited as evidence of a phenomenon known as intertextuality. Perhaps most important, their circular plots and contradictory images are read as destabilizing or "subverting" pat understandings of space and time, the very building blocks of reality. In sending Cole through various time circuits, for example, *12 Monkeys* refuses the happy endings of more traditional Hollywood and television time-travel narratives such as the *Terminator* movies and *Star Trek*. In such productions, moments of stasis, circularity, or chaos related to time travel are ultimately contained and explained away. While these movies and shows tie up loose ends or leave choice ones dangling for sequels, *12 Monkeys* decisively does neither, refusing what Fuchs calls the "(happier) fantasy that [through] time travel everything can be fixed" (51) and leaving no opening at the end for a *12 Monkeys II*. The film asserts a lack of temporal stability, suggesting "that time (and narrative effects) are circular" and that "the nonlinearity of time is inexorable" (12). In sum, rather than looking for a unified meaning through a singular gesture of plot or symbolism, postmodernist film scholars focus on the way contemporary films confound reality and make a number of different meanings for any number of potential viewers.

Two basic assumptions guide the postmodernist approach to textual analysis. The first is that the postmodern aspects of cultural texts are politically progressive or "subversive": *12 Monkeys'* refusal of the "happier fantasy" of time travel, for example, lends it an aura of political and aesthetic sophistication and makes it into a kind of critique of the sci-fi genre and scientific rationality in general. The second assumption is that the questions raised by the postmodern text can be answered within the confines of the text itself. In order to probe the complexities of the postmodern film and to cope with the difficulty of relating the film to an external reality, the critic must delve ever deeper into the text, striving to provide multi-faceted explanations of how the text's internal contradictions open up contradictions or "ruptures" in the narratives, themes and ideologies with which it engages. Reality is not considered directly; rather, the text is analyzed for the "reality effects" that appear within it, usually suspending any detailed or specific consideration of a reality external to the text. Thus is the scholar ironically placed in a rather traditional role of textual explanation, and thus is the problem of the relationship of the text to the real temporarily dispensed with, and perhaps permanently foreclosed.

It is the argument of this chapter that while such a scholarly model can say much about how a film works, it can say little about what a film might actually *mean*. A film's meaning must take into account not only the formal workings of plot and image, but also the circumstances of its production, distribution, and viewing in a particular time and place. It is not at all clear, for example, what the various confusions and destabilizations of *12 Monkeys* add up to in terms of social and political significance. On the one hand, Gilliam explains that for him time travel is a "purely mental state," suggesting that Cole's time travel in the film is an allegory. The confusion around time and sanity would thus seem to be a metaphor, and the film a cautionary tale about what could happen to us all in the future. Yet at the same time, Gilliam states, "Society is so complex now . . . Figuring out how to make things work is really hard. That's why I find it funny when they worry about my dystopic views or my troubles with technology. It's a documentary I'm making!" (quoted in Fuchs 1996: 17). Or as he said in an online interview, "Well, see, [the film] seems to go from now to maybe thirty-five years in the future to the First World War to six years ago to . . . or maybe none of those things. Maybe it's all in the mad man's mind. Who knows . . . I like the idea of keeping it ambiguous. I think we should try to avoid defining things precisely" (quoted in Behar 1996).

We are left, then, with a dilemma: is temporal confusion an empirical fact, or is it a symbolic image of the complicated nature of our lives? At first glance, the clever answer would be that it is both, that the very play of temporality in the film may thus be said to make it both allegorical *and* literal, a premonition of things to come *and* a documentary of current society. Such an answer comports rather well with the postmodernist impulse to embrace contradiction and insist on the inadequacy and obsolescence of "either–or" answers—"the visual techniques of postmodernism include both allegory and realism," as Sharon Zukin observes (1991: 26). Yet to say the film is both documentary and allegorical does not tell us *in what way* it is allegorical, *for whom* it might be a documentary, *in what setting or place* it might be "real" or "unreal," literal or figurative. And if one cannot provide answers to these specific kinds of questions, then one cannot say whether or not a film is progressive or reactionary, establishment or subversive. There is no sure route from a film's aesthetics to its politics.

This essay therefore departs from the postmodernist interpretive model, and instead investigates the relationship of *12 Monkeys* to reality—not only to the "reality" (always placed in scare-quotes in textual analysis) it depicts, but also to the empirical reality in which it was produced, distributed, and viewed. In so doing, this essay will reanimate the question of representation, question the meaning of the concept of postmodernism, and, perhaps most important, reimagine the political and cultural role of the film scholar.

Postmodernism and the urban

> Funny how when Gilliam shows the inner city, it doesn't look much better than the underground, post-apocalypse society.
>
> (FAQ entry, unofficial *12 Monkeys* web site)

The reality of *12 Monkeys* is fundamentally an urban reality. The film's 1990 "past," 1996 "present," and 2035 "future" are all set in (or underneath) either Baltimore or Philadelphia. Late twentieth-century Philadelphia is filthy and full of unsavory characters, symbolizing a corrupt society on the verge of oblivion. It mirrors precisely the corruption and filth of the post-apocalyptic underworld, which is filled with the detritus of human technology, a mishmash of old television monitors, rusty cages, and discarded industrial implements. The future is completely lacking in nature, as Cole repeatedly reminds us when he marvels at the wonders of "fresh" air, grass, trees, and the sky in 1996. At the same time, the urban environs in which much of the plot unfolds are themselves devoid of greenery, natural light and outdoor air. The city of the present is itself an unnatural place.

This dystopic, or nightmarish, urban setting reinforces the lesson of the killer virus: that man's attempts to dominate and manipulate nature will only end in disaster. The film's plot is focused not so much on the end of the world as on the end of humanity. The virus does not extinguish all life, or all animal life, or even mammalian or primate life. It only kills people, "returning the surface to the animals," as Cole's narration says. An early shot of a male lion roaring atop Philadelphia's magisterial city hall uses an easily recognizable King of the Jungle image (the same type of image later used in Disney's *The Lion King*) to drive home the point that nature is back in control in 2035 while humans have been seriously demoted in the food chain—"we live like worms," as Cole says. The virus thus represents a cosmic correction as much as a calamity, the restoration of nature as much as the eclipse of humanity.

At the heart of this postmodernist film thus lies a distinctly old-fashioned, un-postmodern conception of the city as the embodiment of "society," which is in direct opposition to "nature." The opposition of humanity to nature is as old as the Enlightenment, and the symbolic use of the city to represent the filth, corruption, alienation, and disease is nearly as old, a tradition not only in cinema but in literature, philosophy, sociology, and urban policy. In this manner we may glimpse a commonality between postmodernism's view of the world and urban scholarship's view of the city, a commonality of central importance for understanding the socio-political significance of *12 Monkeys*.

Despite different approaches and assumptions,[3] both postmodernist theory and urban scholarship offer similar visions of the places and times they study. As postmodernism has grown from an artistic practice to a critique of aesthetics to a full-blown political theory, it has made increasingly sweeping claims about the nature of reality. This has created a contradiction at the very heart of postmodernism. On the one hand, it claims to be anti-positivist and anti-universalist; that is, it refuses one-size-fits-all ideologies and life-narratives, instead emphasizing relativity, locality, multiplicity, and difference. On the other hand, it is based on a universalizing positivism; that is, in claiming that we now live in a world in which referentiality and facticity are dead, it asserts that this anti-referential, anti-factual state of affairs is *in fact* the *referential truth* of our current situation. It necessarily asserts that postmodernity is a *total* reality: "we," *all* of us, live under the postmodern condition. We all experience temporal disruption and other post-modern phenomena, with a shared fate—no exceptions. It is at this often-overlooked level that postmodernism's *indifference* to difference makes itself apparent. Perhaps the most explicit—and obnoxious—expression of this tendency occurs in Jean-François Lyotard's 1991 volume *The Inhuman*, whose opening chapter, "Can Thought Go On without a Body?," contemplates the role of the body in thought by wondering what will happen to philosophy when the sun explodes. Lyotard's contemplation of the status of

---

3 Postmodernist theory insists on complicating and suspending the relationship of the text to reality, while urban policy—which draws on sociology, economics, history, and anthropology, among other fields—is based on the opposite conviction that we can use observation, statistics and historical documents to produce rational, accurate descriptions of the world. Urban policy is by and large positivist; that is, it believes that singular, definitive answers can be found to social, political, and historical research questions. Postmodernism is decidedly anti-positivist, insisting on multiple possibilities and options, focusing on opening up new questions rather than answering old ones.

humanity in the face of a cataclysmic natural event of course resonates with *12 Monkeys'* use of the killer virus.[4] If the virus spreads or the sun blows up, we are all dead. If the virus is stopped or the sun keeps shining, we are all saved. Humanity for Lyotard, like the city in *12 Monkeys*, is a monolith—seemingly there are no internal contradictions within humanity or the city, no social difference, economic inequality or political power that would allow some people or neighborhoods to flourish while others suffer.

This same sort of thinking makes itself apparent in a broad range of discourses on the city, as scholars, politicians, and pundits have sought to grapple with (or in some cases merely exploit) the decline of industrial cities over the past 30 years. Much of the literature on US cities since World War II has tended to emphasize the urban center as "a 'reservation' for the economically disenfranchised labor force in a monopoly capitalist society" (Hill 1984: 228), with groups of poor people "restricted to deteriorating inner cities" (Sugrue 1993: 110). The resulting image is that of the "Pariah City" (Hill 1978), in which the central city appears as a victim of the suburbs, of economic changes, and of federal neglect. As Carolyn Adams (1988) writes,

> The dramatic population losses suffered by the aging cities of the northeast and midwest in the period after World War II spawned a whole new lexicon of images to describe the central city, including "wasteland," "doughnut," and "bombed-out war zone." The common theme in this postwar urban imagery is the belief that urban life is gradually receding from our inner cities, as residents and business owners flee from the advancing blight, the deteriorating services, and the social pathologies associated with "dying neighborhoods." (2–3)

In such formulations the city appears as a decaying organism: it "ages," it has "suffered," and it is dying as life spatially "recedes" from it. Differences, disparities, and inequalities within the city are nowhere to be found in such unitary and homogenizing narratives. Policy publications take for granted the homogenized view of the city-as-unitary-organism, devising strategies for improving cities' "competitiveness," reducing cities' social service burden relative to the nation as a whole, or otherwise "revitalizing the industrial city" (*Cityscape* 1994; Wharton Real Estate Center 1994; Widner and Wolfgang 1986).

The roles and motivations of scholars and policymakers in reacting to (and helping create) these representations vary widely across the political spectrum. The right has been concerned to demonstrate how the "culture of poverty" (a term coined by anthropologist Oscar Lewis in 1966) has produced an urban "underclass" isolated from market forces and the larger society, unwilling to take the responsibility or action necessary to improve urban America (cf. Murray 1984). The left has used the same negative urban imagery to demonstrate an urgent need for government action in order to save the cities and

---

4 While Lyotard's natural disaster would have the effect of ending all life on earth (and probably of destroying the planet itself), his focus is specifically on the fate of self-conscious human thought—that is, the aspect of humanity that makes us different from all other life forms. In this manner Lyotard's argument contemplates in the abstract realm of philosophy the same humanity–nature opposition that *12 Monkeys* depicts in the more concrete realm of the city.

the populations within them from economic ruin (cf. Wilson 1987). While the political commitments and policy implications vary greatly, however, the underlying logic of homogenization has been pervasive across the board. Katz (1993), writing as editor of the definitive anthology on the subject, notes that "Most American research on poverty and the underclass always has reinforced images of social pathology because it has focused on bad behavior: long-term welfare dependence, drugs, crime, out-of-wedlock pregnancy, low educational achievement, unwillingness to work." As a result, "Areas of concentrated poverty emerge from much of the historical and contemporary underclass literature as monolithic islands of despair and degradation" (21).

In the juxtaposition of postmodernism and urban policy we can thus begin to see how monolithic, universalizing images of humanity and the city work to obscure rather than illuminate the economic, political and cultural dynamics of the society depicted in *12 Monkeys*.

Situating the postmodern

> I think Hollywood's perception of reality—which millions of people seem to buy—
> is so distorted and so crazy that I've always had a problem with it. Compared to
> it, I am a documentary film-maker: I just put on film what I see around me.
>
> Terry Gilliam, as interviewed by Behar (1996)

In order to develop a more concrete understanding of the relationship of a film like *12 Monkeys* to the urban context, we must work to specify and locate—in short to *situate*—the workings of capitalism and the so-called "postmodern condition" that attends it. In other words, we need to ask questions such as: just how universal is the postmodern experience, just how homogeneous is the urban landscape, and just how shared is the fate of urban residents? To help answer these questions we venture outside the confines of the filmic text that is *12 Monkeys*, to the urban environment it stages and in which it was produced. At the same time we keep the focus on the postmodernist themes of *12 Monkeys*, notably the destabilization of time.

We begin with an account provided by Catherine Engle, a member of the Kensington Welfare Rights Union (KWRU) (1993). KWRU is a multiracial direct-action organization in Philadelphia led by poor and homeless people. It works to procure housing, food, and other necessities for poor and homeless people, to "organize a broad-based movement to end poverty," and to insert poor people's voices into the policymaking process, primarily housing (KWRU 1993). Engle became involved with KWRU in 1991 when she met Cheri Honkala, the executive director, who was organizing a tent city in Engle's Kensington neighborhood. Honkala noticed that "there was a SWAT team on Katie's roof" (quoted in Ruben 1995a). Engle was living in her mother's house with her son and daughter because she had recently fled an abusive relationship with her husband. Her son was wanted by the police for allegedly threatening his girlfriend with a gun. His girlfriend was the daughter of a high-ranking official in the police department. Engle recalls that after she told her son to flee rather than risk police retribution when taken into custody, "they would call me and make threats, day and night. When I got up there'd be a call. When I went to bed there'd be a call. The voice would say, 'When we bring him in he's gonna be three colors: black and blue, and red,' from the blood." A poor woman surviving on welfare, Engle had little knowledge of or access to legal resources, and she lived in a neighborhood where intrusive police activity was a constant fact of life. "They would always be in and out [of my house]. There was never a [search] warrant from day one. I had a kitchen full of undercovers." Her son's case even appeared on the television show *America's Most Wanted*. She says she "joined KWRU out of the fact of not being able to help my son . . . I did things with KWRU to keep my mind occupied. All I talked about was my son." During KWRU sit-ins and demonstrations at government housing agencies, Engle would often get up to speak about the injustices of current housing policies, and then begin to cry. "I would always cry [when I spoke]," she says. "All I was thinking about was, 'My son's gone.' It took almost a year before I realized what was going on and what I was doing [with KWRU]" (quoted in Ruben 1995a).

Engle describes herself during this experience as caught in a never-ending cycle of police harassment and terror. Every day was the same as the one before it and the one after it. She felt enveloped by an ordeal whose prehistory she could not effectively remember and whose future she could not really inhabit: "it took almost a year before I realized . . . what I was doing." She represents herself as literally stuck in a particular moment, unable to get on with her life, until KWRU helped get the more serious of the unfounded charges against her son dropped.

The housing policies Engle often spoke about at KWRU demonstrations constitute another instance of disrupted temporality in the city. Because there are insufficient funds available for rehabilitating the large number of abandoned and decaying houses in the city, the city instead resorts to knocking them down. Even demolition funds are woefully inadequate, leading to a situation that produces stagnant housing markets in many poor neighborhoods:

> The unpredictability of welfare income has meant that even a basic rental market is difficult to maintain. In these areas . . . the level of abandonment soars, leading to demolition and/or a simple deterioration in place. At present, Philadelphia's rate of new abandonments matches the rate of demolition, so there is a constant level of 20,000 to 22,000 structures abandoned at any one time, while roughly 1,000 structures a year are being demolished.
>
> (Adams *et al.* 1990: 92)

From the perspective of the landscape of Philadelphia's poor neighborhoods, time seems simultaneously to stand still and to move in a circular fashion. Abandoned buildings disappear from some locales in the landscape, and newly abandoned structures "pop up" out of nowhere to replace them, month after month and year after year. Linear temporal logic is subordinated to a seemingly random series of events in a seemingly endless time loop of abandonment and stagnation.

These two examples resonate strongly with the theme of temporal disruption under postmodernism. Postmodernism's adherents and detractors alike have argued that postmodernity is characterized precisely by the sorts of temporal disruptions and epistemological ruptures that occur in *12 Monkeys*. Fredric Jameson (1984; 1991), in perhaps the most well-known work on the subject, argues that under postmodernism *narrative* gets confounded and deemphasized in favor of *image*. Jameson adopts psychoanalyst Jacques Lacan's use of the term "schizophrenia" to designate a condition in which we cannot "unify the past, present, and future of our own biographical experience or psychic life"

(Jameson 1991: 27).[5] In *12 Monkeys*, schizophrenia is precisely the diagnosis given by psychiatrists to explain Cole's insistence that he is a time traveler, and it is the diagnosis he later wishes to give himself rather than acknowledge the reality that he really does come from a post-apocalyptic, totalitarian society in which he is a prisoner.

This would seem to indicate that Terry Gilliam's claims for the "documentary" nature of his time-bending film may not be so far off the mark. However, the specific historical, economic and geographical conditions of our two examples point away from the universalism of postmodernist accounts of nonlinear time and dystopia. It would be highly problematic, for example, to speak about how Catherine Engle "had the postmodern condition," about how her refusal to be a proper citizen and encourage her son to turn himself in was attributable to a "schizophrenia" that is a part of our postmodern *Zeitgeist*. Such an explanation might be all well and good when speaking allegorically of the universal subject of history as represented by Bruce Willis's Cole, but for a woman living in an impoverished urban neighborhood it would only join neo-conservative ideology, neo-liberal policy and much well-intentioned urban scholarship in reinforcing the association of women and poor people with irrationality and bad citizenship. It is more useful to see how the examples of Engle's experience and Philadelphia's housing market point toward particular state and economic activities that take place in poor neighborhoods, and that disproportionately impact women, children, and people of color. This kind of understanding injects questions of power, class, and place into the discussion. It focuses not on a universal postmodern condition but on a complex, place-specific nexus of governmental and economic practices.

Situating the urban: uneven development in Philadelphia

> The simultaneous emergence of gentrification and displacement, speculative activity and large-scale abandonment provides a schizophrenic image of a city half-phoenix and half-ashes.
>
> (Adams *et al.* 1990: 68)

The totalizing tendencies of postmodernist theory and some urban scholarship tend to make the experiences and consciousness of people like Catherine Engle either invisible or pathological.[6] In the context of current trends in urban development, however, her situation makes more sense.

---

5 While Jameson's formulation is accessible and targeted specifically to questions of postmodernism in the US, Deleuze and Guattari (1983) have produced the primary, if elliptical, non-clinical text on the subject of schizophrenia, and it has spurred a considerable body of work. The main emphasis in all these works is on a Freudian–Lacanian notion of psychosis, in which one's relationship to reality—or the relationship between language/representation and reality—is either severed or collapsed. This is in opposition to neurosis, which is the more traditional concept implicitly employed in critical theory to express the variable, tortured, and mediated relation between language and reality, between the subject and the Social, or between essence and appearance (cf. Horkheimer and Adorno 1972). The switch from neurosis to psychosis mobilizes a shift to a whole new set of theoretical themes and registers: from narrative to image; from linearity to multiplicity; from analysis to performance; from antagonism to incommensurability; from class/identity to difference; from dialectic to rhizome (or back to simple binarisms, depending upon one's point of view); from opposition to displacement; from interest to desire.

6 On the subject of poor people's agency, and its tendency to be overlooked in many academic studies of the poor and cities, see, for example, Coit (1984), Jackson (1993), Kelley (1993), and Piven and Cloward (1979).

Since the 1980s, the tide of disinvestment has been slowed and in some cases even reversed in many US cities. The investment that has come into cities since the 1980s, however, is fundamentally different from the manufacturing-based infrastructure that was destroyed by urban disinvestment in the 1960s and 1970s. The new urban investment model is highly selective, focusing on the development of downtown business districts in which financial, insurance and real estate, or "FIRE" firms congregate to realize economies of scale and efficiencies of proximity that help them serve corporate clients located across the world (cf. Sassen 1991; 1994). These business districts are accompanied by entertainment, shopping, and tourist centers, often collectively referred to as the service economy or the hospitality industry. The new urban economy does not offer the secure, decent-wage employment provided by the older industrial urban economy. Nor is the new economy located in the same neighborhoods in which urban manufacturing industry was based. Instead, municipal governments fund these centralized business and entertainment districts in the hopes that a "trickle down" effect will accrue in the older, neglected, formerly industrial neighborhoods. Rather than targeting investment to stabilize neighborhoods and raise living standards, the new urban economic model redevelops the city as a "growth machine" (Logan and Molotch 1987). It creates landscapes of cultural consumption for suburban residents and tourists, effectively making cities into internal colonies. Poor and working-class people living in these spaces of hyper-investment are displaced, while other poor residential neighborhoods are bypassed by the growth machine and experience the major withdrawal of resources (Adams 1988; Harvey 1996). These neighborhoods typically are located in areas where redlining, industrial withdrawal, and job loss have already created downward mobility, decay of housing stock, population turnover, and the weakening of local civic and community organizations.

In Philadelphia, for example, formerly industrial neighborhoods have decayed, while the banks, insurance companies, law firms, and other producer service firms have located themselves in Center City, the central business district, which has been gentrified, redeveloped and generally renovated. In contrast to the stereotypical image of the city as a "doughnut" with a bleak urban center surrounded by affluent suburbs, Philadelphia now resembles a "double doughnut," with a gentrified urban center surrounded by an inner ring of working-class and impoverished city neighborhoods, and internal and external suburbs at the outskirts (Fig. 17.1).[7] The FIRE/service economy therefore represents not only new investment, but also an economic, cultural and spatial reconstruction of the urban environment. While it raises the profile of certain parts of the city, it actually worsens the situation in many areas that are already in dire straits. Urban geographer Neil Smith (1991) terms this kind of inequality *uneven development.*

The great irony of *12 Monkeys* is that its production took full advantage of this uneven development in Philadelphia. "I overheard the crew talking," said a local woman

---

7 What I refer to here for simplicity's sake as the "double doughnut" is actually the manifestation of a series of economic developments in urban areas, primarily those in the Northeast and Midwest. The historically sequential processes of infrastructural decay, suburbanization, and gentrification have produced in these cities intensely uneven geographical landscapes characterized by large tracts of abandoned or decaying buildings and small pockets of redeveloped commercial and/or residential property. These pockets of gentrification manifest themselves differently in different cities. While Philadelphia offers perhaps the most striking instance of the "double doughnut" or "bull's-eye" effect, cities like Pittsburgh, Cleveland, Kansas City, and of course New York and Los Angeles feature different patterns. On New York, see Smith (1996). On Los Angeles, see Oliver, Johnson and Farrell (1993).

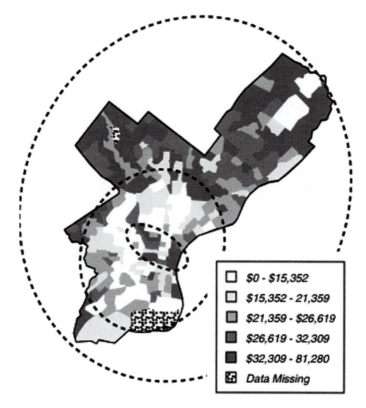

Figure 17.1 The "Double Doughnut": Median Household Income, Philadelphia, 1990

watching a scene being filmed in the impoverished Kensington neighborhood in February 1995. "They said Philly is great because it has shiny Center City and also the slums." The stark contrast between Center City and the "slums" allowed Gilliam to get shots of midtown high-rises, City Hall, and Kensington decay within a convenient 2-mile radius. The official *12 Monkeys* promotional web site is quite explicit about this. Under the heading "Finding Locations in the Urban Mid-Atlantic, The Future is Now," it explains:

> Although Philadelphia and Baltimore have undergone tremendous regrowth in recent years, remn[a]nts of industrial decay remain, serving as reminders of our past as well as outstanding locations for filming. Most important was the use of the old [Port] Richmond and Delaware generating stations [in Philadelphia] which housed outdated machinery which were remodeled into time travel devices for the film. In the 1920s these massive turbine generators burned 2400 tons of coal per day providing hundreds of thousands of kilowatts of energy to Philadelphia. The huge condensers are eighteen feet high with a hollow center. This served as the time machine that Bruce Willis is shoved through to travel back to 1996. (1996)

Beyond the filming of particular scenes and the opportunity to use non-union labor when filming outside Hollywood, a broader benefit of this proximate spatial contrast accrued throughout the production process. Because of uneven development, Gilliam

Figure 17.2   Filming of *12 Monkeys* in Kensington, North Philadelphia, February 1995. Kensington
Avenue was considered an ideal setting for an image of a decadent urban society on
the brink of destruction. The Freedom for Animals Association (FAA) headquarters
was covered with posters and graffiti and served as a cover for the Army of the Twelve
Monkeys, a group of activists led by a mentally unbalanced trust fund baby (Brad
Pitt). Note the tarps hanging from the El overpass, voluminous quantities of steam
and smoke, and construction barriers—all added by the production crew. Photo:
Matthew Ruben

and his producers had at their disposal both a ready-made urban nightmare in which to
film, and a first-rate local film office to help production run smoothly. While much of
the shooting took place in Kensington and other decaying "inner ring" areas, production schedules and other logistics were coordinated in Center City by the Greater
Philadelphia Film Office, which is funded by Greater Philadelphia First, an economic
development corporation run by a consortium of 30 local firms primarily from the FIRE
and technology sectors. The producers brought the stars, director, and other talent from
Hollywood and London, rented or purchased local labor and equipment, obtained local
police officers at no charge for crowd control and traffic management, and saved on
costs by using worthless lots, devalued buildings, and junked equipment for sets, staging, storage, and parking (Fig. 17.2). "We went to Philadelphia looking for rotting
America," Gilliam told *Entertainment Weekly*. "It turned out to be the perfect place"
(Ascher-Walsh 1995: 36). "Throughout their stay," Fuchs writes, "[Gilliam] and production designer Jeffrey Beecroft couldn't believe their good fortune: they found the

city replete with crumbling buildings and beat sites. They were also greeted with enthusiasm by the mayor. Gilliam recalls, 'we met Sharon Pinkenson [executive director of the Film Office], and [Mayor] Ed Rendell, who's a very keen guy. They understand that when films come to your town, it makes your town famous'" (13). An article on the film's economic impact on the city noted that "hotels were chief among the beneficiaries." Yet while the manager of one upscale establishment noted "an increase in room service and dry-cleaning activity," he explained that "film is a small part of our overall business." More important, he stressed, was "the impact on the cachet and positioning of the hotel [which] is invaluable and totally out of proportion to the number of room nights" (quoted in Rickey 1995: D1).

Indeed, *12 Monkeys* has been used, as was *Philadelphia* before it and *Fallen, Beloved* and *The Sixth Sense* after it, to promote Philadelphia's corporations and service industry to a regional, national and international audience of potential investors, tourists, shoppers, and prospective high-skill management employees. In its annual *Report of Progress*, Greater Philadelphia First highlights film production under the headings of both "Communicating Regional Strengths" and "Economic Development." For the years 1992 to 1995, the organization's own figures indicate that film production jobs accounted for between 25 and 75 percent of the total annual job creation for which it takes credit (Greater Philadelphia First 1995: 4–7; 1996: 8; 1997: 13; 1999: 4–5). Like the producers of *12 Monkeys*, Greater Philadelphia First takes advantage of uneven development to craft its own representations and imagery. Temporary film-related employment is added indiscriminately to other numbers to work up a particular picture of "job creation." Film stills from the city's most shamefully depressed areas become promotional images in public relations brochures. And low-wage service businesses happily make do with the indirect benefits of "cachet" and "positioning." All of this occurs in an effort to draw more financial, service, and so-called "knowledge-intensive" industries into the suburbs and Center City, strengthening the geographic stratification characteristic of an economy based more and more on the speedy production of a wide range of commodities, including motion pictures.

These methods and by-products of uneven urban development—temporary work, indirect benefits to local business, the transformation of bleak imagery into promotional imagery—are indicative of the fundamental contradiction urban regions face in an economy in which the management of production and the realization of profit are increasingly determined by the FIRE sector. As the local organ of these types of firms, Greater Philadelphia First enjoys an enhanced position in helping to set the development agenda, especially since the political power of local government, unions, and community organizations generally has been diminished by the same economic processes that have given the FIRE corporations increased influence. However, these same processes have engaged Greater Philadelphia First in an interregional competition for capital investment with other urban regions around the nation and presumably the world.[8] On the one

8 For a concise account of interurban competition in a multinational economic context, see Sassen (1991, 1994). Unfortunately, Sassen's hyperbolic language of "global cities" and "world economy" assumes the obsolescence of nation-based capitals and significantly underemphasizes the continuing role of the state in shaping the dynamics of accumulation and politics within and across localities and nations. Greater Philadelphia First clearly sees one of its roles as drawing multinational capital investment to Philadelphia, and it has had some success in this direction. It is not at all clear, however, that multinational capitalism has a significant ideological function in Philadelphia or Pennsylvania politics.

hand, then, the producer-service economy fosters uneven development, which produces heterogeneous urban space and increases the power of certain kinds of corporations. On the other hand the same forces that give these corporations their increased power also force them to represent somehow the urban region in a unified fashion and to market it as a stable, homogeneous entity offering locational advantages "as lures for a peripatetic capital that values the option of mobility very highly" (Harvey 1989: 303).

As the example of *12 Monkeys* illustrates, one of the most powerful ways of covering over this contradiction is to turn the whole of the city's urban space into a commodity, a set of features that potential investors and high-skill workers can browse through and compare with the amenities offered by other competitive urban spaces. In this context the importance of generating highly *aestheticized* representations of urban space increases as the entire landscape of the city becomes represented less as a site of production and more as an object of consumption. In this regard the aestheticization of the city in *12 Monkeys* fits the bill more or less as well as more traditional forms of promotional literature.

It is important to avoid the error, so often made in postmodernist theory and other fields, of assuming that this situation means production no longer matters, and that we now have a new "consumer society" being thrust upon us. Instead, it should be possible to theorize that recent innovations in production and distribution have helped shape consumption patterns and by extension new forms of what is often termed "culture." These innovations include: sub-contracting, outsourcing, and other organizational shifts away from vertical integration; "just-in-time" delivery systems that eliminate the need for large inventories; small-batch production; highly rationalized techniques of packaging, containerization, and marketing; and the use of electronics to speed up financial services and transactions. David Harvey argues that these techniques "provide a means to accelerate the pace of consumption not only in clothing, ornament, and decoration but also across a wide swathe of lifestyles and recreational activities" (1989: 284–285). These changes occur not because the laws of capitalism have changed or become irrelevant (as postmodernism often asserts), but rather because competition fosters the commodification of urban space, which in turn leads to the increasing integration of lifestyle itself—the act of living in the city—into existing patterns of consumption. It is advantageous for Greater Philadelphia First and others to represent the city in spatialized, ahistorical terms that deemphasize the historical, temporal contradictions of uneven development, and that instead open up the city's landscape to use by shoppers, tourists, and filmmakers.

An example of this sort of representational strategy is *The Greater Philadelphia Story* (1993), a glossy, 70-page coffee table book advertising the "Greater Philadelphia region" to firms and high-level professionals needed to bolster the downtown redevelopment and gentrification projects underway in the city. *The Greater Philadelphia Story* contains the testimony of several dozen individuals employed in the FIRE sector as to the benefits of living in the region. Different vignettes cover different topics: education, recreation, shopping, and so forth. The individuals whose pictures and words appear in the vignettes all are recent transplants, having relocated from other areas during the three years prior to the book's publication. Ron Kozich, Managing Partner at the nationwide law and consulting firm of Ernst and Young, writes:

> From strolling Elfreth's Alley to enjoying a horse and buggy tour through the
> neighborhood where Ben Franklin and Thomas Jefferson helped shape our nation

to exploring some of the world's finest museums, history is so alive and accessible. Although we live here now, we continue to be fascinated tourists in a great city. (9)

Kozich's survey of historic sites is infused with the highly aestheticized and spatialized activities characteristic of commodified urban space—"enjoying a horse and buggy tour," "exploring" museums, and so forth. The body text that accompanies his testimonial represents the city's historic monuments as "America's most historic square mile." "Here, in downtown Philadelphia, just blocks away from department stores and corporate towers, is an endlessly captivating pageant of American History" (9). The impact of these images and activities is reinforced by Kozich's claim that he still feels like a tourist. While a resident lives in a space and is, in an important sense, *of* that space, a tourist enjoys that space by consuming it. Through tourism, all the features of a space— shopping, high culture, architecture, history—are quite literally defined by their commodity function.[9] It is not just that a city's space, architecture and history become incentives for consumption; the city itself becomes defined by its exchange value in a market. The city's distinctive features become more or less interchangeable with those of other cities, and ultimately with one another. And this is precisely the point: Philadelphia's attributes may be listed on a check-off sheet, counted up and totaled against those of any other city, as in the annual *US News and World Report* livability rankings.

In this manner the Philadelphia area is represented as diverse, vital, full of potential, "on the move," and yet paradoxically possessed of a timeless stability. The result is not merely increased profits and expanded markets for locally headquartered corporations; more fundamentally, new wants, needs, and standards of success are created that shape the contours of social life. Consumables—urban amenities, motion pictures, recreational activities—get produced and redefined at ever faster speeds and draw almost at random from a dizzying array of historical sources, influences, and antecedents. As in accounts of the postmodern condition, aesthetic pastiche becomes a primary marketing tool, as linear narrative is replaced by the immediacy of consumer choice, and the ideology of consumption comes to permeate more and more aspects of daily life. "The image, the appearance, the spectacle" of the urban environment and the tourist's paradise, Harvey argues, "can all be experienced with an intensity (joy or terror) made possible only by their appreciation as pure and unrelated presents in time" (1989: 285).

In this context, it is important to note that the speed, immediacy, and pervasiveness of consumer culture extends well beyond specific spaces of consumption, affecting social life in myriad and perhaps unexpected ways. KWRU Executive Director Cheri Honkala relates the effects of the temporal compression and disruption of accelerated consumerism on teenagers in poor communities:

9 Much work in the humanities takes considerable liberties with the term "commodity." While the author is here using the term outside the context of the labor relation *per se*, the intent is still to preserve the strict meaning of the term "commodity." The subsumption of Philadelphia's space under an agenda of competition with other cities for tourist dollars inevitably submits that space to the logic of exchange, which Marx (1990) says is the "mystical character" of the commodity under capitalism, and which distinguishes the commodity from a mere object (163). Philadelphia's historical space competes as a *product* on the basis of its distinctiveness; but the very notion of such a competition implies the potential substitutability, or exchangeability, of this space's distinctiveness for that of any other city's space, according to criteria of "livability," recreation, safety, beauty, availability of land or capital, and so on.

[These] kids have no alternatives . . . [They] have attempted suicide. I['ve] been in so many hospital rooms with mothers with kids trying to kill themselves . . . None of these kids ha[s] any money for movies. They are constantly under harassment for not being up to style in clothing, there's pressure to develop drug addictions— you name it. They're living a hell.

(quoted in Ruben 1995a)

Honkala's narrative resonates with Harvey's account, highlighting the psychic trauma of living under constant pressure to keep up with rapid changes in fashion that follow no logical progression, and with consuming the unending output of cultural products like Hollywood films. In Honkala's account, even drug abuse is subject to the logic of consumption: in the instances to which she refers it is not drugs *per se* that produce the teens' suicide attempts, but rather drug addiction as one more item in a regime of consumption of products with short "life spans" that fit the fast-turnover logic of modern-day capitalism. As the pace, pervasiveness, and social importance of consumption increase, the relative deprivation of the poor rises along with them. Put simply, there are more and more things that one notices one does not have and cannot get, and the increased cultural importance of consumption in the city makes not-having increasingly central to one's identity as a social being. The prototypical consumer, who may go to see *12 Monkeys* and for whom the film may be an allegory of modern life, experiences the acceleration of consumption as a "pageant," an intense spectacle of joy. But the impoverished urban teenager, who cannot afford to see the movie and for whom the film's horrific images constitute a documentary, experiences the flip side of spectacular joy: terror and violence.

Toward a new method

> You only get what you are organized to take.
> (Kensington Welfare Rights Union slogan, quoted in *Poverty Outlaw*)

While Cheri Honkala's account of poor teens' experience is quite powerful, it is also quite depressing. If the only choices are media images of teenagers killing each other for a stylish new pair of sneakers or Honkala's account of teenagers killing themselves because they cannot afford a stylish new pair of sneakers, then the situation seems hopeless and we are stuck back in the debilitating evil villain/passive victim binary that has characterized the "culture of poverty" argument for three decades.[10] It would seem that while modern-day capitalism facilitates the development of agency for certain Philadelphia business interests and for the producers of *12 Monkeys*, it tends to close off possibilities for agency among the women and children who belong to KWRU.

In this context, our own intellectual, political, and *affective* relationship to questions of space and time changes significantly. Instead of trying to make a universal decision about the current status of time or cities, as much postmodernist and urban scholarship asks us to do, we see the divergent fates that await different people and interests in the city. We feel a sense of urgency and hope that Cynthia Fuchs and *12 Monkeys* are wrong in asserting that "nonlinearity is inexorable."

10 For a concise summary of the "culture of poverty" and "underclass" debates, see Katz (1993).

And this, finally, is what is at stake in debates over postmodernism and development in film studies and urban studies. The destabilization of time has widely variable effects, costs and benefits. Harvey's argument, while immensely useful, reaches its limit at this point, when it relegates the difference between consumptive joy and spectacular terror to a parenthetical.[11] In this vein the question of whether postmodernism is anti-referential or referential is the same as the question of whether *12 Monkeys* is a documentary or an allegory. In both cases the answer is that the question itself is misguided. Other questions must immediately interrupt it: "where," "when," "for whom," and "in what context?" For the business community, time-bending means increased profits at the expense of government resources, as firms claim net operating loss carry-forwards from the past and quick amortization of capital from the future. For poor people in Philadelphia, temporal nonlinearity is one way of referring to the effects of the withdrawal of public funding, and more generally to a potential catastrophe that must be resisted.

For Catherine Engle and other members of KWRU, the way out of terror began through an historical and political understanding of the economic and social processes that produce the current conditions of poverty. "The first reason [for KWRU's existence]," Honkala says, "is to meet basic needs. But the game, or the fight, is to provide people with political education."[12]

"Which Way Welfare Rights?," a pamphlet authored in part by Honkala, proposes a way to understand struggle and empowerment for poor people:

> No end or objective can be accomplished without means or resources and their proper utilization . . . [History places] means at the disposal of political leaders . . . in the course of social development. History is the unfolding of the stages of development of society. It is rooted in the constant changes in the economy, changes in the way the necessities of life are produced and distributed. On the basis of these changes, conflicting economic interests of different sections of the population compel them to take up historically evolved forms of struggle and fight it out.
>
> (National Welfare Rights Union 1993)

In postmodernist discourse and urban scholarship, in English departments and sociology programs, this sort of narrative is regularly dismissed for being linear, rigid, retrograde, and masculinist. In fact, it is fair to say that a number of sub-fields, schools of thought, and careers have been founded upon a strict and specific opposition to just this sort of discourse. But when it is *situated*, placed in the context of the confusing and disorienting workings of the economic system it critiques, this linear, teleological narrative, written by and largely for poor women, can be understood as an appropriate tool in a moment characterized not only by its *historical* location but also by its *geographical* one.

Similarly, a KWRU organizing pamphlet (1993) addresses itself to "the victims of poverty," making an appeal across the racial and ethnic lines that often separate neighborhoods from one another:

---

11 Harvey himself has been quite attentive to this limit, and has addressed it thoroughly in his more recent work (1996, 2000).

12 Throughout its seven-year existence, KWRU's ability to provide political education to new members has varied greatly based on available time and resources, the nature of its struggle at particular moments, and the changing priorities of its leadership.

Figure 17.3 A Kensington Welfare Rights Union demonstration. This shot, taken from the documentary *Poverty Outlaw* (Yates and Kinoy 1996), takes place virtually in the same spot where scenes from *12 Monkeys* were filmed. It features youth and adult members of KWRU in a 1992 march leading up to the takeover of an abandoned Kensington Avenue building the group planned to turn into a community center. Courtesy of Skylight Pictures

We as poor people, especially women and youth, are often isolated from one another ...We tend to blame each other, i.e.: poor whites will blame poor blacks, poor blacks blame poor Asians and the cycle goes round and round. And we see this tool of division taking place every day in the Kensington area, even though we all stand in the same soup lines, welfare lines and our children go to school together.

(Kensington Welfare Rights Union 1993)

This passage features neither the ecstatic universalism of postmodernist theory nor the hermetic, agentless pessimism of much cultural criticism and urban policy literature. Rather, it evokes a vision of urban neighborhoods that are different from each other and from the redeveloped city center. It appeals to "the victims of poverty" across the racial lines that often separate neighborhoods from one another. It speaks to poor people who must increasingly avail themselves of the shrinking services of the welfare state, and it uses that shared experience to break the temporal "cycle" that goes "round and round" by organizing poor people across the urban landscape on the basis of *class*. More recently KWRU has attempted to broaden its organizing and educational efforts. *Poverty Outlaw*, a documentary by Pamela Yates and Peter Kinoy, shows KWRU members organizing and marching on the exact same blocks, streets, and sidewalks depicted in *12 Monkeys*, and features testimonials similar to the ones that appear in this essay to educate the general public about the persistence of poverty in urban centers and to help counter the sense of isolation poor people often experience (Fig. 17.3). Since 1998, the organization has embarked on a "Poor People's Economic Human Rights Campaign," using United Nations documents and the internationally recognized discourse of human rights to highlight the dehumanization and repression suffered by poor people across the city, the state of Pennsylvania, and the nation.

Taken together, these passages and activities begin to show how uneven development provides a potential for the formation of political consciousness and agency among the poor people whose bodies and neighborhoods constitute aesthetic fodder for films like *12 Monkeys*. The most dangerous limit to both postmodernist theory and most critical responses to it is that when we are done critiquing we have gained very little practical knowledge of the flip side of the coin of capital accumulation: class formation.

This does not mean that *12 Monkeys'* intervention on behalf of nonlinear time is entirely bankrupt. It does indicate that *12 Monkeys* is a highly ambiguous text. It makes use of an urban landscape of uneven development to tell a homogenizing, universalizing story about global catastrophe. Like most policy pronouncements that emanate from both liberal-centrist and conservative politicians and think tanks, this filmic text can be read as a jarring depiction of reality, or it can be read as one more in a series of suspect discourses that seek to highlight urban depravity and impending social disintegration. It provides us with highly aestheticized images of a decaying society, but omits the antagonistic, contradictory processes that have brought it into being, and the massive social inequality those processes create. *12 Monkeys* thereby erases the conditions under which its own production occurred. Despite its subversive political "content," then, what we have in *12 Monkeys* is the paradigmatic commodity form.

The claim that a major motion picture is a commodity is not an original or interesting conclusion to any argument, to say the least. But it is a crucially important fact that, sadly, has yet to be dealt with adequately by film studies or cultural studies in the US. The commodity form will not go away, and no manner of hermeneutically conjured textual "rupture" will ever undo the commodity to the extent that we can plausibly claim a major trade film to be truly "subversive" of or "resistant" to capitalist social relations.[13]

Politically and methodologically, then, the most important role such a filmic commodity plays is that of a jumping-off point—perhaps simply an occasion—for activists, artists, and scholars and to create and circulate other texts like *Poverty Outlaw* and the narratives constructed by KWRU and its members. Of course, this political role for film does not square well with the priority of textual analysis in the methodological and institutional bases of film studies, cultural studies, and most of the humanities in the US. In the course of presenting and otherwise disseminating portions of this work over the past three years, I have been asked repeatedly why I do not conclude with a new reading of the film that improves upon the postmodernist interpretation with which the essay begins. Why is the reader never presented with a fully formed, alternative reading of *12 Monkeys* that incorporates the arguments and interventions made throughout the essay? While I am not surprised by this sort of question, I am always disheartened by it. "Why don't you come back to the movie at the end?"—as if the work that went into producing the preceding pages were all for the sake of the film. It should be obvious by now that the priority of the text cannot be the ultimate concern of a critical film practice that seeks to address the thorny issue of representation introduced at the outset. It should be equally obvious that traditional film and cultural studies methodologies must be altered, supplemented, and when necessary discarded if humanist scholarship is to regain public relevance as anything more than social capital for well-heeled college graduates who go on to work in the FIRE industries that dominate the contemporary economy of uneven urban development. Perhaps then we might more rigorously situate our readings and ourselves in an ethico-political relation to the struggles of poor people

---

13 For a discussion of the politics and ethics of scholarly analysis of mainstream, big-budget films, see Tobin (1995).

for justice. We might set about trying to help poor people be makers of policy and subjects of cinema rather than their objects, and intensify our efforts to make common cause with those for whom *12 Monkeys* truly is a documentary of the present.

References

Adams, Carolyn Teich (1988) *The Politics of Capital Investment: The Case of Philadelphia*, Albany: State University of New York Press.

Adams, Carolyn, David Bartelt, David Elesh, Ira Goldstein, Nancy Kleniewski, and William Yancey (1990) *Philadelphia: Neighborhoods, Division, and Conflict in a Postindustrial City*, Philadelphia: Temple University Press.

Ascher-Walsh, Rebecca (1995) "Making Monkeys Shine: It's a Pitiful Life in Brad's New World," *Entertainment Weekly*, October 20: 36.

Baudrillard, Jean (1988) *Selected Writings*, edited by Mark Poster, Stanford: Stanford University Press.

Behar, Henry (1996) "A Chat with Terry Gilliam on (and around) 'Twelve Monkeys,'" http://www.filmscouts.com, June 5.

"Business Information for *12 Monkeys*" (1995), Internet Movie Database, Ltd. http://us.imdb.com.

Callinicos, Alex (1990) *Against Postmodernism*, New York: St. Martin's Press.

Cityscape: A Journal of Policy Development and Research (1994) 1 (1) (August), Proceedings of the Regional Growth and Community Development Conference, Washington, DC, November 1993, Washington, DC: US Department of Housing and Urban Development.

Coit, Katharine (1984) "Local Action, not Citizen Participation," in William K. Tabb and Larry Sawers, eds, *Marxism and the Metropolis: New Perspectives in Urban Political Economy*, 2nd edn, New York: Oxford University Press, 297–310.

Davis, Mike (1990) *City of Quartz: Excavating the Future in Los Angeles*, London: Verso.

DeBord, Guy (1994) *The Society of the Spectacle*, New York: Zone Books.

Deleuze, Gilles, and Felix Guattari (1983) *Anti-Oedipus: Capitalism and Schizophrenia*, translated by Robert Hurley, Mark Seem, and Helen R. Lane, Minneapolis: University of Minnesota Press.

Fuchs, Cynthia (1996) "The Monkeys Man"/"*12 Monkeys*" (linked feature and review), *Philadelphia City Paper*, January 5: 16–18, 50–51.

Gilliam, Terry (1995) *12 Monkeys*, Los Angeles: Universal Pictures/Atlas Entertainment.

Greater Philadelphia First (1993) *The Greater Philadelphia Story*, Philadelphia: Greater Philadelphia First Corporation.

—— (1995) *Report of Progress 1994*, Philadelphia: Greater Philadelphia First Corporation.

—— (1996) *Report of Progress 1995*, Philadelphia: Greater Philadelphia First Corporation.

—— (1997) *Report of Progress 1996*, Philadelphia: Greater Philadelphia First Corporation.

—— (1999) *Report of Progress 1998*, Philadelphia: Greater Philadelphia First Corporation.

Harvey, David (1989) *The Condition of Postmodernity*, Cambridge, MA: Blackwell.

—— (1996) *Justice, Nature and the Geography of Difference*, London: Blackwell.

—— (2000) *Spaces of Hope*, Berkeley: University of California Press.

Hay, James (1997) "Piecing Together What Remains of the Cinematic City," in David B. Clarke, ed., *The Cinematic City*, London: Routledge, 209–229.

Hill, Richard Child (1984) "Fiscal Collapse and Political Struggle in Decaying Central Cities in the United States," in William K. Tabb and Larry Sawers, eds, *Marxism and the Metropolis: New Perspectives in Urban Political Economy*, 2nd edn, New York: Oxford University Press, 213–240.

Horkheimer, Max and Adorno, Theodor (1972) *The Dialectic of Enlightenment*, New York: Continuum.

Jackson, Thomas (1993) "The State, the Movement, and the Urban Poor: The War on Poverty and Political Mobilization in the 1960s," in Michael B. Katz, ed., *The "Underclass" Debate: Views from History*, Princeton: Princeton University Press, 403–439.

Jameson, Frederic (1984) "The Cultural Logic of Late Capital," *New Left Review* 146 (July/August): 53–92.

—— (1991) *Postmodernism, or the Cultural Logic of Late Capitalism*, London: Verso.

Jencks, Charles A. (1984) *The Language of Postmodern Architecture*, New York: Rizzoli.

Katz, Michael B. (1993) "The Urban 'Underclass' as a Metaphor of Social Transformation," in Michael B. Katz, ed., *The "Underclass" Debate: Views from History*, Princeton: Princeton University Press, 3–23.

Kelley, Robin D. G. (1993) "The Black Poor and the Politics of Opposition in a New South City, 1929–1970," in Michael B. Katz, ed., *The "Underclass" Debate: Views from History*, Princeton: Princeton University Press, 293–333.

Kensington Welfare Rights Union (1993) "Link Up the Struggle" (pamphlet), Philadelphia: Kensington Welfare Rights Union/United in Strength.

Lewis, Oscar (1966) "The Culture of Poverty," *Scientific American* 215 (4) (October 1966): 19–25.

Logan, John R. and H. Molotch (1987) *Urban Fortunes: The Political Economy of Place*, Berkeley: University of California Press.

Lyotard, Jean-François (1984) *The Postmodern Condition: A Report on Knowledge*, translated by Geoff Bennington and Brian Massumi, Minneapolis: University of Minnesota Press.

—— (1991) *The Inhuman: Reflections on Time*, translated by Geoff Bennington and Rachel Bowlby, Stanford: Stanford University Press.

Murray, Charles (1984) *Losing Ground: American Social Policy, 1950–1980*, New York: Basic Books.

National Welfare Rights Union (1993) "Which Way Welfare Rights?" (pamphlet) Philadelphia: Annie Smart Leadership Institute and *Voices from the Front*.

Oliver, Melvin, James H. Johnson, Jr., and Walter C. Farrell, Jr. (1993) "Anatomy of a Rebellion: A Political-Economic Analysis," in Robert Goode-Williams, ed., *Reading Rodney King, Reading Urban Uprising*, New York: Routledge, 117–141.

Piven, Frances Fox and Richard A. Cloward (1979) *Poor People's Movements: Why They Succeed, How They Fail*, New York: Vintage.

Rickey, Carrie (1995) "*12 Monkeys* Takes the Turnpike: Futuristic Film Leaves Town after Pumping Millions into City's Economy," *Philadelphia Inquirer*, March 27: D1.

Ruben, Matthew (1995a) Interview with Cheri Honkala, March 10.

—— (1995b) Interview with Catherine Engle, March 13.

Sassen, Saskia (1991) *The Global City: New York, London, Tokyo*, Princeton: Princeton University Press.

—— (1994) *Cities in a World Economy*, Thousand Oaks, CA: Pine Forge Press.

Smith, Neil (1991) *Uneven Development*, London: Blackwell.

—— (1996) *The New Urban Frontier: Gentrification and the Revanchist City*, London: Routledge.

Spivak, Gayatri Chakravorty (1986) "Can the Subaltern Speak?" in Cary Nelson and Lawrence Grossberg, eds, *Marxism and the Interpretation of Culture*, Urbana: University of Illinois Press, 271–313.

Sugrue, Thomas J. (1993) "The Structures of Urban Poverty: The Reorganization of Space and Work in Three Periods of American History," in Michael B. Katz, ed., *The "Underclass" Debate: Views from History*, Princeton: Princeton University Press, 85–117.

Tobin, Elayne (1995) "Coffee Talk," *Mediations* 19 (1) (Spring): 66–74.

Wharton Real Estate Center (1994) *Urban Strategy Project* (Urban Audit Working Papers), Philadelphia: Wharton Real Estate Center.

Widner, Ralph R. and Marvin E. Wolfgang, eds (1986) *Revitalizing the Industrial City* (Annals of the American Academy of Political and Social Science 488), Newbury Park, CA: Sage.

Wilson, William Julius (1987) *The Truly Disadvantaged: The Inner City, the Underclass, and Public Policy*, Chicago: University of Chicago Press.

Yates, Pamela and Peter Kinoy (1996) *Poverty Outlaw*, New York: Skylight Pictures.

Zukin, Sharon (1991) *Landscapes of Power: From Detroit to Disney World*, Berkeley: University of California Press.

18 Terminator technology

Hollywood, history, and technology

Paul Smith

The end of the twentieth century came a little bit later, by a decade or so, than the end of the first century of cinema, but the specific character of the twentieth century can hardly be grasped, and imaginaries about the new millennium can hardly be formed without recognizing the crucial function of film and, later, the other visual media, in helping the era be resolved into representations. The visual media (mass media from the very beginning and used deliberately as instruments of mass perception as well as mass distraction) have facilitated and enabled a popular or demotic sense of the world which has been thicker, stronger and more consistent than in any other era. Even if older channels of perception—like books and newspapers—can be said to have been gradually democratized over the course of the nineteenth century, their efficacy was immediately and spectacularly outstripped by the appearance of the technologies of the visual media—those technologies that have marked this century as surely as (or in symbiotic cahoots with) total wars, holocausts, genocides, revolutions, and so on. From the very first exhibited films which terrified audiences with the realism of their representations, to present-day movies like *The Blair Witch Project* that terrify audiences with the realism of their representations, mass visual productions have caught the imagination of subjects and held them in thrall with a thoroughgoing efficiency.

This is one sense in which the cinema can be thought of as a kind of "terminator technology," taking a ruthless hold on our subjectivities while at the same time producing a virtual monopoly on the product and spreading it (whatever its effects) across the world. I'm making an analogy, of course, to the "terminator technology" with which we're probably all familiar by now: the controversial apparatus of the biotechnology industry, led by the corporation Monsanto, which can manufacture seeds whose genes are altered such that they essentially become sterile once they have been grown. The upshot for farmers is that the age-old practice of collecting seeds for re-use is made impossible and so each year they have to order a new set of seeds from their corporate suppliers. This seems to me an apt conceit in several respects for the way in which the American media industry operates, producing commodities whose use-value in the public sphere is confined precisely to allowing the consumer to spend a moment or two in the act of consumption and whose meanings can hardly circulate except in the pre-established world of the entertainment and media industries and whose net result can only be described as an advanced sterility in the body public.

In some areas of media studies one can still find the occasional discussion about how exactly movies have managed to take such a firm grip on subjects. Some of that discussion will be about the primacy of visual perception in the human sensorium, or about our inherent psychological need for realism, and so on. Whatever the merits or demerits of those kinds of discussion, what's usually overlooked in them—and overlooked too in most interpretative work about film—is the simple fact that film was, from the beginning, sold as a commodity and that its power has clearly something to do with the single-mindedness with which an industry was built up around the new and continually renewing technologies of the visual. The film industry has, it almost goes without saying, been America's single most consistent industry in the last hundred years. That's not to say that it has been the most profitable in purely financial terms (although as an export dollar earner it currently ranks second only to the aerospace industry), but to point to its unusual stability and consistent performance in relation to almost any other industry apart from the basic utility industries.

I stress this industrial character of the media not simply because it is an element that is often mysteriously absent from much analysis in media studies, and not just because the history of the industry is in and of itself a fascinating case study in the nature of American capitalism. But I stress it also because I want to argue that the industrial forms of media production inevitably inflect the kinds of meanings manufactured in and as the commodities sold to the mass market. There are few enough political-economic studies of American media which would treat the imbrication of the circumstances of production with the nature or the meaning of the commodity. Even if there are some good studies of the American film industry which concentrate on its economic aspects (such as work by people like Douglas Gomery, or Janet Wasko),[1] there's certainly nothing of the order of Richard Ohmann's book, *Selling Culture*, which takes a properly political-economic kind of approach to the growth of a different industry—that of mass market publications in the late nineteenth and early twentieth century—and by properly I mean that the approach sees the cultural and economic facets of the publishing industry as mutually determining, mutually informing.[2] Ohmann's book offers up a number of hints that could be adopted into a parallel analysis of American visual media. For instance, his proving that the capitalist interest in developing mass market publications was neither ideologically driven nor even especially committed to the nature of the product is particularly important. Rather, his work suggests, these publishing commodities were always mostly accidental in their nature, ephemeral combinations of available discourses, existing and emerging technologies, and available industrial capacities which are then developed willy-nilly into a self-defining industrial endeavor. That kind of observation about forms of production is consistent with a Marxist sense that capitalism is mostly indifferent to the exact nature of the commodity and primarily attends instead to the simple process of converting money to commodity to money.

If carried over to the media generally, this point about the indifference of capital to the exact nature of the commodity might give some comfort to those who nowadays consider the film industry to have abandoned all decency and standards. We've already heard a lot more on that topic in the recent US presidential race, where both major parties sharpened their rhetoric against the dubious morality of public spectacles, and darkly linked that to events such as the Columbine High School massacre. No doubt on some level it's true that the indifference of capital to the commodity habitually fore-

1 Douglas Gomery, *Shared Pleasures: A History of Movie Presentation in the United States* (Madison: University of Wisconsin Press, 1992). See, too, J. Wasko, *Hollywood in the Information Age: Beyond the Silver Screen* (Cambridge: Polity, 1994).
2 R. Ohmann, *Selling Culture* (London: Verso, 1996).

closes on questions of morality and ethics. But I don't mean to join that particular assault on the media right now, since as far as I can see, from their mass beginnings the media have always been charged with some crime of this sort and in any case the tension between, as we might put it, market and community is endemic to American culture and has been ever since the Founding Fathers determined that "we mean to be a commercial people."

But it's also true that the media have chronically in this century been associated with some form of loss, and the more sophisticated assaults on the media's role in American culture will talk of the loss of memory, of affect, of history itself. These kinds of observation have been formulated with especial dignity by Fredric Jameson or with more abandon by the postmodernist likes of Jean Baudrillard.[3] The argument goes, roughly, that the representations produced in and by the media are capable somehow of displacing the real, eradicating the referent of history itself. Here I want to reject the notion that media representations are somehow "hyper-real," or simulacra to be taken for the real, and I rather take the more common sense view that there is nothing more real— certainly nothing excessively real—about them. They are, simply, part of our lives in mediat(is)ed cultures and they have real effects. Once again these effects are the intended and unintended consequences of the business or the industry that sustains any particular media representation and are, in the long run, quite analogous to the effects of consuming any other commodity at all.

To reject the postmodern "hyper-real" theses about the media image and at the same time to reject the liberal view of their decadence and danger: this has certain consequences for thinking about the role of the media as the engine of a set of powerful yet historically located representations. These representations are not just any old representations. That is, what kind of representations they are, what they do to produce meaning, and what effects those meanings have are still of crucial importance. Part of what I want to suggest here is that they are, in one way at least, deeply satisfying representations whereby the world is resolved into images and which therefore help forge memories and identities, but they are representations also turned toward a kind of repeatability: the regime of the action replay and the ideology of sensationalism subventing it are not just psychologically but also socially powerful phenomena which we live with and which forge a general consciousness about how the world works—the world as endlessly repeatable action and renewable sensation, and subject to all the immediacy and ready consumability of the image.

Here I'm half repeating and then somewhat extending what Hayden White has had to say about the media as historical texts, their function as he puts it rather clumsily, as "historiophoty." Responding to some fellow historians who are all in a tizzy about the place of historical discourse in the media century, and about the status of film texts as historical evidence, White points out that there is nothing intrinsically different, still less anything inferior about "historiophoty," and that a historiophotic text is a "text like any other"; he then goes on to argue for the need to analyze carefully the specificity of images as representation and for the need to gauge their ability to predicate historical reflection and not merely complement it.[4] The most immediately useful texts for White's

3 See, for example, Fredric Jameson, *Postmodernism, or the Cultural Logic of Late Capitalism* (Durham: Duke University Press, 1991); and Jean Baudrillard, *Cool Memories,* translated by Chris Turner (London: Verso, 1990).

4 Hayden White, "Historiography and Historiophoty," *American Historical Review* 93 (5) (December 1988), 1193–1199.

discussion would be self-avowedly "historical" productions, such as *Shoah* or *Reds* or *Elizabeth*, and more directly documentaries and testimonial film. But his main point must be taken to extend to all other kinds of media representation so that we can try to see more exactly what place particular kinds of representations play in the construction of our everyday culture and popular memory, and what kind of ideological and rhetorical work they do. Here again for White the crucial task is the study of the production of meaning within the overdetermined formations of contemporary culture and to that I would want to add the sense that it is the industrial formation of American media which informs and inflects the kinds of meanings produced. In that sense the historical matter that is treated in media texts, as well as the historical reflection they can give rise to, must be considered as a function of the scene of their production.

In my book, *Clint Eastwood A Cultural Production*,[5] I tried to describe how those processes of cultural meaning production worked in relation to that one figure. The aim was to demonstrate the thick and complex imbrication of American media practice and production within the particular events and ideologies of particular cultural moments. It was rather usual at that time to see films like those of Eastwood through the lenses of all those over-familiar shibboleths of American mythography (the frontier, vigilantism, the lone heroic savior of the community, the integrity and wholesomeness of small-town America, and so on—all the standard tropes of what I would call a non-materialist brand of American historiography). What I was trying to show, in contrast, was that the meanings embedded in those tropes were by no means mythographic but needed to be specifically co-ordinated with a sense of the industrial work done by—the industrial practices of— contemporary media production, stressing, after Woolacott and Bennett, the "professional ideology" of media production, the professional ideology that sets the range of possibilities for plots and stories, characterization, image construction, production values, and so on.[6] That is, the semantic task of movies like Eastwood's would be to adjust the continually shifting public discourse about America, its history, politics, and culture—civic discourse, in short—back into familiar, manageable and pre-set frames (literally), frames whose calibration to the contexts of contemporaneous circumstances is the only work on meaning that the film industry either wants to do or is capable of undertaking.

In that book, then, I was trying to point to the need to understand the parameters of the industrial production of meaning. This was largely in order to avoid falling into the easy arms of mythographic tropes, but also to try to counter two tendencies in most film/media studies: first, the propensity toward offering "readings" of individual texts in the way of a kind of practical criticism; and second, the then emerging "new audience studies," which seemed to me to fall too easily—perhaps inevitably—into a celebration of audience freedom. Without a sense of the way that professional ideologies and the whole scene of production limit and contain what can be said in films, media criticism will simply continue to replicate the very effort of the media industry itself. That is, critical reflection will not do much more than what is already done by what I call in *Clint Eastwood* the tributary media (those fraternal and co-operative, partially owned and operated branches of Hollywood in the TV networks, entertainment magazines and movie distribution corporations); no more, that is, than subvent

5 P. Smith, *Clint Eastwood: A Cultural Production* (Minneapolis: University of Minnesota Press, 1993).

6 J. Woolacott and T. Bennett, *Bond and Beyond: The Political Career of a Popular Hero* (Basingstoke: Macmillan Education, 1987).

the accommodation of fictional-mythical histories to the ideological demands and parameters of the moment.

Of course the era of Eastwood and of that type of production has waned in many respects. It gave away its predominance first of all to all those action heroes of the 1980s, Sylvester Stallone, Arnold Schwarzenegger, Steven Seagal and the rest, more or less all of whose films' main burden seemed to be to carry on a discursive battle over America's failure in Vietnam and which tried to win that battle in a different decade by way of Body By Jake heroes and Star Wars technology. The more spectacular and brutal the action and the more over-the-top the technology and special effects of that decade's movies, the better; and, of course, the more evident it became that the industry's simple aim was to form a semantic alliance with the Reagan revolution. While many of the films produced at this time specifically addressed the matter of re-fighting the Vietnam war, the consonance between the Hollywood ideological product and the ideological agenda of the Reagan years could be heard in other registers too. Thus, one film of that time stands out for its complaisance and its attempts to resolve the cultural narratives of the 1980s into images: perhaps rather obviously, given my title, I mean *The Terminator*, James Cameron's film starring Arnold Schwarzenegger (1984) (Fig 18.1). This film is interesting on all kinds of levels, but its at-the-time ground-breaking special effects, and its use of special effect technology—that is, to construe a technological time traveling hit-man—were and are especially informative. The film essentially pits an inhuman or inhumane use of technology—time travel, technologically over-endowed cyborgs, novel hi-tech weaponry—against more humane uses in a scenario that is on one level a paradigm for a "just war"; on another an instance of the industrial stand-by of the western. And consonant with its moment of production, the film is also a perverse kind of meditation on abortion, with the Terminator intent on performing a cosmic hi-tech abortion and the humans attempting to save a single baby for future leadership. Along the way the contemporaneous consumer technologies are shown to be weak and ineffectual—an answering machine that doesn't do its job, a shotgun ineffectually used against the Terminator's armory, flimsy and clunky motor vehicles, a Sony Walkman that deafens a victim to signs of danger, and so on. These ordinary technologies of 1980s America are set against the startling technologies of the cyborg terminator and of time travel itself. The film's view and use of technology is just one illustration of the kinds of logical and ideological imaginaries that tend to congeal around technology in US public life and have done so throughout the growth, rise, and supposed triumph of capitalism.

In the last few years, leading up to the millennial moment that we are assured is the moment of fully globalized capitalism, the notion of technology has come to play an almost talismanic role. Not too long ago in Washington, DC, there was an outdoor advertising campaign that provided an ordinary instance of the current technological imaginary in a poster proclaiming that "Technology is changing the face of the World: Washington DC is next" (without, incidentally, telling us what particular technologies might be applied to us, or how they change the face of the world). In our moment of the dotcom economy, we've been bombarded in an especially intense manner with similar claims about how technology is changing or will change the world by changing the very nature of capitalism itself. The most extreme claims of this sort—extreme but nonetheless currently taken as gospel in business, government, and the media—propose that technology can and will advance so drastically that economic value will no longer be produced by labor, or through the exploitation of labor in the way that Marx understood.

Figure 18.1 Arnold Schwarzenegger in *The Terminator* (Orion 1984). Courtesy of the Kobal Collection

Figure 18.2 Arnold Schwarzenegger and Edward Furlong in *Terminator II* (Carolco 1991). Courtesy of the Kobal Collection

Rather, the core of value production in a fully technologized capitalism will be the intangible elements of information and knowledge that are essentially the "content" of our new technologies and that will somehow magically replace labor entirely. That idea seems to me to constitute nothing more than what I've called elsewhere a "millennial dream"—a wish-fulfilling fantasy about a totally whole and wholesome capitalism whose permanent dialectic other, labor, has now been transcended and, along with it, the class struggle that attends capitalism's exploitation of labor. Thus technology becomes a sort of panacea—not just in the everyday sense that suggests that technology can solve all practical problems, but in the sense too that it has rid us of capitalism's central antagonist, labor.[7]

In such a cultural and economic climate where such ideas are taken as commonsense, we need to be especially clear about what role technology *per se* really does play in capitalism—or rather, in the project of capital accumulation. While it's obvious that the development of capitalism's productive capacity is and always has been intimately related to the development of particular technologies, the role those technologies play is not, essentially, the kind of determining role that capitalism's current discourse would have us believe. Traditionally, it hasn't been especially important to capital that technologies should be able to engender "new" commodities, since what has been important usually is the use of technologies as constant capital in the production process and their facilitating cuts in production costs. But since the beginning of the last century Hollywood has, I want to argue, led the way in changes in capital's use of technology in so far as Hollywood's use of new technologies actually continually shifts the nature and meaning of the commodity sold. That is, for media industries, technologies have chronically been less about the logic of production and more about the logic of the commodity itself. When I say Hollywood has led the way in this regard, I mean to point to the now more generalized situation today where capitalist technologies not only directly inflect the nature of the commodity but also more and more frequently become commodities themselves. We now live in the moment where technology-commodities, often developed from state operations like the military or NASA, form a major part of the consumer market and it becomes cheaper and cheaper to purchase say a cell phone and more and more expensive to produce say a ton of steel. This tendency is, I'm suggesting, something that Hollywood has pioneered and which is a now an especially important trend in the millennial moment where production and consumption get closer together.

At the same time as Hollywood leads the way in this process whereby new technologies inflect the nature of the commodity (we've seen this from the birth of sound technologies, through advances like deep focus technology, and on to the development of video, DVD, cable and satellite, and electronic games), Hollywood has always been able to construe the very image of advanced technologies on screen: from Chaplin's assembly line in *Modern Times*, through to Hal the computer in *2001: A Space Odyssey*, and on to Schwarzenegger's *Terminator* and beyond, Hollywood has hung the same kind of imaginary on to these technologies. That is, technologies can always be seen as a threat, they will always be open to abuse, they can be invasive and destructive; but, Hollywood seems to claim, in the way of an industrial template, the proper human control of technologies within the context of the values of patriotism, the family, independence, and heroism is desirable and above all possible.

This is the industrial ideology that crosses all those action films of the 1980s and it might have everything to do with Adorno's notion that the image of the technological world possesses an ahistorical facet that enables it to serve as a mythical mirage of eternity.[8] It is, of course, by means of that "ahistorical" aspect that the real conditions of production and the social relations of production are smothered and denied representation. The "technological world" in that sense comes to elide history, not just in

---

7 P. Smith, *Millennial Dreams* (London: Verso, 1997).
8 My paraphrase.

the service of a transcendent mythology or ideology, but in the service of a kind of wish-fulfillment whereby the central antagonisms of capitalism's history are as it were silenced by the ahistorical, by the "eternal."

But of course, as is clear from even a cursory glance at the varied ideological adventures of Hollywood throughout this century, even eternity is always open to reconfiguration and recalibration under capitalism, and we recall how in fact that industrial template of action movie meanings was, throughout the 1980s, also subvented by a peculiar and apparently decisive stage in US anti-communism. Thus with the fall of actually existing socialism, those action heroes and all their technologies had in their turn to pass the baton, their particular kind of rhetorical task having been transcended by what Francis Fukuyama famously dubbed the "end of history"—by which he meant to point (in another wish-fulfilling millennial dream) to the end of a world-historical dialectical conflict between capitalism and its enemies and to the triumph of capitalism.[9] If the 1980s generally demanded a certain kind of engagement with that world-historical conflict, the 1990s were left, ostensibly, with a little less to do at the overtly political or ideological level. It is that circumstance, perhaps, which best explains the change in Hollywood's mode of operation in the 1990s and its turn toward the kind of familiar tropes and paradigms that enable the emergence of a very different kind of film.

With different films come different kinds of stars and for me the paradigmatic figure in the 1990s is the rather homely one of Tom Hanks. In the course of that decade Hanks steadily became a premium, if not the premium, bankable actor in Hollywood, through films such as *Philadelphia*, *Apollo 13*, *You've Got Mail*, *Saving Private Ryan*, and of course the inimitable Oscar-winning movie, *Forrest Gump*. I'll come back to the last film later, but in the meantime it's interesting to note how each of these Hanks blockbusters of the 1990s assumes a particular relation to recent history. Each of them, that is, can be seen as an instance of how Hollywood "works through" significant historical matter. Even if the 1990s no longer demand a direct confrontation with an ideological enemy, it would seem that there are elements of recent history still to be dealt with—elements that we might think of as domestic matters. Thus, for instance, *Philadelphia* is the first Hollywood movie to tackle directly the arrival of AIDS into American life. Or else, *You've Got Mail* takes as its central diegetic problematic the eradication of small retailers in the path of mega-corporations and their monopolistic power.

In each instance of this sort (and there are of course many others beyond these few Hanks movies) the working through of the historical matter results in a predictable kind of elision or wishing away of the central diegetical or historical material. Thus in *Philadelphia*, to put it very simply, the politics of AIDS and the scarifying consequences of the disease for social relations are swept up into an affirmation of the private values of family life. Similarly in *You've Got Mail*, the big corporation's railroading of small bookshops is turned into the most banal of love stories (and where the Meg Ryan character, the small bookshop owner falling for Hanks's corporate CEO, must now stand as the dictionary definition of "internalizing one's own oppression").

And then of course, there's *Forrest Gump*, the movie that sets the standard for what we might once have called revisionist history with its technological sleights-of-hand and plot devices which place the very face and very figure of Hanks in the midst of the main

---

9 Yet another citation to F. Fukuyama, *The End of History and the Last Man* (London: Hamish Hamilton, 1992)!

events and cultural trends of the last forty years. If the action movies of the 1980s had in a sense refought the Vietnam war, Gump puts a full stop on all of that by taking a sardonic and even playful view of the conflict as well as of the social conflicts that used to be called the war at home. Gump's decades-long relationship with his childhood sweetheart essentially puts an end to the "war at home" in that the girl passes through all the social no-go areas of the 1960s and 1970s (she's a hippie and anti-war protester in the 1960s; a stripper, disco girl, and cocaine addict in the 1970s), only to return to Gump, marry him and produce a child before dying of AIDS. This is, as we might say, all that Hollywood allows: in much the same way as capitalism's millennial dreams have worked to wish away the social contradictions of capitalism and its relation to labor, this film resolves the conflicts and contradictions of the recent American past into an image of continuity lent by the birth of a son. At the end of the film, the son replays Gump's own first school day, getting on the school bus. The film offers, then, a typical Hollywood image of continuity and regeneration through the family—less the regeneration through violence that Richard Slotkin sees as the motor to American life, it's more regeneration through hebetude.[10]

Each of these Hanks movies in its way constitutes, as I've said, a revisionist history of sorts. But it's not exactly their relation to the *truth* of history that is of prime interest here. Rather it's the way that they each resolve a part of American history into images that some would say epitomize the essence of American ideology but which I would say are simply the rhetorical reflexes of an industry indifferent to the nature of its commodities: that is, images of ordinary-Joe heroism, family strife and the affect of reconciliation, the loss of loved ones, and the most quotidian of love stories. Under the guise that the industry has adopted over the years of catering to "ordinary people," each of these films in the end (that's to say, at their end) resolves into images of the gooey clump of sentiment that the industry is fond of calling "the human spirit" (the human spirit, preferably captured in its even gooier phase of "triumph").

It's perhaps here that some of the ideas that I'm trying to suggest are easiest to grasp—the notion that the American media's imposition of a template of industrial meanings on to the material of history incessantly anneals the contradictions of that historical material, and produces a history that is, in essence, domesticated, or rather is the history which will anneal the contradictions of any given contemporaneous moment. And so it is this non-contradictory history which will come to stand in popular memory as a history of our past. If, as Benjamin says, "history resolves itself not into narratives but into images,"[11] it only remains to add that the American media have ensured that the images which elide narrative are images of what is thought of as universal or essential human affect, an appeal to a static set of human values to tame the difficulties and contradictions of narrative.

I'm not intending to be especially critical of this process—at least not as critical as I probably sound. Rather I simply want to mark the way these representations arrive on our doorsteps and the annealing work they have to do to get there. Their dominant and even domineering emergence into the public space of the nation is the result of a specific kind of industrial process used to make a commodity and is fertilized by the

---

10 R. Slotkin, *Regeneration through Violence* (Middletown, CT: Wesleyan University Press, 1973).

11 I have been alluding to this phrase of Benjamin's throughout this essay; see W. Benjamin, "Theses on the Philosophy of History," in *Illumination* (New York: Schocken, 1968), 255.

multifarious tributary media which most of us spend a disproportionate amount of our time attending to (television, radio, popular magazines, and papers, and now the internet). The criticism I have is not of the commodities themselves (I'm almost as indifferent to the different instances of them as is capitalism itself), but rather of the process itself—the process by which capitalism produces its commodities and at the same time tries to transcend, elide or simply wish away the social relations of production. And I'm critical too of the sterility of the public sphere that has been thus induced, a public sphere where all history is ritually represented through the givens, the shibboleths, of an emotive humanism whose terms are not open to debate—or rather which have no forum in which to be debated.

It's with that point that I can return to the title of this chapter, "terminator technology." If there are any benefits to be had from the biotechnology industry, for me the best so far is that they've given us this astonishing metaphor for capitalist production and for the way it works with the trope of technology to elide and wish away the troublesome material base of capitalism's procedures. "Terminator technology" is a metaphor that seems an apt way to talk about Hollywood especially—the locus of technologies that produce commodities which, once they've been purchased and planted in the soil, are effectively consumed once and for all since they're sterile and thus force the consumer to buy them again next year and again the year after, and so on into the new millennium of globalized capitalism. It's into this image, the image of this terminator seed, that I think some part of the history of the twentieth century most tellingly resolves itself.

19 "Compulsory" viewing for every citizen

Mr. Smith and the rhetoric of reception

Eric Smoodin

Defending his 1987 nomination of Robert Bork to the Supreme Court, Ronald Reagan invoked another battle against all odds: "You may remember," his speech ran, "in the movie *Mr. Smith Goes to Washington*, when Jimmy Stewart stands in the well of the Senate and says that lost causes are 'the only causes worth fighting for . . . I'm going to stay right here and fight for this lost cause even if this room . . . is filled with lies.'" Casting himself in Stewart's role, Reagan then asserted, "So will I." Five years later, discussing a politician who himself seemed to be playing a role popularized by Reagan, the *Wall Street Journal* likened presidential candidate Ross Perot to "Jimmy Stewart in *Mr. Smith Goes to Washington*, the pure idealist who triumphs over corrupt insiders." One year after this, in the Los Angeles mayoral race, candidate (and eventual victor) Richard Riordan used his campaign material to characterize his position in the contest "as the Southern California equivalent of *Mr. Smith Goes to Washington*."[1]

Half a century after its 1939 release, then, Frank Capra's film had become a cinematic allusion par excellence in both local and national politics. The story of the ultimate political outsider served as the inspiration for a phenomenally popular president, for one of the richest men in the country, and for a lawyer/investor with a one-hundred-million-dollar fortune.[2] In other words, in this 1980s and 1990s incarnation, Capra's film would be appropriated by powerful mainstream politicians seeking to make voters believe that they were, in reality, virtuous but defenseless Don Quixotes jousting at monolithic institutional windmills. My point is not to argue with this use of *Mr. Smith*. What I find interesting, however, is the absolutely unproblematic interpretation of the film. This same reading gets echoed in numerous movie reviews that use Capra as a kind of shorthand to indicate either the strength or deficiencies of a current film and in newspaper arts page features that discuss Capra's films, Jimmy Stewart's acting style, and Norman Rockwell's paintings as a sort of 1930s American school of representation. In each case, the film becomes an eloquent if somewhat utopian assertion of universally recognized and understood democratic values.[3]

---

1 For Reagan's speech, see the *Washington Post* (14 October 1987), A6. The reference to *Mr. Smith* was eventually dropped from the final version of the president's defense of the Bork nomination; for Ross Perot, see the *New York Times* (6 March 1994), E7, citing the *Wall Street Journal*; for Richard Riordan, see the *Washington Post* (7 June 1993), A5.

2 The report on Riordan's fortune comes from the *Los Angeles Times* (7 June 1993), A6.

3 See, for example, Paul Richard, "Norman Rockwell, American Master (Seriously!)," *Washington Post* (6 June 1993), G1, G8–9. For a more self-conscious and methodologically sophisticated conflation of Capra and Rockwell, see Robert B. Westbrook, "Fighting for the American Family: Private Interests and Political Obligation

Figure 19.1 James Stewart in *Mr. Smith Goes to Washington* (Columbia 1939). Courtesy of the Kobal Collection

When the film first appeared in 1939, this was hardly the case. In fact, perhaps more than any other Hollywood film from the period, *Mr. Smith Goes to Washington* had a deeply charged history in terms of how a variety of audiences interpreted it and also appropriated it. Few other films, for example, so interested the federal government. As much as any other movie, this one had a place in debates about junior high and high school curricula. The subject matter of very few Hollywood products therefore tied into a growing national awareness of the links between history and representation—in this case because this story of the proper exercise of government appeared during an era of major public displays of patriotism and the value of American-style democracy, such as the 1937–1939 celebration of the 150th anniversary of the ratification of the Constitution. During a period when even Eleanor Roosevelt entered the debate over the propriety of playing "The Star-Spangled Banner" at movie screenings, *Mr. Smith* helped define the changing relationship between theaters and the filmgoers who went to them.[4] Finally, to my knowledge, no film from the period elicited anything near the

in World War II," in Richard Wightman Fox and T. J. Jackson Lears, eds, *The Power of Culture: Critical Essays in American History* (Chicago: University of Chicago Press, 1993), 194–221.

4 For a discussion of the "Star-Spangled Banner" debate, see W. C. Ruediger, "Saluting the Flag," *School and Society* (25 February 1939), 249. Mrs. Roosevelt disapproved of playing the anthem at movie theaters.

response from motion picture exhibitors themselves when it came to describing audience reaction.

My project is not so much to study the textual systems of *Mr. Smith Goes to Washington* but rather the reception of Capra's film and also efforts to regulate that reception. Modern film theory and history have only recently begun studying the film audience, and the interaction between audience and film, rather than the film text itself as the site of the production of meaning. In perhaps the most fully worked-out analysis of the interaction of film and film audience, *Star Gazing: Hollywood Cinema and Female Spectatorship*, Jackie Stacey poses the questions that I plan to investigate here: "What do spectators bring to films from their own specific historical and cultural locations which then determine their readings? How do the discourses of particular historical conjunctures limit the possible readings a spectator may make of a film?"[5] In the case of *Mr. Smith*, the answers to these questions disassemble any monolithic interpretation of the text and show that, at least in the years just before the United States entered World War II, "going to the movies" was in actuality a potentially highly volatile activity.

Of course, we can never conclusively reconstruct any film audience, just as we cannot chart all the variations of an audience's interpretation of a film. But we can study a "rhetoric of reception"; that is, the various discursive forms that articulate possible responses to a movie—fan letters, exhibitor reports, government documents, and so on—and also help shape it—advertising and star interviews, for instance. We must also keep in mind the historical specificity of any of these discursive forms and attempt to place them, as well as the members of the film audience, within at least a fairly precise context. For example, 1939 audiences for *Mr. Smith*, familiar as most of them would have been with such New Deal youth mobilizations as the Civilian Conservation Corps and the National Youth Administration, may have paid a far different kind of attention to the film's Boy Rangers than would spectators in the late 1990s and early twenty-first century.

In providing a case study of how films do not simply produce spectators but are also produced by them, I do not want to imply that meaning itself is endlessly deferred as we go from a film to a variety of audiences and then to a variety of sources describing both film and audience. Rather, following Ien Ang in her work on the television audience for *Dallas*, I plan to show that reports on response can be read "symptomatically" and that "we must search for what is behind the explicitly written, for the presuppositions and accepted attitudes concealed within them," so that they come to "be read as texts, as discourses."[6] In Stacey's words, such a reading brings us to a methodology marking the "shift from the textually produced spectator . . . to the spectator as text."[7]

My principal materials come from a variety of industrial, educational, and governmental sources and cover two phases in the reception of *Mr. Smith*: the film's domestic release and then its distribution overseas. When *Mr. Smith Goes to Washington* was released, during the fall and winter of 1939–1940, the *Motion Picture Herald*, a trade journal from the period, provided at least a cautious guide to domestic audience response. Every

5 Jackie Stacey, *Star Gazing: Hollywood Cinema and Female Spectatorship* (London and New York: Routledge, 1994), 49.

6 Ien Ang, *Watching Dallas: Soap Opera and the Melodramatic Imagination* (London: Methuen, 1985), 11 (cited in Stacey, *Star Gazing*, 71).

7 Stacey, *Star Gazing*, 71.

week, the *Herald* ran a column called "What the Picture Did for Me." Here, exhibitors would write in and say how their clientele responded to movies. This column was meant as a guide for exhibitors about how to advertise films and what kind of business to expect, and so the demographic information was fairly precise. The column provided the location of the theater and the kind of audience that came to it; here, race dropped out as a category, but profession was often explicitly stated, and class and ethnicity typically were strongly implied or occasionally clearly expressed (an audience might be categorized as "general," "rural," "mining," or "prisoners," for instance). Typically, descriptions of audience response might run from seventy-five to one hundred words. It is a mark of the special reaction to *Mr. Smith* that many of the entries, sent in by pretty hard-boiled industry types, ran to several hundred words. The *Herald* also offered detailed reports on film ballyhoo, helping us to understand the gimmicks that familiarized people with movies before they saw them.

Coinciding with the 1939 release of the film, Educational and Recreational Guides, Inc., published an edition of *Photoplay Studies* on *Mr. Smith*.[8] These studies were designed for use in junior high and high school film appreciation classes, and came out regularly, typically about films based on "classic" literature or detailing a particularly significant historical period (to my knowledge, the guide to *Mr. Smith* stands out as the only one of its kind; not based on a famous literary source, a momentous event, or the life of a well-known individual). Officially "recommended by the Motion-Picture Committee of the Department of Secondary Teachers of the National Educational Association," these guides functioned in several ways in relation to reception and its regulation. They helped certify the educational value of a film at a time when more than two thousand high schools were teaching motion picture courses or film units in other courses. In addition, they worked to equate film study with aesthetic enjoyment; as the masthead says, the guide served as "a magazine devoted to photoplay appreciation." By so stressing issues of cinematic form and quality, the guide also sought to ensure a reading of *Mr. Smith* on the part of students that made a critique of political systems far less important than narrative plausibility or character motivation.

Finally, State Department documents from 1940 and 1941 that deal with the overseas exhibition of *Mr. Smith Goes to Washington* indicate how a group of government bureaucrats viewed the film. These documents also show how those same bureaucrats imagined that a foreign, often anti-United States audience might receive the film, and then how department officials debated the possibilities for controlling this reception.[9] Indeed, State Department papers point out the perceived problems involved in showing Capra's film to this arguably mythological, almost completely hostile foreign audience; probably only one other film from the period just after the beginning of the war in Europe but still prior to US involvement generated as much governmental concern— Charles Chaplin's *The Great Dictator* in 1940.

8 The Academy of Motion Picture Arts and Sciences Library in Los Angeles has an extensive collection of *Photoplay Studies*. The study guide to *Mr. Smith Goes to Washington* can be found there and also at the Pacific Film Archive in Berkeley, California, in the *Mr. Smith* clippings file.

9 State Department documents about *Mr. Smith Goes to Washington* are stored in the National Archives in Washington, DC, in a file labeled "Adult Education, 1940–44."

"I am filled with song and tears"

Some of our most detailed indications of audience response appear in the "What the Picture Did for Me" column in the *Motion Picture Herald*. According to that column, one of the standard responses to *Mr. Smith* was that of having a transcendental experience, of having life in the United States explained. A theater manager in Waldoboro, Maine, showing movies to a general audience, wrote: "I have just seen one of the greatest emotion [sic] pictures of my life . . . I am filled with song and tears and I am sitting on a mountain peak watching a new sun rising over this land . . . with a new insight on kindness, greatness—a new realization of the meaning of truth and freedom." Similarly, from a theater in Newark, Ohio, catering once again to a general audience, the exhibitor implied that audiences were already tired of the kind of superpatriotic spectacle that we associate with the war years and often assume that audiences were eager to watch. This film, he wrote, "sells more sermon-pure Americanism the hard way than all the star-spangled purpose pictures of the period have managed to instill," and he added that "the picture will bring to your patrons a spirit of patriotism they never thought they would ever have."[10]

This constitutes an extraordinary discussion of how theater managers and their clientele viewed the film. Further, this sense of being a spectator in front of "history" and "patriotism" had, by the time of *Mr. Smith*, become an especially important aspect of both American citizenship and participation in all manner of cultural activities. For at least a seventy-five-year period before Capra's film, as John Bodnar has shown, "public memory" (that is, commemorative and patriotic activity) had become increasingly nationalized and increasingly tied to strategies of representation. At least since the end of the Civil War, expanding business interests, in conjunction with the government, made cultural production the "natural" place to depict the nation's history, to explain its government, and to promote unproblematic loyalty to its institutions. Thus was created an official culture that could be shared by all Americans despite deep ethnic, regional, racial, religious, and class differences.[11]

Among other evidence of the construction of history and patriotism in such a way as to support a corporate and governmental status quo, Bodnar cites the national monuments built in the 1890s to celebrate Civil War soldiers, the emergence of Abraham Lincoln as a symbol of the country's unity during the same period, and also the various celebrations in 1892 of Columbus' landing, celebrations that tended to be organized by businessmen and civic leaders and that stressed the connections between the quadricentennial, military readiness, and social order. Many of these late-nineteenth-century spectacles, however, were as much a tribute to technological progress as to the possibilities for a national culture and shared national history. By the early twentieth century, and particularly during World War I, there was a shift to an official culture that sought to construct consensus in the service primarily of democratic forms, with technology taking a decidedly secondary role.[12] Throughout this period, the central theme of American history, as conceived by parades, Fourth of July celebrations, Civil War commemorations,

10 *Motion Picture Herald* (4 November 1939), 57; (25 November 1939), 51.
11 John Bodnar, *Remaking America: Public Memory, Commemoration, and Patriotism in the Twentieth Century* (Princeton, NJ: Princeton University Press, 1992).
12 Ibid., 83.

and other city, state, and countrywide festivities, was the evolution of a unified nation rather than the development of competing local interests.

Concentrating specifically on the 1930s, Warren Susman has analyzed the construction of a national symbolism aided and abetted by massive technological and communication systems, and with dominant notions of history and patriotism now extending from national monuments and public parks to such everyday entertainments as movies and radio shows.[13] For Susman, the New Deal achieved its success largely from the manipulation of a nationalized signifying practice that dominated not just government documents and activities but popular culture as well: for instance, the NRA eagle, reproduced in the credits of so many movies, functioned as a symbol of restored economic stability, and the fireside chats, broadcast over national radio networks, created a kind of national living room. Thus, Bodnar and Susman suggest that, by the late 1930s, largely because of the convergence of ideological concern and technological possibility, issues relating to citizenship, history, and the country's system of government had consolidated themselves around issues of representation, issues that exhibitors expressed in their commentary on *Mr. Smith Goes to Washington*, and that also marked numerous forms of public display, leisure activity, and popular entertainment.

The 150th anniversary celebration of the ratification of the Constitution, for historical events with parades and ceremonial paintings and even with postage stamps, as the commemorative imprintings of a number of countries, made for frequent news items. Indicating a fully modern mobilization of mass media, advertising, technology, government purpose, and corporate enthusiasm, these celebrations maintained high visibility and effectively reached millions of people in department stores, schools, museums, and other public gathering places (in contrast, the centennial celebration of 1887 to 1889 had been an unqualified failure).[14] The 1939 New York World's Fair performed much the same function of using representational practice to create an official history shared by all citizens, featuring gigantic statues of great Americans like George Washington and regularly screening the film industry's contribution to the fair, Cecil B. De Mille's pastiche of great moments from the country's past, *Land of Liberty*.[15]

In keeping with those efforts described by Susman to sell the New Deal to the American public, the federal government added to this notion of legitimation through representation by finalizing its plans for the mall in Washington, DC, with the construction of the Jefferson Memorial. So important had this project become to arbiters of American culture that in 1939 a work stoppage at the memorial turned into a major news story, with journalists worrying over the prospect of an unfinished representation of the third president.[16] Along with the government, most branches of the entertainment industry also engaged in the conflation of culture, democracy, and history. They did so in part

13 Warren I. Susman, *Culture as History: The Transformation of American Society in the Twentieth Century* (New York: Pantheon Books, 1984). See particularly Chapter 9, "The Culture of the Thirties," 150–183; and Chapter 10, "Culture and Commitment," 184–210.

14 For a discussion and analysis of the 150th anniversary celebrations, see Michael Kammen, *A Machine That Would Go of Itself: The Constitution in American Culture* (New York: Vintage Books, 1987), 282–312.

15 For photographs of the World's Fair statuary, see *Newsweek* (25 March 1940), 18–19; for a discussion of *Land of Liberty*, see Allen W. Palmer, "Cecil B. De Mille Writes America's History for the 1939 World's Fair," *Film History* 5 (1) (March 1993), 36–48.

16 See, for instance, "Jefferson Memorial Woes: Strike Is Latest in the Series of Rows Harassing Project," *Newsweek* (28 August 1939), 22.

because the public often indicated that it could not get enough of this sort of media edification and uplift, at least when the effort seemed serious and sincere, rather than the kind of mindlessly "star-spangled" spectacle that the Newark exhibitor dismissed as tiresome and ineffective. Of course, Kate Smith's radio program was extremely popular. But also, when CBS radio, on its aptly named *Pursuit of Happiness* program, broadcast Paul Robeson's version of "A Ballad of All Americans," a folk epic quoting liberally from the Gettysburg Address and the Declaration of Independence, *Newsweek* reported that "the results were startling. The demonstration in the studio continued for twenty minutes . . . switchboards . . . were deluged with calls; letters poured in."[17]

Finally, merging modern technology and a kind of representational mania, Mount Rushmore neared completion during this period with the unveiling in the summer of 1939 of the fourth and final presidential head, that of Theodore Roosevelt. This unveiling turned Mount Rushmore into something which contained all of American history, as *Newsweek* reported that "Indians performed a pageant depicting the white man's arrival in the Northwest, and Rough Riders who served with Theodore Roosevelt looked on." In addition, the monument itself served to negotiate both modernity and the ancient, with the magazine measuring the mountain sculptures against the Capitol dome as well as the Egyptian Sphinx.[18] Thus, Mount Rushmore typified a 1930s cultural and political context in which it seemed that democracy could in fact be depicted and that representational practice might not simply signify the historical but actually present it, virtually unmediated, to the public.

One motion picture exhibitor, showing films to a general audience, typified this slippage between the monumental, the historical, and the real and the importance of how all of this got represented, and he did so while providing his fellow managers with advice on how to sell the patriotism in *Mr. Smith*: "The Lincoln Memorial scenes alone will sell more America to them than any book or story ever published . . . The crackpots with a torch to burn may have the situation a little foggy, and to offset that just exploit [the film] as though it were [an] actual dramatization of the Declaration of Independence itself."[19] The film, then, practically became an actual historical artifact, providing a representation of the signing of one of the United States' sacred documents.

Some exhibitors did indeed promote this angle in their ballyhoo for Capra's film.[20] The manager of a theater in Buffalo, for instance, "tying in with the local election . . . built an election booth, ballot boxes, etc., for his lobby display" for *Mr. Smith*. "Standings of local candidates were changed daily on the blackboard," and the display "also consisted of [a] regulation voting machine which was loaned by [the] local election board for the occasion." Similarly, for a Chicago showing, "campaign headquarters were set up" advertising the film, with a banner proclaiming, "The people's choice— put Smith in Washington for life!" For another Chicago showing, an exhibitor distributed *Mr. Smith* "business cards . . . with [a] handwritten message on the back reading 'Sorry

17 "Ballad of All Americans," *Newsweek* (25 March 1940), 40.
18 "Four Faces in Granite: Borglum's Black Hills Colossus Is Nearing Completion," *Newsweek* (10 July 1939), 23.
19 "What the Picture Did For Me," *Motion Picture Herald* (25 November 1939), 51.
20 Exhibitors' advertising strategies for *Mr. Smith* were almost certainly influenced by the press kit that Columbia produced for Capra's film. I have not, however, been able to locate such a kit in either of the archival locations I have checked: the Library of Congress and the Academy of Motion Picture Arts and Sciences Library.

you were out when I called. Just wanted to say Goodbye before going to Washington, but you can see me at the Avalon [Theater]."[21]

Through this brand of advertising, theaters stressed the realism of the film, with Jeff Smith himself passing out business cards, with "actual" campaign headquarters being established, and with a blurring of the electioneering in the film and in local neighborhoods. As a result, before ever seeing the film, audiences might be prone not so much to believe unproblematically that which they would see on screen but to view the film as signifying the real, both in terms of a fictional character seeming like an actual one and the film itself embodying the prized values of democracy: the right to vote and to have your opinion count. By serving as a message board about local elections or by simply implying the importance of voting through the establishment of campaign headquarters, these theaters established their own civic spirit and their importance to the community.

Thus the entire viewing context for *Mr. Smith*—including advertising gimmicks and lobby displays—worked to create a specific kind of relationship between the spectator and both the film and the theater, a relationship that assisted in the legitimation of a national culture of patriotism. Typically, film studies have resisted analyzing this kind of spectatorship, one that extends well beyond the time spent viewing a film. Simultaneous to helping construct a reading of the film, however, the advertising campaigns for *Mr. Smith* worked to create a response to the very act of going to the movies. Through advertising, the theater came to be equated with yet another private space where people could feel themselves to be both part of a greater community and also alone—the voting booth. The viewing context for *Mr. Smith* helped to establish a kind of democratic relationship between viewer and film in which watching the movie became the equivalent of exercising the rights of citizenship.

Marvelling at the apparent universal appeal of the film, several managers used variations of such stock phrases as *Mr. Smith* "will click with the masses 100 percent" and do great business in the smallest town or the biggest city. One theater manager, writing from Canada, also stressed the special class appeal of the film, saying that business was "big" and that this was especially telling because his theater was "strictly a class house." These comments stand out as unusual in audience reports from the period; throughout the decade, many managers emphasized the splits between small town and big city entertainments, as well as high-class and working-class films.[22] Many of these same reports also stressed Capra's skills as an artist: "here is proven that the director is the picture," for instance, or "How can you beat that Capra? If there is anyone I would like to meet and talk to in Hollywood, it is Frank Capra!"[23] At this stage in his career, a little more than a year after *Time* magazine certified his celebrity by featuring him on the cover of the issue on 8 August 1938, Capra was being perceived as someone who spoke for "the people" (indeed, as someone a viewer might "like to meet" and

---

21 *Motion Picture Herald* (4 November 1939), 65; (11 May 1940), 68; (3 February 1940), 74.

22 For the "universal" appeal of the film, see *Motion Picture Herald* (18 November 1939), 63: "Will click with the masses 100 per cent"; (2 December 1939), 64: "Pleased 100%"; (30 December 1939), 57: "This picture drew above average and is the kind that builds good will amongst theatregoers." For the comment from the Canadian exhibitor, see *Motion Picture Herald* (25 November 1939), 51. For an indication of the perceived divisions in the audience, and the theater manager's comment about the *Ice Follies of 1939*: "Too much dialogue for small town," *Motion Picture Herald* (2 December 1939), 64.

23 *Motion Picture Herald* (23 December 1939), 51; (16 December 1939), 59.

"talk to"). His work seemed to transcend class and regional differences and to create consensus (a trait he shared with very few other filmmakers from this period—only Walt Disney comes immediately to mind).

These reports from exhibitors give a clear indication that audiences wanted more motion pictures like *Mr. Smith*, but also that they certainly did not expect them, primarily because of the motion picture industry itself. Despite the triumph of the nationalized representational practices described by Bodnar and Susman and manipulated by business and government interests, Capra's film shows how the conflation of popular culture, history, and patriotism could in fact mobilize audiences to voice displeasure with corporate and elected leaders. For many viewers, *Mr. Smith* emerged not as a triumph for the film business but as a triumph in spite of it. One exhibitor wrote: "For once, and it is a rare occasion indeed, I am proud to be connected with the cinema industry; thankful of the privilege to be one of that army of theater managers whose duty it now is to make certain that every citizen in his community is on hand when *Mr. Smith* comes to town."[24] Thus the reception of the film points out the manner in which low-level members of the industry—exhibitors—and probably many audiences, too, felt deeply dissatisfied with the industry. This dissatisfaction was different from the one historians associate with perhaps the dominant antimovie movement of the 1930s, that of the Catholic Legion of Decency, and was fueled by such studies as those commissioned by the Payne Fund.[25] This 1939-style sensibility about the cinema had nothing to do with the perceived licentiousness of movies or with their deleterious effects on children. Rather it implied that the film industry should play a role as a liaison between citizens and government and had been derelict in its civic duty to the American public. But the attitude toward *Mr. Smith* also shows the level to which many members of the industry sought to mobilize around products they believed in, to the extent that they could consider themselves a kind of people's "army," in the exhibitor's words, bringing light to the masses. Capra's film, which itself typified the manner in which issues of government and issues of representation merged, also became a symbolic call to arms, demonstrating the possibilities during the period for a kind of evangelical merging of government purpose and industrial practice.

Just as the reception of *Mr. Smith* evidenced unhappiness with what the film industry had become, so too did it show dissatisfaction with what the federal government had turned into; and also how representational issues seemed to crystallize, for the audience, their own uneasy relations with their national leaders. One exhibitor praised Jimmy Stewart for "pitching *Mr. Smith* down the throats of frantic Washington." Another lumped Washington, the film industry, and the rest of the media together as the combined enemy of the people: "*Mr. Smith Goes to Washington* should be shown to every member of the Senate and Congress," and there should be a law making it "compulsory" viewing for every citizen, "even if an extra 10 percent of the gross were exacted by the Government to go toward supporting not only those nearsighted men of movies who continue to feel the public must be treated as though possessing their own ignorance, but also those who . . . have attempted to poison the roots of our democracy."[26] He added that no

24 *Motion Picture Herald* (4 December 1939), 57.
25 For a discussion of the Payne Fund Studies and the relationship between the movies and the Legion of Decency, see G. Jowett, *Film: The Democratic Art*, 220–259.
26 *Motion Picture Herald* (25 November 1939), 51; (4 November 1939), 57.

one saw any insult to the United States in this film until newspapers started complaining about it (he referred here to newspaper criticism of the representation of journalists in the film and to coverage of the Senate's own disapprobation after a special screening).[27] So even within the industry itself there existed a sense of a conspiracy of which movies and the other mass media were all a part, with *Mr. Smith* standing out as something of a miracle, as that which got made in spite of a governmental/media monolith that opposed the "common person."

Education for democracy

Besides the hyperbole of proposing laws to make the film compulsory viewing, exhibitors made some very practical suggestions for ensuring the largest audience possible for *Mr. Smith*. One exhibitor wrote, "Play it and plug it 100 per cent over your usual budget. It will come back with interest. Your school teachers will send their pupils for one of the greatest lessons in the 'American Way of Thinking' they will ever get anywhere." Similarly, the review of the film in the *Motion Picture Herald* stressed the educational value of *Mr. Smith*, turning the film into an exhibitor's dream come true because of how it functioned as "a spectacle, a lesson and an entertainment" all at the same time.[28] Throughout this period, exhibitors typically tried to tie motion pictures into educational concerns, but the connection rarely seemed as self-evident as it did with *Mr. Smith*, and the exhibitors' conviction rarely so heartfelt.

By asserting the educational value of Capra's film, exhibitors were in fact entering a much larger debate about the practicality and efficacy of teaching democratic values to adolescents and children. Between August 1939 and January 1940, the national media made significant news stories out of Columbia University's Congress on Education for Democracy, a high-brow journal's special issue on "the challenge of democracy to education," the White House Conference on Children in a Democracy, and the potential of the National Council for the Social Studies to devise a method of building better citizens through education.[29] In addition, just as the media during this period became a site for depicting "democracy," so too were they expected not simply to entertain the masses but to educate them as well, and frequently about issues of perceived particular importance to Americans. In 1939, for instance, both the CBS and NBC radio networks began ambitious art appreciation programs, *What's Art to Me?* and *Art for Your Sake*. A program on the NBC Blue Network, *America's Town Meeting of the Air*, regularly broadcast programs around such special issues as "How Can We Defend Democracy in America Now?," while composer and public intellectual Deems Taylor

27 The Production Code administration film of *Mr. Smith*, stored at the Academy of Motion Picture Arts and Sciences Library in Los Angeles, includes memos about the feelings of journalists toward the film, see Frank Knox to Will Hays, 14 November 1939, and Joseph Breen to Will Hays, 6 December 1939. For coverage of the screening for the Senate, see "Mr. Smith Riles Washington," *Time* (30 October 1939), 49.

28 *Motion Picture Herald* (25 November 1939), 51; (7 October 1939), 38.

29 "Ideas Swapped by 3,000 at the 'Country Store' Forum on Education for Democracy," *Newsweek* (28 August 1939), 25; "Challenge," *Time* (9 October 1939), 46. The journal under consideration was the October 1939 issue of the *Survey Graphic*; "Compulsory Schooling up to 16 Urged at White House Parley," *Newsweek* (29 January 1940), 36; "For Better Citizens," *Time* (6 November 1939), 61.

broadcast a weekly NBC program, *Musical Americana*, that *Newsweek* said "flourishes a frank bias in favor of musical nationalism."[30]

In the late 1930s, specialized journals aimed at educators engaged in a serious discussion of the possibility of teaching democratic values to young children. Articles such as "Educational Planning in a Democracy," "Education for Democracy," "The Unique Function of Education in American Democracy," and "Propaganda, Democracy and Education" generally supported the notion of education-as-indoctrination into American values, and even President Roosevelt weighed in on the issue. In an address to the National Education Association in 1938, he said that "for many years I, like you, have been a pedagogue, striving to inculcate in the youth of America a greater knowledge of and interest in the problems which, with such force, strike the whole world in the face to-day."[31] Certainly, the exhibitors who stressed the educational value of *Mr. Smith*, and in particular its lessons for youngsters in "The American Way of Thinking," were interested in the box office possibilities of selling the film to students.

But they participated in a project that could seemingly be shared by all Americans and by all forms of cultural production. All adults, from film exhibitors to presidents, had a responsibility to instruct kids in the marvel of democracy, and all popular culture entertainments could be judged and enjoyed in relation to the political lessons that they taught.

The *Photoplay Studies* guide for *Mr. Smith Goes to Washington*, however, shows that the discourse about education at this time did not unproblematically concern itself with the necessity of teaching democracy to the masses. In its seventeen pages, the guide introduced students to the plot of the film and its production history, and provided "Questions for Classes in Civics" as well as "Questions about Washington" and "Questions on Cinematic Treatment." All of the sections were prepared by "experts"— a high school principal, the president of the New York City Association of Civics Teachers, and National Education Association officials. Immediately, in its opening paragraphs, the guide sought to persuade students not to view the film politically:

> *Mr. Smith Goes to Washington* stands or falls solely on its cinema merits. Even the dialogue should be considered first of all as a contribution to cinematographic qualities: and so too should be judged the complications and interweavings of the plot, the motivation of the characters, the realistic truth of the background. To classes and students of movie enjoyment and appreciation, consequently, this first advice should be given: consider *Mr. Smith Goes to Washington* as a movie.

---

30 "Art Via the Air Waves: Both CBS and NBC Starting New Cultural Programs," *Newsweek* (6 November 1939), 30; "War of Words: Town Meeting Opens Fifth Explosive Season," *Newsweek* (9 October 1939), 39; "All-American Program: Deems Taylor and a Symphony to Wave Musical Flag," *Newsweek* (29 January 1940), 44.

31 All of the articles mentioned appeared in *School and Society*, Floyd S. Gove, "Educational Planning in a Democracy" (25 June 1938), 829–830; William F. Russell, "Education for Democracy" (31 December 1938), 862–864; J. Cayce Morrison, "The Unique Function of Education in American Democracy" (30 July 1938), 132–137; William H. Kilpatrick, "Propaganda, Democracy and Education" (1 April 1939), 405–409. President Roosevelt's address, given on 30 June 1938, was reprinted in *School and Society* (9 July 1938), 29–31.

Then, in an implicit critique of the film's apparent ideological position (and of the more overtly political projects of the film education movement from earlier in the decade), the guide instructed each student to disregard any possible link between *Mr. Smith* and contemporary events. The film undoubtedly had a basis in "many recent occurrences enacted on the American scene and reported in newspapers." But students should ask themselves "whether the process of highlighting [these occurrences] has been carried too far, whether the total result is plausible, whether a wrong impression of American political life is given, and whether the total effect has been exaggeration rather than a truly artistic effect."[32]

So the study guide attempted to control any student's reading of *Mr. Smith* and prevent an interpretation that might question the workings of Congress. For the study guide, the film's criticism of governmental systems could only be judged aesthetically, with students learning about narrative plausibility and with the language of the guide itself suggesting that *Mr. Smith* had indeed gone "too far."

The study guide questions inspired by the film seem dryly informational ("Why was a successor to the late Senator Foley not elected immediately by the people?" "Who is the Senior Senator from your state?" "How did it happen that Washington was made the nation's capital?" "In what noted but still unfinished cathedral is Woodrow Wilson, the World War president, buried?").[33] Other parts of the guide pose an early auteurist discourse about the film's director ("more important than the presence of a competent acting cast is the fact that the whole production has been under the guidance of Frank Capra").[34] The project of the guide, then, confirms and expands upon Lauren Berlant's thesis on the Washington discourse in general. In her analysis of a 1990s appropriation of *Mr. Smith*, an episode of *The Simpsons* television program called "Mr. Lisa Goes to Washington," Berlant writes that this discourse "is already all about the activitiy of national pedagogy, the production of national culture, and the constitution of competent citizens," particularly among young children and adolescents.[35] *Photoplay Studies* provided just this kind of training (although, of course, it is impossible to tell how seriously any student took this instruction). The guide to *Mr. Smith* gave students a seemingly thorough instruction in citizenship—who senators are, for instance, and how they are elected—and in the history that all citizens needed to know. But the guide also added an aesthetic dimension to that citizenship with its questions and commentary about cathedral architecture and Capra's direction. In this "construction of a patriotic youth culture," to use Berlant's phrase,[36] the study guide insisted that "Washington" and "American history" and "aesthetic accomplishment" were in fact complementary categories that created a logical, non-threatening, smoothly working system of power relations between people and institutions.

---

32 *Photoplay Studies: A Magazine Devoted to Photoplay Appreciation* (Educational and Recreational Guides, 1939), 3.

33 Ibid., 7, 10, and 12. It is quite possible that some aspects of the film itself encouraged the rather narrow, fact-based civics lesson approach of the study guide. I am thinking here of the scene in which Saunders "teaches" Skith all about the process through which a Senate bill is written, introduced, and passed.

34 Ibid., 5.

35 Lauren Berlant, "The Theory of Infantile Citizenship," *Public Culture* 5 (3) (Spring 1993), 395–410. The quotation comes from page 397.

36 Ibid., 407.

The problem "below the Rio Grande"

Reviewing *Mr. Smith* for overseas exhibition, particularly in Latin America, State Department officials also expressed an interest in the educational value of the film. They concentrated, however, much more on what the film might teach a national body politic rather than an adolescent one. But first I should point out that the very fact of the State Department's interest indicates a special status for *Mr. Smith*. Of course, the federal government regularly looked for ways to use the film industry to further foreign policy (arranging star tours of various countries, for instance, or producing propaganda films for countries perceived to be within the United States' "sphere of influence").[37] And the State Department worked, in particularly fraught exhibition cases, as a liaison between the American movie studios and foreign governments. On a film-by-film basis, however, the State Department did not involve itself in the overseas details of the United States film business. Only when a private citizen or government bureaucrat brought a problem to the department's attention did officials start to weigh in on the merits of an individual movie. In the case of Capra's film, the documents provide an indication of how the State Department assumed the film would be received, but give a much more thorough account of how department officials themselves interpreted the film; and their language in discussing *Mr. Smith* indicates their own anxiety about the place of the United States in global politics.

The documents show much the same anti-Washington tension that the exhibitors wrote about in "What the Picture Did for Me." The issue, though, was not that of Washington versus "typical" US citizens but rather Washington against the world and, more specifically, those developing countries in Latin America that may not have made the kind of commitment to democracy that the United States government would have liked. In this debate about relations with Latin America, *Mr. Smith* became a lightning rod through which State Department officials could register concerns with the film industry and censorship, and about exporting US-style capitalism and political systems.

In March 1940, Thomas Burke, the chief of the Division of International Communications, composed a memo that discussed the problems facing the film industry and the federal government, and the contradictions that emerged from them. He wrote that motion picture markets overseas had dried up considerably, largely because of the war and foreign censorship restrictions. He went on to say that "censorship is one of the main threats that confronts the motion picture industry on the western hemisphere" and that the industry had "called upon the [State] Department for assistance perhaps more frequently than ever before in its history." He added that

> it seems reasonable to say that our ability to ride successfully through the morass of censorship is in no small measure based upon the respect and confidence which we have instilled in the minds of both governments and governed in the Latin American area . . . [where] democracy is ridiculed as an impractical device by certain of the totalitarian governments.

---

37 For an analysis of the relations during this period between the federal government and the motion picture industry in terms of furthering foreign policy, see *Animating Culture*, Chapter Five.

Then the memo cautioned that "it seems incredibly inconsistent for any American commercial enterprise which thrives on United States prestige to abet the hostile propagandists
by ridiculing democratic systems."[38]

Thus the State Department's perception of Latin America created a puzzle.
Censorship was an evil that threatened the film industry. But in places where democracy was ridiculed, why allow US-made, arguably antidemocratic artifacts to flourish?
And this was where Capra's film came to the department's attention and where different kinds of reception practice would be acknowledged. The author of the memo and
his associates saw the film as "a bit of buffoonery." But they were not convinced that
the film would be received in this manner in Latin America. In fact, the memo pointed
out "the serious damage that might result from showing such a film outside the United
States and particularly below the Rio Grande."[39]

The same sentiments turned up in a number of memos. In September, for instance,
the chargé d'affaires in Bangkok wrote that, while *Mr. Smith* constituted excellent entertainment "for home consumption . . . [it] should never be permitted to be shown outside
of the borders of the United States."[40] Even when officials decided to oppose censoring the film, they viewed *Mr. Smith* as a dangerous movie, and their language shows
how the film spoke quite directly to nationalist, masculinist concerns. A few days after
he wrote his first memo about *Mr. Smith* (and subsequently having a department official
question his call for banning the film), Burke reversed his resistance to Capra's movie.[41]
Nevertheless, he added that "in order to establish our national virility," the United States
need not go out of its way "to establish our susceptibility to sin," as *Mr. Smith* seemed
to do. For Burke, the film demonstrated to "our neighbors the fact that we are 'muy
hombre,'" but did so in the worst possible way, by implying that the United States was
"basically corrupt."[42]

What I find especially interesting here is not so much a concern with how "natives"
might receive the film but with how the United States itself would be "received" in
Latin America; the entire southern hemisphere seemed to mobilize northern fears of
being feminized among the Latinos, of not being quite "virile" enough. In this
instance, the discourse of at least some government officials created a kind of homosocial sphere of influence, where "our" men must be shown to be more manly than
"theirs." If this were true, this might give us a better understanding of the discomfort
with Capra's film, which takes the shape of an Oedipal drama about sons slaying fathers
and which ends with the male hero having passed out, and then, a few moments later,
Clarissa Saunders—the woman who acts as Senator Smith's political mentor—screaming
"yippee."

Anticensorship sentiment prevailed at the State Department, although most of the
memos discussed sitting down and talking with Will Hays about how such a movie could
have been made in the first place. Typically, the tone was friendly but firm: "It is my
understanding that it has been our policy to bring to the attention of Mr. Hays

38 Thomas Burke to Mr. Long, Mr. Briggs, Mr. Bonsal, and Mr. Duggan, 21 March 1940.
39 Ibid.
40 J. Holbrook Chapman to Secretary of State Cordell Hull, 29 July 1940.
41 For the memo questioning Burke's judgment, see Mr. Bonsal to Mr. Briggs and Mr. Daniels, 19 March
    1940.
42 Thomas Burke to Mr. Long, Mr. Briggs, Mr. Bonsal, and Mr. Duggan, 21 March 1940.

instances where the Department . . . considered that the susceptibilities of our friends south of the Rio Grande have been offended by American-made motion pictures. I believe that this policy is absolutely sound and should be continued."[43] State Department and diplomatic officials generally disapproved of the film, citing, among other things, its "malicious ridicule" of US governmental institutions and the manner in which it worked to "distort the facts in regard to American life."[44] But most of these officials also tended to doubt that they should routinely "express views concerning specific commercial pictures."[45] Moreover, they worried whether it would not be "highly undesirable if a member of the Congress used the personal opinions of our officers as the main basis for an arraignment of the motion picture industry?"[46] Many members of Congress criticized the film industry for everything from block-booking practices to producing interventionist propaganda to moral lapses, and the official State Department action against *Mr. Smith* might allow them to assume that they had the backing of the federal government in their attacks against Hollywood (indeed, after the 1939 Washington preview of *Mr. Smith*, a number of senators vowed to pursue with new interest a variety of antitrust measures against the film studios).[47]

Thus the case of *Mr. Smith* pointed out the delicate balance between various segments of the industry and the government, and the strains caused by conflicting goals: promoting the film industry versus promoting the United States' interests around the world. The Hollywood studios needed the State Department's help in dealing with overseas markets and so might have been susceptible to pressure concerning film content. But the department itself had to be careful to maintain the appearance of a hands-off rather than a regulatory relationship with private corporate production; indeed, one of the sustaining myths of American capitalism has been that of the laissez-faire attitude of the government toward business, even during a century of increasing regulation. Furthermore, the State Department, at least in 1940, sought to separate itself from those members of Congress who vigorously agitated for increased government supervision of film production. And besides, in 1940 the department had better ways to spend its time than monitoring individual movies.

Even so, the decision to permit the overseas exhibition of *Mr. Smith* was a difficult one for department officials. Much of the evidence that convinced them came from the American Consulate in Switzerland where the reception of the film demonstrated its potential for promoting democracy rather than the opposite. The American Consul General there (felicitously named James Stewart) wrote to the State Department, saying that the film had been playing to packed houses and had "achieved a position as a symbol of democracy in this country, probably never enjoyed by any other character originating in the United States. In fact, progressive leaders in Switzerland decided to use the film "to attack . . . the antiquated principles of the Federal Parliament" and to work for "parliamentary reform."[48] In the State Department's understanding of reception, then, *Mr. Smith* functioned to criticize the United States only in "uncivilized" places. But in

43 Laurance Duggan to Mr. Long, Mr. Burke, and Mr. Thomson, 21 March 1940.
44 For the complaints about *Mr. Smith*, see Burke to Long *et al.* and Bangkok Legation to Secretary of State Cordell Hull, 2 January 1941.
45 Bonsal to Mr. Daniels and Mr. Briggs, 19 March 1940.
46 Thomas Burke to Mr. Thomson, 11 February 1941.
47 "*Mr. Smith* Riles Washington," 49.
48 James B. Stewart to Secretary of State Cordell Hull, 30 January 1941.

"civilized" ones like Switzerland, the film served to posit the United States as a model of the possibility for democratic reform.

Assessing reception

How can we make sense out of these multiple discourses? Two of them seem in absolute opposition to each other: the exhibitors' discussion of the film, which primarily detailed a domestic response, and the analyses from the federal government, which speculated upon a potential global reception of the film. Clearly, both demonstrated a deeply felt, though contradictory, antagonism toward the motion picture industry. Exhibitors were furious that this kind of film rarely got made; State Department officials were upset that this type of film got made at all. Everyone felt that this film raised issues of the efficacy of democracy, but in different ways in different places, and to different ends.

All the discussions about *Mr. Smith* demonstrated a consensus in terms of method and goal; that is, motion pictures possessed a powerful ability to indoctrinate, and the spread of democratic institutions constituted a fitting national project. But they demonstrated absolute fracture when it came to determining the best way to indoctrinate and discern the meaning of democracy. That break became apparent in the tension between the industry and "the people." But it was no less evident in the interactions between those institutions that we might tend to think of as monolithically conforming to a dominant ideology, the motion picture industry and the federal government, even as the country moved toward a period of war marked by increased efforts on the part of government and business to build consensus.

In the final analysis, this rhetoric of *Mr. Smith*'s reception may well construct interpretations that are "false"—simple binary oppositions between the "little people" and the federal government, as in the case of the film exhibitors, or irrational concerns about degrees of manliness, which we find in the State Department documents. But these interpretations are themselves nonetheless "real," that is, deeply felt and capable of mobilizing a great deal of activity. Here, we might follow Paul Virilio and keep in mind that the conflation of representation and government that held such a central role in the exhibitors' reports had its full effect in a devastating global war that started in the same year that *Mr. Smith* was released.[49] And certainly, concerns about US virility versus that of the Third World continue to be played out, not only discursively, as in the memos about *Mr. Smith*, but also in the implementation of US global policy.

---

49 Paul Virilio, *War and Cinema: The Logistics of Perception*, translated by Patrick Camiller (London: Verso, 1989).

20 Standardizing professionalism and showmanship

The performance of motion picture projectionists during the early sync-sound era

Steve Wurtzler

Many of the policies of the US film industry during its so-called "classic" period (spanning roughly the 1920s through the late 1950s) were motivated by a desire to ensure profits through institutional practices premised on efficiency and standardization. Film is, however, an "intangible" commodity, never entirely susceptible to the mass production protocols and/or ethos that yield the serial production of identical consumer goods. Nonetheless, the US film industry aggressively sought to standardize methods of producing, distributing, and exhibiting films. In *The Classical Hollywood Cinema*, Janet Staiger describes in some detail the motivation behind and methods pursued by the film industry in an attempt to achieve this standardization at the level of film production.[1] Such standardization did, of course, necessarily co-exist with efforts to achieve innovation in the form of product differentiation. While production practices could be efficiently managed and regulated, each commodity produced—that is each film—had to show some degree of difference from every other.

Staiger's account, in keeping with the focus of the volume as a whole, largely stresses standardization efforts within the *production* of films. Contemporary film historians often follow the logic of the film industry itself in conceptualizing business practices according to the tripartite distinction between production, distribution, and exhibition. "Production," in Bordwell, Staiger, and Thompson's book, and indeed in film studies in general, emphasizes those practices that culminate in a film text prior to its *distribution* to movie theaters. In a largely uninterrogated move, historians take the *product* of film production to be a single, definitive film text, as if the productive labor of the Hollywood system culminated prior to the physical distribution of films nationally; in this scheme, the text arrived at the local theater in finished form. Such an assumption conforms to and echoes the *goals* of the US film industry, if not its actual historical practices. US film history is characterized by recurring tensions between numerous practices that sought to guarantee a single, definitive film text or to standardize the exhibition of film commodities and countervailing tendencies in which the film text became subject to local variation.

The imposition of the Production Code, or rather its more public enforcement following 1934, should be understood not only as part of a larger public relations campaign designed to cultivate a socially responsible image for Hollywood or, as Richard

1 David Bordwell, Janet Staiger, and Kristin Thompson, *The Classical Hollywood Cinema: Film Style and Mode of Production to 1960* (New York: Columbia University Press, 1985), 87–112.

Maltby has argued, as an attempt to foreclose federal intervention into Hollywood's discriminatory trade practices, but also as an attempt to achieve the efficient, national circulation of identical versions of films by superseding the vagaries of locally imposed, geographically specific censorship restrictions.[2] The Production Code Administration, like standardized production practices, had as *one* of its goals the standardization of each film text as a commodity.

Similarly, the development and design of exhibitors' pressbooks and studio-orchestrated national advertising campaigns should be seen as part of a larger attempt to exert centralized control over local retail practices.[3] For example, the pressbook accompanying Warner Bros.' *Little Caesar* (1931) advised movie theater owners:

> *Little Caesar*, while it depicts the graphic and hair-raising episodes in the lives of members of gangland, does not in any way glorify the gangsters. All your campaign should be geared to the theme of the picture. Do not in any way attempt to glorify the gangster or racketeer. In fact it would be well to stress the helplessness of gangland to the law. Follow the ad copy and illustrations in this press sheet to the letter and you will be on the safe side. (No pagination)

Here Warner Bros.' national distribution office sought to foreclose local and regional versions of the public outcry against Hollywood's representations of gangsters by standardizing local film advertising and promotion.

Simultaneously however, some countervailing practices attest to the extent to which the US cinema's business practices often resulted in the production and, importantly, the exhibition of geographically and temporally contingent texts. Newsreels during the early 1930s, for example, were designed so that potentially problematic segments might be eliminated at the discretion of local theater managers. William Fox, founder of the Fox Film Corporation, encouraged managers of his corporation's theaters in 1931 to exercise their own judgment in excising segments from nationally released newsreels. Insisting that managers pre-empt "demonstrations or irritation" inside their theaters, Fox instructed:

> You are not only authorized, but you are herewith very pointedly instructed to delete all subjects of a controversial nature on prohibition, pro or con; all subjects which can be construed as Bolshevist propaganda; all political speeches which take sides on matters of public interest; shots showing breadlines; and economic discussions on which the country or your particular patronage is divided.[4]

---

2 On the relationship between the Production Code and Hollywood's trade practices, see Richard Maltby, "The Production Code and the Hays Office," in Tino Balio, ed., *Grand Design: Hollywood as a Modern Business Enterprise, 1930–1939* (Berkeley: University of California Press, 1993), 37–72. See also Richard Maltby, " 'Grief in the Limelight': Al Capone, Howard Hughes, the Hays Code and the Politics of the Unstable Text," *Movies and Politics: The Dynamic Relationship* (New York: Garland, 1993), 133–181.

3 The nature and function of pressbooks, also known as exhibitors' campaign books, are described in Mark S. Miller, "Helping Exhibitors: Pressbooks at Warner Bros. in the late 1930s," *Film History* 6 (1994), 188–196.

4 "Fox Warns Mgrs. to Keep an Eagle Eye on Newsreels," *Motion Picture Herald* (March 7, 1931), 54. Fox's final instruction, "Lastly, bear in mind that anything clipped from the newsreel must be carefully guarded and preserved and must be reinserted and returned to the exchange when you return the rest of the reel," reasserted the industry's desire for a standardized commodity to be exhibited elsewhere.

Theater managers appropriately disciplined by Fox's 'pointed instructions' became active agents of textual production, producing through their editorial decisions a different local textual commodity from that which was distributed nationally.

Film studios and theater owners clashed throughout the silent film era over the speed at which local exhibitors and projectionists presented films. While some film producers and cinematographers sought to standardize camera speeds (an admittedly difficult task given the use of hand-cranked cameras), projectionists, often at the prompting of theater owners and managers seeking to fit an overly long program of films into a predetermined schedule of starting times, operated film projectors at a much faster rate. Some period accounts suggest that while camera speeds were "standardized" around 60 feet per minute, projection speeds varied between 45 and 70 feet per minute.[5] This practice of "over-cranking" or "film racing" could have unintentionally comic results. According to one period account, "In the *Passion Play* [the projectionist] can make Peter act the part of a jumping jack and he can turn a horse race into a howling farce, by over-speeding and under-speeding . . . Imagine the figure of the Savior carrying the cross at a gallop."[6] While it is doubtful that any projectionist who transformed Peter into a jumping jack or theater manager who insisted that Christ gallop with the cross to Calvary would have maintained his employment for long, disparities between the speeds at which films were exposed and were projected attest to an essential technological instability of the silent film text.[7]

For some time, revisionist film histories have begun to address this instability of the cinematic text, exploring a series of local exhibition and film accompaniment patterns.[8] In a recent essay, Tim Anderson examines the manner in which sound accompaniment for nickelodeon-era silent films was identified as a problem requiring a move *toward* the standardization of the performative aspects of film exhibition. Examining the trade journal *Exhibitors Herald World*, Anderson tracks attempts to discipline musical and sound-effects practices in nickelodeons. Local exhibition practices threatened more than a film's

5 F. H. Richardson, "Lessons for Operators: Chapter IX. The Picture," *Moving Picture World* (May 9, 1908), 413. The Silent Film Bookshelf website provides a useful introduction to and overview of the debates surrounding projection speeds for silent film. Richardson's article is reprinted there as are a number of other period documents (http://cinemaweb.com/silentfilm/bookshelf May 26, 2000). Interestingly, the Society of Motion Picture Engineers eventually established standards of 60 feet per minute for camera operation and 80 feet per minute for projection operation immediately prior to the industry's conversion to sound, thereby institutionalizing in word if not in deed the disparity between filming and projection speeds.

6 F. H. Richardson, "Projection Department," *The Moving Picture World* (December 2, 1911), 721.

7 If we expand the notion of textuality beyond the feature-centric bounds of single narrative films to include instead the range of filmic and other live performative practices that constituted an evening at the movies throughout much of the studio system era, the nature of the cinematic commodity becomes increasingly plural and increasingly the product of locally contingent practices. A given feature film could be interpolated within a larger locally or regionally designed program of newsreels, animation, and entertainment short subjects then currently in distribution as well as live performances, local contests, the projection of radio broadcasts through theater loudspeakers, etc.

8 Some examples of this historical work include Rick Altman, "The Silence of the Silents," *Musical Quarterly* 80 (Winter 1996), 648–718; Mary Carbine, "'The Finest Outside the Loop': Motion Picture Exhibition in Chicago's Black Metropolis, 1905–1928," *Camera Obscura* 23 (May 1990), 9–41; Gregory A. Waller, *Main Street Amusements: Movies and Commercial Entertainment in a Southern City, 1896–1930* (Washington, DC: Smithsonian Institution Press, 1995); and Gregory A. Waller, "Hillbilly Music and Will Rogers: Small-town Picture Shows in the 1930s," in Melvyn Stokes and Richard Maltby, eds, *American Movie Audiences: From the Turn of the Century to the Early Sound Era* (London: British Film Institute, 1999), 164–179.

status as a stable, nationally distributed commodity, however, and Anderson notes that "the popularity and prevalence of inappropriate, 'jackass' music among some audiences existed because it yielded other sets of semantic pleasures that were *not* sanctioned by the dominant narrative."[9] Also at issue for nickelodeon music reformers was both a perceived threat to the admittedly precarious social standing of the cinema and a threat to the ability of film texts to circumscribe textual meaning and ways of viewing.

Simultaneous with research like Anderson's that acknowledges the historical contingency of film texts, film restoration efforts struggle to recover and to restore crucial components of cinematic history from the ravages of time and technological decay. Film restoration's "salvage paradigm," often celebrated at the same film studies conferences that include learned papers detailing the contingency of cinematic texts, presupposes an original, identifiable textual artifact ultimately stabilized through the act of restoration.[10] Indeed much of the crucial and invaluable labor of film restoration involves assembling from disparate and dispersed archival collections the fragments through which a stable artifact is reconstructed.[11] But what was the "original" for a film like Paramount's *The Wild Party* (1929)? National advertising copy like "Whether you see *The Wild Party* as an all-talking picture or 'silent' it's *great entertainment* because with Paramount the *story* is the thing," point not only to the multiple versions of individual films released during Hollywood's conversion to synchronous sound, but also to the problematic and largely unaddressed process through which an "authentic" text is retrospectively identified and then salvaged from the path of destructive historical change.[12] Promotional claims in 1929 such as "It doesn't matter if you see a Paramount Picture with sound and talking, or the *same picture* 'silent'—it's the last word in *entertainment*," attest by their very denial to the existence of multiple "originals" of the same film.[13]

9 Tim Anderson, "Reforming 'Jackass Music': The Problematic Aesthetics of Early American Film Music Accompaniment," *Cinema Journal* 37 (1) (Fall 1997), 12.

10 The term "salvage paradigm" is intended to invoke debates on museum curatorship, cultural displays, and multiculturalism that have interrogated a series of ethnographic and anthropological practices seeking to salvage traces of, or evidence concerning, "vanishing" peoples and cultures. The "salvage paradigm" debates within and surrounding anthropology address the process through which an object attains the discursively elevated and perhaps fetishized status of artifact. Although it is linked to early twentieth-century anthropology and collecting, James Clifford, for one, claims that the salvage paradigm reflects "a desire to rescue 'authenticity' out of the path of destructive historical change" and that the practice "is alive and well . . . found not only in ethnographic writing but also in the connoisseurships and collections of the art world and in a range of familiar nostalgias" (James Clifford, "Of Other Peoples: Beyond the 'Salvage' Paradigm," in Hal Foster, ed., *Discussions in Contemporary Culture*, No. 1, Seattle: Bay Press, 1987, 121). Such a "salvage paradigm" rhetorically underwrites our film restoration efforts and the discursive framing that seeks to label historical film objects as authentic. These debates from outside of film studies might provide a framework for further consideration of the often problematic process whereby an "authentic" film object is identified. Despite the rhetorical efforts of various labels accompanying restored films to identify them as "authentic," questions regarding the criteria through which we define such authenticity remain frequently unposed. Paolo Cherchi Usai, for one, has begun to address these issues in terms of silent film. See Paolo Cherchi Usai, *Burning Passions: An Introduction to the Study of Silent Cinema* (London: British Film Institute, 1994), especially 18–19, 52–53, 67 *passim*.

11 See, for example, Robert Gitt, "Restoring Vitaphone Films," in Mary Lea Bandy, ed., *The Dawn of Sound* (New York: Museum of Modern Art, 1989), 11–13, and Robert Gitt, "Bringing Vitaphone Back to Life," *Film History* 5 (1993), 262–274. Gitt describes the reconstruction of early synchronous sound films using rediscovered soundtrack discs and picture elements assembled from a variety of US and international archives.

12 Advertising copy from *The Saturday Evening Post* (6 April, 1929), 48.

13 Advertising copy from *The Saturday Evening Post* (23 March, 1929), 82.

The period surrounding Hollywood's conversion to synchronous sound provides a particularly rich moment in which to explore the historical and textual implications of the clash between the industry's desire to achieve and to enforce standardization and various countervailing local practices. This technological change held the *promise* of eliminating locally divergent, often idiosyncratic film exhibition practices by standardizing the acoustic accompaniment of films and by "synchronizing" the rate of film projection with that of film exposure. However, in the short term at least, the conversion to synchronous sound obstructed the industry's drive toward standardization, exacerbating the possibility of local variation in motion picture presentation. The conversion to synchronous sound transformed the motion picture projectionist into a *performer* of sound, displacing in a sense live acoustic performance from the orchestra pit to the projection booth. For a brief period in the history of American cinema, the projectionist became an active and audible performer in motion picture theaters across the country.

> He approaches his task, not from the standpoint of a worker who is to receive a monetary consideration in the form of wages for a given number of hours of service, but rather from the standpoint of an artist, mechanically etching upon the silver screen a series of beautiful photographic images that are unfolding to his movie audience a visual impression of a beautiful story told with the aid of his mechanical pen.
>
> (William F. Canavan)[14]

Such glowing descriptions of cinema artisans were typically reserved for the film director artfully orchestrating the combined talents of cast and crew, or less often for the cinematographer who, "painting with light," skillfully used the motion picture camera as his "mechanical pen." Surprisingly though, the film artist described above was in fact the movie projectionist anonymously practicing his craft out of public sight in the projection booth. William F. Canavan, at the time president of the International Alliance of Theatrical and Stage Employees and Moving Picture Operators (IATSE), sought in November 1929 to reinforce an increased importance for projectionists within the US film industry. In the midst of an industry-wide technological change—the conversion to synchronous sound—Canavan glowingly emphasized the projectionist's daily contribution to the industry. Canavan labeled the projectionist both an artist and a showman, claiming that "real showmanship is one of the most essential qualities for the real projectionist. He must be show-minded in all that the term implies, with a background of theatrical experience which will imbue him with that inherent theatrical spirit—'The Show Must Go On,' no matter what may happen."[15] Not surprisingly, the president of the projectionists' union also emphasized the professionalism of the membership he represented. Canavan described an army of under-appreciated projectionists actively preparing themselves for the conversion to sound through "intensive training and study" despite inconsistent technical support from equipment manufacturers. IATSE members were embracing technological change despite the inherent inadequacies of both laboratory-developed equipment and "far from perfect" installations of that equipment in movie theaters. In Canavan's words, "the projectionist is more of an idealist than a

---

14 William F. Canavan, "Motion Picture Projection," *Projection Engineering* 1 (4) (December 1929), 31.
15 Ibid., 31–32.

working man. He looks upon motion picture projection as a 'Specialized Art' and is ever striving to improve the quality of screen entertainment even though it entails a personal sacrifice."[16]

Canavan's depiction of the motion picture projectionist as a skilled artisan might be readily dismissed as an example of relatively transparent self-interest and self-promotion —the president of a powerful union celebrating that union's membership. Yet the labelling of projectionists as skilled professional artisans in the midst of the American cinema's conversion to synchronous sound was far more widespread than can be explained away as simply self-aggrandizing rhetoric. Instead, the period surrounding Hollywood's conversion to sound exhibited an industry-wide concern with both the labor and the identity of the motion picture projectionist.

Technological change exacerbated pre-existing concerns about both the performance and the professional identity of the projectionist. Although these concerns did not originate from the technology itself, they were directly related to it because Hollywood's conversion to sound required projectionists to become, quite literally, performers of reproduced sound. Sync-sound technology promised increased standardization in motion picture presentation, but at least during the period in which the industry adopted the new sound technology (1926–1932), such standardization of reproduction could only be approximated rather than achieved, and even then approached only through careful supervision, management, and control of the labor of motion picture projectionists.

In the gap between the film industry's desire for standardization and the realities of both sound-recording and sound-reproducing technology, the identity of the projectionist and the nature of his labor became a site of rhetorical struggle. Such a rhetorical struggle, common to instances of technological change, involved attempts to shape and to discipline both the identity of the emerging technology and the industry employees operating it. Technological change within US film, like any other technology-intensive industry, required not only shifts in "manufacturing" processes, but also the negotiated adaptation of the workforce to new conditions of labor. The effect of Hollywood's conversion to sound on the hierarchical division of labor within the film production component of the industry has been documented elsewhere.[17] During the conversion of movie theaters to recorded film sound, not only did local musicians lose their employment, but also film projectionists suddenly took on increased responsibilities for the successful presentation of films. For a time, at least, motion picture projectionists became more than operators of machinery and a discourse of professionalism and responsibility sought to encourage these historically elided laborers to inhabit a new workplace subjectivity.

Widespread discussion of the labor of film projectionists did not originate with Hollywood's conversion to sound. Prior to the full-scale diffusion of sync-sound technology, motion picture projection practices were defined as a problem because of a perceived lack of performance standards, an apparent absence of an implicit code of

---

16 Ibid., 31.
17 Historians like Jim Lastra and Donald Crafton have recently revised the received wisdom that technological change affected Hollywood labor by requiring "quiet on the set" and abruptly terminating the careers of several silent-era stars whose voices were found to be unsuitable to recording. Jim Lastra, "Standards and Practices: Aesthetic Norm and Technological Innovation in the American Cinema," in Janet Staiger, ed., *The Studio System* (New Brunswick, NJ: Rutgers University Press, 1995), 200–225; Donald Crafton *The Talkies: American Cinema's Transition to Sound, 1926–1931* (New York: Charles Scribners' Sons, 1999).

conduct for projectionists and consequent fears of irresponsible behavior, and a resulting pattern of inadequate film presentations to the public. Frequently citing the lack of
standardization in film presentation, representatives of film production companies and
advocates of "better" film exhibition called for an industry-wide concern with the labor
of projectionists. Among the most active advocates for projection reform, F. H.
Richardson, technical editor of the trade publication *Moving Picture World*, argued in
a series of public presentations and trade-press articles for careful attention to the often
overlooked work of the projectionist.[18] Citing such improper practices as inadequate or
careless maintenance of projectors, damage to release prints through both routine care-
lessness and excessive lubrication, inattention to the dimensions of the projected image
and the effects of auditorium lighting upon the screen image, and the waste of elec-
tricity through inefficient operation, Richardson cautioned the industry about the need
to enforce standards for public presentations of films. Calls for reform by Richardson
and others invoked both economic and artistic damage done to the industry through
inattention to the role of the projectionist in presenting films to the public. Period accounts
frequently cited not only under-motivated and unskilled motion picture operators but
also a resulting damage to films, to projection equipment, and, most importantly, to
the box office revenues of theaters.

Proposed solutions to the "problem" of projection hinged on fostering a sense of
professionalism among these anonymous theater employees. In addition to providing
consistent and well informed oversight of their labor (through, for example, establishing a "supervisor of projection" within theater chains), proposed solutions focused on
the need to establish an identity for projectionists and, importantly, to institutionalize
labor practices that would grow out of that identity. While the formation of projectionist
societies or educational committees by union locals could play a role in improving the
quality of film presentations, the most frequently cited solution for projection reform
involved a new identity for the projectionist. Prior to the conversion to sound, some
industry voices argued loudly for a reconceptualization of the projectionist from a "mere"
operator of machinery to an essential component, an active participant, in the production of entertainment. "If we wish to secure the best possible results, we must raise the
standard of projection. To raise the standard of projection, we must raise the standing of
the projectionist."[19] The quality of projection could be improved and the presentation

18 See, for example, F. H. Richardson, "Why Expert Knowledge and High Grade Intelligence is essential in
the Theater Projection Room," *Transactions of the SMPE* 11 (31) (1927), 500–511. Richardson's concern with the labor of projectionists dated to at least 1908 and the inauguration of his regular column in
Moving Picture World. As noted above (see note 5), he was a frequent advocate of controlling silent film
projection speeds.

19 McGuire, in a discussion of F. H. Richardson, "Why Expert Knowledge and High Grade Intelligence is
Essential in the Theater Projection Room," *Transactions of the SMPE* 11 (31) (1927), 508. McGuire
strikingly echoes both Richardson's silent-era rhetoric about projection speeds and the arguments of those
concerned with reforming nickelodeon-era musical accompaniment. Although largely undeveloped in his
essay, Tim Anderson notes that one site of intervention in the problem of live accompaniment was the
professionalization of the musician (9, 17–18). Anderson acknowledges that for some exhibitors the desire
for professionalism in musical performance clashed with the desire to maximize profits, with that profit
motive foreclosing the participation of more costly, unionized professional musicians in early film exhibition.
The innovation of synchronous sound rendered mute this particular point as recorded sound eliminated
musicians from theater orchestra pits thereby offering exhibitors a financial incentive to embrace technological change.

of films standardized, some claimed, by inculcating projectionists with professional attitudes about their labor.

For Richardson, the projection problem extended beyond individual projectionists to the larger attitudes of the industry as a whole. Noting "the almost total lack of any sort of publicly expressed appreciation of the work of the projectionist" as well as the tendency to label them "operators," Richardson argued that the attitude throughout the industry was "acting to stifle all pride in work and incentives to excel in it."[20] Richardson even went so far as to advocate a publicity campaign to educate the public about the importance of film projection—a campaign that would include movie star testimonials to the important work done by projectionists.[21]

The film industry's adoption of synchronous sound technology exacerbated these pre-existing concerns about projection and rendered more urgent the accompanying rhetorical appeals. The introduction of new technology into the projection booth caused such urgency precisely because the goal of standardizing the presentation of motion pictures became even more elusive as the tasks of projectionists underwent dramatic change. With the new technology came new responsibilities for the motion picture operator and implicitly new power within the industry.[22] Hollywood's conversion to sound introduced a variety of new tasks into the everyday labor of the projectionist. Many of these new procedures remained essentially inaudible and largely dissimulated, unless something went awry. Besides routine maintenance and troubleshooting of the new acoustic equipment, projectionists had to check and successfully cue soundtracks recorded on discs as well as be prepared to improvise should the sound-on-disc system fall out of synchronization with the projected images. For the sound-on-film system, projectionists exercised great care to keep the film itself clean, as any accumulated dirt or oil could clog the delicate reproducing slits necessary for converting the encoded soundtrack into electrical signals.[23] Projecting sync-sound films sometimes involved installing a new aperture mask when showing films with the Movietone sound-on-film system. The location of the soundtrack alongside the image required a mask to prevent the on-screen projection of the photographically encoded soundtrack. The soundtrack's presence on the celluloid consequently changed the aspect ratio of the film. In addition to changing this aperture mask, projectionists also often changed the projector lens to restore the on-screen image

20 F. H. Richardson, "The Importance of Good Projection to the Producer," *Transactions of the SMPE* 12 (34) (1928), 360–361.

21 Richardson, "The Importance," 359–360. Anderson also cites at least one letter to *Moving Picture World* that addressed the lack of praise and appreciation received by appropriately disciplined nickelodeon accompanists ("Reforming 'Jackass Music,'" 15). Again, many of the issues surrounding concerns about film projection in the early sync-sound era echo similar issues surrounding live accompaniment in the nickelodeon era.

22 Crafton notes that the conversion to sound, in the short run at least, allowed projectionists to demand successfully increases in wages and additional staff in the projection booths. *The Talkies*, 217–218.

23 Synchronous sound film was commercially introduced through competing and not entirely compatible formats. Western Electric's Vitaphone system, introduced in 1926, reproduced sound recorded on large circular discs, essentially enlarged phonograph records. The Fox-Case Corporation introduced its Movietone system in 1927 in which the soundtrack was encoded photographically on the same strip of celluloid as the image. RCA's Photophone system (1927) also recorded sound on film as did a competing Western Electric system. While sound-on-film became the industry standard, the initial period of conversion required many projectionists to become adept at operating *both* sound-on-disc and sound-on-film systems and switching smoothly from one to another during a performance.

to its "proper" size.[24] Among the most difficult tasks initially faced by projectionists involved successfully navigating changeovers from one projector to the next during reel changes. Until cues for such changeovers were standardized on release prints, projectionists developed a variety of individual strategies to guarantee smooth shifts from one reel to the next. These strategies extended from careful rehearsals to even punching holes in release prints.[25]

Period accounts of these new responsibilities often invoked the financial interest of individual or chains of theaters as well as the industry as a whole. Noting that poor or inconsistent projection detracted from the labor of all who worked on a film, calls for a new attitude of professionalism addressed not only the projectionists themselves but also, importantly, theater managers and owners. Warren Nolan, a publicist for United Artists Corporation, emphasized the urgency of improved projection standards in light of technological change: "The gentlemen in charge of projection of sound pictures— to say nothing of those who record them—have been constituted individual showmen by this new form of presentation. They have been given power, and they have been given responsibility. Timing and tone are in their hands, and artists on the screen and audiences in the seats are at their mercy."[26] The conversion to sound was held up not only as an opportunity to improve the knowledge and skill of the projectionist and thereby institute improved projection practice, but also as an opportunity for the industry as a whole to re-examine the importance of improved standards of showmanship.

While the conversion to sound upped the ante for efforts to improve projection, this technological change was also seen as a potential solution to the projection problem. Richardson frequently suggested that the conversion to sync-sound provided projectionists with a renewed interest and increased commitment to the quality of their labor. For Richardson, one important effect of synchronized sound was "to supply the projectionist with a much greater personal interest in his work."[27] Because of the new technology and the new responsibilities it entailed, "Projectionists who up to that time had turned an absolutely deaf ear to all pleadings that they study the technique of projection, suddenly and rather violently bestirred themselves."[28] From this perspective, the conversion to

---

24 H. Rubin, "Some Problems in the Projection of Sound Movies," *Transactions of the SMPE* 12 (35) (1928), 867–871.

25 Nickelodeon music reformers also cited the necessity of rehearsal for accompaniment much as advocates of professional standards for projectionists would argue some twenty years later, see Anderson ("Reforming 'Jackass Music,'" 14). Reel changes required projectionists to shift from one projector to another in order to guarantee the continuous presentation of a film. A successful reel change dissimulated the labor of the projectionist, rendering invisible and inaudible the very fact that a shift from one projector to another had taken place. Idiosyncratic marking mechanisms such as the punching of holes in a film so that the consequent flash of white light on the screen could cue the projectionist when to start the next projector and prepare for the changeover, not only undermined the industry goal of standardization of practice but also damaged the film print that would be shipped from one venue to the next. Without standardized methods of indicating changeovers, film prints would bear a physical trace of one projectionist's labor, carrying that trace to subsequent projection rooms and film venues.

26 Warren Nolan, "Talking Pictures and the Public," *Transactions of the SMPE* 13 (37) (1929), 132–133.

27 F. H. Richardson, "The Effect of Sound Synchronization upon Projection," *Transactions of the SMPE* 12 (35) (1928), 874.

28 Richardson, "The Effect of Sound Synchronization," 873. This perspective that technological change improved the performance of projectionists was widely echoed in the period. See also, for example, Harold B. Franklin, *Sound Motion Pictures: From the Laboratory to Their Presentation* (Garden City, NY: Doubleday, Doran & Co., 1929), 62.

sound could end complacency and the inaccurate assumption that film projection involved simply operating a machine, thereby abruptly terminating an era in which the work done in projection booths functioned as an almost textbook case of alienated labor. "The silent picture was, to the great number of projectionists, a sort of impersonal thing. He felt that so long as it was steady and well lighted his interest ceased. He felt that audiences regarded him and his work as of little or no importance, and that he was merely the necessary attendant or operator of a machine."[29]

Part of the industrial context within which Hollywood converted to sound was an ongoing economic consolidation and an increased emphasis on standardizing the product offered to consumers. Technological change promised, on the surface, both to cut theater owners' operating expenses and to standardize the presentation of films. Writing in 1929, Harold Franklin, president of Fox West Coast Theatres, noted the musical benefits of sync-sound technology:

> Music, as synchronized, is in closer unity with the situations pictured than was the case in former times. There is not, moreover, the distraction caused by the close proximity of musicians to the screen. The small towns, where inadequate orchestras used to render their ineffectual accompaniments to the silent pictures, have reaped the special benefits of musical synchronization. Music of the best calibre becomes available to every type of theatre.[30]

Because of their potential to eliminate idiosyncratic live musical accompaniment and with it the employment of musicians in individual movie theaters, synchronous soundtracks promised both economic savings in the long run and greater standardization of exhibition practices.[31]

This desire for standardized film presentations directly clashed with some of the design features of the initial sync-sound reproduction devices. Technological systems bear within them assumptions about their appropriate use. These preconceptions affect the design of an artifact and often shape how a device can be used. While a technology cannot *inevitably* determine the uses to which it is put, technological design can constrain potential uses of an artifact, predisposing a device to one or more set of applications instead of other competing approaches. While the film industry and movie exhibitors sought to dissimulate the work of putting on the show and to standardize motion picture performances, sound film equipment had embedded within it a different conception of the motion picture operator. The technology initially installed in projection booths arose from a presumption that the operator would be a *performer* of reproduced sound. The design of the apparatus itself provided an obstacle to the larger industry goal of standardizing projection practice.

The conception of sound reproduction as a performance originated in some of the components of film sound projection devices. Western Electric's initial Vitaphone sound

29 Richardson, "The Effect of Sound Synchronization," 874.
30 Franklin, *Sound Motion Pictures*, 361.
31 James P. Kraft provides a useful perspective on the conversion to sound from the perspective of employment practices of musicians, see James P. Kraft, *Stage to Studio: Musicians and the Sound Revolution, 1890–1950* (Baltimore: Johns Hopkins University Press, 1996). See especially Chapter 2, "Boom and Bust in Early Movie Theaters," 33–58.

reproduction system incorporated developments from public address devices designed within the Bell System and introduced and refined during the early 1920s.[32] Not only were individual components of the public address systems reapplied to motion picture sound projection, but so too were the assumptions surrounding the role of the public address sound engineer in performing electrically mediated sound. Western Electric's public address system provided the sound engineer with flexibility in operating the device since many public address situations required that the system be readjusted during performances. Especially in outdoor presentations, the public address engineer had to respond to changing conditions by varying the system's performance such as increasing or decreasing the acoustic output of loudspeaker horns. As a provision of system design, AT&T engineers were dispersed throughout a large crowd for the purpose of monitoring sound levels and signalling the system's operator to make volume adjustments as needed during that presentation. Public address sound projection was thus conceptualized as a live technological performance with volume adjustments used to maintain a consistent, audible "broadcast."[33] Flexibility in acoustic projection and a consequent perception that the operator was an active performer of electrically augmented sound were thus built into the public address system itself.

AT&T conceptualized sound reinforcement and acoustic projection as not fully automated processes but instead as the product of ongoing monitoring and adjustment, a live performance undertaken by appropriately trained engineers. The same conception initially informed the design, installation, and operation of synchronous sound film equipment. In the Western Electric Vitaphone sound-on-disc system, volume was controlled in the projection booth through a fader which attenuated the power in the circuit between the reproducing device and the main amplifying system.[34] In period descriptions of the Western Electric sound projector, manipulations of volume during the course of a sync-sound film presentation (called "riding gain") were described as a matter of course. These accounts cited four reasons for projectionists to "ride gain" during a show. Sound volume levels had to be modulated, first, because of variations in sound energy requirements in the theater and, second, owing to variations in the size of the audience at any given time during a performance. While these first two reasons for riding gain emphasize the projectionist's response to changing acoustic conditions in the performance space (much like the public address apparatus designed and marketed by Western Electric), the other two reasons for volume variation during a film more overtly constituted the projectionist as a performer of sound who contributed to the aesthetics of the motion picture. Projectionists using the Western Electric system also rode gain in response to variations in the levels of recorded sound and, finally, it was "necessary to have some means of varying sound level in theaters because of . . . the desirability of level control during reproduction for the purpose of emphasis."[35] Through volume adjustments during a performance the projectionist both compensated for potential deficiencies in the recorded soundtrack and introduced acoustic effects.

32 E. C. Wente, "Contributions of Telephone Research to Sound Pictures," *Journal of the SMPE* 27 (August 1936), 188–194.
33 I. W. Green and J. P. Maxfield, "Public Address Systems," *Bell System Technical Journal* 2 (1923), 138–139.
34 Coke Flannagan, "Servicing Sound Picture Projection Equipment in Theatres," *Transactions of the SMPE* 13 (38) (1929), 294.
35 S. K. Wolf, "The Western Electric Reproducing System," in Lester Cowan, ed., *Recording Sound for Motion Pictures* (New York: McGraw-Hill, 1931), 301.

The competing RCA Photophone sound-on-film system was also designed on the assumption that "the control of volume level is the chief concern of the projectionist during the operation of sound-reproducing equipment" and consequently the system provided a fader between the projector pick-up circuit and the first stage of amplification.[36] Period descriptions took volume manipulation for granted during the presentation of a synchronous sound film as "few pictures are so recorded that they can be run through at a single fader setting."[37] Cue sheets, either provided by the film distribution company or developed autonomously by the projectionist after the appropriate rehearsal, indicated when and how the necessary changes to volume should be performed during a presentation. The projectionist's cue sheets for Paramount's 1928 baseball film *Warming Up* indicated that the projectionist was to vary sound volume throughout six of the film's eight reels. Indicating a "normal" fader (volume) setting of "11," the cue sheet instructed projectionists to adjust the "Fader up one point at Baseball Scenes [and] after Baseball Scenes back to 11." In addition, at several points during the film, projectionists were to adjust the "Fader down two points at singing—then back to 11 after singing."[38] The practice of requiring volume changes during the projection of films continued at least as late as the 1933–1934 film season. In its exhibitor's pressbook for *Golddiggers of 1933*, Warner Bros. instructed exhibitors to "tell your operator—for best results move Fader up two points for the musical production numbers on 'Golddiggers of 1933' and also on the Trailer."

Throughout the early sync-sound era, projectionists labored to establish and then maintain appropriate volume levels during sound reproduction. (In Richardson's words, "To [the projectionist] the 'fader' is literally the 'throttle.'")[39] That task was not as simple as it might at first appear. In describing the maintenance program provided to theaters by Western Electric's subsidiary, Electrical Research Products, Inc. (ERPI), Coke Flannagan informed the Society of Motion Picture Engineers that as of 1929, deficiencies in the operation of projector and sound systems posed a greater threat to performances than mechanical failures. According to the ERPI engineer, the weak link in the Western Electric sound film system was the projectionist—specifically in terms of volume levels. "Operation [of Western Electric projectors] and showmanship are so closely related as to be inseparable, the operation of the equipment presents a greater problem than is presented by apparatus failures. Although the system may function perfectly the effect in the theater can be unpleasant and unnatural because of improper sound level. In fact undistorted sound when too loud is at times more objectionable than distorted sound at proper level."[40] Sound reproduced with too much volume exacerbated any acoustic flaws of a particular theater. Excessive reverberation was rendered "further aggravating" when the system was operated at greater energy—sounds were sustained longer, reflecting from surface to surface before being absorbed to inaudibility. Excessive

36 R. H. McCullough, "Practice and Problems of Sound Projection," in Lester Cowan, ed., *Recording Sound for Motion Pictures* (New York: McGraw-Hill, 1931), 330.

37 McCullough, "Practice and Problems," 331.

38 I am grateful to Martin Barnier for providing me with copies of the projectionist's cue sheet for *Warming Up*. Barnier apparently obtained the document at the Film Study Center, Museum of Modern Art, New York ("Sound Files 1927–1935"). The cue sheet is appended to a memo from M. H. Lewis entitled "Additional Instructions Regarding Sound Pictures and Discs," July 26, 1928.

39 Richardson, "The Effect of Sound Synchronization," 874.

40 Flannagan, "Servicing Sound Picture Projection Equipment," 294.

volume led to "unpleasant effects" and inaudible dialogue. Projectionists were cautioned to operate the Western Electric system at the minimum power level to ensure "comfortable audition."

In October 1930, H. M. Wilcox, operating manager of ERPI, suggested that one of the greatest current obstacles to nearly perfect reproduction was a tendency to keep the volume too loud. Cautioning against establishing projection volume levels by starting out too loud and then lowering the fader to an appropriate setting, Wilcox suggested that volume levels be determined by starting the fader too low and then raising volume until an appropriate setting was reached. Establishing the "proper" volume thus ultimately became an imprecise matter resolved by the judgment of the theater manager, the projectionist, or both. (In fact, the cue sheet for *Warming Up* indicated that "The fader markings shown herein were made at sound test in a fair sized Reviewing Room, where fader setting '11' proved satisfactory. This setting will possibly have to be changed to suit acoustics and other conditions at various theatres. This should be watched.") Wilcox further cautioned against adjusting volume to achieve adequate results for the worst seats in a house, such as in the rear of the balcony. The resulting excessive power would both increase surface noise and render volume too loud for the majority of seats in a theater.[41] In addition to establishing appropriate volume levels, the sound film projectionist had to modulate volume and the system's output energy in relation to the size of the audience at any given performance or as that audience size changed during a specific performance. Audience members functioned as acoustic absorbing material and different fader settings had to be determined for empty, half or full houses.[42]

Although period technical and trade journals indicate that manipulation of sound volume was part of the projectionist's task during the early sync-sound era, the rhetoric of professionalism and showmanship surrounding sound projection sought to limit "riding gain." Shifts in volume were to serve larger aesthetic purposes and not to occur simply at the whim of a projectionist or house manager, no matter how well meaning. In November 1929, Haviland Wessells cautioned against every theater manager or projectionist attempting to become his own musical conductor. Wessells described an anonymous house manager rushing back and forth to the monitor button to lower the volume of the music whenever the "action of a picture pepped up and music became a bit louder," and then increasing the power "when the music dropped down with a slowing of action."[43] The same manager, claimed Wessells, "raises a whisper to a shout," effectively ruining planned diminution of volume during dramatic scenes. Such apocryphal cautionary tales suggested that, when possible, prevailing standards of showmanship

41 "Volume Too Loud," *Projection Engineering* 2 (10) (October 1930), 28.
42 Flannagan, "Servicing Sound Picture Projection Equipment," 294; J. Garrick Eisenberg, "Technique of Sound-Picture Projection," *Projection Engineering* 1 (4) (December 1929), 25.
43 Haviland Wessells, "Sound—As the Customers Hear It," *Projection Engineering* 1 (3) (November 1929), 13. Here volume variations echo the rationale for variations in projection speed during the silent era, a practice that drew similar scorn from the production end of the industry. In 1920, even Richardson admitted that "there are occasional exceptions where a scene may actually be improved by moderate overspeeding of projection. Such scenes are, however, rare. As a rule they are those where speeding automobiles are involved, with no animate figures other than those in the machines. Such scenes merely form the exception which proves the rule." F. H. Richardson, "The Various Effects of Over-Speeding Projection," *Transactions of the SMPE* 10 (1920) reprinted on the website of Silent Film Bookshelf, see note 5.

dictated that house managers and projectionists should defer to the recording levels encoded on the soundtrack.

The active manipulation of sound volume described above was generally designed to guarantee the audibility of recorded soundtracks. But volume control involved more than merely ensuring comfortable audition and/or minimizing the potentially deleterious effects of excessive reverberation. Despite the concerns expressed by Wessells, period accounts indicate that the operation of sound apparatus frequently involved careful monitoring and the introduction of acoustic effects intended to enhance the aesthetics of the recorded sounds. Both conditions of sound recording at the time and representational protocols, then currently undergoing formulation, constructed sound reproduction as potentially a compensatory activity. It was through the performance of reproduced sound that inadequacies in the recorded soundtrack could be disguised. In addition, both "realistic" effects as well as acoustic embellishments could be added by projectionists to the synchronous sound film. "Serious attention is being directed to the importance of controlling sound level of music and speech to insure naturalness and *to augment the effect* of the action or dialogue upon the emotions of the audience" (my emphasis).[44] Such acoustic augmentation included not only volume effects, but also frequency attenuation and compensation in projection for acoustic defects introduced during recording.

During the period surrounding Hollywood's conversion to sound, the film industry's trade publications featured advertisements for acoustic equipment like the Samson Qualpensator, a device offering not merely volume control but also the ability to accentuate or diminish different acoustic frequencies. Acknowledging differences in acoustic taste, advertising copy noted that "Some like the bass notes emphasized; others prefer them softened. Still others prefer the treble, others both treble and bass notes or even the middle register notes modified to their taste."[45] The Qualpensator could vary acoustic output "to please in any one of these ranges" and further "[it] will do much to compensate for the poor acoustical properties of a room."

RCA's Photophone sound film system included in its normal amplification circuits a variable low frequency attenuator, called a "compensator," that was designed to diminish low frequency signals and thereby accentuate the higher frequency sounds of any recording. Through listening tests at the time of installation in movie theaters, RCA engineers established a normal setting for the compensator using a test recording, but thereafter, the compensator could be varied at any time by the operator. The device allowed projectionists to compensate for so-called "boomy" recordings (those in which lower frequencies predominated) and thus "with this device it is possible to increase the intelligibility of reproduced speech which for any reason is lacking in high frequencies."[46] Devices like the Samson Qualpensator or RCA's compensator allowed sound film projectionists to accentuate or to diminish the range of audible frequencies reaching the film audience.

Besides adjusting the frequency response of sound film projection systems either to suit the public and their supervisor's tastes or to render more audible so-called "boomy"

44 Flannagan, "Servicing Sound Picture Projection Equipment," 295.
45 Samson Qualpensator advertisement, *Projection Engineering* 2 (4) (April 1930), 1.
46 John O. Aalberg, "Theater Reproduction by RCA Photophone System," in Lester Cowan, ed., *Recording Sound for Motion Pictures* (New York: McGraw-Hill, 1931), 311.

recordings, the appropriately disciplined film projectionist also manipulated volume to compensate for acoustic problems encoded on to recorded soundtracks. "Only half the mixing is done in the studio . . . the projection room must do the rest," or so announced a January 1930 advertisement for Hardwick, Hindle volume faders published in motion picture industry trade publications.[47] In December 1929, J. Garrick Eisenberg, sound recording engineer at Tiffany Studios, explicitly outlined a series of instances in which the projectionist's showmanship responsibilities included careful acoustic performance to render inaudible a variety of deficiencies in recorded soundtracks. Eisenberg claimed that the projectionist was "responsible also to a large degree for the artistic rendition of the sound accompaniment."[48] Among the specific recording deficiencies cited by Eisenberg were abrupt differences in volume level from one reel to the next and problems in scale matching such that "when the close-up of an individual player is shown, quite often the sound level is not increased proportionately, with the result that the close-up illusion is destroyed."[49] He also described inadequate differentiation of recorded volume levels for special effects. In this latter case, Eisenberg noted that recorded levels for sound effects might be either too loud or too soft. "Sometimes when some loud, terrifying noise is intended to accompany the action, the relatively small difference in recording levels allowed enfeebles the effect: one hears loud, raucous conversation, commands, shouts, then a supposedly huge explosion goes off with only a slightly louder 'pop.' The result is ludicrous. Equally bad are such effects as footsteps approaching along a gravel path which sound like a herd of pachyderms trampling down a forest of young bamboo, in comparison to the dialogue level."[50] Again, the projectionist's cue sheet for *Warming Up* reveals a trace of early sound-era projection practice. In Reel 8, the projectionist was instructed to increase volume in step with narrative developments. "At scene where Tolliver strikes out McRoe bring fade up one point at each strike—and hold till end of baseball scene—then back to Fader '11' for indoor scene." Here the projectionist manipulated volume to accentuate the increasing tension of narrative events.

Under such conditions as those described by Eisenberg and codified by the instructions for *Warming Up*, the projectionist literally became a performer of sound, carefully attending to the presentation of recorded sound so as to disguise recording errors, manipulating the volume of reproduction either for the sake of realism (achieving approximate acoustic matching for shifts in shot scale, like diminishing unduly loud footsteps) or for the sake of dramatic effects (acoustically accentuating the abrupt sound of an explosion or the increasing crowd noise at a baseball game). Although often assisted in these representational tasks by cue sheets provided by film distributors, the projectionist also

47 Hardwick, Hindle Volume Faders, advertisement, *Projection Engineering* 2 (1) (January 1930), 35.
48 Eisenberg, "Technique of Sound-Picture Projection," 25.
49 Eisenberg's presumption that a cut to a closeup should be accompanied by a concomitant increase in volume was not universally shared throughout the film industry. In fact, during this period such representational issues as the relationship between shot scale and sound volume were the subject of intense debate within the film industry. For analyses of these debates, see Rick Altman, "Sound Space," in Rick Altman, ed., *Sound Theory/Sound Practice* (New York: Routledge, 1992), 46–64, and Jim Lastra "Reading, Writing and Representing Sound," in Altman, ed., 75–78. I also briefly discuss this debate among Hollywood sound practitioners in "'She Sang Live, but the Microphone Was Turned Off': The Live, the Recorded, and the *Subject* of Representation," in Altman, ed., 96–99.
50 Eisenberg, "Technique of Sound-Picture Projection," 24.

had to be guided by, in Eisenberg's words, "some sense of artistic appreciation."[51] An appropriately disciplined projectionist of the early sync-sound era necessarily combined electro-mechanical proficiency with aesthetic judgment. The professional identity that projectionists were encouraged to inhabit combined the routinized labor of attending to a machine with the creative performance of sound reproduction.

Period accounts by Eisenberg and others that described the production difficulties surrounding sound recording and the irregular and inadequate sound levels that resulted, consistently framed such deficiencies in production practice as temporary aberrations caused by hurried production conditions in Hollywood or by the ongoing development of recording techniques. While projectionists were thus charged with compensating for recording inadequacies, those inadequacies were nearly always carefully framed as temporary in nature with refinement and standardization of production and reproduction techniques the inevitable goal.[52] In Eisenberg's words, "Meanwhile the burden of carrying on under present conditions falls largely upon the projectionist, and if he is at all worthy of his salt, he will make every effort to cover up by skillful handing of the gain controls, the present limitations of the art."[53] In the short term, however, it fell to the motion picture projectionist to perform sound reproduction and actively contribute to industry standards of showmanship. Such professionalism was indeed a short-term solution. Far more efficient in terms of the goal of standardization would be refinements to the recording process whereby the performative labor required of projectionists in the early sync-sound era could instead be successfully encoded into the recorded soundtrack, rendering them yet again mere operators of a machines. Besides offering national standardization or movement toward the goal of national standardization, such a process would also "de-skill" the projectionist workforce, providing leverage for theater owners seeking more restrictive and exploitative contracts.

Although standardization of film performances was a goal expressed within the film industry, variations in theater acoustics, standards of sound projection equipment, quality and volume of recorded soundtracks, and recording practices all made such a goal initially unattainable. In a 1930 editorial of the recently inaugurated trade journal *Projection Engineering*, Don McNicol clearly described both the desire for standardization and obstacles to accomplishing that goal:

> If all theatres were alike in acoustics, if all projection equipment was in the same first rate condition, and if all projectionists were equally familiar with the artistic effects desired in a given picture, there would be little complaint in regard to lack of uniform results. That such variations do exist signifies that every exhibitor should

---

51 Ibid., 22. Similar associations between film projection and artistry also characterized some film industry rhetoric surrounding disparities in projection speed. "The operator 'renders' a film, if he is a real opertor, exactly as does the musician render a piece of music, in that, within limits, the action of the scene being portrayed depends entirely on his judgement." F. H. Richardson, "Projection Department," *The Moving Picture World* (December 2, 1911), 721–722.

52 See also J. Garrick Eisenberg, "Mechanics of the Talking Movie," *Projection Engineering* 1 (3) (November 1929), 22–24.

53 Ibid., 24.

take all reasonable precaution to compensate for irregularities or inaccuracies peculiar to the auditorium and his projection facilities.[54]

Into the gap between standardization as an industry goal and the realities of equipment, theater acoustics, and recorded soundtracks, professionalism arose as an alternative way of framing and disciplining the labor of the motion picture projectionist. This rhetoric of professionalism invoked standards of education and training as well as renewed pride in one's work, and it framed the labor of the projectionist as an artistic contribution to the industry, in some ways equal to the contributions of those engaged in film production. The projectionist was, for a time, categorized as a motion picture performer, instrumental in the creation of aesthetic effects.

At important moments in US film history, the labor of textual production did not cease with the national distribution of copies of films. Instead, a range of exhibition practices might be usefully reconsidered as constitutive of the Hollywood text. These include a variety of live performance methods that accompanied silent films. Hollywood's adoption of recorded soundtracks offered the possibility of standardizing and indeed eliminating much of this "post-distribution" labor in textual production, but the innovation of synchronous sound technology did not guarantee standardized acoustic practices.

A reconsideration of the performative aspects of projectionists' labor should qualify, if not actually change, our notions of film texts and textuality during Hollywood's conversion to synchronous sound. Our contemporary understanding of the early sync-sound film owes much to the Herculean efforts of ongoing film restoration. Film restoration and the "salvage paradigm" on which it is based have begun to render visible and audible perhaps the most widely discussed, theorized and historicized yet unheard and underviewed period of cinema's ongoing technological change. But film restoration is in some ways ideologically complicit with Hollywood's industrial desire for standardization. By retrospectively valorizing the carefully controlled labor of film production, it sometimes elides the labor of projectionists and other instances of what we might call the "post-distribution" labor of textual production, that is, the labor of textual *performance*. For some films, it is only through film restoration that a no-longer-existing US film industry achieves its goal of textual stability and standardization.

A closer look at the technology of motion picture projection and the labor of projectionists in the early sync-sound era illustrates that the soundtracks for these films were not finally and ultimately determined by Hollywood's recording engineers, but were instead acoustically contingent on a number of factors, not the least of which was, in the words of the literature of the period, the level of professionalism and showmanship exhibited by long forgotten projectionist-performers. Volume adjustments for the sake of audibility of dialogue, for example, compensated for sound technology's and sound recordists' inability to serve perceived narrative needs while volume adjustments for the sake of "creating effects" supplemented and indeed usurped the signifying potential of

---

54 Donald McNicol, "Editorial: Picture Rehearsals in the Theater," *Projection Engineering* 2 (12) (December 1930), 4.

the sync-sound film by often emphasizing the spectacular qualities of recorded sounds. When the properly disciplined motion picture projectionist "rode gain" or attenuated the frequency of recorded soundtracks, he became temporarily an enunciator collaborating with, or potentially undermining, the textual work of enunciation.[55]

A greater historical awareness that US cinema's production practices often yielded an indeterminant text, or rather several simultaneously co-existing versions of a film, might productively contextualize approaches to contemporary cinema. Contemporary trips to our local video venue confront us with multiple versions of the same film: the theatrical release (often panned and scanned), letterboxed or other "widescreen" versions, and even potentially a "director's cut." The contemporary practice of encoding multiple versions of the same film on a single DVD (with, in some instances, a choice of acoustic accompaniment that includes spoken commentary) underscores the contingent nature of film studies' ostensible object. The "director's cut," for example, might be viewed as an almost fetishistic holdover from film studies' auteurist past, but the practice also plays off and invokes a desire to see and to hear that which has been hidden or presumed lost. The "director's cut" offers us "restored" and/or "previously unseen" footage promising to deliver an experience previously denied even as it implicitly attests to the industrial conditions and the corporate division of labor that resulted in that original denial. The notion of a single, original version of a film becomes even more tenuous, even more obviously a necessary heuristic, with efforts like the restoration of *Touch of Evil* or the remastered soundtrack for the rerelease of *Vertigo*. Rather than being simply the product of new and emerging technologies of restoration or of distribution formats, multiple versions of contemporary and "restored" films have a long history in the US cinema.

55 I invoke the term "enunciation" here to indicate the manner in which a reconsideration of textual production at the site of exhibition could enliven an increasingly eclipsed framework from film studies' intellectual history. When careful attention to film history causes us to reconsider filmic representation as, in part, a live performance, we must also re-examine the presumption of a stable, knowable film artifact that underwrites close textual analysis.

21 States of emergency

Patricia R. Zimmermann

To flourish in defiance

The valiant members of the National Alliance of Media Arts and Culture (NAMAC) fight on the front lines in the civil war to keep public media arts culture truly popular.[1] These museum curators, festival directors, grants agencies, foundations, distributors, alternative exhibitors, and media production groups together sustain a viable, dynamic media arts culture despite the intensification of the transnational media sector that robs us all of any place to argue and be with people other than ourselves. These warriors, together with NAMAC, carve out places and spaces for public culture in these terribly privatized times. Despite the headaches and heartaches of keeping the non-profit sector alive in a zeitgeist wherein popular equals commercial, these various cultural workers perform the hard work of organizing a popular resistance to commercial media. This transnational corporate media sector more often than not deprives us of creativity and collectivity, two modes of action that define the popular as that which energizes action beyond the self.[2]

All scholars and educators owe a large debt to these cultural workers who hold up the infrastructures that keep hope alive for a democratic media culture. We benefit directly and indirectly from their often invisible and under-heralded work. As front-line troops blazing a trail through the amazing art practices, debates, and work pushing through the cultural lethargy dragging like seaweed on the bottom of a sailboat keel, we need them. And we also need to be part of this movement to reclaim the popular for people, to wrest it away from the corporations who define the popular through marketing and grosses.

Against all that says no to public culture, the non-profit media arts sector provides space for radical—and popular—media art to flourish in defiance. Its cultural work opens up ideas and new media practices for all of us, even when all we can do to participate is read the massive amounts of brochures and flyers announcing its programs that flood our campus mailboxes. Its foraging through the complex, ever-shifting terrain of contemporary work leads us to artists, movements and practices that we want to think about, teach, write about, and program. It provokes us. It makes us feel less alone in the quickly corporatizing academy. It gives us hope.

---

1 The National Alliance of Media Arts and Culture is perhaps the largest organization of its kind in the US, representing the institutions and foundations that comprise the infrastructure and administrative sector for media arts. Its website is at www.namac.org.

2 For an elaboration of this notion of popular, see John Fiske, *Reading the Popular* (Boston: Unwin Hyman, 1989) and Jane Shattuc, *The Talking Cure: Talk Shows and Popular Culture* (New York: Routledge, 1997).

Emergency: thinking about media arts

This chapter seeks to navigate something I have called the "states of emergency" in the media arts world.[3] I use the plural—states—to suggest that we are currently not in the midst of one, easy-to-understand state of emergency, but in a multi-layered, poly-vocal complexity comprised of many states, as in states of the union from New York to Ohio, to Montana, to Texas, and to Utah. But it is also many states, as in conditions of engagement. I use this term "states" to suggest—perhaps in an invocation of femin-ist thinking originating in the 1970s—states of consciousness or unconsciousness, words I marshall not to describe a medical or drug-induced condition, but rather invoke to describe our level of political and social/historical analysis. Thus, states of emergency can operate as a way to suggest that our responses to arts defunding, corporatization, annihilation of truly popular radical culture, and end of public debate must perform swift acts of triage—we can't wait or it will all die.[4]

These states of emergency in the end don't have all that much to do with state, federal, or private foundation funding, although parts of them certainly do. States of emergency, as I am using this construct, are more identified with what I see as a state of emergency in how we think about media, media arts, and arts practices. There is a state of emergency in how we decide what is popular and what is not.

Given this current state of affairs and the globalization expanding exponentially around us, we need completely new, risky epistemologies—a fancy, perhaps overly the-oretical word for thinking about thinking, for the structure of knowledge—that can account for the complexities of our current era and aggressively imagine ways to carve out some public space in it.[5]

There is, then, a state of emergency not only in the material, infrastructural realms we all occupy but also in how we think. And compared to procuring $100,000 operat-ing budgets from non-profit agencies for programs and operating costs, new thinking is so much easier to come by if we can just let go and reimagine the universe. Popular media, then, is redefined from its corporatized marketing, product tie-ins, and individ-ualistic fantasies to a more collective, energized engagement with both the world and others. In other words, we need to think of the popular as that which fuels passion with others and energizes new thought and practices.[6]

It is too easy in the twenty-first century to bemoan the horrific state of affairs that is the non-profit media arts sector. Reduced budgets, declining attendance, political assaults,

3 For a fuller explication of the various material and discursive formations of this state of affairs, see Patricia R. Zimmermann, *States of Emergency: Documentaries, Wars, Democracies* (Minneapolis: University of Minnesota Press, 2000).

4 For an analysis of the growth of media transnationals and their gutting of public culture, see Erik Barnouw *et al.*, *Conglomerates and the Media* (New York: New Press, 1997); Robert McChesney, *Corporate Media and the Threat to Democracy* (New York: Seven Stories, 1997); and John Hess and Patricia R. Zimmermann, "Transnational Documentaries: A Manifesto," *Afterimage* (January/February 1997), 10–14.

5 In his *Hypertext 2.0: The Convergence of Contemporary Critical Theory and Technology* (Baltimore: Johns Hopkins University Press, 1997), George Landow argues that the new media technologies and hypertextual modes reorient linearity and deductive reasoning, requiring new navigational tools to think through these new formations.

6 In his *Cultural Democracy: Politics, Media, New Technology* (Albany: State University of New York Press, 1997), David Trend surveys the contemporary media fields and argues that the political, the populist, and the popular need to be reunited.

isolation, and creeping commercialization can make it all seem like a remnant of some 1970s fantasy of communal living and organic farming. Fixating too much on funding or defunding the arts infrastructures obliterates the vivid histories of organizations that thrived without any arts agency or private foundation support at all during the 1950s and 1960s: The Flaherty Seminar, Cinema 16, and Art in Cinema, to name just a few.[7]

These organizations did not simply invent ways to survive and get resuscitated, a language more appropriate perhaps to hospital cardiac units. More importantly for my argument here, they *imagined* the future, which meant, quite simply, unsettling and rewiring the universe with every program, every idea, and every event. They insisted that the popular can be produced and not simply consumed. And this rewiring, we now know from historical reclamation projects by scholars, meant *thinking differently* all the time. And it also meant constantly redefining the popular away from the fantasies of the so-called "mass market" to the realities of creating fantasies that move spectators beyond themselves in a space that insisted by its very existence that things can be different. In our field of film/media/visual/cultural studies, far too much attention has been paid to textual analysis and not enough to the ways in which distribution and exhibition creates spaces for popular culture to emerge.[8]

As that great champion of independent media Erik Barnouw once told me, this rewiring meant knowing that the most important thing any public popular media event can do is "boil over."[9] By that term, Barnouw meant that what is repressed in our culture and our politics and our lives can come out furiously in a public way, boil over the confines of the pot, get people talking and energized, and create conflict out of which can emerge change and even, sometimes, solidarities.

For most academics who interact with undergraduates and graduate students daily, I would suspect it is a rare event that any "boiling over" of any kind happens. Right now, on my campus where *almost any* debate and controversy about *almost anything* is framed as impolite, loud, and above all to be averted, I would be happy with a low simmer of any kind. Somewhere, someplace, there must be room for an unofficial, samizdat culture of hope where things can "boil over," where people can connect to each other through public conversations and collective actions, and where ideas and art truly matter and truly make a difference.[10]

7 Erik Barnouw and Patricia R. Zimmermann, "The Flaherty: Four Decades in the Cause of Independent Cinema," Special Quadruple Issue of *Wide Angle*, nos 1–4, 1995; and Scott MacDonald, "Cinema 16," Special Double Issue of *Wide Angle*, nos 1 and 2, 1997.

8 Diane Waldman and Janet Walker, eds, *Feminism and Documentary* (Minneapolis: University of Minnesota Press, 1999). Most of the essays in this anthology locate the nexus of feminism and documentary within the social circulation of work, figuring their interactions with political/social structures and the structures of distribution created as equally critical as the texts themselves.

9 During the 1994 Flaherty Seminar (where Barnouw and I curated a homage to its 40th anniversary), in private conversation discussing my fears that our programs would precipitate vicious arguments, Barnouw encouraged me not to worry, contending that good curating should be a provocation for ideas and debates that were repressed and percolated to "boil up" and "boil over" so that they would be rendered public.

10 Toni Morrison, "The Site of Memory," in Russell Ferguson, Martha Gever, Trinh T. Minh-ha, and Cornel West, eds, *Out There: Marginalization and Contemporary Cultures* (Cambridge, MA: MIT Press, 1990), 299–305.

Histories of civil wars

Historically, all of us—educators, curators, artists, and administrators—have been engaged in this civil war against difference and public culture for more than ten years. Although, to be accurate, its origins should be located in the early years of the Reagan administration's attacks on politically engaged documentaries like *From the Ashes: Nicaragua Today* and *El Salvador: Another Vietnam* in 1981.[11] For example, my entire professional life in media arts and critical writing over the last twenty-plus years has been flogged by arts defunding, political attacks against academics, artists, and our colleagues in the media arts sector, embattled infrastructures, and the end of public space. The privatization is so bad that in my home state of New York, garbage in state parks has even been privatized. We now have to carry out our trash ourselves.

The overused term "culture war," with its high culture, elitist connotations, seems grossly inadequate.[12] We are not simply embattled over culture as art production, but over social, historical, economic, and political shifts and reorganizations of what constitutes the popular that are absolutely monumental in scope. The entire globe is being reorganized and reengineered. The entire globe—as well as the entire media arts field in every country—is up for sale like used household appliances at a yard sale.[13]

We can map how bad it is when the Hollywood transnationals see economies of scale by producing feature films in places racked by nationalist genocide, like Bosnia or places where the transition from communism to neo-liberalization and the free market has left national film industries either in ruins or dead, like Russia, Hungary, and Poland. The vultures are no longer circling the corpses but eating them as appetizers.

Most of us just happen to live in the US, but similar trends of defunding and privatization can be discerned in Asia, western and eastern Europe, Latin America, and Canada.[14] We are therefore poised on a crumbling, frightening precipice as we edge into the enigmatic, morphing media landscapes of the twenty-first century.

Therefore, I prefer the term "civil war" rather than "culture war," language coined by neo-conservatives like Newt Gingrich, Hilton Kramer, Congressman Danenmeyer and their buddies.[15] It is intellectually and politically dangerous to allow the forces of privatization to frame what is our debate and what marks our lives. The term "civil war" is much more applicable and useful: we are, of course, fighting about borders, about north/south divides across the globe, about the place of genders, races, sexualities, regional identities, and the differently-abled within the reordered white nation, about annihilation of difference and heterogeneity—not just of people, but of a whole range of places, spaces, practices, and popular media movements.

11 Patricia R. Zimmermann, "Public Television, Independent Documentary Producers, and Public Policy," *Journal of the University Film and Video Association* 34 (3) (Summer 1982), 9–25.

12 For examples of the neo-conservative attacks, see David Horowitz and Laurence Jarvik, eds, *Public Broadcasting and the Public Trust* (Los Angeles: Second Thoughts, 1995); and Hilton Kramer and Roger Kimball, eds, *Against the Grain: The New Criterion on Art and Intellect at the End of the Twentieth Century* (Chicago: Ivan R. Dee, 1995).

13 Herbert I. Schiller, *Culture, Inc.: The Corporate Takeover of Public Expression* (Oxford: Oxford University Press, 1989).

14 Zillah Eisenstein, *Global Obscenities: Patriarchy Capitalism and the Lure of Cyberfantasy* (New York: New York University, 1998).

15 For a substantive tracking of the origins and debates about the "culture wars," see Richard Bolton, ed., *Culture Wars: Documents from the Recent Controversies in the Arts* (New York: New Press, 1992).

We have been engaged in this civil war about who and what will survive and who will define the nation for so long that our energies are flagging. Many of us feel tired and lonely. There is now a whole generation of students and new media arts professionals and artists who do not even see this situation as a crisis, but as business as usual, de rigeur, common place, what is, reality.

If you are a 20-year-old film and digital media student now, more than likely all you have experienced as popular culture is commercial film screenings of *Robocop*, *The Matrix*, and *Raiders of the Lost Ark* on campus, with diminished appearances by edgy, outrageous visiting artists, an explosion of white male agents from the transnational media corporations preaching the ecstasy of free-market media fun, and a limited non-profit sector that looks a little boring, a little too self-important, and more than a little too retro in Birkenstocks and tie-dye shirts.

Who can blame these students for thinking that their future is limited to menial jobs at Time Warner and Disney or slaving as production assistants on Clairol commercials? Who can blame them for looking for low-end, entry level transnational media jobs with high-powered computers with fast internet connections so they can surf for web installation art when the boss is off to Korea hiring workers for animation *maquiladoras*?

Even the word *independent* media has a different meaning from how I would guess most of us who have participated in this movement of popular political media would define it from living in it and watching it. The first year of Reagan's unraveling of the arts infrastructure, the welfare state, and federal regulatory controls of media—1981— set in motion the intensive economic and political restructurings encircling us now. This same year also represented a significant turning point for US feature-length, narrative independent cinema, for it was during this period that these films first reached larger audiences in art cinemas and festivals, culminating in nearly 15 years of agitation across many different formats and genres.[16] Yet this work failed to expand our vision of the possibilities of cinema: it simply replaced international art cinema with subtitle-free, English-only productions that did not, for the most part, interrogate the language of cinema but instead embraced classical Hollywood style, only with younger casts and wilder clothes.[17]

Nearly two decades later, the transnational media companies and their boutique distributors raid independent media, looking for low-budget work to attract new untapped niche audiences with hefty amounts of disposable income and time, and to generate large profit margins. The independent films so heralded by journalists simply function as hip upgrades adorned with tattoos, nose rings, and designer jeans to the old B-picture system developed during the classical Hollywood studio era. Once the elaborate rock and roll sound mixes and special effects are stripped away, it is difficult to discern many significant distinctions between "indie film" and a Hollywood studio production because, first of all, the Hollywood studios no longer exist. Hollywood films and these independents are merely two sides of the same old/new global Hollywood: a perpetual quest for deals, dollars, and undeveloped niche markets. The independent media has

16 For an insider's view of the development of commercial independent cinema in the 1980s and 1990s, see John Pierson, *Mike, Spike, Slackers and Dykes: A Guided Tour across a Decade of Independent American Cinema* (London: Faber, 1996).

17 In his *The Cinema of Outsiders: The Rise of American Independent Cinema* (New York: New York University Press, 1999), Emanuel Levy shows how the decline of "art cinema" is directly related to the "rise" of the American independent narrative film in English which replaced it.

simply been transformed from an articulation of popular culture—that is, a media of the people by the people—into a farm team for the big leagues.[18]

Reclaiming independent media

Therefore it is vital for our field—again, scholars, media arts cultural workers, and audiences—to engage in an historical reclamation project for the term "independent media." We need to reroute the current commodification of the term and insist we are not a market niche. We need to revive the independent media's oppositional political heritage from the anti-war, women's, and civil rights movements but we can't get stuck in the 1960s. We need to recuperate the term "popular," stripping it of its marketized, commercial veneers to revitalize the people and passions that should define it.

We need to reclaim the parts that still work and recycle them, such as the idea of a committed arts practice where the larger world outside the self matters. This should not be read as a nostalgic evocation of paradise lost, a time when politics, art, and the community served the more lofty ideals of social and political revolution through 16 mm and porta-paks. Rather, we need to locate the independent media and its supporting organizations within their historical, popular legacies and their evolving futures in order to rethink how the dramatic contradictions of the new global politics, new wars, new technologies, and new forms can recharge its purpose.

In the transnational economic era, culture matters but differently and in new ways. Culture is no longer the place where the nation state revitalizes itself away from the instrumentality of capital. It is now the place where transnational capital defines itself. In other words, transnational capital has subsumed culture.[19] In older formations of the nation, culture was where dreams and nightmares, fantasies and realities resided. Now, these same discourses resurface as problematic sites, eruptions, and disturbances.

The fronts upon which this civil war is waged also look different from earlier periods of independent media. Previously, radical media was defined in a series of oppositions, with independents located within alternative media against the corporate networks, a conflict pitched between the commercial and the non-commercial, between the monumental, historical sweep and breadth of public interest, and the limitations of private interests.[20]

But in the new millennium and beyond, these very oppositions that have guided the independent film community and alternative media are being dramatically altered by a dizzying myriad of changes: increased concentration across industries in telecommunications; a more fluid, layered transnational media flow; the emergence of media products and telecommunications technologies as central players in geopolitical trade negotiations like the General Agreement on Tariffs and Trade (GATT); deregulations and privatizations of public telecommunications across the globe; and aggressive state

18 See Justin Wyatt, "The Formation of the 'Major Independent': Miramax, New Line and the New Hollywood," in Stephen Neale and Murray Smith, eds, *Contemporary Hollywood Cinema* (New York: Routledge, 1998), 74–90.
19 Masao Miyoshi, "A Borderless World? From Colonialism to Transnationalism and the Decline of the Nation-State," *Critical Inquiry* 19 (4) (1993), 736.
20 See, for example, Deirdre Boyle, *Subject to Change: Guerrilla Television Revisited* (Oxford: Oxford University Press, 1997).

and federal arts defunding. Yet at the same time, the proliferation of new technologies like camcorders and digital media loosen up the borders between high- and low-end productions to create new, unregulated public spaces with promise.[21]

We need to think about independent media not as Quentin Tarantino and Miramax, but as work and places which envision public space as volatile and necessary. We need to define independent media and the media arts fields as places where, to refer to Erik Barnouw again, the great pathfinder in this field, *things boil over.*

Layers of contradictions

At this juncture, I want to propose six provisional layers of contradictions that perhaps can open up a possible rethinking of the media and can help us get to that boiling over point. We need to start our new thinking about these states of emergency from these contradictions, not from criteria generated from a previous historical formation, or from a lingering nostalgia for the good old days. Certainly, this list is not conclusive, and there are many more sectors to unravel. I will explore all of these contradictions through some of the sedimentary layers of the media arts field. I elaborate these ideas not as fully resolved positions but as detonation points to open up discussion, and to loosen up old ways of conceiving media arts.

Contradiction 1: The transnational versus the local

First, it is vital not to think solely in terms of nation states and national arts funding policies anymore. The nation state has transformed into a transnational nodal point for cultural capital. The media transnationals like Time Warner, Bertelsman, and Disney are larger than most nation states across the globe. They are completely unregulated. They constantly mutate along with changing social and political conditions. They depend on new technologies like computers and satellites to move data and images, transmuting the relationship between space and time, and shearing capital away from any location. We have experienced the most intensive decade of cross-media merger activity in history, with Time-Warner-Turner-AOL reigning as the largest media company in the world.[22] It is the new Ottoman Empire. Let us not forget that 1989, the year of the now notorious Mapplethorpe controversy, was also the year of the Time Warner merger, the Tiananmen Square massacre, and the fall of the Berlin Wall.

In some theoretical arguments, the local has now taken on more importance as a place where difference can survive. Yet even the local is crisscrossed by the transnationals, and by the diasporas and displacements of large numbers of people.[23] As Trinh T. Minh-ha

---

21 For a discussion of how low-end camcorders have been utilized by the reproductive rights movement in the United States, see *States of Emergency: Documentaries, Wars, Democracies* (Minneapolis: University of Minnesota Press, 2000), 119–153.

22 Edward S. Herman, *Triumph of the Market: Essays on Economics, Politics and the Media* (Boston: South End Press, 1995) and Herbert I. Schiller, *Information Inequality: The Deepening Social Crisis in America* (New York: Routledge, 1986).

23 Caren Kaplan, *Questions of Travel: Postmodern Discourse of Displacement* (Durham, NC: Duke University Press, 1996) and Arjun Appadurai, *Modernity at Large: Cultural Dimensions of Globalization* (Minneapolis: University of Minnesota Press, 1996).

has said, the First World is in the Third World and the Third World is in the First World.[24] The contradictions between the transnationals and the local are always laced with these diasporas.

This economic and social reorganization has shifted the role, function, and purpose of media arts. And because the nation state is withering and morphing into some new kind of economic cyborg, the cultural sector no longer serves the purpose of national identity formation—that is, pluralizing the nation, and expanding its histories. This is an argument we in the media arts field have been making for many years. Only the nation state in its old formations needs history and culture. New transnational nation states need something else: free markets.

So we urgently need to start thinking about the relationship between the transnational and the local just to know where we are, and to plot where we might like to go. The difficulties with this navigational problem are that all these locations are constantly shifting, and therefore require provisional assessments and agile responses.

Contradiction 2: The public versus the private

Public space is being decimated while privatization gobbles up everything. The entire globe is up for sale, and privatized. In the twenty-first century, privatization breeds multiple meanings: the decline of the welfare state, the triumph of the market economy, a retreat into the self, and sitting alone at a computer. We are all in effect grounded, staying home alone where we can't make any trouble. We need to retake public space, wherever we are, whenever we can. In whatever is left of public space, we must delete all forms of privatization in any and all ways we can dream up: showing films for free; creating digital *osterias* for web surfing, eating and flirting; and doing screenings of cut and mix images and sound in dance clubs.

If Newt Gingrich, in decrying public television, can exclaim "we need to privatize it all," then we need to counter, as often and as loudly as we can: "we need to publicize it all."

Contradiction 3: Commercial culture versus public arts funding

After thirty years of contemporary film theory, I would assume the arguments that commercial image culture depends on turning its audience into passive consumers for commodity culture, voyeurism, and mystification and also the cultural studies counter arguments that viewers can actively engage popular cultures and remake them are quite familiar, even trite, for most intellectuals. After thirty years of independent media arts, the argument that public arts funding was designed in order to provide an antidote to the enervating compulsion of commerce to invigorate democracy has achieved mantra-like status. In the cusp of the new millennium, however, these borders between the commercial sectors and the media arts sectors, between theory and practice, are blurry, shape-shifting, fluid.

Miramax picked up *Welcome to Sarajevo*, a compelling humanist, anti-nationalist film about the ravages of the Bosnian war and the morally driven journalists who covered

---

24 Trinh T. Minh-ha, *Woman, Native, Other: Writing Postcoloniality and Feminism* (Bloomington: Indiana University Press, 1989), 119.

it. NBC and then Fox ran Michael Moore's searing political news magazine series *TV Nation*. Even though it was pulled off the air, it recirculates in film festivals, video stores, and classrooms. And the big bad computer companies like Microsoft have joined forces with hackers, librarians, and developing countries of the south to fight the ending of the fair use provision in international copyright law.

As the National Endowment for the Arts and the National Endowment for the Humanities are shells of their former robust selves, and very few foundations or agencies are funding artists, the entire concept of public arts funding seems like a hallucination left over from the 1960s. Commercial, transnational media culture has invaded nearly all public arenas: grammar schools, public libraries, parks, universities, film festivals, and even the most august of museums who curry favors from the Phillip Morris Company and The Gap.

The beleaguered and sexually exposed President Clinton, an early proselytizer for the information superhighway, has been underwritten by the media transnationals, his largest campaign contributors. Despite the impeachment hearings, he stayed in office, bolstered by the new czars of the media transnationals, Steven Spielberg, Jeffrey Katzenberg, and Michael Eisner.

Instead of configuring a binary opposition between big bad corporate media and pure and holy public culture, a paradigm shift, borrowed from digital subcultures, is desperately required. We no longer need a position in one camp or the other. We need instead to hack into all media sectors to obtain, metaphorically speaking, the freeware and shareware we need to produce work, show it, and think about it. In other words, we need to torque everything—with wit, irony, and imagination. We need to reclaim the very notion of popular culture.

Contradiction 4: Analog versus digital/single technology versus convergence

I have heard various "film" people, rhapsodizing about the transcendent possibilities and beauty of celluloid above all else, proclaim, "who wants to see art on a computer screen?" Yet after their retro-analog invocations, they retreat home to edit their works on Avids or Media 100s or Macintosh computers, sending email around the globe to other cineastes.

Our field must, whether we like it or not, figure out how we will interface with digitality in an emancipatory and popular way. It is not only inevitable, it is necessary, as digitality motors the transnational world order and reorganizes all labor.[25]

However, the digital is not separate from material, lived worlds, analog forms, the real, or psychic traumas. As artists like Philip Mallory Jones, Reginald Woolery, Branda Miller, Muntadas, Melanie Printup Hope, and others have so astutely taught us, the analog and the digital are enfolded, wrapped into each other like a braid. These artists have also shown how the digital is not only one technology or way of thinking, but is in itself multiple, including CD-ROMs' web sites, installations, chat rooms, Computer Graphics Interface (CGI), and the internet.[26]

25 For a compelling argument on the way digitality motors new social and economic formations, see Dan Schiller, *Digital Capitalism: Networking the Global Market System* (Cambridge, MA: MIT Press, 1999).
26 Many digital culture writers posit that the digital is defined by its very multiplicity of forms, for example, see Peter Lunenfeld, *Snap to Grid: A User's Guide to Digital Arts, Media and Cultures* (Cambridge, MA: MIT Press, 2000).

We need to figure out how to curate and exhibit this wide, diverse range of digital work by inventing new forms of access, distribution, and exhibition for it. We need to refuse to allow it to be privatized and individualized by imagining ways to make it public and collective. For example, museums could take out ads in local newspapers alerting the populace to artists' web sites.

This move from private to public digitality is as urgent as creating cable access centers in the 1970s. It is an exciting battle, and one where media arts centers and organizations as custodians of the last public spaces can make an enormous difference: they can construct portals where computers and digitality open up to the public beyond the borders defined by Microsoft. Digital theorists Arthur and Marilouise Kroker have argued that computers hem us in and dumb us down. Therefore we need to decipher how to render digitality a vital part of our common public space, rather than an invisible and embedded capitalist surveillance machine.[27]

This trajectory is urgent as digital apartheid emerges. Only 25 percent of all US households have a modem, and those users are predominantly, white, male, and upper middle class. Ninety percent of all the world's computers are in 35 countries of the north. The US has as many phone lines as all of Asia. In Africa, some countries have only one phone line per 1,000. Yet, there are more phone lines in Manhattan than in all of Africa. In the US, less than 40 percent of public libraries are wired.[28]

In this context, media arts groups with public space, computers, CD-ROM drives and web access could combine analog and digital to imagine new forms of public and popular culture. Convergence might even change its meaning from the confluence of technologies to popular, energizing alliances between people. After all, few are willing to dispose of bodytime altogether.

Contradiction 5: The individual versus the collective/art versus politics/ academics versus practitioners/despair versus hope

A whole panoply of contradictions unfold in these arenas that essentially graph the same phenomenon. Twenty years ago, many of us in the independent media arts sector debated all these issues until we drew blood. We argued violently over whether avant-garde or social activist media was more political and called each other "apolitical" or "anti-art, overly realist." We argued over who was more political and courageous, theorists or artists, academics or activists, and wondered what sector held the most utopian promise for popular, organized resistance to the hegemonic formations that stifled us.

Then, in 1981, Paper Tiger TV settled that debate by deconstructing it: its collective put scholars and activists together to create newsreels about the contradictions of media consciousness. Feminist, queer, and racialized film and video in the 1980s created hybrid forms that rejected the limiting monikers of avant-garde or social activist.[29]

27 Arthur and Marilouise Kroker, eds, *Digital Delirium* (New York: St. Martin's Press, 1997).

28 Bryan D. Loader, *Cyberspace Divide: Equality, Agency, and Policy in the Information Society* (London: Routledge, 1998); Brij Tankha, ed., *Communications and Democracy: Ensuring Plurality* (Penang: Southbound Press, 1995); and *Our Creative Diversity: Report of the World Commission on Culture and Development* (Paris: UNESCO, 1996), 104.

29 Bill Nichols, *Representing Reality: Issues and Concepts in Documentary* (Bloomington: Indiana University Press, 1991); Diane Waldman and Janet Walker, eds, *Feminism and Documentary* (Minneapolis: University of Minnesota Press, 1999); Chris Holmlund and Cynthia Fuchs, eds, *Between the Sheets, in the Streets: Queer, Lesbian, Gay Documentary* (Minneapolis: University of Minnesota Press, 1997).

Currently, most of us shuttle daily between despair and hope: there's no money but programs and distributors figure out how to recycle and cut costs. There's no public space so artists take over dance clubs or alter voice boxes in Barbie dolls or pirate commercial media images. There's no money for completely unsettling radical analysis in a 90-minute feature-length film, so artists make radical web sites with activists like the McSpotlight, Cyberfeminism, and Digital Diaspora sites.[30] My undergraduate students scrounge for old abandoned media technologies to recycle like Pixelvision cameras and Super 8 just so they can create work after college. As DeeDee Halleck once told a master class at Ithaca College, anyone with two VCRs and a Blockbuster Video store can become an artist. The tools and means to transforms media arts into a truly popular form of engagement with the world are here.

Despite the myriad formations this recycled hope occupies, I would wager that the massive privatization of our culture *still* conspires to make us all feel alone and even more lonely. I would suspect most media arts veterans now are thrilled to find just one or two other people who think public art matters, whether they are avant-gardist or social activist. For those newer to the "field" like my students, these categories from the 1960s, 1970s, 1980s, and 1990s matter much less than finding anyone who will tell them they are not alone and not crazy to think media means more than Miramax.

Contradiction 6: History versus the future

As a historian, I become really nervous when anyone talks about "history." History is usually marshaled to create the mythologies nation states use to annihilate everyone who doesn't fit. History is usually dug out of its grave when those with power—governments, academic administrators, programmers, foundations, and Gingrich—need to quell the masses by erasing our collective hard drives to avoid critique and uprisings.[31] A summons to an immobilized and fantasized past is usually a way to preserve the future for control by the wrong people.

Instead, the independent media arts sector—and that includes professors and students—needs a concept of histories in the plural rather than a limited version of a more singular, monolithic history. All of these histories seem buried, and, given our states of emergency, urgently require archaeology. Film and media studies academics have spent entire careers analyzing Warner Bros., David O. Selznick, MGM, Disney and other studios to understand the political economy of image culture. Now, more than ever, our media arts comrades need academics to cross over and work with them to recover these lost, ephemeral histories, not as nostalgia for old war stories, but to see how our field was continuously formed as an unsettled, contentious, and shape-shifting site. We need to historicize how media arts provided public space to sustain popular culture of the people. As Michel Foucault, the French poststructuralist, has argued, all historical archaeology should be driven by the political questions located in the present. As Jacques Derrida, the French promulgator of deconstruction, has written, "the archive always opens out towards the future."[32]

---

30 For example, see http://www.mcspotlight.org, http://brandon.guggenheim.org, and http://obn.org, http://thing.at/face.

31 For wide-ranging discussions on the relationship between history and nation building, see the essays in Anne McClintock, Aamir Mufti, and Ella Shohat, *Dangerous Liaisons: Gender Nation and Postcolonial Perspectives* (Minneapolis: University of Minnesota Press, 1997).

32 Jacques Derrida, *Archive Fever* (Chicago: University of Chicago Press, 1997), 19.

To translate: radical histories always create new ways to think about and change the future. To translate again: media academics spend far too much time in the area of cultural studies analyzing commercial culture like the Brady Bunch, and far too little time working with, analyzing, and showing the critical media emerging all around them. Writing, of course, is one powerful way to take back some public space, but it is not the only way and should never be privileged. Another way to reinvent public space is through creating public exhibitions of work, showing unseen cinemas, and creating room for repressed dialogues to be made visible. The ultimate act of political intervention these days may be simply to provide a space where people can be with each other off-line. To translate again: I would urge my academic colleagues in cultural studies to turn off their 50-channel cable televisions, get on down to their local media arts centers, museums, or film festivals to see some new work, show it, and start writing about it.

Zones of contestation

In closing, I would propose that it is not viable to pick one side of these contradictions any more, to argue for the virtues of collective, publicly-funded media art in public spaces that is entirely digital and local, or some such silly formulation derived from the cyber-fantasies of repression currently circulating.

We must be honest that we live and work within these contradictions, linked together like hypertext on the World Wide Web. We can't get out of them. The only way to deconstruct them is to surf them and understand their oscillations as places, nodal points, if you will, where we can confront this closed down universe we live in. We need to open it up to contradictions which can be hashed out together and hack it all into something new. We need to create zones of contestation where there aren't any.

It seems to me, then, that our job is not to resolve these contradictions, but to let them rip, so we can invent a future that we would all want to live in. If we can do anything differently from Time Warner or Disney, it is that we can remake, reimagine, and reclaim public spaces where these contradictions can be exposed in our programming, our art events, our artwork, our writing, our curating, our administrating, and our teaching. Our collective job, then, is to carve out space where the future can be imagined, rather than sold.

No matter what, our current states of emergency demand new thinking. No matter what, our current states of emergency require the energy and courage to let these contradictions be explored and exploded. No matter what, our current states of emergency require that we summon our energy, find other people of passion, and take over some space from the privatizers. No matter what, we must reach out and create a larger community of people that crosses all kinds of borders: national, sexual, ethnic, gender, arts administrators, academics, curators, makers, and analog and digital artists. No matter what, we can't get stuck in any one technology, but must pluralize them all and reimagine how to reprogram public space with them.

It is only by surfing the folds of these contradictions with the passion with which we surf the Web that we will create the greatest arts funders of all: imagination and hope. It is only then that Erik Barnouw's call to action can be answered. It is only then that things will boil over.

Afterthoughts: June 2000

How, exactly, can academics and other non-profit sectors of the media arts world create and enact public spaces that boil over? The very notion of salvaging the term "public" seems like a nearly indomitable task in these increasingly privatized and corporatized times in which we labor, as the public is no longer one place but many, and no longer stable but provisional. Yet to imagine how those newly fashioned public spaces can be configured as popular seems even more daunting. The construct of the "public" and the "popular" are increasingly figured as utopian fantasies rather than lived realities: these concepts have been so detached from our everyday reality that they have been cast as ephemeral ghosts wafting through the antechambers of our libraries.

However, perhaps we commit a tactical error by lingering too long in the lofty realms of the abstract, the remote, the unattainable, and the fantasy of the mass political cultural movement as we analyze and materialize these conceptions of the public and the popular. In the end, the notions of the public and popular are pedagogical in that they depend on some engagement with altered epistemological structures propelled by interactions with people and objects.

If we confine ourselves and our hopes to thinking that this reclamation of public space is an all or nothing proposition, our pedagogical goals to create dynamic spaces of dialogical exchange will flounder. Yet, if we borrow some strategies from hackers and think about the cracks, fissures, and places that can be nudged, reworked, widened, and energized, then our successes may in fact bloom into something larger as they coordinate with others staging similar strategies to recapture a popular public. We are not in the business of indoctrination, but in the dialectic of engagement: we must accept that opening up a plurality of discourses will mean that our students and audiences will more likely than not disagree with our own positions.

A revealing anecdote may perhaps anchor these claims to site our interventions in more particularized zones. One of my good friends, another film scholar, was invited to give a talk at an upstate New York graduate program conference dedicated to considering the relationships between politics and the academy. My friend related the despair the graduate student organizers felt about the end of all public spheres and politics. The graduate students agonized over how to enact an energized, ethically driven pedagogy in the classes they offered to undergraduates and in their own pursuit of degrees and jobs. My friend diagnosed a pervasive, immobilizing denial in their observations: everything was elsewhere, when in fact, everything was there.

My friend explained that they could actually find the "political" and "the public" by simply deploying their analytical skills to decipher the tributaries of their students' desires in popular culture. She related the story of an undergraduate who used his fantasies about a Hollywood actor to perform his queer identity which was only just emerging. They could, she countered, create spaces in their classrooms for work that was repressed by mass cultural practices and the exchange economy, and could reroute the mass cultural film formation for real desires that exceeded normative behaviors and forms.

Rather than entering into the unstable terrains of dialectical exchanges that often entail a "boiling over" that may not fit the lesson plan, we both worried that the students were repressing the very locales in which they labored in order to function within a phantasmatic of total intellectual and political control. We then listed how film/media culture could be revitalized in concrete, specific ways that edged the popular into the classroom as a viable desire rather than as a training camp for theoretically correct language and exegesis or professionally normative indoctrination.

We agreed that it is the role of academics and programmers to create new meanings for the concept "popular" by expanding their programming repertoires to include non-commercial work produced by the media arts sector along with the classics. By borrowing from Soviet film theory from the 1920s, academics could, as every good programmer knows, forge new dialectical montages between works and across histories and nations by creating combinations designed for maximum intellectual disturbance that link the past to the needs of the present.

For example, George Kuchar's *Hold Me While I'm Naked*, which refers to Hitchcock, could be programmed with *Psycho*, or *Notorious*. Or *Man with a Movie Camera* could be paired with Craig Baldwin's manifesto to the anti-copyright movement *Sonic Outlaws*. Or Martin Arnold's *Piece Touchee* could be paired with *Battleship Potemkin* to show how graphic montage is updated. The list is endless.

This kind of rather aggressive and not so obvious screening strategy means revising how we think about teaching cinemas. It demands that the faculty consider its film screenings as something more than the prelude to theoretical exegesis or the cinematic incarnation of the frog splayed for dissection in the biology lab. Screenings function as theory in action: they show rather than tell, and promote the sensuousness of visual and aural experience in a deeply phenomenological way that we desperately need to recover in this posthuman cyberage. We must not rob our students of those initial experiences of unsettled pleasure and passionate inquiry that drew us all to this field in the first place.

Rather than dictating the canon, or even a revised multicultural canon, the faculty could work as editors to create space for concepts, and to link these newer works to older ones by showing how they are in conversation with each other as debates and polemics that students and more public audiences can join and contribute to. Even though we may have taught *The Cabinet of Dr. Caligari* so much we have merged with Cesar himself, we must always check our cynicism at the door and ensure that our students can experience the painted shadows on the sets through fresh eyes. Who knows what they may find if released from our paradigms and our cynicism?

Conceptualizing our film/media screenings as programming, rather than as time-worn examples, may provide space to breathe life into these films, rather than to see these films as remnants of a wilted but glorified cinematic past.[33] Classes can "boil over" when the faculty organizes screenings that show that debates about culture and art matter. Through programming, we can disturb the mass cultural mythologies and fantasies surrounding cinematic practices which promote the idea that reading *Premiere* magazine and watching the Entertainment Channel constitute critical discourse about cinema.

Film screenings on college campuses perhaps survive as one of the few public spaces where our students watch films with others as a form of intellectual engagement rather than alone with their remote control. This situation represents a significant cultural shift

33 Scott MacDonald must be credited for inspiring this pedagogical style. In many conversations over the years, he has discussed how immersing students in fresh experiences with the texts without initial professorial mediation produces powerful intellectual engagement and movement. He has always underscored that a professor's conceptual grid should undergird the selection and organization of films screened, rather than provide predetermined readings. My colleague Gina Marchetti should also be credited for her contribution to elaborating this strategy to disturb preconceptions about cinema in the two-plus-years we have been team teaching our Introduction to Film Aesthetics course to freshmen/women at Ithaca College.

that demands our attention and our action. We need to treat our screenings as sacred places where we can enlighten viewers how to read cinema, expand the very forms of cinema that students know, and let a wide range of debate, anxiety, and passion unfurl without penalties. As public culture closes down everywhere, this strategy is a pedagogical imperative. In other words, we need to provide a distinctly public service that differentiates itself from Blockbuster Video by making public space for works that students do not have access to via commercial outlets.

But we also need to analyze our audiences—student and public alike—to figure out how to lure them in with all the critical means in our arsenals rather than push them away through our pedantry and erudition. This may mean anchoring more experimental texts to more accessible narrative feature films, or drawing out formal and political connections in unusual ways through alarming juxtapositions. In many ways, we need to function more as cut and mix film DJs than as pundits, creating pulsating environments that seduce and push as we respond to the crowd in our classroom. We can no longer work within covert nationalist paradigms that separate national cinemas from each other, create distinctions between high and low, and fashion ghettoes for women's, black, documentary, experimental, and hybrid forms. Our screenings, both curatorially and pedagogically, need to perform the polyvocalities, pluralities, border crossings, and hybridities which mobilize our theoretical practices. We need to mess things up so that new intellectual knots can be formed which require collective unraveling. We need to pose problems rather than provide answers. We need to provide space, as well as grades. Even though most of our students will most likely work for the media transnationals or dotcom start-ups, we still owe them the experience of cinema as a public art form that moves one to argue, as Salman Rushdie has said, with the world.

No matter what, we need to program against the multiplex, the video store and the cable TV stations by providing something different, more explosive, more demanding and more unique. We need to provide a "value added" experience for our students and for our audiences. And we need to reinstall affect and emotion, entrées into critical thinking and engagement that can often open doors that rationality inhibits. I do not want to mistake advocacy for passion as a return to the romantic, but rather to argue that the binary between emotional connection and intellectual distance be expunged.

By advocating an exploration of truly independent international media, I do not want to suggest jettisoning popular cinematic forms, as every teacher I know understands the power of deconstructing *Aladdin* or *The Matrix*. One of our favorites in the Introduction to Film Aesthetics class at Ithaca College is the pairing of *Singing in the Rain* with Kenneth Anger's *Scorpio Rising* and Bruce Conner's *Mongoloid* for the first class. We ask students simply to explain to us how all three films are similar.

My point here is that programming in whatever venue we function should always push the edge and put spectators on the most exciting rockface so that they have to figure their own way down. In our classrooms and our public programs, we need to support this media arts culture, and we need to see ourselves as a vital part of its infrastructure, even if we are not curators by trade and prefer sitting in archives reading old David O. Selznick memos or crouched at Steenbeck editing machines doing shot-by-shot analysis of *North by Northwest*.

It is no longer ethical to sever the connection between the media arts realms occupying the real world and the academy often figured as distant and remote, especially when so much film/media education has transformed into preprofessional training grounds for the media transnationals at all but the very elite institutions. The technocrats, as

Pierre Bourdieu has argued, have captured enormous discursive and material territory in the post-cold war era.[34]

Film programs at university level have not been immune: increasingly, they are ruled by technocrats who argue the value of very instrumental education in the service of capital and consumerism (students, they claim, want production skills courses, new technology, and jobs, so it is mandatory to meet the market need and to extinguish all contentions about redesigning for a more critical curriculum) as a cover for silencing the humanities and debates about cultural practice and its intellectual foundations. Film and media programs constantly must navigate the ever-shifting borders between collaboration with the media transnationals and intellectual inquiry, and even dissent. These are stormy seas indeed; pitched battles are inevitable. Film/media programs are marked by covert regimes that regulate and control student and faculty imaginations alike and require constant vigilance. Despite those retrograde conservatives who condemn it as an ivory tower, higher education nonetheless constitutes the front lines of debates about the public sphere. Therefore we need to insist on our own kind of professional connections, ones that insist that intellectual critique, artistic engagement, and understanding the non-profit media arts infrastructure are as essential skills as threading Aton cameras and working Avid editors.

Two areas worth exploring as nodal points that crystallize this regime of technocracy are the issues of technology and media piracy. As we move into what some have called the "post-film" era of new technologies, it is vital for film scholars and programmers to theorize ways to explore pluralizing technologies rather than privileging celluloid as a holy grail. Many venues in the media arts world have already done this, mixing up technologies from film, video, CD-ROM, web, and installation to investigate visual culture's multiple interfaces.

Image culture is now a mobile formation that fluidly migrates across and between technologies: we need to unpack the possibilities inherent in analyzing technology as an important component of media arts. Rather than focusing only on images and their structures, we need to move toward analyzing interfaces. And we need to think about creating spaces for multiple interfaces in our screening spaces and classrooms, integrating the technologies and also pluralizing them. The fact that most film students now own large collections of classics on video suggests that there are all kinds of ways to reimagine our classrooms and screening spaces. First, provide them with work they can't order online. Second, suggest that visiting artists sell students their tapes at a low cost so that the media arts world can become part of everyone's personal library.

One vital area that weaves the technological with the popular and the public is media piracy. New technologies like video, camcorders, VCRs, and computers have made it easier and easier to pirate images from commercial media culture to remake them and liberate them from their ideological constraints and consumerist functions. In fact, the area of copyright has emerged as a major battleground in the new economy of cyberspace, with corporations attempting to limit fair use provisions by extending the concept that images function as property. The counter argument, put forward by artists, librarians, and scholars, contends that images and ideas need some protection via fair use provisions to ensure democratic exchange of ideas for critique, parody, and cultural interventions.

---

34 Pierre Bourdieu, *Acts of Resistance: Against the Tyranny of the Market* (New York: New York University Press, 1998), 41.

This work activates images designed for consumption by remaking them into means of production of new critical modalities. A huge amount of media pirate work has been produced in the last ten years, often remaking images from popular Hollywood films via critical analysis and parody. For example, Joan Braderman's *Joan Sees Stars* recycles Hollywood films through her own desires for women stars. Tracey Moffat's *Lip* re-edits films with black maids to unwind the covert racism embedded in commercial media. Brian Springer's *Spin* downloads satellite feeds from CNN during the 1992 election and re-edits them to demonstrate the disconnect between public performance and ideology among politicians and newscasters. Martin Arnold reworks classical Hollywood films with Andy Rooney and Judy Garland to uncover the latent sexual psychic formations realism disguises. Craig Baldwin's *Sonic Outlaws* steals images from everywhere to make an argument that piracy motors democracy in an era of the media transnationals. Alex Rivera's *Dia de la independencia* pirates footage from *Independence Day* and racializes it as Latino.

Obviously this work can be easily programmed with Hollywood films as it cannibalizes them. It is also work that animates the deep pleasures of the popular culture text within critical dialogues and politically destabilized theorizations that provoke debate among audiences. Pirate work sustains the argument that it is impossible to separate various cultural practices so therefore the only strategy left is to intermingle them via technological interventions. Pirates often combine many different aesthetic strategies within a piece, demonstrating that what was popular can be remade into public discourse, and that which was repressed and silenced in images can become a popular public reinvention.

In the context of the rollbacks to higher education, the attempts to disembowel the humanities in favor of professional education which is a cover for insider trading within the corporate world, and the depletion of budgets for arts programming, this strategy of muddying the borders between the media arts world and the academy requires cleverness, administrative navigational skills, and, above all, optimistic moxie.[35]

In an ideal world where budgets enacted our intellectual goals without conflict and the memos from administrators and arts agencies informing us we were not funded would evaporate, we would have unlimited budgets and good projection. The reality, of course, is that we barely manage to salvage any of these proposals or create any of these new spaces within the intensity of the work speed-ups and the blurred borders between home and job infiltrate most of our academic workplaces.

However, rather than encasing ourselves in despondency we need to see anything that we can make happen that produces anything resembling public dialogue as a step in the right direction. Concretely, we might ask for budgets to bring in visiting media artists to show that media culture lives outside corporations. Or we might simply work with our university libraries' acquisitions staffs to enlarge their concepts of what videos and films to buy, encouraging them to take a closer look at the catalogs of the non-profit distributors. Or we might redesign our courses to center on debates rather than canons, on volatile ideas and dialectics rather than methods, on transnational and inter-genre explorations rather than the nationalisms embedded in separating cinematic practices from each other.

Most of all, we need to know that our reclamation of the popular and the public will require our labor power as well as our imaginations. In many ways, we need to, as the title of a book suggests, "reinvent film studies," not simply by teaching new paradigms

---

35 See Bill Readings, *The University in Ruins* (Cambridge, MA: Harvard University Press, 1996).

to replace the old triad of Marxism, psychoanalysis, and structuralism, but by reconfiguring ways to reinvent public film/media culture in the places we spend most of our work time—libraries, screening rooms, and classrooms.[36] We need to take what some of those graduate students told my friend was elsewhere and deposit it right here, where we work, where we think, and where we play.

Dedication

This chapter, in a slightly different form and style sans the afterthoughts section, was originally delivered as a plenary address at the 1998 annual meeting of the National Association of Media Arts and Culture in Pittsburgh. I would like to thank Helen DeMichiel for her help and inspiration. It is reprinted with the permission of NAMAC. For this volume, the chapter has been re-edited and revised with an afterthoughts section. I would like to thank Amy Villarejo for her encouragement to write an afterthoughts section that connected these ideas to our pedagogy. As a speech, it was dedicated to my good friend, Leslie Schwartz Burgevin, a visionary curator and arts advocate at the Johnson Museum of Art in Ithaca, New York. Leslie died in February 1998 after a ten-year fight against cancer.

36 I borrow this term to describe the "post-film era" from Christine Gledhill and Linda Williams, eds, *Reinventing Film Studies* (London: Arnold Press, 2000).

Index